CHRISTIAN
ETHICS

CHRISTIAN ETHICS

The
Issues
of
Life
and
Death

Edited by

Larry Chouinard, David Fiensy & George Pickens

WIPF & STOCK · Eugene, Oregon

Wipf and Stock Publishers
199 W 8th Ave, Suite 3
Eugene, OR 97401

Christian Ethics
The Issues of Life and Death
By Chouinard, Larry and Fiensy, David
Copyright©2003 by Chouinard, Larry
ISBN 13: 978-1-60899-499-1
Publication date 3/15/2010
Previously published by Parma Press, 2003

Dedication

To the Memory of
Charles R. Gresham
Colleague, mentor and friend

TABLE OF CONTENTS

Introduction[GFP]   1

Ethical Foundations

1.1   God's Commands and Christian Ethics:
      A Theology of Christian Life[RH]   7

1.2   Education and Moral Development[IRE]   29

1.3   Ethics in a Postmodern World[MSK]   51

1.4   Using the Old Testament for Ethical Guidance[RRM]   72

1.5   Using the New Testament for Ethical Guidance[RFH]   102

1.6   The Church and Culture: Paul's Alternative Vision[LC]   122

Social Ethical Issues

2.1   The Bible and Social Justice[LC & MMcL]   155

2.2   You Cannot Serve God and Mammon:
      Christians in an Age of Affluence[PP]   185

2.3   The Earth Is the Lord's: The Christian and the
      Environment[GP]   207

2.4   A Christian Perspective on Capital Punishment[DF]   233

2.5   Violence in the Name of God: Israel's Holy Wars[GH]   261

2.6   The Nonviolent Reign of God[LCC]   285

The Family and Ethical Choices

3.1   Divorce and Remarriage[LK]   319

3.2   Homosexuality and the Biblical Witness[IMH]   354

3.3   Sexual Ethics in the New Testament[GL]   379

The Christian and Medical Ethics

4.1   Medical and Ethical Guidance on Abortion[LC, DF & GW]   411

4.2   Biomedical Issues Facing the Modern Church[DM]   434

4.3   To Care for the Dying Is to Affirm Life[GR]   457

List of Contributing Authors

Lee C. Camp, Ph.D. (Notre Dame University)
Assistant Professor of Christian Ethics
David Lipscomb University

Larry Chouinard, Ph.D. (Fuller Theological
  Seminary)
Professor of New Testament
Kentucky Christian College

James R. Estep, Ph.D. (Trinity Evangelical
  Divinity School)
Professor of Christian Education
Lincoln Christian Seminary

David Fiensy, Ph.D. (Duke University)
Professor of New Testament
Kentucky Christian College

Gary Hall, Ph.D. (Union Theological
  Seminary)
Professor of Old Testament
Lincoln Christian Seminary

John Mark Hicks, Ph.D. (Westminster
  Theological Seminary)
Professor of Bible
David Lipscomb University

Ronald Highfield, Ph.D (Rice University)
Professor of Religion
Pepperdine University

Robert F. Hull, Ph.D. (Princeton Theological
  Seminary)
Dean and Professor of New Testament
Emmanuel School of Religion

Leonard Knight, Ph.D. (Oakland University)
Professor Counseling Psychology
Kentucky Christian College

Mark S. Krause, Ph.D. (Trinity Evangelical
  Divinity School)
Provost and Professor of Biblical Studies
Puget Sound Christian College

Gregory Linton, Ph.D. (Duke University)
Professor of New Testament
Great Lakes Christian College

Margaret McLaughlin, MSW (Louisiana State
  University)
Professor and Social Work Program Director
Kentucky Christian College

Rick R. Marrs, Ph.D. (The Johns Hopkins
  University)
Professor of Religion, Division Chair
Pepperdine University

David Musick, Ph.D. (University of Kentucky)
Vice Chair of Education and Development,
  Assistant Professor
Associate, Center for Bioethics
University of Pennsylvania School of
  Medicine

George Pickens, Ph.D. (University of
  Birmingham)
Professor and Program Director of
  Intercultural Studies
Kentucky Christian College

Paul Prill, Ph.D. (Indiana University)
Professor of Communication
David Lipscomb University

Greg Rutecki, MD (University of Illinois)
E. Stephen Kurtides Chair of Medical
  Education and Professor of Medicine
The Feinberg School of Medicine
Northwestern University

Gail Wise, Ed.D., MSN (University of
  Kentucky)
Professor and Department of Nursing
  Chairperson
Kentucky Christian College

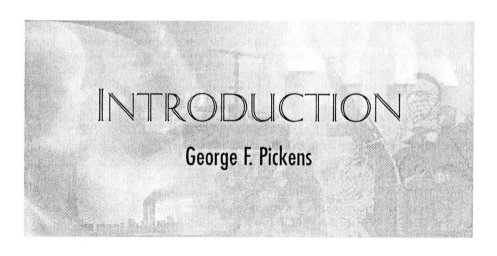

INTRODUCTION

George F. Pickens

The crucial significance of ethics in our time is illustrated in a poignant scene from the movie, *Jurassic Park*. Returning from an introductory tour of the theme park teeming with dinosaur clones, the awestruck visiting scientists are asked to share their impressions. While John Hammond, played by Richard Attenborough, celebrates the scientific successes they had just witnessed, an angry Dr. Malcolm, played by Jeff Goldblum, interrupts with an alarming ethical observation. "Your scientists were so preoccupied with whether or not they could, they never stopped to think if they should." As the story unfolds and the havoc and terror created by the escaped dinosaurs spreads to destroy the theme park, the viewer wonders who the most lethal beasts really are. Are they the extinct creatures that are only doing what instinct tells them to do, or are they the unethical humans who are guided only by thirsts for money and scientific "progress," oblivious to or uncaring about the consequences of their decisions and actions? Driven by greed and fascination for innovation, the *Jurassic Park* scientists were concerned only with what they *could* do to the tragic neglect of what they *should* do. Ethics were overshadowed by expediency.

> All too often in our world, expediency is given more attention and resources than ethics.

In this case fiction most definitely mirrors reality. All too often in our world, expediency is given more attention and resources than ethics. Driven by the gods of greed, "progress," convenience, and self-interest, human decisions are being made more upon the behavior that is possible than upon the behavior

1

that is ethical. Scientists, wrestling with questions of quality and quantity of life, often turn to expediency rather than ethics. Legislators, vying for votes in an increasingly relativistic society, are tempted to choose the way of popularity over the way of values. And common citizens, yearning for the "good life," frequently choose what is easy, comfortable, and convenient rather than what is right. Our time is characterized by a fascination and preoccupation with the "can" questions, and consequently the "should" questions are becoming increasingly unpopular, viewed by an increasing number of people as irrelevant and unimportant.

Ethics deals with the "should" questions, and their rarity in our time highlights their need for greater attention. The long-term quality of our lives and witness demand that thinking and action become more ethical, asking alongside the "can" questions the overriding "should" questions. Even so, a preoccupation with expedient behavior is only one of the challenges related to ethics. Another accompanying and perhaps more serious challenge to living ethical lives in our day is the lack of agreement on common standards for right, moral, and proper action. In a world that is becoming increasingly more relativistic, and where accepted standards for behavior and guidelines for decisions are being questioned, the search for common ethical foundations is crucial. Where can one turn for assistance in deciding what is ethical? Are there universal principles for ethical behavior, and who directs the definitions and standards for right and wrong?

> Where can one turn for assistance in deciding what is ethical?

Christian ethics offers answers to these questions. Christianity is certainly about beliefs that are correct and right, but it is also (and some would say primarily) about a way of life that is informed and guided by specific principles and values. The Christian life, therefore, is an ethical life, governed by the standards for behavior and lifestyle that are communicated through Scripture. Drawing upon the Hebrew Scriptures, the example of Jesus, and the New Testament, Christians are called to manage their lives according to the teachings of the Bible. These Christian ethical standards are pervasive, affecting every aspect of individual and social life. So, Christian ethics provide not only a common starting point for a quest for what is moral, but Christian ethics also informs and determines that search.

This volume seeks to make a contribution to this search for Christian ethical decisions and actions. While the contributors come from various institutions, academic disciplines, and regions of the United States, they share at least three convictions. One, the contributors believe that the standards for ethics must be rooted in the Christian Scriptures. Second, they share a conviction that Christians are called to live ethical lives, and consequently, Christians will be identified as distinctly different from those guided by other ethical standards. Third, the authors of the following chapters communicate approaches to Scripture and community reflective of parts of the Stone-Campbell Movement. The contributors represent both the independent Christian Churches/Churches of Christ and the a capella Churches of Christ. This volume, then, demonstrates an ethical discussion that is taking place within these two streams of the Stone-Campbell Movement.

> *Christian ethics provide not only a common starting point for a quest for what is moral, but Christian ethics also informs and determines that search.*

However, the **views expressed are solely those of the authors themselves.** The contributors were given liberty to express their own positions, so the editors have not attempted to forge harmony on the difficult and controversial issues that are addressed. Rather, it has been the intention of the editors to allow the book to reflect the difficulty, diversity, and tension that characterize the often-perilous task of articulating Christian ethics in our time. This book, then, represents a necessary yet risky journey towards understanding and living an ethical Christian life. As such, it is to be understood as a map, not a creed; it reflects the directions of individual and communal journeys, not yet destinations.

The book is organized around four related sections. The first set of articles focuses on broader, more general and foundational issues for Christian ethics. The remaining three sections are more specific, focusing on particular issues that are crucial for our time. The second section deals with social ethics, the third section highlights central ethical issues related to the family and ethical choices, and the final section contains three articles reflecting Christian perspectives on the crucial area of medical ethics. The articles are meant to encourage and facilitate discussion. It is hoped that, at the least, these chapters will assist in Christian lives becoming more reflective, deliberate, and consistent with the perfect truth of Scripture.

Finally, the editors wish to thank those who assisted in this project. Mrs. Terry Golightly, the administrative assistant for the Sack School of Bible and Ministry at Kentucky Christian College, typed several of the manuscripts. Ms. Andrea Bugglin, undergraduate assistant, proofread many of the manuscripts to check for form. And of course, we are especially indebted to our teaching colleagues at Kentucky Christian College, to the library staff, and to the technological support staff for their assistance and encouragement in this undertaking.

ETHICAL
FOUNDATIONS

In This Section

Ronald Highfield

**God's Commands and Christian Ethics:
A Theology of Christian Life**

James R. Estep

Education and Moral Development

Mark S. Krause

Ethics in a Postmodern World

Rich R. Marrs

Using the Old Testament for Ethical Guidance

Robert F. Hull

Using the New Testament for Ethical Guidance

Larry Chouinard

The Church and Culture: Paul's Alternative Vision

GOD'S COMMANDS AND CHRISTIAN ETHICS
A THEOLOGY OF CHRISTIAN LIFE
Ron Highfield

A Parable of Modern Morality

Once upon a time human society decided that science and technology had brought great evil on humankind. To rid themselves of this curse, the people burned science books, destroyed laboratories, smashed machines, and forbade the study of science. Many centuries later, with science long forgotten, curiosity drove individuals to assemble bits of machinery, bind scorched scraps of textbooks and scientific articles together, and collect confused oral traditions. They assembled machines from the pieces. They wove leaflets of scientific literature together in "books." They tried to make sense of the differing strands of tradition. None of the machines worked, however, for the would-be scientists had stuck parts of different kinds of machines together arbitrarily. The new "books" consisted of incoherent patchworks of fragments from general textbooks, popular magazines, and technical articles; and worse, the pieces belonged to different sciences and pseudosciences—from physics, biology, computer science, phrenology, and astrology. Something irretrievable had been lost. Gone forever was a community of people with the shared beliefs, values, institutions, and skills needed to sustain science. Without a living tradition, coherence, wholeness, clarity, and a common language evaporate. Science degenerates into arbitrary rules, fragments of knowledge, and pieces of unusable machinery.

Moral philosopher Alasdair MacIntyre relates this parable to help us understand the present state of ethics in the western, post-Christian world.[1] The neopaganism of the Renaissance, the divisive-

> *The neopaganism of the Renaissance, the divisiveness of the Reformation era, and the rationalism of the Enlightenment together smashed the 1500-year-old ethical vision that had made Christendom possible.*

ness of the Reformation era, and the rationalism of the Enlightenment together smashed the 1500-year-old ethical vision that had made Christendom possible. Torn asunder was the web of shared beliefs, authorities, traditions, and ethical practices that had made possible a common ethical language and a coherent understanding of the good life. Today, and for some 200 years past, we live amidst the fragments of that once-coherent ethical vision. Only in isolated cultural pockets, in a few communities, is a memory of that vision precariously preserved. The immense majority has no recollection of those bygone days. Rather, individuals arbitrarily piece together a rule here, a principle there, a feeling, an out-of-context proverb, or a pithy saying to cobble together something that resembles a life. They mine the most disparate sources—the Bible, Buddhism, Hinduism, Stoicism, Native American religions, transcendentalism, romanticism, pragmatism, utilitarianism, TV advertisements, and celebrity endorsements—to construct a part-time, short-term rationalization for the current phase of their shifting life preferences.

Secular ethicists can assemble a coherent ethical vision no more effectively than can secular couch potatoes. They merely raise the incoherence of the average person to the level of theory, which exposes the tragicomic nature of modern culture to plain view. Contemporary medical ethicists, for example, find themselves so overwhelmed by the lack of an ethical vision shared by the culture that they are reduced, for the most part, to casuistry, to making decisions based on analogy to past decisions: "If we did that then, we can do this now." "Do no harm" and other such principles, when appealed to at all, derive their authority only from their wide acceptance. Disputes over issues such as

> *Secular ethicists can assemble a coherent ethical vision no more effectively than can secular couch potatoes.*

abortion, cloning, euthanasia, physician-assisted suicide, genetic manipulation, and other "difficult" issues are addressed more and more in the courts where robed elites impose their preferences on the public in the name of the ever more elastic Constitution of the

United States.[2] The underlying chaos is barely concealed by the curtain of ethical agreements based on the temporary will of the majority divined by a method resembling political polling.

We live in a culture saturated with moral nihilism and ethical chaos. Living as a Christian today demands that we remain conscious of this fact and not adopt unthinkingly the eclectic ways of the world. Vigilance is doubly required of would-be Christian ethicists. Many current discussions of ethical issues presuppose ethical pluralism and demand acquiescence to this pluralism as the price of being heard. Hence, we are tempted to disguise our Christian identity by translating our Christian "principles" into secular language. We make ethical arguments that differ little from those of our secular colleagues, arguments that focus on the consequences of an action, or the utility of an end, on assumed rights, or some fashionable notion of justice. Only by doing this, we rationalize, can Christians participate in public forums and have an impact on how these issues are decided.

> Vigilance is doubly required of would-be Christian ethicists.

Christians that follow the tactic just described are not acting as Christian ethicists. Perhaps, in a spirit of magnanimity we could call them "Christians in ethics." Christian ethics, however, is something completely different. In this chapter, I will argue that Christian ethics is a form of Christian theology and cannot be secularized without being destroyed. I will begin with a brief discussion of general ethics to give us some orientation. I will then set out the basic approach of Christian ethics, followed by a discussion of the parody that always accompanies it as a shadow ethics. I will then clarify some confusion about the problem that makes Christian ethics necessary. Finally, we ask how Christian ethics might apply to the Christian life in concrete ways.

> Christian ethics is a form of Christian theology and cannot be secularized without being destroyed.

General Ethics[3]

Ethics concerns human action—not merely a few special "moral" or "immoral" actions—all human actions. An action is an intentional activity that uses means to achieve ends. Actions are complex, however, and ethics does not attempt to craft a complete theory of action. Ethics is not concerned directly with the physical, biological, psychological, or social aspects of the action. It focuses, rather, on a particular aspect of action, the quality of being good or evil, right or wrong.

We can consider the ethical aspect of an action from at least three vantage points. First, we can ask what gives an action an ethical quality. What is the origin and ground of the distinction between good or evil? What do we mean by the words good and evil? Philosophers call the discipline that addresses these questions, *metaethics*. Second, we can ask how we know what we are to do and avoid doing. What are the general moral guidelines for property ownership, for human sexual relations, or for the exercise of violence? We are seeking here some general norms for behavior; hence, ethicists often refer to this area of study as *normative ethics*. Third, we can ask how metaethical and normative principles apply to specific, often new or controversial, actions. Is it right, for example, to create embryos for possible implantation in the womb knowing that some of them will not be used and hence are likely to be destroyed? Under what circumstances is it permissible to destroy frozen embryos? Is it permissible to use organs from aborted babies for research or therapy? Not surprisingly, this approach to ethics is called *applied ethics*.

Let us consider these three general areas in a bit more detail. Philosophers distinguish at least two types of metaethics: moral realism and moral skepticism. Moral realism asserts that moral distinctions are grounded in an objective reality; they are not merely subjective human inventions. Some realists (for example, Plato) understand this objective reality as a realm of "spiritual objects," laws, or relationships. Others ground the objectivity of morality in God's commands. Moral skepticism, on the other hand, denies any objective basis to moral distinctions. Skeptics often find the origin of morality in necessities of social life. Since moral skeptics understand the needs of societies as differing widely from society to society and from age to age, they are usually also moral relativists.

Normative ethics proposes one principle or one "set of principles" by which to determine whether a proposed action is right or wrong. Three types of normative ethical theories contend for our allegiance: virtue theory, duty theories, and consequentialist theories. Rooted in the culture of ancient Greece, virtue theory emphasizes acquiring a good character and forming good habits. Rather than obeying rules by a mere act of will or calculating the consequences of a proposed action, the good person will act spontaneously in a way consistent with his good character. Having acquired wisdom, he will act wisely. Having attained justice, she will act justly. Having become courageous, he will act courageously. The virtuous

---

Determining Right from Wrong:
1. **Virtue theory**—Developing good characters produces good actions.
2. **Duty theories**—"Right" is achieved by fulfilling externally determined obligations.
3. **Consequential theories**—An action is "right" if the ends produced are for the greater good.

---

person will avoid bad character traits or vices, such as vanity, injustice, and cowardice. Virtues can be acquired through discipline and practice. Hence, education holds a central place in virtue theory. Aristotle's *Nichomachean Ethics* was the first sustained treatment of virtue ethics. Christian theologians in the Medieval West developed Christian virtue theories. Thomas Aquinas (1225–1274) supplemented the Greek "natural" virtues with three "supernatural" virtues: faith, hope, and love.[4]

A second type of normative ethics proposes that we follow one or more rules that we acknowledge as our self-evident duty. In all duty theories (also called "deontological theories," so named from the Greek word for duty, *deon*), behaving ethically means doing one's duty. We do certain things because we are obligated to do them, not because we are so inclined or foresee a favorable outcome. The seventeenth-century moral thinkers, Hugo Grotius and Samuel Pufendorf, divided scores of duties into three categories: duties to God, to oneself, and to others. John Locke coordinated duties and rights. Human beings have certain God-given rights: life, liberty, and property. And everyone is duty bound to respect those rights. Immanuel Kant reduced earlier lists of duties to one "categorical imperative." All moral actions, Kant contended, can be measured by the duty to treat people as ends only and never as means to ends; that is, we should love people and use things but never love things and use people.

The third type of normative ethics attempts to measure the moral quality of an action solely by the consequences it produces. Consequentialism, as this theory is called, asserts that the right course to take is the one that produces more good than bad consequences. This theory has been attractive to many modern moralists because it appeals to observable, measurable experience rather than to an internal, moral sense. Three types of consequentialism break out according to how we measure the consequences. Ethical Egoism makes its decision based on the projected consequences of the action for the agent alone. What good or bad will likely happen to *me* if I cheat on my income taxes? Ethical Altruism asks about the amount of good and bad produced for everyone but the agent. What will happen to *others* if I drink and drive? Utilitarianism focuses on the good and bad consequences for everyone. Will the good that comes to *me and everyone else* outweigh the bad that comes from genetically altering plants and animals to increase agricultural production?

Applied ethics constitutes the third major "branch of ethics." When they hear the word ethics, most people think first of the issues dealt with in applied ethics. Political and legal controversies over physician-assisted suicide and abortion, and constant media attention to the genetic experimentation, cloning, and stem cell research focuses our attention on the practical side of ethics. Clearly, just as it is necessary to ground normative principles in a metaethical theory, it is necessary to apply normative principles to the concrete issues of life: homosexuality, adultery, insider trading, false advertising, race relations, animal rights, pollution, endangered species, war, guns, and welfare. Unfortunately, many discussions about these matters display a woeful ignorance of the normative and metaethical aspects of ethics. The parties assert one ungrounded opinion against another. Neither side is clear about normative principles and their metaethical grounds. Hence, it is not possible to come to an agreement about what should be done (except by a lucky accident) or even to understand the true nature and source of the disagreement.

In a way that contrasts sharply with the exposition of Christian ethics to follow, general ethics, in all its different branches and theories, circles about one problem: how do we discover what to do? It assumes that the human situation is one of ignorance about how we ought to act but that we have the capacity to discover the good way. As soon as we discover how we ought to act, the work of ethics is done. Only obliquely does general ethics deal with whether or not human beings have the power or will to act rightly.

Christian Ethics[5]

The Command of God

Christian ethics is an aspect of Christian theology and is (I believe) best understood as the doctrine of the command of God.[6] Or, put another way, Christian ethics is the theology of the Christian life. Hence, we should not draw a sharp distinction between ethics and doctrine.[7] Our view of human action should not be divorced from our understanding of God any more than our deeds separated from our relationship to God. Christian ethics is as much a theological task as is thinking about God, Christ, and the atonement. Christian ethics, like other aspects of Christian theology, must begin from faith and seek to understand the faith. Christian ethics, as I conceive it, seeks to understand the truth, justice, and moral excellence of the commands of God.

> *Christian ethics is the theology of the Christian life and seeks to understand the truth, justice, and moral excellence of the commands of God.*

Why am I so insistent that we approach Christian ethics as the doctrine of God's command? First, we define ethics as the doctrine of the command of God because that is what Scripture does. Think of the Old Testament Law. Think of the Ten Commandments (Exod 20:1-17): "And God spoke all these words: 'I am the LORD your God, who brought you out of Egypt, out of the land of slavery. You shall have no other gods before me. . . .You shall not commit adultery. . . .'" Consider Psalm 1 and 119:

> Blessed is the man
>   who does not walk in the counsel of the wicked
> or stand in the way of sinners
>   or sit in the seat of mockers.
> But his delight is in the law of the LORD,
>   and on his law he meditates day and night (Ps 1:1-2).
>
> Blessed are they whose ways are blameless,
>   who walk according to the law of the LORD.
> Blessed are they who keep his statutes
>   and seek him with all their heart.
> They do nothing wrong;
>   they walk in his ways.
> You have laid down precepts
>   that are to be fully obeyed (Ps 119:1-4).

Things are much the same in the New Testament. Think about Jesus' teaching in the Sermon on the Mount. "You have heard that it was said to the people long ago, 'Do not murder, and anyone who murders will be subject to judgment.' But I tell you that anyone who is angry with his brother will be subject to judgment" (Matt 5:21-22). Reflect on Jesus' call to costly discipleship in the Gospel of Mark. In the farewell discourses of John 13–17, Jesus, far from renouncing the commands of God, gives a new command: "A new command I give you: Love one another. As I have loved you, so you must love one another" (13:34). Consider Paul's ethical teaching. Though Paul argues against those who wish to be saved by law keeping, he is clear that we are under the rule of Christ. Note the ethical sections of Galatians, Ephesians, and Colossians. Think of the Book of James's practical ethics.

Scripture roots the qualitative distinction between good and evil in the nature and will of God, and it grounds our knowledge of good and evil in the command of God. Nowhere does Scripture give us the right to make this distinction for ourselves, nor does it teach that we have the capacity to discern good and evil on our own. How could we justify taking another path?

Second, we must approach Christian ethics as the command of God because any other approach would be inconsistent with the Christian doctrines of God, Christ, the Holy Spirit, sin, salvation, sanctification, etc. It would be inconsistent to allow human beings to judge good and evil and not allow human beings to judge God. Who is God? Our Creator! Our gracious Savior! Our Lord! Who is Christ? Our Redeemer! Our Lord! Our substitute! Who are human beings? Creatures! Sinners! Rebels! Can we, may we then also become the judges of good and evil? Impossible.

Third, from the vantage point of Christian ethics, other approaches to ethics, in which human beings decide between good and evil, are not only wrong but also are manifestations of rebellion against God. Adam and Eve are the founders of general ethics, for they presumed to judge between good and evil. As Bonhoeffer observes, "Already in the possibility of the knowledge of good and evil Christian ethics discerns a falling away from the origin."[8]

The Structure of Christian Ethics

Since God is one and the Christian faith takes God for its object, the whole of the faith is present in every part and every part mirrors the whole. Each attribute of God, for example, can be expressed as an aspect of every other attribute. Since God is both infinite and loving, he exists as infinite love and loving infinity. Since God is both just and merciful, he lives as just mercy and merciful justice. We must think in terms of a trinitarian doctrine of the church and a churchly doctrine of the Trinity. In the same way, each Christian doctrine can be expressed in relation to all the others. Moreover, every other Christian doctrine must find expression in the doctrine of the Christian life or Christian ethics. Every doctrine has implications for the Christian life. In the following paragraphs, we will indicate the basic ethical implications of four major doctrinal aspects of Christian theology: the doctrine of God, Creation, Reconciliation, and Redemption.

The Doctrine of God. God is the origin, measure, and end of all things. God is greater than anything we can imagine. Consider the majestic heavens. He is more glorious. Behold the mysteries of the ocean depths. He is deeper. Think of the most beautiful deeds done by human beings. His are more beautiful. God is eternal. The oldest mountain range, the most ancient star, and the universe itself are no more permanent, compared to him, than your breath on a January morning. God knows every existing being and every possibility. The past, present, and future are open to him. God's justice is perfect. His love is pure. All the good things we enjoy or can imagine enjoying have their model in him. He is the Good in all goods.[9]

> God is the fundamental, eternal fact. Hence, worship is the fundamental ethical act, and it finds its natural place in the doctrine of God.

What should be our response to such a God? To fall on our faces and worship! Moving into God's presence, we are compelled to praise him. Worship is our appropriate response to the existence and being of God. God is the fundamental, eternal fact. Hence, worship is the fundamental ethical act, and it finds its natural place in the doctrine of God. Thinking of God leads us to exclaim with the psalmist, "Great is the LORD and most worthy of praise; his greatness no one can fathom" (Ps 145:3). Before God we must cry along with the four living creatures, "You are worthy, our Lord and God, to receive glory and honor and power, for you created all things, and by your will they were created and have their being" (Rev 4:11). Augustine of Hippo (AD 354–430) rightly observed long ago:

Man is one of your creatures, Lord, and his instinct is to praise you . . . since he is part of your creation, he wishes to praise you. The thought of you stirs him so deeply that he cannot be content unless he praises you, because you made us for yourself and our hearts find no peace until they rest in you.[10]

It may seem strange at first to include worship in Christian ethics.[11] We tend to think of Christian ethics as concerned only with a limited set of actions; for example, we focus on those things addressed in the last six of the Ten Commandments: family, property, sex, and life. The first three commandments we usually think of as "religious" and not ethical. Christian ethics, however, brings all human action under its scrutiny. Worship is the fundamental human action. We will worship something! Worshiping something that is not God (Baal, the Rolling Stones, money, pleasure, sex) will corrupt our other actions (see Romans 1!). Genuine worship of the true God will issue forth in thankfulness, humility, and joyful obedience.

The Doctrine of Creation.[12] "In the beginning God created the heavens and the earth" (Gen 1:1). God created the world out of nothing. The affirmation of "creation from nothing" (*creato ex nihilo*) is a central component of the Christian doctrine of creation. It asserts what every reader of the Bible knows: nothing forced or made it necessary for God to create. There was no preexisting material or pattern that constrained God in any way. God's act of creation was free, loving, gracious, and very good. God freely gave us our being. We came into existence, not because of any power we had or anything we did, but because God's love overflowed in the generosity of creation. God created a world full of good and beautiful things for us to enjoy.

When you receive a gift, your first feeling is gratitude and your first impulse is to give thanks. In creation, God gave us the most basic gift, existence—and all that is needed to sustain it. We can enjoy nothing else without existence. Hence, gratitude and thanksgiving are the fundamental ethical acts that correspond to God's act of creation. When we are overwhelmed with gratitude toward God for what he has given us, we will not envy what he has given to our neighbor. We will exercise a generosity toward others like the generosity God has toward us. Ingratitude is incomprehensible in view of what God has done for us in creation.

The Doctrine of Reconciliation. In God's action of reconciliation we discover the depths of the grace of God we first met in creation.

The reconciling activity of God presupposes the sin and alienation of humanity. Despite knowing God's greatness and benefiting from his generosity, humanity plunged itself into sin. Fallen human beings refuse to worship God as God. They turn away from him who is worthy and seek their good in lower things. Outrageously, humanity feels no gratitude and offers no thanksgiving to its creator. "I owe no one for myself. I am my own," the blind sinner says in his heart. Enjoying God's gifts, the ungrateful creature boasts, "I need thank no one. I provided these things."

If we have no right to demand that God create us, how much more have we no right to expect forgiveness and reconciliation! Sin is the human "No!" to God. In sin, we refuse God and his gifts. We want to be free of him so that we can possess ourselves and do as we please. If God were to take our "no" seriously and let us have our way, we would be doomed. For there is no life, no good—indeed nothing at all—apart from God. But, in a costly move we can never fully understand, God ignores our refusals and demonstrates his love to sinners. In Christ, God overcomes our silly "no" with his profound "yes." "For God so loved the world that he gave his one and only Son, that whoever believes in him shall not perish but have eternal life" (John 3:16). The giving God of creation is revealed as the forgiving God in reconciliation. In Christ, God forgives the idolatrous and ungrateful sinner. In the death and resurrection of Christ, God puts to death the old sinful humanity and resurrects a new humanity pleasing to God.

Repentance toward God and love toward others is the twofold ethical act required of humanity in response to God's act of reconciliation. Since God has put the old human to death in Christ, we must renounce our past life of sin and treat that sinner as dead and gone. In Christ, Paul reminds the Romans, "we died to sin" (Rom 6:2). We must now take up that new life in Christ. Paul concludes: "Since, then, you have been raised with Christ, set your hearts on things above, where Christ is seated at the right hand of God. Set your minds on things above, not on earthly things. For you died, and your life is now hidden with Christ in God" (Col 3:1-3). "We love because He first loved us" (1 John 4:19). We forgive because He forgave us. We are to follow Christ (Phil 2:1-11). We are to be like our Master (John 13:1-17).

The reconciliation we now experience by faith in Christ anticipates our future redemption. Sadly, here and now we can still be plagued by sin, tormented by evil, and intimidated by death. At best, our worship is impure, our gratitude halfhearted, and our love weak. Of ourselves we do not have the power required to rise to the high call-

> Christian ethics is an important part of the doctrine of the Holy Spirit.

ing of God. But even now the Holy Spirit, who gives life to all things, raised Jesus from the dead—and in the future will renew the world— lives in us, and empowers us for holy living. Through the Spirit, Christ lives in us now. Christ lives and loves in and through us. The Christian life is life in the Spirit and led by the Spirit. Apart from the Spirit we cannot please God (Rom 8:7-9). Christian ethics is an important part of the doctrine of the Holy Spirit.

The Doctrine of Redemption. The reconciliation and salvation God has accomplished in Christ is now hidden to the world. In the future, God's salvation will become a world historical event in God's final redemption. God will raise the dead, and sin and evil will be banished from his sight. The saved will share in the eternal life of God and sin will no longer be possible for them. Everything begun in creation and advanced in reconciliation will be completed in redemption. The good creation we experience now will be saved and intensified, and all evil will be removed from it. God's glory will fill creation, and creation itself will be glorified (Romans 8).

Hope is the basic ethical act that corresponds to the Redeemer God. We live in anticipation of the future that God will bring to creation. Hope and courage characterize the Christian life. Hope frees us to give without expecting something in return. It liberates us to love even those that would threaten us with injury and death. It enables us to resist the temptations of the moment and invest our lives in things that will last. Christian hope gives us the strength to accept whatever joy or sorrow God gives us without a hint of that godless despair that hides

> Hope is the basic ethical act that corresponds to the Redeemer God.

under the name of resignation. Hope frees us to live daring lives without the presumption that drives the faithless to a frantic search for pleasure today or for security against the evils of tomorrow.[13] In hope, we can believe we will not miss the good God has for us today and we will not be destroyed by the evil tomorrow may bring.

Worship, gratitude, thanksgiving, repentance, love, and hope are the basic ethical acts of the Christian life. After showing how these foundational activities flow out of a heart attuned to the character and action of God, Christian ethics can then explore the many ways these attitudes must permeate every detail of our lives before God. Before we can take up that task, however, we must deal with the sad reality that consideration of God's character and action does not always produce a reaction of worship, thanksgiving, repentance, love, and hope. Sometimes it produces the opposite of these.

Shadow Ethics

In this fallen world, a shadow ethics (a negative image) always follows on the heels of Christian ethics. God's commands always elicit rebellion from sinful humanity. Whatever good God commands, sinful man finds repugnant, and whatever evil God forbids, sinful man finds attractive (see Romans 7). This ethics reverses the relationships found in Christian ethics. Whereas Christian ethics begins in the knowledge that God is the origin, measure, and end of all things, shadow ethics assumes that we can act as our own gods. We refuse to acknowledge God as the measure of all things. Therefore we refuse to worship God. We cannot really believe that God is worthy of praise, that God really is greater than we. Instead, we worship ourselves and place ourselves in the center of the universe. All things must

> *Shadow ethics assumes that we can act as our own gods.*

serve us! For obedience, which we view openly or secretly as beneath our dignity, we substitute a distorted concept of freedom. Shadow ethics understands freedom, not as the power to live according to our true being before God, but as freedom from restrictions on our chaotic, momentary impulses. Christian ethics considers shadow freedom to be more like slavery than true freedom and more like death than life.

Whereas Christian ethics recognizes God's gift of creation with gratitude and thankfulness, shadow ethics cannot feel grateful for God's gifts. It does not give thanks. In our sin, we either take God's generosity for granted or convince ourselves that we are entitled to it. We find fault with God's good creation and chafe at our limitations. Whether in our dreams or in our technology, we seek to remake God's world to our specifications. Whether we imagine we can build a tower to heaven, clone our way to immortality, or become omnipresent through the Internet, we cannot escape our limits. We are God's creatures. That is our glory. We can have no other.

Whereas Christian ethics cultivates a broken spirit and imitates the love of Christ, shadow ethics, reacts to God's reconciling love and forgiveness with intensified hatred. Being exposed as a self-destructive sinner, sinful man protests his innocence all the louder. Things must not be as bad as all that. Our problems—surely not our fault!—must lie within our capacities to solve. If we are our own gods and creators, we can save ourselves as well! Just as we invent technology to overcome our limitations, we invent religions and therapies to deal with our spiritual and emotional problems. We refuse to imitate the divine model set forth in Jesus. We project, rather, an image of the human self as a self-defining god, and then we attempt to imitate it.

Whereas Christian ethics bids us hope in God and the future he has promised, shadow ethics asks us to hope in ourselves. We can find in ourselves, however, no real basis of hope and courage, for, as time-bound creatures, we have no power to guarantee the future for which we wish. And so we invent the myth of human progress; that is, the future must turn out better than the past. But the myth is a lie, and its falsehood is always on the edge of human consciousness. Sinful man becomes angry and venomous as his impending destruction approaches. Hopelessness, futility, and despair alternate with groundless optimism, frantic activity, and giddy excitement. The exponents of shadow ethics lash out at the representatives of the coming redemption.

The Problem of Ethics

The problem of a discipline is the central issue that created the need for the discipline. As I have already indicated, general ethics always returns to the central problem of how to determine what is right. It presupposes that we have the right and the capacity to make

> The real problem of Christian ethics is that human beings knowingly reject the good and right and are not able to do them even when they see them.

this determination, and it tacitly assumes that—when we discover the answer to the problem—we will have the capacity to do the right thing. Christian ethics approaches the question differently. Unlike general ethics, Christian ethics does not treat the problem of determining what is right as the central issue. The real problem of Christian ethics is that human beings knowingly reject the good and right and are not able to do them even when they see them.[14]

Since, for Christian ethics, doing right means obeying God's commands, it seems odd to make determining what is right its central task. Hence, the first question we must ask is: Are God's commands so unclear that clarifying them must be the main point of our ethical work? Surely, we must answer no. In the Bible, when God commands a person to do something, we get the impression that the command was clear enough for that person to know what to do. It is reasonable, therefore, to assume that God has the ability to help *you* know what he wants *you* to do today. Of course, some biblical commands are obscure to modern readers. We do not know what they meant, and we are not sure of their exact application. For most of us, however, the commands, "You shall not steal," "You shall not kill," and "You shall not covet" are clear—all too clear.

I am suggesting that we stand before God in the same relation to God as those in the Bible whom he commands with clarity and specificity. Jesus told the parable of the Good Samaritan (Luke 10:25-37) to a scribe who was trying to obscure God's command to "Love thy neighbor." "Who is my neighbor?" the professional interpreter asked. Jesus told him, in effect, "God's commands are not general principles subject to endless discussions about interpretation, which allow us in the meantime to ignore God's command. When you meet someone who needs you, you will know at that time what God commands you to do." God's commands will be clear to those to whom he directs them at the time he commands them. In the specific situations of our lives, when the Devil tempts us, whether with seductive whispers or threatening shrieks, we do not live in a fog of interpretive ambiguity.[15] We cannot claim uncertainty or

> *We cannot claim uncertainty or obscurity as an excuse for disobedience.*

obscurity as an excuse for disobedience. Yes, you must prepare yourself to hear God's command with Bible study, communal discernment, prayer, and invocation of the Spirit's leading. Do not think, however, that you can avoid responsibility for your actions by feigning ignorance and blaming God for his lack of clarity.

Second, let us consider why Christian ethics, unlike general ethics, questions the human capacity for doing good and treats it as

> For Christian ethics, the problem is not something more information could remedy, greater intellectual effort could penetrate, and further calculations resolve.

the central problem. The Bible addresses the problem of how the idolatrous and ungrateful rebel can be turned back to God, of how the slave of sin can be liberated to serve righteousness, and of how the dead can be raised. These are the central problems God addresses in the history of salvation. For Christian ethics, the problem is not something more information could remedy, greater intellectual effort could penetrate, and further calculations resolve. The problem of Christian ethics is that sinful humans cannot—because they will not!—obey God's command. The problem is not that we lack knowledge we can obtain for ourselves through further ethical reflection. The problem is that we habitually and stubbornly reject the one thing that can open the good way before us: the command of God.

In the New Testament, God solves the problem of ethics by justifying sinners through Jesus Christ and sanctifying the unholy by the Holy Spirit. How can human beings be righteous before God? Only by faith in Jesus Christ. What we were powerless to do "God did by sending his own Son in the likeness of sinful man to be a sin offering" (Rom 8:3). How can human beings truly obey God's commands (Romans 7)? Only in the power of the Holy Spirit. "And so he condemned sin in sinful man, in order that the righteous requirements of the law might be fully met in us, who do not live according to the sinful nature but according to the Spirit" (Rom 8:3-4). We can obey God truly and from the core of our being only in the power of the Spirit. For the Spirit controls us and thus frees us for heartfelt obedience.

Now let us consider the day-to-day living of the Christian life that becomes possible with the help of the living Word and Holy Spirit.

Practical Christian Living

At this point, we may be tempted to abandon the path taken so far. We are inclined to view the work of justification and sanctification as doctrinal theory, as a mere prelude to practical application. We are prone to think, "We've looked at what God has done, so we must now figure out what we should do in response." Reasoning this way, we begin treating God's commands, Jesus' teaching and example, and the apostolic teaching as if they were dead letters, spoken on other occasions to other people, and in need of being made relevant to our day and time. "That's what they said then to that situation, but what would they say now to our situation?" we ask. Or we view them as abstract rules or principles from which to deduct further applications in a legalistic and rationalistic manner. Either way, we place a chasm between God's commands and our obedience. We conclude that we can and must bridge this gulf with our interpretive strategies and rational powers. God must now speak his commands through human interpreters.

In this way, we fall back into the pattern of general ethics, searching for what we should do and using various human-centered ethical theories to help us decide. How tempting it is, as the interpreter of God's commands, to substitute our own preferences, opinions, wishes, and dreams for God's command! While honoring God theoretically as the judge of good and evil, as God's interpreters we can sit on the bench and pronounce a very human judgment on ourselves.

Resisting all these temptations, however, Christian ethics must fight against the tendency to substitute human judgment for God's command. For God is alive. God speaks, commands, and leads today. Christ is risen and resides among his people. He has

> God is alive. God speaks, commands, and leads today.

not delegated his lordship to another. The Holy Spirit makes God's word of comfort and command an active power in our lives today. The Christian life is to be lived in the power of the Holy Spirit and under the guidance of the living word of God.

Perhaps I should deal with a possible misunderstanding at this point. Am I arguing that on every occasion where you are faced with an ethical decision, the Holy Spirit will whisper God's command in your ear or cause you to think it in your mind or feel it in your heart? Not exactly. This approach artificially separates the work of the Spirit in the life of the Christian from the Spirit's work in revealing the Word recorded in Scripture. It leaves us vulnerable to subjective fantasies in which we mistake our own shifting feelings for the Spirit's promptings. Scripture knows no such dichotomy. In Scripture, the word is always the "Word of the Spirit" and the Spirit is always the "Spirit of the Word." The Spirit is never pitted against

God's law as such but only against the "written code" (Rom 2:29; 7:6) or "works of the law" (Gal 3:3). Notice again the relationship between the Spirit and God's commands articulated by Paul in Romans 8:3,4: "And so he condemned sin in sinful man, in order that the righteous requirements of the law might be fully met in us, who do not live according to the sinful nature but according to the Spirit." Keeping the preceding cautionary note in mind, we continue with the theme of living the Christian life in the power of the Word and Spirit.

The very idea of the Christian life presupposes that we live in the Christian community, the church, the body of Christ. Here we worship, offer thanksgiving, love one another, and live in hope of God's future. Here we listen to the word of God. In the church we meditate on the Old Testament Scriptures, the teaching and example of our Lord Jesus Christ, and the apostolic teaching. In the church, the word of Scripture speaks, not as a dead letter, a document of history, but as the living word of God speaking here and now. The words of the commandments, "Honor thy father and thy mother," "Do not kill," "Do not commit adultery," resonate as concretely today as on the day when God first spoke them to Moses. Jesus' words of comfort, "Do not be afraid" (Luke 12:32), have power in themselves to do what they say, just as the words of a mother whispered in her child's ear comforts him. For the one who spoke, speaks, and, in the power of the Spirit, he becomes present again in his words. For Jesus said in the Great Commission: "Therefore go and make disciples of all nations, baptizing them in the name of the Father and of the Son and of the Holy Spirit, and teaching them to obey everything I have commanded you. And surely I am with you always, to the very end of the age" (Matt 28:19-20).

For the individual Christian, living a Christian life begins with acknowledging that God is God and obeying his command to worship him alone. It is premised on the attitudes of thanksgiving for the gift of creation and repentance for sin. It grows out of a life of prayer: "Thy will be done on earth . . . and lead us not into temptation" (Matt 6:19-13). If we are sincere in that prayer, we will listen to God's commands, we will ponder Jesus' teaching, and we will give ear to the apostolic teaching. If we have God's word stored up in our hearts and we seek the Spirit's guidance, we will know what God commands us to do when the time comes. When we are faced with an enemy, we will be able to hear God's command, "Love your enemies!" (Matt 5:44). When others tell us how much more convenient it would be to abort a baby rather than bring it into the world, we will be able to hear the Holy Spirit say above the confusion of the world, "Love your neighbor" and "You shall not kill." When we feel an illicit or perverted sexual passion rising in our flesh, we will not allow our minds to

> For the person led by the Spirit, the difference between worshiping God and playing God is clear and stark.

think up ingenious rationalizations for its indulgence. However complicated medical technology gets, we will be able to see the difference between letting God have a loved one he is calling home and speeding someone's death for our selfish purposes. For the person led by the Spirit, the difference between worshiping God and playing God is clear and stark.

Conclusion

This leads us back to MacIntyre's parable. Our semipagan or half-Christian contemporaries are confused about ethics. They are confused about ethics because they are confused about God. And they are confused about God because they refuse to obey God. Christians need not be confused, for our faith provides us with a full and consistent understanding of the world. Like Jesus and because of Jesus, "I know where I came from and where I am going" (John 8:14). We have no need to patch together bits and pieces of wisdom from here and there to find a way to get along in life. We have the incarnation of God's Wisdom as our head. We have the Living Word himself to show us how to live. We have the life-giving Spirit as our intimate guide. Let us listen to him and obey.

Notes

[1]Alasdair MacIntyre, *After Virtue: A Study in Moral Theory*, 2nd ed. (Notre Dame, IN: University of Notre Dame Press, 1984) 1-5. MacIntyre is one of the foremost contemporary moral philosophers. See also his *Whose Justice? Which Rationality?* (Notre Dame, IN: University of Notre Dame Press, 1988); and his *Three Rival Versions of Moral Enquiry: Encyclopaedia, Genealogy, and Tradition* (Notre Dame, IN: University of Notre Dame Press, 1990).

[2]For a provocative discussion of the ethical chaos of recent Supreme Court decisions, see *First Things* (November 1996). This issue can be found on the *First Things* web site at http://www.firstthings.com/ftissues/ft9611/articles/eodmaster.html. This journal, edited by Richard John Neuhaus, is the most influential American journal providing a Christian perspective on religion and public policy. A search of the back issues will reveal many helpful articles on abortion, homosexuality, and medical ethics. See also my essay, "Justice Kennedy's Rhetoric of Abortion Rights," on my web page at http://seaver.pepperdine.edu/religion/faculty/Highfield/mystery.htm. The Supreme Court case I am discussing in this article, *Planned*

Parenthood v. Casey, can be found at http://supct.law.cornell.edu/supct/html/91-744.ZO.html.

[3]This section summarizes, James Fieser, "Ethics," n.p. [cited December 2002]. Online: http://www.utm.edu/research/iep/e/ethics.htm. All quoted phrases and technical terms in this section are cited from Fieser. I did not put quotes around the very common terms used by Fieser. I borrowed the term "general ethics" from Karl Barth, *The Doctrine of God*, Vol. 2:2, in Church Dogmatics, ed. and trans. by G.W. Bromiley, J.C. Campbell, et al. (Edinburgh: T & T Clark, 1957) 525.

[4]See *Summa Theologica*, Q. LXII. Art. 1-4. You can find this text on-line at: http://www.newadvent.org/summa/206200.htm. The New Advent site has placed the entire *Summa* on-line and houses *The Catholic Encyclopedia*, which has to date 11,000 historical, ethical, philosophical, and theological articles. Mark this cite in your web browser.

[5]In this section, my debt to Karl Barth will be evident to anyone who has read the sections on ethics in his *Church Dogmatics*. See especially, *The Doctrine of God*, vol. 2. part 2, 509-781. See also Karl Barth, *The Holy Spirit and the Christian Life: The Theological Basis of Ethics*, trans. by R. Birch Hoyle (Louisville, KY: Westminster John Knox, 1993).

[6]The Protestant Reformers and their post-Reformation followers dealt with Christian ethics in the form of studies of the Ten Commandments. See, for example, the *Heidelberg Catechism* (1563). You can find it on-line at: http://pijnacker-nootdorp.gkv.nl/english/heidcate.htm. One of its authors, Zacharius Ursinus, wrote a commentary on the *Heidelberg Catechism*. His commentary on the Catechism's teaching on the Ten Commandments runs over 130 pages. See *Commentary on the Heidelberg Catechism*, trans. by Rev. G.W. Williard (Phillipsburg, NJ: Presbyterian and Reformed, n.d.) 488-618.

[7]See Otto Weber, *Foundations of Dogmatics*, vol. 1, trans. by Darrell L. Gruder (Grand Rapids: Eerdmans, 1981) 63-69. In this section, "Dogmatics and Ethics," Weber discusses the history of the relationship between theology and ethics, and gives reasons why they must not be separated.

[8]Dietrich Bonhoeffer, *Ethics*, ed. by Eberhard Bethge, trans. by Neville Smith (New York: Touchstone, 1995) 21.

[9]The work of the Romanian Orthodox theologian Dumitru Staniloae is permeated with the theme of how everything in nature and in God's revelation points us to God and draws us into the life of the Trinity. See his systematic theology, *The Experience of God*, ed. and trans. by Ioan Ionita and Robert Barringer (Brookline, MA: Holy Cross Orthodox Press, 1998).

[10]Augustine of Hippo, *Confessions*, trans. by R.S. Pine-Coffin (London: Penguin Books, 1961) 21.

[11]Consider, however, the advice Thomas à Kempis (AD 1380-1471) gave in his *The Imitation of Christ*. "What good does it do to speak learnedly about the Trinity if, lacking humility, you displease the Trinity? Indeed it is not learning that makes a man holy and just, but a virtuous life makes him pleasing to God. I would rather feel contrition than know how to define it. For what would it profit us to know the whole Bible by heart and the principles of all the philosophers if we live without grace and the love of God? Vanity of vanities and all is vanity, except to love God and serve Him alone" (cited February 8, 2003). Online: http://www.ccel.org/k/kempis/imitation/imitation.htm.

[12]In a concise and insightful section, Robert W. Jenson discusses six propositions on the Christian doctrine of Creation. See his book, *The Works of God*, vol. 2, Systematic Theology (New York: Oxford, 1999) 3-16. In addition, see his chapter on "Human Personhood" in the same volume, 95-111, for a good discussion of human freedom and other ethical fundamentals. For more on creation from nothing and its implications, see Colin E. Gunton, *The One, the Three, and the Many: God, Creation, and Culture of Modernity* (Cambridge: Cambridge University Press, 1993); and idem., *The Triune Creator* (Grand Rapids: Eerdmans, 1998).

[13]See Craig Gay's section entitled "Christian Hope as a Political Virtue" (73-78) in his excellent analysis of Christian belief in modern culture: *The Way of the (Modern) World: Or, Why It's Tempting to Live as if God Doesn't Exist* (Grand Rapids: Eerdmans, 1998).

[14]Dietrich Bonhoeffer makes this point repeatedly and with great power in his *Ethics*. His words are worth quoting extensively: "The knowledge of good and evil seems to be the aim of all ethical reflection. The first task of Christian ethics is to invalidate this knowledge. In launching this attack on the underlying

assumptions of all other ethics, Christian ethics stands so completely alone that it becomes questionable whether there is any purpose in speaking of Christian ethics at all. But if one does so notwithstanding, that can only mean that Christian ethics claims to discuss the origin of the whole problem of ethics, and thus professes to be a critique of all ethics simply as ethics.

"Already in the possibility of the knowledge of good and evil Christian ethics discerns a falling away from the origin. Man at this origin knows only one thing: God. It is only in the unity of his knowledge of God that he knows of other men, of things, and of himself. He knows all things only in God, and God in all things. The knowledge of good and evil shows that he is no longer at one with this origin.

"In the knowledge of good and evil man does not understand himself in the reality of the destiny appointed in his origin, but rather in his own possibilities, his possibility of being good or evil. He knows himself now as something apart from God, outside God, and this means that he now knows only himself and no longer knows God at all; for he can know God only if he knows only God. The knowledge of good and evil is therefore a separation from God. Only against God can man know good and evil" (21-22).

[15]First Corinthians 10:12-13 also supports my thesis: "So, if you think you are standing firm, be careful that you don't fall! No temptation has seized you except what is common to man. And God is faithful; he will not let you be tempted beyond what you can bear. But when you are tempted, he will also provide a way out so that you can stand up under it."

Bibliography

Barth, Karl. *The Doctrine of God.* Vol. 2. Pt. 2 of *Church Dogmatics.* Ed. and trans. by G.W. Bromiley, J.C. Campbell, et al. Edinburgh: T & T Clark, 1957.

Barth's chapter entitled "The Command of God" (509-781) is the best exposition of Christian Ethics I have ever read. He roots Christian ethics in the nature of God and contrasts his view with the major alternatives.

Bauckham, Richard. *God and the Crisis of Freedom: Biblical and Contemporary Perspectives.* Louisville, KY: Westminster John Knox Press, 2002.

In this new book Bauckham, of the University of St. Andrews in Scotland, argues that true human freedom can be attained only "by dependence, belonging, relationship, community, and—importantly and most controversially—divine authority" (quoted from the back cover of the book). This is a very important theme for ethics today.

Bonhoeffer, Dietrich. *Ethics.* Ed. by Eberhard Bethge. Trans. by Neville Smith. New York: Touchstone, 1995.

Bonhoeffer follows Barth's basic approach to ethics. He roots Christian ethics in the commands of God and shows how they apply to issues of life and death. If you cannot make your way through Barth, read this book.

Helm, Paul, ed. *Divine Commands and Morality.* New York: Oxford University Press, 1981.

This collection of essays from some of the foremost contemporary philosophers looks at the divine command theory from a philosophical perspective.

Jenson, Robert W. *Systematic Theology.* 2 Vols. New York: Oxford University Press, 1997–99.

Jenson's theology represents the very best of the recent Trinitarian thinking. In dialogue with the Church Fathers and contemporary Orthodox theologians, Jenson develops a theology that sees everything as coming from the Father, through the Son, and in the Holy Spirit. He understands the human person in light of the Trinitarian life of personal love among the members of the Trinity.

MacIntyre, Alasdair. *After Virtue: A Study in Moral Theory.* 2nd ed. Notre Dame, IN: University of Notre Dame Press, 1984.

In this work, moral philosopher Alasdair MacIntyre lays the groundwork for his alternative to the ethical chaos he finds in modern culture. Most useful is his analysis and critique of modern ethics.

Staniloae, Dumitru. *The Experience of God: Orthodox Dogmatic Theology.* 2 Vols. Trans. and ed. by Ioan Ionita and Robert Barringer. Brookline, MA: Holy Cross Orthodox Press, 1994–2000.

The work of Staniloae represents the best of contemporary Orthodox theology. He draws on the riches of the Orthodox tradition in explaining the Christian faith in a way understandable to modern westerners. His thought is permeated with a spirituality that makes it ethical through and through. If you want to read Orthodox theology, start with Staniloae.

Werpehowski, William. "Command and History in the Ethics of Karl Barth." *Journal of Religious Ethics* 9 (1981) 298-320.

This article helps explain some difficult aspects of Barth's ethics.

EDUCATION AND MORAL DEVELOPMENT

James Riley Estep, Jr., Ph.D.

It is obvious even to the casual observer that moral formation is a critical concern not only for the community of faith but for society and culture as well. Many of the best selling nonfiction books of the last decade address the concern for moral formation in children, particularly those by such authors as William Bennett and Robert Coles. Similarly, the moral confusion that is ordinarily present throughout our culture occasionally rises to the surface following a catastrophic human injustice or momentous social dilemma, and usually gives rise to questions such as, "What were they thinking?" "How can someone justify that kind of behavior?" "Where are their values?" Or, "And they call themselves religious! How?"

> It is obvious even to the casual observer that moral formation is a critical concern not only for the community of faith but for society and culture as well.

Nothing illustrates this more than the 2001 HBO special "Conspiracy." It is an historical docudrama regarding perhaps the most infamous meeting of the twentieth century. In a two-hour meeting on January 20, 1942, fifteen high ranking Nazi military, political, and economic representatives gathered to discuss the "Jewish question." Within a two-hour period the participants, sitting around a large meeting table in an exquisite home with storybook-like grounds, determined the fate of over six million human beings. The Jews were to be "evacuated," a comfortable euphemism for extermination. As one watches the drama unfold, you hear a full range of moral arguments for their attitudes, decisions, and actions.

Appeals to survival of their race, German nationalism, affirmations of the legality of their decisions (based on laws they themselves had written and enforced), the eventual historical vindication for their actions, and even appeals to the defense of the Christian faith typify the meeting's deliberations.[1] Once again, the same questions arise: "What were they thinking?" and "How can someone justify that kind of behavior?" These same questions are also present in our everyday life, typically as moral assumptions and more overtly during times of moral indecision and predicament.

This chapter is perhaps unlike others in this book. Whereas other chapters tend to address topics of ethical concern such as war, racism, abortion, or euthanasia; this chapter addresses a *process*. It will not seek to view educational issues through an ethical lens, such as rights to privacy (e.g., Family Education Rights and Privacy Act [FERPA]), race and affirmative action in higher education, nor will it endeavor to address the issues of economic inequities of the public school system or issues of religion's place in the public school classroom. While all of these are valid concerns, and even related to both ethics and education, the design of this chapter is simply different. This chapter will endeavor to comprehend the process whereby individuals form a moral sense. *How does education influence the formation of ethical individuals? Can it? What are its limitations?* In so doing, it will address the subject through four prominent questions to the Christian educator:

> *This chapter will endeavor to comprehend the process whereby individuals form a moral sense.*

- How do Christian educators understand morals?
- What are the various conceptualizations of how morals are formed?
- How can education facilitate moral formation? More specifically, can Christian education facilitate moral formation?
- How does moral development theory influence the practice of Christian education?

One underlying piece of our investigation into these matters will be the place of the Christian faith, and specifically Scripture, in moral formation. How does Christianity influence our understanding of morality? How does faith in Christ influence moral growth in the individual? How can education that is Christian aid in moral formation?

How Do Educators Understand Morals?
Ethics and Moral Development: Connecting Points

How does one define *morals*? What does it mean to *be* moral? How does one determine this? It is important to bear in mind that definitions always impose limitations. Without a sound concept of morality, it is impossible to understand how moral development occurs. Each of the four major theories of moral development contain within them an implied fundamental definition of morality, and hence each has its own self-imposed limitation on the subject. For example, behaviorists associate morality with behaviors, whereas cognitive theorists equate morality with moral reasoning or decision-making. Similarly, psychoanalytical theorists view morality as an internal, subconscious struggle for self-identity and mental harmony, whereas humanists see morality as an innate quality of being human, focusing on the moral potential within humanity. Hence, each of their subsequent approaches to moral development are going to reflect their definitions of morality. *So, how do Christian educators understand morals?*

> *Different views of moral development*
> 1. Behaviorist
> 2. Cognitive theory
> 3. Psychoanalytical
> 4. Humanist

Morality is not a monodimensional concept but rather is multidimensional. Christian educators have presented morality as having three interrelated dimensions: cognitive, affective, and behavioral.[2] Ted Ward, professor emeritus of both Michigan State University and Trinity Evangelical Divinity School, describes morality as a "bridge" consisting of "moral reasoning," moral will," and "moral strength" leading us from "moral truth" to "moral action."[3] The *moral reasoning* elements of morality have been described as moral judgments, choices, decisions, all of which reflect the mental or thinking aspect of morality.[4] One can readily see the connection between morality and knowledge or cognition in Scripture (Ps 119:34; John 13:7; Eph 2:12; Phil 4:9; Jas 3:17). Developmental theorists such as Jean Piaget, Lawrence Kohlberg, and Carol Gilligan represent models of moral development exclusively focused on this dimension.

Second, *moral affect* refers to the sense of valuing and character formation, addressing the affective domain. This is perhaps the most neglected aspect of moral formation. As Robert Cooper observes, "[Moral] formation is not only a matter of forming thought but is also *a matter of forming affect*, of forming feeling among a community of persons, of forming ourselves in accordance with a vision of the God, who, in Jesus, has made us friends, who has given us to each other as gifts."[5] While not addressing the subject of moral development, educational theorist David Krathwohl's learning taxonomy describes the third level of affect as "Valuing" which is "sufficiently consistent and stable to have taken on the characteristics of a belief or an attitude. . . . At this level, we are not concerned with the relationships among values but rather with *the internalization of a set of specified, ideal values*."[6] Scripture does indeed reflect such a moral affect (Gal 5:22; 1 John 4:7-8). Theorists such as Anna Freud, Erick Erikson, and Robert Coles would represent those advocating this dimension of moral development.

Finally, *moral behavior* refers to moral actions, the behaviors of an ethical person.[7] This is perhaps the most commonly held concept of morality, particularly in regard to children. Being "good" is a matter of having the proper and expected behaviors. Once again, Scripture seems to bear witness to the connection of morality to expected standards of conduct (Ps 15:1-4; Amos 5:11-12,21,22; Jas 1-2; Matt 25:31-40). For example, an individual's strong character "gives the power to do what one believes is right."[8] Hence, behavior is the exhibitor of both moral reasoning and moral affect. Understanding morality as three-dimensional paradigm provides a comprehensive concept of morality as being a matter of ethical cognition, affect, and behavior that is sound scripturally and consistent with the social sciences.

How Are Morals Formed?
Survey of Moral Development Theories

Bonnidell Clouse identified four main theoretical clusters on moral development, each representing a different approach to the subject: Psychoanalytical, Conditioning, Moral Potential, and Cognitive/Moral Reasoning.[9] The first approach, *psychoanalytical*, was proposed by Sigmund Freud and his successors. In it, morality develops through psychological conflict between the ego, superego, and the id, elements of the conscious and subconscious mind. Hence, moral development is a psychological process of creating mental harmony. *Conditioning*, favored by B.F. Skinner and subsequent behaviorist theorists, means that moral development occurs through external stimuli, and hence morality is understood as a behavioral reaction produced by an external stimulus in any given situation. Rather than an internalizing process, it is morality as a conditioned response to external stimuli. Humanist theorists, such as Carl Rogers and Abraham Maslow, regard the basis for morality as the *human moral potential*. Morals are regarded as innate to human beings, developing as one's fundamental and advanced needs are fulfilled, and results in one advancing toward self-actualization.

However, educators, Christian and otherwise, tend to lean more heavily on those theories that are allied more closely with theories of cognitive development, known as *cognitive-moral reasoning*. For example, in his treatment of "moral development" in the *Harper's Encyclopedia of Religious Education*, Donald Joy comments only on the cognitive-moral reasoning theories of developmentalists Jean Piaget and Lawrence Kohlberg.[10] This approach unites cognitive development with the advancement of moral decision-making. In so doing, educators are provided with familiar territory—human development—as a means of describing moral formation. Three main theorists represent the cognitive–moral reasoning approach to moral development: Jean Piaget, Lawrence Kohlberg, and Carol Gilligan (Figure 1).[11] This section will briefly summarize each of their theories and then provide a general critique of the cognitive-moral reasoning approach to moral development.

Figure 1: Moral Cognitive Development Models

Age	Piaget's Modes	Kohlberg's Levels	Gilligan's Levels
13+	Moral Autonomy	Level 3: Postconventional	Level 3: Postconventional Morality (interdependent concern for self and others)
13		Level 2: Conventional	Level 2: Conventional Morality (concern for others)
12			
11			
10		Level 1: Preconventional	Level 1: Preconventional Morality (concern for self)
9	Transitional Phase, both modes present		
8			
7	Heteronomy (Moral Realism)		
6			
5			
4			
3	"Pre" or "Proto" moral development; foundations for development being established		
2			
1			

Jean Piaget (1896–1980) postulated that "all morality consists in a system of rules, and the essence of all morality is to be sought for in the respect which individuals acquire for those rules."[12] For Piaget, two general modes or stages of moral cognition were present in children between the ages of six and twelve: *heteronomy*, or moral realism, and *moral autonomy*. In the first stage, rules are immutable and external, established by an outside authority figure, such as parents, teachers, civic authorities, or religious authorities. However, the second stage of moral development signals the internalization of these rules. The rules are adopted and accepted as one's own internal morality, and rather than being obeyed simply as the orders of a superior; they are accepted as a necessity for maintaining relationships and community life.[13]

Lawrence Kohlberg (1927–1987) based his moral development theory not on the acquisition of rules, but on the moral reason behind human behavior. He did not ask, "Is an action moral or immoral?" nor "Is a motive moral?" or even ask "*Why* is something moral or immoral?" Rather, he asked, "At what level of reasoning does one justify or explain one's moral decisions?" Right and wrong, moral or immoral are categories that simply do not apply to Kohlberg; rather, it is simply a matter of level of moral reasoning. To ascertain this, Kohlberg used moral dilemmas to facilitate moral reasoning in a given moral predicament. It was not the answer provided by the subjects that made it right or wrong, but why they believed it to be right or wrong. For example, "Is it right or wrong to steal?" Kohlberg offers no answer. However, he would argue that the reason to steal or not to steal would reflect a different level of moral reasoning, but the act, motive, or reason would not be regarded as a moral or immoral regardless of the response. Hence, no judgment was made on the decision or the outcome, but simply on the presumed level of moral reasoning used to make this decision.

Kohlberg proposed three basic levels of moral reasoning, with each level composed of two stages. Level I moral reasoning, preconventional morality, bases moral decision on a personal criteria. On this level, right or wrong is determined by the personal implications of the decision. For example "Should I cheat on the ethics exam?" Once again, for Kohlberg this is not a yes or no subject, rather it is the reason provided for the decision. "Yes, because I need to pass the exam!" or "No, because I'd get caught and be in trouble!" Notice the active word in both is "I," right and wrong determined by the individual on the basis of the positive or negative effect on the individual.[14]

The second level, conventional morality, contains the elements associated with Level 1, *but* another line of thought is added. Level 2 maintains that moral decisions are dictated by an outside authority, i.e., laws, rules, guidelines are adhered to to gain favor from another. The individual focus in Level 1 is replaced by a concern for being regarded as "good" or "bad" by an authority figure, such as parents, teachers, or pastor; seeking the affirmation of a respected individual. For example, "Should I cheat on the ethics exam?" Such a dilemma might be answered in the affirmative, "Yes, think of what my frat buddies would think of me!" or in the negative, "No, think of what Professor Tanner would think of me." In short, the key to right and wrong is the opinion of a respected other and the desire to gain approval from them.[15]

Kohlberg's Level 3, postconventional morality, is a level of individual moral autonomy. Unlike the previous two levels, which were always dependent upon the response or affirmation of another individual, moral decisions at level three are based on individually applied principles. These principles are beyond personal self-interest (Level 1) or laws (Level 2), calling for selflessness and reasoning beyond the limitations of the law. For Kohlberg, the ultimate moral principle was *justice*, a personal commitment to fairness to all regardless of personal loss/gain or legalities. "Should I cheat on the ethics exam?" "No, because regardless of the impact on my grade or what Dr. Tanner thinks of me, it is simply wrong. It is a matter of personal honor and trust between the professor and students, and the integrity of the institution is more important than my grade." Or, an admittedly more difficult answer to conceive, "Yes, because regardless of the possibility of getting caught or what Dr. Tanner thinks of me, if I do, I'll let down the whole class and reflect poorly on Dr. Tanner's abilities as an instructor." Level 3 almost always carries with it a sense of inner conflict between the universal principles and the lower levels of moral reasoning (i.e., self-interest and permissible requirements). It represents a laying aside of the thoughts of personal gain or acceptance in order to follow a higher ethical principle.

Carol Gilligan (1936-) was Kohlberg's assistant, and applied his research methodology to the study of women's moral development, which Kohlberg had inadvertently omitted from his studies.

"Men feel secure alone at the top of the hierarchy, securely separate from the challenge of others. Women feel secure in the middle of a web of relationships; to be at the top of a hierarchy is seen as disconnected."[16] Without dismissing Gilligan too rapidly, her proposed levels of moral reasoning in women parallel the same levels for Kohlberg's moral development in men. Perhaps the one significant distinction is that the ultimate moral principle for women was not justice, as with men, rather it was caring. However, justice and caring have one common thread that does signal a moral tone: The ultimate moral principle is to regard others before one's self, whether that is expressed in terms of justice or caring.

Assessment of Cognitive-Moral Reasoning Theories

Can Christian educators use these theories? Is this approach to moral development alien to the Christian community? While this section will endeavor to provide a general critique of the cognitive-moral reasoning approach to moral development, it will tend to focus on Kohlberg's theory since his is considered the most advanced and the most widely recognized. This approach to moral formation does find some warrant in Scripture. As previously noted, the connection between knowledge and moral behavior is evident in the Scriptures (Ps 119:34; John 13:7; Eph 2:12; Phil 4:9; Jas 3:17), as well as many evangelical theological tenets such as revelation (both special and general) and the *imago dei*. Similarly, Duska and Whelen comment that, "If the highest level of moral reasoning is on a principled level, and if the highest principles are justice and love, one is hard pressed to find a more consistent statement of such principles than in the New Testament."[17] Perry Downs affirms Kohlberg's "compatibility with Scripture," explaining "clearly Scripture makes appeals on all three levels of moral development," i.e., conditional promises, appeals to authority, or universal principles. Figure 2 contains a catalog of Scriptures that generally reflect the moral development theory presented by Kohlberg and Gilligan.[18] Hence, such theories as presented by Piaget, Kohlberg, and Gilligan may be *critically applied* to Christian education without a loss of theological integrity.

Figure 2: Kohlberg and Gilligan's Moral Development Theory and Scripture

Kohlberg/Gilligan's	Kohlberg's Stages	Scripture References
Level 1 Preconventional Ages 4–10	Stage 1: Punishment Orientation	"I will bless those . . . I will curse those . . ." (Gen 12:3); Gen 6:11; 9:11; Deut 28:1-3, 8,11,15-16,20; 2 Chr 7:14; Job 4:7-9, Matt 6:14-15.
	Stage 2: Naïve Reward Orientation	
Level 2 Conventional Ages 10–13	Stage 3: Good-boy/Good-girl Orientation	"Thus saith the Lord . . ." "It is written . . ." Exod 20:12; Ps 19:7-8; Matt 16:24, 1 Cor 10:32–11:1; Eph 6:1-3; Col 3:20; 1 Thess 5:22.
	Stage 4: Authority Orientation	
Level 3 Postconventional Ages 13+	Stage 5: Social Contract Orientation	"I delight in loyalty rather than sacrifice, and in the knowledge of God rather than burnt offerings" (Hos 6:6; cf. Matt 9:13; 12:17); Isa 11:9; Micah 6:8; Matt 22:36-40; Mark 2:27; Luke 4:18; 10:25-27; John 14:15; Rom 7:6; 13:8; 1 Cor 13:13; Gal 5:14; Col 1:15-20.
	Stage 6: Universal Moral Principles	

However, evangelicals, such as those mentioned above, have several cautions regarding the wholehearted, uncritical acceptance of the cognitive-moral reasoning approach to moral development. While numerous authorities have critiqued Kohlberg's approach to moral development, two general criticisms seem to rest at the heart of their concerns. First is the severe limitation placed on this definition of moral development. While morality must include motive or decision-making, as this approach suggests, morality cannot be limited exclusively to the issue of moral reasoning. As previously noted by Perry Downs, morality is multidimensional, including more than just the cognitive reasoning process of moral decision-making.[19] Hence, while all morality does reflect a moral decision, there is more to morality than the decision itself. If Kohlberg's definition is flawed, or at least incomplete, then his entire approach is similarly limited in its ability to address the subject of moral development comprehensively. A possi-

> *Morality cannot be limited exclusively to the issue of moral reasoning.*

ble reason for the more comprehensive understanding of moral formation is the addition of theological perspective with those provided from the social sciences. Hence, moral formation cannot be conceived as consisting of just a process of cognitive-mental reasoning, but must include the dimensions of moral affect and behavior.

The second general criticism is philosophical in nature.

Kohlberg's moral development theory is driven not simply by empirical evidence, but ideological concerns.[20] For example, Kohlberg's rejection of religion as a positive influence on moral development was *not* done on the basis of empirical evidence or social science precedent.[21] Similarly, Iris Cully notes that "The Christian could not affirm, with level [stage] five thinking, that the social contract is an ultimate form of morality," since Christianity is often countercultural and called to a higher allegiance.[22] One factor which is emphasized by Christian educators, but minimized by non-Christians, is the role of religious belief in the formation of morals. However, the development of morals and faith are intertwined in the Christian approaches to development. As Perry Downs comments, "The church has always been concerned with morality because it is an important corollary to faith."[23] Additionally, due to an evangelical concept of the nature of humanity (e.g., human brokenness), Christian educators tend to present moral development more as a process of *formation* than one of a sequential, automatic developmental process innate to human beings, such as physical development or structuralism in cognitive development. In short, Kohlberg's basis for moral decisions is incomplete for the Christian educator.

How Can Education Facilitate Moral Formation?
Moral Education for Ethical Formation

The idea that ethics and education are related is both ancient and contemporary. Moral education, character formation, and more recently values clarification all reflect attempts to facilitate moral development through the educational process. What has in effect changed over the centuries, and particularly within the twentieth century, is the basis for morality and our understanding of its development. Michael Peterson of the University of Notre Dame comments that, "In a sense, the debate is over the basis of moral education," arguing that Christian education has a unique basis in Christian theism, Scripture, "historical reflections of the believing community," and humanity's common experience.[24] Arthur F. Holmes comments that the appeal to authority in traditional, secular moral education is typically made to "com-

> The idea that ethics and education are related is both ancient and contemporary.

mon morality," conscience, institutionalization, duty, or natural law.[25] What is indeed the more sufficient basis for morality and moral education is an appeal to God as Revealer, through both His special instruction (Scripture) and His creation (general revelation).[26]

Toward an Education for Christian Moral Formation

Moral formation has always been an objective of Christian education. "Christian morality is clearly a morality in response to God. . . . It thus follows that Christian religious education must not isolate the doctrinal and the moral dimensions of the faith but handle both dimensions together as it initiates people of any age into an intelligent informed understanding of their faith."[27] Christian educators have not simply been critical or silent on moral development theory. Several prominent educators have formulated models of moral development within the context of a Christian worldview. Figure 3 contains a summary of the five leading Christian approaches to moral development.

Figure 3: Christian Approaches to Moral Formation

Theorist	Metaphor/Idea	Description
Donald Joy	"Pilgrimage"	Movement from terror and fear of taboos toward reverence and respect of God; via law, principles, and ultimately values. Three levels of moral formation are egocentric (self-centered), heterocentric (law centered), and Logocentric (Christ-centered).
Gabriel Moran	"Religious Imagery"	Virtue, care, character, and community; religious tradition is held by a religious community, which has a community narrative and life, and hence provides moral exemplars to influence moral formation.
Craig Dykstra	"Visional Ethics"	Moral formation requires a perspective beyond one's own life (hence Kohlberg's dilemmas are not sufficient for moral formation), which is provided by God's revelation to provide reliable moral insights, moral integrity, and a sense of oughtness.
Bonnidell Clouse	Synthesis of the four prominent moral development theories	Moral formation is a process of conflict, action, knowledge, and, human potential, as described by modern theorists and exemplified in the Bible, but rather than just one process it is accomplished through a synthesis of all four.
Ted Ward	"Bridge"	Moral truth results in moral action, and they are connected (i.e., the bridge) by moral reasoning (cognition), moral will (volition), and moral strength (character).

The following section is designed to present a model of moral formation from a Christian perspective, including the nature of ethics and morality as well as how education can facilitate moral formation. It will address this subject in three parts: (1) the basis for Christian ethics and morality, (2) the process of moral formation, and finally (3) an educational agenda designed to advance moral formation (cognitive, affective, and behavioral).

An underlying principle of Christian moral formation is our acknowledged dependence on the influence of the Holy Spirit in the life of the individual to aid in the process of moral formation. He is influential within the individual prior to conversion (John 16:8), in conversion (Acts 2:38; 1 Cor 2:10-16; Rom 8:1ff), and after conversion (1 Cor 12:1ff; 2 Cor 13:14; Gal 5:2; Eph 4:3; Phil 2:1). As Ferré describes him, the Holy Spirit challenges the spiritual *status quo*, "behind all pedagogy is the prompting of the Spirit."[28] While spirituality and morality are indeed two different concerns, they are not independent from one another.

> *An underlying principle of Christian moral formation is our acknowledged dependence on the influence of the Holy Spirit in the life of the individual to aid in the process of moral formation.*

The Basis of Christian Ethics and Morality

As previously noted, it is often the basis of ethical and moral formation that separates Christian educators from their counterparts. For example, Kohlberg views the subject of morality as a matter of decision-making or moral reasoning, but this is only one dimensional. Ethics are more than the mental process of the decisions; their scope includes affect and behavior. Ethics and morality imply the presence of norms. The pertinent question becomes *who establishes the norms? From where do they come?* For Christian educators, ethics and morality are not simply a human or societal product; rather, they are *dependent* on God. Figure 4 endeavors to illustrate the nature of Christian ethics and morality. In it, ultimately, ethical standards are attributed to God, revealed to humanity through creation and Scripture. Morality is a process of internalizing these ethical principles (see Eph 6:6, "doing the will of God from the heart," Matt 5:1ff). Several theo-

> *Ethics and morality imply the presence of norms. The pertinent question becomes who establishes the norms?*

logically informed frameworks for ethics and morality have been presented by the community of faith, based on a variety of central Christian tenets, such as follows: Creation and Conversion,[29] Sanctification,[30] and as previously mentioned the *imago dei* and Revelation. Hence, the general concept of Christian morality is the

> *The general concept of Christian morality is the integration of God-given principles into one's life, and ultimately society and culture.*

integration of God-given principles into one's life, and ultimately society and culture. This integration likewise implies part of the concern for the process of moral formation.

Figure 4: Morals and Ethics

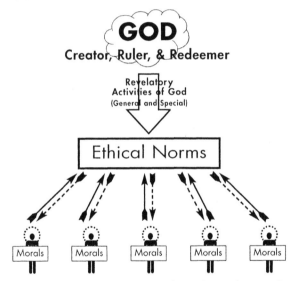

Humanity created as the imago dei, with moral potential

The Process of Moral Formation

Scripture does present a metaphor of *growth* to denote moral formation, and hence seems to favor the idea of an outside force leading the formation rather than an innate process of development within the individual (1 Cor 2:1ff; 13:11; Heb 5:12-14; Phil 2:14; Eph 4:15). Hence, the notion of a purely *developmental* approach to morality would be insufficient to the broader growth or formation approach presented in Scripture. The New Testament calls us to a *transformational morality*, such as Romans 12:2 (NASB), "And do not be conformed to this world, but be transformed by the renewing of your mind, that you may prove what the will of God is, that which is good and acceptable and perfect." While this transformation is similar to what has been advocated by Piaget, Kohlberg, or Gilligan, it differs in that moral formation is not formless, having a pattern of individual or societal design. Rather, it is the integration of a transcendently prescribed pattern. Individuals must progress beyond their own ego (self) past a societal or relational concern (often expressed in laws) and on toward the transcendent ethical principles universally applicable to everyone, the God-given ethical frameworks. Donald Joy's model of Christian moral formation would apply in this instance, as one moves from such moral "controls" as taboos, terror, and fear through an approach to morality typified by law (e.g., the Decalogue), then principles (e.g., the Greatest Commandment), and ultimately values (e.g., faithfulness, steadfastness, love, righteousness) that reverence (rather than terror) and respect (rather than fear) God.[31] According to Joy we progress through this through stages:

> *Moral formation is not formless; it is the integration of a transcendently prescribed pattern.*

- Egocentrism—centering morality on self interest, e.g., taboos
- Heterocentrism—centering morality on external authorities, e.g., laws
- Logocentrism—centering morality on the principles/values of the Logos (Christ).

Hence, it is a matter of using moral reasoning, affect, and behavior to integrate theologically derived ethical principles into one's life.

An Educational Agenda to Advance Moral Formation

This section will address the factors that aid and advance the process of moral formation first by discussing strategies for cognitive, affective, and behavioral moral formation. *Cognitive moral formation* is best advanced through facilitating moral reasoning. Christian educator Catherine Stonehouse comments that there is a correlation between the level of thinking and moral reasoning.[32] Figure 5 demonstrates this relationship, noting that as a child and adolescent's cognitive abilities increase, so increases their capacity to understand and reason through moral dilemmas. Ultimately, moral reasoning requires the capacity of abstract thought, which is not attained until early adolescence. Hence, one factor that contributes to moral formation is engaging the minds of students to think.

Figure 5: Cognition and Moral Reasoning
Based on Catherine Stonehouse, Patterns in Moral Development (Eugene, OR: Wipf and Stock, 2000) 63.

Level	Level of Thinking	Description	Moral Reasoning
1	Abstract	Children's actions equal their thoughts, reactions to environment	Morality is behavioral, reactionary, reflected in actions
2	Pre-logical	Children's thoughts are unorganized, isolated thoughts, unaware of significance of event sequences	Morality is behavioral, situational; no consistent moral reasoning or action.
3	Action	Children think in logical, concrete terms that are egocentric	Morality is cognitive, sense of absolute right and wrong, but based on personal consequence.
4	Concrete	Children think in logical, concrete terms, but are able to think outside the box of personal experience	Morality is cognitive, sense of right and wrong, but not as absolute; able to understand the actions of others and base morality beyond personal consequence.

How does one use the Bible in determining ethical or moral decision, affect, or behavior? Charles Cosgrove's *Appealing to Scripture in Moral Debate* notes five "rules" of using the Bible in moral reasoning:[33]

- *The Rule of Purpose*—"the purpose (or justification) behind a biblical moral code carries more weight than the rule itself."
- *The Rule of Analogy*—"Analogical reasoning is an appropriate and necessary method for applying scripture to contemporary moral issues."
- *The Rule of Countercultural Witness*—"greater weight to countercultural tendencies in scripture than to those tendencies that echo the dominant culture of their time."
- *The Rule of Nonscientific Scope*—"scientific (or 'empirical') knowledge stands outside the scope of scripture."
- *Moral-Theological Adjudication*—"moral-theological considerations should guide hermeneutical choices between conflicting plausible interpretations."

While an appeal to authority for moral clarity appears to be a Kohlberg Level 2 approach to moral development, in fact it is different. By appeal to Scripture as described above, it is not a matter of following an external law to gain favor, but rather to internalize and increase our cognitive attention on moral questions.

Christian education happens when moral decision-making, personal faith, tradition, and experience come together, which can be done through instruction and providing an encouraging context for moral formation. Downs identifies two kinds of moral teaching: (1) "teaching moral behavior," focusing on actions, which is of short-term value; and (2) "teaching moral content," meaning teaching right-and-wrong (Decalogue, John 14:15), which seems to have a longer influence.[34] *How can I teach so as to facilitate moral formation?* The following are some teaching strategies for advancing moral formation:

- Utilize biblical instruction, precedent, and examples in moral discussion.
- Avoid providing simple answers to moral dilemmas.
- Clarify and analyze moral issues.
- Reflect critically on moral reasoning (sources of authority, line of reason, base issue).
- Cite biblical, historical, personal, and practical examples of moral solutions.
- Distinguish facts, opinions, and judgments on moral issues.
- Develop moral principles reflecting Christian beliefs and commitments.
- Consider consequences and implications of moral choices.

Affective moral formation is best facilitated through relationships in healthy contexts. Catherine Stonehouse comments that moral formation is fostered when the atmosphere is one of respect, belonging, justice, and openness.[35] Downs, once again, speaks of the influence of participation in a just or moral community, typically the church or Christian institutions.[36] "The things you have learned and received and heard and seen in me *practice these things,* and the God of peace will be with you" (Phil 4:9, NASB). It is in these contexts that the previously mentioned moral relationships are formed, and hence are critical for the formation of moral affect with one's self, others, society, and ultimately God (see Figure 6).

Figure 6: Contexts of Moral Relationships

Adapted from Tom Wallace, "Values and Spirituality: Enhancing Character Develpment and Teaching/Learning Processes for a New Millennium," *Journal of Christian Education* 43.1 (2000) 44.

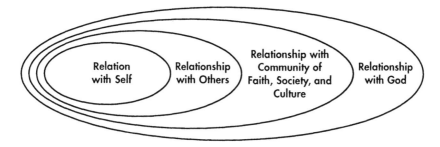

Finally, the affective dimension of *personal faith* is a potent influence on moral formation. Faith focuses us on the future, hope for what is to come, and a genuine sense of trust. Stonehouse comments that Kohlberg did acknowledge that religion or faith was one possible reason to be moral, and that Coles "came to believe that religious faith contributed greatly to that [moral] strength."[37] While faith and morality are two distinct concerns, faith is the broader context in which moral formation can occur.

Behavioral moral formation is advanced through *human relations*. Mentoring and peer relationships provide an intimate context in which moral formation may occur. Downs speaks of the value of "modeling morality," citing 1 Corinthians 15:33, "Do not be deceived: 'Bad company corrupts good morals.'"[38] Family, neighborhood, school, and church can all provide positive relationships. Perhaps an extension of this factor is that of *moral exemplars* that serve as models for not only behavior but also moral reasoning and moral affect. In so doing, the Church can be an aid to parents and other caregivers in moral formation as a means of additional and supportive nurture.[39] Historically, this has been the general approach to moral education in the church and school, with a variety of individuals to serve as models from throughout the Bible and history (allowing for culturally specific exemplars to be selected).

How Does Moral Development Theory Change the Practice of Christian Education?

The Benefit of Moral Formation in the Practice of Christian Education

What are the implications of moral development theory and Christian education? How does the Christian educator make use of the insights provided by moral development theory? In this conclusion, the possible implications of moral development theory will be presented in relation to Christian education in the classroom (curriculum, teaching-learning, teacher-student relations) and the community of faith.

Moral Formation and the Classroom

Moral reasoning does place an emphasis on the "why" of morality. In Christian education, far too often the "why" is omitted from our considerations. The content of instruction is stressed but not the process of assimilating God's truth into the life of the student. Hence, morals are often taught as moral precepts or codes, but without any internalization on the part of the student. As Nels Ferré critiques, "The direct learning of social, moral, and spiritual wisdom is seldom applied by the learner because it has not been personally appropriated. Education suffers from a chronic indigestion of unassimilated propositional truths."[40]

> *In Christian education, far too often the "why" is omitted from our considerations.*

Teachers could readily use dilemmas as a means of facilitating cognitive moral formation by simply encouraging students to ask the "why" related questions to morally complex decisions or situations. Unlike Kohlberg's laboratory contexts, students could be presented with moral situations that are relevant to their actual lives. Similarly, students would be encouraged to provide theologically based rationales for moral decisions, hence aiding in the integration of faith and moral formation, and necessitating the use of Scripture in Christian learning and instruction. Even within the context of the classroom or group itself, students could develop community rules

> *"Education suffers from a chronic indigestion of unassimilated propositional truths."*

with biblical/theological rationales for each of them. Thus, the Scriptures become a relevant part of the student's daily life. All of this concern over instruction and learning also hinges on the understanding of the teacher-learner relationship, advancing moral affect and behavior. Teachers must understand that

> *Teachers must serve not only as exemplars of Christian moral behavior and character, but provide an example of moral reasoning.*

students are in the process of moral formation, with students functioning at various levels within a single class. Similarly, teachers must serve not only as exemplars of Christian moral behavior and character, but provide an example of moral reasoning.

Moral Formation and the Faith Community

The Church as a community of faith can provide an excellent context for the formation of morals. Through relationships, instruction, service, and worship individuals can be presented a moral vision or image (such as that presented by Moran and Dykstra), so as to promote moral formation. As such, moral development theory has provided insights into the approach and practice of ministry within congregations.

Clouse comments that, "Problems within the church may occur because Christians at one stage or level are unable to understand Christians at a different stage or level."[41] Similarly, Jack Pressau, in his book *I'm Saved, You're Saved . . . Maybe?* uses the insights gained from Kohlberg to address a wide variety of ministry issues, including its possible contributions to our understanding of "Christian maturation" and proposes ministry interventions at the preconventional, conventional, and postconventional level to facilitate the maturation process.[42] He maintains that the "ideal Christians are those who function in thought, and to a degree, in behavior, at all moral Levels at once."[43]

Moral development theory also reminds the Christian community of the differences between gender-related ministry. For example, Stonehouse makes use of Gilligan's approach to moral development in women so as to provide a perspective upon congregational ministry that is more conducive specifically to moral formation in Christian women.[44] How many ministries or programs that are designed for the "whole church" are in fact reflective of only the male Christian and not the female Christian? How might a moral appeal be received differently by males and females in a congregation?

Donald Joy even notes how Kohlberg's levels of development can provide insight into conflicts over the interpretation of Scripture, since the reader enters on a particular level and tends to interpret passages along given parameters, e.g., the Level 1 reader approaches the Bible with superstition, while the Level 2 sees it as being doctrinaire, and the Level 3 reader sees affirmations of truth. Hence, Christians may differ on their interpretation of Scripture due to an intrinsically personal reason (i.e., level of moral development) rather than an innate difficulty with the biblical text.[45] Moral formation is a critical concern for Christian educators, both in theory and practice. By gleaning insights from both Scripture and the social sciences, we are better able to fashion a more complete understanding of moral formation, as well as provide improved ministry to congregations and individuals.

Notes

[1]"Conspiracy" was based on a set of notes from the meeting taken by Dr. Martin Luther that were discovered in 1947. The notes were discovered by American investigators preparing for the Nuremburg trials in which some of the meeting's participants were on trial. The evidence contained in these notes provided sufficient evidence to convict them of war crimes and crimes against humanity.

[2]Cf. Catherine Stonehouse, "Moral Development," *Evangelical Dictionary of Christian Education* (Grand Rapids: Baker, 2002) 484-488.

[3]Ted Ward, *Values Begin at Home* (Wheaton, IL: Victor Books, 1989) 108-109.

[4]Perry Downs, "Promoting Moral Growth and Development," *Street Children* (Monrovia, CA: MARC, 1997) 66.

[5]Robert M. Cooper, "Moral Formation in the Parish Church," *Anglican Theological Review* 69.3 (1987) 283.

[6]David R. Krathwohl, Benjamin S. Bloom, and Bertram B. Masic, *Taxonomy of Educational Objectives: Handbook 2—Affective Domain* (White Plains, NY: Longman, 1964) 180 [emphasis added].

[7]Ibid.

[8]Stonehouse, "Moral Development," 488.

[9]Cf. Bonnidell Clouse, *Teaching for Moral Growth* (Downers Grove, IL: Victor/Bridgepoint, 1993).

[10]Donald Joy, "Moral Development," *Harper's Encyclopedia of Religious Education* (New York: Harper and Row, 1990) 425-426. It should be noted that Stonehouse, ("Moral Development") while providing a broader perspective on moral development than the cognitive model does devote the majority of her article to the cognitive model.

[11]Cf. James Riley Estep Jr. and Alvin W. Kuest, "Moral Development," *Introducing Christian Education: Foundations for the 21st Century*, ed. by Michael Anthony (Grand Rapids: Baker, 2001) 73-82.

[12]Jean Piaget, *The Moral Judgement of the Child* (New York: Free Press, 1965) 13.

[13]Cf. Ronald Duska and Mariellen Whelan, *Moral Development: A Guide to Piaget and Kohlberg* (New York: Paulist Press, 1975) 8-11.

[14]Lawrence Kohlberg and P. Turiel, "Moral Development and Moral Education," in *Psychology and Educational Practice*, ed. by G. Lesser (Glenview, IL: Scott Foreman, 1971) 415.

[15]Ibid.

[16]Carol Gilligan, *In a Different Voice* (Cambridge, MA: Harvard University Press, 1982) 42.

[17]Ronald Duska and Mariellen Whelan, *Moral Development: A Guide to Piaget and Kohlberg* (New York: Paulist Press, 1975) 99.

[18]Cf. Estep and Kuest, "Moral Development," 73-82.

[19]Downs, "Promoting," 66

[20]Paul Vitz, "The Kohlberg Phenomenon," *Pastoral Renewal* 7.8 (1982) 64-65.

[21]Cf. James Michael Lee, "Christian Religious Education and Moral Development," in *Moral Development, Moral Education, and Kohlberg*, ed. by Brenda Munsey (Birmingham, AL: Religious Education Press, 1980) 333-336.

[22]Iris V. Cully, *Christian Child Development* (San Francisco: Harper and Row, 1979) 86.

[23]Perry Downs, *Teaching for Spiritual Growth* (Grand Rapids: Zondervan, 1994) 95.

[24]Michael L. Peterson, *With All Your Mind: A Christian Philosophy of Education* (Notre Dame, IN: University of Notre Dame Press, 2001) 143.

[25]Arthur F. Holmes, *Ethics: Approaching Moral Decisions* (Downers Grove, IL: Inter-Varsity, 1984) 57-63.

[26]Ibid, 63-67.

[27]John E. Greer, "Moral and Religious Education: A Christian Approach," *Christian Perspectives for Education*, ed. by Leslie Francis and Adrian Thatcher (Leominster, England: Gracewing, 1990) 332-333.

[28]Nels F.S. Ferré, *A Theology for Christian Education* (Philadelphia: Westminster, 1967) 146.

[29]Samuel F. Rowan, "Testing Validity: Moral Development and Biblical Faith," *Moral Development Foundations*, ed. by Donald Joy (New York: Abingdon Press, 1983) 111-137.

[30]Joel Brondos, "Sanctification and Moral Development," *Concordia Journal* (October 1991) 219-439.

[31]Donald Joy, ed., *Moral Development Foundations: Judeo-Christian Alternatives to Piaget/Kohlberg* (New York: Abingdon Press, 1983) 33-34.

[32]Catherine M. Stonehouse, *Patterns of Moral Development* (Eugene, OR: Wipf and Stock, 2000) 63.

[33]Charles H. Cosgrove, *Appealing to Scripture in Moral Debate* (Grand Rapids: Eerdmans, 2002) 3.

[34]Downs, "Promoting," 73-75.

[35]Stonehouse, "Moral Development," 67-85.

[36]Downs, "Promoting," 75-76.

[37]Stonehouse, "Moral Development," 488.

[38]Downs, "Promoting," 75.

[39]Cf. Donald B. Rogers, "Christian Formation: The Neglected Mandate," *Religious Education* 96.3 (1991) 427-440.

[40]Nels F.S. Ferré, *Christian Faith and Higher Education* (New York: Harper and Brothers, 1954) 80.

[41]Clouse, *Teaching*, 281.

[42]Jack Renard Pressau, *I'm Saved, You're Saved . . . Maybe?* (Atlanta: John Knox Press, 1977) 103-111.

[43]Ibid., 111.

[44]Catherine Stonehouse, "The Church: A Place Where All God's Children Grow?" *Christian Education Journal* 13.1 (1992) 33-48.

[45]Joy, *Foundations*, 33-34.

Bibliography

Clouse, Bonnidell. *Teaching for Moral Growth*. Wheaton, IL: BridgePoint Books, 1993.
   Excellent text presenting a comprehensive Christian model of moral development.

Duska, Ronald, and Mariellen Whelan. *Moral Development: A Guide to Piaget and Kohlberg*. New York: Paulist Press, 1975.
   A Guide to Piaget and Kohlberg seeks to introduce the reader to the moral development theories of these two leading theorists and critically apply them to education in the church.

Joy, Donald M., ed. *Moral Development Foundations: Judeo-Christian Alternatives to Piaget/Kohlberg.* Nashville: Abingdon Press, 1983.

A multiauthored volume that critiques Kohlberg's theory of moral development from an evangelical perspective (Wesleyan) and presents a Christian alternative to the formation of morals.

Kuhmerker, Lisa, ed. *The Kohlberg Legacy for the Helping Professions.* Birmingham, AL: Doxa Books, 1991.

A multiauthored book that favorably views Kohlberg's theory of moral development, with application made to education, religious education, and counseling.

ETHICS IN A POSTMODERN WORLD

Mark S. Krause, Ph.D.

As I put the finishing touches on this chapter, the United States has begun the Second Gulf War with Iraq. By the time you read this, this war will doubtlessly be past and probably renamed. President George W. Bush issued a strong statement before the war began, warning the President of Iraq, Saddam Hussein, that he must flee the country within forty-eight hours to avoid his own death. Bush also advised the armed forces of Iraq not to resist the coming American and British armed forces.

What does this have to do with postmodernity and ethics? Surprisingly, the unlikely postmodernist Bush included a very post-modern ethical warning to the Iraqi troops. He cautioned, "War criminals will be punished. And it will be no defense to say, 'I was just following orders.'"[1] Many postmodern thinkers would reluctant-ly nod their heads in agreement. In the postmodern age we are called to make ethical decisions on something more substantial than simply *following orders.*

This way of thinking is very threatening to evangelical Christians, most of whom believe themselves to have been resistant to the influ-ences of postmodernity. After all, isn't the ethical side of our faith a matter of determining God's standards through study of the Bible, and then maintaining this code of conduct in our lives? It is not for us to determine what is right and what is wrong, we say. We live lives that are pleasing to God by following God's orders, don't we?

Defining Ethics

Ethics, simply put, is the study of what constitutes right and wrong behavior. Such study usually hopes to arrive at rules of con-

> Ethics, simply put, is the study of what constitutes right and wrong behavior.

duct defining proper actions for those subject to the rules. Sometimes, however, making a list is the easiest part. The hardest part is determining the basis whereby a valid list can be made. Ethicists have identified two primary categories for ethical systems.[2] They are:

1. **Consequential.**[3] This approach says that an action is judged to be good or bad on the basis of its outcome. If the outcome is favorable, the action was good. If the outcome is unfavorable, the action was bad. The huge question, of course, is how to achieve consensus as to what is a favorable outcome and what is an unfavorable outcome. This is one of the sticky issues of postmodern ethics and will be discussed in further detail below.

2. **Deontological.**[4] In contrast to the consequentialist approach, a deontologicalist ethic would determine right and wrong behavior on the basis of some absolute standard. Thus, in any situation that requires an ethical choice, that choice is made on the basis of what one *ought to do*, and this action should be consistent and not vary according to different circumstances. The raging issue with deontological ethics advocates is how to agree upon an absolute standard that would determine one's duty. This, too, will be discussed at greater length below.

Simply put, the *consequential* approach says, "I will do that which will be good." The *deontological* approach says, "What is good, I will do."

But why be ethical? Assuming we are able to come up with some standard for determining what is ethical behavior, what compels us to follow this standard? Michael Josephson outlines five possible reasons for being ethical:

- There is *inner benefit*. Virtue is its own reward.
- There is *personal advantage*. It is prudent to be ethical. It's good business.
- There is *approval*. Being ethical leads to self-esteem, the admiration of loved ones, and the respect of peers.

- There is *religion*. Good behavior can please or help serve a deity.
- There is *habit*. Ethical actions can fit in with upbringing or training.[5]

Cursory analysis notes that all of these lean toward a consequentialist approach to ethics. Josephson cannot bring himself to say that ethics are based on following an absolute standard because it is true. The closest he comes is in saying that ethical behavior may seem to please or serve a deity for a religious person or that it may be habitual because of upbringing.

Defining Postmodernity

Postmodernity's definition has been hotly debated for the last decade. Many authors have merely seen postmodernity as a reaction to the Enlightenment and its offspring, the modern era. In this analysis, postmodernity becomes a type of antithesis to modernity (as the Enlightenment was a reaction to medieval thinking). Postmodernity *is* everything modernity *is not*. This type of analysis demands that the inquirer thoroughly understand modernity in order even to begin to understand postmodernity. The result is that many discussions of postmodernity focus more on the characteristics of modernity than postmodernity. While such an approach may have been adequate (or even necessary) in the 1990s, it wears thin as we move further into the twenty-first century. It is akin to saying that the best way to understand love is to do a rigorous study of hate.

While it may be too early to be exhaustive or conclusive in proposing a definition of postmodernity, I would like to give six contrasts to serve as hooks on which the hats of postmodernity may hang.[6] While there is some overlap in these contrasts, each presents an important aspect of postmodernity.

Fluid rather than Foundational

A first contrast is that postmodernity is *fluid* rather than *foundational*. That is, while it is possible to build a small philosophic system for an individual or community, it need not share universal, unquestioned principles with all other systems. Moreover, building a universal system is an improbable and probably impossible task. It is also possible to live a life perfectly oblivious to history, even recent history. The typical thinking is, "My life is not controlled by the past,

> *Postmodernity is a web of belief more than a belief structure.*

but by the present. I am not bound by tradition, no matter how old and glorious it may seem to others. I may have some foundational principles within my system, but I may also change them when they no longer serve me. My system must be fluid." All parts of the system are important and related. Such a system has been described as a *web of knowledge* (or *belief*) rather than a *building*. There are no foundations for a spider web. There are anchor points, but there are several of these and none is individually crucial for the integrity of the web. If part of the web is damaged, it can continue to function and be modified at the same time. But these modifications will affect the entire web, not just a section.[7] The parallels to the Internet as "World Wide Web" are obvious and appropriate.

The ramifications of nonfoundationalism are profound. In the postmodern world unquestioned foundational principles of knowledge are not possible, not desirable, and not necessary. Even in the so-called "hard sciences" there is a growing recognition of the inadequacy of a foundationalist approach to everything. An example will illustrate this trend. I once spoke at a church in a college town and mentioned that relativism and the rejection of absolutes had become rampant upon most university campuses, permeating every academic discipline. Afterward this claim of universal relativism was challenged by a church member who was a physics professor at the local college. Although I knew I was in way over my head, I asked him to give me an unquestioned,

> *In the postmodern world unquestioned foundational principles of knowledge are not possible, not desirable, and not necessary.*

absolute truth from the field of physics. His answer? "There is no fixed place in the universe." As soon as these words left his mouth, he realized the irony of his statement, and quickly closed the conversation. His answer was the equivalent of a philosopher saying that the only absolute truth of philosophy is that there is no such thing as absolute truth. In other words, the nonfoundationalist perspective says, "I base my system on fluidity rather than foundation."

Furthermore, in the postmodern world there is not simply a rejection of absolute truth as a foundation, there is a rejection of objective truth. There is a growing recognition that we cannot do science objectively, whether that be experimentation with chemical reactions or interpretation of texts, because we always come to any scientific task with pre-understandings, biases, and personal agendas. Postmodernists see the category of "objective truth" as a chimera foisted upon the western world as a necessary part of the Enlightenment agenda.[8] The postmodern person is not surprised, therefore, that crashing jet airliners into the twin towers of New York City caused outpourings of national grief in

> In the postmodern world there is not simply a rejection of **absolute** truth as a foundation, there is a rejection of **objective** truth.

America and dancing in the streets in Palestinian cities. Can the same event cause sorrow and celebration? Well, of course, says the postmodernist, it's all a matter of your point of view. Stanley Fish represented postmodernity well in his *New York Times* editorial published a few weeks after September 11th:

> How many times have we heard these new mantras: "We have seen the face of evil"; "these are irrational madmen"; "we are at war against international terrorism." Each is at once inaccurate and unhelpful. We have not seen the face of evil; we have seen the face of an enemy who comes at us with a full roster of grievances, goals and strategies. If we reduce that enemy to "evil," we conjure up a shape-shifting demon, a wild-card moral anarchist beyond our comprehension and therefore beyond the reach of any counter-strategies.[9]

Multiconnective rather than Sequential

A second contrast is that postmodernity is *multiconnective* rather than *sequential*. My friend, Milton Jones, illustrates this in two ways. First, Jones says that we have a couple of generations who grew up watching Sesame Street and its "number for the day." Rather than learn numbers as part of a sequential counting scheme (1, 2, 3, 4 . . .) we learned to value each number as an individual regardless of its place in the sequence. We don't need to go from 1 through 2 to get to 3, because while 3 might be today's number, yesterday's number might have been 7 and tomorrow's number might be 5. Second, Jones points to the way video and computer games are played. Most experienced players are not concerned with advancing to the end of the game by successively beating each level. They are likely to obtain a code that lets them go from level one to level twelve right away, because "that's where the good stuff is." But they are likely to go back and play the other levels later.

Linear thinking was the rationalistic hallmark of the Enlightenment and of modernity. Sequential planning and implementation were methodologically assumed in the twentieth century for entities ranging from the central government bureaus of the Soviet Union to the elder boards of the local church. We were told to "plan the work and work the plan." Yet these plans seemed to produce disaster as regularly as they produced success: witness the continually ruinous five-year plans in the twentieth-century's planned-economy countries. Contrast this with current business models where "long-range" planning may be for the next 12–24 months, where careers are developed using "networking" as much as accomplishment, where strategic alliances may be more important than strategic planning, and where the flexibility to react and adjust quickly to changing markets is prized far above institutional stability, traditions, and history.[10]

This characteristic of postmodernity should not be mistaken for lack of organization and sheer randomness. The organization may be nonsequential, but the connections will be valid. If no foundation is recognized, there is no obvious starting place or ending place. We may organize to fit our needs at a given time and reorganize on the fly.

Holistic rather than Compartmental

A third contrast is that postmodernity is *holistic* rather than *compartmental*. The ability for individuals to keep job, school, family, and church in nice tidy and separate packages is no longer possible or desirable. Postmoderns often have the perception that the church is rampant with hypocrites, and they despise "phoniness" and "phonies." They long for authenticity in relationships and in people. From the postmodern perspective, when we compartmentalize aspects of our lives, we live in a state of constant hypocrisy. We live separate, conflicting lives. Postmoderns see no need to do this. Loss of confidence in absolutes lessens any fear of social stigma or disapproval. If I am not really a Christian believer, why pretend? I will not hide parts of my life simply because they might offend someone else.

The greatest social error in the postmodern world is not offensive or vulgar behavior, but to show disrespect. And any criticism may be viewed as disrespect. Offensive behavior is a problem for the offended, not the offender. We are called to accept and tolerate others without being judgmental. Our acceptance must be unconditional and entire. It must be holistic and sincere. So while a holistic emphasis may be the enemy of phoniness and hypocrisy, it may also be used to justify behaviors long considered offensive or even taboo in the Western world.

> *The greatest social error in the postmodern world is not offensive or vulgar behavior, but to show disrespect. And any criticism may be viewed as disrespect.*

Spiritual rather than Scientific

A fourth contrast is that postmodernity is *spiritual* rather than *scientific*. A common misconception of postmodern Generation X is that it is either nonreligious or antireligious. This is incorrect. Generation X is spiritually more sincere than the Boom Generation and spiritually deeper than the Builder Generation. The difference is that this spirituality is not necessarily oriented toward Christianity or the institutional church. An anonymous Internet citizen voiced this orientation when he said:

> I believe in a God. But not to the point of heaven and hell and Christ on a cross. Not anymore. I've found that I am much happier with myself when I try and do what is right for me. . . .

Those who despair, mistakenly thinking there is a lack of spirituality of the rising postmodern generations, might have their eyes opened by spending some time analyzing the music videos presented on MTV and other cable channels.[11] The mix of spirituality and sexuality one encounters may be quite disturbing, but that does not negate the spiritual dimension of these influential and popular media.[12] One is surprised at the common practice of music video actors wearing crosses, which are often large and prominent. There is a spiritual hunger that overshadows any rationalistic or scientific bent. An example is found in the lyrics of the David Gray song, "The Other Side," a dirgelike paean crying out for spiritual peace in the face of depression and suicidal thoughts. Gray sings:

> Meet me on the other side,
> Meet me on the other side,

I'll see you on the other side,
See you on the other side.[13]

When assessing Enlightenment science, postmodern citizens are generally unimpressed with scientific and technological advances. Technological progress is seen as inevitable and probably economically conspiratorial. That computer that impressed you so much ten years ago is now useful only as a doorstop. Science and technology are not the answers to our problems; they solve and create problems at the same time.

Personal Story rather than Metanarrative

A unifying factor in most communities has historically been some type of *metanarrative*. This is a comprehensive explanation for why things are the way they are, particularly why humans beings find themselves in the human condition. Traditionally, such metanarratives had religious roots and were seen as originating from a divine source (the *metanarrator*). In European history the church became the arbiter and interpreter of the metanarrative, the Bible. The Bible, as seen through the eyes of church tradition, provided answers to all questions of human origins, human purpose, and the ultimate goals of humans.

Even with the rise of scientific methodology and its rejection of the supernatural, there was still concern for a metanarrative. In the twentieth century Stephen Hawking, Carl Sagan, and others attempted to provide a comprehensive naturalistic explanation for all things. In this pursuit a divine metanarrator was disallowed.

In postmodernity even the metanarrative is called into question. Mark E. Dever analyzes this shift by noting that in postmodernity

> . . . there is not only no metanarrator, but there is no meta-narrative either. There is only my narrative. . . . The self in postmodernism is unable finally to be judged by any other, except in terms of power. The self becomes the ultimate; the self is divinized.[14]

One unknown Internet contributor named Lavonda put it this way:

> What the hell's going to church for? These days you've got to take religion in your own hands.

So we find that each person must have his or her own story, a tale in which that person is the central figure, the hero, the victim, but usually not the villain. I narrate my story. I do not need God to do that for me. I do not have to make sense or explain everything, only explain it in a way that makes sense to me. I use the Bible to help me tell my story sometimes, but not as a source for the plot or to explain the meaning of my life. Such is the postmodern perspective.

Interiorizing rather than Externalizing

With Descartes and his agenda of methodological doubt, the locus of authority in the Western world shifted from external sources (such as the church or the Bible) to the individual. Authority became interiorized, internal. Because of rational method we had the ability, even the obligation to doubt everything. This doubting right trumped any type of external claims to authority in the realm of ideas. No one could force me to believe when I still harbored doubts.

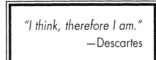

"I think, therefore I am."
—Descartes

This characteristic of Enlightenment modernity has been continued in postmodern thinking, with one important difference. In modernity one was always required to subject truth claims to the canons of rationality. Ideas and arguments needed to be consistent and coherent to be valid. Graeme Codrington has explained the goals of modernity as an "algorithm of explanation." According to Codrington modernity proceeded in this fashion:

- The more we study, the more we learn.
- The more we learn, the more we understand.
- The more we understand, the more control we have.
- The more control we have, the better the world we can create.[15]

But this agenda has been rejected in postmodernity. In postmodernity, rationality is treated with distrust. After all, weren't the Nazis the most coldly rational people in the history of humanity? So the postmodern continues to doubt, to be suspicious, but feels no obligation to be logically consistent. Postmodern belief systems may contain glaring contradictions and inconsistencies, but the one holding these beliefs is answerable to no one but herself or himself. My job, as an outsider, is to respect and tolerate everyone else's beliefs, no matter how wacky or dangerous.

⇢⊨⊙ ⊙⊨⊰

As we approach the area of ethics more specifically, we should remember these six contrasts. Postmodernity is:

- Fluid rather than Foundational
- Multiconnective rather than Sequential
- Holistic rather than Compartmental
- Spiritual rather than Scientific
- Personal Story rather than Metanarrative
- Interiorizing rather than Externalizing

With these things in mind, we are ready to discuss the possibility of ethics in this postmodern milieu. The first step, however, is not to look at postmodern systems of ethics but rather to ask whether or not postmodernity even allows for the possibility of ethics. The primary issue in this regard is to explore the postmodern concept of good and evil.

Evil in Postmodern Perspective

Classical Christian doctrine has usually defined *evil* as rebellion against God. This is the theological lesson of the Garden narrative, the human desire for the knowledge of good and evil in disobedience to God's express command to the contrary. But postmodernity either rejects or neglects metanarrative and external sources of authority as the basis for truth claims. What, then, is evil in the postmodern world?

Michel Foucault

Certainly one of the most influential thinkers in the development of postmodernity was the French philosopher and historian, Michel Foucault. For Foucault the central element to his philosophy was the necessity of freedom in all things and from all external coercive influences. Foucault asked, ". . . what is ethics, if not the practice of freedom, the conscious practice of freedom. . . . Freedom is the ontological condition of ethics. But ethics is the considered form that freedom takes when it is informed by reflection."[16] This emphasis on personal freedom is essential to the postmodern trend to interiorize all authority.

Therefore, for Foucault concepts of truth (and therefore evil) are never absolute. They are imposed by elements of the society which is in power and are used to maintain such power. The ultimate virtue for Foucault is "care of self." Evil, then would seem to be anything that hindered one's "care of self," or the personal neglect of such. Foucault sees this as standing in opposition to Christianity on the one hand, but ultimately in harmony with Christianity. That is, ". . . in Christianity salvation is attained through the renunciation of self." But, ironically, according to Foucault the bottom line in Christianity is ". . . achieving one's salvation [which] is also a way of caring for oneself."[17]

Many postmodern thinkers have followed Foucault in this. One critic, Roger Shattuck, has noted that "Without limits, our actions could have no naughtiness."[18] This expresses the construct of many postmodern thinkers who have redefined what traditionalists called "sin" as "transgressing." Transgression is the identification of boundaries (rules) and then moving beyond these boundaries. For Foucault and others, such "transgressing" is empowering and invigorating. Those who would repress an individual's potential for transgressing are deniers of freedom. In this the biblical concept of "sin" is transformed into a positive term and any notion of evil is completely stood on its head.[19] Such a conclusion would have doubtlessly pleased Foucault!

Jean Baudrillard

Jean Baudrillard's *The Transparency of Evil* is one of the most thorough postmodern explorations of the issue of evil. It was first published as *La Transparence du Mal* in 1990 and translated into English in 1993. Baudrillard sees absolute values of good and evil as no longer viable.

> Once again we are put in mind of microphysics: it is as impossible to make estimations between beautiful and ugly, true and false, or good and evil, as it is simultaneously to calculate a particle's speed and position. Good is no longer the opposite of evil . . .[20]

Baudrillard sees good/evil as a type of Moebius strip, opposites yet a dependent unity.[21] Both will change as a society's norms and needs change and develop. But there is no independent sense of evil or of good. Each depends on its opposite for its existence. Furthermore, Baudrillard no longer believes that evil can be overcome by good. It doesn't work that way any more.

> [T]here is no longer such a thing as a strategy of Good against Evil, there is only the pitting of Evil against Evil—a strategy of last resort.[22]

Baudrillard does see a difference between good and evil. He explains it this way:

The Good consists in a dialectic of Good and Evil. Evil consists in the negation of this dialectic. . . .[23]

In this view Baudrillard joins the general postmodern consensus that evil is a limiting of freedom, a roadblock to the possibility of transgressing boundaries. As long as current standards of good and evil are in competition, the dialectic continues freely. In Baudrillard's presentation of evil, there are no longer absolute standards for evil. Evil is not the crossing of boundaries, the breaking of rules. Such rules no longer exist. Baudrillard now speaks of evil in terms of a virus, whether in the human body or in a computer network. Evil/virus is the infection or invasion of the unwanted other.

Reactions to Postmodern Concepts of Evil

Shattering world events such as the atrocities of September 11, 2001, have caused lively discussion and challenge to this postmodern concept of evil as limiting personal freedom. Some still resist any attempt to label people or actions in any absolute way. For example columnist Alexander Cockburn is able to do no better than observe that after 9/11 "Evil" is the current term for "awfulness beyond our comprehension."[24] In other words, evil is a matter of perspective, and ours may be limited and inadequate.

Conservative pundit Kathleen Parker editorialized in response to the death of *Wall Street Journal* reporter Daniel Pearl in Pakistan. In this essay Parker explores the question as to whether or not the President of the United States is justified in labeling other nations or people as "evil." Parker has a conservative agenda to defend the President but gives a clear presentation of evil from a postmodern perspective (perhaps unwittingly). Notice some of her statements:

> Anyone who has followed Pearl's story knows his bio by now. To the words already delivered, I would add only this: Pearl was killed by evil. *Not* by people with legitimate political concerns; not by "folks" who are at cultural odds with the United States; not by disenfranchised victims of American imperialism. But by evil.

Parker's analysis of this evil gets specific in the article. She believes that the United States has the moral authority to label other countries as evil because they deny freedom.

What gives us moral authority in the war against terrorism

isn't the fact that we're bigger and stronger. Our authority comes from the fact that we protect and nurture freedom. In human history, that's a biggie.[25]

So she becomes the flip side of the Foucault coin. Foucault saw evil as the limiting of evil. Parker sees good as the protection and promotion of freedom. Postmodernity's view of evil has triumphed.

Postmodern Ethics

Consider long-time Utah Jazz star Karl Malone and his flying elbows. The NBA rulebook states that an elbow that makes contact above the shoulders is ground for immediate ejection of a player. Yet Karl Malone has made a career out of intimidating other players with elbows to the head, sometimes with major injuries. Question: after years of throwing elbows, but not being penalized, *is Karl Malone breaking the rules?* Are there any rules?

Is identification of ethical behavior possible in the postmodern world? If there are no absolutes, and all claims to truth or authority may be arbitrarily doubted, where can we find a basis for ethics?

If we follow our stated contrasts that characterize postmodernity, we can shape the contours of what a postmodern ethical perspective might be. It should be fluid, multiconnective, personally holistic, spiritually related, part of one's personal story, and based on

> *Is identification of ethical behavior possible in the postmodern world if there are no absolutes?*

interiorized authority. We can quickly note that this mix disallows a truly deontological basis for ethics, at least from a traditional, religious source. As postmodern spokesman Michel Foucault said, ". . . most of us no longer believe that ethics is founded in religion."[26] It is also worth noting that there is a general hostility toward ethics among some postmoderns. As one Internet denizen quipped, "Ethics is about the restrictions of freedom."

Richard Rorty

American Richard Rorty, who represents an important stream of postmodern thought, finds a need for ethics and morals. In Rorty's case, however, it is reasonable to simply use the ethical system that is basic to one's cultural tradition. Rorty is willing to use the basic Judeo-Christian ethical system of America, because this is his tradition. In this he describes himself as a "freeloading atheist."[27]

This approach meets several of the characteristics of post-modernity outlined above. In particular, it bows to the requirement of interiorized authority. Rorty does not particularly recognize the authority of traditional Judeo-Christian (biblical?) ethics. He has simply exercised his own freedom and personal authority to opt for this system. He, therefore, brings a nonfoundationalist approach to loot and exploit an ultimately foundationalist system.

> As a "freeloading atheist," Rorty brings a nonfoundationalist approach to loot and exploit an ultimately foundationalist system.

This answer to the problems of ethics in the postmodern environment is both intellectually lazy and disturbing because of its temporary nature. As American society distances itself more and more from any connections to a system of ethics derived from Scripture, where will Rorty go? Rorty seems a likely target for David Tracy's observation that ". . . postmodern thinkers often seem, at best, ethically underdeveloped."[28]

Zygmunt Bauman

The postmodernist who has done the most focused work in the area of ethics is Polish sociologist Zygmunt Bauman.[29] According to Bauman, one of the characteristics of late modernity is that traditional sources of moral authority (rules, principles, commandments) have collapsed. Postmodern ethics is thus, to use Bauman's phrase, "morality without ethical code."[30] Bauman calls us to return to a position of unconditional responsibility to our fellow humans, minus the crutch of a set of rules determined by ethical experts.

But can we be ethical without rules? How will we recognize ethical behavior without standards? Are we left sharing the future with the potential Iraqi war criminals, where (as President Bush stated), ". . . it will be no defense to say, 'I was just following orders.'" Bauman does have a rule, however. He calls for unconditional responsibility toward others. As popularly phrased, we are called to treat all others with respect and dignity. This "Golden Rule" philosophy certainly has Judeo-Christian roots (Matt 7:12, cf. Lev 19:18).

Friedrich Nietzsche

To some, Bauman sounds suspiciously like protopostmodernist Friedrich Nietzsche's claim of an ultimate virtue. In the nineteenth century Nietzsche dismissed the authority of society to make pro-nouncements concerning ethical behavior. "That which an age con-siders evil is usually an unseasonable echo of what was formerly considered good."[31] Yet after dismissing such traditional rules as a constantly moving target, Nietzsche proclaimed, "What is done out of love always takes place beyond good and evil."[32] So there are no rules, but don't forget rule #1: Always be motivated by love.

Aside from the inconsistency of this position, Nietzsche's def-inition of "love" should terrify Christian believers. Remember that Nietzsche was also the philosophic basis for Nazi Germany's agen-da of eugenics and ethnic genocide. In Nietzsche's last great work, *The Antichrist*, he said:

> What is good?—Whatever augments the feeling of power, the will to power, power itself, in man.
>
> What is evil?—Whatever springs from weakness.
>
> What is happiness?—The feeling that power *increases*—that resistance is overcome.
>
> Not contentment, but more power; not peace at any price, but war; *not* virtue, but efficiency (virtue in the Renaissance sense, *virtu*, virtue free of moral acid).
>
> The weak and the botched shall perish: first principle of *our* charity. And one should help them to it.
>
> What is more harmful than any vice?—Practical sympathy for the botched and the weak—Christianity. . . .[33]

So our greatest act of love for "all the botched and the weak" [*allen Missratenen und Schwachen*] is to put them out of their misery and euthanize (kill) them. This is a very strange love, even in the post-modern context.

Other Voices

Recently the sports world has had furious discussion concern-ing Pete Rose and his aspiration to be inducted into Major League Baseball's Hall of Fame. Rose was banned from baseball because of allegations that he placed wagers on his team, the Cincinnati Reds, while he was the manager. So although he holds the record for the most base hits in a career, he is not eligible to receive the ultimate acknowledgment of this feat, the Hall of Fame. Those who approach this issue unemotionally realize that Rose has violated the one car-dinal principle of competitive sports: you cannot allow gambling on games by those who have the power to influence the outcome of those games. To do so destroys the core belief of baseball fans, namely that teams win games fair and square, that outcomes of games are not predetermined. Rose apparently did this, and has refused to admit it or show any sort of contrition. An editorial appearing in the *Seattle Times* had this to say about the Rose affair:

> Any decent tale of contrition comes with a lesson to be passed on to young fans. Here is the one taking shape: Rules are flexible, based on income, achievement and connections.
>
> The lesson is, pray for the blessings of robust athletic skills. Physical gifts and special aptitudes might translate into academic dispensations in high school, the burying of assault charges in college and the profitable restoration of a reputation in adulthood.
>
> Better yet, keep the Hall of Fame for those who excelled at the sport and did not disgrace the game.[34]

In effect the editorial writers are lamenting the postmodern world's approach to ethics. They want to say, "We have a rule. You cannot gamble on your own team." But the system doesn't seem to work that way any more, because "rules are flexible." Ethical boundaries are flexed by reason of money, ability, and status.

If there is any emerging consensus, I would describe it like this.

- Ethical behavior must be approached consequentially.
- I am expected to respect other individuals in all that I do and say, but this respect will be evaluated by each person.
- Respect may have various expectations in different relationships.

David Tracy has phrased it like this:

> The real face of postmodernity, as Emmanuel Levinas sees with such clarity, is the face of the other, the face that commands "Do not kill me," the face that insists, beyond Levinas, do not reduce me or anyone else to your grand narrative.[35]

Consider also the words of Adrian Mihalache, the editor of the web journal, *spark-online*.

> The main figures of cyberspace—the cyber-surfer who explores the Web, the cyber-smith who builds up its places and founds its institutional sites, and the cyber-evangelist

who promotes ideas, invites attention, and lures passers-by—are no longer the stable, coherent and rational selves of the Modern School, but the petulant, playful, multicentered, disembodied 'spirits' of postmodernism. They do not recognize such thing[s] as 'universal truth' and reject the belief that reason and science offer a stable foundation for knowledge and ethical behavior.[36]

Paul Feyerabend puts it more bluntly when he says,

> . . . there is only *one* principle that can be defended under *all* circumstances and in *all* stages of human development. It is the principle: *anything goes* [emphases in original].[37]

A Biblical Response to Postmodern Ethics

To live in a world that celebrates "anything goes" is ultimately self-destructive. It is not only postmodern, it is postethical. For the Christian believer, this approach is inadequate and cannot be accepted. A Christian worldview, if based on the Bible, need not be tied to the rationalistic mind-set of the nineteenth and twentieth centuries, but there are certain cardinal principles that are essential. As Leonard Sweet has written, "We need to admit the problem of absolutist thinking without giving up the belief in absolutes."[38]

> "We need to admit the problem of absolutist thinking without giving up the belief in absolutes."

The attempt of postmoderns to develop a consequential ethic based on respect for individuals and individuality is not completely foreign to the Bible. We are called to treat our fellow men and women with care, justice, and respect. Where this differs is at the level of motivation. Above, we noted five reasons offered by Michael Josephson for being ethical. All of these fail from a biblical perspective for one simple reason: they leave God out. Even Josephson's suggestion that there might be a religious reason for being ethical goes no further than to imply that this may serve a delusional need to please a (nonexistent?) deity. The biblical reason for respecting others is that each person has been created in the image of God (cf. Gen 9:6).

It is for others in this volume to deal specifically with biblical material related to the issue of ethics. However, I would like to offer a few observations on postmodernity and the Bible. Nearly three millennia ago the prophet Isaiah said this:

> Destruction is certain for those who say that evil is good and good is evil; that dark is light and light is dark; that bitter is sweet and sweet is bitter. Destruction is certain for those who think they are wise and consider themselves to be clever (Isa 5:20,21, NLT).

Ancient but timeless words. We are in the postmodern world whether we like it or not. Not everything about this is bad, but in the area of ethics, postmodernity offers nothing but disaster for Christians. Furthermore, a Foucaultian who sees evil as any attempt to control what was once called "sin" or "transgression" is not even within hearing distance of the gospel. In the end it is the job of the Holy Spirit to convict the world of sin.

> And when he comes, he will convince the world of its sin, and of God's righteousness, and of the coming judgment (John 16:8, NLT).

A ray of hope in the postmodern context comes from the spiritual hunger of many people today. They are left high and dry by the technology and the overhyped consumerism of our culture. They flounder in a stormy, bottomless sea of ethical choices with no solid rocks to save them. They are like the author of Ecclesiastes, who looked back at his life and said, "Anything I wanted, I took. Anything I wanted to do, I did . . . and all of it was meaningless, a chasing after the wind" (Eccl 2:10-11, my paraphrase). Even the thoroughgoing postmodern may be open to the gospel when his or her feelings of alienation become overwhelming.

> *A ray of hope in the postmodern context comes from the spiritual hunger of many people today*

We offer a truth that cannot be doubted: God loves us. He loves us so much that he was willing to have his only Son die for us. He loves us so much that he took the initiative to restore a relationship that we messed up. That was good news in the first century and is good news in the twenty-first century.

Notes

[1]The full text of this speech may be found at "Iraq: Denial and Deception," the White House web site, accessed March 19, 2003, http://www.whitehouse.gov/news/releases/2003/03/20030317-7.html.

[2]While many handbooks of philosophy or ethics discuss these two approaches, a useful, nontechnical summary may be found in the chapter "The Ethics of Being" by Cheryl Bridges Johns and Vardaman W. White, in *Elements of a Christian Worldview*, ed. by Michael D. Palmer (Springfield, MO: Logion Press, 1998) 286, 287, 289.

[3]Consequentialism is also known as utilitarianism or as a teleological approach to ethics. While utilitarianism carefully defined is a subset of consequentialism, both are teleological in method.

[4]As with consequentialism, some ethicists use different names for this approach. Sometimes it is referred to as nonutilitarianism or nonconsequentialist. It has also been called obligationalness or duty-based ethics.

[5]Michael Josephson, "Making Sense of Ethics," from the Josephson Institute of Ethics web site, http://www.josephsoninstitute.org/MED/MED-1makingsense.htm, accessed March 19, 2003.

[6]Obviously these contrasts pit postmodernity against modernity to some degree. So much for consistency!

[7]The postmodern model of knowledge as a web or net probably originated with Harvard philosopher W.V.O. Quine in the 1950s. For an excellent presentation of Quine's theory and others who have advanced the web-of-knowledge model see Nancey Murphy, *Beyond Liberalism & Fundamentalism* (Valley Forge, PA: Trinity Press, 1996) particularly chapter 4, "Epistemological Holism and Theological Method," 85-109.

[8]See Philip D. Kenneson, "Can the Christian Faith Survive If Belief in Objective Truth Is Abandoned? A Reply to John Castelein," *Stone-Campbell Journal* 2 (Spring, 1999) 43-56.

[9]Stanley Fish, "Condemnation without Absolutes," *New York Times* (October 15, 2001).

[10]An interesting manifestation of this postmodern phenomenon is the recent shift in the North American Christian Convention to become "The Connecting Place," recognizing that networking is more key to career success than "how-to" seminars on church growth methodology. This may be observed even in the new name for the NACC's web site, www.nacctheconnectingplace.org.

[11]In my "Global Issues" class (a capstone course for our General Education component) we did this last semester, and I can testify that I learned a great deal from MTV analysis as assisted by my wonderful students.

[12]The best exploration of the spirituality of Generation X and of music videos can be found in Tom Beaudoin, *Virtual Faith: The Irreverent Spiritual Quest of Generation X* (San Francisco: Jossey-Bass, 1998).

[13]Full lyrics are found at http://www.lyricsspot.com/song.php?s=24656.

[14]Mark E. Dever, "Communicating Sin in a Postmodern World," in *Telling the Truth: Evangelizing Postmoderns*, ed. by D.A. Carson (Grand Rapids: Zondervan, 2000) 142.

[15]Graeme Codrington, "Postmodernism," from the Internet site http://www.geocities.com/athens/pantheon/3675/graeme.htm, accessed March 21, 2003.

[16]Michel Foucault, *Ethics: Subjectivity and Truth*, vol. 1, Essential Works of Foucault 1954-1984, ed. by Paul Rabinow, trans. by Robert Hurley et al. (New York: The New Press, 1994) 284.

[17]Ibid., 285.

[18]Roger Shattuck, *Forbidden Knowledge* (New York: St. Martin's Press, 1996) 28.

[19]See Charles Colson, "How Evil Became Good," *Christianity Today* (August 9, 1999) 80.

[20]Jean Baudrillard, *The Transparency of Evil: Essays on Extreme Phenomena*, trans. by James Benedict (London: Verso, 1993) 5-6.

[21]See ibid., 43.

[22]Ibid., 139.

[23]Ibid.

[24]Alexander Cockburn, "Why more journalists are being exposed to attack," *The Seattle Times* (February 28, 2002).

[25]Kathleen Parker, "Journalist's death a lesson in evil," *The Seattle Times* (February 26, 2002).

[26]Michel Foucault, *The Foucault Reader*, ed. by Paul Rabinow (New York: Pantheon Books, 1984) 342.

[27]See the discussion of Rorty and his proposal for ethics in Douglas Groothuis, *Truth Decay: Defending Christianity against the Challenge of Postmodernism* (Downers Grove, IL: InterVarsity, 2000) 187 ff.

[28]David Tracy, "Theology and the Many Faces of Postmodernity," *Theology Today* 51 (April 1994) 107.

[29]See Zygmunt Bauman, *Postmodern Ethics* (Oxford: Blackwell, 1993).

[30]Ibid., 31.

[31]Friedrich Nietzsche, *Beyond Good and Evil*, trans. by Helen Zimmern (New York: The Modern Library, n.d.; German original, 1885) IV:149.

[32]Ibid., IV:153.

[33]Friedrich Nietzsche, *The Antichrist*, trans. H.L. Mencken. German original published 1895. Mencken translation published 1920. Found at **http://www.fns.org.uk/ac.htm**, section 2. I am struck by the parallels to Nietzsche in

the archvillain of the Harry Potter books, Lord Voldemort. See the words of Voldemort's mouthpiece, Professor Quirrell in J.K. Rowling, *Harry Potter and the Sorcerer's Stone* (New York: Scholastic, 1997), 291.

[34]"Charlie Liar," *The Seattle Times* (January 25, 2003). May be accessed at **www.seattletimes.nwsource.com.**

[35]Tracy, "Theology," 108.

[36]Adrian Mihalache, "the postmodernity of cyberspace," from the online journal, *spark-online*. issue 13.0. **http://www.spark-online.com/october00/discourse/mihalache.html** (accessed March 19, 2003).

[37]Paul Feyerabend, "Anything Goes," in *The Truth about the Truth: De-confusing and Re-constructing the Postmodern World*, ed. by Walter Truett Anderson (New York: Tarcher/Putman, 1995) 200.

[38]Leonard Sweet, *Postmodern Pilgrims: First Century Passion for the 21st Century World* (Nashville: Broadman & Holman, 2000) 154.

Bibliography

Baudrillard, Jean. *The Transparency of Evil*. Trans. by James Benedict. London: Verso, 1993.

Perhaps the most thorough exploration of the problem of evil by an influential French postmodernist. Baudrillard's general thesis is that "evil" in the postmodern world is the limiting of freedom.

Bauman, Zygmunt. *Postmodern Ethics*. Oxford: Blackwell, 1993.

Although now somewhat dated, this is a thoroughgoing work exploring the possibility of a workable and practical ethical system in the postmodern context.

Erickson, Millard J. *Postmodernizing the Faith: Evangelical Responses to the Challenge of Postmodernism*. Grand Rapids: Baker, 1998.

Although somewhat predictable and reactionary, Erickson takes on various prominent members of the evangelical camp who have embraced elements of postmodernity. He does not seem to realize that his critique is tied to the classical Enlightenment model of twentieth-century evangelicalism, and is therefore unconvincing to postmoderns.

Grenz, Stanley J. *A Primer on Postmodernism*. Grand Rapids: Eerdmans, 1996.

Always a fresh thinker, Grenz takes a cautious look at both the promises and the dangers of postmodernity for evangelicals.

Jones, Milton. *Christ No More, No Less: How to be a Christian in a Postmodern World*. Orange, CA: New Leaf Books, 2001.

This is a passionate work from a pastor who has devoted himself to understanding the postmodern generation so that he can communicate the gospel of Jesus Christ to them. It offers both analysis and practical insights.

Josephson, Michael. "Making Ethical Decisions." Josephson Institute of Ethics web site. Accessed March 20, 2003. **http://www.josephsoninstitute.org/MED/MED-intro+toc.htm**.

This web site contains a wealth of material for teaching ethics, particularly in a business environment. While not overtly religious, Christians will find much to appreciate in this resource.

Robinson, Dave, and Christ Garratt. *Introducing Ethics*. Cambridge: Totem Books/Icon Books, 1997.

While very simple in its presentation (using many cartoons) this insightful little book is valuable for students entering the study of ethics from the philosophy side of the house. In particular, Robinson and Garratt move into the problems of doing ethics in the postmodern context, something most handbooks on ethics don't get to.

Sweet, Leonard. *Post-Modern Pilgrims: First Century Passion for the 21st Century World*. Nashville: Broadman & Holman, 2000.

Always stimulating, Sweet pushes Christians to come to grips with living in the postmodern world. There is much criticism of the church and of twentieth-century Christianity in Sweet's work (and it does get tiresome at times), but he challenges in ways no other Christian writer is doing at the beginning of the twenty-first century.

Using the Old Testament for Ethical Guidance

Rick R. Marrs, Ph.D.

Utilizing the Old Testament in contemporary ethical discussions is highly complicated and fraught with peril. So begin many scholarly treatises attempting to delineate the role and value of the Old Testament materials for contemporary Christian ethics. Often these works never graduate beyond a delineation of the multiple dangers and pitfalls involved in incorporating the Old Testament into the discussion. In many ways, for those conversant with the difficulties involved in attempting to articulate a comprehensive presentation of the *theology* of the Old Testament, similar issues (in perhaps even greater magnitude) confront the Old Testament *ethicist*. Questions arise regarding the "center" (if any) of Old Testament ethics, the tensions between the normative vs. the descriptive nature of the task, the lengthy historical span from which the materials derive, and the multiple forms and purposes of the texts. Each of these questions (and more) forces itself upon us.

Ethics, like theology, addresses the fundamental issues of life. Both concern the deep questions of what we believe and how we behave; perhaps more importantly, both address the question of rationale—why we believe what we do and why we behave the way we do. Both must be kept in dialogue with the other. The old adage remains true—"bad theology results in bad behavior."[1] Simply put, Scripture boldly proclaims that our view of God informs our decisions and our behaviors; our view of God informs our views of ourselves and others; our view of God informs our treatment of the world in which we live, God's creatures with whom we interact, the values we hold, and the goals to which we aspire.

Without a doubt, the difficulties confronting us when we attempt to incorporate the Old Testament into our ethical decision-making are substantial and complex. Immediately the magnitude of the task looms before us. Will we incorporate the entire Old Testament canon into our discussion, or will we be

> The difficulties confronting us when we attempt to incorporate the Old Testament into our ethical decision-making are substantial and complex.

selective? If we are selective, how will we determine what materials warrant consideration? Put differently, will we work from a canon within a canon? Although at first blush this sounds offensive, in actual practice this is the mode of operation for many contemporary Christians. If the Old Testament is utilized at all in contemporary ethical decision-making, it is often used selectively to justify preestablished ethical positions.[2] If the size of the corpus is daunting, more intimidating is the historical span embraced by that corpus and the plethora of genres represented within that corpus. The materials span a period prior to the patriarchal age (early second millennium) to the Hellenistic era (ca. 300 B.C.). They derive from decidedly different socioeconomic and political systems. In Genesis 12–50 we encounter ethical behavior within a tribal society, in Samuel and Kings we meet ethical activities within a monarchical system. We are privy to the behaviors of people at the height of power (the United Monarchy) and in the depths of despair (the Babylonian exile).

We also must grapple with how we utilize these various materials for ethical input. On the one hand, some of the material may seem predisposed (if not pre-packaged) for ethical analysis. A significant amount of the Pentateuch contains *legal dicta* articulating rules and regulations for community life. However, as Christians, we are immediately driven to determine which of those legal pronouncements remain applicable for today's readers. While "you shall honor your father and mother" resonates to this day, "you shall not boil a kid in its mother's milk" seems far-removed from contemporary life.[3] To complicate matters, some scholars argue that legal materials are themselves highly problematic, since they are rooted in the notion of obedience, and obedience in and of itself is morally neutral! That is, the "goodness" or "badness" of obedience is determined ultimately by the ethics of the one demanding the obedience.[4]

Further, much of the material labeled "Law" (*Torah*) in the Old

Testament appears formally in a genre we would more appropriately label narrative.[5] This realization is not without consequence. In what way is narrative "law?" Put differently, in what way does (should) narrative discourse function ethically for us? Are the narratives of the patriarchs normative? Should Abraham (and his treatment of Sarah and Hagar) function for us as an ethical role model? What is (or should be) our valuation of the behavior of Lot, his wife, and his daughters? How do we view David, "the man after God's own heart" in his affair with Bathsheba and murder of Uriah?

Often at this point the discussion returns to the scope of the task before us. Is our task descriptive or declarative (i.e., normative)?[6] Should we content ourselves simply with describing the ethical premises and behaviors of the Old Testament materials, or should these materials prove normative for us today? If the latter, hermeneutical questions rush to the fore alongside theological questions![7]

> Should we content ourselves simply with describing the ethical premises and behaviors of the Old Testament materials, or should these materials prove normative for us today?

Against a larger backdrop, two issues require clarification. The first concerns the nature of the Old Testament materials. The second concerns the sociological dynamics of the Old Testament materials. Regarding the first, it is much easier to state what the Old Testament materials are *not* than what they are. First and foremost, the Old Testament is neither a moral guidebook nor a theological tractate. Rather, it contains *occasional* materials.[8] They span a lengthy historical period and reflect a multitude of social, political, cultural, and economic circumstances. Although this may at first seem to complicate our task unnecessarily, in the end it enhances and enriches our ethical understanding. The difficulties created by the diversity of the Old Testament also create numerous valuable and valid windows through which we can observe divine–human interaction and behavior. We are privy to ethical behavior (and misbehavior) in situations of slavery and punishing exile, in circumstances of power and prestige; we observe the activities of God, his people, and the nations in incredibly diverse arenas. If theology provides the backdrop and rationale for ethical behavior, ethics manifests the implementation and actualization of that theology in the multiple dimensions of daily life (e.g., in the family, in government, in the marketplace, in worship, etc.).[9]

The sociological dynamics of the world behind the text of Scripture also demands consideration. When we read Scripture, we realize that we are often reading the "minority report." Although we can often reconstruct the "popular morality" of the day, the ethical valuations placed on that morality typically derive from a small group called by God to critique and criticize those ethical values and behaviors. When we choose to read the Old Testament as *Christian Scripture* and fully a part of the canon (as did the early church), we at the same time cast our ethical lot with those voices that produced this Scripture.[10]

Against this backdrop, I propose the following. Rather than immersing myself in the numerous ethical conundrums that dot the Old Testament landscape, I will concentrate on several selected ethical principles articulated across the Old Testament that may serve usefully for further ethical discussion. I will focus less on the nuts and bolts of "how to use the Old Testament for contemporary ethical decision-making" and more on the major theological underpinnings upon which much of the ethics in the Old Testament rests. My focus will first and foremost be upon the implications of Old Testament ethics for contemporary communities of faith. I am most interested in addressing what can be said positively, i.e., in articulating those pervasive and prominent theological themes that can inform our contemporary discussions of ethics. In the Old Testament, ethical thought and behavior is inextricably rooted in two great theological doctrines: 1) the nature of God; 2) the covenant relationship between God and his people. The nature of God informs our view of the nature of humanity and the world in which humans dwell. Covenant theology shapes our treatment of others.

> In the OT, ethical thought and behavior is inextricably rooted in two great theological doctrines: 1) the nature of God; 2) the covenant relationship between God and his people.

The organizational principle for my discussion will be the canon in its original tripartite form as evinced in the Hebrew Bible (*Tanakh*). I will first discuss the ethical value of the Law (*Torah*). The focus will be twofold, dealing with the significance of narrative discourse and *legal dicta* for OT ethical thought. Second, I will elucidate possible ethical contributions from the Prophets (*Nebi'im*). Since prophecy was quintessentially the proclamation of the Word of God, reflecting upon the ethical substance of this proclamation deserves attention. Finally, I will present ethical value provided by the third section of the corpus, the Writings (*Kethubim*). Given the bulk and diversity of these materials, I will limit my focus to the hymnic (Psalms) and proverbial literature (Book of Proverbs). The focus throughout will concern the underlying theological principles that inform the ethical thought evidenced in these selected materials, and how these theological principles might elucidate and enrich contemporary ethical discussions among Christians.

The Law (*Torah*) and Ethics

The Pentateuch opens with a majestic vision of the sovereign Creator of the universe. As Creator, God inexplicably chooses to "image" himself in one (and only one) specter of his creation—humanity. While the full ontological implications of this concept elude us, the functional implications are clear. As creatures in the image of God, we have power and responsibility. We have been commissioned to "be fruitful and multiply, fill the earth and subdue it."

> As creatures in the image of God, we have power and responsibility.

Made in the image of God, we are to attend responsibly to maintaining and nurturing our immediate created order. To speak in clichés, to whom much is entrusted, much is expected. As divine image bearers, we are creatures of dignity and worth, since the all-powerful Lord of the universe has declared his creation "good." The Old Testament roots our treatment of each other ethically in this doctrine. After the flood, the Lord enlarges the human domain (animals now become part of the human diet [Gen 9:3-4]), but reasserts the original ethical intent of his creation of humans in his own image:

> Whoever sheds the blood of a human,
>   by a human shall that person's blood be shed;
> for in his own image
>   God made humankind (Gen 9:6).[11]

Created in the image of God, we are to reflect in our ethical actions and attitudes toward others the very character and nature of God.[12]

When we read the Pentateuch, we realize that ancient Israel embedded her *legal dicta* within the larger narrative story of her history and relationship with God.[13] This observation is of no small conse-

> *Israel never released her legal formulations apart from her larger story.*

quence for ethics. Whereas other ancient Near Eastern peoples produced self-standing law codes,[14] Israel never released her legal formulations apart from her larger story. The implication is obvious. For Israel, one could only understand the legal regulations imposed by God within the context of the larger narrative of God's merciful salvific acts in the choosing and guidance of Abraham, the deliverance from Egypt at the Red Sea, and the gracious provisioning during the desert wanderings.[15] Exodus 19 seamlessly interweaves theology and ethics:

> Then Moses went up to God; the LORD called to him from the mountain saying, "Thus you shall say to the house of Jacob, and tell the Israelites: You have seen what I did to the Egyptians, and how I bore you on eagles' wings and brought you to myself. Now therefore, if you obey my voice and keep my covenant, you shall be my treasured possession out of all the peoples. Indeed, the whole earth is mine, but you shall be for me a priestly kingdom and a holy nation. These are the words that you shall speak to the Israelites" (Exod 19:3-6).

Moses begins by affirming the initiating and decisive actions of God on behalf of his people. Against this prior unmerited divine act, God calls his people to obedience. Obedience carries heavy ethical consequences. The people will be a kingdom of priests (i.e., servants) and a holy nation (i.e., unique and distinct). The ensuing legal statements in Exodus specify the ways in which this service and distinctiveness will play out in daily life.

Within the Pentateuch, the book of Deuteronomy eloquently integrates theology and ethics.[16] Set against the historical and geographical backdrop of imminent entrance into the Promised Land, Moses powerfully explicates the ethical expectations God has for Israel. Theologically, the covenant dominates the landscape. God rescued his people from Egypt and led them to Sinai to consummate the covenant relationship. To use ancient Near Eastern treaty language, the almighty Suzerain of the universe expects his vassal Israel to behave ethically in accordance with the covenant stipulations; her ethical standards must mirror the standards of the Lord.

For the LORD your God is God of gods and Lord of lords, the great God, mighty and awesome, who is not partial and takes no bribe, who executes justice for the orphan and the widow, and who loves the strangers, providing them food and clothing. *You shall also love the stranger, for you were strangers in the land of Egypt* (Deut 10:17-19).[17]

The book of Deuteronomy addresses three fundamental questions that carry far-reaching ethical implications: Who are we? Why do we do what we do? Why do we have what we have? The answer to the first question is obvious. Deuteronomy repeatedly reminds its listeners that they are the undeserving recipients of the magnanimous grace of the sustaining Lord of the universe. Though wholly undeserved, they have been chosen by God. Their choice has nothing whatsoever to do with any inherent qualities they possess. Rather, their choice is rooted solely in the nature and character of God. This merciful God has delivered them and is bringing them into the land beyond the Jordan for two principal reasons—he loves them, and he is keeping his promise to their ancestors (Deut 7:7-9; 9:6-7). Election reflects clearly the ethical nature of God—he is a faithful lover and promise keeper.[18]

Against this backdrop, the second question arises—why do we do what we do? Deuteronomy 6:20-25 replies:

When your children ask you in time to come, "What is the meaning of the decrees and the statutes and the ordinances that the LORD our God has commanded you?" then you shall say to your children, "We were Pharaoh's slaves in Egypt, but the LORD brought us out of Egypt with a mighty hand. The LORD displayed before our eyes great and awesome signs and wonders against Egypt, against Pharaoh and all his household. He brought us out from there in order to bring us in, to give us the land that he promised on oath to our ancestors. Then the LORD commanded us to observe all these statutes, to fear the LORD our God, *for our lasting good*, so as to keep us alive, as is now the case. If we diligently observe this entire commandment before the LORD our God, as he has commanded us, we will be *in the right*."

The scene is poignant. The child comes to the parent seeking a rationale for keeping the divine injunctions. Strikingly, Moses provides the parent theological instruction. In response to the question,

Moses instructs the parent to begin *not* with human obligation, but with the divine initiative. Theologically and ethically, Scripture *always* begins with God's actions on our behalf.[19] It is

> Theologically and ethically, Scripture always begins with God's actions on our behalf.

God's saving and life-giving actions on our behalf that contextualize and make sense of our response of faithful obedience.[20]

Deuteronomy also addresses the ethical implications of the question, why do we have what we have? In response to this question, Moses answers:

> Remember the long way that the LORD your God has led you these forty years in the wilderness, in order to humble you, testing you to know what was in your heart . . . in order to make you know that one does not live by bread alone, but by every word that comes from the mouth of the LORD. . . . Take care that you do not forget the LORD your God, by failing to keep his commandments, his ordinances, and his statutes . . . when you have eaten your fill and have built fine houses and live in them, and when your herds and flocks have multiplied, and all that you have is multiplied, then do not exalt yourself, forgetting the LORD your God. . . . Do not say to yourself, "My power and the might of my own hand have gotten me this wealth." But remember the LORD your God, for it is he who gives you power to get wealth, so that he may confirm his covenant that he swore to your ancestors, as he is doing today (Deut 8:2-3, 11-12, 17-18).

This third question also carries ethical weight. How we handle our possessions inevitably corresponds to our understanding of the *source* of our possessions. Like Israel, if we succumb to the temptation to consider our wealth and belongings the result of our own endeavors, we behave differently. We see our belongings as *our* belongings and tend to hoard and behave ethically in ways that serve ourselves. In contrast, to see our possessions as gracious gifts from a benevolent Lord frees us to mirror the ethics of this Lord and share these gifts from God freely with others.[21] Ultimately, our ethical stance toward our personal resources and the resources of God's world in which we live is anchored firmly in our theological vision of God as Creator and Sustainer of our universe.[22]

The Prophets (*Nebi'im*) and Ethics

The prophets, though unfamiliar terrain for many Christians, provide rich ethical resources. From one vantage point, the prophetic literature allows us to see the inseparable connection between theological reflection and ethical application. The prophets demonstrate "ethics in action." They show the practical outworking of ethics in the daily life. Though numerous prophets could be selected, I will simply highlight a few of the ethical riches present in three eighth-century prophets—Amos, Micah, and Isaiah.

> The prophetic literature allows us to see the inseparable connection between theological reflection and ethical application.

The eighth century B.C., though in many ways dramatically different from our modern world, presents us with numerous social and cultural analogies. In the latter half of that century, Israel and Judah found themselves repeatedly confronted with ethical dilemmas both domestically and internationally. On the one hand, during much of that period the economy was robust, allowing both countries to increase military spending and operations, to enlarge borders and dwellings, and to expand the business sector. With these increases came consequences. During this period, a significant rift developed between the haves and the have-nots. Though a time of prosperity, increasing numbers of the community found themselves reduced to poverty and forced to divest themselves of land and cherished possessions. Specifically, the agrarian (rural) sector of the community found itself at the mercy (or lack thereof!) of the rising mercantile (urban) sector. Into this context God injected his prophets. He sent Amos from his small southern village to preach in the urban marketplaces of North Israel. He sent Micah from his small southern village to speak against the social abuses rampant in Jerusalem. He commissioned Isaiah to call his people back to faithful ethical living. Each prophet roots his ethical message in a theological vision of God and the relationship to which God has called his covenant people.

The Lord called Amos to restore a vision of the sovereignty of God to a northern kingdom out of control ethically. Although Amos frequently is depicted simply as a preacher of social justice, it is essential that we realize that his social criticisms are centrally rooted in his vision of God's all-encompassing sovereignty. For Amos, there is no arena of life outside Yahweh's control. Amos finds himself called to preach to a successful community with a flourishing economy, and yet a society that regards religious activity as a means of self-justification before God. Amos derides the absurd disconnect that has occurred between worship and ethics:

> Come to Bethel—and transgress;
> to Gilgal—and multiply transgression;
> bring your sacrifices every morning,
> your tithes every three days;
> bring a thank offering of leavened bread,
> and proclaim freewill offerings, publish them;
> for so you love to do, O people of Israel!
> says the Lord GOD.
> Hear this, you that trample on the needy,
> and bring to ruin the poor of the land,
> saying, "When will the new moon be over
> so that we may sell grain;
> and the sabbath,
> so that we may offer wheat for sale?
> We will make the ephah small and the shekel great,
> and practice deceit with false balances,
> buying the poor for silver
> and the needy for a pair of sandals,
> and selling the sweepings of the wheat" (Amos 4:4-5;
> 8:4-6).[23]

Social ethics informs Amos's message throughout. His book opens with an extensive cataloguing of the social abuses practiced by the foreign neighbors surrounding Israel. In dramatic fashion he lists the war crimes these foreign nations have committed. Each nation is guilty of serious crimes of inhumanity. As he concludes his devastating critique of international criminals, he saves his most blistering critique for that nation guilty of the most flagrant violations of social injustice. That nation is none other than Israel!

> Thus says the LORD:
> "For three transgressions of Israel,
> and for four, I will not revoke the punishment;[24]
> because they sell the righteous for silver,
> and the needy for a pair of shoes—
> they that trample the head of the poor into the dust of the
> earth,

and turn aside the way of the afflicted;
a man and his father go in to the same maiden,
   so that my holy name is profaned;
they lay themselves down beside every altar
   upon garments taken in pledge;
and in the house of their God they drink
   the wine of those who have been fined[25]

(Amos 2:6-8, RSV).

Perhaps nowhere in Scripture is complete disregard for the rights of others and an absence of community more tellingly depicted. The rights of the poor and the values of various groups are being man-handled while religious activities continue unabated. Such is the society that results when ethical behavior and worship are severed theologically. For Amos, Israel's ethical atrocities are doubly tragic. On the one hand, she has numerous advantages not afforded other peoples (note the recital of Israel's salvation history in 2:6-11). Clearly, increased privileges carry increased attentiveness to social responsibilities. On the other hand, Israel's social crimes are more heinous than those of the previous nations, for she commits these outrages *against her own community!*[26]

In this environment, Amos stridently calls Israel to return to God's original intent for her. Amos fearlessly reestablishes the inte-gral connection between theology and ethics, and the inseparable linkage between worship and ethical behavior. Radically, Amos affirms that the sovereign Lord of the universe pays more attention to one's daily ethical deeds than to one's cultic activities! Or better, ethical misdeeds during the week negate religious activities. Amos 5 presents the importance of integrating ethical behavior and worship:

Therefore because you trample on the poor
   and take from them levies of grain,
you have built houses of hewn stone,
   but you shall not live in them;
you have planted pleasant vineyards,
   but you shall not drink their wine.
For I know how many are your transgressions,
   and how great are your sins—
you who afflict the righteous, who take a bribe,
   and push aside the needy in the gate. . . .[27]
Seek good[28] and not evil,
   that you may live;

and so the LORD, the God of hosts, will be with you,
    just as you have said.
Hate evil and love good,
    and establish justice in the gate;
it may be that the LORD, the God of hosts,
    will be gracious to the remnant of Joseph
                                    (Amos 5:11-12,14-15).

If Amos 5 exhibits the disastrous consequences of mollifying a concern for social justice with a productive and energetic cult, Amos 6 depicts the dangerous lack of sensitivity to the plight of others that may result from luxurious contentment (see Amos 6:1-6,12-13).[29] Amos reminds us that ethical apathy often results when we disregard God's sovereign oversight of all facets of our lives. In contrast, Amos declares that a community that has experienced repeated and profuse manifestations of God's unmerited acts of grace can appropriately respond ethically only with justice and righteousness to all. Religious activities, no matter how extensive or elaborate, can never substitute for God's all-consuming passion for right ethical action:

> *Amos reminds us that ethical apathy often results when we disregard God's sovereign oversight of all facets of our lives.*

I hate, I despise your festivals,
    and I take no delight in your solemn assemblies.
Even though you offer me your burnt offerings and grain
        offerings,
    I will not accept them;
and the offerings of well-being of your fatted animals
    I will not look upon.
Take away from me the noise of your songs:
    I will not listen to the melody of your harps.
But let justice roll down like waters,
    and righteousness like an ever-flowing stream (Amos 5:21-24).

Micah receives an equally difficult commission from the Lord. Although from the rural village of Moresheth, God sends him to urban Jerusalem to proclaim God's judgment upon the abusive ethical practices of the powerful elite of that city.[30] Like Amos, Micah decried the abusive injustices manifested in policies and activities detrimental to the poor and oppressed.

Alas for those who devise wickedness
　　and evil deeds on their beds!
When the morning dawns, they perform it,
　　because it is in their power.
They covet fields, and seize them;
　　houses, and take them away;
they oppress householder and house,
　　people and their inheritance.
Therefore thus says the LORD:
Now, I am devising against this family an evil
　　from which you cannot remove your necks;
and you shall not walk haughtily,
　　for it will be an evil time.
On that day they will take up a taunt song against you,
　　and wail with bitter lamentation,
and say, "We are utterly ruined;
　　the LORD alters the inheritance of my people;
how he removes it far from me!
　　Among out captors he parcels out our fields"
　　　　　　　　　　　　　　　　(Micah 2:1-4).[31]

Micah excoriates the rich and powerful who plot to take land from the poor. Perhaps most interesting is Micah's choice of theological language to describe these acts—these land barons "covet" (חמד, *ḥāmad*: the only key term used twice in the Decalogue) the "inheritance" (נחלה, *naḥălāh*: the term used for God's gift to each family upon entrance into the Promised Land) of their neighbors! For Micah, these ethical moves are not simply ethical misdeeds; they are none other than crimes against God! Micah's use of theologically laden vocabulary is most significant, for it demonstrates that his social critique is thoroughly informed by his theological vision.

Inculcating within a community a sense of theological perspective hopefully results in justice becoming central to daily life. For Micah, justice is the norm by which all of life must be critiqued. In Micah 3, he affirms the importance of justice in the life of a people.[32] Micah is not content simply to catalogue specific crimes; rather, he addresses himself to the fundamental social structures that allow such actions to continue. He decries the rampant abuse of justice in the treatment of the weak both by the

> For Micah, justice is the norm by which all of life must be critiqued.

legal system (3:1-4) and by the religious establishment (3:5-8). For Micah, justice is truth activated; it must be implemented and practiced at all levels and in all sectors of society.

Micah, like Amos, articulates the demanding and threatening task of viewing all of life theologically. Religious activities cannot be severed from daily social practices. Micah demonstrates the tremendous importance of applying a

> Religious activities cannot be severed from daily social practices.

comprehensive theological vision of God's all-encompassing justice to daily social acts. Micah forced those in power to grapple with the ethical implications of their policies and actions upon the powerless.[33] Micah pushes the Jerusalem elite to grapple with the implications of their actions upon the poor and powerless. Clearly the policies and programs of the capital city affected (disastrously) the villages of the Judean countryside. Life is never lived in a vacuum. Micah demonstrates that right ethical behavior cannot content itself merely with criticizing unethical acts; it may need to condemn the systems that perpetuate those acts and allow them to flourish.[34]

Isaiah, perhaps the best known of the eighth-century prophets, fully links ethics, theology, and worship. Although Isaiah offers several justifiably famous ethical passages, to understand fully Isaiah's ethical message we must begin with his vision of God in chapter 6. Upon entering the temple precinct, Isaiah sees God "high and lifted up." His robe engulfs the inner sanctuary. Isaiah hears the seraphs crying out, "Holy, holy, holy is the LORD of hosts." Upon seeing the Lord, he exclaims, "Woe is me! I am lost . . . yet my eyes have seen the King, the LORD of hosts!" That day Isaiah saw the Lord as King and as the Holy One of Israel. To be somewhat simplistic, we would suggest that his vision of God as King fully informed his political outlook (see Isaiah 7–9), his vision of God as Holy fully informed his view of worship and ethics (see Isaiah 1–5). Isaiah's vision informs and elucidates his ethical message and ministry in two crucial ways. First, seeing the Lord as Holy and as King means that his subjects owe him exclusive allegiance and unshakable trust. Exclusive and comprehensive allegiance involves every aspect of life (e.g., political, social, religious, economic). Ethically, this certainly entails a lifestyle reflective of the Lord's own holiness. Second, all worship begins with a recognition of an individual's and community's complete inadequacy before God. Religious activity, no matter how extensive, elaborate, or flawlessly conducted, can never substitute for right behavior.

Against this backdrop, the opening covenant lawsuit (Isaiah 1) receives added meaning. To a community proud of its religious activities and sanguine about its (un)ethical behavior, Isaiah charges breach of covenant. Israel, the favored child, is guilty of rebellion (1:2-3). Rebellious Israel behaves more stupidly than draught animals ("Israel does not *know* . . . *offspring* of evildoers")! Although public worship is in high gear, the covenant is in complete disarray.

> Hear the word of the LORD,
>> you rulers of Sodom!
> Listen to the teaching of our God,
>> you people of Gomorrah!
> What to me is the multitude of your sacrifices?
>> says the LORD;
> I have had enough of burnt offerings of rams
>> and the fat of fed beasts;
> I do not delight in the blood of bulls,
>> or of lambs, or of goats.
> When you come to appear before me,
>> who asked this from your hand?
>> Trample my courts no more;
> bringing offerings is futile;
>> incense is an abomination to me.
> New moon and sabbath and calling of convocation—
>> I cannot endure solemn assemblies with iniquity.
> Your new moons and your appointed festivals
>> my soul hates;
> they have become a burden to me,
>> I am weary of bearing them.
> When you stretch out your hands,
>> I will hide my eyes from you;
> even though you make many prayers,
>> I will not listen;
>> your hands are full of blood.
> Wash yourselves; make yourselves clean;
>> remove the evil of your doings
>> from before my eyes;
> *cease to do evil,*
>> *learn to do good;*

> *seek justice,*
> > *rescue the oppressed,*
> *defend the orphan,*
> > *plead for the widow* (Isaiah 1:10-17).

The contrast is striking: Judah offers religious fervor; the Lord seeks ethical rightness. Worship devoid of ethical propriety misses the core element to God's call. Isaiah reminds us that the religious dimension of our lives can never be divorced from the ethical dimension. The two dimensions are inseparably inter-twined. The implications for contem-porary ethical reflection are obvious.

> No area of life stands outside the purview of God's vision.

For Christians, life is holistic. No area of life stands outside the purview of God's vision. God's intent for his people is to live lives that are singular in focus and purpose. Our ethical dealings enrich or diminish our religious endeavors. Our worship should inform and enhance our vision of daily life; unethical behavior diminishes (or negates) the validity and integrity of our worship (see below, the discussion of Psalms 15, 24, 73).

The devastating impact that unethical behavior can have upon a community of faith is amply evidenced in Isaiah 5:8-23. Isaiah laments the presence in his community of those who mistreat the poor (vv. 8,22-23), who engage in self-enjoyment with no concern for the plight of others (vv. 11-17), who attempt to manipulate God to their own purposes (vv. 18-19), who have inverted values (v. 20), and who are proud (v. 21). Like Amos and Micah, the heart of the problem lies in a severed covenant.[35]

Although Isaiah paints a somewhat depressing picture of cur-rent ethical life in Judah, he does not content himself with simply castigating the offenders. Rather, he also paints a picture of what Jerusalem could again become ethically.

> How the faithful city
> > has become a whore!
> > She that was full of justice,
> righteousness lodged in her—
> > but now murderers! . . .
> I will turn my hand against you;
> > I will smelt away your dross as with lye,
> > and remove all your alloy.

And I will restore your judges as at the first,
  And your counselors as at the beginning.
Afterward you shall be called the city of righteousness,
  the faithful city (Isa 1:21,25-26).

Isaiah contrasts the current ethical deterioration of Jerusalem ("whore . . . murderers") with what the Lord intended his community of faith to embody ("city of faithfulness"). Violence and exploitation have supplanted justice and integrity. This is the ethical character of a community severed from covenant relationship with God. Yet Isaiah envisions a future for Jerusalem in which justice and righteousness again dominate the landscape. Isaiah knows such a transformation will not be easy. He uses the imagery of smelting to capture the rigor of the transformation. Just as pure silver only emerges from the refiner's fire, so justice and righteousness only come through intense effort and painful soul-searching. For Isaiah, the presence of ethical integrity (viz., righteousness, faithfulness, justice) results from two factors: a renewed vision of the sovereignty of God (v. 24) and a disciplined response (smelting).

The prophetic literature provides a wealth of resources for contemporary ethical reflection. The prophets remind us of the necessity of grounding our ethical decisions and attitudes in serious theological reflection. They also challenge us to maintain a fundamental integrity to our lives—an integrity that inseparably connects our religious lives (e.g., worship) with our daily ethical behaviors. They call us to active stances on behalf of the poor and dispossessed, to confront uncompromisingly those unethical behaviors and attitudes that would exploit or diminish the lives of the other. Such are the ethical promises and challenges of this portion of Scripture.

The Writings (*Kethubim*) and Ethics

Like the Law and the Prophets, the Writings typically link ethics to worship and root ethical thought and practice within the context of community life. Although this section of Scripture offers numerous resources for ethical reflection; I will concentrate on two areas. First, some discussion will concentrate on the interrelation of ethics and worship in the Psalter. Second, attention will be given to the place of ethics in Proverbs.

The Psalter provides a rich resource for contemporary ethical thought. Containing psalms for a variety of worship experiences, it offers psalms that address the relation of worship and daily (ethical) life. On the one hand, it provides us with psalms that articulate the importance our daily ethical decisions have upon our gathering for corporate worship (e.g., Psalms 15, 24). On the other hand, it provides us with psalms that reflect the importance gathering for worship has for daily ethical living (e.g., Psalm 73).

Psalms 15 and 24 are entrance liturgies. They were likely sung as worshipers ascended the temple mount to worship the Lord.

> O LORD, who may abide in your tent?
>   Who may dwell on your holy hill?
> Those who walk blamelessly, and do what is right,
>   and speak the truth from their heart;
> who do not slander with their tongue,
>   and do no evil to their friends,
>   nor take up a reproach against their neighbors;
> in whose eyes the wicked are despised,
>   but who honor those who fear the LORD;
> who stand by their oath even to their hurt;
> who do not lend money at interest,
>   and do not take a bribe against the innocent.
> Those who do these things shall never be moved
>   (Psalm 15).[36]

Psalms 15 and 24 sound strikingly similar to the ethical calls found in the prophets. Like the prophets, these psalmists understand worship as the offering of our lives to the Sovereign Lord. Since worship is first and foremost the offering of our lives (often captured tellingly in the quality of the sacrificial gifts offered), then the ethical quality of our lives matters! These psalms do not breathe the air of legalism. The psalmists knew that entrance into the presence of God could never be earned or justified.[37] Like Isaiah, they knew that entering God's presence was a "death-defying" act. However, they also knew that their God called them to serious self-examination and self-reflection upon entrance to the sanctuary. Simply put, if worship was the offering of one's life to God, then the quality of that offering mattered. A sacrifice marred by disingenuous speech, slander, false business transactions, and disregard for one's neighbor spoke volumes about one's relationship with God. Psalm 15 raises the question of who we are and what we should be as we enter God's presence (v. 1), and then proceeds to answer that question (vv. 2-5).

These psalms provide helpful resources for contemporary ethical reflection. They remind us that worship can function powerfully as an agent in introspection and self-inventory. They remind us that, if our ethical behavior is to mirror that of the God we worship, entrance into the presence of that God can never be casual or routine. As R. Davidson states, "To live in the light of this steadfast love is to accept a discipline, the discipline to demonstrate the same steadfast love in daily relationships with other people."[38] P. Craigie captures the ethical importance of worship well:

> *Worship can function powerfully as an agent in introspection and self-inventory.*

> What transforms the psalm from a barrier to a gateway is the realization that the preparation for worship illuminates also the necessity for worship. On the one hand, we must live in such a way that we may prepare for worship with integrity, without hypocrisy; on the other hand, the introspection involved, prior to worship, clarifies beyond any doubt the need for forgiveness. Failing to have fulfilled the ten conditions, we require forgiveness before we can enter divine presence. Only then do we realize that the privilege may never be casually exploited and also that the Holy God is not inaccessible.[39]

Like Psalms 15 and 24, Psalm 73 addresses the integral relation of ethics and worship, but from the opposite direction. Psalm 73 speaks to the impact our worship has upon our ethical outlook. The psalm introduces us to a psalmist truly striving to live faithfully to God's will. He engages in serious self-analysis and strives to live a life of integrity. He finds himself surrounded by those flouting God's law and engaging in repeated unethical acts. He becomes dispirited when he sees that not only do they go unpunished, they actually flourish and prosper! He struggles, but in vain, to find an intellectually satisfying solution to this moral dilemma. Experiencing such situations repeatedly, he realizes that even he, a teacher of the faithful, finds his faith slipping. At that point when he can no longer live with such unresolved tension, he enters the sanctuary (v. 17). There he finds resolution, for there he sees clearly the "true end" of all things.

> *"We must live in such a way that we may prepare for worship with integrity . . . ."*

The message of Psalm 73 and its ethical implications are powerful. Psalm 73 acknowledges that serious intellectual effort will not fully resolve the apparent injustices in the world in which we live.[40] It is only in the presence of the almighty Lord of the universe that we "see" life as God truly intended it. Simply put, we bring our ethical quandaries with us to the sanctuary, for it is there that God moves powerfully to aid us in our struggle to live lives of faithfulness and holiness in a world prone to unethical behavior. One function of corporate worship is to allow God to refocus our vision![41] In worship, we discover that our faith depends not primarily on our fragile and often vulnerable grasp of God, but on God's grasp of us ("you hold my right hand" [v. 23], "you guide me" [v. 24], "God is the rock of my heart" [v. 26]).[42] Surrounded constantly by ethical dilemmas and at times seemingly powerless to explain the rampant injustices in our world, we gather regularly with the faithful so that God may again remind us not only *who we are, but whose we are, and why we are.*

> One function of corporate worship is to allow God to refocus our vision: we gather so that God may again remind us who we are, whose we are, and why we are.

The book of Proverbs addresses ethics from start to finish. The book is a veritable treasure trove for serious reflection on the ethics of speech and sexual behavior (Proverbs 1–9).[43] Although frequently reflecting ancient conditions and a cultural outlook perhaps foreign to moderns, the principles underlying the proverbial maxims deserve serious consideration. The book of Proverbs speaks eloquently and extensively about the character and nature of a wise person.[44] It talks of the life of the wise person from three vantage points: the wise person in relation to God, the wise person in relation to others, and the wise person in relation to self.

Proverbs 10:9-12 provides a portrait of the ethical life of the wise:

Whoever walks in integrity walks securely,
  but whoever follows perverse ways will be found out.
Whoever winks the eye causes trouble,
  but the one who rebukes boldly makes peace.
The mouth of the righteous is a fountain of life,
  but the mouth of the wicked conceals violence.

Hatred stirs up strife,
but love covers all offenses.

The life of wisdom manifests righteousness, integrity, conviction, courage, and compassion. The wise person presents an ethical stance in which all life is viewed against the backdrop of the sovereignty of God (Prov 16:1-11; 19:21; 21:30-31; cf. Jas 4:13-17).[45] To live wisely in relation to God means realizing that all of life is a gift from God. However, with this gift comes responsibility. Thus, the wise person is the responsible (note the frequent references in the book of Proverbs to discipline and diligence). The wise person also realizes that worship is integrally related to ethics (Prov 15:8; 21:3 [cf. Matt 23:23-24]; 3:9-10 [cf. Matt 6:33-34]).

> To live wisely in relation to God means realizing that all of life is a gift from God and with this gift comes responsibility.

The ethical dimensions of the life of the wise can also be seen in relation to others. The wise person manifests compassionate concern for the other. Like the rest of Scripture, this ethical concern is grounded theologically (Prov 14:31; 17:5; note the converse in 22:22-23). The wise person treats the other with justice (Prov 29:7; 31:9), kindness (Prov 14:21; 19:17), and generosity (Prov 11:24-25; 28:27). Wisdom carries ethical benefits for the other. It is worthy of note that wisdom demonstrates its value clearly in situations with potential conflict. Proverbs contrasts the ethical character of the fool, who is given to retaliation and strife, versus the ethical response of the wise, who demonstrates

> The wise person manifests compassionate concern for the other.

forgiveness (see Prov 19:11; 24:29 vs. 25:21-22 [cf. Rom 12:20; Matt 5:44-45]; 26:20-21; 29:22). The ethical behavior attendant in the life of a wise person creates a healthy community (Prov 11:11; 14:34; 29:2,4,14,16,18) and results in blessings to the other (Prov 13:14,20).

Finally, the book of Proverbs talks of the wise person in relation to self. The wise person takes criticism seriously. The wise person is a careful listener (Prov 18:2; 17:10; 19:25) and is improved by criticism (Prov 27:17). The wise person takes relationships seriously, knowing that one both influences and is influenced by those relationships (Prov 13:20; 17:17; 18:24). The ethical qualities of the wise person enumerated in the book of Proverbs are striking. The wise person is a person of humility (Prov 25:6-7; cf. Luke 14:7-11) who lives a disciplined life of moderation (Prov 25:16; cf. 21:17; 23:29-35), self-control (Prov 25:28; 29:11), and dependability (Prov 6:6-11; 26:13-15; 28:19). The wise person is value-oriented, manifesting a concern for loyalty and fidelity (Prov 3:3), social sensitivity (Prov 21:13; cf. Exod 22:22-24), and integrity (Prov 11:1; 16:11; 22:10,23; 24:23-26).

Conclusion

The preceding comments have attempted to demonstrate the positive and constructive role the Old Testament can play in contemporary ethical thought and discussion. Whereas the Old Testament is often viewed simply as an overwhelming mass of controverted, questionable, and insoluble ethical dilemmas, I would contend that we first begin with the theological and ethical riches these materials provide. The Old Testament eloquently reminds us that our ethical stance can never be separated from our theology. It calls us to take seriously all aspects of our lives when we think of the ethical dimensions of the divine-human relationship. Ethically, our religious acts impact and are impacted by our ethical behavior. The Old Testament poignantly reminds us how often we miss God's true intent for our lives, and the all-encompassing nature of the divine call.

> *The OT poignantly reminds us how often we miss God's true intent for our lives, and the all-encompassing nature of the divine call.*

Perhaps no passage better captures the ethical distance between God and us than Micah 6:6-8:

"With what shall I come before the LORD,
   and bow myself before God on high?
Shall I come before him with burnt offerings,
   with calves a year old?
Will the LORD be pleased with thousands of rams,
   with ten thousands of rivers of oil?
Shall I give my firstborn for my transgression,
   the fruit of my body for the sin of my soul?"
He has told you, O mortal, what is good;
   and what does the LORD require of you

But to do justice, and to love kindness,
and to walk humbly with your God?

On behalf of God, Micah indicts the people for failing miserably to capture the essence of the divine-human relationship. In response to the apparent divine unhappiness, the people suggest they might assuage his hurt by increasing the amount of their gifts. They even suggest ridiculous amounts. In complete and utter contrast, Micah replies that God's people have completely misunderstood the nature of the relationship. They have lost all sense of the unique holiness to which a uniquely holy God has called them. The "offering" he desires is not an offering of some*thing*, but first and foremost an offering of the *self*! The quintessence of right ethical living is captured in the eloquent finale—ethical rightness involves doing justice, manifesting steadfast love, and walking humbly with God.[46] A. Hunter expresses the thought well:

> The good that Yahweh seeks in every person among his people is rooted in making justice and steadfast love the controlling interests in all of life, thereby fostering a relationship with Yahweh that is characterized by paying careful and judicious attention to honoring his claim on all of life. This is the offering Yahweh accepts.[47]

At the beginning of this chapter, we noted the numerous difficulties, complexities, and seemingly unanswerable questions that repeatedly surface in discussions of Old Testament ethics. While those questions and concerns are neither insubstantial nor inconsequential, I hope I have shown that they may ironically fall victim to the very thinking present in Micah's day. Micah's audience missed the forest for the trees. They majored in minors, not realizing that the weightier matters of truth and justice were left undone. What may appear initially as weaknesses for use of the Old Testament in ethical discussion may in reality be strengths. The Old Testament provides us with a plethora of ethical material spanning a lengthy historical era, deriving from a multitude of social contexts, and evincing a variety of forms. Though complex, we compound the difficulties when we decide simply to choose one set of Old Testament materials to the exclusion of other material. What I have suggested is that we take seriously the entire canon of Scripture and put as much of it as relevant in dialogue with our contemporary worldview and social setting. Such an approach allows us to engage in serious ethical reflection on important concerns of our day with *more* data rather than *less*. More often than not, it enriches the discussion rather than simply complicating it. Two examples, often considered problematic, will suffice.

An ethical principle enumerated in Scripture is "honor your father and mother." We earlier alluded to a possible difficulty applying that ethical principle in our modern world of child abuse and irresponsible parenting. However, from another vantage point, the Old Testament is a rich resource for us in this contemporary discussion of what it means to honor parents. First, we noted earlier that the *legal setting* of this law most plausibly addresses the ethical behavior of *adult* children. Second, the extensive narratives of the Old Testament provide us valuable and valid examples of children honoring parents in difficult circumstances. In I Samuel, we read of Jonathan's interaction with his father Saul and his best friend David. Jonathan provides a parade example of an adult child who honored his father while simultaneously protecting the life of his friend! Third, in the book of Proverbs, ethical maxims abound addressing the nature and character of the "honorable child."

A second example treats the Old Testament social practice of polygamy. Often ethical discussions will cite this practice as evidence of the difficulty of utilizing the Old Testament in contemporary ethical reflection. I would argue the opposite. The first (and only) reference we have to the nature of the male–female relationship as God intended occurs in Genesis 2:22-24. From that union—one male and one female—"one flesh" results. The ethical norm for the marriage relationship is clearly fidelity and exclusive unity between two individuals. However, the Old Testament narratives document cases of bigamy and polygamy. Though often no explicit condemnation is provided in these early materials, *every* instance of these marital relationships evidences a problematic marital and family situation. In every instance, tension, animosity, and conflict seem the order of the day. I would suggest that the Old Testament materials provide us significant *implicit* ethical data to warrant the conclusion that Genesis 2 provides the only valid marital relationship. These exceptional cases reflect the nature of skewed life in a fallen world. The wisdom literature also gives an inordinate amount of attention to the problems, sufferings, and tragedies that arise from relationships that veer from the divinely intended norm. These materials, rather than presenting a problem, prove rich resources for a contemporary society given to serial monogamy and a laissez-faire attitude toward sexual relationships.

We would not suggest that the task before us is either simple or easy. Like anything that truly matters, it involves rigorous reflection and a humble willingness to place ourselves under the Word of God. The task before us may become either overwhelming or empowering. For those with ears to hear, the Old Testament raises compelling ethical questions we must address.

> The task before us may become either overwhelming or empowering.

To what degree are our ethical decisions informed by our theological vision? To what degree do we maintain the inseparable link between worship and ethical behavior? To what degree are our ethical lives informed by our vision of a sovereign God of the universe? To what degree are our ethical behaviors and attitudes a manifestation of our covenant response to a glorious and gracious God? To what degree do we allow God's justice to inform our ethical stance? At the heart of OT ethical thought is a vision of the covenant relationship to which God has called us. We can do no better than heed the ethical charge in the stirring words of our Lord in the prophetic Psalm 50:

> "Gather to me my faithful ones,
> who made a covenant with me by sacrifice!"
> The heavens declare his righteousness,
> for God himself is judge.
> "Hear, O my people, and I will speak,"
> O Israel, I will testify against you.
> I am God, your God.
> Not for your sacrifices do I rebuke you;
> your burnt offerings are continually before me. . . .
> Those who bring thanksgiving as their sacrifice honor me;
> to those who go the right way
> I will show the salvation of God" (vv. 5-8,23).

Notes

[1] In the New Testament, we see this dramatically exemplified in a misinterpreted Paul resulting in the opposite ethical lifestyles of libertinism and rigid asceticism. I would not suggest that the opposite is true, viz., that simply because one has a sound theology good behavior automatically follows.

[2] Numerous examples could be given, from justifying capital punishment to justifying wars of aggression. Interestingly, seldom (if

ever) have I encountered someone arguing for capital punishment for all the capital crimes in the Old Testament (e.g., adultery, truculent children).

³A popular approach distinguishes between moral and ritual or ceremonial law. (Some even suggest this distinction goes back to the rabbis.) However, no such distinction is made within the Old Testament itself. Further, while "honor your father and mother" initially sounds attractive, working out the specific "look" of this law in a society prone to physical and verbal child abuse complicates matters considerably. (As a side note, we must first determine the age and sociocultural context of the "child" being addressed in this law [every other injunction in the Decalogue addresses adults]!)

⁴Simply put, to give a cup of cold water to a thirsty person in obedience to the claim of Jesus Christ is a morally right act because of the ethical rightness of the one to whom obedience is given; in like manner, to gas people in obedience to a tyrant is morally wrong because of the abysmal character of the one to whom obedience is given.

⁵The Pentateuch is labeled "Law" (*Torah*) in the Hebrew Bible. Clearly our modern narrow definition of "law" solely as legal rules and regulations needs broadening.

⁶As mentioned previously, ethical treatments share numerous commonalities with contemporary studies in Old Testament theology. In theological studies, the descriptive task often utilizes the nomenclature "history of Israelite religion," leaving the declarative and normative discussion to Old Testament theology.

⁷Issues of genre become increasingly important at this stage. The manner and method in which such diverse materials, from widely divergent social settings, can be brought to bear upon ethical issues, is daunting. For example, how do originally liturgical materials (Psalms) inform ethical decision-making? How does one apply prophetic proclamations delivered in specific historical and social settings (e.g., eighth-century northern Israel) to contemporary Christians in the modern western hemisphere? Can one apply directly and universally proverbial adages and maxims?

⁸This in no way implies that occasional materials do not possess continuing authority. It simply assumes these ancient documents, written for an audience other than the contemporary church, must be transferred hermeneutically to the modern setting.

⁹Against this backdrop, the hermeneutical task (viz., determining the normativeness of these various accounts) becomes most crucial.

¹⁰To clarify, this means we side with the ethical stance of Jeremiah rather than the opposing prophets of his day, we align ourselves with Micah rather than the prophets of weal of his day.

¹¹Proverbs 14:31 echoes this vision: "Those who oppress the poor insult their Maker, but those who are kind to the needy honor him."

¹²This understanding is compellingly articulated in the book of Deuteronomy (see below), where our actions toward and treatment of others should mirror God's actions toward and treatment of the other.

¹³A discussion of the ethical dimension of narrative is beyond the scope of this essay. Suffice it to say, a significant amount of recent study has engaged the question of how narrative has a norming quality. That is, the biblical narratives are written in such a manner that they do not simply narrate past events of importance solely for antiquarian value; rather, they are written so that they might form and shape current community identity and behavior. Simply put, Abraham's story becomes my story, his ethical successes and failures inform and shape my ethical life and actions.

¹⁴See, for example, the Sumerian Code of Ur-Nammu or the Babylonian Code of Hammurapi. The well-known law code of Hammurapi contains 282 codified laws on a stele.

¹⁵A helpful analogy might be to reflect on the view others might have of a parent if only told the rules imposed by that parent upon the children. Apart from the context of the larger relationship, such rules could likely seem illogical and capricious.

¹⁶We could use the book of Leviticus equally profitably to develop the integration of theological vision and ethical consequence. In Leviticus it is the nature of God as holy that illuminates the ethical horizon rather than the covenant. The decisive ethical refrain in Leviticus is "you shall be holy, as I, the LORD your God, am holy."

¹⁷Deuteronomy provides numerous examples of this theological anchoring of law. The

Deuteronomistic rendering of Sabbath observance offers an excellent example. Deuteronomy ties Sabbath keeping with the Lord's deliverance of his people from Egyptian servitude. These former slaves now must weekly mirror God's treatment of them by "setting free" their hired help from Sabbath labor (Deut 5:12-15).

[18]These passages provide further testimony grounding ethical attitudes and acts in the nature of God. In response to the perennial question, "how then should we live?" Deuteronomy offers a resounding response: treat others as God has treated you. It is no accident and of no small significance that Jesus reintroduces such an ethical vision in the Sermon on the Mount.

[19]Stated globally, in the Old Testament, the Exodus (deliverance) always precedes Sinai (obligation); in the New Testament, the cross (divine initiative) always precedes Pentecost (human response).

[20]In Deut 4:5-8 faithful observance of the divine will is labeled "wise, discerning, and just."

[21]Deuteronomy stands in striking contrast to the modern American view regarding possessions. For most modern Americans, possessions and wealth are the result of hard work, good education, entrepreneurial ingenuity, and self-interest. In Deuteronomy, wealth and possessions are gifts from God; hard work and responsible behavior are simply faithful responses to God's gracious bestowal of his gifts.

[22]In Exodus 20, the Sabbath rest is rooted squarely in the theology of creation. Because God created the world in six days and rested on day seven, his faithful followers acknowledge his creative power by "resting" each seventh day. By not engaging in ceaseless feverish activity, faithful followers of this all-powerful God acknowledge that the world is safely in the hands of this sovereign Lord. This theology of work has significant ethical implications for how we understand our vocational lives.

[23]Amos surely intends sarcasm—these people, though religiously active, make no connection between their religious lives and their ethical actions. Amazingly, they can plot unethical business moves while sitting in worship!

[24]This language has covenant overtones. Simply put, these social atrocities result from a shattered covenant. M. Barre ("The Meaning

of לֹא אֲשִׁיבֶנּוּ in Amos 1:3–2:6," JBL 105 [1986] 611-631) demonstrates that the refrain "I will not revoke the punishment" is better read, "I will not restore the (covenant) relationship."

[25]Perhaps the ultimate atrocity is the using of goods, *acquired unethically*, for religious purposes!

[26]R. Coote (*Amos among the Prophets* [Philadelphia: Fortress, 1981] 323) cites three ways the ruling class "waged war" upon the poor: through excessive taxation and exorbitant interest rates; through venality; through the manipulation of the market economy.

[27]The "gate" is a stock designation for the judicial system in the prophets. Court cases were regularly conducted at the city gate.

[28]To "seek the Lord" is elsewhere in the Old Testament a stock expression for gathering to worship God. Here Amos dramatically redefines it, making it synonymous with "doing good." To seek God is to engage in just and right ethical behavior with one's fellow citizens.

[29]Just as the rich man failed to care for Lazarus (Luke 16:19-31), even though he knew him by name, so the wealthy in Amos's day were apparently oblivious to the plight of the poor (the "ruin of Joseph"). As J. Ward (*Amos–Hosea* [Atlanta: John Knox, 1981] 30-31) reminds us, "no political or economic system distributes wealth, power, and privilege fairly." The "haves" among us must constantly examine our lifestyles and ethical decisions to make sure we manifest compassion and mercy to the less fortunate.

[30]For a fuller discussion of the social dynamics underlying the message of Micah, see R. Marrs, "Micah and a Theological Critique of Worship," in *Worship and the Hebrew Bible: Essays in Honor of John T. Willis*, ed. by M.P. Graham, R. Marrs, and S. McKenzie, JSOT 284 (Sheffield: Sheffield Academic Press, 1999) 184-203; "Micah and the Task of Ministry," RQ 30 (1988) 1-16. Because of the diverse social settings of his larger community, Micah proclaimed strikingly different messages to these various constituencies. To the powerful and self-secure, he proclaimed withering doom oracles; to the poor and hopeless, he proclaimed the sustaining gracious presence of a Lord intervening on their behalf.

[31]Micah's proclamation carries rhetorical power. While the abusive land grabbers

"devise evil" (unethical acts) upon their beds at night, God "devises evil" (punishment) for them!

[32]Micah treats justice in ch. 3 in a threefold context: in vv. 1-4 it concerns the administration of justice in the courts; in vv. 5-8 it concerns the absence of justice in the ministry of the false prophets; in vv. 9-12 it concerns justice with respect to the actions of Judah's entire governmental system.

[33]In Micah 1:10-16 Micah documents the disastrous consequences Jerusalem policies are having upon the surrounding countryside.

[34]Such a message is hard medicine to swallow. Not surprisingly, the book of Micah notes several occasions when Micah received stinging rebuke from his prophetic contemporaries (e.g., 2:6-11; 3:5-8). Interestingly, they argue that matters of politics and economics have no place in preaching! Micah rejoins with a scathing critique of their ministry—they are false prophets offering simply what the people want to hear so that they might live lives of comfort and luxury! Micah charges his opponents with willingly accepting God's gracious treatment of them, but refusing to extend the same gracious treatment to the defenseless poor. Micah struggles against his opponents, for they piously justify their position with Scripture (see 2:6-11)! Micah addresses the true nature and function of "hearing the Word of the LORD." For Micah, openness to God's gracious call necessarily entails hearing God's demanding critique of all aspects of social behavior. One cannot claim God's goodness for oneself while simultaneously denying it to others! H. Wolff (*Micah the Prophet* [Philadelphia: Fortress, 1981], 50) states it well: "For Micah, Jesus Christ did not bear our iniquities and guilt so that we might treat with indifference those exploited."

[35]The indicting oracles of vv. 8-23 are preceded by the song of the vineyard (5:1-7). There, Isaiah likens God's people to a failed vineyard, a "vineyard" that produced social bloodshed and oppression rather than justice and righteousness!

[36]Psalm 24 is similar, but possibly reflects a more specific liturgical setting. In Ps 24:7-10, the "gates" of the city are called to "lift up their heads" so that the King of Glory may enter. These verses can plausibly be interpreted as reflecting a liturgical ceremony in which the ark of the Lord was transported about the city and then reentered the city-gates and transported again to its abode in the sanctuary.

[37]The attributes listed here are sometimes called the "Ten Commandments for Admission." Both negative and positive attributes are cited, reflecting that ethically the absence of evil must be coupled with the presence of good. One might suggest that the New Testament equivalent for a proper understanding of these psalms would be to hear the Sermon on the Mount as "entrance admission" to the presence of God! None would suggest that the Sermon on the Mount reflects unhealthy legalism. Rather, these psalms, like the teachings of Jesus, remind us that a central purpose for coming into the presence of God is so that the purpose and power of God can come to bear on our daily identity and character formation.

[38]R. Davidson, *The Vitality of Worship* (Grand Rapids: Eerdmans, 1998) 57. These psalms allow us to avoid two unhealthy ethical extremes. At one extreme, we avoid a stress on the holiness of God that results in a stance of utter despair at ever entering the presence of God. At the other extreme, we avoid a cavalier thoughtlessness that considers admission into God's presence a guarantee.

[39]P. Craigie, *Psalms 1-50*, WBC, 19 (Waco, TX: Word, 1983) 153.

[40]This is in no way intended to suggest that worship is a substitute for serious intellectual effort. The sanctuary is no place for the notion that pious simplicity can take the place of serious reflection and deep searching for God. As M. Tate (*Psalms 51-100*, WBC 20 [Dallas: Word, 1990] 238) rightly observes, the psalmist's sanctuary experience occurred *only after* serious intellectual effort.

[41]The psalmist's spiritual experience here seems analogous to the modern experience we might have as the ophthalmologist flips lenses before our eyes, or as we manually focus a 35mm camera.

[42]R. Davidson (*Vitality*, 235-236) eloquently states, ". . . the heart of our faith is not our grasp of God but God's sure grasp of us." He cites 1 John 4:10: "not that we loved God but that he loved us and sent his Son. . . ."

[43]A discussion of these ethical topics is beyond the scope of this paper. However, the book of Proverbs provides rich resources for contemporary Christians grappling with the ethics of proper speech and proper sexual

conduct. In a society beset with the ills of inappropriate speech and an obsession with sexual expression, the book holds eloquent practical ethical advice for the community of faith.

[44]As is well known, but worth repeating, biblical wisdom is not synonymous with intelligence. Wisdom is manifested in behavior (ethics) and attitude rather than IQ. James 3:13-18 articulates succinctly and eloquently the decisive difference between godly wisdom and earthly wisdom, and the ethical consequences of each.

[45]To be wise involves viewing life not as a random series of haphazard events, but as the unfolding purposes of a gracious and loving God.

[46]To do justice is to actualize the will of God in all facets of our daily lives—to act, not according to personal advantage or comfort, but according to God's will. To love kindness is to manifest loyalty. It involves feeling a sense of solidarity (community) with the weak and disenfranchised. To walk humbly is to attend carefully to the will and way of God, rather than to go presumptuously on our own way.

[47]A. Hunter, *Seek the Lord* (Baltimore: St. Mary's Press, 1982) 252.

Bibliography

Barton, John. "Approaches to Ethics in the Old Testament." In *Beginning Old Testament Study,* ed. by John Rogerson, 113-130. Philadelphia: Westminster Press, 1982. (For an earlier rendering of this article, see "Understanding Old Testament Ethics," *JSOT* 9 [1978] 44-64.)

Barton reviews several of the issues involved in determining the ethical place of the OT in contemporary biblical studies. He addresses the issues of moral norms, the basis of ethics, motives, and incentives to ethical conduct, and the continuing impact of the OT.

Birch, Bruce. *Let Justice Roll Down: The Old Testament, Ethics, and Christian Life.* Louisville, KY: Westminster John Knox Press, 1991. (For an earlier work, see Bruce Birch and Larry Rasmussen. *Bible and Ethics in the Christian Life.* Minneapolis: Augsburg Press, 1976; rev. 1989.)

This is an invaluable work. Birch addresses methodology, approach, and using the OT as a moral resource. His scope is comprehensive; he attempts to grapple with the whole OT corpus.

Clements, R.E. "Christian Ethics and the Old Testament." *Modern Churchman* 26 (1984) 13-26.

Clements provides a useful discussion of using the OT as an ethical norm, the sociology of law in the OT, and the OT as an ethical system.

Gustafson, James. "The Place of Scripture in Christian Ethics: A Methodological Study." *In* 24 (1970) 430-455.

Gustafson, a noted ethicist, provides a valuable discussion of the issues related to using Scripture in contemporary ethical reflection. He argues that Christian ethics must be informed by biblical theology. For Christians, ethical judgments should be consistent, consonant, and coherent with the theological themes that are primary and pervasive in the biblical witness.

Hamilton, Victor. "The Ethics of the Old Testament." In *Christian Ethics: An Inquiry into Christian Ethics from a Biblical Theological Perspective*, ed. by L. Hynson and L. Scott. Anderson, IN: Warner Press, 1983.

Hamilton offers a succinct overview of ethics in various sections of the OT, including creation theology, the patriarchal narratives, the covenant and law, the prophets, and the wisdom literature.

Janzen, Waldemar. *Old Testament Ethics*. Louisville, KY: Westminster John Knox Press, 1994.

Janzen utilizes the OT stories as paradigms for correct ethical behavior. He articulates five paradigms: the holy life (priestly paradigm); the wise life (the sapiential paradigm); the just life (the royal paradigm); the serving and suffering life (the prophetic paradigm); the familial paradigm. He links the five paradigms through the familial paradigm, and then creatively links them to the NT presentation of Jesus' "five offices"—priest, sage, king, prophet, and God-imaging human.

Kaiser, Walter, Jr. *Toward Old Testament Ethics*. Grand Rapids: Zondervan, 1983.

Kaiser's work provides a useful resource for assessing the current state of ethics among conservative evangelicals. The tone is typically dogmatic and the style apologetic, the approach somewhat propositional. Kaiser attempts to reclaim the validity of the OT for contemporary ethical discussion, and to discount the negative assessments of OT ethics prevalent among numerous scholars.

Wilson, Robert. "Approaches to Old Testament Ethics." In *Canon, Theology, and Old Testament Interpretation: Essays in Honor of Brevard S. Childs*, ed. by G. Tucker, D. Petersen, and R. Wilson, 62-74. Philadelphia: Fortress Press, 1988.

This short article nicely summarizes the several approaches to OT ethics and the issues that need further discussion.

USING THE NEW TESTAMENT FOR ETHICAL GUIDANCE

Robert F. Hull, Jr., Ph.D.

Approaching the Task

"Dear Editor" letters to my hometown newspaper often quote or refer to the Bible in reference to moral/ethical issues. What counts as an ethical issue may vary from place to place, but in the "Bible Belt" state-sponsored lotteries, liquor-by-the-drink, abortion, homosexual practice, affirmative action, R-rated movies, divorce and remarriage, gender equality, and military service are ethical concerns important enough to be addressed by means of quotations from the Bible, especially the New Testament. Many letter-writers so take for granted the authority of Scripture that they assume that all they need to do is quote a text in order to settle an issue. The result is predictable: Sometimes a short "Bible war" breaks out, as another letter to the editor quotes a Bible text to refute the first letter-writer. Occasionally a writer who is not a Christian joins the fray, pointing out that if "Bible-believing" people cannot agree on the texts they read, they cannot hope to convince others to take the Bible seriously.

This scenario, which is played out in other places besides newspapers, suggests both how important and how difficult it is to approach the Bible for ethical guidance. As I have hinted above, even defining the most serious ethical concerns is not always easy. Although the issues mentioned there seem to draw the most predictable mail and to reflect the strongest feelings in the town where I live,

> Even defining the most serious ethical concerns is not always easy.

persons in other places (and even some people where I live) might identify a different set of issues they feel just as strongly about: poverty, homelessness, corporate greed, racism, environmental destruction, militarism.

It is important that we think deeply, carefully, and clearly about our need for ethical guidance and about how the New Testament functions in our search for such guidance. If your experience is anything like mine, you have been taught to treasure the New Testament, to regard it as a source of morally absolute teachings and a sure guide to ethics, but your teachers may have been unable to say exactly how and why the New Testament is authoritative in one respect, but not in another. For example, we would probably all agree that the apostle Paul's condemnation of the incestuous relationship in I Corinthians 5:1-5 is ethically binding on believers everywhere and at all times, but I would guess that the vast majority of Christians would not regard Paul's instructions in 6:1-8 in quite the same way. Here he forbids a believer to take a fellow-believer to a civil court to have an issue decided. Some church bodies and some Christians do follow the rule of not bringing suit against a fellow believer,[1] but you might wish to test the proposition for yourself: If you were defrauded out of several thousand dollars by another Christian, would you be willing to take the offender to court to recover your losses? If you have already begun explaining in your own mind why incest is always wrong but litigation by Christians in a civil court is not always wrong, or if you are remembering how a former teacher told you to reason out such matters, you are illustrating the problem: The ethical function of the New Testament is not self-evident; we do often have to reason out, explain, decide, adjudicate issues of ethical importance. How and why this is so will be explained in due course.

Scripture Interpretation and Ethical Decision-Making

This essay is not a study of "New Testament ethics," for that would be an accounting of the behavior of the people in the NT in relation to their historical and social environment. It would need to take account, not only of the OT and other literature that guided the ethics of Jews,[2] but also the vast amount of Greek and Roman philosophy devoted to ethics, since a fair amount of ethical teaching in the NT parallels that of contemporary philosophy.[3] We sometimes forget that the people *in* the New Testament did not themselves have a New Testament to guide them!

> We sometimes forget that the people *in* the New Testament did not themselves have a New Testament to guide them.

What we are interested in is how the NT informs and authorizes our own ethical decisions and practices. We are really dealing with how the NT is interpreted so that it, an ancient (and in some ways very strange) set of writings can be brought to bear on contemporary ethical issues. This means that we have to ask about ethical matters such questions as the following: (1) Which texts in the NT speak authoritatively to this issue and how can the connection be clearly shown? (2) Are we limited to Scriptures that speak *directly* to the kind of situation with which we are dealing? If not, how can we show the logical force of the texts we cite in reference to issues that were not in the purview of the ancient author? (3) What should we do when equally well-informed and well-meaning Christians disagree on the applicability of the NT to a particular issue?[4]

An illustration will suggest how difficult it is to move directly back from contemporary ethical concerns to the Bible. In 1970 James M. Gustafson wrote an essay on "The Place of Scripture in Christian Ethics,"[5] using as a test case a "hot-button" issue of his time, namely whether the United States military should have invaded Cambodia, an action that occurred in late April 1970 during the Vietnam War. Clearly, no text in the Bible speaks directly to that issue. Gustafson showed that all parties in the debate, to the extent they used the Bible to make their case, not only drew upon different texts, but also invoked other arguments having to do with politics, economics, military strategy, and the like. In the spring of 2003, there was an international debate concerning whether the U.S. military (by itself or with allies) should invade Iraq in order to force compliance with a United Nations mandate that Iraq destroy its weapons of mass destruction. The Associated Press carried a story dated 30 January 2003 in which it quoted a bishop in the United Methodist Church, speaking on behalf of the National Council of Churches in saying that such an attack would be contrary to "God's law."[6] The bishop made it clear that he hoped to influence President George Bush, himself a United Methodist. The same report, however, summarized a contrary view from the president of the Southern Baptist Convention's Ethics and Religious Liberty Committee, who defended war against Iraq as justified. Indeed, it is not difficult to find op-ed pieces by thoughtful and well-informed Christians writing for the national and international media on the one hand in support of, and on the other in opposition to, war with Iraq. The proper place of the Bible in this debate is not easy to specify. Aware of our capacity for self-deception and our tendency to co-opt the Bible to support our own point of view, we have to realize that it is possible to be unethical even in the ways we interpret Scripture.[7] Clearly, we cannot cut ourselves loose from Scripture in our ethical decision-making. What we need are some understandings of how the NT ought to function as a guide to ethics *even if we cannot always agree on what a proper course of action would be.*

> *What we need are some understandings of how the NT ought to function as a guide to ethics even if we cannot always agree on what a proper course of action would be.*

The New Testament and Ethics: A Variety of Approaches

Recent studies have helpfully summarized a variety of approaches to the NT (and the Bible in general) as guides to ethics. The most thorough of these is Jeffrey Siker's book *Scripture and Ethics: Twentieth-Century Portraits.*[8] By examining the texts used by eight theologians and the ways they use them, Siker illustrates that there is no self-evidently "correct" way of applying Scripture to ethical concerns. The influential liberal Protestant theologian Reinhold Niebuhr[9] did his ethical reflections on the basis of quite different assumptions, and perhaps different texts, than does Stanley Hauerwas,[10] with his emphasis on ethics as the life of the church in community, or James Cone,[11] whose standpoint is African-American liberation. Richard Hays has worked out a similar typology, investigating the writings of five theologians in answer to the question "How do ethicists use Scripture?"[12] As Hays notes, despite the differences in standpoints, methods, and outcomes, people who use the NT for ethical reasoning generally demonstrate four "modes of appeal to Scripture." Theologians (and other people, for that matter) find in Scripture a source of (1) *rules* (direct commands), (2) *principles* (general considerations governing specific actions), (3) *paradigms* (examples of positive or negative actions), or (4) *a symbolic world* (the ambiguity of the "human condition" and of the character of God).[13] In due course I will draw upon some of these in giving examples of ethical decision-making.

Another very helpful analysis of the ways in which we interpret Scripture for ethical purposes looks at the assumptions that are often hidden behind the arguments we make.[14] Because the cases I will shortly cite illustrate some of these assumptions, I will summarize them here:

The Rule of Purpose holds that the purpose for a moral rule in the Bible is more important than the rule itself. Cosgrove cites the biblical rule against lending at interest, which was so important that it is found multiple times in the Bible (Exod 22:25; Deut 23:19-20; cf. Ezek 18:8; Prov 28:8; Luke 6:34-35). Up through the Middle Ages Christians treated lending money at interest as sinful; nowadays many ethicists would claim that the *purpose* of the rule was to protect the poor from being exploited. Some would "lighten up" on the rule by prohibiting *excessive* interest (usury); others might simply say that the modern Western economic system benefits more people, even the poor, by its banking and lending system than did the biblical-era agrarian economy.

The Rule of Analogy says that, even if some contemporary moral issues were not problems during the biblical era, we can find analogies in the Bible that provide us principles to help in deciding the contemporary issue. For example, genetic manipulation, organ transplants, in-vitro fertilization, and other examples of high-tech human engineering are not mentioned in the Bible, but one might find analogies there that can help us make ethical decisions about these newer technologies. Here is one possibility: One could say that the Bible treats childbearing as so important that sometimes extreme measures (such as "levirate marriage," [Gen 38:6-11,26; Deut 25:5-10; Mark 12:18-27]) are justified in order to prevent a woman's remaining childless. Might the use of a sperm donor and artificial insemination be a valid analogy?[15]

The Rule of Countercultural Witness holds that, in general, greater weight should be given to the tendencies in Scripture in favor of the weak and marginalized than to those that represent the powerful and dominant. This rule requires that the reader be able to identify and "discount" the expression of the dominant culture and to reveal and magnify the voices of the weaker. This rule claims that God's ultimate will is always imperfectly expressed by human beings (even inspired writers of Scripture), but is more likely to be found standing against dominant ideologies than in support of them. For example, although Scripture always presupposes, and never directly opposes, slavery, greater weight should be given to texts supporting freedom (1 Cor 7:21; Phlm 15-21) and equality before God (Gal 3:28) than those reflecting the status quo (Col 3:22-25; 1 Pet 3:18-19). I will deal with the case of slavery at greater length below.

The Rule of Nonscientific Scope asserts that theology and the empirical sciences are different ways of knowing and that it is not the aim (the *scope*) of Scripture to give its readers what we today would call "scientific" information. In its various uses, this rule can have a bearing, not only on such issues as cosmology, but also on certain applications of the social sciences. For instance, the picture of the woman in 1 Timothy 2:13 as second to be created and first to be deceived rests for its cogency both on a literal reading of the narrative of Genesis 2–3 and the widespread generalization that women are more easily led away by passions than are men. The rule of nonscientific scope says that we know, empirically, that the ancient generalizations about the natural inferiority of women are wrong, and we are not ethically bound by the understandings reflected in those ancient texts even if their authors understood themselves to be asserting facts.[16]

The Rule of Moral-Theological Adjudication says that when there are two plausible ways of understanding the same text, we should apply the text in the way that agrees with what we have already judged to be morally or theologically desirable. In a rough-and-ready way, we encounter this rule when a reader opts for an understanding that agrees with his or her moral sensibilities. In a more disciplined way ancient writers insist on the "analogy of faith," that is, ambiguous texts are interpreted to agree with orthodox faith. In all applications of this rule certain moral-theological convictions are held to be so basic that they incline us to understand ambiguous texts in agreement with those basic convictions. Obviously, persons with differing moral value judgments may well disagree on their interpretation of particular texts, but each will still be applying the rule. Consider, for example, Matthew 5:44: "Love your enemies and pray for those who persecute you." A firm pacifist, such as John Yoder, would take the text as requiring the church *as a whole* not to engage in war, since peacemaking is an overriding moral value for Yoder; Paul Ramsey, a "just war" ethicist, would see the same text as applying only to individuals in their conflicts, since one of his "baseline" values is that force must sometimes be used to help the "neighbor" against tyrannical powers.[17]

Before looking at some model ethical problems, I think it only fair for me to lay out my own "baseline" convictions about the use of the NT for ethics. I do not by any means offer these points as a comprehensive guide, but only as a suggestive approach. I intend also that they be seen, not as independent beads on a string, but more as facets of a cut diamond, not only bounding each other on several sides, but with angles of each facet visible through other facets.

Foundational Convictions for Using the New Testament for Ethics

Ethics based on the New Testament will be:

Communal. Although one's personal moral/ethical practice ought to be shaped by the NT, the formation of Christian character occurs in relation to the community of faith, the church.[18] Not a single writing in the NT is intended for individual consumption. The most personal letters in the NT, those to Timothy, are replete with references to the church's traditional beliefs and practices and with exhortations that are meaningless outside a communal context. Even the letter to Philemon is addressed also "to Apphia our sister and Archippus our fellow soldier *and the church in your house*" (v. 1).

> *Not a single writing in the NT is intended for individual consumption.*

The Roman Christians Paul described as "full of goodness, filled with all knowledge, and able to instruct one another" (Rom 15:14, RSV)[19] did not have a NT to guide them. Paul, who had not founded that church, acknowledged that, without his teaching, they already had communal resources to enable the continual transformation he writes about in Romans 12:1-2. The formation of character is not a lonely occupation for a brave soul alone in a room with a New Testament.

This ethical shaping is not a function of formal teaching alone but is part of the give-and-take of personal relations within local congregations and is signaled in the NT by the "one-another" texts, from the "love one another" of the Gospel of John (13:34-35) to

Paul's "when you come together to eat, wait for one another" (1 Cor 11:33). Christian ethical living not only reflects the values and commitments of the church community, but also helps to shape community.[20] The church's worship life is crucially important in shaping ethical practice. Every occasion of baptism is a reminder to believers to "remember your baptism"

> The church's worship life is crucially important in shaping ethical practice.

and the "newness of life" marked by that cleansing (Rom 6:5-7; 1 Cor 6:9-11; Col 3:1-17). Every celebration of the Lord's Supper is a reminder that "because there is one loaf, we who are many are one body" (1 Cor 10:17), and when we partake, we should "discern the body" (1 Cor 11:29) not only of the Lord, but of the church.[21]

Imitative. The pattern of Christian ethical behavior has models. The OT injunction "You shall be holy; for I, the LORD your God, am holy" (Lev 19:2) is probably the basis of Jesus' call to perfection "as your heavenly Father is perfect" (Matt 5:48). What is sometimes overlooked is that this maxim concludes a section (vv. 43-47) showing the ways in which God is to be imitated, namely in doing good to both the righteous and the unrighteous. God is to be imitated specifically as God is made known in the love of Christ (Eph 5:1-2).

The imitation of Christ is absolutely central to ethical formation in the NT. It is Paul's conviction that believers are those who have been chosen by God to be "conformed to the image of his son" (Rom 8:29). In their baptism, believers have been "united with Christ" (Rom 6:3), and "clothed with Christ" (Gal 3:27), just as Paul could claim to have been "crucified with Christ" (Gal 2:19).[22] Those who had "learned

> The imitation of Christ is absolutely central to ethical formation in the NT.

Christ" (Eph 4:20) were presumed to "have the mind of Christ" (1 Cor 2:16). Rather than a laundry list of specific acts ("What would Jesus do?"), it is the humble, obedient death on the cross which sets the pattern for Christ-imitation (Phil 2:1-11). It is the story of the serving, suffering, and crucified Jesus that lies at the heart of Christian ethics.[23] Presumably, therefore, the early churches knew not only the "gospel message," but also some of the teachings of Jesus when he set himself before his followers as model and mentor (Mark 10:35-45; Luke 22:24-27; John 13:12-17).

Like a good moral teacher of Hellenistic times, Paul encourages his readers to imitate him insofar as he imitates Christ (1 Cor 11:1). He acknowledges that the Thessalonians "became imitators of us and of the Lord" (1 Thess 1:6) and encourages them to continue to follow his example (2 Thess 3:7-9).

The circle is closed when the imitator becomes the model for others: "Join in imitating me and mark those who so live as you have an example in us" (Phil 3:17). Timothy is reminded of what he has seen and heard from Paul (2 Tim 3:10-11; 2:2) and instructed to convey the teachings to "faithful people" who will, in turn, share them with others (2 Tim 2:2). The readers of Hebrews are encouraged to imitate the faith of their leaders (13:7) and the example of those who "through faith and patience inherit the promises" (6:12). Indeed, a whole group of churches can be held up as a model for imitation, as the churches of Judea (1 Thess 2:14), who bore persecution faithfully, and the Macedonians, who gave generously to the poor saints in Jerusalem (2 Cor 8:1-6).

Gospel-Centered. The "good news" of the salvation of God in Jesus Christ is the central theme of the NT and a crucial thematic link with the OT.[24] Just as the gospel, not the law, is the motive power for salvation, so also it is the gospel, not law, which is the driving force for ethical living: "Let your manner of life be worthy of the gospel of Christ" (Phil 1:27). When Mark referred to his story of Jesus as "the beginning of the gospel," he made it clear that the advent of Jesus into the world was good news. Any Greek-speaking Jewish reader would have linked the Greek word *euangelion,* "gospel," with its usage in the Greek translation of Isaiah 52:7-10, which refers to the announcement that God was bringing his people back from captivity as the "good news" of peace, redemption, and salvation. Ethical living, living that is "worthy of the gospel of Christ," will be living that honors the saving message of Jesus and aims to be an instrument of God's continuing work of freeing captives.

> As the gospel is the motive power for salvation, so it is the driving force for ethical living.

Paul goes on to illustrate a "manner of life worthy of the gospel of Christ"[25] by telling, first, of the descent of the Messiah to the "slave's death" of a cross (Phil 2:6-11), and secondly, his own story of descent from high position in Judaism to conformity with the death of Jesus (3:4-10). Peter's refusal to share table fellowship with Gentile believers (Gal 2:11-12) was a failure to live up to the ethical demands of the gospel ("the truth of the gospel," 2:14). In other words, more was at stake than the question, "Is the gospel for Gentiles as well as Jews?" Equality in salvation implied the ethical decision of togetherness at table as well.

Luke's accounting of Jesus' "inaugural sermon" in the synagogue at Nazareth (Luke 4:17-21) focuses on the "good news" as summarized in Isaiah 61:1-3, with its emphasis on help for the poor, release for captives, sight for the blind, liberty for the oppressed. As the story of the early church reveals, wherever the gospel was taken, charity for the poor, ministry to the imprisoned, and other "saving" deeds followed. By claiming that ethics based on the NT will be "gospel-centered," I am asserting that Christian people ought to act in ways that tend to support people who need to be freed or "saved" in all kinds of ways, not only from sinful rebellion against God, but also from addictions, from abuse by those more powerful than

> Christian people ought to act in ways that tend to support people who need to be freed or "saved" in all kinds of ways.

they, from the fear of using their spiritual gifts, and from the law-based theology that often cripples our churches.

Three Case Studies

In what follows I will sketch out briefly three case studies involving ethical decision-making. The first is a summary of a famous case in the NT itself. I cite it as an example of how the earliest churches worked through the most difficult problem they faced in the first several generations. The second is a hypothetical case, although the "pieces" of it are easily paralleled by real-life situations. I will refer back to the various "rules" that might be (or were) invoked in the decision-making, as well as how my own "foundational convictions" come into play. The third focuses on a remarkable moral/ethical accomplishment of the nineteenth century. Obviously, all I can do in the limited space here is to lay out the essential elements of each case and some suggestions of how the NT serves as ethical guide.

The Case of Gentiles and the Law

The case itself is disclosed in Acts 15:1 in these words: "Certain individuals came down from Judea and were teaching the brothers, 'Unless you are circumcised according to the custom of Moses, you cannot be saved'" (NRSV). The question whether Gentiles had to follow the Torah, including having their males circumcised, was not simply a "theological" matter, but a "grace versus works" issue. To be an "Israelite" said something about not only how one worshiped, but also what one ate, with whom one associated and under what circumstances, and countless matters of custom and culture. In the eyes of many Jews it was perfectly appropriate to include with the word "Gentile" the characterization "sinner" ("We who are Jews by birth and not Gentile sinners . . ." Gal 2:15); conversely, many Greeks and Romans would have found it just as natural to refer to Jews as "superstitious" and "clannish."

The theological issue looks to us to be clear-cut. The condensed version is given in Acts 10:34-43, which makes it clear that God shows no partiality, offers forgiveness to all people through Jesus Christ, and calls all to repentance and baptism. For many Jews, however, what this meant was that the ranks of God's chosen people, to whom the Messiah had finally come, were now opened up to the Gentiles—provided, of course, they take on themselves the "yoke of the covenant," including circumcision and fidelity to the sacred Scriptures. Even if one could solve the theological problem (which is the hardest nut Paul ever had to crack—see the whole of Galatians and much of Romans), there were still the practical issues of table fellowship, cultural differences, tradition.

Luke Timothy Johnson has masterfully summarized the Lukan attention to this problem in Acts, where the issue dominates the story from chapter 10 on.[26] Johnson points out the various "players" in this case: The Holy Spirit, Simon Peter, Cornelius, Jewish believers in Jerusalem and Antioch, Paul, and Barnabas. He also details the moves and strategies necessary to reach consensus: simply agreeing on the theological point was not enough. Eventually a council was called in Jerusalem (Acts 15:1-29), to which elders from the Jerusalem church, apostles, Paul, and Barnabas were invited. They not only quoted Scripture (vv. 16-18), they also summarized past events and interpreted their meaning theologically (vv. 7-14); they listened, they discussed, and they sought the will of the Holy Spirit (15:28). Finally, they reached a decision that represented a genuine compromise: The Gentiles were admitted to the church without circumcision or Torah-keeping; *but* they were required "to abstain from what has been sacrificed to idols and from what is strangled and from unchastity" (v. 29, RSV). This seems to us unfair; judging strictly by the gospel, it was. Of all the laws in the Torah, why single out "unchastity"?—because Jews tended to characterize Gentiles as sexual profligates, since they had no law to keep their passions in check. All the prohibitions were, quite frankly, concessions to Jewish sensibilities; thus, the stricture against meat offered to idols was put in so as not to offend those whom Paul later called "the weak" (1 Cor 8:1-10), that is, believers who were not mature enough in their faith to ignore the so-called "gods" at the shrines that also served as local butcher shops, where meat was routinely dedicated to some deity. The rule against blood must have seemed particularly arbitrary to Gentiles. Nevertheless, all this "seemed good to the Holy Spirit and to us" (v. 28). When the decision was communicated to all the churches by means of a circular letter carried by a delegation, there was pastoral work being done, drawing the churches together around this new agreement.[27]

There are many ethical implications of this "case." (1) This was a communal process, wrought out by means of discussion, discernment, and decision. (2) It was "gospel-centered" in that the theological basis for the decision was the fact that Gentiles and Jews both had to come to God through response to Jesus Christ and that Gentiles were freed from the "yoke" (v. 10) of the Torah. (3) Scripture was necessary to the decision, but not sufficient to clear up the issues. No objection was raised to Peter's choice of texts (Jer 12:15; Amos 9:11-12) nor his application of those texts to the issue at hand, but just quoting the Bible was not enough. (4) The compromise that was reached was justified on the basis of how the new practice would "play out" on the field; James frankly noted that—put in our own terms—"there are synagogues all over the place" (v. 21); in other words, Gentile believers ought to have a care for Jewish sensibilities if they want to win a hearing for the gospel. (5) The compromise was a temporary expedient. Although the Jew/Gentile issue continued to bedevil the church for several generations, Christians in general today do not believe themselves to be bound by the decision reached in Jerusalem. A steak eaten rare might bother our stomachs, but probably not our consciences.

The Case of the Overbearing Husband

Hazel and Coleman married right out of high school. She grew up in the church; Coleman did not, but was a star athlete and good-looking. Coleman is intensely possessive of Hazel. He wants her to stay home and especially dislikes it when she goes out shopping, or even to church, all dressed up and with her hair done nicely. He says she is just trying to attract other men. Lately he has become physically and verbally abusive, especially if he comes home drunk. After ten years it looks like their marriage has had it. She's tried to get Coleman to go to a marriage counselor, but he refuses. She knows the teaching of her church is against divorce, but she has asked her minister to help her with a decision.

Obviously, there are some prudential considerations in this make-believe case. She can get some protection from the law if he is abusive, but this doesn't solve the larger question: given their history and his obstinacy, is she justified in divorcing him?

Scripture will weigh very heavily in the decision, but which texts? A strict "hard-liner" could conclude on the basis of Mark 10:2-12 (cf. Matt 5:31; 19:3-9) divorce is not an option; in any case, should she divorce Coleman, she would be forbidden to remarry. First Corinthians 7:15 takes up the problem of a believing wife married to an unbelieving husband and allows divorce, but only if the unbelieving partner wants to separate. Coleman doesn't want to separate. She asks her minister about 1 Peter 3:1-6. This text counsels wives to be submissive to their husbands so that unbelieving men can be won to faith by their wives' good behavior. Moreover, it appears to support her husband in his displeasure at her "dressing up." The text says, "Let not yours be the outward adorning with braiding of hair, decoration of gold, and wearing of fine clothing, but let it be the hidden person of the heart. . . ." (1 Pet 3:3, RSV; cf. 1 Tim 2:9-10). A strict "biblicist" might counsel Hazel to go home, obey Coleman, and hope to win him over to Christ.

Her minister, however, believes an ethical decision will require the use of some of the "rules of interpretation" mentioned above. Does the "rule of purpose" have any bearing on the divorce/remarriage texts? Some historical research shows that Jewish women didn't even have the right to divorce. Perhaps the Matthaean text is partly an effort to give wives some protection from frivolous divorces. Greek and Roman women could divorce their husbands, which seems to be the situation envisioned in Mark 10. Probably all of the divorce texts have as one purpose fostering attitudes toward marriage among believers that will run counter to the norm in the pagan world, as well as to casual divorce of women by Jewish men.

If the purpose of the rule is more important than the rule, would it be legitimate to inquire of Paul with respect to marriage of believers to unbelievers, "Are there no circumstances under which the believer can divorce the unbeliever, even if the unbeliever wants to stay married? Should she stay in an abusive relationship?" The 1 Peter text is even more troubling, because it presupposes that the wives are suffering some level of abuse (the whole context is about undeserved suffering by the godly at the hands of the ungodly). Again, the social/historical context of

> "Are there no circumstances under which the believer can divorce the unbeliever, even if the unbeliever wants to stay married?"

1 Peter is important, because the churches of Asia Minor are suffering a lot of social pressure because of their "countercultural" lifestyle. One of the purposes of the advice to wives in this section might be to encourage them not to appear too "countercultural"; if the dominant culture expected wives to be submissive, dowdy-looking, and quiet, perhaps the churches would not be under such threat if they made some accommodation to the cultural expectations.

On the other hand, the purpose of the gospel seems to be to free people from oppression, not to force them simply to "take it," no matter what. The "rule of countercultural witness" suggests that the ethical thing to do is generally to come to the side of the weak and marginalized (Hazel) against the dominant (Coleman). Although 1 Peter sets up the example of Jesus' undeserved suffering as a model for his readers to imitate, does the "imitation of Christ" in Hazel's case trump all other considerations?

One might draw other concerns into the conversation, especially with regard to the difference between the legal and social conventions regulating marriage in the ancient Mediterranean world and our own. One would also need to ask what is the role of the wider church community in helping Hazel reach a decision in this case? Unfortunately, the congregation is often "the last to know" when a divorce finally occurs. This may be an indictment of how poorly equipped congregations are to do critical pastoral work, how prone to gossip and to rush to judgment. It may be that not nearly enough is done to salvage marriage in some cases and that other marriages which are not ended should have been ended long ago. We cannot know at this point whether more effort on Hazel's part to love her husband and gently try to overcome his domineering ways might bring him around. Assuming she does all within her power to try to bring him around, and he does not change, I think it would be an ethical thing to do for Hazel to divorce Coleman and remarry.

The Case of the American Debate over Slavery

The thirteenth amendment to the Constitution, formally abolishing slavery within the United States of America, represented what has been called "an extraordinary shift in moral vision,"[28] because human slavery was a social convention traceable to the beginning of human records. As unthinkable as slave-holding is today, it is sobering to realize how relatively recently the ethics of the slave system were being debated by religious leaders in this country.[29]

Briefly, the pro-slavery defenders could easily show that the practice of slavery is assumed throughout the Bible and is never directly condemned; in fact, instructions regarding its practice are found both in the Torah (Exod 21:1-11; Lev 25:43-46) and the NT (Col 3:22–4:1; Eph 6:5-9; 1 Pet 2:18-20; 1 Tim 6:1-2). A "Professor Dew" of Virginia observes: "When we turn to the New Testament, we find not one single passage at all calculated to disturb the conscience of an honest slaveholder."[30] No other ethical issue illustrates more powerfully the perils of proof-texting; it is impossible to refute the claim of the pro-slavery people that the Bible at most condemns abusive treatment of slaves, but does not judge slave-holding to be, by nature, abusive. The abolitionists, on the other hand, had to turn to more indirect arguments from Scripture. In fact, without saying so, they used some of the "hermeneutical rules" or assumptions identified above. For example, Albert Barnes argued that "the gospel, if fairly applied, would remove slavery from the world; it is therefore wrong."[31] Barnes was insisting that the *principle* of the gospel was more important than the *texts* controlling, but not abolishing, slavery. Abolitionists also tended to favor the "rule of countercultural witness" by emphasizing those texts in which God acts in favor of the weak and marginalized against the dominant.

> As unthinkable as slave-holding is today, it is sobering to realize how relatively recently the ethics of the slave system were being debated by religious leaders in this country.

The case of slavery also shows the importance of reading the text in light of its historical/social context. People who are shocked

that the authors of Scripture do not flatly condemn slavery fail to reckon with
the extent to which slavery was woven
into the fabric of ancient life. Not only
was it a part of the economic system
taken for granted, but it was also, from
Aristotle on, seen to be part of the natural order of things.[32] Although an

> *One could almost say
> that, absent a miracle, a
> world without slavery was
> literally beyond the power
> of people in the ancient
> Roman world to conceive.*

occasional philosopher asserted that slaves were human beings, not
simply "living tools," no social commentator of antiquity advocated
the abolition of the slave system. One could almost say that, absent
a miracle, a world without slavery was literally beyond the power of
people in the ancient Roman world to conceive.

Compared to much of what we read about slavery in secular
sources, the NT texts that require Christian masters to treat their
slaves "justly and fairly" (Col 4:1) and not to "threaten" them (Eph
6:9) are somewhat "countercultural." Even so, the matter-of-fact
acceptance of slavery in the NT rightly presents an ethical dilemma
to thoughtful people. The portrait in 1 Pet 2:18 is especially troubling, for here slaves are told to be submissive "not only to the kind
and gentle but also to the overbearing (the Greek word is *skoliois*,
'twisted')." The most hopeful sign of progress is the little letter to
Philemon, in which Paul all but asks Philemon to grant freedom to
Onesimus, his slave-turned-brother-in-Christ ("I write to you,
knowing that you will do even more than I say"—v. 21). The circumstance that American slave-owners routinely sent ministers
down to their slave cabins to preach from these biblical texts counseling obedience to masters makes one wonder how it was that so
many slaves became Christians!

Since the biblical texts directly relating to slavery are uniform-
ly accepting of the practice, what process of ethical reflection
enabled such a massive "shift in moral vision"? Above all, it seems
to me, the message of the gospel itself, if heard long enough and
taken seriously enough, is simply incompatible with the ownership
of one human being by another.[33] One could say that the germ of
emancipation is already there in Galatians 3:28, where we learn that
"in Christ . . . there is neither slave nor free," but it was many centuries before the full implications of that text were realized (if,
indeed, they have been realized yet). A "gospel-centered" ethic cannot, finally, tolerate slavery. Perhaps the "rule of purpose" even

comes into play. If we acknowledge that the texts in Colossians and Ephesians relativized the harshness of slavery, acknowledged Christian slaves as brothers, and mitigated the absoluteness of the master's power, perhaps we should see that the *purpose* of these "rules" was ultimately to support the equality of all social classes before the God whose Son "took on himself the form of a slave" (Phil 2:7) and humbled himself to the obedience of death for the sake of all people. Surely the "rule of countercultural witness" speaks powerfully in support of these weakest and most marginalized of all.[34]

In the final analysis, the case of slavery and its eventual outlawing should serve as a warning against an ethic that simply strings together texts that seem to deal directly with the moral/ethical problem. Even putting the best possible construction on the NT texts about slavery, their "solution" to the harshness of the institution is only a contingent answer. There is no way to "rescue" these texts so as to make slavery still acceptable, as some of the most famous theologians of the nineteenth century tried to do. Indeed, I think that the application of the Colossians and Ephesians texts to the employer/employee relationship (a fairly common sermonic practice) is also unjustified. From an ethical standpoint, we cannot make a "biblical" case for slavery. Some texts, and some principles, such as the imitation of Christ, simply trump other texts, or else the gospel holds no real power to make a new creation. "If anyone is in Christ, there is a new creation; old things have passed away. Look, all things have become new" (2 Cor 5:17). If it took so long for the implications of the gospel to be worked out in relation to slavery, might there be other ethical issues still waiting for the people of God to work out in the churches where we work and worship?

> From an ethical standpoint, we cannot make a "biblical" case for slavery.

Notes

[1]Mennonites, for example, do not sue at law.

[2]Much of the so-called "Second Temple Literature" ("Intertestamental Literature") is full of moral/ethical teachings, including important materials from the Dead Sea Scrolls.

[3]For examples see Abraham J. Malherbe, *Moral Exhortation: A Greco-Roman Sourcebook* (Philadelphia: Westminster, 1986); and Wayne A. Meeks, *The Origins of Christian Morality* (New Haven: Yale University Press, 1993). For an interesting comparison see Robert P. Seesengood, "Rules for an Ancient Philadelphian Religious Organization and Early Christian Ethical Teaching," *Stone-Campbell Journal* 5 (2002) 217-233.

[4]David Kelsey raised similar questions in a very influential book, *The Uses of Scripture in Recent Theology* (Philadelphia: Fortress, 1975) 2-3.

[5]James M. Gustafson, "The Place of Scripture in Christian Ethics," *Interpretation* 24 (1970) 430-455.

[6]Reported in the *Johnson City Press* (Johnson City, TN) 30 January 2003.

[7]See Daniel Patte, *Ethics of Biblical Interpretation: A Reevaluation* (Louisville, KY: Westminster John Knox, 1995).

[8]Jeffrey Siker, *Scripture and Ethics: Twentieth-Century Portraits,* (New York: Oxford, 1997).

[9]Ibid., 8-24.

[10]Ibid., 97-125.

[11]Ibid., 149-169.

[12]Richard Hays, *Moral Vision of the New Testament* (San Francisco: HarperSanFrancisco, 1996) 207-290. The theologians are Reinhold Niebuhr, Karl Barth, John Howard Yoder, Stanley Hauerwas, and Elisabeth Schuessler Fiorenza.

[13]Ibid., 208-209.

[14]These are found in Charles H. Cosgrove, *Appealing to Scripture in Moral Debate: Five Hermeneutical Rules* (Grand Rapids: Eerdmans, 2002).

[15]The Rule of Analogy is extremely complex, as is shown by Cosgrove's devoting 38 pages to it (ibid., 51-89).

[16]I borrow this example also from Cosgrove, *Appealing to Scripture,* 143-145.

[17]See Siker's sketch of Ramsey's ethics, *Scripture and Ethics,* 80-96; and Hays's analysis of Yoder, *Moral Vision,* 239-253.

[18]The emphasis on "living out the story of the faith" within a Christian community is connected especially with the writings of Stanley Hauerwas, beginning with *A Community of Character* (Notre Dame: University of Notre Dame Press, 1981); see also Allen Verhey, *The Great Reversal: Ethics and the New Testament* (Grand Rapids: Eerdmans, 1984); and Stephen E. Fowl and Gregory Jones, *Reading in Communion: Scripture and Ethics in Christian Life* (Grand Rapids: Eerdmans, 1991).

[19]This is a key text in Allen Verhey, *Remembering Jesus* (Grand Rapids: Eerdmans, 2002).

[20]Hays's treatment of "community" as one of the "focal images" for Christian ethics makes this point powerfully (*The Moral Vision,* 196-197).

[21]These are reasons why the acts of breaking the "one bread," pouring the "one cup," and speaking aloud the words of Jesus are so symbolically powerful in the community's worship.

[22]Michael J. Gorman has coined the term "cruciformity" to describe the "cross-shaped" life of the believer; see *Cruciformity: Paul's Narrative Spirituality of the Cross* (Grand Rapids: Eerdmans, 2001).

[23]Thus, Hays's second "focal image" of the cross (*The Moral Vision,* 197) and Gorman's reference to Paul's "master story" (*Cruciformity,* 23) as his identity with the crucified Jesus. In Luke Timothy Johnson's memorable phrasing, "The story of Jesus is the norm for the moral character of the community" (*Living Jesus* [San Francisco: HarperSanFrancisco, 1999] 111).

[24]Bruce Shields, "New Testament Hermeneutics," *Christian Standard* 132/12 (March, 1997) 4-6, points out the centrality of the gospel for NT interpretation.

[25]It is important to note that the word translated "let your manner of life" is *politeuesthe,* which summarizes one's civic obligations, in this case, not as a citizen of Philippi, but as one whose "citizenship is in heaven" (Phil 3:20), but who must live faithfully to the gospel on this earth.

[26]Luke Timothy Johnson, *Scripture and Discernment: Decision Making in the Church* (Nashville: Abingdon, 1996).

[27]Ibid., 105-106.

[28]Bruce C. Birch and Larry L. Rasmussen, *Bible and Ethics in the Christian Life* (Minneapolis: Augsburg, 1989) 60.

[29]Willard Swartley has summarized the arguments in these debates in *Slavery, Sabbath, War, and Women* (Scottdale, PA: Herald Press, 1983) 31-53.

[30]From a book entitled *The Pro-Slavery Argument,* published in 1852; quotation from Swartley, *Slavery,* 35.

[31]Albert Barnes, *An Inquiry into the Scriptural Views of Slavery* (New York: Negro Universities Press, 1969 [orig. pub. 1857]) 365; quotation from Swartley, *Slavery,* 45.

[32]See Thomas Wiedemann, *Greek and Roman Slavery: A Sourcebook* (Baltimore: Johns Hopkins University Press, 1981). Aristotle

119

memorably defined a slave as "living property" (*Politics* 1.2.4-5).

[33]As Albert Barnes (n. 31) had already observed.

[34]See above, 106-107 (where I summarize this rule).

Bibliography

Birch, Bruce C., and Larry L. Rasmussen. *Bible and Ethics in the Christian Life.* 2nd ed. Minneapolis: Augsburg, 1989.

This widely-used textbook introduces ethical theories and relates them to Christian practice. It explores the nature and function of biblical authority and shows how the Bible can function as a resource for the moral life. Clearly outlined and written with the student in mind.

Cosgrove, Charles. *Appealing to Scripture in Moral Debate: Five Hermeneutical Rules.* Grand Rapids: Eerdmans, 2002.

Deals with the importance of how one makes and supports arguments in moral debate. Uncovers the unspoken assumptions that underlie many common ways of using the Bible in moral debate. My summary of these hermeneutical rules (in the essay above) demonstrates how important this book is.

Hays, Richard B. *The Moral Vision of the New Testament: A Contemporary Introduction to New Testament Ethics.* San Francisco: HarperSanFrancisco, 1996.

The best guide I have read to the ethical use of the New Testament. Hays first describes the moral/ethical contents of the NT writings, then suggests three "focal images" (community, cross, and new creation) by which to evaluate the work of five contemporary ethicists in using the NT. Lastly, he works through five test cases to show how the NT helps in making ethical decisions.

Johnson, Luke Timothy. *Scripture and Discernment: Decision Making in the Church.* Nashville: Abingdon, 1996.

This little guide walks the reader through theory, exegesis, and practice in working through tough ethical problems. Firmly committed to the decision-making as a group process, Johnson uses the "Jerusalem Council" of Acts 15 as a model for the contemporary church. He selects three test cases: leadership (women in the church), fellowship (homosexuals in the church), and stewardship (the use of possessions) and suggests the kinds of questions needed for group decision-making.

McDonald, J. Ian H. *The Crucible of Christian Morality*. New York: Routledge, 1998.

The merit of this book is that it focuses on the roots of Christian ethics, including the Jewish and Greco-Roman "social world" of moral thought and practice. His deft summaries of the ethos of the communities from which various NT writings derive sets this book apart.

Verhey, Allen. *Remembering Jesus: Christian Community, Scripture, and the Moral Life*. Grand Rapids: Eerdmans, 2002.

Construes Christian ethics as the process of "remembering" Jesus along with the early Christian communities that preserved his teaching and shaped their characters by that story. Elegantly written, full of illustrations from the author's long experience of teaching undergraduate students.

THE CHURCH AND CULTURE
PAUL'S ALTERNATIVE VISION
Larry Chouinard, Ph.D.

Introduction

As observed by Walter Brueggemann, the community of faith never lives in a cultural vacuum, but always in the "shadow of the Empire."[1] Though the empires take diverse forms, each in their own way present both challenges and inevitable tensions among those who have been called to embody an alternative story and extol a radically different ethic. Whether the nations appear tolerant or intolerant of those who voice the language of faith, there is always the tendency for secular forces to use religious commitment as a vehicle for its own agendas, while at the same time marginalizing those who appear to conflict with the dominant cultural convictions and values. Certainly, there have always been some cultural forms that will not hesitate to resort to violent means in the attempt to exert conformity to the spirit of the age. However, all too often people of faith have offered little resistance and have surrendered willingly to the prevailing cultural trends. The ease with which faith is often subordinated and forced to support secular agendas has effectively silenced prophetic voices and has left the religious community with, in the words of Hauerwas and Willimon, "the saccharine residue of theism in demise."[2]

> All too often people of faith have offered little resistance and have surrendered willingly to the prevailing cultural trends.

In Israel's case they often struggled to maintain their distinctive identity and sense of community in the midst of extraordinarily powerful cultural forces. Each of the great empires to whom Israel was subjected presented its own unique challenge to a self-conscious intentional community intent on preserving both identity and praxis. As witnessed in the prophetic literature, their struggle often succumbed to syncretistic patterns in which they compromised their unique calling and peculiar practices. The problem facing every faith-based community is how to exhibit a discerning spirit that balances creative engagement with the prevailing culture without compromising the narrative that both informs and shapes the character of the community.

Culture and Faith

It has been observed that much of the Old Testament was written to give guidance to Israel, as a minority culture living in the midst of the nations, on how to preserve their sacred heritage while at the same time embodying the vision of God's creative and redemptive purposes for all humanity.[3] George Lindbeck has argued the case that the modern church should use Israel's story as a template for an "Israel-like" understanding of the church.[4] It certainly is the case that the early church saw Israel's history as their own (Rom 1:16-17; 4:18ff.; 1 Cor 10:1-11; Gal 3:14-25; 6:15; Eph 2:11). As we will see, for Paul the church's story is simply the ongoing story of God's faithfulness to the Abrahamic covenant now fulfilled in Jesus and the mission of the church. Accordingly, like Israel, Christians have their own sacred texts, rituals, peculiar symbolic forms, patterns of behavior, and even a distinctive language that in effect generate a unique cultural expression.[5] Even though the experience of the early church shared a common narrative with Israel, the experience of early Christians in the midst of the Roman Empire differs from the way Israel encountered the nations. Based upon the analysis of 1 Peter, Miroslav Volf observes an important distinction with respect to a Christian's relationship to the non-Christian environment:

> Christians do not come into their social world from outside seeking either to accommodate to their new home (like second generation immigrants would), shape it in the image of the one they have left behind (like colonizers would), or establish a little haven in the strange new world reminiscent of the old (as resident aliens would). . . . Christians do not have such a vantage point since they have experienced a new

birth as *inhabitants* of a particular culture. Hence, they are in an important sense insiders. As those who are a part of the environment from which they have diverted by having been born again and whose difference is therefore internal to that environment, Christians ask, "which beliefs and practices of the culture that is ours must we reject now that our self has been reconstituted by new birth? Which can we retain? What must we reshape to reflect better the values of God's new creation?[6]

The difficulty of exercising real spiritual discernment rests on the failure to adequately understand how the narrative that informs and shapes the Christian community differs from the dominant cultural convictions and practices of the broader society. Critical questions need to be addressed: What is peculiar to a Christian identity or way of life that does not find expression in any other cultural form? Is there anything distinctive in Christian identity and practice that both defines and delineates distinctive cultural boundaries between the church and its social environment? Does the Christian way of life exhibit shared beliefs and values that are by necessity both subversive and threatening to a secular society? These are questions not often posed by modern Christians, at least those living in the Western world.

The work of H. Richard Niebuhr built upon the social theory of Ernst Troeltsch in an attempt to offer possible models depicting the relationship of the church to the world according to five categories: Christ against culture, Christ of culture, Christ above culture, Christ and culture in paradox, and Christ the transformer of culture.[7] Niebuhr defines culture as an "artificial secondary environment which man superimposes on the natural. It comprises language, habits, ideas, beliefs, customs, social organization, inherited artifacts, technical processes, and values."[8] Within Niebuhr's paradigm, culture takes on a monolithic quality that demands that the believer must fall under the rubric of one or the other of his categories. Because one may reject certain aspects of a cultural expression does not necessitate the total rejection of culture, as implied in his category "Christ against culture." But an even more serious flaw in Niebuhr's approach surfaces in the following:

> . . . cultures are forever seeking to combine peace and prosperity, justice with order, freedom with welfare, truth and

beauty, scientific truth with moral good, technical proficiency with practical wisdom, holiness with life, and all of these with all the rest. Among the many values the Kingdom of God may be included—*though scarcely as the one pearl of great price. Jesus Christ and God the Father, the gospel, the church, and eternal life may find places in the cultural complex, but only as elements in the great pluralism* [italics mine].[9]

While Niebuhr opts for the "Christ that transforms culture" he obviously does not take seriously the possibility that Christ may himself offer a cultural option. Therefore, it is not a matter of how Christ fits into a preexistent culture, but rather which cultural paradigm provides an intelligent and coherent reading of reality. Although Niebuhr's categories offer general categorical constructs, they are not adequate for understanding the complex relationship of the church to our world today.[10]

A Counterculture Community

The articulation of a moral vision must begin with constructive reflection on the identity and mission of the church in the midst of the contemporary world setting. Participation in the Christian community necessarily involves a peculiar way of thinking and living in a given social environment. Hays has effectively argued that Paul's ethical vision is fundamentally ecclesial in character. In other words, Paul's ethical vision provides "no basis for a general ethic applicable to those outside the church," but rather Paul's instructions "are aimed at defining and maintaining a corporate identity for his young churches, which are emphatically countercultural communities."[11] While some social historians prefer to use the designation "sect" or "sectarian" to describe the social forms and strategies used by the early church to maintain its distinctive identity and purpose,[12] the language may be somewhat anachronistic for a movement that saw themselves not as a mere sect or faction of Judaism, but as the embodiment of the fulfillment of God's promises to Israel.[13] Neither did the early church's effort to maintain a distinctive identity and community mean a total withdrawal from societal engagement, like might be seen with the Qumran dissenters.

> *Participation in the Christian community necessarily involves a peculiar way of thinking and living in a given social environment.*

125

In fact the social dimension of the Christian movement is highlighted by the very term Paul used to describe these new local communities, i.e., the term *ekklesia*. Horsley highlights the significance of Paul's use of this term:

> By general consensus, while *ekklesia* comes to Paul from the Septuagint (the Jewish Bible in Greek) with strong connotations of the "assembly" of (all) Israel, its primary meaning in the Greek-speaking eastern Roman empire was the citizen "assembly" of the Greek *polis*. *Ekklesia* is thus a political term with certain religious overtones. It is misleading to continue to translate *ekklesia* as *"church,"* particularly insofar as that implies worship or ritual activity. On the other hand, the "assembly" of the Greek *polis* certainly involved praise, acclamation, and discussion of issues of concern to the citizenry, which were also some of the principal activities that Paul's communities carried on at gatherings of the "assemblies." . . . Paul, moreover, understood that in catalyzing local assemblies among the peoples and cities, he was building an . . . alternative society to the Roman imperial order.[14]

In a time when the church has largely acquiesced to modernity's effort to marginalize religious faith by relegating it to private feelings and personal experience, with little relevance to the "real" world, it is refreshing that several scholars have challenged such notions with a new ecclesial model that takes seriously the church's responsibility to embody "a distinct social/political alternative."[15] Philip Kenneson has argued persuasively that the modern church needs "different models for conceptualizing its own identity and its relationship to the rest of society."[16] He calls upon the believing community to "re-imagine" the church as a "contrast-society," whose "life is animated by a different spirit—a difference manifested in its material practices and institutions, as well as in the narratives and convictions that give them shape and intelligibility."[17] Therefore, our conflict with the world is best understood as a conflict of narratives that inform and encourage different practices and convictions. A narrative grounded in God's redemptive work in Christ results in the following scenario:

> Churches are rightly understood as alternative communities to the extent that they offer a way of ordering life—an alternative way of telling and embodying their stories. . . . Within

a Christian narrative ordering, however, there is a conscious resistance to Christian convictions and practices being compartmentalized, privatized, and therefore trivialized, because this is seen as denying these convictions and practices precisely the status that they are supposed to have within that narrative, where they are *the* ordering and controlling convictions and practices of Christians' lives.[18]

> "Churches are rightly understood as alternative communities to the extent that they offer a way of ordering life . . . ."

Stanley Hauerwas and William H. Willimon in their provocative book, *Resident Aliens*, understand discipleship as "a joyful call to be adopted by an alien people to join a countercultural phenomenon, a new *polis* called church."[19] Rather than "suppress its peculiarities in order to participate responsibly in the culture . . . the political task of Christians is to be the church rather than transform the world."[20] The church makes its best contribution to the wider society by providing a community capable of developing a people of virtue. The church as an alternative *polis* engages in theological politics, that is, a politics anchored in the reality of the presence of God's Kingdom. Therefore, for Hauerwas and Willimon, the Christian's endorsement or rejection of the politics of the state is always subordinate to the church's call to embody the ethics and mission of the Kingdom.

> The church makes its best contribution to the wider society by providing a community capable of developing a people of virtue.

According to Rodney Clapp, the "original Christians . . . were about creating and sustaining a unique culture—a way of life that would shape character in the image of their God."[21] As a unique and coherent "culture," the church constitutes a distinctive *polis* "embodying and passing along a story that provides the symbols through which its people gain their identity and their way of seeing the world. The church as a culture has its own language and grammar, in which words such as 'love' and 'service' are crucial and are used correctly only according to certain rules."[22] The church as a culture carries and sustains its own way of life which includes (1) a particular way of eating, learned through the Eucharist; (2) a particular way of handling conflict, the peculiar politics called "forgiveness" and learned through the example and practice of Jesus and the cross; (3) a particular way of perpetuating itself through evangelism rather than biological propagation.[23]

From the Mennonite tradition, John H. Yoder articulates a similar view of the church when he describes the call of the disciples as a "calling into being a community of *voluntary* commitment, willing for the sake of its calling to take upon itself the hostility of the given society. . . . What matters is the quality of life to which the disciple is called. The answer is that to be a disciple is to share in that style of life of which the cross is the culmination."[24] For Yoder the radical revolution to which Jesus has called his disciples is not one that advances by the edge of the sword, but by the "politics of Jesus [wherein] the Christian learns to identify and disarm the real enemy, identified as the 'principalities and powers'" (see ch. 8). Accordingly, "although immersed in this world, the church by her way of being represents the promises of another world. . . . The church cultivates an alternative consciousness."[25]

In a similar vein, Duane Friesen argues that the church as an alternative community can be a potent force in the world.[26] Primarily, Friesen has in mind the "local, gathered congregation, a believing community that seeks to model an alternative society in faithfulness to Christ."[27] For Friesen, in contrast to Hauerwas and Willimon, being the church does involve transforming the world, as believers seek, in the words of Jeremiah to an exiled Israel, "the *shalom* of the city" (Jer 29:7).

The descriptive model which sees the church as an "alternative community," a "countercultural movement," or a "new *polis*" should not be construed as implying that the church withdraw from the public arena in pursuit of some form of transcendental redemption. In fact, the terminology is intended to offer an ecclesial vision that understands the church as the embodiment of Kingdom values and priorities and therefore the only effective witness to expose the world's fallenness and the futility of its strategies. In the words of Hauerwas, "the church serves the world by giving the world the means to see itself truthfully," and to offer creative alternatives.[28]

> "The church serves the world by giving the world the means to see itself truthfully," and to offer creative alternatives.

Yoder argues that while the church should serve the world, its service is modeled after a "revolutionary subordination" that renounces all domineering claims and voluntarily assumes a position of servanthood.[29] In Jesus and his Kingdom a new political reality has dawned, exhibiting an alternative order that directly engages and challenges the old order by its embodiment of the spirit of Christ. Therefore, the church, based upon the "politics of Jesus" witnesses to an alternative way of thinking and being. When the church is truly *the church*, an alternative culture is manifested that does not entail social withdrawal or sectarian isolationism. Instead, the church exercises a spirit of discernment to determine the form that faithful discipleship must take, given the societal context in which it finds itself.

Rather than embracing secular notions that equate the public arena with the secular, while religious faith is relegated to the sphere of the private, the vision articulated above understands the church as a new *public order* offering an alternative cultural expression grounded in the reality of God's Reign. Because this new cultural expression transcends ethnic and national boundaries, it is critical that the church not simply mirror the dominant national culture in which it finds itself. The American civic cultural expression, for example, has exerted tremendous pressure to reshape the Christian story in a way that reinforces and supports the American story. Too often the language of the church has been hijacked and twisted to fit the agendas of national policies. And the church, rather than being a witness to an alternative reality, has acquiesced by endowing with sacred value America's symbols (e.g., the flag, Constitution, national monuments, etc.), solemn civic liturgies (e.g., pledging allegiance to the flag, voting, national holidays, singing national hymns, and possibly "shopping"), and civic notions of virtue (e.g., patriotism, service in the Armed Forces, capitalistic consumerism). The question that must be asked is how the church's sacred symbol of the cross, the liturgy of a common meal uniting all humanity, and the core virtues of love, forgiveness, and non-violence can be made to square with America's civic "religious" ideology? The issue can only be resolved in terms of one's ultimate allegiance and which metanarrative will be the determining factor in shaping ethical choices. Sadly, in the Western world the faith of many Christians has

> The faith of many Christians has become so aligned with a particular economic system (e.g., capitalism) and/or nationalistic peculiarities that a Kingdom perspective is never seriously evaluated.

become so aligned with a particular economic system (e.g., capitalism) and/or nationalistic peculiarities that a Kingdom perspective is never seriously evaluated.

Although there are considerable differences between living in the first century under the domination of the Roman Empire and living in our modern Western world, we can nevertheless learn a great deal about how the early church saw itself in relationship to the broader culture. In order to appreciate the church as a distinct countercultural movement, we will look at Paul's letter to the Corinthians and his strategy for cultivating a cultural expression radically at odds with their broader culture. As recent New Testament research has indicated, Paul's ecclesial vision is much more concerned with questions about identity and the social integrity of the *ekklesia* than individual salvation issues that have often dominated Christian discussions. As Hays observes:

> The advice that he offers is not merely generic and conventional, as though he were a first-century Ann Landers, answering everybody's cards and letters in terms of a lowest common denominator of common sense. Rather, he is seeking to shape the life of a particular community in accordance with his vision; his exhortations are aimed at defining and maintaining a corporate identity for his young churches, which are emphatically countercultural communities. Thus, his letters should be read primarily as instruments of community formation.[30]

Paul's Alternative Vision

Of course, the struggle to exhibit a distinctive countercultural stance is not peculiar to the modern church. The earliest Christian churches all struggled with the cultural implications of the explosive message they were charged to proclaim. As Wright observes, the Christian community knew quite early that the message they proclaimed demanded "an allegiance that might very well involve not only a previously unimagined self-denial, but also social ostracism, imprisonment, torture and death. Early Christianity certainly does not look as if it spread because demands were being trimmed to the hearers' expec-

> The struggle to exhibit a distinctive countercultural stance is not peculiar to the modern church.

tations or wishes."[31] The letters of Paul give evidence of his pastoral efforts to assist these fragile Christian communities to articulate and model a response to their general social environment.

For Paul, two fundamental stories coalesce to form the foundation for Christian identity and praxis.[32] First, as suggested earlier, Paul taught his Christian communities, which were composed largely of Gentiles, that their identity was deeply rooted in the story of Israel, and the message they told reflected their conviction that in Jesus God had brought "Israel's history to its appointed destiny."[33] Hence, the early church saw itself as continuing the sacred history of Israel in the light of its culmination in Jesus. This, therefore, will become critical for Paul's effort to construct a solidified community in Corinth, with clearly identifiable boundaries and a sense of embodying a distinct ethos reflective of their unique story, symbols, and communal identity and purpose.

For Paul, however, it is critical that the story of Israel be subsumed under the Jesus story which gives the former its coherency and climactic fulfillment. As noted by Wright, "Israel's destiny has been fulfilled, her exile finished, her salvation won, but in a manner which undermines the Jewish ethnic and nationalistic hope that Paul had once formerly espoused."[34] While Paul recognizes that the message of a crucified Messiah/King is offensive to the Jew and a point of ridicule by the Gentile (1 Cor 1:22-23), he nevertheless makes "solidarity with the crucified"[35] the core of his gospel proclamation (cf. 1 Cor 2:1-5).

So on the one hand, the gospel Paul preaches challenges Israel with the "good news" that Yahweh's promises to Israel have their fulfillment in the crucified and risen Lord Jesus. Therefore, any attempt to reinstate Jewish national peculiarities as binding upon Gentiles is nothing more than "cultural imperialism."[36] Certainly the pressures of synagogue conformity had to weigh heavily upon the early Christians, whether they be Jew or Gentile. But, on the other hand, Paul's gospel also confronted the pagan world with a Lord and King that rivaled the claims of Caesar and the Empire. Paul knows that his gospel is subversive and undermines any claim of absolute allegiance that the Empire might make. If the communities that Paul addresses are to be an effective witness to an alternative Kingdom characterized by a radically different ethos, they must thoroughly catch Paul's vision and theological framework driving his gospel proclamation. These new communities are the *ekklesia* of God called

> *Paul knows that the life of the church depends on not being absorbed into the broader culture, whether it be pagan or the synagogue.*

to witness to the sovereignty of God's Reign. Paul's letters provide a window through which we can catch a glimpse of his sensitive pastoral strategy to enable his people to understand their identity and the social and ideological boundaries that separate the church from its social and cultural environment. Paul knows that the life of the church depends on not being absorbed into the broader culture, whether it be pagan or the synagogue.

Corinth: Climbing the Social Ladder of Clout and Prestige

In this section we will take a brief glimpse at the dynamics of Paul's efforts to create community cohesiveness and solidarity in the midst of cultural tensions. In his letter to the Corinthians Paul brings all his pastoral and rhetorical skills to bear in order to help his readers inculcate a response to their cultural and social environment. Paul is sensitive to his reader's sociohistorical situation, and thus he seeks to impress upon his readers a clear sense of their identity and the ideological boundaries that distinguish the Christian community from their wider social environment. He knows that if the Christian communities he addresses are to have an effective witness which creatively engages their cultural setting, they will need to view themselves and their congregational life in new and different ways, consistent, not with the spirit of the age, but with the message of the crucified Messiah.[37]

According to Luke (Acts 18:11), Paul spent eighteen months in Corinth (sometime between A.D. 50 and 52), having come to the city as he says "in weakness and fear, and with much trembling" (1 Cor 2:3). Horsley highlights the cultural difficulties confronting Paul upon entering the metropolis of Corinth:

> Having been shaped by a different cultural background than were the Corinthians . . . Paul's situation in Corinth resembles that of a modern European Christian missionary in a colonial situation, only in reverse. In modern times missionaries from the imperial metropolis and dominant culture went to colonized people in order to 'convert' them to the colonizers' metropolitan religion and culture. By contrast . . .

Paul was a missionary from a subjected 'backward' people and culture attempting to 'evangelize' people who shared the culture of the imperial metropolis.[38]

Although classical Corinth (6th to 4th centuries B.C.), once rivaled Athens as the supreme Greek city-state, Roman military might destroyed the city in 146 B.C., and one hundred years later Julius Caesar, recognizing its strategic location, rebuilt the city as a Roman colony. The resettlement of Corinth was not with Roman army veterans (cf. Philippi), but with former slaves, Roman freedmen, and diverse ethnic groups from throughout the eastern Mediterranean (e.g., Syrians, Egyptians, Romanized Greeks, etc.). But whatever their ethnic origins and economic status, "their shared goals were now civic honor and material success through assimilation into the Roman order."[39] Accordingly, "a competitive spirit of social upward mobility was more than usually prevalent in this city."[40]

Imperial Roman order was maintained primarily through intimidation and a steady stream of Roman propaganda designed to impress Rome's subjects with the positive benefits of imperial rule. Since the emperor was the bringer of peace and order to the Mediterranean world, and since such benefits could never be repaid in kind, "the reciprocity ethic dictated that they make a return in the form of deference, respect, and loyalty."[41] In many cities throughout the empire, including Corinth, the imperial Roman cult emerged as the central factor shaping civic pride and community ideology. The forum in Corinth was dominated by the imperial presence in the form of statues, shrines, and inscriptions.[42] The city celebrated on an annual basis festivals that honored the emperor, and the famous Isthmian games were restored as an additional means to honor the emperor and his family. Everything about Corinth (architecture, coins, symbols, and monuments) underscored in the mind of Corinthian citizens that the emperor is to be honored as Corinth's chief benefactor or patron. And as Danker notes, it was well understood in antiquity "that receipt of benefits from a head of state puts one under obligation and loyalty."[43]

Along with sheer terror and propaganda, the system of patronage was the means whereby the Romans were able to construct a network of relationships assuring loyalty and an ongoing power structure designed to keep subservients in line. With the emperor

being the primary *patron* who has provided various goods and services, the recipient was honor bound to express gratitude by various
forms of public homage and acts of devotion. The system became the
means of imperial manipulation and control by assuming that the
subjects of the emperor would acknowledge and advertise the
emperor's generosity and supreme power. The system permeated
the empire, because like the emperor, the elite of every major city
sought a patronal role, thereby ordering social relationships according to a system of power and dependency. In an honor-shame culture like Corinth, "public recognition was often more important than
facts and . . . the worst thing that could happen was for one's reputation to be tarnished."[44] It was the obligation of those indebted to a
patron "to enhance the prestige, reputation, and honor of his or her
patron in public and private life." As Elliott further notes, the forms
of service owed the patron are diverse: ". . . the client favors the
patron with daily early-morning salutations, supports his political
campaigns, pays his fines, furnishes his ransom, supplies him information, does not testify against him in the courts, and gives constant
public attestation and memorials of the patron's benefactions, generosity, and virtue."[45]

In a city that had made self-promotion an art, one's sense of
self-worth in Corinth was dependent upon public recognition and
the exhibition of social clout. In order to successfully climb the lad-
der of fame and public recognition in Corinth it was critical to cultivate a network of relationships that assured the enhancement of
social status and civic honor. It must be kept in mind that the benefits afforded by the patron were not performed out of a benevolent
care of those less fortunate but were calculated to promote one's
political ambitions and to enhance one's civic reputation. As such,
the system promoted competitiveness, rivalries, inequalities, and
pride. Since such notions permeated life at Corinth, is it any wonder
that Paul felt compelled to undermine such thinking with a radically
different view of community and service?

No doubt Paul had occasion to address the implications of
such thinking on the life of the Christian community during his
eighteen-month stay in Corinth. But it should be kept in mind that
from the time Paul established the small and diverse community of
believers in Corinth (Acts 18:1-18) until the time he settled in
Ephesus and wrote 1 Corinthians (Acts 19; cf., 1 Cor 16:8) was only
at the most three to five years. It is therefore not surprising that,

although they had been "washed . . . sanctified . . . [and] justified in the name of the Lord Jesus" (6:11), the permeating influence of Corinthian culture had begun to distort and radically reshape their understanding and involvement in the Christian community. As Winter observes: "They had grown up in, and imbibed the culture before they became Christians. They reacted to some issues that arose after Paul left on the basis of the learnt conventions and cultural mores of Corinthian *Romanitas*."[46]

It appears then, that in only a few short years there had developed a rift between Paul's understanding of life in solidarity with "Christ and him crucified," and the Corinthian capitulation to the social values and practices dominant in their wider culture. It may be, as argued by John Barclay, that the reason the church did not suffer social ostracism or hostility from outsiders is because they tailored their faith and Christian experiences in order to foster social status, while playing down those elements of faith that may be socially offensive and countercultural.[47] Barclay's assessment of the Corinthian church sounds remarkably like many American congregations:

> The church is not a cohesive community but a club, whose meetings provide important moments of spiritual insight and exaltation, but do not have global implications of moral or social change. The Corinthians could gladly participate in this church as one segment of their lives. But the segment, however important is not the whole and not the centre. Their perception of their church and of the significance of their faith could correlate well with a lifestyle which remained fully integrated in Corinthian society.[48]

From Paul's perspective, the church at Corinth had compromised its social and ideological distinctiveness. Paul writes 1 Corinthians to confront his readers with a sustained critique and exposure of Corinthian cultural influences in the light of his original message of "Christ and him crucified" (2:2). Like their *Jewish forefathers* they lived in the midst of dangerous cultural influences that threatened to undermine their identity as God's people. Like Israel their identity as the elect of God must be shaped by Scripture, not their broader cultural environment. Therefore, as noted by Cousar, they must embrace "a new epistemology commensurate with the message of the cross, [and] appropriate to the eschatological times."[49] While these factors would contribute to a cohesive community, with clearly defined ideological boundaries, Paul's ongoing "concern for all the churches" (2 Cor 11:28) is indicative of what must have been a perennial question that haunted the Apostle: i.e., ". . . how much did [his] converts' original . . . socialization persist during their resocialization into the Christian social world and threaten community boundaries and cohesion?"[50] No doubt, in Corinth, some in the church were "defining the lines of demarcation between the church and the surrounding society far too loosely for Paul's liking." Therefore, part of Paul's burden in 1 Corinthians is "to strengthen the social and ideological boundaries of the church."[51]

Space will allow only a cursory survey of how Paul responds to Corinthian aberrations in his letter. Essentially, he writes to persuade his readers to abandon aspects of Corinthian identity and status defining conduct, and to replace such thinking with a sense of identity grounded in a very different story, i.e., what God accomplished in the cross. If they are to counter the influences of the broader Corinthian culture, they must rediscover their sense of community, shaped by a radically different epistemological foundation: (1) the story of Israel, (2) eschatological realities, and (3) the wisdom of the cross.

The Corinthians and Israel's Story

Paul opens his letter with the language of election and holiness, clearly reminiscent of God's choice of Israel as his covenant people (1:2,9,26-28, cf. Exod 19:6). Like Israel, the Corinthian Christians are "called to be holy" (1:2), which is further described as a calling "into fellowship with his son Jesus Christ our Lord" (1:9). Such language reminds his largely Gentile readers that in Christ, the God of Israel has assembled (*ekklesia*) a new and holy nation, a people where the categories of Jew and Gentile are irrelevant. Since these readers have been incorporated into the story of Israel, Paul will speak of their past life in terms that imply the passing of ethnic distinctions: "You know *when you were Gentile* [italics mine] you were influenced and led astray by mute idols" (12:2). When Paul draws from Israel's stories and cites from their Hebrew Bible, the Corinthians are to hear and heed these Scriptures as their own. Although the Corinthians may not always have fully followed Paul's reasoning from Jewish Scriptures, his use of Scripture addresses them as Israel and is intended "to reshape their consciousness so that they take corporate responsibility for the holiness of their community. . . ."[52] A brief overview of Paul's reasoning from the OT helps the modern reader to appreciate how essential it was for the Corinthians to see themselves as continuing Israel's story, and thereby embody a unique cultural expression.

When Paul addresses the issue of eating meat in the context of a pagan idolatrous temple (8:1–10:33), he draws upon a scene from Israel's wilderness experience (Exodus 32) and speaks of that generation as the Corinthian's "forefathers" (10:1). Hence, Paul's argument against eating and drinking in pagan temples is reinforced by reminding the Corinthians what happened to their *forefathers* when they flirted with idolatry and were led into "pagan revelry," and "sexual immorality" (10:7-8). Dining in the pagan temples of Corinth not only subjected the participants to idolatrous worship, it also exposed believers to tremendous pressure to indulge in promiscuous behavior.[53] In spite of the fact that great social prestige was attached to receiving an invitation to feast in the temples, Paul is more concerned with community purity and solidarity than he is in advancing one's social standing. Therefore, the Corinthians are to identify with Israel and resist any activities that undermine corporate holiness and solidarity.

It is significant that when Paul addresses Corinthian behavioral aberrations his focus remains on the "health and integrity of the church as a corporate body."[54] With respect to the incestuous relationship described in 5:1-8, it is the community's failure to take action that most disturbs Paul. They have been called to be an "unleaven" community purged of all impurity (5:7; cf. 1:2), yet they have allowed such deviant behavior to persist in their midst. Their failure to address the situation may reflect a greater sensitivity to Roman social etiquette, and a consequent loss of social standing if they heed Paul's instructions to "expel the wicked man from among you" (5:13).[55] But Paul is not concerned about the social implications, rather the contaminating influence such conduct would have on the community of believers. In a sign of solidarity reminiscent of Israel's responsibility to exercise group discipline, the Christian community is to "assemble in the name of our Lord Jesus" (5:4; cf. Josh 7; Lev 18:24-30; 20:22-24; Deuteronomy 28), and expurgate the offender from their fellowship (5:2; cf. 1:9). Paul's instructions echo the expulsion language found throughout Deuteronomy (cf., 13:5; 19:19; 21:21; 22:23; 23:1; 24:7),[56] and are primarily motivated to maintain the "unitary holiness of community."[57] However, Paul is careful to clarify that his position should not be construed as a "ghetto-like" withdrawal into a form of isolationism from the wider society (5:9-13). Yet, Paul does clearly distinguish the "people of the world" (5:10) from the one "who *calls himself a brother* [italics mine] but is sexually immoral" (5:11). And, he expects the Corinthian church to model values and practices that witness to the new reality to which they belong, even though they may conflict with the social order of honor and power.

In a move that may have been difficult for his Gentile readers to follow, Paul reinforces his call for community action by a subtle invocation of Passover imagery (5:6-8). In preparation for the partaking of the Passover feast, Israelites were to remove all leaven from their homes, thus symbolizing their purification before Yahweh (Exod 12:14-20). The Corinthian community is to be an "unleaven community," purged from all impurity in light of the fact that "Christ our Passover lamb, has been sacrificed" (5:7). As Hays observes: "The result is that the community itself will be like the unleaven bread prepared for the feast. . . . The incestuous man, on the other hand, is to be excluded from the household whose door is marked by the blood of Jesus, the Passover lamb; thus he is left outside, exposed to the power of the destroyer (1 Cor 5:5; cf., Exod 12:12-13)."[58] Accordingly, Paul seeks to solidify their Christian identity by setting boundaries that clearly set apart their community as a unique cultural expression.

Although it is true that explicit scriptural citations in 1 Corinthians to support ethical counsel are few,[59] the letter does cultivate a community consciousness and identity rooted in the call to identify with Israel's story. As Roetzel has argued, Paul's "grammar of election and holiness"[60] underscores much of Paul's ethical vision in 1 Corinthians. Conceptually, the language reinforces their commonality based upon the redemptive work of Christ and their shared corporate vocation. It should be recalled, as articulated by Hays, that Paul's ethical instructions are not directed to "individuals in isolation," but rather are the "outworking of an ecclesiologically-centered ethic."[61] Their identity and sense of self-worth must be centered in their participation in the called community of God, and not in those individualistic claims of power and status typical of their broader culture. In fact, it is their focus on individual status and personal claims of spiritual fulfillment that has fractured the community into competitive rivalries. At no time is this more concretely exhibited than when they assemble together.

The Corinthian practices with respect to the Lord's Supper (11:17-22) were typical of a status-oriented culture where "higher-status individuals would normally expect more and better food than lower-status persons who might be present."[62] In Paul's estimation, an assembly characterized by the reinforcement of such social inequities, replicated the practices of a typical Roman dinner party, not the egalitarian affirmations associated with the Lord's Supper (cf. 11:20). As Winter observes, their practice, "had degenerated into a 'private dinner' where the social 'haves' devoured their own meal and drank themselves into a stupor with their own wine, while the hungry low-class 'have-nots' were left looking on as slaves did at private dinners. . . . In behaving thus some Christians replicated the dinner 'etiquette' of their secular counterparts."[63] Rather than "discerning the body" (i.e., by celebrating their ecclesial oneness), they used the occasion to reinforce their social distinctions and standings in the social world of Corinth. Consequently, like the Israelites who experienced God's displeasure when their conduct undermined community holiness and solidarity (cf. Num 11:1-3; 12:1-16; 15:32-36; 16:1-50), so the Corinthians seem to be experiencing a kind of plague as a result of their "despising the church of God and humiliating those who have not" (11:22): "many among you are weak and sick, and a number of you have fallen asleep" (11:30).

It appears that even the problems associated with spiritual gifts can be traced to their cultural sensitivities to look for any avenue to enhance their social standing. In spite of the fact that all have been "baptized by one Spirit into one body" (12:13), and all have been gifted by the one Spirit (12:4-11), they have undermined communal unity by extolling certain gifts as the mark of true spirituality, and therefore an indicator of social power and prestige. It may be, as argued by some, that "glossolalia provided an alternative means to achieve status through speech for those untrained in rhetoric."[64] Paul therefore articulates an alternative ordering and ranking of gifts in terms of their contribution to the upbuilding of the body (cf. 12:27-31; 14:4-5). His ecclesial reflection compares the church to the human body, thus accenting the worth and value of every member regardless of their social conditions. Unlike the contemporary use of body imagery which reinforced a social hierarchy, where the elite is served by those of lesser status, Paul envisions a community where those "we think are less honorable we treat with special honor" (12:23), and all the members of the body "have equal concern for each other" (12:25). Solidarity is such that "if one part suffers, every part suffers with it; if one part is honored, every part rejoices with it" (12:26).

The ease with which they have accommodated their faith to the value system and social ordering typical of the Corinthian culture has contributed to the diluting of group solidarity and identity. They have failed to understand a concept basic to Israel's sense of election and call to holiness, i.e., corporate solidarity and accountability.[65] Paul shatters their hyperindividualism by identifying the church as the holy temple of God (3:16-17). It is nothing short of amazing that Paul can depict this largely Gentile assembly as the *locus* of God's dwelling on earth. Thus he understands the church as replacing the Jerusalem temple as the place where God's glory now resides. With this one stunning metaphorical reference Paul has seriously undermined all individualistic claims to a superior holiness or spirituality. Hence Israel's stories, symbols, and rituals have all become pivotal for Paul as he constructs in Corinth a community subverting the normal social and cultural life of the city with a radical vision of an alternative community.

Eschatological Realities

Paul addresses the Corinthians as the people of God gathered in the last days to eagerly "wait for our Lord Jesus Christ to be revealed" (1:7). The revelation of Jesus in his coming is further described, in distinctly Jewish terms, as "the day of our Lord Jesus Christ" (1:8; cf. *Yom Yahweh*). The imagery suggests that "the day of Christ" is to be understood as a day of judgment in which all will be held accountable. Only in Christ can they find the strength needed to be found "blameless" on that day (1:8). Thus, early in the letter Paul constructs an eschatological foundation pivotal for his ethical vision and strategy for cultivating a healthy understanding of the church as God's end-time community.

As the eschatological people of God, the Corinthians must hear Paul's gospel as the "good news" that God has indeed acted to fulfill his promises, and thus these Gentile readers have become participants in a story coming to a climactic closure. For Paul, Christ's death, resurrection, and subsequent outpouring of God's eschatological Spirit (1:7; 13:8-10; cf. Ezek 36–37; Joel 2:28-32), signals the ushering in of a new world order wherein God's reign in Christ has begun (15:20-28). Therefore, Paul's gospel announces the "good news" that the imperial violence directed at God's anointed has been overcome by Jesus' resurrection and ascension to the throne (15:25). Ultimately, his powerful reign will be victorious over all forces, whether cosmic or political, and all things will be returned to their rightful subordination to God's sovereignty (15:24-28). The implications of Paul's words are rightly noted by Hays:

> For the inhabitants of the Roman colony Corinth—who walk about a city replete with statues and temples dedicated to the glory of the Roman rulers—Paul's words serve as one more summons to a conversion of the imagination, seeing the world as standing ultimately under the authority of another who will overturn the arrangements of power that now exist. Resurrection of the dead is a subversive belief, because it declares that God alone is sovereign over the created world.[66]

Although Paul's readers "live at the time when this age is drawing to a close" (10:11, NLT), they must be vigilant since "only at the still-future parousia will all the powers finally be destroyed" (15:23-26; cf. 2:6-8).[67] Between now and then the community at Corinth must cultivate a strategy for survival that takes seriously the tensions between an "'already/not yet' eschatological dialectic."[68] Certainly in their presumptuous judging of one another (4:4-6), and their arrogant boasting of wisdom and social status (1:18–3:23), they foolishly forget that it is only the Lord's judgment that will "bring to light all things now hidden in darkness and disclose the purpose of the heart" (4:5).

In contrast to the prevalent Greco-Roman understanding of an eternal world, coupled with the Roman propaganda that the Roman Republic launched a world-everlasting,[69] Paul trivializes the importance of the world: "For this world in its present form is passing away" (7:31). As noted by Wimbush, Paul's statement "serves as a model of existence *in* the world without granting any importance to the world."[70] It should be noted that for Paul this cosmic change has already begun (note the present tense of παράγω). A discerning community is necessary in order to develop a measure of detachment that does not become too intertwined with this present evil age.

Paul's eschatological vision radically challenges the Corinthian believers to reconsider their effort to replicate the social world and values of a depraved and fallen cultural expression. They must come to see themselves as the embodiment of a new order, with its own distinctive ethos, shaped by its unique identity-defining stories, with its own understanding of the virtuous life, and a community understanding whose life embodies values and an ethical vision quite alien to the dominant culture. And, in the words of J. Louis Martyn: "Those who recognize their life to be God's gift at the juncture of the ages recognize also that until they are completely and exclusively in the new age, their knowing by the Spirit can occur only in the form of knowing by the power of the cross."[71]

Solidarity with the Crucified One

Foundational to Paul's response to the Corinthian crisis is the development of an alternative story that challenges human wisdom and provides his readers with a new lens through which they are to see themselves and construct distinctive patterns for living and community involvement. For Paul, the message of the cross both shapes their corporate identity and solidarity, and establishes a way of conduct that challenges social norms and conventional practices.

> For Paul, the message of the cross both shapes their corporate identity and solidarity, and establishes a way of conduct that challenges social norms and conventional practices.

First, his readers must understand that their communal relationships are not determined by allegiance to the one who baptized them, but to the one who was crucified for them (1:10-17). Their baptism served as a boundary marker signaling their initiation into a new reality which takes priority over old social distinctions and values. Paul is emphatic that any notion that assigns honor, prestige, or loyalty to the one who baptizes necessarily detracts from the honor due the one who was "crucified for you," and in whose name you were baptized (1:13-14). As Paul will further argue, since such notions lead to competitive boasting in human leaders, and "taking pride in people" (4:6), he urges his readers to "boast only in the Lord" (1:31).

At the root of the Corinthian problem is their tendency to highly esteem the messenger, based upon conventional standards of rhetorical eloquence and *persona*, while downplaying a message that might be offensive to the dominant ethos of Corinth. Paul challenges such thinking by insisting that a gospel strained through human wisdom undermines the centrality of the cross and nullifies its life-changing power (1:17). As noted by Hays, Paul understands the cross "as the lens through which all human experience must be projected and thereby seen afresh. The cross becomes the starting point for an *epistemological revolution* [italics mine]."[72] Therefore, Paul confronts their factious spirit and infatuation with human personalities with a radically different way of viewing their life in community, i.e., as an alternative order that embodies God's redemptive call of the "weak," the "lowly," and those whom the world "despises" (1:27-28).

Paul's effort to challenge and reshape the thinking of his readers includes his own concrete example of what it means to "have the mind of Christ" (2:16). However, what is ironic about Paul's caricature of himself is that at virtually every point his life and values seem to stand at odds with those virtues and accomplishments admired in the broader social world of Corinth: He admits his lack of eloquence and rhetorical skill (2:1ff.; 2 Cor 10:10; 11:6); he seems to acknowledge that his "bodily presence" may not measure up to contemporary expectations of respected orators (2 Cor 10:10);[73] he grants that according to aristocratic standards his presence and ministry may be assessed as "weak" and "foolish" (1 Cor. 4:10); after all, no accomplished sophist would freely embrace manual labor (4:12; 9:15-18), homelessness (4:11), brutal treatment (4:11), and in general, the world's disgust (4:9,13). Such language clearly contrasts with the Corinthians who pursue "social and cultural integration," not the "social alienation and dislocation" experienced by Paul and his associates. As long as the dominant ethos of Corinth shapes their sense of identity and social values, the church will never comprehend or appreciate the countercultural impact a cruciformed life entails.

Instead of identifying leaders in terms of worldly credentials and secular status, Paul answers the questions, "What is Paul?" and "What is Apollos?" by identifying their respective roles of service on behalf of the Corinthian church (4:5-9; cf. 16:15-18). Rather than rivals, Paul and Apollos serve a common purpose and their respective roles complement one another. In 4:1 Paul urges the Corinthians to "regard us as servants of Christ and as those entrusted with the secret things of God." Paul uses the metaphor of "steward" (οἰκόνομος), and thus compares himself to a slave put in charge of the house in the absence of the master.[74] The imagery highlights Paul's sense that both he and Apollos are ultimately accountable to the Lord, not the Corinthians. And, unlike some teachers who may tailor their message to please their audiences, Paul was not free to compromise the message of the cross in order to proclaim a gospel that would please the social elite of Corinth. Therefore, he affirms in 2:2: "For I resolved *to know* nothing while I was with you except Jesus Christ and him crucified." Paul's point is that when he labored in Corinth, the paradigm of the cross, and the mind-set associated with that sacrificial act is what gave shape to his preaching and ministry, not the conventional thinking in Corinth.

The paradigm of the cross not only encourages sacrificial service, but also led Paul to embrace a positive nonviolent form of resistance toward those who were abusive: "when we are cursed, we bless . . . when we are slandered we answer kindly" (4:12-13). Such responses are reflective of Jesus' example (cf. 1 Pet 2:23-24) and are reminiscent of his teachings (Luke 6:28; cf. Rom 12:14; 15:3). Paul had so identified with the crucified Lord that virtually every relationship had been transformed. It is in this light that he can appeal to his readers to become imitators of his lifestyle and mind-set (4:16; 11:1). In contrast "to those models of leadership which were prevalent in Graeco-Roman society, Paul's legitimation comes not from his own qualities which might have commanded respect, but rather he defers to Christ alone."[75] The attitude of Christ that Paul highlights, and which is so desperately needed in the Corinthian church, is spelled out in 10:33:

> Rather than alignment with a culture that values self-promotion and the pursuit of power, Paul lives a countercultural way of life in accord with his message of a crucified Messiah.

"For I am not seeking my own good but the good of the many, so that they may be saved." Therefore, rather than alignment with a culture that values self-promotion and the pursuit of power, Paul lives a countercultural way of life in accord with his message of a crucified Messiah. Within this paradigm, values that promote self-boasting and assessing others in terms of how they promote personal and social aspirations have no part in the *ekklesia* of God.

144

Conclusion

If our reading of Paul's letter to the Corinthians is defensible, then certainly Paul's ecclesial vision challenges the modern church to "think carefully and critically from a solid biblical and theological foundation about how to discern its relationship to culture, not simply to respond from the political preference of either the left or the right."[76] In fact, once one perceives the church as embodying an alternative cultural vision, then discernment is fundamentally concerned with "building up the church in holiness" . . . by focusing on "those elements in the church's identity that make it truly 'other' than the world."[77] Certainly, there are many values and practices characteristic of our broader Western culture that Christians would share in and endorse participation. Yet, as a distinct cultural expression embodying a new public order in the midst of the nations, the identity and integrity of the *ekklesia* demand a discerning spirit that effectively resists the tendency of the dominant culture to control and reshape our ecclesial vision in terms of what furthers and promotes nationalistic or secular interests. The poignant observations of Friesen on this point are helpful:

> The church does not depend for its life on a particular form of government or economic system. It seeks to be obedient to God and seek the welfare of the city even in totalitarian and repressive systems. But every land is also a foreign land. Christians have an allegiance to another city. They belong to Jesus Christ. Thus, loyalties and commitments transcend narrow national identities.[78]

> "But every land is also a foreign land."

Accordingly, I will close with a few observations on what a counter-cultural church might look like.

First, the church is for Paul a distinct community whose "meaning" and "alternative polity" are quite alien to the life of the nations.[79] The self-deprecating way of the cross does not resonate in a culture consumed with self-image and material success. Humility and self-sacrifice does not seem to be a recipe for success in the hardball world of American politics. The willingness to forgo revenge or the pursuit of personal rights do not have much appeal in a culture shaped by stories of revenge and retaliation. How would the message of self-denial, fundamental in the story of the cross, appeal to a culture where the "gospel of consumerism" assigns ultimate priority to "consumer needs"? Accordingly, the legitimacy and success of the church is determined "by the popularity of its product and the share of the religious market it acquires."[80] In a culture that almost deifies competition, is it any wonder that pastors and churches see themselves as competitive providers of services and goods, each rushing to outdo the other in meeting consumer demands? Rather than embodying a different story grounded in "Christ and him crucified," the church has often mirrored the Corinthian story, aptly summed up by Johnson:

> We and they are primarily concerned with ourselves. We like them, indulge our individualism and elitism, seek some way to measure ourselves against one another, plot our progress toward God by means of greater knowledge, or freedom, or greater physical exertion (asceticism if not circumcision), or more fastidious keeping of rules, or more spectacular varieties of spiritual gifts, or more exalted versions of mysticism.[81]

Second, fundamental to Paul's ethical vision is the recognition that in continuity with covenantal Israel, whose identity and way of life was learned and lived together as community, so life in Christ entails a particular pattern of community living.[82] While it is not disputed that Paul expects every believer to embody the story of Jesus, "the call to cruciformity is . . . a call that no one can fulfill in isolation."[83] Neither Paul's message or mission were concerned to enhance individual spirituality isolated from the life of the Christian community. His letters are concerned to cultivate a faithful communal life, and thereby establish a network of visible alternative communities that effectively witness to a counter reality. Hence, the language of personal piety or spiritual fulfillment, so characteristic of American evangelicalism, ultimately reflects the faulty ideology of the Corinthians, and in Paul's estimation seriously undermines the integrity and value of life in the body of believers.

> "The call to cruciformity is a call that no one can fulfill in isolation."

Third, Fowl and Jones have effectively argued that apart from the "routines of everyday life," the church needs to create separate spaces where we can instruct and form each other to be disciples and wise readers of Scripture. As they emphasize:

> . . . we need to participate in the friendships and practices of

Christian communities in order to become wise readers of Scripture who can link the words we use with the Word whom we follow. . . . Hence Christian communities provide the contexts whereby we learn—as the body of Christ through the power of the Holy Spirit—to interpret, and to have our lives interrogated by, the scriptural texts such that we are formed and transformed in the moral judgement necessary for us to live faithfully before God.[84]

When the Corinthians modeled their assemblies after the dominant ethos of their culture, it was disastrous for cultivating healthy relationships. In their assemblies they desperately needed to *"unlearn* the ancient culture of honor and status and to learn what it means to exist as an exclusive alternative community, worshiping the one God, grounded in the cross of Christ, and infused by the cruciform Spirit."[85] Instead, they used their gatherings to promote status and personal agendas at the expense of the body solidarity. The atmosphere of their assemblies simply could not generate the "conversations and practices" necessary to help them overcome those features that frustrate and undermine the desire to live faithfully before God.[86] Of course, questions might be raised about the viability of our modern form of assembly to contribute to the development of a level of commitment and discernment necessary to equip the community to withstand the subtleties of secular inculturation. Developing a "space" conducive to the development of character and discernment may require more than an hour a week, with an occasional potluck thrown in under the guise of fellowship. As Friesen observes: "The key issue for the church is how people can be morally formed to live by an alternative vision of life in a culture where the forces of modernity are eroding the very elements essential to the development of character."[87]

Fourth, such an undertaking calls for the best of biblical and theological scholarship to be an intricate part of the life and teachings of the contemporary Christian communities. If the church is to cultivate depth of character and "wise readers of Scripture" it must "nurture and develop people who are capable of exercising the critical virtues of professional biblical scholarship."[88] However, it must be remembered that "the most faithful interpretation of the Messiah's story is not a letter or argument but a living body, one whose life unfolds step-by-step in ways analogous to Messiah

Jesus."[89] Therefore, in the Christian community we need concrete examples of those who embody those virtues and quality of character fundamental to the Christian way of life. As Friesen observes:

> We learn (i.e., are "disciples") by experiencing the modeling of others, by practicing the discipline with others who seek to be practitioners. These practices are "bodied" in visible, concrete ways of living that can be observed and evaluated by others, even those outside the circle of the community of faith.[90]

So if the Christian communities are to be faithful to their identity and vocation we must take our cues from our "countercultural Lord," and not the pragmatic world of corporate America, or the ideology of American imperialism.[91]

Notes

[1]Walter Brueggemann, "Always in the Shadow of the Empire," in *The Church as Counterculture*, ed. by Michael L. Budde and Robert W. Brimlow (New York: State University of New York Press, 2000) 38-58.

[2]Stanley Hauerwas and William H. Willimon, *Resident Aliens* (Nashville: Abingdon Press, 1989) 121.

[3]For a good survey of this theme see Paul D. Hanson, *The People Called: The Growth of Community in the Bible* (San Francisco: Harper & Row, 1987).

[4]George Lindbeck, *Scriptural Authority and Narrative Interpretation*, ed. by Garrett Green (Philadelphia: Fortress Press, 1987) 165.

[5]For discussions on culture see, C. Geertz, *The Interpretation of Cultures: Selected Essays by Clifford Geertz* (Hutchinson: London, 1975); see Kathryn Tanner, *Theories of Culture: A New Agenda for Theology* (Minneapolis: Fortress Press, 1997) 93-122, for a comprehensive overview of the notion of Christianity as culture; however, Duane Friesen, *Artists, Citizens, Philosophers: Seeking the Peace of the City* (Scottdale, PA: Herald Press, 2000) 23-63, responds that her analysis did not adequately deal with the distinctive marks of Christian identity and does not take seriously that Christ represents a cultural vision; see also Lucien Legrand, *The Bible on Culture* (Maryknoll, NY: Orbis Books, 2000).

[6]Miroslav Volf, "Theological Reflections on the Relation between Church and Culture in 1 Peter," *Ex Audit* 10 (1994) 5.

[7]H. Richard Niebuhr, *Christ and Culture* (New York: Harper Torchbooks, 1951).

[8]Ibid., 32.

[9]Ibid., 38-39.

[10]Friesen, *Artists*, 60-61, lists nine possible ways the church can relate to the surrounding culture, and even hold all these positions simultaneously.

[11]Richard B. Hays, "Ecclesiology and Ethics in 1 Corinthians," *Ex Auditu* 10 (1994) 2-3.

[12]See, e.g., John H. Elliott, "The Jewish Messianic Movement: From Faction to Sect," in *Modeling Early Christianity*, ed. by Philip F. Esler (London: Routledge, 1995) 75-95.

[13]Richard A. Horsley, "Building an Alternative Society: Introduction," in *Paul and Empire: Religion and Power in Roman Imperial Society*, ed. by Richard A. Horsley (Harrisburg, PA: Trinity Press, 1997) 206.

[14]See ibid., 208-209.

[15]In the restoration tradition see the works of C. Leonard Allen, Richard T. Hughes, Michael R. Weed, *The Worldly Church: A Call for Biblical Renewal* (Abilene, TX: ACU Press, 1988); C. Leonard Allen, *The Cruciform Church: Becoming a Cross-Shaped People in a Secular World* (Abilene, TX: ACU Press, 1990).

[16]Philip D. Kenneson, *Beyond Sectarianism: Re-Imagining Church and World* (Harrisburg, PA: Trinity Press, 1999) 2.

[17]Ibid., 87.

[18]Ibid., 88.

[19]Hauerwas and Willimon, *Resident Aliens*, 30; see also their *Where Resident Aliens Live* (Nashville: Abingdon Press, 1996).

[20]Hauerwas and Willimon, *Resident Aliens*, 38-41.

[21]Rodney Clapp, *A Peculiar People: The Church as Culture in a Post-Christian Society* (Downers Grove, IL: InterVarsity, 1996) 82.

[22]Ibid., 89.

[23]Ibid., 89-90.

[24]John Howard Yoder, *The Politics of Jesus* (Grand Rapids: Eerdmans, 1994) 37-38.

[25]Ibid., 94.

[26]Friesen, *Artists*, see ch. 2.

[27]Ibid., 150.

[28]Stanley Hauerwas, *The Peaceable Kingdom* (Notre Dame, IN: Notre Dame Press, 1983) 101.

[29]Yoder, *Politics*, see ch. 9.

[30]Hays, "Ecclesiology," 2.

[31]N.T. Wright, *The New Testament and the People of God* (Minneapolis: Fortress Press, 1992) 445.

[32]Richard Hays has perhaps done more than anyone to argue for a basic narrative foundation undergirding Paul's letters. For Hays, Paul's story-shaped theology was grounded in his reading of the phrase "faith of Christ" (πίστιν Ἰησοῦ Χριστοῦ) as a shorthand reference to Christ's faithfulness, rather than a reference to the faith of the believer. Thus, the phrase conjures up the imagery of the Jesus story every time it is encountered. See Richard B. Hays, *The Faith of Jesus Christ: The Narrative Substructure of Galatians 3:1-4:11*, 2nd ed. (Grand Rapids: Eerdmans, 2002). See also Bruce W. Longenecker, ed. *Narrative Dynamics in Paul* (Louisville, KY: Westminster John Knox Press, 2002), for a critical assessment.

[33]Wright, *New Testament and the People of God*, 447.

[34]N.T. Wright, "Gospel and Theology in Galatians," in *Gospel in Paul: Studies on Corinthians, Galatians and Romans for Richard N. Longenecker*, ed. by L. Ann Jervis and Peter Richardson, JSNTSS 108 (Sheffield: Sheffield Academic Press, 1994) 232.

[35]Language of Neil Elliott, *Liberating Paul: The Justice of God and the Politics of the Apostle* (Maryknoll, NY: Orbis Books, 1994) 198f.

[36]John M.G. Barclay, *Obeying the Truth: A Study of Paul's Ethics in Galatians*, SNTW (Edinburgh: T & T Clark, 1988) 250. As noted by Rodney Stark, *The Rise of Christianity* (Princeton, NJ: Princeton University Press, 1996) 213: ". . . a major way in which Christianity served as a revitalization movement within the empire was in offering a coherent culture that was *entirely stripped of ethnicity*."

[37]Paul's encounter with the risen Lord brought to a halt his involvement in sacred violence against the Christian community. In the words of Robert Hamerton-Kelly, *Sacred Violence: Paul's Hermeneutic of the Cross* (Minneapolis: Fortress Press, 1992) 82, "he went over to the side of the victim. Instead of continuing the crucifixion he joined the crucified."

[38]Richard A. Horsley, "Rhetoric and Empire—And 1 Corinthians," in *Paul and Politics: Essays in Honor of Krister Stendahl*, ed. by Richard A. Horsley (Harrisburg, PA: Trinity Press, 2000) 84.

[39]Richard A. Horsley and Neil Asher Silberman, *The Message and the Kingdom* (Minneapolis: Fortress Press, 1997) 164.

[40]Andrew D. Clarke, *Serve the Community of the Church: Christians as Leaders and Ministers* (Grand Rapids: Eerdmans, 2000) 174; see also Dimitris J. Kyrtatas, "Modes and Relations of Production," in *Handbook of Early Christianity*, ed. by Anthony J. Blasi, Jean Duhaime, Paul-Andre Turcotte (Oxford: Altamira Press, 2002) 547: "The Roman world was full of freedmen seeking to improve their position and move into the upper classes."

[41]Peter Garnsey and Richard Saller, "Patronal Power Relations," in *Paul and Empire*, 97.

[42]For discussion see J. Murphy-O'Connor, *St. Paul's Corinth* (Delaware: Michael Glazier, 1983).

[43]Frederick W. Danker, *Benefactor: An Epigraphic Study of a Graeco-Roman and New Testament Semantic Field* (St. Louis, MO: Clayton Publishing House, 1982) 450.

[44]Ben Witherington, *Conflict & Community in Corinth* (Grand Rapids: Eerdmans, 1995) 8.

[45]John H. Elliott, "Patronage and Clientage," in *The Social Sciences and New Testament Interpretation*, ed. by Richard Rohrbaugh (Peabody, MA: Hendrickson, 1996) 149.

[46]Bruce W. Winter, *After Paul Left Corinth* (Grand Rapids: Eerdmans, 2001) 27.

[47]John Barclay, "Social Contrast in Pauline Christianity," *JSNT* 47 (1992) 69.

[48]Ibid., 71. According to Niebuhr's categories the Corinthian church would reflect the "Christ of Culture" category.

[49]Charles B. Cousar, "The Theological Task of 1 Corinthians," in *Pauline Theology*, vol. 2, ed. by David M. Hay (Minneapolis: Fortress Press, 1993) 97.

[50]Harold Remus, "Persecution," in *Handbook of Early Christianity*, 441.

[51]As observed by Edward Adams, *Constructing the World: A Study in Paul's Cosmological Language*, ed. by John Barclay, Joel Marcus, and John Riches (Edinburgh: T & T Clark, 2000) 87.

[52]Richard B. Hays, "The Conversion of the Imagination: Scripture and Eschatology in 1 Corinthians," *NTS* 45 (1999) 411.

[53]As noted by Brian S. Rosner, "Temple Prostitution in 1 Corinthians 6:12-20," *NovT* 40 (1998) 337, "pagan temples were the restaurants of antiquity where prostitutes . . . offered their services on such festive occasions."

[54]As noted by Richard B. Hays, *First Corinthians*, Interpretation (Louisville, KY: John Knox Press, 1997) 80; and Cousar, "Theological Tasks," 98.

[55]Clarke, *Serving the Community*, 182, suggests that the "community's reluctance to take action against this man would . . . have been out of deference to his superior status coupled with the fear of loss of benefit from this patron figure"; Elliott, *Liberating Paul*, 213, postulates that the violator(s) may have been "members of the city's elite."

[56]See Brian Rosner, *Paul, Scripture, & Ethics: A Study of 1 Corinthians 5-7* (Grand Rapids: Baker, 1994) 61-93.

[57]Hays, "Ecclesiology," 10-11.

[58]Hays, "Conversion of the Imagination," 412.

[59]As noted by Victor Furnish, "Belonging to Christ: A Paradigm for Ethics in First Corinthians," *Int* 44 (1990) 148.

[60]See Calvin J. Roetzel, "The Grammar of Election in Four Pauline Letters," in *Pauline Theology*, vol. 2, ed. by David M. Hay (Minneapolis: Fortress Press, 1993) 211-233.

[61]Hays, "Ecclesiology," 5,7.

[62]Elliott, *Liberating Paul*, 206.

[63]Winter, *After Paul Left Corinth*, 158.

[64]Elliott, *Liberating Paul*, 206; see also Dale Martin, "Tongues of Angels and Other Social Status Indicators," *JAAR* 59 (1992) 547-589.

[65]Bruce J. Malina, "Understanding New Testament Persons," in *The Social Sciences and New Testament Interpretation*, 41-61; Malina notes that "the Mediterranean selves we read about in the Bible could not have been individualistic selves in that way we are. Rather they were all group-oriented selves, very concerned to adopt the viewpoints of the groups (their in-groups) whose fate they shared. They would have never considered Jesus as a personal Lord and Savior or as a personal Redeemer. If anything, Jesus was the church's (the group's) Lord and Savior, and it was by belonging to the church (the group) that one experienced the presence of the Lord" (45).

[66]Hays, *First Corinthians*, 265.

[67]Gordon D. Fee, "Toward a Theology of 1 Corinthians," in *Pauline Theology*, 57.

[68]Hays, *First Corinthians*, 10.

[69]See Winter, *After Paul Left Corinth*, 251-260; and Elliott, *Liberating Paul*, 189, who notes that for Paul "the rhapsodies of a 'golden age' are a fraud."

[70]Vincent L. Wimbush, *Paul, the Worldly Ascetic: Response to the World and Self-understanding according to 1 Corinthians 7* (Macon, GA: Mercer University Press, 1987) 47.

[71]J. Louis Martyn, *Theological Issues in the Letters of Paul* (Nashville: Abingdon Press, 1997) 208.

[72]Hays, *First Corinthians*, 27.

[73]As Winter, *After Paul Left Corinth*, 35, notes: "For more than two centuries 'rhetorical delivery' had encompassed both speech and 'bodily presence.' . . ."

[74]Witherington, *Conflict and Community in Corinth*, 138.

[75]Clarke, *Serve the Community*, 221.

[76]Friesen, *Artist*, 35-36; for an excellent overview of the task and goal of discernment in the church see Luke Timothy Johnson, *Scripture & Discernment: Decision Making in the*

Church (Nashville: Abingdon Press, 1996) 109-132.

[77]Johnson, *Scripture & Discernment*, 124.

[78]Friesen, *Artists*, 37.

[79]See David S. Yeago, "Messiah's People: The Culture of the Church in the Midst of the Nations," *Pro Ecclesia* 6 (1997) 160, 171.

[80]Ibid., 167. Yeago goes on to point out: "When these assumptions hold sway large, wealthy congregations and denominations will be perceived as more *important*, indeed more *legitimate*, than small, impoverished ones; the former will seem as 'successful' and therefore exemplary."

[81]Johnson, *Scripture & Discernment*, 113. Stephen E. Fowl, *The Story of Christ in the Ethics of Paul*, JSNTSS 36 (Sheffield: JSOT Press, 1990), 200, observes that, "The intelligibility of any community's moral discourse will . . . depend on the power of its narratives to provide a truthful account of the community's existence and identity, and on the community's faithfulness in ordering its own practice in a manner appropriate to such narratives."

[82]See Larry L. Rasmussen, *Moral Fragments and Moral Community: A Proposal for Church in Society* (Minneapolis: Fortress Press, 1993) 138-140.

[83]See the insightful study of Michael J. Gorman, *Cruciformity: Paul's Narrative Spirituality of the Cross* (Grand Rapids: Eerdmans, 2001) 385; Gorman observes that, "Much of Western Christianity, as many have lamented, is decidedly private and individualistic. We find a spirituality that is narrowly focused on 'me and Jesus,' and the corollary convictions that the Church is optional and that salvation is a private, 'spiritual' matter" (384).

[84]Stephen E. Fowl and L. Gregory Jones, *Reading in Communion: Scripture and Ethics in Christian Life* (Eugene, OR: Wipf and Stock, 1998) 34.

[85]Gorman, *Cruciformity*, 356.

[86]Fowl & Jones, *Reading in Communion*, 35.

[87]Friesen, *Artists*, 135.

[88]Fowl & Jones, *Reading in Communion*, 43.

[89]Gorman, *Cruciformity*, 367.

[90]Friesen, *Artists*, 139.

[91]For a cogently argued assessment of the parallels between the imperialism of the ancient Roman empire and modern America see, Richard A. Horsley, *Jesus and Empire: The Kingdom of God and the New World Disorder* (Minneapolis: Fortress Press, 2003).

Bibliography

Clapp, Rodney. *A Peculiar People: The Church as Culture in a Post-Christian Society*. Downers Grove, IL: InterVarsity, 1996.
Clapp powerfully argues that faithfulness necessitates embodying a lifestyle that witnesses to an alternative reality and community that is in many respects counter to the popular American culture.

Fowl, Stephen E., and L. Gregory Jones. *Reading in Communion: Scripture and Ethics in Christian Life*. Eugene, OR: Wipf and Stock, 1998.
Fowl and Jones offer a solid rationale for reading and practicing Scripture in the context of the life of the Church.

Gorman, Michael J. *Cruciformity: Paul's Narrated Spirituality of the Cross*. Grand Rapids: Eerdmans, 2001.

Gorman makes a compelling case that conformity to Christ, the crucified One, is the "all encompassing, integrating narrative reality of Paul's life and thought." Gorman's work is noteworthy for its detailed and extensive exegetical work and theological reflection on the centrality of the cross in Paul's thought and mission.

Kenneson, Philip D. *Beyond Sectarianism: Re-Imagining Church and World*. Harrisburg, PA: Trinity Press, 1999.

Kenneson sets forth a model of the church that describes its role and vision as a "contrast-society" that operates with its own understanding of rationality, culture, politics, and religious hope. As such it embodies a life and practice that function as a witness to the non-Christian world.

SOCIAL

ETHICAL ISSUES

IN THIS SECTION

Larry Chouinard & Margaret McLaughlin

The Bible and Social Justice

Paul Prill

**You Cannot Serve God and Mammon:
Christians in an Age of Affluence**

George Pickens

**The Earth Is the Lord's:
The Christian and the Environment**

David Fiensy

A Christian Perspective on the Death Penalty

Gary Hall

Violence in the Name of God: Israel's Holy Wars

Lee C. Camp

The Nonviolent Reign of God

THE BIBLE AND SOCIAL JUSTICE

Larry Chouinard, Ph.D. and Margaret McLaughlin, MSW

Introduction

In an age that has promoted a secularizing split between the private realm of faith and the public arena of social action, it is not surprising that for many Christians social justice issues are relegated to secular or political authorities having little to do with the Kingdom of God or discipleship.[1] Churches often seem eager to promote an individual spirituality or piety that speaks to personal "felt needs" but are strangely silent about the need to confront social injustices. Furthermore, popular Christian notions of evil have largely failed to articulate a coherent worldview that adequately interprets spiritual realities with the concreteness of world events, secular institutions, or political realities. In fact, the modern church's view of the realm of evil has been more informed by Hollywood horror movies than the witness of Scripture. Sin is something we talk about on a personal level, but seldom on a corporate, institutional, or global scale.[2] This reality testifies to the success of current cultural trends to push religious faith to the margins, confined to private or individual convictions, never to be taken seriously in

> Churches often seem eager to promote an individual spirituality or piety that speaks to personal "felt needs" but are strangely silent about the need to confront social injustices.

> The modern church's view of the realm of evil has been more informed by Hollywood horror movies than the witness of Scripture.

the public arena. In many ways the church has acquiesced to such notions, as evidenced by the deafening silence on the varied forms of social injustice (e.g., institutional greed, racism, poverty, and the plight of various groups marginalized by social pressures and oppression).

Not only have we not been a voice for the oppressed and those suffering injustice, many Christians have actually contributed to furthering the alienation and injustice experienced by several groups by our unthinking lack of sensitivity and immoral condoning of popular notions that are both demeaning and dehumanizing of people for whom Christ died. This paper is an attempt both to educate and sensitize the believer concerning the plight and forms of oppression experienced by several at risk groups within our society. We take seriously the biblical call to promote and practice "justice and mercy" (cf. Matt 23:23), and therefore if we are to avoid secular ideologies and a stereotypical dismissal of various people groups, we must recover a biblical understanding of justice. In what follows we want to propose a public ethic grounded in the paradigmatic embodiment of God's justice demonstrated in Jesus. It's time we "get out of the salt-shaker," and truly become the "salt of the earth" (Matt 5:16).

> *English translations often obscure the extent that the language of "justice" permeates both Old and New Testaments.*

The Biblical Vision of Justice [3]

In spite of the fact that the Greek and Hebrew terms translated "justice" (Hebrew: *mishpat* and *tsedaqah*; Greek: *dikaiosune* and *krisis*) occur over 1,000 times in biblical literature, English translations often obscure the extent that the language of "justice" permeates both Old and New Testaments. When the Hebrew terms *mishpat* and *tsedaqah* are repeatedly translated "righteousness" or "judgment," the English reader often fails to see that the terms accent God's delivering, restorative power that moves to set things right by vindicating the oppressed. Even when the terms are translated "justice," all too often Western notions of justice are read into the terms. Visions of justice that focus solely on "retribution," whereby offenders get what is coming to them, or a "distributive" form of justice that renders to each according to their merit, often fail to do "justice" to the nuances associated with the biblical idea. As we will see in our overview of biblical texts, the term most frequently translated "justice" in the OT (*mishpat*, 422×), does not seem to focus primarily upon vindictive retribution, but upon God's saving action to restore *shalom* by making things right.[4] The fact is, both God's love and justice emerge from a covenantal relationship, and are intended primarily to transform a situation through restorative and corrective means. God's justice thus moves to eliminate those factors that contribute to the absence of God's *shalom*. Biblical justice is therefore a response that relieves oppression and all forms of injustice that result in a distortion of the way things should be. Hence, the modern notion behind the sentiment that "justice must be satisfied," or that justice demands that the offender must "repay his/her debt to society," may not adequately reflect the biblical perspective that seems less focused upon "punitive retribution" and more upon a "restorative justice," whereby order is restored (*shalom*). As observed by Perry Yoder:

> Righteousness, *tsedaqah*, is the proper order, while justice, *mishpat*, is doing justice to achieve the just order, which results in *shalom*. Seen this way, justice, to be true justice must be both substantive—bring about a right order in the society—and procedural, it must bring about this right end through fair and equitable means.[5]

An overview of key texts highlighting the distinctive biblical vision of God's justice, and how it should be embodied by the community of believers will serve as a correction to modern knee-jerk reactions that often pursue vengeance and retaliation in the name of justice.

Israel's God is distinguished from the gods of the nations by the indictment that pagan gods fail to "defend the cause of the weak and fatherless; [and] maintain the rights of the poor and oppressed" (Ps 82:1-3). In contrast, the Lord of Israel "is known by his justice" (Ps. 9:16). He "loves righteousness and justice" (Ps 32:5; 99:4; Isa 61:8), and "they are the foundation of his throne" (Ps 89:14). Yahweh's love of justice is manifested in "secur[ing] justice for the poor and uphold[ing] the cause of the needy" (Ps 140:12; cf. 99:4; 105:6). Furthermore, "his justice upholds the cause of the oppressed and gives food to the hungry" (Ps 146:7). The justice of God despises "bloodshed" (Isa 5:7) and calls for his people to "give up your violence and oppression and do what is just and right" (Ezek 45:9). In the end, it is justice manifested by Israel's God that becomes "a light to the nations" (Isa 51:4).

In the Law Israel is called to embody God's justice by emulating his just treatment of those most vulnerable. They are not to "deny justice to your poor people in their lawsuits" (Exod 23:6). They are warned not to "pervert justice" (Lev 19:15), and that includes how they treat the "alien" and the "native-born" (Num 9:14; 15:16): "Do not deprive the alien or the fatherless of justice" (Deut 24:17; cf. 27:19). As J.G. McConville observes, "The whole concept of the behavior of Israelite man towards his fellow-man in Deuteronomy is explicated by the analogy of the behavior of Yahweh towards his people."[6]

Ironically, later when Ezekiel rehearses the sins of Jerusalem he observes that the exiled people "oppress the poor and needy and mistreat the alien, denying them justice" (22:29). Earlier Isaiah had pled with Israel to "seek justice, encourage the oppressed. Defend the cause of the fatherless, plead the case of the widow" (1:17). Jeremiah indicts the "royal house of Judah" for their failure to "administer justice" (21:11-12). Ezekiel speaks out against their oppressive violence: "You have gone far enough, O princes of Israel! Give up your violence and oppression and do what is just and right" (45:9). Amos charges the "house of Israel" with "turning justice into bitterness and [casting] righteousness to the ground" (5:7). They "trample on the poor" by forcing them to give up their grain (5:11), and "deprive the poor of justice in the courts" (5:12). Therefore, Amos pleads, "let justice roll on like a river, righteousness like a never-failing stream" (5:24). In the words of Micah: "What does the LORD require of you? To act justly and to love mercy and to walk humbly with your God" (6:8). In the end, God's judgment awaits those "who oppress the widows and the fatherless and deprive aliens of justice" (Mal 3:5).

Our overview of *mishpat*/justice demonstrates that justice is most often viewed as an *act* whereby the marginal and oppressed are delivered, restored, and extended relief in the midst of an oppressive situation (cf. Ps 7:9; 9:6-9; 76:9; 96:10; 97:2; 116:5; 146:7; Isa 16:5; 28:6,17; 51:4; Jer 9:24). The oppressed call upon God to "decree justice" (Ps 7:6), and in their deliverance they sing of God's "love and justice" (Ps 101:1). God's love and mercy is never contrasted with his justice as if they stand opposed to one another. Modern notions that would say "we want God's mercy not his justice," fail to realize that

God's justice merges with such concepts as his steadfast love, compassion,
kindness, and mercy (cf. Ps 36:5-6; Jer
9:24; Micah 6:8; Hos 12:6). That's why
Jeremiah can pray, "Correct me, LORD,
but only with justice—not in your

> God's love and mercy is
> never contrasted with his
> justice as if they stand
> opposed to one another.

anger, lest you reduce me to nothing" (10:24). The exhibition of
shalom-justice meant both the transformation of the condition of the
oppressed, and God's judgment upon the oppressor. God's judgment
always stands against oppressive structures that bring distress and
chaotic conditions among those most vulnerable.

The highest task for Israel's king is the pursuit of shalom-justice. The Psalmist entreats God: "Endow the king with your justice, O
God, the royal son with your righteousness. He will judge your people in righteousness, your afflicted ones with justice. . . . He will
defend the afflicted among the people and save the children of the
needy; he will crush the oppressor" (72:1-4). According to 2 Samuel
8:15, "David reigned over all Israel, doing what was just and right for
all his people." However, by the time of Jeremiah, the prophet must
warn the evil kings of Judah: "Do what is just and right. Rescue from
the hand of the oppressor the one who has been robbed. Do no
wrong or violence to the alien, the fatherless or the widow, and do not
shed innocent blood in this place" (22:3). Isaiah indicts Israel's Kings
for making "unjust laws," "oppressive decrees" that "deprive the poor
of their rights and withhold justice from the oppressed of my people,
making widows their prey and robbing the fatherless" (10:1-2).
Contemporary with Isaiah, Micah addresses the Northern Kings and
condemns the rulers for despising "justice," and distorting "all that is
right." They "build Zion with bloodshed and Jerusalem with wickedness" (3:9). Is it any wonder that the prophetic critique of Israel's
leaders led to a future hope that one day God would raise up a figure
who would rule his people with justice and righteousness. The language of the prophets points to an ideal ruler who will truly reign in
a manner that embodies God's shalom-justice:

> For to us a child is born,
>   to us a son is given,
>   and the government will be on his shoulders.
> And he will be called
>   Wonderful Counselor, Mighty God,
>   Everlasting Father, Prince of Peace.

Of the increase of his government and peace
   there will be no end.
He will reign on David's throne
   and over his kingdom,
establishing and upholding it
   with *justice and righteousness*
   from that time on and forever.
The zeal of the LORD Almighty
   will accomplish this (Isa 9:6-7).

"In those days and at that time
   I will make a righteous Branch sprout from David's line,
   he will do what is *just* and *right* in the land.
In those days Judah will be saved
   and Jerusalem will live in safety.
This is the name by which it will be called:
   The LORD Our Righteousness (Jer 33:15-16; cf. 23:5-6).

Here is my servant, whom I uphold,
   my chosen one in whom I delight;
I will put my Spirit on him
   and he will *bring justice to the nations*.
He will not shout or cry out,
   or raise his voice in the streets.
A bruised reed he will not break,
   a smoldering wick he will not snuff out.
In faithfulness *he will bring forth justice*;
   he will not falter or be discouraged
till *he establishes justice on earth*
               (Isa 42:1-4; cf. 11:1-9; 32:1ff.).

It is our contention that Jesus embodied the ideal vision of a promised Davidic king who would come in fulfillment of the promises associated with the exhibition of God's *shalom*-justice on behalf of his people. In Jesus, God's justice worked its redemptive power to break the cycle of oppression, restore order out of chaos, and repair the damage that sin has done to human relationships. Luke highlights this intention with his portrayal of Jesus' first public act in his hometown Nazareth:

He went to Nazareth, where he had been brought up, and on the Sabbath day he went into the synagogue, as was his custom. And he stood up to read. The scroll of the prophet

Isaiah was handed to him. Unrolling it, he found the place where it is written:

The Spirit of the Lord is on me,
   because he has anointed me
   to preach good news to the poor.
He has sent me to proclaim freedom for the prisoners
   and recovery of sight for the blind,
to release the oppressed,
   to proclaim the year of the Lord's favor (4:16-19).

In Matthew's Gospel Jesus' ministry is emphatically linked to God's chosen Servant who enacts "justice among the Nations," and "brings justice to victory" (12:18-22; Isa 42:1-4). In the proclamation of God's Kingdom Jesus envisioned the inauguration of social structures that promote the prophetic vision of justice highlighted earlier. In Jesus, God's mercy moves to "take pity on the weak and needy" (cf. Ps 72:1-4). When those deemed as "unclean" and "impure," by royal and cultic standards, are made whole, the oppressive forces that marginalized and tyrannized are neutralized by a superior ethical authority. Twice, in Matthew's Gospel, Jesus cites Hosea 6:6 (cf. 9:13; 12:7, "I desire mercy not sacrifice") to counter Pharisaic understanding of Torah which lent itself to the unjust treatment of those whom Jesus described as "harassed and helpless" (9:36), "weary and burdened" (11:28), "the innocent" (12:7), and "sheep without a shepherd" (9:36). In Jesus we truly see the fulfillment of God's transforming justice that brings restoration and wholeness to his people by placing a priority on the centrality of "justice" (see Matt 23:23).

Jesus not only embodied God's justice, he brought into existence a "messianic community that was to live in a manner consistent with the demands of the new age in the midst of the old, challenging the unjust status quo by its very existence as a dissident community of equals."[7] The disciples are called to share in God's liberating power and to participate in the execution of his *shalom*-justice on behalf of the oppressed (see Matt 10:5-6). But they must avoid the model of secular rule, which was driven by the quest for power and self-promotion (Matt 20:25-27). Pagan rulers and their high officials promote a structure that lends itself to exploitation and abuse of others. In contrast, the radical "politics of Jesus"[8] pursue the welfare of the marginalized (Matt 18:2-6), value the restorations of relationships

(Matt 5:21-25; 18:15-20), and exhibit unlimited readiness to forgive (Matt 6:9-15; 18:21-35). It is clear in the teachings of Jesus that he expected his disciples to practice social justice by exhibiting a caring spirit toward those in need (Matt 25:31-46).[9] It is precisely those oppressed and not valued by the dominant society that Jesus calls his disciples to serve and value in the same way they value their Lord. Their eschatological fate is determined by such service.

Biblical justice certainly moves far beyond retributive sources of justice in that it is fundamentally "restorative," seeking the well being both of the violator and the victim. As Jeffrey Hammond has rightly observed, *reconciliation* is an important component of biblical justice:

> *Biblical justice certainly moves beyond retributive aims to restorative.*

Justice then, is a function of reconciliation, which itself is a function of love. To be reconciled with another person is to declare that 'justice has been done.' This is the irony of justice. Reconciliation is an act made in love, emanating from the freedom the believer has in Christ. To seek reconciliation one must be empowered by the Holy Spirit to scale the walls of bitterness, regret, and desire for revenge that keeps a person locked into retributive ideas of punishment.[10]

It is the prior initiative of God in Christ to reconcile his creation by restoring *shalom*-justice that is foundational for the believer's practice of justice. It is through Christ that we find the motives and resources to become a community in pursuit of justice. As Paul affirms, we have been "reconciled to God" so that we might embody the reconciling justice of God (2 Cor 5:21). This reconciliation with God necessarily demands an honest reflection upon the way of sin in our own lives. Before we can constructively labor for social justice, we must confront our own prejudices and stereotypical categories with which we assess those marginalized by dominant social structures. If we are to be an agent for healing and reconciliation in a broken and defensive world we must first acknowledge both our need to forgive and to be forgiven. Howard Zehr highlights the liberating power of forgiveness:

> *It is through Christ that we find the motives and resources to become a community in pursuit of justice.*

> Forgiveness is letting go of the power the offense and the offender have over a person. It means no longer letting that offense and offender dominate. Without the experience of forgiveness, without this closure, the wound festers, the violation takes over our consciousness, our lives. It, and the offender, are in control. Real forgiveness then is an act of empowerment and healing. It allows one to move from victim to survivor.[11]

Forgiveness necessarily entails a penitent spirit, willingly acknowledging the subtle ways we participate in injustices. Sometimes our participation may not even be consciously understood. As a member of a dominant group that has practiced oppression, a giant step toward reconciliation is the acknowledgment of our sin, either as an active participant in the oppression of others, or in our failure to be a voice critical of the many forms injustice may take.[12] Acknowledging personal prejudice and behaviors that have tended to dehumanize or devalue those who are socially oppressed is a first step toward recovery from the destructive harm of bigotry and bitterness. However, the work of reconciliation and the restoration of biblical justice do not come without personal sacrifice, and sometimes rejection and alienation from those we thought to be friends. In our refusal to participate, or find humor in demeaning jokes or racist practices, we place a higher priority and allegiance to the just Reign of the Lord Jesus than our desire to be socially accepted (cf. Matt 10:34-39). Perhaps the words of David, when overcome with the enormity of his own sin, could form the words of our petition as we ask God to help us overcome our bigotry and general lack of sensitivity toward those less fortunate or different from ourselves: "Create in me a clean heart, O God. Renew a right spirit within me" (Ps 51:10).

We turn now to a brief overview of the threefold dimension of the practice of justice as suggested by our overview of the biblical witness: (1) Economic Justice, (2) Justice and the Vulnerable, and (3) Justice and Racial Equality. Obviously, some groups that are at risk for social injustice may in fact experience oppressive tactics that overlap into all three areas (e.g., poverty and the oppression of minority groups certainly overlap). We are not attempting to give a detailed analysis of the causal factors that may have put certain groups at risk for injustice. Our effort is simply to sensitize those who take seriously biblical justice and the way of the Kingdom in the world, to certain forms of injustice not usually addressed in mainstream Christian thought. If we are to be a voice for the oppressed and model an alternative ethical consciousness grounded in Jesus' Lordship, we need to become aware of the insidious forms injustice may take.

Economic Justice

Biblical Reflection

Certainly one of the more striking features of biblical justice is the special attention given to the plight of the poor and needy. Literally hundreds of texts address this concern.[13] It is clear in both Israel's legal code and the collection of prophetic writings that not only is the *justness* of Israel's society determined by their treatment of the weak and vulnerable, their sacred literature portrays Yahweh as an advocate and deliverer of those in need of care. Furthermore, as the embodiment of divine justice, Jesus identifies with the poor and proclaims a message characterized as "good news for the poor" (Luke 4:18-21; Isaiah 61). It would seem that a profound regard for the biblical vision of social justice necessitates reflection on the perennial problem of the injustice of poverty in the midst of abundance.[14] An overview of the biblical materials evokes a concern for the poor in at least four different ways.[15]

First, God is presented in Scripture as one who defends the cause of the poor. Especially in the Psalms, the poor and needy look to God for his saving power (Ps 70:5; 86:1). The poor of Israel are those without sustenance, and who have cast their dependency upon God. They express a resolve that in the midst of their poverty, God will hear their plea (Ps 34:6; 35:10; 68:10; 69:33; 113:7) and secure "justice and uphold the cause of the needy" (Ps 140:12). This confidence rests in the conviction that unlike the gods or the nations their Lord defends "the cause of the weak and fatherless . . . [and] . . . maintains the rights of the poor and the oppressed" (Ps 82:3-4). In fact, in the prophetic literature, Yahweh holds the "leaders of the people" accountable with the indictment that "the plunder from the poor is in your houses" (Isa 3:14); therefore, through the prophet God inquires, "What do you mean by crushing my people and grinding the bones of the poor?" (Isa 3:15). God is therefore seen as "a refuge for the poor, a refuge for the needy in his distress" (Isa 25:4). The Scriptures are clear: God is truly an advocate and defender of the poor (cf. Isa 41:17).

Second, as observed by Mott and Sider,[16] the laws of Israel contained in the Pentateuch have "at least five important provisions designed to help those who could not help themselves": (1) Every three years tithes are to be collected in various cities of Israel to aid the aliens, fatherless, and poor widows (Deut 14:28-29). (2) Harvesting laws stipulated that the corners of the grain fields, along with any fruit left over after harvest be left for the poor and needy (Lev 19:9-10; Deut 24:19-21). (3) Every seventh year they are to allow the fields to lie fallow so that the poor may have access to all natural growth (Exod 23:10-11; Lev 25:1-7). (4) A zero-interest loan should characterize loans to fellow Israelites who have fallen into poverty and cannot support themselves. If they are unable to repay the balance owed by the Sabbatical year, all debts should be forgiven (Exod 22:25; Lev 25:35; Deut 14:1-11). (5) Israelites who serve as slaves to pay off debts are allowed to go free in the seventh year; they are to "be openhanded toward your brothers and toward the poor and needy" in order that there "be no poor among you" (Deuteronomy 15; Exod 21:1-11; Lev 25:47-53).

Few issues are so potentially destructive of community cohesiveness and solidarity as an extreme disparity in personal wealth and income among its members. It is significant that at the close of Old Testament history, Nehemiah is confronted with an outcry of desperation and frustration as some within the community felt threatened with economic ruin because their Jewish brothers failed to be observant of the laws concerning land requisition, enslavement of fellow Israelites, and the practice of usury (Neh 5:1-5). Nehemiah responds to their abuse with two proposals: Any land they have seized as collateral or because of failure to pay debts must be returned unconditionally. They were also to cease the practice of charging interest on loans (5:11). The people are compliant to Nehemiah's request: "We will give it back . . . And we will not demand anything more from them. We will do as you say" (5:12). Later the people promise, "every sev-

> *Few issues are so potentially destructive of community cohesiveness and solidarity as an extreme disparity in personal wealth and income among its members.*

enth year we will forgo working the land and will cancel all debts"
(10:31).

Sider sums up the normative principle that emerges from the
biblical witness on the just treatment of the poor and needy:

> Justice demands that every person or family has access to
> the productive resources (land, money, knowledge) so they
> have the opportunity to earn a generous sufficiency of mate-
> rial necessities. And be dignified participating members of
> the community.[17]

In his treatment of Deuteronomy 15, Jeffries Hamilton observes
that this text interprets "rights" in terms of obligations, "more particularly as a set of obligations which the powerful owe to the powerless."[18] He contrasts these laws with the assumptions behind our
modern Bill of Rights:

> The Bill of Rights tends to safeguard the liberty of the indi-
> vidual by spelling out what government or the powerful in
> society should *refrain* from doing—limiting peaceful assem-
> bly, censoring the press, etc. This view of rights defines those
> things which individuals do which should not be placed in
> jeopardy.
> The view of Deuteronomy, as we have seen, is more active.
> It defines that treatment which the dependent has a right to
> *expect* of society and that treatment which society *owes* to the
> dependent.[19]

Third, God identifies with the poor so profoundly that his people must model his concern if they are to be loyal to their covenantal relationship. Mistreatment of the alien or taking advantage of the
poor widow arouses the Lord's anger, and like the Egyptians who
mistreated Israel were destroyed, so Israel will meet the Lord's wrath
if they exhibit a callous disregard for the poor in their midst (Exod
22:21-24). Jeremiah is emphatic that God will destroy Judah because
"they do not defend the rights of the poor" (5:28). On the other hand,
Josiah was considered a good king because "he defended the cause
of the poor and needy and so all went well." The prophet concludes,
"Is that not what it means to know me?" (22:16). Isaiah compares
his generation to "Sodom and Gomorrah" because their sacrificial
system lacked a corresponding pursuit of justice that defended "the
cause of the fatherless, or pleaded the cause of the widow" (1:10-

17). As Amos effectively argues, worship is nothing more than a sham without a deep concern for the practice of justice (5:21-24), which brings relief to the poor and oppressed (4:1; 5:11-12; 8:4-6). Therefore, no matter how frequent our worship or orthodox our practice, without a corresponding care for the poor we can make no claim to be the people of God.

Fourth, the New Testament builds on the prophetic tradition, as Jesus announces his intention "to preach good news to the poor" (Matt 11:5; Luke 4:18; 7:22) and is portrayed (especially in Luke) as an advocate for the poor (Luke 14:13-14; 19:8; 21:1-2). Jesus upholds the Deuteronomic principles that the rich and powerful have an obligation to care for those less fortunate (Luke 18:18-30; 14:13; 19:8; 21:2-3).[20] The early church exhibited the same positive regard for the poor (see Acts 9:36; 10:4,31). The ministry of Paul, in particular, is prefaced by the encouragement to "remember the poor" (Gal 2:10). His efforts to raise funds on behalf of "the poor among the saints in Jerusalem" (cf. Rom 15:26; Acts 24:17) occupied a major portion of his work (cf. 2 Corinthians 8-9). Finally, James certainly stands in the prophetic tradition in his diatribe directed at the rich in their practice of injustice toward the poor (2:1-11; 5:1-6). There can be no doubt that the New Testament mirrors the Old in the pursuit of the welfare of the poor.

> *No matter how frequent our worship or orthodox our practice, without a corresponding care for the poor we can make no claim to be the people of God.*

Applying the Biblical Model

Our overview of the biblical perspective on poverty, and the means by which they sought to alleviate the problem, provides for the modern reader a vision of values and responsibilities that God's people are to take seriously. Given the differences between the sociopolitical world of the Bible and our world today, it may be that specific mechanisms for relief of the poor need to be modified in light of a different culture and economy. Nevertheless, as noted by Hamilton, "the primary task of the exegete is not naming of policy but the identification of attitude."[21] Accordingly, an overview of the biblical vision of a just society should stimulate significant questions concerning our treatment of the poor and those who lack economic and political clout:

How are we to feel about the poor? Is there a point at which our neighborly obligation ends? What sort of attitude does the community represent to the world at large when it comes to these issues? *These* are the difficult questions, even more than the specifics of cost-effectiveness and effective empowerment.[22]

It is easy to dismiss poverty as solely the result of a lazy neglect of one's responsibilities. It is true that laziness, and sinful choices concerning alcohol and drug abuse, and even sexual misconduct may precipitate a spiral into poverty and economic distress.[23] However, it is entirely too simplistic to reduce the causal factors producing poverty to any one factor. There are very real social and societal structures that have contributed significantly to the unjust treatment of the poor and dependent within our society.[24] But even if a single factor could be named contributing to another's impoverishment, that by no means alleviates personal responsibility to help those in need. The sin of the rich man with respect to Lazarus was not that he was made rich by his oppression of Lazarus, but rather he found himself in torment at death because he failed to use his wealth to alleviate the suffering of one in need (Luke 16:19-31). In our refusal to take personal responsibility for the relief of another, we have aligned ourselves with unjust structures that promote poverty and oppression.

> *It is entirely too simplistic to reduce the causal factors producing poverty to any one factor, nor would this alleviate personal responsibility to help those in need.*

We live in an affluent nation that has accepted a way of life that often undermines a genuine concern for the poor. While we may cherish the principles of capitalism and democracy, we must not downplay the systemic problems and tensions associated with such systems. As Haltermann rightly observes:

> *We have accepted a way of life that often undermines a genuine concern for the poor.*

Capitalism and democracy are uneasy partners and a balance between them must be struck in any nation that tries to live by both creeds. The driving force behind capitalism is inequality—the dream of making more money than other people. The driving force behind democracy is equality—one person, one vote. If a democrat is born equal, a capitalist intends to die as unequal as possible. In the balance between these two great strivings lies the health of nations.[25]

While we may espouse the benefits of a democratic-capitalistic market-driven economy, the system has not always worked fairly among those with little political and economic influence. The gap between the affluent elite and those who are economically deprived continues to widen. The competitive nature of Western capitalism favors the corporate world, often at the expense of procedural justice and legal obligations toward those of limited resources. In our rush to propagate the "American dream," many Christians have failed to articulate a balance that exposes the downside of a totally unrestricted market economy. Merely extolling the virtues of competition and consumerism reflects an uncritical embracing of the corporate world of big business and their subtle ways of exploitation that often drive people to bankruptcy and economic despair. After all, the hardball world of global capitalism is driven by competitive and sophisticated enticements not only to buy certain products, but also to embrace a consumer way of life. The relentless bombardment of marketing appeals, commercial ads, and sales pitches ("the average American experiences nearly sixteen thousand encoun-

> The hardball world of global capitalism is driven by enticements to embrace a consumer way of life.

ters *per day*[26]) encourages the American people "to buy, spend and borrow to obtain the ever-growing supply of goods, novelties, and services, lest the market economy grind to a halt."[27] As Stassen and Gushee so aptly put it: "If Christian ethics is following Jesus, it must involve a clear-eyed analysis and finally repudiation of an economic ethos that ratifies the 'deceitfulness of wealth' and makes Mammon the virtual idol."[28]

The Church and Poverty

In the final analysis, the church must model the role of Yahweh in Israel and become an advocate for the poor and the dependent.[29] We must, like Zacchaeus, repent of our involvement or uncritical endorsement of sinful economic structures that perpetuate economic injustice. As noted by Sider, Zacchaeus "never supposed that he could come to Jesus and still continue enjoying all the economic benefits of that systematic evil. Coming to Jesus meant repenting of his complicity in social injustice. It meant publicly giving reparations. And it meant a whole new lifestyle. . . ."[30]

Based on the biblical vision of a just and caring society, the church should model among its own and before all humanity, a value system that ultimately pursues for all the basic need for inclusion in the broader community and improvement in ways that encourage self-dignity, responsibility, and well-being. Our modeling of Yahweh's care for the poor may go far beyond a financial response, and include an investment of one's time to listen to the story of another. Giving of one's time to work in a homeless shelter or serve at a soup kitchen would certainly be a major step in getting us out of our insulated comfort zone. The church should work creatively to help provide the tools, education, and employment opportunities to empower the poor to overcome their situation. As an advocate for the poor, our prophetic voice should be directed toward those who have the power and resources to bring meaningful relief and change on behalf of those who have little. In the prophetic tradition, the church should challenge those with wealth and power to use their resources to the increase of a *just* society. As effectively argued by Hamilton:

> The church should work creatively to empower the poor to overcome their situation.

> The suggestion that the church serve as advocate for the dependent is an attempt to do this. Such a role transfers to the people of YHWH in a secular society the role that YHWH played in a theocentric society. As such, the church makes what could otherwise be a secular undertaking, providing for the welfare and empowerment of the poor, into a sacred undertaking. . . .[31]

> The church makes a secular undertaking into a sacred undertaking.

The vision of the kingdom and the pursuit of justice require nothing less.

Justice and the Vulnerable

As noted in the previous section, biblical justice entails a kind of obligation owed to those in special need and care. Although the secular world may "see rights as things to be safeguarded from encroachment rather than as a set of obligations owed,"[32] the church must model an alternative ethos. As observed in the Deuteronomic Code, "how Israel treated the sojourner, the orphan, the widow, the indebted one, the slave, all of them completely dependent in the end on a God who sees to their care, was in this sense a reflection on the extent to which they respected themselves in their position of dependence on a God who answers the cry of the oppressed with compassion."[33] In Israel's community these were the most vulnerable, and their treatment was the most important barometer of the justness of their society. It is clear that those with economic power were to use their resources for the welfare of those less fortunate, in order to contribute to an increase in *shalom*-justice.

Jesus' enactment of the presence of God's Reign in his ministry vividly accented the value that God placed upon those who occupy the fringe of societal boundaries. When those deemed as "unclean" and "impure" by social and cultic standards (cf. Lev 21:16-23) are made whole, the oppressive forces that marginalized and tyrannized them are thereby challenged with a superior claim of authority and power. Those limited by debilitating illnesses and deformities not only suffered the physical burden of their condition, they found themselves ostracized from the community, unable to participate as a full Israelite (cf. Deut 21:1-6). Therefore, Tom Wright aptly spells out the significance of Jesus' healings:

> The effect of these cares, therefore, was not merely to bring physical healing; not merely to give humans, within a far less individualistic society than our modern one, a renewed sense of community membership; but to reconstitute those healed as members of the people of Israel's god [sic]. In other words, these healings, at the deepest level of understanding on the part of Jesus and his contemporaries, would be seen as part of his total ministry, specifically, part of that open welcome which went with the inauguration of the kingdom—and, consequently, part of his subversive work, which was likely to get him into trouble.[34]

Jesus' ongoing concern for those vulnerable to societal oppression is seen in his effort to get the disciples to identify with and care for those he terms, "harassed and helpless, like sheep without a shepherd" (Matt 9:36). Jesus embodies the ideal Shepherd King who in the words of Ezekiel comes to "search for the lost and bring back the strays . . . bind up the injured and strengthen the weak . . . [and] shepherd the flock with justice" (Ezek 34:16). In his outreach to so-called "sinners" (cf. Matt 9:11; Luke 15:2) he was ridiculed as a "friend of sinners" (cf. Matt 11:19). On another occasion he is chastised by Simon the Pharisee for allowing a sinful woman to freely have contact with him (Luke 7:36-50). He characterized his ministry as a conscientious effort to call "sinners" not the "righteous" (Matt 9:13; Luke 19:20). It is precisely those rejected by Jewish orthodoxy as notoriously sinful that Jesus invites to live under the Reign of God. They are the ones "burdened" by legal niceties and "wearied" by Pharisaic casuistry (Matt 11:28-30) and therefore are "scattered because there was no Shepherd and when they were scattered they became food for all the wild animals" (Ezek 34:5). Jesus responds to their vulnerable condition by offering them the healing gift of God's *shalom* and thereby enacting God's restorative justice.

Today's Vulnerable

Who are those in our modern society that are particularly vulnerable to oppressive social structures or vicious cycles of neglect and abuse? The church has often been guilty of a kind of "moral myopia" because we have been socialized into the acceptance of certain ways of seeing people and interpreting their social condition. It is critical that people of faith learn to identify social patterns that lend themselves to exploitation and oppression. As a people rooted in the biblical tradition, we must take seriously the reality of the fallen nature of all social structures and their potential for evil or good. Institutions and the social order can function either to enslave or liberate and bring relief to the human condition. Stephen Mott challenges the Christian community to struggle with evil in terms of "the geography of evil." He perceptively writes:

> In combating evil in the heart through evangelism and Christian nurture we deal with a crucial aspect of evil, but only one aspect. Dealing with the evil of the social order and the worldly powers involves social action, action in the world. Christian social reform has been effective when there has been a sense of a stronghold of evil in society that must be resisted.[35]

It is critical that the community of faith learn to identify those groups that are particularly at risk, and learn to weep with those who are victimized by the powers that be. A profound "hunger and thirst for justice" enables us to be moved by the anguish of human suffering. Why would we ever think genuine Christian piety is best exhibited by merely occu-

> A profound "hunger and thirst for justice" enables us to be moved by the anguish of human suffering.

pying a pew and singing a few hymns once or twice a week? Jesus' call to discipleship necessarily involves social action and consequences that will manifest themtselves in a vigorous and systematic involvement in the lives of those who are hurting.

Children: As it was in the ancient world, so today children are extremely vulnerable and at risk for neglect and abuse. Children in the ancient world, while cherished within the family unit, were extremely vulnerable to the harshness of life within Palestinian peasantry. Various types of sickness stemming from malnutrition and poverty made childhood in the ancient world extremely precarious. Infant mortality rates were extremely high within peasant communities.[36] Concerned parents bringing their children to Jesus in hope of healing and protection is reflective of their deep concern (Matt 18:3-4; 19:13-15). Repeatedly, for Jesus the conditions of childhood become a model of dependency and humility that are reflective of a mind-set and quality of life fundamental to the kingdom of God.

Has our modern society successfully assured the well-being and protection of our children? It may be surprising to realize that approximately 36% of those suffering in poverty are children.[37] Every night, 300,000 children must sleep in the streets because of homelessness. Over 7,000 children under sixteen will sleep tonight in an adult correctional facility. It is estimated that between one and three million children—both boys and girls—are making their living through child prostitution.[38] But even within what

> Approximately 36% of those suffering in poverty are children.

should be a safe environment, children are often subject to adult sexual abuse. The church must be committed to being an advocate and refuge for these, our most vulnerable. Certainly, the community of faith can creatively offer preventive and nurturing programs that not only protect our children, but also offer them an environment of nurture and love.

Women: All will agree that women have come a long way since the women's suffrage movement of the 1920s secured the right to vote. Nevertheless, there has always been the tendency for males to assert their masculine identity by claiming superiority over women. To reinforce the fragile male ego, many males assert their dominance by reliance upon a Victorian sexist stereotype of the subordinate woman.[39] However, as more women entered college and pursued professions once dominated by males, there emerged what some have termed the "battle of the sexes," along with an escalation of rhetorical labels that only further intensify the conflict (e.g., chauvinism, misogynist, feminazi). Without addressing all the social and religious influences of the extremes of feminism, alongside an entrenched patriarchalism, certainly the biblical vision challenges the modern church to work toward maximizing the opportunities for women to develop their potential to the fullest. We must affirm that men and women are fundamentally equal in worth, potential, and social rights. We must stand opposed to any effort to devalue or undermine the worth or contribution the woman may bring to the work place.[40] And, as Jesus held Jewish males accountable for their demeaning lustful looks that reduced women to mere sex objects (Matt 5:27-30), so we must deplore degrading sexual innuendoes and advances made upon women in the work place.

> We must affirm that men and women are fundamentally equal in worth, potential, and social rights.

Certainly there are recognizable gender distinctions. Nevertheless, "the primary issue is not specifying gender role but maximizing mission, effectiveness and impact."[41] Both Jesus and Paul offer a servant model of leadership that refuses to assign authority merely to gender. It is this vision of women that offers the best paradigm for addressing the injustice often perpetrated upon women, both in the broader society, and sadly to say, also in the church.

Disabled: Other groups that often experience various forms of injustice include people with disabilities and the aged. When the disciples encountered a man born blind, they immediately assumed that the plight of the man was the result of sin (John 9:2). Jesus, however, saw the man's condition as an opportunity to exhibit the power and presence of God in his life (9:3). In other words, Jesus saw his potential not his limitations and ministered to the man's need. Only when we see people through a different lens can we be effective in service. Rather than focusing on limitations we must train ourselves to allow those with disabilities to function at their highest level without placing even well-meaning artificial limits on them. Certainly an advocate for social justice would strongly support any legislation that prohibited discrimination against qualified workers with disabilities who

> Only when we see people through a different lens can we be effective in service.

are able to perform essential job functions with or without reasonable accommodations (e.g., Americans with Disabilities Act).[42] Structural or institutional policies that dehumanize or devalue the worth of another must be opposed.

Aged: David Gil points out that "contemporary discrimination against aged persons reflects a recent challenge to, and partial reversal of, early societal tendencies toward domination of younger people by their elders. . . ."[43] Today's youth may find the words of

> There is something humiliating about measuring the worth of a life simply in terms of physical health and social productivity.

Leviticus 19:32 somewhat archaic: "Show your fear of God by standing up in the presence of elderly people and showing respect for the aged." The tension is heightened by the feeling that old people are competing with younger people for the health dollar.[44] An aging population is seen as an economic burden because their productive years are behind them, and now with the deterioration of health they are viewed as a drain on society's limited resources. Yet, there is something humiliating about measuring the worth of a life simply in terms of physical health and social productivity. Justice demands we oppose all bureaucratic efforts to limit one based upon age and societal usefulness. As the theologian Karl Barth argued some years ago:

> A man [*sic*] who is not or is no longer, capable of working, of earning, of enjoyment and even perhaps of communication, is not for this reason unfit to live, least of all because he cannot render to the existence of the State any notable or active contribution, but can only directly or indirectly burden it.[45]

Rather than labeling the aged as a "burden" and then avoiding responsibility, the biblical vision responds to elderly fears, pain, and suffering by gladly "carrying their burdens, and in this way fulfill the law of Christ" (Gal 6:2). A concern for justice for the elderly not only involves providing for their physical needs, but also "our community needs to rediscover the healing properties of touch, voice, companionship, and the simple art of listening."[46] Furthermore, "when all care is categorized as 'therapy' with a dollar value, we fail to see the simple, unobtrusive acts of kindness which are indispensable to our humanity."[47] In the kingdom, justice takes the form of genuine care to lift the burdens of another.

Homosexual: Does a "hunger and thirst for justice" include being an advocate for justice on behalf of those of whose lifestyle we may disapprove? Should one's sexual orientation be sufficient reason to deny basic human rights and social services? Should a voice of justice be heard against discriminating policies and random acts of violence directed toward those who have embraced a gay or lesbian lifestyle? Presently there is no federal legislation protecting gays and lesbians from discrimination in the workplace. Only eight states and 110 municipalities have statutes barring discrimination against gays. Although many gays and lesbians will not be satisfied until all people accept their lifestyle as normal and healthy, perhaps we can strive for some common ground based on accepting a person's basic right to dignity and humane treatment.

While some seem consumed with making the homosexual the target of abuse and hateful rhetoric, certainly we can expect better from those who take seriously Christ's compassionate ministry and his redemptive death. In spite of the diverse ways that sin has distorted and stained all human lives, all persons, nevertheless, reflect God's image and are precious in his sight. Those who follow the example of Christ find no justification for dehumanizing and demeaning behavior directed toward certain groups that undermine their basic humanity, dignity, and right to humane treatment.

> Harsh and unjust treatment of any sinner cannot be reconciled with the ethics of the kingdom and the virtues of love, kindness, peace, and humility.

These observations should not be construed as an endorsement of homosexual behavior or a proposal for a revised reading of the texts that clearly take issue with homosexual acts or practices.[48] But we do contend that harsh and unjust treatment of the homosexual cannot be reconciled with the ethics of the kingdom and the virtues of love, kindness, peace, and humility. Furthermore we agree with Stassen and Gushee who argue,

Looking for ways to deny homosexuals personal safety and security, access to jobs, housing, government services, or other basic rights of participation in American society is abhorrent. On the other hand, supporting efforts by churches to enable homosexuals to deal with their sexuality in a redemptive way within the parameters offered by Scripture is certainly to be encouraged. We must love homosexual persons while remaining clear on our convictions about God's intention for human sexuality—and equally clear that all of us stand guilty and in need of redemption.[49]

Clearly certain groups are especially vulnerable to abuse and unjust forms of discrimination. Shall our voices remain silent when human dignity and value are undermined by the brutal forces of injustice?

Justice and Racial Equality

Although the last few decades have witnessed a growing awareness of the injustices perpetuated by the evils of racism, the chasm between white and black America continues to widen. As one African-American author put it: "Ever since I can remember, it has been almost axiomatic that if we blacks took a stand on an issue, conservative, evangelical Christians would line up on the opposite side of the street, blocking our way. The gulf between us is so deep that it is hard to imagine us on the same side of an issue."[50] Although laws have been passed prohibiting discrimination, and various faith-based efforts have affirmed the need for racial reconciliation, we are still a country sharply divided along racial lines.[51]

As the United States becomes more ethnically diverse,[52] a growing ethnocentrism has emerged that evaluates other cultural expressions solely in terms of the practices and convictions of one's own group, resulting in evaluative assessments that exclude certain people from opportunities based upon their peculiar racial, cultural, or ethnic grouping. Racism has led to atrocities against Native Americans in the nineteenth century, the wholesale extermination of Jews during the Holocaust, ethnic cleansing in former Yugoslavia, and the tragedies of South African apartheid. While we deplore the injustices that have been perpetrated upon various minority groups, our focus will be upon the African-American experience for understanding the sin of racism. This form of racism is largely based upon the assumption that physiological differences (e.g., skin color pigmentation) imply also one's superiority or inferiority in terms of intellectual capacity, ethical inclinations, human potential, and social worth. Racist ideology, therefore, moves from a biological definition of race to an evaluative judgment about people's inherent worth as human beings. The results are prejudicial attitudes founded upon faulty and inflexible generalizations, not on solid evidence or experience. Other components of prejudice may be identified:

> Prejudice . . . has an emotional component connected with it. It is characterized by a rigid or inflexible attitude or predisposition to respond in a certain way to its object. When the object of prejudice is a group, the individuals included in it may be viewed as a group only in the mind of the prejudiced despite the fact that its individual members may have little similarity or interaction with each other. Prejudice entails systematic misjudgment as the facts.
>
> Characteristic of prejudice is the tendency to select certain facts for emphasis, while downplaying others. New experiences are made to fit old categories through selection of only those ones that harmonize with a prejudgment or stereotype.
>
> Prejudice is learned. It is not usually acquired through direct contact with its object, however, but with prevailing *attitudes* toward it.[53]

Certainly, part of the problem contributing to our division along racial lines stems from the failure to adequately read and interpret one another's story. Whites are largely in denial concerning the extent that the legacy of racism continues to disadvantage members of the black community. But why would we assume that the wrongs of the past, such as the institution of slavery, followed by over a century of segregation, which continued to exploit blacks as socially and intellectually inferior, would not create a generation lacking the same advantages as white Americans? There may be some dispute concerning how to remedy the situation, but there can be no dispute that simply sweeping such historic injustices under the rug, and with a shrug telling black Americans to simply "get over

> *Part of the problem contributing to our division along racial lines stems from the failure to adequately read and interpret one another's story.*

it," adequately addresses the problem or is conducive to reconciliation. We also need to listen to an ongoing story of injustice as people of color continue to experience discriminating practices based upon race. Stassen and Gushee document several areas where black Americans experience injustices, not often noticed or taken seriously by white Americans. To highlight just a few of their observations:

- Black men are seven times more likely to die as murder victims than are white men.
- Blacks are less likely to receive prompt police attention when victimized as opposed to whites.
- Blacks are victimized by reported hate crimes more than any other group, whether racist, ethnic, religious or sexual.
- A black convicted of murder is more likely to be sentenced to death, all things being equal, than a white convicted of murder.
- Black women can expect to live five years less than white women.
- Black men can expect to live seven years less than white men.
- In 1998, the median income for a black household was $25,351 and for a white household $40,912.
- A higher percentage of blacks than whites live in poverty at every level of educational attainment.
- Blacks are more likely to experience police harassment, excessive use of force, brutality, racial profiling, differential treatment in law enforcement, and in the courts.
- Blacks still experience discrimination when it comes to hiring, voting, and inclusion in voluntary associations.[54]

Certainly, there are those instances where some inequities can be traced to poor choices or a lack of initiative to take advantage of opportunities that may be available. But, it is naïve to assume, all things being equal, that blacks are extended the same privileges and opportunities, as are whites. Establishing friendships across ethnic and racial lines, and truly listening to their stories and first-hand experiences can only overcome

> *It is naïve to assume, all things being equal, that blacks are extended the same privileges and opportunities, as are whites.*

these faulty assumptions. Few whites have ever experienced, on a daily basis, the hurt and frustration of discriminatory policies and prejudicial treatment based upon racial inequalities. An inability or refusal to recognize systematic racial injustice makes meaningful racial reconciliation all but impossible. As noted by Stassen and Gushee, "white social isolation from blacks and theological individualism"[55] has contributed to a reading of biblical texts that has failed to sensitize one to the presence of injustice. We have failed to understand how Jesus' ministry includes a proclamation of "justice to the nations" (Matt 12:18). Understanding the gospel solely in terms of the enhancement of one's personal spiritual life has trained us to be oblivious to social injustice. On the other hand, the black community has often nurtured a general suspicion that all whites are racists and not to be trusted. Such broad generalizations are also not helpful in producing reconciliation. Perhaps the greatest gift that could be extended by the black community is a willingness to forgive their white oppressors and work for healing. In the spirit of Martin Luther King and many who worked to overthrow apartheid in South Africa, ongoing

> *Perhaps the greatest gift that could be extended by the black community is a willingness to forgive their white oppressors and work for healing.*

hostilities and injustices dividing white and black Americans can only be overcome with a common vision of grace and forgiveness. That seems to be the way the early church was able to address the social and ethnic barriers confronting and threatening their fellowship.

Although "there is no evidence in antiquity of widespread prejudice against a particular group of people simply because of their color, or the combination of their color and distinctive ethnic features (hair, facial feature, etc.),"[56] that is not to say that one's ethnic background, social status, and even gender, were not a basis of discriminating ideology. Jesus repeatedly crossed ethnic and social boundaries deeply entrenched in the Palestinian culture of the first century. He seemed willing to extend his healing mercies beyond his fellow Jews by recognizing a Gentile centurion as having a faith he had not found within Israel (Matt 8:10) and praising a Canaanite woman as one with "great faith" (Matt 15:28). His willingness to engage in conversation a Samaritan woman (John 4:1-26), and his use of a "good Samaritan" to teach a vital lesson (Luke 10:25-37), certainly flew in the face of anti-Samaritan religio-racism typical of most first-century Jews. Ultimately, Jesus' disciples were commissioned to a mission without racial or ethnic boundaries (Matt 28:18-

20, *ethnoi* = all ethnic groups). Jesus, therefore, established a paradigm of mercy and compassion that transcended all racial and ethnic barriers.

Although it was not easy, his followers worked successfully to shatter racial and ethnic barriers by means of a mission that spread throughout the Mediterranean world. Both Jew and Gentile were to be accepted on equal terms as part of a new community where ethnic distinctions are no longer relevant or determinative in one's relationship with God or in their involvement in community (Gal 3:28). They were simply emulating the one who "came and preached peace, to you who were far away and peace to those who were near" (Eph 2:17). The result was a community described as "one new man out of two," a "family," and a "dwelling place where God lives by his Spirit" (Eph 2:19-21). The boundaries of this new community are "religio-moral rather than racial-ethnic."[57] It is time that the churches witness to God's creative powers by dissolving racial tensions and working for a truly just society. In the words of Stephen Mott: "Because the church is a manifestation of the Reign of God, the norms that guide it must exemplify the highest vision of human community."[58]

> *"Because the church is a manifestation of the Reign of God, the norms that guide it must exemplify the highest vision of human community."*

Notes

[1] Glen H. Stassen and David P. Gushee, *Kingdom Ethics: Following Jesus in Contemporary Context* (Downers Grove, IL: InterVarsity, 2003) 355: "One can hear persons who, influenced by the secularizing two realms split between private and public, say Jesus taught only love for individuals and not justice in relation to political and economic powers and authorities. Perhaps they think Rome was the government and the high priests were only religious. Perhaps they forget that state, church, and economic wealth were not separated but very much mixed together on the same hill and in the same temple in Jerusalem, and that Rome allowed the Jewish authorities to do most of the daily ruling. When Jesus confronted the representatives of the temple authority, he was confronting the public authorities of his time."

[2] See the extensive treatment of this theme in the three volumes by Walter Wink: *Naming the Powers: The Language of Power in the New Testament*, vol. 1 (Philadelphia: Fortress Press, 1984); *Unmasking the Powers: The Invisible Forces that Determine Human Existence*, vol. 2 (Philadelphia: Fortress Press, 1986); *Engaging the Powers: Discernment and Resistance in a World of Domination*, vol. 3 (Philadelphia: Fortress Press, 1992). See also the balanced appraisal by Marva Dawn, *Powers, Weakness, and Tabernacling of God* (Grand Rapids: Eerdmans, 2001) 1-34.

[3] Much of the material that follows comes from the forthcoming article, Larry Chouinard, "The Kingdom of God and the Pursuit of Justice in Matthew," *Restoration Quarterly* (2003).

[4] As noted by Christopher D. Marshall, *Beyond Retribution* (Grand Rapids: Eerdmans,

2001) 53: "The justice of God is not primarily or normatively a retributive justice or a distributive justice but a restorative justice, a saving action by God that recreates *shalom* and makes things right." In Jewish thought the restoration of *shalom* (well-being, restored order, peace) cannot be realized without justice, since justice removes all things that hinder the realization of *shalom*.

[5]Perry B. Yoder, *Shalom: The Bible's Word for Salvation, Justice and Peace* (Nappanee, IN: Evangel Publishing, 1987) 97.

[6]J.G. McConville, *Law and Theology in Deuteronomy*, JSOT Supplement 33 (England: Sheffield, 1984) 37.

[7]Marshall, *Beyond Retribution*, 71.

[8]Drawn from the influential work by John H. Yoder, *The Politics of Jesus* (Grand Rapids: Eerdmans, 1994).

[9]The question concerning who are those described as "the least of these brothers of mine" [(1) *all* who are poor, needy, and hungry, or (2) followers of Jesus who are poor, needy, and hungry], has been in much dispute; see Warren Carter, *Matthew and the Margins* (Maryknoll, NY: Orbis Books, 2000) 492, for a concise discussion.

[10]Jeffrey Hammond, "The Irony of Justice," *Wineskins* (May/June 2000) 14.

[11]Howard Zehr, *Changing Lenses: A New Focus for Crime and Justice* (Scottdale, PA: Herald Press, 1990) 47.

[12]Some positive efforts leading to racial healing and reconciliation can be seen in the National Association of Evangelicals, which called together black and white evangelicals for confession and a vow to work together for new multiracial relationships. The same confession and commitment was made in 1995 at the Southern Baptist Convention. Of course it remains to be seen how such actions will result in social change.

[13]See Ronald J. Sider, *For They Shall Be Fed* (Dallas: Word, 1997).

[14]See the article by Paul Prill, "Christians in an Age of Affluence," in this volume.

[15]These observations are an adaptation from Stephen Mott and Ronald J. Sider, "Economic Justice: A Biblical Paradigm," in *Toward a Just and Caring Society*, ed. by David P. Gushee (Grand Rapids: Baker, 1999) 27-30.

[16]Ibid., 40-41.

[17]Ibid.

[18]Jeffries Hamilton, *Social Justice and Deuteronomy: The Case of Deuteronomy 15* (Atlanta: Society of Biblical Literature, 1992) 145.

[19]Ibid., 145.

[20]Several authors have argued that Jesus intended his mission as outlined in Luke 4:18-19 (Isa 61:1-2), to be a call for his "followers to live 'as if' the Jubilee (see Leviticus 25) were being enacted"; see Tom Wright, *Jesus and the Victory of God* (Minneapolis: Fortress Press, 1996) 295; Yoder, *Politics of Jesus*, 64-77; Robert Sloan, *The Acceptable Year of the Lord* (Austin: Scholars Press, 1977).

[21]Hamilton, *Social Justice*, 157.

[22]Ibid., 157.

[23]For example, Stephen V. Monsma, "Poverty, Civil Society and the Public Policy Impasse," in *Toward a Just and Caring Society*, 46-71, observes that one-third of all single mothers live in poverty. Poverty is especially high among African Americans; and one cannot ignore the fact that only 45% of African-American families are headed by a married couple.

[24]See Ronald J. Sider, "Structural Evil and World Hunger," in *Readings in Christian Ethics*, vol. 2, ed. by David K. Clark and Robert V. Rakestraw (Grand Rapids: Baker, 1996) 367-376.

[25]James Haltemann, "The Market System, the Poor and Economic Theory," in *Toward a Just and Caring Society*, 72.

[26]See Michael Budde and Robert Brimlow, *Christianity Incorporated: How Big Business Is Buying the Church* (Grand Rapids: Brazos Press, 2002) 14.

[27]Ibid., 14. One need only recall that after 9/11 one of the exhortations of our President was to continue to shop.

[28]Stassen and Gushee, *Kingdom Ethics*, 426.

[29]As noted by Hamilton, *Social Justice in Deuteronomy*, esp. 155-157.

[30]See Sider, "Structural Evil and World Hunger," 376.

[31]Hamilton, *Social Justice and Deuteronomy*, 149.

[32]Ibid., 145.

[33]Ibid., 153.

[34]Wright, *Jesus and the Victory of God*, 192.

[35]Mott, *Biblical Ethics and Social Change*, 16.

[36]See discussion in R.L. Rohrbaugh, "Introduction," in *The Social Sciences and New*

Testament Interpretation, ed. by R.L. Rohrbaugh (Peabody, MA: Hendrickson, 1996) 4-5.

[37]U.S. Census Bureau, *Income and Poverty 2001*; consult **http://ferret.bls.census.gov**.

[38]Eileen W. Lindner, "The Child Advocacy Calling: Writing the Vision Plainly," *Church and State* (September/October 2000) 7.

[39]See the discussion in Carroll Osburn, *Women in the Church: Reclaiming the Ideal* (Abilene: ACU Press, 2001) 1-18.

[40]According to a recent study by Margaret Gibelman, "So How Far Have We Come? Pestilent and Persistent Gender Gap in Pay," *Social Work Journal* 48 (January 2003) 23: "The Bureau of Labor Statistics (BLS) reported that the median weekly pay of full-time working women was 75 percent of the median pay for men in 1996." According to another study, "women who leave the workplace [e.g., maternal leave] experience a 33 percent drop in wages when they return, and their pay never catches up again." Kathrine Esty et al., *Workplace Diversity* (Adams Media Corporation, 1995) 13. In a survey conducted in March 2002 by the Census Bureau, it was found that women, especially older women, are far more likely than men to live in poverty. For instance, 12 percent of women age 65 and older lived in poverty; 7 percent of men did (see **www.census.gov/Press-Release/www/2003/cb03-53.html**).

[41]See discussion by Stassen and Gushee, *Kingdom Ethics*, 323.

[42]See discussion in Esty, *Workplace Diversity*, 156-157.

[43]David G. Gil, *Confronting Injustice and Oppression: Concepts and Strategies for Social Workers* (New York: Columbia University Press, 1998) 30.

[44]In what follows I am indebted to the article by Rosalie Hudson, "The Economic Burden of Aged Care: Some Theological Reflections," *St. Mark's Review* (Autumn 2000) 16-23.

[45]Karl Barth, *Church Dogmatics*, vol. III, 4 (Edinburgh: T. & T. Clark, 1960) 423; cited in Hudson, "Economic Burden," 17.

[46]Hudson, "Economic Burden," 20.

[47]Ibid., 22.

[48]See the article in this volume by John Mark Hicks, "Homosexuality and the Biblical Witness."

[49]Stassen and Gushee, *Kingdom Ethics*, 311.

[50]Spencer Perkins, "The Prolife Credibility Gap," *Christianity Today* 21 (April 1989) 21.

[51]Stassen and Gushee, *Kingdom Ethics*, 389-390, point to the "voting patterns in the 2000 presidential election" as illustrating the gap in political loyalties dividing black and white Christians.

[52]The 2000 census revealed that Hispanic Americans have now pulled even with African Americans in population at around 35 million each. Cited in ibid., 405.

[53]Cited in "Racism and the Church: Overcoming Idolatry," A Report of the Commission on Theology and Church Relations of The Lutheran Church—Missouri Synod (February 1994) 15. **www.icms.org/ctcr/docs/pdf/racism.pdf**.

[54]Stassen and Gushee, *Kingdom Ethics*, 391-398.

[55]Ibid., 406.

[56]Ben Witherington, *The Acts of the Apostles: A Socio-Rhetorical Commentary* (Grand Rapids: Eerdmans, 1998) 295.

[57]Stassen and Gushee, *Kingdom* Ethics, 404.

[58]Mott, *Social Ethics and Social Change*, 131. Sociologist, David Gil, *Confronting Injustice and Oppression*, 39, acknowledges: "Transformation of unjust and oppressive societies into just and nonoppressive ones would require major changes in patterns of people's actions, intentions, and social relations. In turn, such changes seem to depend on changes of people's consciousness, which would be conducive to alternative patterns of actions and relations."

Bibliography

Marshall, Christopher D. *Beyond Retribution: A New Testament Vision for Justice, Crime, and Punishment.* Grand Rapids: Eerdmans, 2001.

Although this book deals primarily with the death penalty, it offers a thorough theological basis for moving from retributive justice to restorative justice. It is the best available for a sustained evaluation of the criminal justice system and an alternative vision for an improved system that comes closer to the biblical model of justice.

Mott, Stephen Charles. *Biblical Ethics and Social Change.* New York: Oxford University Press, 1982.

Mott offers a synthesis of biblical studies and ethics. His work argues persuasively for the church as a countercommunity providing a powerful witness and incentive for both character and social change.

Mott, Stephen, and Ronald Sider. *Toward a Just and Caring Society.* Grand Rapids: Baker, 1999.

This book is a collection of essays from sixteen evangelicals addressing societal issues from a biblical perspective. The book examines complex issues such as poverty, the market system, health policies, business, and welfare reform. The book moves beyond partisan arguments and polarization to offer real solutions and hope.

Zehr, Howard. *Changing Lenses: A New Focus for Crime and Justice.* Scottdale, PA: Herald Press, 1990.

An important study that proposes a "restorative model" that takes seriously the needs of both offenders and victims.

YOU CANNOT SERVE GOD AND MAMMON
CHRISTIANS IN AN AGE OF AFFLUENCE
Paul Prill, Ph.D.

Paradox characterizes much of the teaching of Jesus. Consider three of his most well-known statements: "The first shall be last and the last first." "If anyone wants to be great in the kingdom of heaven, he must become a servant." "If you want to keep your life, you must lose it." All three of these statements disorient the listener/reader and create a tension of thought and action, the hallmark of paradox. It is a tension which we cannot resolve, but one within which we must live.

The presence of paradox is most evident in the way in which the Bible approaches the issue of money and the relationship of the believer to it. On the one hand the Bible affirms that the material world is good and that God promises wealth as an evidence of his blessing. On the other hand, one is hard-pressed to find examples of people who consistently use their wealth well, prompting Jesus to say, "You cannot serve God and Mammon." In the next few pages we will explore three ideas. First, we will look at the paradox of wealth as it develops in the Bible. Second, we will look at the ways in which money works to shape our values, priorities, and commitments. Finally, we will look at ways in which we can overcome the power of Mammon in our lives and in our churches. The overriding principle which governs this discussion is that the way we use the wealth which God has given us is a measure of the reality of our faithfulness to him in all areas of our life.

> The way we use the wealth which God has given us is a measure of the reality of our faithfulness to him in all areas of our life.

Movies always begin with an establishing shot, a way to create a mind-set and tone for the picture as well as provide an introduction for the film. To begin our discussion of money and the Christian, we should remember the "establishing shot" of the Bible.

> In the beginning, . . . God created the heavens and the earth. . . . And God said to [Adam and Eve], "Be fruitful and multiply, and fill the earth and subdue it. . . . See, I have given you every plant yielding seed that is upon the face of the earth, and every tree with seed in its fruit; you shall have them for food." . . . God saw everything that he had made, and indeed, it was very good (Genesis 1, passim).

Everything which takes place in Scripture has this beginning somehow in mind, either as a reminder of how far we have strayed from God's perfection or as an anticipation of what God has in store for us at the end of the age.

The vision we encounter in the opening two chapters of Genesis reminds us of the incredible goodness and abundance of God's love for humankind. This vision forms the basis for James's statement that every good and perfect gift comes down to us from the Father of lights (Jas 1:17) and Paul's claim that all of creation is good and fit for human use provided it is received with thanksgiving (1 Tim 3:4-5). Adam and Eve had everything that they needed and more. All creatures great and small, and all plants, lived in perfect peace and harmony. No one lacked for anything. There is a sense of delight and joy only slightly below the surface of the text, but so unmistakable that C.S. Lewis could capture it in his novel *Perelandra*. The protagonist, Ransom, finds himself in a second Eden on the planet Venus. As he walks, he encounters some food and, upon tasting it, has the most extraordinary sensation.

> It was, of course, a taste, just as his thirst and hunger had been thirst and hunger. But then it was so different from every other taste that it seemed mere pedantry to call it a taste at all. It was like the discovery of a totally new genus of pleasures, something unheard of among all men, out of all reckoning beyond all covenant. . . . As he let the empty gourd fall from his hand and was about to pick a second one, it came into his head that he was neither hungry nor thirsty.[1]

Abundance and satisfaction. Appreciation and admiration. This is what God declared in the beginning to be very good and what he intended and intends for his creatures.

This vision of abundance persists and finds fulfillment in the book of Revelation. There we read descriptions of all kinds of precious metals and jewels adorning the streets and gates and buildings. We encounter a Jesus whose appearance smacks of opulence with his golden sash and his brasslike feet. One possible way to read these descriptions is to see how meaningless all of our possessions are in light of the resplendent glory of God. Robert Royalty compares the images in Revelation with their antecedents in Greco-Roman culture and in the Old Testament. His analysis leads him to conclude that what John does is to depict God as phenomenally wealthy, with each vision wealthier than its literary or historical source.[2] This wealth, then, legitimates the power of God as opposed to any other power. More importantly for our purposes, God intends for us to inhabit the new heaven and the new earth with all of its abundance and wealth, a return to Eden.

The story of the patriarchs and of the nation of Israel continues this theme of abundance. Abraham becomes a rich man. He passes much of his wealth to his son Isaac. Isaac's son Jacob flees to Laban's country where he too accumulates a great deal of wealth. Jacob's son Joseph becomes a wealthy man in Egypt, and Israel and his descendants enjoy prosperity for a time while they are in Egypt. Despite all of the intrigues and adventures of these patriarchs, despite all of the ways in which they fail God at times, they are his chosen people, and God grants them material wealth as a sign of his blessing.

After the nation of Israel has experienced a long period of slavery in Egypt, God again demonstrates his faithfulness to his people. He hears their cries from captivity and delivers them powerfully from the hand of Pharaoh, and as they leave for the land of promise, the Egyptians heap upon them treasures. When they arrive at the border of the land and send in the spies, they discover a land flowing with milk and honey containing grapes so large that a single cluster required two men to carry it on a pole between them (Numbers 13). Finally, when they prepare to occupy the land after their forty years of wandering in the wilderness, Moses speaks to the people about the promise of God:

> For the LORD your God is bringing you into a good land, a
> land with flowing streams, with springs and underground

waters welling up in valleys and hills, a land of wheat and
barley, of vines and fig trees and pomegranates, a land of
olive trees and honey, a land where you may eat bread without scarcity, where you will lack nothing, a land whose
stones are iron and from whose hills you may mine copper.
You shall eat your fill and bless the LORD your God for the
good land he has given you (Deut 8:7-10).

Moreover, this was not a one time gift, but was a promise from God
that he would continue to bless the people if they were faithful to
him, to give them more and more material blessings in response to
their obedience.

If you heed these ordinances [the Torah], by diligently
observing them, the LORD your God will maintain you with
the covenant loyalty that he swore to your ancestors; he will
love you, bless you, and multiply you; he will bless the fruit
of your womb and the fruit of your ground, your grain and
your wine and your oil, the increase of your cattle and the
issue of your flock, in the land that he swore to your ancestors to give to you. You shall be the most blessed of peoples . . . (Deut 7:12-14a).

We know how the story continues. The people are not faithful,
just as they were not faithful in the wilderness of Sin. The northern
kingdom and the ten tribes which inhabit it fall to the conquests of
Assyria; the southern kingdom and its two tribes fall to Babylon.
There they stay until they have paid double for all of their sins (Isa
40:2). Nevertheless, the notion of God's steadfast love and his promise to Abraham, Isaac, and Jacob persists. The prophets share many
themes, and one of the more prominent ones is the notion that the
people will return to the land and that they will enjoy the wealth of
the nations. Isaiah presents this clearly in the later visions of the
book. "Then you shall see and be radiant; your heart shall thrill and
rejoice, because the abundance of the sea shall be brought to you.
. . . Your gates shall always be open; day and night they shall not be
shut, so that the nations shall bring you their wealth, with their
kings in procession" (60:5,11). Like Job, Israel shall receive all that it
had lost and gain even more because God wants to share his abundance and bless them materially as a sign of their status as God's
chosen people.

What then can we say about the notion of wealth as it is presented in the Old Testament? First, God has made a good earth, which continues to be good even after the sin of Adam and Eve. Second, God intends to bless the chosen people with an abundance unparalleled in the rest of the world. Third, these blessings will continue so long as the people of God remain faithful to their calling.

At this point, one can understand the thinking of those who espouse a gospel of wealth. How can one deny the Deuteronomic principles and the promises of God? Doesn't Jesus even promise that whoever gives will receive "pressed down, shaken together, running over . . ." (Luke 6:38)? Should we not, like the Israelites fleeing Egypt, pray for and accept the transfer of wealth from those who are not the people of God to those who are? Should we not rejoice and delight in the goodness of what God has made and given to us? These conclusions would seem to make sense were it not for one prominent statement of Jesus in the Sermon on the Mount, a statement which establishes the paradox of biblical teaching about money. Jesus says very simply and categorically, "You cannot serve God and Mammon." Now we must turn our attention to the negative side of wealth.

This statement of Jesus strikes us as a bit odd, anachronistic. We wonder sometimes if Jesus would say the same thing today, given the change from the economic system of his day. Our culture and large parts of our world tout the virtues of a capitalist economy. Charles Handy notes that capitalism has several moral benefits as well as economic ones, a sentiment seconded by economists from Adam Smith in 1776 to Michael Novak in 1982 and most recently by theologian John Schneider.[3] At its best, capitalism encourages productive work and thrift, virtues which are consistent with the advice found throughout the book of Proverbs. Moreover, in those countries which have adopted entirely or mostly capitalist economies, the standard of living, the life expectancy, and the quality of life are all the highest in the world.[4] Finally, the emergence of global capitalism has produced the same positive benefits in the developing world. Even the poorest of the poor nations have seen the quality of life in their countries improve as they adopt some form of market-based economies.[5] Is this not the return to *shalom* which the prophets envisioned? While we may live in the "not yet," we can still see move-

> *Our culture and large parts of our world tout the virtues of a capitalist economy.*

ment toward some kind of economic well-being and improved quality of life for all people in all countries.

Why, then, would Jesus place Mammon (wealth) in the same category as false gods like Baal, Molech, Asherah, or Marduk? Why make Mammon into a god with the power to control our behavior, to command our allegiance, to order our lives? For us in America and for that matter those in most of the world, money is just a tool, a means to an end. Surely no one would call a shovel a god. Nor would one call a computer a god. They are both tools which allow us to work and enjoy the benefits of our labor. Moreover, in the United States the inscription on our money ("In God We Trust") even bears witness to its intended place in our society. We are not the servants of money. We receive it in abundance as an indication of the blessing of God. We save money and we invest it wisely so that we may be good stewards of what God has given us. We own money; money does not own us.

Interestingly, Mammon is derived from an Aramaic word meaning "that in which one trusts."[6] From this definition, it becomes clear why Jesus considers it an idol. Mammon deflects our attention and our trust away from God. Instead of the Almighty God, we pursue the Almighty Dollar. Instead of trusting in God to secure our future, we accumulate stocks and bonds, which are classified in our economy as "securities." Like the ring of power in J.R.R. Tolkien's trilogy (*The Lord of the Rings*), Mammon seems to take possession of those who would possess it. Few have the character of Frodo Baggins to resist its power, especially as its power grows.

> Instead of the Almighty God, we pursue the Almighty Dollar.

Here is the essential paradox about money in the Bible. While the Old Testament establishes the sacramental nature of wealth, it has virtually nothing good to say about the wealthy outside of the Patriarchs.[7] Beginning with Solomon and continuing through the end of the Old Testament story, the historians and the prophets point to the cares of the world and the lure of wealth which choke out the budding fruitfulness of the Word of God. Consider the reasons why Israel and Judah went into captivity. Certainly it was because of their idolatry, culminating in Manasseh's sacrifice of one of his own children. Additionally, it was because money relationships and the consequent injustices which resulted had corrupted the community.

While the Jews continued to make their burnt offerings to God and observed the holy days and fasts, they neglected their responsibilities to economic justice inside their communities. When they cry out to God, "Why do we fast, but you do not see? We humble ourselves, but you do not notice?" God responds simply "you fast only to serve your own interest on your fast day. . . . Is this not the fast that I choose: to loose the bonds of injustice, to undo the thong of the yoke, to let the oppressed go free . . . ? Is it not to share your bread with the hungry, and bring the homeless poor into your house; when you see the naked to cover them, and not hide yourself from your own kin?" (Isa 58:5-6).

It is not the case that Israel lacked resources, but those resources were wrongly used. First, the gold and silver which might have helped the poor were used to make idols (Isa 2:7-8 and Hos 2:8). Second, their desire for possessions beyond what God had intended and their seeking after security in things other than God had driven them to injustices and lack of compassion for the needy in their midst. Amos describes how some people lived in great houses of ivory while at the same time oppressing the poor and crushing the needy (4:2). Those same people threw lavish parties with musicians and wine, dressing in all of their finery and wearing expensive perfume, to which God says, "I abhor the pride of Jacob . . . and I will deliver up the city and all that it is in it" (6:8). They even trade in human flesh, buying and selling their fellow Israelites to fit their needs (8:4-6). There is little to commend the use of wealth among the Israelites during the reign of the kings.

The teaching about money and the wealthy is more nuanced in the New Testament, but underlying the entire discussion is an attitude consistent with the prophetic warnings of the Old Testament. A few passages will suffice to establish the tone of the discourse about Mammon. "It will be hard for a rich person to enter the kingdom of heaven" (Matt 19:23). "The cares of the world and the lure of wealth choke the word, and it yields nothing" (Matt 13:22). "What will it profit them if they gain the whole world but forfeit their life?" (Matt 16:26). "Do not store up for yourselves treasures on the earth . . . for where your treasure is, there your heart will be also" (Matt 6:19-21). James warns against the intrusions of the rich into the life of the church (2:1-6) and tells the rich to weep and mourn, since they have apparently deprived the poor of a living wage (5:1-6). Paul adds that "those who want to be rich fall into temptation and are trapped by the many senseless and harmful desires that plunge people into ruin and destruction. For the love of money is a root of all kinds of evil, and in their eagerness to be rich some have wandered away from the faith . . ." (1 Tim 6:9-10).

If the teaching of the Bible clearly warns against the abuses of wealth, why is it that we fail to heed the warnings? A quick review of some random statistics reveals some startling truths about what we do with the money we have received. Americans have clearly gotten wealthier over the past four decades, doubling income during that time. As we have become wealthier, our lives have become more comfortable, with larger, better appointed houses and cars, better diets, and more access to health care. And as we have grown wealthier, our spending has increased dramatically. Juliet Schor estimates that our spending has increased at a minimum by 30 percent between 1979 and 1995, and, taking into account changes in the consumer price index, a maximum of 70 percent.[8] Well and good. We have worked hard, and we are delighting in the bounty which God has given us. We are practicing "godly materialism."[9] Yet at the same time our incomes and spending have gone up, our giving as a percentage of our income has gone down dramatically. In 1968, evangelical Christians gave just over six percent of their incomes to churches and charities. By the mid-1990s that had fallen to just over two percent.[10]

> *Yet at the same time our incomes and spending have gone up, our giving as a percentage of our income has gone down dramatically.*

More revealing is where we Americans spend our money. As you read the following list, think about what values our choices represent.

- $17 billion on pet food, $4 billion more than needed to provide basic health and nutrition for everyone in the world
- $8 billion on cosmetics, $2 billion more than needed to provide basic education for everyone in the world[11]
- twice as much on cut flowers as on overseas Protestant ministries
- twice as much on panty hose and stockings as on overseas Protestant ministries
- three times as much on video games and pinball machines as on overseas Protestant ministries

- three times as much on swimming pools and accessories as on overseas Protestant ministries
- seven times as much on sweets as on overseas Protestant ministries
- seventeen times as much on diets and diet-related products as on overseas Protestant ministries
- twenty times as much on sports activities as on overseas Protestant ministries
- twenty-six times as much on soft drinks as on overseas Protestant ministries
- 140 times as much on legalized gambling activities as on overseas Protestant ministries[12]

All of these statistics suggest the same question. Who or what determines the spending priorities for Americans and for American Christians? Is it God or Mammon? Quite clearly, the values which determine our purchasing decisions are skewed. How did that happen? How did Mammon triumph?

Adam Smith published *An Inquiry into the Nature and Causes of the Wealth of Nations* in 1776 and with it introduced his audience and later ones to a systematic way of thinking about capital and its uses in producing wealth. One of the basic premises for Smith's understanding of capitalism was value. Gold was in shorter supply than iron and so had more value. Any able-bodied person could dig a ditch, but only a skilled person could perform surgery. So the surgeon had more value in the job market than did the ditch digger. One could, from Smith's perspective, determine the value of any good, service, or piece of information and thus could establish its role in the general economy. Smith did not, however, render economics an autonomous discipline, unanswerable to ethics, politics, and religion. Smith's body of writings include large works on law and on ethics. Thus Smith continues the tradition of the church Fathers, believing that economic behavior must take place in the larger context of faith.

Nevertheless, Smith's work on value set the stage for a view of economic behavior which eventually led to our current understanding of a consumerism divorced from ethics. A generation before Smith, in 1729, the satirist Jonathan Swift wrote "A Modest Proposal." Swift assumed the persona of a social scientist and imagined what would happen if all human relationships fell under the umbrella of value and profitability. Noticing that raising children always results in economic loss for a family, Swift suggested, modestly, that families begin seeing children according to their economic value. To perpetuate the species, families should raise some children for breeding purposes. Then to ensure that the family turns a profit on its enterprise, it should raise most of its children to be slaughtered like cattle or sheep, selling the meat for ragouts and fricassees and the flesh for coats and hats or, one might add, for kid gloves. Obviously Swift never intended for individuals to engage in such behavior, but his proposal anticipated a time when all relationships would be measured by their economic profits and costs.

> The definition of value has shifted from the religious sphere to the economic one.

The majority of evidence from recent times seems to point to Swift as an astute observer of human nature. The definition of value has shifted from the religious sphere to the economic one. As John Boli argues in his essay, "The Economic Absorption of the Sacred," "the sacred order identifies, among other things, the cultural sources of value or worth. If God is the only sacred, everything of value comes from God; if the individual is sacred, value is presumed to flow from individual action. The sacredness of the economy implies, with only slight exaggeration, that only economic value has any reality."[13] How does this play out in practical terms? Do not other values count? We still go to church. We still fall in love and get married. Surely these are important activities in our lives. They have value, but they are priceless; and, as Boli continues, "pricelessness is neither here nor there."[14] Since faith and family cannot be figured into any equation, they become less relevant in making calculations and incidentally less relevant to our personal choices.[15]

Charles Handy documents well the pervasiveness of economic values in his book *The Hungry Spirit*. Handy has spent his entire career working in industry and is a champion of a capitalism which has a humane base to it. But the capitalism which he has observed so far believes that "anything which is unpriced is ignored by the market." He offers air as a good example. We cannot place a value on air. In fact, we all treat air as if it were free. We are learning that the chemicals which we place into the air adversely affect the quality of our lives, yet the consequent debate over air pollution and how to deal with it is fierce and often convoluted by the inability to quantify the harms caused, the market-value of air quality. After considering several other examples like this, Handy concludes, "By ignoring what is eventually unpriced, the market can distort our values."[16] This seems increasingly true in human relationships. Theologian Nicholas Wolterstorff argues that the ethical means of defining human relationships have given way to economic ones, concluding "an *ethic* of personal relations has been replaced by a *calling* to work for that impersonal thing called 'money.' All that is left by way of an ethic . . . is the ethic of the contract."[17]

Like the Laodiceans, our values are distorted. They claimed to be rich, but Jesus said that they were poor. Their riches led them into a kind of spiritual lethargy so repugnant that Jesus threatened to vomit them out of his mouth (Rev 3:14-22). Unlike the Laodiceans, though, we refuse even to admit that we are rich. Our standard is not the rest of the world, nor even the median income in the United States. When most of us think of being rich and having the good life, we think in terms of the top five percent of incomes in the United States, currently about a $250,000 annual income. It would seem, then, that we need to rethink our relationship to money and look for ways to make friends for ourselves with "the Mammon of unrighteousness" (Luke 16:9).

Godly contentment offers the best starting point for dealing with the power of Mammon. When Paul warns against the desire to become rich, he does so in the context of contentment, writing, "There is great gain in godliness combined with contentment, for we brought nothing into this world, so that we can take nothing out of it; but if we have

> *Godly contentment offers the best starting point for dealing with the power of Mammon.*

food and clothing, we will be content with these" (1 Tim 6:6-7). Paul refers to the same principle in his letter to the church at Philippi, but the context is slightly altered, as Paul recalls the economic circumstances of his life. Sometimes he has had little economic support and little material advantage; at other times, he has had plenty. In both circumstances, he remembers, he has learned to be content. Psalm 131 captures well this spirit of godly contentment: "O Lord, my heart is not lifted up, my eyes are not raised too high; I do not occupy myself with things too great and too marvelous for me. But I have calmed and quieted my soul, like a weaned child with its mother . . ." (vv. 1-2). Perhaps Proverbs best expresses the idea: "give me neither poverty nor riches; feed me with the food that I need, or I shall be full and deny you, and say, 'Who is the LORD?' or I shall be poor, and steal, and profane the name of my God" (30:8-9).

At the heart of godly contentment is the trust that God will supply us our daily bread (Matt 6:11), that God will not forsake the righteous, causing their children to beg (Ps 37:25). There is a trust that the God who cares for the birds of the air and the lilies of the fields will provide us with those things that we need to live in this world. There is also a recognition that God is the answer to our greatest hunger. This does not deny our daily hunger, our material needs. Rather it recognizes that we have two hungers. The physiological, biological hunger for food and drink and shelter which comes from the fact that we are material beings, created from the dust of the ground. And the spiritual hunger, the need to understand why we are here and what claims The Holy Other makes on our lives. As Augustine so aptly puts it in the beginning of his *Confessions*, "You have made us for yourself, Lord. You have made us for yourself, and our hearts are restless until they rest in you."[18]

Unfortunately, while it is easy to articulate a principle of godly contentment, it is difficult to live it. Charles Handy points to an African saying about our two hungers, material and spiritual, and then laments, "In capitalist societies, however, it has been our comfortable assumption, so far, that we can best satisfy the greater hunger by appeasing the lesser hunger."[19] One of the most remarkable and shameful statements of the twentieth century underscoring this assumption was made by John Maynard Keynes, architect of the economic recovery following World War II, who said that if we wanted to get the economy back on track we would need to institutionalize greed.[20] Anyone familiar with the New Testament would recognize that greed is idolatry (Eph 5:5). Do we really want to say that we would practice idolatry because economic conditions (Mammon) required it?

> We say that we are not greedy, yet we are seldom satisfied.

The Greek word for greed is *pleonexia*, and it defines a kind of insatiability, an appetite which can never get enough. We say that we are not greedy, yet we are seldom satisfied. Robert Wuthnow has studied extensively our ambivalence about materialism, and he concludes, while an overwhelming majority of people think that materialism is a serious problem in our country, an equal number would like to have more money so that their lives would be more comfortable.[21] Juliet Schor reports that only 15 percent of Americans are happy with being neither rich nor poor. The remaining 85 percent would like to have the incomes equivalent to the top 18 percent of wage earners.[22]

Try as we might, we have a hard time resisting "all that is in the world—the desire of the flesh, the desire of the eyes, the pride in riches" none of which comes from the Father but from the world (1 John 2:16). Moreover, we live in a world which constantly places before us the options to consume well beyond our needs and, as our increasing personal debt burden would indicate, beyond our means. In 1995, commercial interests around the world spent $385 billion for advertising.[23] This year, 2003, a sixty-second slot during the Super Bowl cost $2 million. Advertisers and their critics agree that we do not typically get solid product information, though many commercials do contain useful information. Instead, we are being sold an identity, a definition of who we are, a sense of security, an opportunity to create our own worlds in ways that seem right in our own eyes. We are being sold the desire to desire, the need to need, not an object which meets one of our basic needs.[24] We should not be surprised by this need to need. Commenting on the book of Ecclesiastes, Miroslav Volf traces the biblical descriptions of desire, concluding that insatiability is part and parcel of who we are.[25] Because this is and has been true of human nature, the desire for simplicity, for contentment, may be insufficient for most of us to overcome the power of Mammon.

To guard against selfish consumption, we need to practice the discipline of generosity. One of the fundamental teachings of both the Old and the New Testaments supports the idea that how we use our money is a measure of our discipleship. All of the economic laws of the Old Testament (Sabbath, Gleanings, Jubilee) were designed to ensure

> To guard against selfish consumption, we need to practice the discipline of generosity.

economic justice among the people of God. As we have already argued, the voices of the prophets condemned the practices of the people in this regard. Their use of money demonstrated their basic faithlessness before God. We must now face the same test. James says that the test of faith is not just piety, but the treatment of our brother in need (Jas 2:14-17). John seconds James's statement insist-

ing that we cannot say we love God if we fail to deal compassion-
ately with the material needs of our poor brothers and sisters (1 John
3:16). Jesus himself insists that the criteria for judgment will involve
how we treat the least of those who are nonetheless his brothers and
sisters (Matthew 25). What we as Christians do with our money
matters to God.

We only need look to the example of the early church to see
how the discipline of generosity applied. At Pentecost believers sold
their possessions to care for the new converts who stayed behind in
Jerusalem. Luke says that they practiced *koinonia*; that is, they had
everything in common.[26] A lot of misunderstanding surrounds this
early practice. Invoking the story of the rich young ruler, some have
claimed that they sold all that they had and put the proceeds in a
common treasury from which the apostles and later the deacons met
the material needs of the Jerusalem community. A few have even
suggested that their practice, along with the command to the young
ruler, prohibits Christians from owning any property, from having
savings or retirement accounts, from having life or health insurance.
Must we all sell what we have in order to follow Christ? Is financial
planning, even at its most rudimentary level, a sin? The answer is an
emphatic "No."

What really happened in Jerusalem we can never know exactly. Clearly people sold some of their possessions. Just as clearly,
people did not sell, nor were they required to sell, everything. The
sin of Ananias and Sapphira was not that they didn't sell everything,
but that they lied about what they had done. Peter makes it perfectly clear to Ananias that his property belonged to him to do with as
he saw fit and that there was no need to lie about having only sold
some things at that particular moment (Acts 5:1-11). More likely
what happened in those early days of Christianity is that the believers sold some of their possessions at one time and some at a later
time as needs arose.[27]

Paul will extend this principle when he writes to the church at
Corinth about their need to contribute to the well-being of the saints
in Jerusalem.[28] Here he clearly lays out the need for generosity from
believers who have benefited greatly from God's abundant material
blessings, and Paul is not above guilt manipulation.[29] First, he says
that the poor believers in Macedonia, who begged for the privilege of
sharing in this contribution, dug deep into their pockets to give
beyond their means. Second, he adds the example of Christ's gen-

erosity who "though he was rich, yet for your sakes he became poor, so that through his poverty you might become rich" (2 Cor 8:9). What he wants the Corinthians to understand is that this sharing is not to disadvantage them; they are not required to give what they do not have (v. 12). Rather they are to give from their abundance (affluence, if you will) so that there might be a fair balance, that their brothers and sisters will not suffer while they enjoy prosperity.

Furthermore, Paul articulates a general principle in the next chapter which applies not only to this one particular contribution, but he generalizes the notion of how we ought to give throughout our lives. "The point is this: the one who sows sparingly will also reap sparingly, and the who sows bountifully will also reap bountifully" (9:6). One might be tempted to read this as supporting a gospel of prosperity: the more I give, the more I get to use as I see fit. But Paul continues, "And God is able to provide you with every blessing in abundance, so that by always having enough of everything, you may share abundantly in every good work. . . . He who supplies seed for the sower and bread for food *will supply and multiply your seed for sowing and increase the harvest of your righteousness* (vv. 8 and 10, italics mine). God may bless the Corinthians materially, but if he does so, it will be so that they can become even more generous, their generosity becoming a witness to the extravagant love and mercy of God (vv. 12-13).

Affluence should prompt us to become even more generous. Paul will say simply that those who are rich in this present age need "to do good, to be rich in good works, generous, and ready to share, thus storing up for themselves the treasure of a good foundation for the future, so that they may take hold of the life that is really life" (1 Tim 6:18-19). Jesus tells a parable about the

> *Affluence should prompt us to become even more generous.*

foolish manager put in charge of his master's possessions, just as humans have been put in charge of the creation which belongs to God. But this manager mistreats his fellows and lives a luxurious life. As the master sends him away to be cut into pieces, he says, "From everyone to whom much has been given, much more is expected; and from the one to whom much has been entrusted, even more will be demanded" (Luke 12:48). Instead of allowing our giving to decline precipitously over the past four decades, Christians to whom much more has been entrusted should have, according to these teachings from Scripture, dramatically increased their charitable giving.[30]

One of the best suggestions for practicing disciplined generosity is the graduated tithe.[31] As Ron Sider envisioned it, each person would set a standard of living as a base line. Let's take the median income for a family of four, currently around $42,000, as the standard.[32] From that, the family would give a tenth and use the rest to cover household expenses. When the income increased to $43,000, the family would give 15 percent of the extra $1000 or $4350. When the income went to $44,000, the family would give 20 percent of the extra $1000 or $4550. After 18 years, assuming 5 percent increases each year, the family would give away 100 percent of each subsequent raise. Thus a family which began by giving $4200, 10 percent of their income would, after 18 years, eventually be giving $14,550 out of $60,000, or about 25 percent of their income. Of course, if you establish your standard as the median income and start out making much more than that, then you should adjust your initial giving accordingly. What the graduated tithe enables you to do is to enjoy much of the early raises to improve your standard of living, to save for education and/or retirement, to eat celebratory dinners, or to take some weekend sabbatical retreats. At the same time you acknowledge that God has provided the abundance, has entrusted you with more, and therefore expects more from you.

Can this really be done? Some stories indicate that people are already doing it. Rodney Clapp relates the story of Malcolm Street, a banker in Texas. Street's work taught him that affluence did not bring happiness. He decided that God needed to work a change in him, and now he lives in a middle-income community, as opposed to a gated one, where he participates in a weekly Bible study and a monthly men's prayer breakfast, and he gives away 30 percent of his income.[33] Craig Blomberg, who is a teacher at Denver Seminary gives away 30 percent of his income and lives in an affluent suburb of Denver.[34]

My own story is a bit more tortured. When I came to faith, I was an antimaterialist, borderline-Marxist hippie at Western Illinois University in Macomb, Illinois. One of the first questions that I had back in 1972 when I became a disciple was about money. I read the New Testament several times and concluded as others have that our relationship to money is not a neutral one. I have been reading about and thinking about wealth from various perspectives ever since that time. I come from a lower middle-class background and now find myself in the top twenty percent of wage earners in the United

States. When my wife and I became disciples, we already had one child and had made many foolish financial decisions. Yet we managed to give between five and ten percent of our income away every year. When we both finally finished our degrees (we both have Ph.D.s) and began to escape from the debt we had accumulated, we began to increase our giving each year. We now live in a median-priced home in a quiet subdivision in Nashville, and we each have a car. We have made five trips to Europe over the past 15 years. This year we will give 20 percent of our after-tax income, and our goal is to get to 20 percent of our gross income. So, you see, it can be done.

Will disciplined generosity make a difference? The math is not hard to do. One estimate puts the increase from tithing in churches alone at $131 billion.[35] Each year!!! Think of what could be done with that money. Of the 2.5 billion of the world's poorest citizens, 200 million are Christians of one variety or another, and as such deserving of special attention (Gal 6:10). Whether money comes to them in the form of food, seeds, microloans, animals, or housing, they could enjoy a better standard of living until their national economies can produce enough wealth to sustain them.[36] The net result would be thanksgiving to God and a witness to the world that Christians see to it that there is no one needy in the family of God. What a witness that would be! Some of that $131 billion could be used to establish additional affordable day care and health care for the poor and the single parents in our churches and communities. Some might be used to bolster the endowments of our struggling Christian colleges and universities. Since it would be available each year, there is no end to the good which Christians could do in the world if we would recognize that how we spend our money, and more importantly, how we give our money are indicators of our commitment to God.

Obviously no one can tell *you* what to do. The circumstances of your birth, the way in which you grew up, your choice of occupations which may carry with it some expectations of how you will dress and where you will live, your own hobbies and interests, all of these will determine where you draw that base line. Right now, few of you as college students have any money to speak of. But I can assure you that one day most of you will make more than you ever dreamed of making, and, unless you are careful, you will wonder where it all went and goes. Before you know it, you may not be giving as you have been prospered, as the standard collection prayer goes. That's why you need to decide early that you will give your tithes and offerings to God and that, as an indication of faithfulness, you will practice the discipline of generosity to temper the demon of insatiability.[37]

One more idea recommends itself as a means of learning how to use money. Robert Wuthnow writes that, though money is one of the most frequent topics in the Bible, it is one of the least discussed topics at church, and I would add in our Christian schools. One unintended result, according to Fred Clark, is that we are more likely to produce careerists instead of disciples, teaching our students and parishioners how to assimilate to the culture rather than transform it.[38] But Wuthnow is quick to add that in those churches where substantial teaching about giving takes place, members give at 6 percent, three times the national average.[39] It is still not a tithe, but it is a giant step in that direction. Teaching has to be more than the "Budget Sunday" sermon. The list of books in the recommended readings following the essay would take about one year to get through carefully and thoughtfully. Moreover, this teaching needs to take place at all levels in the church from the youngest to the oldest. Right now, our *Christian* understanding of money is deeply informed by our *cultural* understanding of money. Only a sustained and persistent attempt to change our patterns of thinking is likely to work.

> Though money is one of the most frequent topics in the Bible, it is one of the least discussed topics at church.

Is wealth bad? No. And yes. Money is not inherently bad, but too few people have demonstrated that they can use money in a godly way. We cannot just say, "I don't love money," or "I am seeking first the kingdom of heaven." We have to live out faith in very practical ways each day. We do that by choosing to go to church regularly, by engaging in private quiet times of prayer and Bible study, by going on mission trips, by volunteering at charitable organizations in our communities. All of these are good things, and we should continue to do them, but we cannot avoid the strong teaching of the Bible on the subject of money. The way we use money is a test of our discipleship, a test of where we put our trust. Do we trust in Mammon or do we trust in God?

> The way we use money is a test of our discipleship, a test of where we put our trust.

Notes

[1]C.S. Lewis, *Perelandra, A Novel* (New York: Macmillan, 1944).

[2]Robert M. Royalty, Jr., *The Streets of Heaven: The Ideology of Wealth in the Apocalypse of John.* (Macon, GA: Mercer University Press, 1998).

[3]Adam Smith, *An Inquiry into the Nature and Causes of the Wealth of Nations,* 2 vol. (Indianapolis: Liberty Fund, 1981); Michael Novak, *The Spirit of Democratic Capitalism* (New York: Simon & Schuster, 1982); John Schneider, *The Good of Affluence: Seeking God in a Culture of Wealth* (Grand Rapids: Eerdmans, 2002).

[4]Ronald J. Sider, *Rich Christians in an Age of Hunger: Moving from Affluence to Generosity* (Dallas: Word, 1997) xiii.

[5]Ibid.

[6]Gerhard Kittel, ed., *Theological Dictionary of the New Testament* (Grand Rapids: Zondervan, 1967) 4:388.

[7]Jacques Ellul, *Money & Power* (Downers Grove, IL: InterVarsity, 1984) 62-69.

[8]Juliet B. Schor, *The Overspent American: Why We Want What We Don't Need* (New York: HarperPerennial, 1998) 11-12.

[9]John Schneider, *Godly Materialism: Rethinking Money & Possessions* (Downers Grove, IL: InterVarsity, 1994). Schneider coins this term to express the notion that rich Christians should not feel guilty because God has blessed them. Rather they should delight in his bounty.

[10]Sider, *Rich Christians,* 204-205. See also a news item in *Christian Century,* 118/4 (January 31, 2001) 8-9.

[11]The first two items come from Martin F. Camroux, "On Making Christianity Too Easy," *Expository Times* 111 (2000) 412.

[12]The remaining items in the list are cited in Craig L. Blomberg, *Neither Poverty nor Riches: A Biblical Theology of Material Possessions* (Grand Rapids: Eerdmans, 1999) 19.

[13]John Boli, "The Economic Absorption of the Sacred," in *Rethinking Materialism: Perspectives on the Spiritual Dimension of Economic Behavior,* ed. by Robert Wuthnow (Grand Rapids: Eerdmans, 1995) 106. See also, J. Philip Wagaman, *Economics and Ethics: A Christian Inquiry* (Philadelphia: Fortress Press, 1986).

[14]Boli, "Economic Absorption," 106.

[15]Evy McDonald cites a study which concluded that we spend about six hours a week on average shopping and only forty minutes talking with our children. "Spending Money as if Life Really Mattered," in *Simpler Living, Compassionate Life: A Christian Perspective,* ed. by Michael Schut (Denver: Living the Good News, 1999).

[16]Charles Handy, *The Hungry Spirit. Beyond Capitalism: The Quest for Purpose in the Modern World.* (New York: Broadway Books, 1998) 13-15.

[17]Nicholas Wolterstorff, "Has the Cloak Become a Cage? Charity, Justice and Economic Activity," in Wuthnow, *Rethinking Materialism,* 161. Other writers worth consulting here are Christopher Lasch, *The Culture of Narcissism: American Life in an Age of Diminishing Returns* (New York: Norton, 1978); Robert Wuthnow, "A Good Life and a Good Society: The Debate over Materialism," in *Rethinking Materialism,* 1-17. Robert Shorris, *A Nation of Salesmen: The Tyranny of the Market and the Subversion of Culture* (New York: W.W. Norton & Co., 1994).

[18]Augustine, *Confessions.* Also in connection with the idea of contentment, see Richard Foster, *Freedom of Simplicity* (San Francisco: Harper and Row, 1981).

[19]Handy, *The Hungry Spirit,* 3.

[20]Cited in E.F. Shumaker, *Small Is Beautiful: Economics as if People Mattered* (New York: HarperCollins, 1989).

[21]Wuthnow, "A Good Life," 1-11.

[22]Schor, *The Overspent American,* 13.

[23]Sider, *Rich Christians,* 21.

[24]Schor, *The Overspent American,* 27-42. See also Michael Jessup, "Truth: The First Casualty of Postmodern Consumerism," *Christian Scholar's Review* 30 (Spring 2001) 293. Jean Kilbourne, *Deadly Persuasion: Why Women and Girls Must Fight the Addictive Power of Advertising* (New York: Free Press, 1999).

[25]Miroslav Volf, "In the Cage of Vanities: Christian Faith and the Dynamics of Economic Progress," in *Rethinking Materialism,* 171-175.

[26]Interestingly, Christians understand *koinonia* first as the common life they have in God and Christ. Flowing from that common life, then, is the responsibility to care for one another. This would seem to follow the pattern I have laid out here, contentment in God

followed by the discipline of generosity. See Kittel, *TDNT*, 3:801-802; and also Colin Brown, ed., *The New International Dictionary of New Testament Theology* (Grand Rapids: Zondervan, 1967) 1:643.

[27]Blomberg reviews the arguments for and against total divestiture; *Neither Poverty nor Riches*, 161-164.

[28]Paul has to plead with them about their economic behavior in relationship to their practice of the love feast and the Lord's Supper, where the rich were coming early and eating all of the food, thus depriving their poor brothers and sisters of their share of the common meal (1 Cor 11:17-22). The Corinthians fail the test of money the first time, and that failure becomes another indication of their immaturity and divisiveness. Paul seems to want to ensure that they don't fail it a second time.

[29]Schneider does not want wealthy Christians to feel guilty about their wealth. But clearly Paul believes that when it is appropriate Christians should be reminded not of guilt feelings but of real guilt. If rich Christians are being generous, well and good. But if they are giving at the average rate of 2 percent while buying more expensive houses and cars, then perhaps they should be made to feel guilty.

[30]Two recent articles detail the economic pathways which evangelicals have taken over the past two decades and some of the attendant faith-related problems which have accompanied that choice: Michael S. Hamilton, "We're in the Money! How Did Evangelicals Get So Wealthy, and What Has It Done to Us?" *Christianity Today* 44 (June 12, 2000) 36-

43; and Martin Marty, "Will Success Spoil Evangelicalism?" *Christian Century* 117 (July 19-26, 2000) 757-761.

[31]Sider, *Rich Christians*, 193-196. For a variation on Sider's idea, see Robert W. McClelland, *Worldly Spirituality: Biblical Reflections on Money, Politics & Sex* (St. Louis: CBP Press, 1990) 24-34.

[32]www.infoplease.com/ipa/A0104688.html (as of Nov. 2003).

[33]Rodney Clapp, "Why the Devil Takes Visa," *Christianity Today* 40 (October 7, 1996) 30.

[34]Blomberg, *Neither Poverty nor Riches*, 247-249.

[35]*Christian Century* (January 21, 2001) 9.

[36]John Schneider, citing the work of Hernando de Soto, believes that there is sufficient wealth in second- and third-world countries to make them economically stable provided that property laws can be established and enforced; *The Good of Affluence*, 211-220.

[37]Almost all charitable organizations have overhead costs. As a general rule, you should not give to an organization which passes on less that 70 percent of your donation to its intended beneficiary. You can ask for an audited financial statement from an organization to which you would like to contribute or you can check sources like http://www.give.org/ (as of Nov. 2003) and http://www.guidestar.org/ (as of Nov. 2003).

[38]Fred Clark, "Christianizing Christian Education," February 1995, www.libertynet.org/esa/prism/education.html (as of Nov. 2003).

[39]Robert Wuthnow, *God and Mammon in America* (New York: The Free Press, 1994).

Bibliography

Blomberg, Craig L. *Neither Poverty nor Riches: A Biblical Theology of Material Possessions*. Grand Rapids: Eerdmans, 1999.

This is the most important book with which anyone interested in this subject should begin. Blomberg offers a thorough and nuanced treatment of the topic of wealth and its use in both testaments. His bibliography runs to thirty-eight pages, reflecting the depth of scholarship on the subject which you will find there.

More importantly, he is not concerned about the agendas of the evangelical left or right, though he understands both of them. Instead he is concerned about whether or not we understand how it is that money becomes a test of our faithfulness to God.

Gonzalez, Justo. *Faith and Wealth: A History of Early Christian Ideas on the Origin, Significance and Use of Money.* San Francisco: Harper and Row, 1990.

Next, I would suggest this book. Gonzalez also reviews the biblical literature on money, though with a less nuanced approach than Blomberg. The most important contribution which he makes is to document how the church in the second through the fourth centuries dealt with the issue of wealth and the wealthy, especially after Christianity had become the official religion of the Roman Empire. His analysis complements that of Blomberg quite well.

The remaining books can be read in any order. They are listed here in alphabetical order by author.

Clapp, Rodney, ed. *The Consuming Passion: Christianity & the Consumer Culture.* Downers Grove, IL: InterVarsity, 1998.

I have used essays from this book in my Media Criticism class to show students how the idea of conspicuous consumption has become so dominant in our culture. The book consists of eleven essays from differing practical and theological perspectives, and, as such, it offers a good introduction to modern consumer culture and its effects.

Schneider, John R. *The Good of Affluence: Seeking God in a Culture of Wealth.* Grand Rapids: Eerdmans, 2002.

A complete reworking of Schneider's earlier work, *Godly Materialism: Rethinking Money & Possessions*, it makes the case for democratic capitalism and for the accumulation of wealth among Christians on the premise that the economic realities which prevailed in the Old and New Testaments no longer prevail and thus are not normative for our current behavior. Like the two authors from whom he heavily borrows, Michael Novak and Dinesh D'Souza, Schneider believes that "capitalism is the greatest liberating power in human history" and that it will usher in a new age of faith beginning with the rich (2-4). It stands as a critique of the work of the other authors included in this list.

Schor, Juliet B. *The Overspent American: Why We Want What We Don't Need.* New York: HarperPerennial, 1998.

This follow-up to her previous book, also worth reading, *The Overworked American*, examines our patterns of consumption, how they are shaped and how they contribute to our present dissatisfaction with our lives. As is true with all economic statistics and forecasts, one can find other economists drawing slightly to dramatically different conclusions from the same economic data.

Sider, Ronald J. *Rich Christians in an Age of Hunger: Moving from Affluence to Generosity.* Dallas: Word Publishing. 1997.

When this book first appeared in 1977, it changed the way that evangelicals thought about hunger and also evoked considerable criticism. It also changed my own approach to money. Sider has revised some of his ideas in the anniversary edition here cited, but his essential analysis remains the same. As long as there is oppressive poverty in the world, Christians have an obligation to become more generous givers.

_____. *Just Generosity: A New Vision for Overcoming Poverty in America.* Grand Rapids: Baker, 1999.

A companion volume to the previous book, this book offers more concrete ways in which Christians can become involved in changing communities locally and globally.

THE EARTH IS THE LORD'S
THE CHRISTIAN AND THE ENVIRONMENT
George F. Pickens

Long ago the Psalmist observed, "The heavens declare the glory of God, the skies proclaim the work of his hands" (Ps 19:1). Yet, as I looked out the window of my high-rise hotel room in Beijing, the glory of God reflected in the skies was almost impossible to recognize. Even at that early morning hour the smog was so thick that it clouded my view of the sky and the streets below. Rather than the glory of God's handiwork, what was most obvious was the pollution produced by humans and their machines. While it remains true that God's glory can be seen in creation, in the modern world the relationship between the environment and its Divine Creator is becoming increasingly more difficult to detect. Given the environmental degradation that plagues our planet, it can be argued that today the heavens declare more the irresponsibility of humans than the grandeur of God.

> Given the environmental degradation that plagues our planet, it can be argued that today the heavens declare more the irresponsibility of humans than the grandeur of God.

Because environmental problems are now becoming so globally common and obvious, awareness and concern have been mounting. The state of the environment that was considered a crisis as early as the 1960s[1] is today considered by many to be the most pressing single issue facing humanity.[2] Environmental degradation impacts every other global problem: it causes disease, creates shortages, sparks wars, kills and maims, eradicates entire species, and it even increases the cost of living for the average affluent person normally isolated from other environmental problems.

Need of Creation Care

Social Integrity

Integrity of Nature

...nship between global prob-
... red to as the "Tragedy of the
... way in which the world holds
... ecifically, the world's oceans,
... d the atmosphere are shared
... atures, and when any part of
this global ecosystem is damaged, ... s at the expense of the entire globe and its inhabitants. Degradation of the global environment is tragic because of its pervasive impact; however, it has also been tragic because of the late arrival of awareness and responsible action.

Nations have only recently begun to address the global environmental crisis. While many European and a few Asian countries began to respond more responsibly to the environment earlier, the United States began to give broad governmental attention to the environment only during the 1970s. Indeed the 1970s have been referred to as the "Decade of the Environment," and it was in 1970 that President Richard Nixon signed into law the National Environmental Policy Act (NEPA) and the Environmental Quality Act (EQA). That year also witnessed the creation of the Environmental Protection Agency (EPA), and the first "Earth Day" was celebrated on April 22, 1970.[4]

Unfortunately the following decade brought environmental reversals in the United States. During the 1980s concern for the economy took precedence over sensitivity to the environment, and the decade ended with "a grim reminder of the price of environmental carelessness." On March 24, 1989, the Exxon tanker *Valdez* ran aground on the Bligh Reef in Alaska. The consequent oil spill brought unprecedented environmental damage, as "ecosystems whose integrity had been as uncompromised as any in the world had been radically and unpredictably altered."[5] This disaster alarmed even the most reluctant environmentalists, and ecological issues were again brought to the fore of national attention. While Earth Day had not been officially recognized in the U.S. since the first in 1970, it was again celebrated on April 22, 1990. The 1990s witnessed an environmental movement that grew in both size and influence. From Washington to the fifty state capitols the environment has now become an issue given at least lip service by every serious politician. "Green" organizations and organizations involved in environmental issues have become more common and vocal, and even though much more responsible action must be taken, environmental concerns are now being raised in the public mind.[6]

The environment has also received the attention of international organizations,[7] and it has been the focus of at least four international conferences sponsored by the United Nations. The first world conference on the environment was held in Stockholm, Sweden, in 1972. While little was accomplished at this conference in the way of international resolutions on the environment, primary issues and positions were shared and frameworks for communication were established. The second world conference on the environment was held ten years later, in 1982, in Nairobi, Kenya. This conference witnessed greater international partnership and dedication to global environmental concerns. A third world conference on the environment met in Rio de Janeiro, Brazil, in 1992. The largest number of world leaders in history attended this conference, and two treaties with global environmental impact were signed.[8] In September 2002 the United Nations sponsored the World Summit on Sustainable Development in Johannesburg, South Africa. One focus of this conference was the relationship between sustainable economic growth and the environment. Through these gatherings the nations of the world are demonstrating with varying degrees of resolve their intention to act in environmentally responsible ways.[9]

Unfortunately, while the world has slowly awakened to the environmental crisis, many Christians have neglected the issue, and the world has noticed. Indeed, a generation ago it was observed, "most Christians simply do not care about the beauty of nature, or nature as such."[10] Going even further, rather than having anything constructive to offer, it has been argued that Christianity is responsible for the modern environmental crisis. In an influential 1967 article entitled "The Historical Roots of our Ecological Crisis,"[11] Lynn White argued that Christianity gave rise to at least two intellectual developments that have led to the "rape of the world." Modern science, a product of Christianity's natural theology, and modern technology, a result of the Christian view that humans are to exert mastery over nature, have together produced the modern environmental crisis.[12] According to White, environmental destruction "cannot be understood

> *While the world has slowly awakened to the environmental crisis, many Christians have neglected the issue, and the world has noticed.*

historically apart from distinctive attitudes toward nature which are deeply grounded in Christian dogma."[13] More recently, *Time* magazine echoed this view that Christianity was at least partly to blame for the global environmental crisis.[14]

These critiques of Christianity's environmental record have given rise to a recent Christian discussion about creation care.[15] While serious, modern evangelical Christian reflection on the environment can be traced at least to 1970,[16] the most recent discussion began as a reaction to the 1985 publication of *God in Creation* by the German theologian, Jürgen Moltmann.[17] Scores of books and articles representing various Christian views of creation care were subsequently published.[18] Then, after almost a decade of critical thinking and discussions, the first "Evangelical Declaration on the Care of Creation" appeared in 1994.[19] These publications represent the increased attention being given to this central yet long neglected area of Christian theology and ethics.

Even so, a disturbing 1980 survey conducted by the U.S. Fish and Wildlife Service revealed that those with the highest rate of church attendance "had the lowest knowledge of environmental concerns." The survey also found that "those who attended church services most regularly had the most dominionistic and utilitarian attitudes toward the creation around them."[20] Indications are that little has changed, so clearly much more needs to be accomplished, especially in encouraging deeper biblical reflection on the environment and in formulating Christian ethical behavior in relationship to creation.

It is the purpose of this chapter to facilitate such reflection and action. Environmental concern and action are central to the Christian faith, and consequently it is a crucial ethical issue for all Christians. Creation care represents the will of God for all humans, and Christians—of all people— must be concerned with choices and lifestyles that honor God's intentions in all areas of life, including environmental issues. Thus, respectfully caring for God's creation is part of what it means to be a Christian, and the ethical life for the Christian must be characterized by an approach to the environment that includes at least three elements: sensitivity to the global environmental condition; dynamic appropriation of the Christian sources for environ-

> *Respectfully caring for God's creation is part of what it means to be a Christian.*

mental ethics; and, concrete actions in daily life which demonstrate Christian ethical behavior towards creation.

In order to provide an overview of these basic elements of Christian environmental ethics, in the sections that follow a more specific review of the environmental crisis will be presented. Then, with a sense of urgency provided by this modern global context of environmental decay and disaster, the fundamental Christian sources available for approaching environmental issues will be summarized. Finally, specific suggestions for guiding Christian ethical responses in creation care will be offered.

The Need for Creation Care

The growing attention of national and world governments summarized above attest to the obvious need for responsible environmental policies. The recent awakening of interest in creation care by Christians is also partly due to blatant environmental decay and destruction. It is virtually impossible to ignore any longer the myriad environmental problems that impact daily life as unwelcome yet stark reminders of hazards that will only worsen with neglect.

Many Christians are not shocked by the corruption of creation witnessed in our day. For example, Scripture speaks of an ecocrisis, in part, when it portrays creation "groaning" under the weight of sin's consequences (Rom 8:22). And, in a passage from John's vision that foresees environmental destruction, a frightful message of judgment is pronounced upon those who have destroyed the earth (Rev 11:18). Yet simply not being surprised by the current crisis in creation is not necessarily helpful; hearing a warning and heeding it are two very different responses. Becoming informed about the nature and causes of current environmental degradation is the basis for responsible and obedient action.

> *Becoming informed about the nature and causes of current environmental degradation is the basis for responsible and obedient action.*

Yet some still refuse to acknowledge that creation is seriously threatened. In part this denial is a result of the gargantuan nature and global dimensions of the problems. The lethal pollution that exists in the city or on the other side of the planet is often either unknown or its seriousness is unappreciated by those living outside these immediate areas. The destruction of the rain forests in the tropics appears as only a minor footnote to news considered more relevant to daily life in temperate climes. But perhaps the most significant obstacle to the recognition of the current environmental crisis is

> . . . its insidious nature. It is subtle and gradual, like a cancerous cell, involving the seemingly innocuous activities of everybody on earth. It creeps upon us daily so that we become used to environmental decay and ecological diminishment, so much so that many people even deny that it is occurring. Like true addicts, we find every available avenue to deny what a few others ([environmentalists and] primal peoples, for example) can clearly see. . . .[21]

In spite of these obstacles to acknowledging the current crisis in creation, it is clear to those who are most informed that "life on earth is diminishing both in quantity and quality."[22]

A better understanding of the scope and nature of the current environmental crisis, ironically, resulted from the two most environmentally destructive chapters in human history: the two world wars of the twentieth century. The massive demand for materials that was a part of both wars underscored and intensified the unequal distribution and fragile limits of the world's resources. Shortages that were part of the war experiences for many of the world's peoples initiated a competition for scarce resources that continued after the wars were over. Consequently, frustration, safeguarding, hoarding, fear, panic, and subsequent wars on a global scale have resulted as peoples have sought to control ever-diminishing supplies of the world's resources. Within this historical context, three characteristics of the global environment become apparent.

Natural Resources Are Limited and Dwindling

First, the world's natural resources are limited and dwindling. While certain resources are renewable (for example, solar, water, and wind energy, and to a certain extent, wood supplies), the energy sources that are in greatest demand are nonrenewable. Fossil fuels (oil, natural gas, coal), which provide the bulk of the energy used in motor vehicles and to produce electricity, are found in limited supplies. During the 1990s the global oil reserves were estimated to allow production at 1989 levels for forty additional years. Proven world natural gas reserves will permit production at 1987 levels for approximately fifty-five years. World coal reserves, while much more abundant than either oil or gas, are also limited. Accurate estimates for the quantity of existing global supplies of coal are difficult to obtain, yet even coal-wealthy nations like the U.S. recognize environmental hazards from overreliance upon coal (pollution, land degradation, etc.), thus limiting its widespread use.[23] These indicators from the world's energy supplies also apply to other resources. For example, water is increasingly a contested global resource that is dwindling. According to the United Nations and the World Bank, about forty percent of the world's population in some eighty countries face severe water shortages. In the Middle East and North Africa, for example, if present demands for water continue, there will be an eighty percent decrease in per capita water supply by 2025. It is predicted that many of the wars waged in the twenty-first century will be over water.[24]

These examples highlight a core characteristic of the current environmental crisis and "an elementary lesson of ecology . . . that we live on a finite, essentially self-contained planet. There are no infinite bounties or inexhaustible resources."[25] This limited and dwindling supply of the world's resources highlights the need for creation care.

The Earth's Ability to Support Life Is Limited

A second characteristic of the global environment is the earth's exhaustible ability to support life, human or otherwise. "Carrying capacity," a term borrowed from biology, is used to guide research into the limits of the earth's life-support system. Carrying capacity is "the number of individuals of a certain species that can be sustained indefinitely in a particular area."[26] When it is used to focus on environmental issues, carrying capacity is the estimated ability of the earth to sustain life. While many factors about the earth's carrying capacity are unknown and debatable, it is agreed that the earth's carrying capacity is exhaustible. In trying to determine the exact limits of the earth's life-support system, answers to certain questions are sought. For example, how many people can the earth support? What is the quality of life under review? What are the values, living standards and habits, and expectations of the population? Additionally, carrying capacity is related to nonhuman life. What, then, are the limits of the world's animals and plants to adapt to a given human population? How many nonhuman species can become extinct without seriously altering the earth's carrying capacity?

It is difficult, if not impossible, to definitively answer these questions, but certain observations about the earth's limited carrying capacity can be made:[27]

1. It is possible to increase the carrying capacity of the earth, at least in some places, at some times, under certain circumstances. An example would be the abilities of human ingenuity during the Agricultural and Industrial Revolutions to provide more efficient use of certain resources, thus increasing global food supplies.

2. It is known that when the carrying capacity of the earth is exceeded, disaster results. Wars, famines, droughts, and pestilence result, in part, from a population living above the ability of the earth to support human life.

3. Consequently, when carrying capacity is surpassed, population declines, and often there is a subsequent decrease in the earth's carrying capacity itself. Excessive population leads to disastrous conditions (famine, wars, etc.), which often result in environmental destruction. An example would be the long-standing conflicts in parts of the Middle East and Africa that have precipitated ecological disasters.

It is the informed belief of many environmentalists that the earth's carrying capacity has already been reached and even exceeded in places. The "Evangelical Declaration on the Care of Creation" reflects this conviction, stating, "Many of these [environmental] degradations are signs that we are pressing against the finite limits God has set for creation. With continued population growth, these degradations will become more severe."[28]

> It is the informed belief of many environmentalists that the earth's carrying capacity has already been reached and even exceeded in places.

A major factor in arriving at this position is the global inequities in standard of living. Even if it is true, as some argue, that the earth currently has the carrying capacity for several more billion human beings, "it cannot, however, support even its current human population living as its richest tenth do now."[29] All creatures share the earth's finite life-support system, and if some draw from it in excess, others will experience shortages. The human suffering that results from this imbalance in the world's use of resources should be a Christian concern, and it thus amplifies the call for creation care.

The Earth's Ability to Absorb Waste Is Limited

A third observation about the global environmental condition places further limits on the two previously discussed. While it can be optimistically argued that human ingenuity expressed in future technological advancements will discover and harness sufficient resources and increase the earth's carrying capacity, the problems of waste management remain. Even if sufficient resources become accessible to support human life well into the future, what is to be done with the by-products of human consumption? "The waste products of human society are overwhelming the earth's ability to absorb them."[30] Environmental degradation on a global scale related to the disposal of waste materials are beginning to create serious problems. Irresponsible waste disposal produces water, air, and land pollution, and the disposal of toxic wastes is especially problematic, in part due to the horrendous amounts being produced annually. In the early 1990s the EPA estimated that industry in the U.S. produced nearly 1 trillion tons of new toxic wastes each year.[31] Nontoxic solid wastes are also growing at alarming rates. "Between 1970 and 1988 the annual amount of solid wastes generated in the United States grew by about 25 percent, until it reached about 1,500 pounds per person."[32] These wastes cause disease and have the potential to kill masses of people.[33] The threats posed by these ever-increasing amounts of waste highlight another mandate for creation care.

The need for creation care can also be realized by reviewing the specific types of environmental degradation that are occurring in the modern world. Lists of global environmental problems differ according to perspective and degree of specificity. One group of Christian environmental scientists group ecological problems into three broad categories:[34] (1) the threats to the earth's life support system from global warming and ozone depletion; (2) the threats from species extinction through the loss of natural habitat and the subsequent extermination of the plants, animals, and humans native to them (massive deforestation and loss of natural wetlands and tundra are examples of this threat); (3) threats from human pollution and overconsumption (problems in this category include water and land pollution, and issues related to waste creation and disposal).

Other descriptions group the dimensions of the modern environmental crisis into more specific categories. For example, one list describes the current environmental crisis as having eight dimensions: pollution, global warming, ozone depletion, overpopulation, resource exhaustion, maldistribution of global resources, reductions and extinctions of global species, and threats posed by genetic engineering.[35] The "Evangelical Declaration on the Care of Creation" acknowledges "seven degradations of creation": land degradation, deforestation, species extinction, water degradation, global toxification, the alteration of the atmosphere, and human and cultural degradation.[36]

While it is beyond the scope of this article to provide a discussion of each of these environmental degradations, it is hoped that sufficient evidence has been presented to acknowledge that a global environmental crisis exists and that this crisis poses serious threats to all creation. These threats represent an urgent call for attention and action. The remainder of this chapter will chart the parameters for Christian environmental action, first through highlighting the primary Christian sources available for creation care, and then through suggesting specific types of ethical responses to the environmental crisis.

Christian Environmental Reflection and Action

An encouraging dimension of the current debate over the environmental crisis is the growing number of environmentalists—even those who themselves are not religious—who recognize the inability of science and public policy alone to provide long-term solutions. It is widely recognized that lasting resolutions to the environmental crisis must include contributions from religion. For example, Lynn White, the environmentalist who alleged Christianity's complicity in environmental degradation, recognized the need for a religious remedy. "Since the roots of our trouble are so largely religious, the remedy must also be essentially religious. . . ."[37] Growing recognition is emerging that current environmental problems represent not just a challenge for science and government, but also for the religious community. The problems and the solutions are not merely physical and material, they are also spiritual in nature. "What we call the environmental crisis is not merely a crisis in the natural environment of human beings. It is nothing less than a crisis in human beings themselves."[38]

> The problems and the solutions are not merely physical and material, they are also spiritual in nature.

This perspective not only resonates with the Christian belief that inner, spiritual issues are at the center of all humanity's problems, but it also provides exciting opportunities for Christian witness through creation care. In spite of the criticisms leveled against Christianity's alleged lack of environmental concern, Christians have a wealth of resources that mandate, inform, and guide responsible environmental action. As the world looks to the Church for participation and even leadership in creation care, Christians have a rich tradition to guide their belief and action.

Below, a summary of the primary Christian sources available for thinking biblically about environmental issues will be offered. The teachings of Scripture will be at the core of our discussion, which will highlight dominant themes central to biblical thinking about the environment. First, however, in order to encourage and inform our own serious biblical reflection on the environment, a reminder of the importance given to understanding the relationships between humans, God, and nature in Christian history will be offered.

Historical Christian Reflection on Nature

Recent Christian thinking about the environment has been plagued with certain misconceptions that persist, often dominating and obscuring the issue. One popular misunderstanding is that Christian concern for the environment is recent, lacking the depth and grounding of historical Christian precedence. The misconception is that, historically, Christians haven't considered nature worthy of serious theological reflection. This misunderstanding views modern Christian attention to the environment as a compliant reaction to a recent liberal, or New Age agenda. Further, it is argued that the Church's recent concern for environmental issues reflects a distraction from historic orthodoxy. The position is that concern for creation represents a minor, even absent, issue in historical Christian theology and ethics. Chris Sugden describes but doesn't share this view:

> It is hard for evangelicals to take the environment seriously as a mission concern. Evangelicals are "gospel people," and the gospel is focused on the salvation of people from sin. Ideas that the trees and the land and the rivers, let alone the foxes and the butterflies are worth the time, attention, and resources of the Christian constituency have struggled to find acceptance in evangelical churches.[39]

However, the truth is that historically Christian theologians have given a great deal of attention to nature. "In traditional Christian thought . . . the rudiments for a rich theology of nature are not lacking. Indeed . . . the tradition is dramatically suggestive, for those who have eyes to see."[40] While the writings of the early Church Fathers were influenced by a Platonic view of nature (the spiritual is superior to the physical), and were essentially reacting to widespread pantheism and Gnosticism, still nature was considered a necessary, fundamental subject for Christian attention. Even Origen, who was especially influenced by a Platonic view of nature, did not view nature as an evil to be ignored, neglected, or abused, and accordingly he gave significant attention to the relationship between humans, God, and nature. Origen and Irenaeus each developed a theology of nature to refute Gnostic teachings that God was removed from nature, maintaining God's presence in and revelation through the natural world. Irenaeus "saw nature as he perceived the Scriptures to see it, as humanity's God-given home—blessed, embraced, and cared for by the very God who took flesh in order to redeem a fallen humanity and thereby also to initiate a final renewal of the whole creation."[41] Later Christian writers like Augustine, Aquinas, Bonaventura, Francis of Assisi, Luther, Calvin, and Wesley all recognized nature as worthy of attention and a theology of nature as central to Christian theology. Each reflects this recognition in their writings, and these sources represent a rich heritage from which current theologizing about the environment can draw.

Concern for nature is thus not recent to the Christian story. The relationship between humans, God, and creation has been a topic of reflection throughout Christian history, as influential theologians across time have made important contributions to the Christian view of nature and humanity's role in creation care.[42] The Bible was the source from which these theologians have drawn their conclusions, and it is now necessary to turn attention to the scriptural resources available for Christian environmental reflection and action.

The Bible and the Environment

The Bible is the primary source for Christian environmental reflection and action, and "people who ground their faith in the Bible will, if they are consistent, be passionate environmentalists."[43] It is significant that the biblical record begins with nature, and throughout Scripture the natural environment mediates God's revelation and human responses as God works within and through the natural world. Indeed, nature is more than the mere backdrop or setting for the Bible's salvation story; rather, it is an integral component of God's unfolding plan for salvation that extends to all creation. God's purposes then, as revealed in Scripture, not only have a vertical (human to God/theological) dimension, but also accompanying and interdependent horizontal (human to human/social and human to nature/ecological) dimensions.

While certain biblical passages provide direct and explicit references to the environment, several fundamental Christian doctrines that are developed throughout Scripture also have significant implications for Christian environmental reflection and action. While it is impossible to either list or discuss at length all the Christian doctrines with implications for creation care here, six foundational Christian doctrines that have direct, scriptural, and practical implications for creation care will be highlighted.[44]

Creation. A beginning and primary doctrine of the Bible is that God is the Creator of everything, and that he continues to be active in monitoring and sustaining his entire creation. God is revealed first as benevolent Creator and Sustainer of the rest of nature before He is revealed as the Creator and Sustainer of humanity. Indeed, humans appear later in the creation story, within the broader context of God's concern for all creation. "Humankind is created from the dust of the earth, emphasizing that people are directly related to the environment, and in spite of their perceived status, are themselves an intrinsic part of nature."[45]

> God is revealed first as benevolent Creator and Sustainer of the rest of nature before He is revealed as the Creator and Sustainer of humanity.

From the biblical doctrine of creation three affirmations can be made which have direct implications for creation care:

1. *The earth is not god.* The creation narrative (Genesis 1–3) makes it clear that God is the Creator, and that everything else that exists has been created and is thus subservient to him. While God is present in his creation, and indeed is even revealed in and through his creation (e.g., Ps 19:1), nevertheless, creation remains just that—that which has been created. While an inti-

mate relationship exists between all creation and its Creator, the creation is not the same as the Creator. Indeed, it is this distinction, in part, which is to be commemorated through the biblical prohibition against idolatry. No image should ever be worshiped because no part of creation should ever be confused with the Creator.

This sharp biblical distinction between creation and Creator challenges the views of pantheism, animism, and their modern heir, the New Age Movement. These view nature or parts of nature as divine, and it is this fear of seeming to worship nature rather than its Creator that causes many Christians to suspect and even avoid environmental issues. "The environmental movement has . . . sometimes been clubbed together with the 'New Age' and other heretical concerns as traps to ensnare people from coming to believe in the truth. . . ."[46] Yet, such an overreaction must not keep us from honoring creation's other affirmations.

> It is the fear of seeming to worship nature rather than its Creator that causes many Christians to suspect and even avoid environmental issues.

2. *The earth is the LORD's.* While the earth is not to be worshiped, the Bible makes it clear that the earth belongs to its Creator. "The earth is the LORD's, and everything in it, the world and all who live in it," declares the Psalmist (24:1). This means that creation should not be approached in a cavalier way, as if it were the property of humanity. Creation is not to be ignored, ravaged, misused, or taken for granted. All creation belongs to God, and any approach to it must include reverence, recognizing its ultimate ownership by God. Creation is not ours.

It belongs to God, and we are to exercise our dominion over these things not as though entitled to exploit them, but as things borrowed or held in trust, which we are to use realizing that they are not ours intrinsically. Man's dominion is under God's dominion and under God's domain.[47]

> Creation is not ours.

3. *Humans are creatures and caretakers of creation.* God created humans, and thus they share a common origin with the rest of creation. Recognizing this shared beginning, St. Chrysostom

wrote of the animals, "Surely we ought to show them great kindness and gentleness for many reasons, but, above all, because they are the same origin as ourselves."[48]

The order of creation is also extremely significant in this regard. Humans are created last, and a common explanation is that humans were so prominent in God's plan that he went to great lengths to prepare for their creation. However, a more consistent interpretation of the creation narrative provides another view. Humans are created last because all that came before was so loved and delicate that it required a caretaker. Thus, humans enter the creation story, in part, to fulfill the role of extending God's care for the rest of creation.

So, humans are introduced in Scripture as creatures, created with a purpose of caring for the rest of creation (Gen 1:26-31; 2:15). Humans were created to "work and take care of" the garden (Gen 2:15), and the word for "work" used here means "to serve," and its related nouns actually mean "slave" or "servant." The word translated "take care of" "suggests watchful care and preservation of the earth." It is the word used repeatedly to describe the way God watches over his people in Psalm 121.[49] Thus, when humans responsibly care for creation, they are not only fulfilling one of the central reasons for their own creation, but they are also demonstrating their love and obedience for their Creator, the central purpose for their existence. "God intends our work [in creation] to be an expression of our worship, and our care of the creation to reflect our love for the Creator."[50]

Creation care is also a reflection of the divine image that is borne by humans. According to the creation narrative, unlike the rest of God's creatures, humans were created in the image or likeness of God (Gen 1:26,27). This designation is not only descriptive of humanity's identity, but also of the nature of human responsibility to the rest of creation. Surely, the divine image in humanity refers to the spiritual, aesthetic, and rational capacities that distinguish humans from the rest of creation; these are the implications of the divine image that are most often recognized. Even so, the divine image also dictates the ways humans are to relate to the rest of God's creation. In short, men and women are to relate to creation in ways that mirror or imitate God. This human role and responsibility to the rest of creation mandated by the image of God includes at least three activities:[51]

1. Like God, humans are to be keepers of creation, assisting in God's work of sustaining creation. Thus, conservation and

proper treatment of animals are activities that reflect the image of God.

2. Like God, humans are to recognize the balance that is a part of creation, and respect, honor, and perpetuate it. In the beginning God ordained the Sabbath to protect the limits of all creation, and he directed humans to honor this creation-renewing practice.[52] When the limits of creation are respected, for example through responsible farming practices and balanced and regulated consumption of the earth's resources, the image of God is being reflected.

3. Like God, humans are to facilitate the fecundity of the earth. Creation was designed with the ability to renew and replenish itself (within limits), and God pronounced these abilities good. His initial charge to humans included the direction to "be fruitful" (Gen 1:28), and this commission has implications for enjoying, respecting, and protecting the earth's fecundity. Human fruitfulness depends upon the fecundity of the rest of creation. Rather than eradicating species and degrading the earth to the point that it cannot renew or replenish itself, humans are to reflect the image of God through honoring the natural productivity of the earth.

Thus, the image of God "is not a special status as the sole bearer of intrinsic value or a special sanction to destroy with impunity, but rather a special role or function—a vocation, calling, task, commission, or assignment."[53] When humans accurately live out the image of God that is upon them, they will be involved in creation care.

> When humans accurately live out the image of God that is upon them, they will be involved in creation care.

Another implication for the environment that is included in the biblical doctrine of creation is found in the specific charge given to humans. At their creation, humans were told to "rule over" or "have dominion over" creation (Gen 1:28), and in modern times some Christians have interpreted this directive as permission to exploit creation at will, without limits. However, premodern Jews and Christians saw this commission as a dominion of benevolence rather than a dominion of exploitation. Taken within the

> Dominion cannot mean selfish and unrestrained exploitation.

broader context of the entire creation narrative and interpreted within the parameters for creation care discussed above, dominion cannot mean selfish and unrestrained exploitation. Dominion means "just governance," and "humans practice dominion properly when they care for God's creation benevolently and justly in accord with the will of the ultimate Owner."[54]

Covenant. The Bible reveals God as a covenant-making God, and each of the major covenants God enters into in Scripture includes an integral element related to nature.[55] As noted above, God's covenant with Adam in creation included a provision for the care of all creation, as well as a demonstration of obedience that reflected a proper relationship to nature (eating certain foods and not eating another). Thus, the Adamic covenant was forged on the proper relationship between God, humans, and nature.

The covenant with Noah emerges from a corrupted then reformed relationship between God, humans, and nature, yet the environmental destruction of the flood is not the only implication for creation. God's concern was for the salvation of animals—illustrated by their presence in the ark—as well as humans, and after the flood, the terms of the covenant included revised relationships with the land, plants, and animals. The covenant was even signified and sealed through a phenomenon in nature (see Genesis 6–9, esp. 9:1–17). Central to the Abrahamic covenant was the promise of land (Gen 12:7; 15:7), and the interplay between God, humans, and nature (the land) is the focus of the remainder of the Old Testament.

In the Mosaic covenant God commemorated human dependency upon nature. It was only through the provisions of nature, namely animals and crops and the natural environment that supports them, that the sacrificial system could be maintained. Thus, human obedience and righteousness was conditioned by proper relationships with nature. The Mosaic covenant also included expanded human responsibilities to the environment. Much of the levitical code is conditioned by responsibility to all nature. With their obvious vertical and horizontal implications and purposes, the principles of Sabbath and Jubilee are central to the understanding of human identity and responsibility to God and the rest of creation. "The sabbath is the true hallmark of every biblical doctrine of creation."[58]

Thus the Bible teaches a concept of sabbath much broader than most people today would make it. We are called to keep the sabbath [principle] not only personally but also for the land and for its other inhabitants. Our motive is to demonstrate love and obedience to God, the Creator and owner of all, and so to affirm our lasting linkage with him and with his creation.[59]

While the new covenant in Jesus Christ exceeds the land boundaries of the Old Testament, nevertheless it includes both present and future implications that directly relate to all creation. "The witness of the New Testament is, therefore, twofold: it transcends the land, Jerusalem, the Temple. Yes, but its history and theology demand a concern with these realities also."[60] The inaugural event of the new covenant also has direct environmental implications.

Incarnation. The means God used to introduce the new covenant is the incarnation, and this doctrine also has direct implications for creation care. When he became flesh through natural means (human birth), God entered into solidarity with the physical and material world, highlighting his intimate presence and activity in and through the natural world. The means God used to mediate the new covenant, the incarnation, reflects God's continuing preference to work in and through nature to reveal his will and accomplish his purposes.

> "The incarnation confers dignity not only on humankind, but on everything and everyone . . . with which humankind is united in interdependence."

"The incarnation confers dignity not only on humankind, but on everything and everyone . . . with which humankind is united in interdependence." John of Damascus long ago realized this fundamental relationship God was perpetuating between himself, humanity, and the rest of nature in the incarnation, when he observed, "through it [the natural world] my salvation has come to me."[61]

The Presence of God's Spirit in the World. Scripture declares the presence and activity of God's Spirit in and through nature (e.g., Isa 6:3; Ps 19:1). Paul said that God reveals himself through nature's seasons (Acts 14:17), and later in Athens he said that God created the natural world, in part, so that humans might desire him (Acts 17:26,27). To the Romans, Paul wrote that God could be understood through the things that he has made (Rom 1:19,20). The entire material world is "an effective medium of revelation and a vehicle of communion with God. . . ."[62] Therefore, the revelation of God through nature—natural or general revelation—is a foundational doctrine of the Christian faith.[63] Within this context, creation care can be understood as a way to engage in God's ongoing self-revelation through the natural world.

> Creation care can be understood as a way to engage in God's ongoing self-revelation through the natural world.

The Effects of Sin on All Creation. Scripture highlights the relationship between God, humans, and nature in Genesis 3 in a narrative about the consequences of sin. After the humans sinned and judgment was pronounced, it had consequences for all creation, not just for humans.

> If man obeyed God, he would be the means of blessing to the earth; but in his insatiable greed, in his scorn for the balances built into the created order and in his shortsighted selfishness he pollutes and destroys it. He turns a garden into a desert (cf. Rev. 11:18). That is the main thrust of the curse in Genesis 3.[64]

Paul's understanding of the consequences of sin also includes nature. He asserts that the effects of sin extend to all creation, and he contends that, not only humanity has been corrupted by disobedience, but also all creation is groaning under the weight of sin (Rom 8:22). Sin has thus had a pervasive negative impact upon the environment. Through sin, humans have failed to relate to nature in God-ordained ways, either through benign or malicious neglect, or through willful destructive exploitation. Environmental degradation, therefore, is a visible reminder of the fallen nature of humanity, and indeed, of all creation.

Cosmic Redemption. Sin's consequences for all creation, however, are not the last word of Scripture. Just as salvation means restored relationships with God and others, so it should also mean a corrected relationship with all creation. John Howard Yoder has discussed the environmental implications of Jesus' ministry and message within the context of the proclamation of the year of jubilee. According to Yoder, current practices and understandings of Jesus' day would have meant that a strong environmental message would have been understood when Jesus applied Isaiah's prophecy to himself (Luke 4:16-21).[65] As a devout Jew in first century Palestine, Jesus' lifestyle would have also demonstrated creation care.[66]

According to Paul, salvation will ultimately extend to all creation. In his words creation "will be liberated from its bondage to decay and brought into the glorious freedom of the children of God" (Rom 8:21). The vision of the end times given through John also portrays a restoration of the created order, including a new heaven and a new earth (Rev 21:1). God's original plan in creation included a world in harmony with itself and with him, and his will is for nothing less than a restoration of this plan. Thus, the introduction and restoration of proper relationships between God, humanity, and nature are themes woven and developed consistently throughout Scripture.

> God's original plan in creation included a world in harmony with itself and with him, and his will is for nothing less than a restoration of this plan.

Christian Environmental Action

Another foundational doctrine with direct implications for environmental stewardship is the biblical understanding of the Church as an alternative community, called to serve as God's agent and imagination in the world, demonstrating the way of Jesus Christ.[67] From this doctrine emerge several practical implications for creation care, and this chapter concludes with a list of suggestions for Christian environmental action for individuals and congregations.

The Environment and the Individual Christian. The beginning point for responsible environmental action is for the individual Christian to acknowledge that creation care is a Christian responsibility. Like other duties—loving our neighbor, forgiving our enemies, etc.—caring for the environment is not an option; it is part of our committed discipleship. Included in this acknowledgment is the Christian responsibility to become informed about the global environmental condition, and then to become agents for the environmental education of others. Christians' consciences should be sensitive to environmental issues because of our faith, and Christians should also become the environmental conscience for society. Indeed, the current environmental crisis provides countless opportunities for Christian witness.

> Christians' consciences should be sensitive to environmental issues because of our faith, and Christians should also become the environmental conscience for society.

After accepting the Christian responsibility for creation care, a two-dimensional strategy for creation care should be practiced in daily life. This strategy is summed up in the phrase coined by Rene Dubos, "Think global-

> "Think globally, act locally."

ly, act locally."[68] While daily decisions and actions impact most directly our local communities, Christians must become more aware of the global implications of their lifestyle choices. Concern for the environment and our fellow creatures must produce limits on our consumption of the world resources. For example, while gasoline may be very affordable and plentiful at this time in one local community, this must not be allowed to cloud the global condition that is radical-

> While affluent Christians may have the ability to afford everything "bigger and better," concern for global neighbors must guide our consumption of the world's resources.

ly different. While affluent Christians may have the ability to afford everything "bigger and better," concern for global neighbors must guide our consumption of the world's resources. Lifestyle questions of affordability must be expanded to include the environment, for the costs of our consumption have implications that go beyond our bank balances. Questions about the environmental cost of our decisions must also be asked. Our practice of Christian stewardship must extend to all areas of our life so that our choices and habits begin to reflect love for God and our neighbors.

Conservation of the world's resources must also become a priority in our lives. A major Harvard University study concluded that "conservation, rather than coal or nuclear energy, is the major alternative to imported oil" in the U.S. However, to many, the term "conservation means deprivation, a doing without something; but the Harvard study . . . has shown that much . . . conservation can take place without causing any real hard-

ship."[69] In fact, conservation can actually improve quality of life for the individual as well as for the environment. Walking instead of driving for those short trips will not only benefit the environment through reduced levels of

> Conservation can actually improve quality of life for the individual as well as for the environment.

pollution, but developing this habit will also save money and provide exercise that can prolong life. Turning off the lights in unoccupied rooms, placing water heaters and climate controls on timers, and eating less and healthier are all ways of improving the quality of life while caring for creation.[70]

Rediscovering the biblical principle of Sabbath will assist in limiting consumption and practicing conservation. The teachings of Sabbath transcend the selection of one day for corporate worship. The principle involves taking time to rest and enjoy the blessings of God around us, especially in creation. "When people celebrate the Sabbath [principle] they perceive the world as God's creation, for in the Sabbath quiet it is God's creation that they are permitting the world to be."[71] Setting aside regular "sabbath" times in our lives will allow us to reconnect with ourselves, God, our families, and creation. It is through ceasing activity that we not only mirror God's response to creation, but it is in stopping that we also truly live the countercultural lives to which God has called us.[72]

The Environment and Christian Congregations. Congregations must also be involved in creation care. The biblical doctrines of creation and accompanying issues of environmental concern should be part of our regular preaching plans and Christian education curricula. Summer youth camps and related adult programs are natural opportunities to teach Christian responsibility for the environment.

> *Congregations should also conduct regular "environmental audits" of their lives and ministries.*

Congregations should also conduct regular "environmental audits" of their lives and ministries. This congregational assessment would include:[73]

1. Investigating the missions and ministries that the congregation supports to assure that they are environmentally responsible.
2. Using only recycled paper in the church office.
3. Ensuring that the church take advantage of local waste recycling programs.
4. Selecting reusable or at least environmentally friendly (not Styrofoam) cups, plates, and tableware for congregational functions.
5. Using environmentally friendly cleaning products.
6. Planning menus for church dinners that are easy on the world's resources.
7. Ensuring that church-owned buildings are energy efficient.
8. Investing church funds in ways that reflect creation care.

As the congregation raises the awareness of creation care in its communal life, individual members will become educated and become more environmentally responsible in their lifestyles and choices.

The environmental crisis is real and present, and Christians not only have the historical and scriptural resources to respond effectively, we also have the responsibility. "The Judaeo-Christian tradition has historically stressed responsibility for nature," and these resources "allow us to cope with these [environmental] problems" in ways non-Christians cannot.[74] Through individual and congregational action, the ancient declaration of the Psalmist—"The earth is the LORD's"—again can be recalled and celebrated.

Notes

[1]Modern attention was drawn to the ecological crisis by the seminal article by Lynn White, "The Historical Roots of our Ecological Crisis," reprinted in *The Care of Creation*, ed. R.J. Berry (Downers Grove, IL: InterVarsity, 2000) 31-42.

[2]An example of an organization which draws attention to the modern environmental crisis and its relationship to other global problems is the Worldwatch Institute (as of this writing, www.worldwatch.org), best known for its annual "State of the World" publications.

[3]The biologist, Garrett Hardin, first coined this term in 1968, and an expanded discussion of this concept can be found in John L. Seitz, *Global Issues*, 2nd ed. (Malden, MA: Blackwell, 2002) 213-215.

[4]Fred Van Dyke et al., eds., *Redeeming Creation: The Biblical Basis for Environmental Stewardship* (Downers Grove, IL: InterVarsity, 1996) 17-18.

[5]Ibid., 18.

[6]Ibid., 18-19.

[7]The best example is the United Nations Environmental Program (UNEP) (as of this writing, www.unep.org).

[8]The treaties related to curbing greenhouse gases (signed by the US) and protecting biodiversity (rejected by the US). An excellent summary of these conferences can be found in Seitz, *Global Issues*, 158-161.

[9]For more information on the 2002 World Summit, visit (as of this writing, www.europa. eu.int/comm/environment/agend21/).

[10]Francis A. Schaeffer, *Pollution and the Death of Man* (Wheaton, IL: Tyndale, 1970) 85.

[11]White, "Historical Roots." The article first appeared as a lecture given to the American Association for the Advancement of Science in 1966.

[12]Ibid., 40.

[13]Ibid., 42.

[14]*Time* (January 2, 1989) 29-30.

[15]The Christian perspective is best communicated through the term "creation" as opposed to "nature" or "the environment." "Creation" carries the reminder of the role of the Creator and the subsequent role of humans as created beings and fellow creatures. See Van Dyke, *Redeeming Creation*, 39-40. Components for a Christian theology of creation care will be discussed later in this chapter.

[16]The publication of Francis A. Schaeffer's *Pollution and the Death of Man* introduced creation care into the evangelical debate for a time.

[17]Jürgen Moltmann, *God In Creation* (San Francisco: Harper & Row, 1985).

[18]An excellent overview and summary of evangelical thinking on creation care is Chris Sugden, "Evangelicals and the Environment in Process," *Evangelical Review of Theology* 17 (1993) 119-121. The entire April/June 1993 (10:2) issue of *Transformation* was dedicated to creation care. An excellent bibliography of significant Christian works on creation care published in the last 30 years is Joseph K.

Sheldon, "Christians and the Environment in the 1990s: A Selective Bibliography," *Transformation* 10 (1993): 21-23; and a more complete bibliography can be found in Joseph K. Sheldon, *Rediscovery of Creation: A Bibliographical Study of the Church's Response to the Environmental Crisis* (Metuchen, NJ: Scarecrow Press, 1992).

[19]The declaration was first published in *Christianity Today*, and the full text can be found in Berry, *Care*, 17-22, and at www.creationcare.org/Resources/Declaration/declaration.html.

[20]Van Dyke, *Redeeming Creation*, 132.

[21]Gene Wilhelm, "Theology and Ecology," in *Ecology and Religion*, ed. by John E. Carroll and Keith Warner (Quincy, IL: Franciscan Press, 1998) 260.

[22]Ibid.

[23]Seitz, *Global Issues*, 133-134.

[24]Ibid., 63-64. The U.S. is not immune from limited and dwindling supplies of water. For example, during the drought of 2001, more than half of Kentucky's counties experienced water shortages. This and other details about the water crisis in the U.S. can be learned from an August 12, 2001, article in the *Toronto Star* (as of this writing, http://www.commondreams.org/headlines01/0812-04.htm).

[25]James A. Nash, *Loving Nature* (Nashville: Abingdon Press, 1991) 40.

[26]Seitz, *Global Issues*, 59.

[27]This summary is taken from an excellent discussion of carrying capacity as it relates to environmental issues in ibid., 59-65.

[28]Berry, *Care*, 18.

[29]Loren and Mary Ruth Wilkinson, "The Depth of the Danger," *Transformation* 10 (1993) 4.

[30]Van Dyke, *Redeeming Creation*, 123.

[31]Seitz, *Global Issues*, 176.

[32]Ibid., 175.

[33]For example, in the 1950s and 1960s hundreds in Japan were killed from eating mercury-contaminated fish; see ibid., 176.

[34]Van Dyke, *Redeeming Creation*, 19-20.

[35]Nash, *Loving Nature*, 23-24. Chapters 1 and 2 (23-67) survey these environmental problems in depth.

[36]Berry, *Care*, 18. Lengthy discussions of these problems with specific documentation is included in Calvin B. DeWitt, "Creation's Environmental Challenge to Evangelical Christianity," *Care*, 60-73; and in C.B. DeWitt, "Seven Degradations of Creation," in *The Environment and the Christian*, ed. by C.B. DeWitt (Grand Rapids: Baker, 1991) 13-23.

[37]White, "Historical Roots," 42.

[38]Moltmann, *God in Creation*, xi.

[39]Sugden, "Evangelicals," 119.

[40]Paul H. Santmire, *The Travail of Nature* (Minneapolis: Fortress Press, 1985) 8.

[41]Ibid., 35. A brief yet helpful summary of Origen and Irenaeus's theologies of nature can be found in Berry, *Care*, 25-30. Santmire provides a more detailed discussion; Santmire, *Travail*, 31-53.

[42]Santmire, *Travail*, 1-73, provides an excellent historical overview of Christian thinking about the environment from the Church Fathers to present day. A solid discussion is also included in Nash, *Loving Nature*, 125ff.

[43]Ronald J. Sider, "Biblical Foundations for Creation Care," *Care*, 45.

[44]These foundational doctrines are based upon the discussion found in Nash, *Loving Nature*, 93-138. I have also heavily relied upon Moltmann, *God in Creation*, and Santmire, *Travail*, for this section.

[45]John Drane, "Defining a Biblical Theology of Creation," *Transformation* 10 (1993) 7-11.

[46]Sugden, "Evangelicals," 119.

[47]Schaeffer, *Pollution*, 70.

[48]Quoted in Robin Attfield, *The Ethics of Environmental Concern* (Athens, GA: The University of Georgia Press, 1991) 35.

[49]Sider, "Biblical Foundations," 48.

[50]Stott, "Foreword," *Care*, 9.

[51]These three "fundamental ecological principles" are adapted from Alister E. McGrath, "The Stewardship of the Creation: An Evangelical Affirmation," in *Care*, 87.

[52]A further discussion of the environmental implications of Sabbath is included later in this chapter.

[53]Nash, *Loving Nature*, 105.

[54]Ibid.

[55]An excellent discussion of the environmental implications of the biblical doctrine of covenant is found in Van Dyke, *Redeeming Creation*, 71-88. Also, Santmire, *Travail*, 189-218, proposed an "ecological reading of biblical theology," which seeks to keep all creation

central to the salvation story that unfolds in Scripture.

[58]Moltmann, *God in Creation*, 6.

[59]Van Dyke, *Redeeming Creation*, 68.

[60]W.D. Davies, *The Gospel and the Land* (Berkeley, CA: The University of California Press, 1974) 367.

[61]Both quotes are from Nash, *Loving Nature*, 109.

[62]Davies, *The Gospel*, 367. Davies also includes an excellent discussion of general or natural revelation.

[63]An excellent summary of the historical and scriptural backgrounds to a theology of natural revelation is found in Gerald R. McDermott, *Can Evangelicals Learn from World Religions?* (Downers Grove, IL: InterVarsity, 2000) 49-54. His discussion focuses on the works of John Calvin, Jonathan Edwards, and Karl Barth.

[64]Henri Blocher, *In the Beginning* (Downers Grove, IL: InterVarsity, 1984) 184. See Genesis 3:17-24.

[65]John Howard Yoder, *The Politics of Jesus* (Grand Rapids: Eerdmans, 1995) 60-75.

[66]Vernon Visick, "Creation's Care and Keeping in the Life of Jesus," in DeWitt, *Environment*, 93-106.

[67]A basic discussion of the environmental implications of the biblical doctrine of the Church is found in Nash, *Loving Nature*, 126-128. The chapter in this volume by Dr. Larry Chouinard provides a detailed presentation of the Church as an alternative community.

[68]Seitz, *Global Issues*, 235.

[69]Ibid., 141.

[70]An excellent list of practical suggestions for implementing creation care in the individual lives of Christians is found in Tony Campolo, *How to Rescue the Earth without Worshiping Nature* (Nashville: Thomas Nelson, 1992) 155-171.

[71]Moltmann, *God in Creation*, 276. Moltmann devotes a chapter to the role of the Sabbath principle in creation care; see 276-296.

[72]Larry L. Rasmussen, *Earth Community Earth Ethics* (Maryknoll, NY: Orbis Books, 1996) 224.

[73]The idea and parameters for the congregational environmental audit is taken from Campolo, *How to Rescue*, 141. His eleventh chapter, "The Greening of the Church," 134-153, provides many excellent, practical suggestions for implementing creation care through the local church.

[74]Attfield, *Ethics*, 34.

Bibliography

Berry, R.J., ed. *The Care of Creation*. Downers Grove, IL: InterVarsity, 2000.

A collection of essays focusing on the 1994 "Evangelical Declaration on the Care of Creation." The full text of the Declaration is included and is supported by articles which provide context and commentary.

Davies, W.D. *The Gospel and the Land*. Berkeley, CA: The University of California Press, 1974.

A monumental work which examines the significance of the earth in the development of biblical theology. While the emphasis is on the promise of the land within the Old Testament and its review in the New Testament, Davies' "territorial theology" reflects the biblical understanding of God's plan to reconnect all of creation and to accomplish His plan within the context of wider creation.

DeWitt, C.B., ed. *The Environment and the Christian*. Grand Rapids: Baker, 1991.

The editor, a Christian environmental scientist at the University of Wisconsin, Madison, leads a group of evangelical contributors in examining the role of creation care in the New Testament. A Christian theology of creation care is developed. Especially valuable is an appendix review of environmental stewardship literature and the New Testament.

Moltmann, Jürgen. *God in Creation*. San Francisco: Harper & Row, 1985.

First presented as the 1985 Gifford Lectures at the University of Edinburgh, the prominent German theologian develops a Christian theology of creation. This is a must-read for anyone interested in pursuing a biblical understanding of God, humans, and nature.

Nash, James A. *Loving Nature*. Nashville: Abingdon Press, 1991.

An excellent primer on Christian ecological ethics. In this interdisciplinary study, the author draws upon history, theology, biblical studies, ecological sciences, social sciences, and philosophical ethics to develop a Christian approach to the environment.

Santmire, H. Paul. *The Travail of Nature*. Minneapolis: Fortress Press, 1985.

A helpful overview of Christian ecological theology. An assessment of views of nature within the tradition of Christian theology is presented from the Church Fathers to present thinkers. An especially stimulating chapter is included on an ecological understanding of biblical theology. Extensive notes also supply rich bibliographical resources for serious study of a Christian theology of the environment.

Van Dyke, Fred, et al., eds. *Redeeming Creation*. Downers Grove, IL: InterVarsity, 1996.

A popular introduction to the biblical basis for environmental stewardship, suitable for small group study. Especially valuable are the reflection questions at the end of each chapter and an appendix list of Christian organizations that focus on creation care.

A Christian Perspective on Capital Punishment

David A. Fiensy, Ph.D.

Is capital punishment an instrument of justice or a tool of vengeance?[1] Is it mandated in the Bible—a no-brainer for any Bible believing Christian—or is it a vestige of an age of hardened hearts which under Christ should be discarded? Would a Christian repudiation of capital punishment be tantamount to the abandonment of moral values, or would it be an affirmation of one of the most important moral values: the sanctity of human life?

Although 70% of the people in the United States support the death penalty,[2] the churches are having second thoughts. The Catholic bishops, the Presbyterians, the United Methodists, the American Baptists, the Friends, the Evangelical Lutherans, the Disciples of Christ, and the United Church of Christ oppose the death penalty. Recently even the voice of evangelicals, *Christianity Today*, stated its opposition to the death penalty.[3] The

> Although 70% of the people in the United States support the death penalty, the churches are having second thoughts.

execution of born-again Christian Karla Faye Tucker has caused many evangelical Christians to reconsider the death penalty and think more about the rehabilitation of criminals.[4]

When we speak of the death penalty in the United States, what are we talking about in terms of human lives? In the year 2000, 85 persons were executed (80 of them by lethal injection and 5 by electrocution). Of those executed 49 were white, 35 were black, and one was Native American. Thus, although African Americans make up around 13% of the population, they comprised 41% of those execut-

> In the year 2000, 85 persons were executed and at the end of the year there were 3,593 persons on death row awaiting execution.

ed. In addition to those executed each year, one must bear in mind those on death row. At the end of 2000 there were 3,593 persons on death row awaiting execution, an increase of 1.5% over the previous year. Of those on death row 1,990 were white, 1,535 were African American, 29 were Native American, 27 were Asian, and 12 were of unknown race. Hispanics (some of which were white and some of which were black) numbered 339. Again, the African Americans comprised a conspicuously disproportionate percentage of the total on death row (43%). In addition, some estimate that over one-third of all of those on death row are mentally retarded.[5] Those arguing either side of the issue may appeal to these figures to indicate the injustice of the system. Those in favor of capital punishment decry the backlog of murderers on death row waiting to be executed and the slowness of justice. Those opposed to capital punishment point to the obvious bias of a system that sentences a disproportionate segment of the population to death.

Most of those condemned to death in America have been convicted of murder. Nevertheless, other crimes have been considered worthy of the death penalty as well. These crimes include: treason, hindering preparations for war, perjury resulting in the death penalty, kidnapping, sexual battery, capital rape, aircraft hijacking, espionage, mutiny, desertion, and assaulting or willfully disobeying a superior officer.[6]

These statistics indicate to us the question that this essay will attempt to answer. What should we do with these three thousand or so souls that have been condemned to death and indeed with others who may be so condemned in the future? We will first of all quickly list the arguments made on both sides of the issue that are based on public policy considerations. These will furnish us with some background into which we can place our main study: the biblical and theological arguments for and against capital punishment. It is the thesis of this paper that Christians should oppose the death penalty.

Public Policy Arguments
Concerning the Death Penalty

This essay will argue the Christian basis for opposing capital punishment. As such, most of the arguments below are irrelevant. Nevertheless, since many Christians seem unable or unwilling to separate Christian theology from that given as American constitutional or pragmatic reasons for or against capital punishment, we will survey these reasons below. The standard arguments in the public or political arena for retaining capital punishment are as follows:

1. Capital punishment deters crime. When potential murderers realize they will have to pay for their crimes with their own lives, they will refrain from committing them.
2. Capital punishment is more economical than life imprisonment. It costs less than keeping someone in prison for the rest of his or her life.
3. Capital punishment gives the offender what he/she deserves and "balances the scales of justice." It furnishes retribution for taking a life and shows respect for life in so doing.
4. Executing murderers is the only way to prevent some crimes. If some criminals such as war criminals or revolutionaries (take Hitler for instance) are allowed to live, they will continue to cause evil in prison.
5. Since most Americans favor the death penalty according to recent polls (see above), we should retain it.[7]

Probably the most cited reasons today are numbers 1 and 3 above, the deterrence and retribution arguments. Advocates of the deterrence argument maintain that the death penalty makes future murderers think twice before they commit capital crimes. There are problems with this argument, however. First, the statistics have not established that where the death penalty is in force, murder rates decrease.[8] The taking of a human life is too important an event to base it on an argument that the statistical information does not support. Second, it assumes that potential murderers calculate the consequences of their actions. In reality, many if not most murders are committed in the heat of anger or hatred, by professional criminals who do not expect to be apprehended, or by persons under the influence of drugs. These people will not take time to count the cost of their intended action. Third, even if the statistical evidence did support this argument and even if we could show that the prospect of the death penalty did make people stop to think twice before murdering, it would be immoral for a Christian to accept deterrence as a reason for maintaining the death penalty.

The deterrence argument is based on the philosophy of utilitarianism, not Christian morality. Utilitarianism maintains that one should do what is the greatest good for the greatest number of people. Thus, if your execution benefits a group of persons in the future, then you should be executed. If one responds that the criminal deserves to be executed, then one is leaving the deterrence argument and posing the argument from retribution. The deterrence argument standing by itself is an argument from utilitarianism. But such a view of the person devalues the worth of the individual and exalts the worth of the crowd. A person's death according to this way of thinking becomes an example for others but ignores the one who is executed. One's life is only of value if it is beneficial to the society as a whole according to this line of reasoning.[9]

The second argument, that it is too costly to keep people in prison for life, is also questionable. By the time one adds up the trial expenses involved in a capital murder case and the appeals process that must be allowed since a person's life is at stake, it usually costs more to execute someone than to keep him in prison for life.[10] Again, even if it were the case that it is more costly to keep a person in prison than to execute him, that would not be a valid argument for a Christian. We do not kill people because they are costing us money.

The third argument, the retribution argument, is another of the popular justifications for capital punishment that some Christians cite. Christians seek to find this argument in Scripture, especially Genesis 9:6, and see it as the bulwark in protecting respect for human life. One must pay life for life. We must postpone the analysis of this proposition until our discussion of scriptural evidence for and against the death penalty. For now, let it be said that in the public policy arena such an argument often amounts to little more than seeking revenge.

The fourth argument in my opinion has merit. If one believes (as I do) that the only justification for taking a human life is in the immediate protection of another human life, there could be exceptional circumstances (but rare) in which even those in general opposed to capital punishment could favor it. But these are exceptional circumstances. How many times do we find someone like Hitler (the leader of an international hate group and a mass murderer) in one of our prisons? One should not use rare exceptions to determine the conclusions in this matter.

The fifth argument, that most Americans want capital punishment, is based on the popularity of the practice. While poll-taking is sufficient for some ethicists, it can never be an adequate basis for Christian ethics. We do not simply do what the majority of a group wants. We are asking what is right, not what is common.

The public policy arguments in favor of capital punishment do not satisfy the adherent of Christian ethics. We want to know the will of God in this matter not the will of the masses. In this case Christians may be called on to lead the crowd instead of falling in step with what is common American thinking.

The standard public policy arguments against capital punishment are as follows:

1. Capital punishment affects disproportionately the poor and racial minorities. There seems to be a class and race bias in the application of the death penalty since those groups are executed in far greater numbers proportionally than the wealthy and white populations.

2. Too many mistakes are made in the application of the death penalty. With the invention of new DNA methods in crime detection, it is becoming clear that many innocent people have been sentenced to death.

3. Capital punishment ends the possibility of reform of the criminal. Instead of restoring a criminal to society, the death penalty compounds one terrible act with yet another act of killing.

4. Capital punishment actually makes it more difficult to obtain a guilty verdict in murder cases since juries are far less prone to convict a person that will be executed. Thus the death penalty may harm the judicial system.[11]

Proponents of capital punishment answer arguments 1, 2, and 4 with the same counter: Improper application of the penalty does not mean the penalty itself it wrong. The solution is to clean up the process so that it is not racially biased, does not make so many mistakes, and does not tend to hinder the judicial system. In principle, these counter arguments are correct. Of course, while we are in the process of cleaning up the system—a process that may take quite a while—innocent people may suffer and the law may be unfairly applied.

Argument number 3 turns on the reason for punishment. Here we are again confronted with Christian ethics as opposed to some other ethical system or worldview. In the Christian system there is no place for revenge. Vengeance belongs only to God. But this is an ethic based on a Christian faith commitment, not one that can be founded on reason alone. Thus we again must await our analysis of Scripture for further consideration of this point.

Arguments either for or against capital punishment that are based only on reason or practicality—in other words, arguments in the political arena—fail. To settle issues of life and death, we need more than statistics and appeals to what "works." Christians should not be satisfied with such evidence anyway. We want to know what God's will is by understanding clearly what his word says. To this end, we now turn to the biblical texts.

> To settle issues of life and death, we need more than statistics and appeals to what "works."

Old Testament Teaching on Capital Punishment

It is typical for proponents of capital punishment to cite the many Old Testament texts that command execution for crimes. The assertion is that if God commanded execution in the Old Testament, it must be in his will. The Mosaic Law commands the death penalty (usually by stoning but also by burning, by the sword, and by other means) for several offenses. Scholars' lists of capital crimes in the Torah vary from about 15 to 25 different offenses. Below is a fair representation of such crimes that were considered worthy of the death penalty:[12]

Family Laws

Cursing or striking one's parents	Exod 21:15, 17; Lev 20:9; Deut 21:18-21

Sexual Laws

Bestiality	Exod 22:19; Lev 20:15-16
Adultery	Lev 20:10; Deut 22:15-16
Incest	Lev 20:11-13
Homosexuality	Lev 20:13
Prostitution	Lev 21:9; Deut 22:13-21
Rape	Deut 22:25

Religious Crimes

Trespassing sacred precinct	Exod 19:12-13; Num 1:51

Witchcraft	Exod 22:18; Lev 20:27
Idolatry	Exod 22:20; Deut 13:1-19, 18:20
Profaning the Sabbath	Exod 31:14
Blaspheming the Name	Lev 24:16
False prophecy	Deut 18:20
Child sacrifice	Lev 21:9

Violent Crimes

Murder	Exod 21:12; Lev 24:17
Kidnapping	Exod 21:16; Deut 24:7
Perjury in a capital case	Deut 19:16-21
Negligence that results in death	Exod 21:28-29; Deut 22:8

Proponents of the death penalty maintain that these texts at least prove that capital punishment is not inherently wrong or else God would never have commanded it. Also the texts show, they maintain, that civil government is ordained by God to perform the executions. While these particular laws may not be timeless, the idea of capital punishment, they say, is timeless.[13]

One should make two observations about the use of these texts. First, although some Christian interpreters want to argue for a wider application for the death penalty today,[14] most want to reserve it only for murderers. By a legal casuistry they seek to demonstrate that God only wants murderers to be executed today, that requiring the death penalty for murder only is a timeless truth. Thus, they say the Mosaic Law demonstrates to us that murderers should be executed, but not the perpetrators of other crimes for which execution was demanded. In other words, they sense some problems with executing persons for most of the crimes listed above. But such a use of the Mosaic Law is selective. It is admitting that one cannot really take the law literally. For example, no one is advocating the death penalty, as far as I know, for false prophecy or profaning the Sabbath. This use of the Mosaic Law is a tacit acceptance that the Israelite civil law is not for Christians.

Second, the Mosaic Law was the covenant between God and Israel. As such, the Christian has to ask legitimately whether this law can or should govern society today. Israel lived in a theocracy; Christians have not made such a covenant and do not live in such a society. Rather, we live in many different kinds of societies: democracies, monarchies, and oligarchies. We have no basis for trying to reestablish the old Israelite theocracy. Thus, the cases of capital punishment in the Mosaic Law are mostly irrelevant to the Christian.

> We have no basis for trying to reestablish the old Israelite theocracy.

By far the most cited Old Testament text to support capital punishment is Genesis 9:6:

> The one shedding the blood of a human being;
>> by a human being his blood will be shed,
> because in the image of God
>> he made the human being (author's translation).

This text is considered very important for proponents of the death penalty because: a) It is pre-Mosaic and thus apparently supposed to be accepted by all humanity. b) It is based on the principles of the sanctity of human life since humans are created in the image of God c) and on the just retribution of life for life, like the so called *lex talionis* or law of retaliation given in Exodus 21:24-27; Leviticus 24:19-22; and Deuteronomy 19:19-21. Advocates of the death penalty maintain that this text is a timeless mandate for the execution of murderers. Bible believers have no choice, they maintain, but to obey this mandate.[15]

The opponents of capital punishment often respond that Genesis 9:6 is not legislation, not a command, but a wisdom statement or a prediction of what happens in that society when one takes a human life.[16]

It would be helpful to look at this verse in context. The verse comes after Noah and his family emerge from the ark. The language of Genesis 9:1-7 is the language of the creation story of Genesis 1: "Be fruitful and multiply" (Gen 9:1,7; cf. Gen 1:28); "In the image of God" (Gen 9:6; cf. Gen 1:26-27). The world after the flood is in almost the same state as at its beginning. It is like a new creation. Yet there is one significant difference. In the first creation (Gen 1:29-30) human beings were allowed to eat only plants. Now (Gen 9:3-4) humans may eat both plants and animal flesh. But since the נֶפֶשׁ (*nepheš*) "life," is in the blood of an animal, the blood must be respected. Thus animals' blood is respected by not being eaten. One may eat the meat but not the blood. The blood of human beings is respected by not shedding it, and God will demand (דָּרַשׁ, *dāraš*) an account for it if it is shed. The talk of demanding an account then leads to the verse in question, Genesis 9:6.

It is observed by nearly all interpreters that Genesis 9:6 is a very skillfully written Hebrew poem in chiasm.[17] As such, it tends to read more like a proverb than a legal decree. Further, nothing is said in the proverb about who has the power and authority to take vengeance for murder. The text simply says that God will demand an accounting of those who shed human blood. Finally, the brief poem shifts from the first person ("I will demand an account," 9:5) to the third person ("his blood will be shed," 9:6) in the passive voice (niphal). Thus one could plausibly argue that Genesis 9:6 is an old proverb that the narrator has inserted into the narrative as his interpretation and not to be understood as the words of God speaking directly to Noah.

According to this understanding, the text is saying the following: In the newly created order after the flood, humans may eat animal flesh only if they respect the sanctity of life (*nepheš*) that is in the blood (9:4). This thought leads to a statement about human blood. God "will require it" (9:5) or demand a reckoning. To this statement the narrator added a proverbial statement rather like Matthew 26:52. Killers will meet their end in the same way their victims did. This is the regular feature of blood-feud cultures (see below).

At any rate, whether this understanding is correct or not, the text is not commanding one to execute people. It certainly does not set up civil governments or institutions to do the executing. The only thing that is commanded or "mandated" is the prohibition against eating blood, a commandment that few modern non-Jews seem interested in keeping. I conclude that Genesis 9:6 hardly presents us with a timeless mandate for capital punishment. It does present us with an important text for the sanctity of human life. All human life is sacred since all humans are created in the image of God.

There is distinct difficulty in using this text the way proponents of capital punishment use it. In the first place, it does not clearly refer to murderers (with premeditation) but to shedders of blood. This could refer to persons who have accidentally killed, to children who have killed, even to executioners.[18] Anyone who sheds human blood by this dictum will have his blood shed (how and when are not indicated). Again, in blood-feud cultures, the relatives of the dead person do not care whether the death was accidental or not. They want to exact blood for blood.

The Old Testament hardly furnishes the Christian with justification for the death penalty. The Mosaic Law is the covenant law between God and Israel, not the civil law for all societies and for all times. Genesis 9:6 is found in the context of prohibiting the consumption of animal blood and may only contain a proverbial statement about how violent people usually meet their end. These texts provide, then, an uncertain basis for the justification of the taking of a human life in execution.

On the other hand, opponents of the death penalty point out that the Old Testament conception of murder (shedding blood) is that it pollutes the holy land of Israel (Num 35:33; Judg 24:7; 2 Sam 21:1-9). Belief that blood polluted one's land was common in the ancient near east. The only way to cleanse the land, according to this ideology, was by cultic execution of the offender. But this conception is not the same as the basis for capital punishment in modern societies. Thus, attempting to translate ancient Hebrew law into modern societies fails because the ideological basis for each is different.[19]

Further, opponents of the death penalty note that capital punishment was not always enforced in the Old Testament. Cain, Moses, and David committed murder but were not executed (Gen 4:15; Exod 1:12; 2 Sam 12:13). Joseph's brothers should have been executed for attempting murder but were not (Gen 50:15-21). People profaned the Sabbath but were not executed (Neh 13:15-21). Adulterers are said to be lacking in judgment but are not condemned to die (Prov 6:32) just as Hosea's adulterous wife was not executed (Hos 3:1). Finally, some Old Testament texts urge mercy and rehabilitation of the offender:

> *Capital punishment was not always enforced in the Old Testament.*

Rescue those taken away to death (Prov 24:11).

As I live, says my Lord Yahweh, if I take delight in the death of the wicked—on the contrary (I delight) in the repentance of the wicked from his way, and he will live (Ezek 33:11).[20]

One should always be cautious in proof-texting. A few exceptions to the laws do not prove that the laws of capital punishment were not enforced. Yet these few exceptions do give us reason to pause. Perhaps the death penalties "mandated" were not seen as immutable and timeless by the ancient Hebrews. Such a caution is even more justified when we consider the way the rabbis of the Mishnah handled the death penalty laws.

Mishnaic Teaching about the Death Penalty

The rabbinic texts, especially the Mishnah,[21] place severe restrictions on the application of the death penalty. In the first place, the courts did not accept circumstantial evidence.[22] Only the testimony of two eyewitnesses to the crime were able to convict (in accordance with Num 35:30 and Deut 19:15). Further, witnesses could only attest to what they had seen with their own eyes (thus no hearsay evidence was admitted). A person could not be convicted unless he/she had acted with malice. To ensure that the offender had acted with malicious intent, it had to be proven that someone had warned him/her of the deed and that the offender had acknowledged that he/she was acting maliciously. Witnesses to a crime were questioned about the facts and any disagreements caused the case to be dismissed.[23] The result of all of these measures was obviously that conviction in a capital case was next to impossible. Evidently that was the rabbis' intention. One section of the Mishnah has this to say about capital punishment:

> The Sanhedrin that executes one person in seven years is called cruel.[24] Rabbi El'azar ben Azariah (c. AD 100) said, "One in seventy years." Rabbi Tarfon (c. AD 120) and Rabbi Aqiba (c. AD 120) said, "Had we been in the Sanhedrin, not a person ever would have been executed." Rabbi Simeon ben Gamliel (c. AD 140) said, "They would increase the shedders of blood in Israel." (m. Makkot 1:10) (author's translation).

The Mishnah made it very difficult to execute anyone. This difficulty was no accident as the text from Makkot demonstrates. Many of the rabbis were opposed to the free use of the death penalty and some were opposed to it altogether, a viewpoint criticized by Rabbi Simeon ben Gamliel as threatening the safety of society. True, a proponent of the death penalty could respond that the rabbis of the second century A.D. were living in the protective bubble of the rabbinic academy, without the harsh responsibilities of the Sanhedrin of the first century. Thus they could afford to be lenient with respect to the death penalty. But the problem with *ad hominem* arguments is that they always cut both ways. Perhaps it took the quiet environment of the academy in the second century for Jewish Old Testament scholars to travel to the end of the road in their reflections. One is tempted to conclude that many of the rabbis were simply following the tendency of the Old Testament to its logical conclusion. The respect for all human life as made in the image of God (Gen 1:27; 9:6) if followed reflectively, can lead to opposition to the death penalty. The rabbis teach in m. Sanhedrin 4:5 that anyone who causes a human being to perish has caused a world of humans (i.e., his/her descendants) to perish.[25]

New Testament Texts

Advocates of either side of this issue often engage in proof-texting in their use of both Old and New Testaments. Most of these texts are unimpressive as far as deciding this important question.[26] One substantial text, however, that is frequently cited in support of capital punishment is Romans 13:1-7:

> Let every person [ψυχη] *submit* to higher authorities [εξουσι-αις]. I say this because there is no authority except by God. Those (authorities) that exist have been ordained by God. [2]The result is that the one who opposes the authority, resists the ordinance of God and those that have resisted them will receive judgment. [3]For leaders are not fearful to someone doing a good deed but to someone doing a bad deed. Do you want to be free from fear of the authority? *Do good* and you will have praise from it. [4]For it is a servant of God (intended) for a good purpose for you. But if you do evil, be afraid. For it does not carry the sword [μαχαιραν] for no reason. For it is God's servant of justice to direct wrath toward the evildoer. [5]Therefore, it is necessary to *submit* not only because of the wrath but also because of your conscience. [6]Also, because of this *pay* your taxes. For they [the tax collectors?] are ministers of God who are devoted to this very task. [7]*Pay back* to every one what is owed. To the one to whom you owe a tax, (pay) the tax; to the one to whom you owe revenue, (pay) the revenue; to the one to whom you owe respect, (show) respect; to the one to whom you owe honor, (give) honor (author's translation).

Proponents of capital punishment join this text with Genesis 9:6 to maintain that God's timeless plan is retributive justice as in "an eye for an eye." Romans 13 shows us how this justice is to be administered: by the civil government. "The purpose of government is justice, not mercy."[27] Thus the Christian reason for capital punishment, it is maintained, is retribution which in their view is not the same as revenge. The "sword" of Romans 13:4 is in this understanding the sword of capital punishment. God has ordained civil government to punish (render justice to) criminals, especially to carry out executions: "eye for eye, life for life." Genesis 9:6 is God's timeless plan (which in this understanding is a mandate for execution) and Romans 13:1-7 indicates how God wants the plan to be put into action.[28]

As it was with our examination of Genesis 9, so it will be in our investigation of Romans 13. A close inspection of this text will show that it cannot bear the burden that proponents of capital punishment have put on it. There are many important questions that we could ask of this text, but in an essay of this nature we must restrict our questions to those which speak to our subject. Thus we ask the following: What was the historical situation behind this text? What is the immediate literary context of Romans 13:4 (or in other words, what specifically is commanded in this text?) Finally, what is the meaning of the word "sword" in verse 4?

Over the years several suggestions have been made about the historical situation behind Romans 13:1-7. A Jewish revolution was brewing in the background, maintain some interpreters, and Paul wanted to warn Christians (especially Jewish Christians) not to participate.[29] Others suggest early Christians in their zeal and enthusiasm refused to recognize the legitimacy of any government and Paul is counseling them to reflect further on this immature view.[30] Still others have suggested that the problem had to do with excessive taxation and the general problems with the greedy tax collectors.[31] There are texts from this period which indicate that taxation was a growing problem[32] and Romans 13:1-7 does refer to taxes several times. Thus, given both the historical evidence that complaints about taxation and greedy tax collectors were becoming more and more frequent and given the references in Romans 13 to taxes, I would conclude that Paul was teaching the Roman Christians to pay their taxes in spite of perhaps justified complaints.

The second question we are asking this text is what is the context of Romans 13:4: "the sword." Another way of asking this question is to ask what specifically is commanded. The translation given above has sought to highlight the things commanded in Romans 13:1-7. The readers are instructed to submit to authorities (twice), to do good, to pay taxes (twice), to pay revenue, to show respect, and to give honor. The two references to taxes and the one reference to paying revenue would seem to argue that this text is giving instructions (commands) about submission to civil government by paying taxes. The text is not (or at least not primarily) about the proper role of government or about government's divine mandate to execute criminals. It is mainly about the Christian's obligation as a child of God to give whatever one owes, especially taxes. Such a context fits nicely with our suggested historical background.

Finally, we ask to what does the word μαχαιρα "sword" refer? Here the date of the lexical tool makes a difference.[33] Some of the proponents of capital punishment have gotten the impression that the sword of Romans 13:4 is the equivalent of the Latin expression *ius gladii* "the right of the sword" or the power of capital punishment that all higher Roman magistrates possessed.[34] In other words, this would be, according to this understanding, the sword used for beheading criminals and thus symbolize the right of civil government to execute people. Thus, Paul would be saying that civil government has a divinely appointed right, even a mandate, to execute wrongdoers.

But such an understanding of the sword in Romans 13:4, it would seem, is inaccurate. More recent lexical work has emphasized that: 1) The word used for sword in Romans 13:4, μαχαιρα, denoted a short sword or dagger, thus unsuitable for beheading someone in execution.[35] 2) The Greek equivalent of the Latin *ius gladii* was not μαχαιραν φορειν which we have in Romans 13:4.[36] 3) When μαχαιρα was used in official contexts it referred not to executions but to the police force.[37] Thus, Paul is referring to the civil government's power to force compliance in paying taxes. If one does not pay his taxes, the police will force him/her to do so.

Romans 13:1-7 cannot bear the weight that proponents of capital punishment have put on it. Once again, one of the main supports for the Christian belief in the death penalty is weakened, if not destroyed, when we attend to the historical situation and the context. A text instructing Christians to pay their taxes can hardly be appropriated to defend maintenance of the death penalty. And if the two main props for capital punishment (Gen 9:6 and Rom 13:1-7) are removed, why would one want to advocate the death penalty any further?

Opponents of the death penalty often cite John 7:53–8:11, the story of the adulteress, as evidence that Jesus rejected capital punishment. According to the Mosaic Law, adulterers should be executed (see above), but Jesus sent the woman away and told her to sin no more. Surely, this indicates his abrogation of the Old Testament death penalty laws, so it is argued.[38]

One could perhaps make a weak case from this text to oppose capital punishment. This case is weak because we would only have to conclude that Jesus rejected the death penalty for adultery. Such a conclusion would not prove that Jesus also annulled the death penalty for other crimes such as murder.

But even this weak case is quite impossible due to the profound textual problems with this pericope. One can still find a few scholars that want to argue the genuineness of this story, but the vast majority assess the evidence and conclude that this story was not originally a part of the Gospel of John (or any other part of the New Testament).[39] Therefore, although it would support my position somewhat, I must disallow its use.

Other opponents of capital punishment—rightly in my judgment—appeal to the Sermon on the Mount, especially to Matthew 5:38-39 and the reiteration of Jesus' words in Paul's and Peter's letters. In this teaching Jesus contrasts the righteousness of the Kingdom of God with the Mosaic Law of retaliation. The Old Testament *lex talionis* or law of retaliation is found in three places in the Mosaic Law:

> If there should be a mortal wound, you will give life for life: *eye for eye, tooth for tooth*, hand for hand, foot for foot, scar for scar, bruise for bruise, wound for wound (Exod 21:23-25).

> Each one when he causes a disfigurement to his fellow—as he has done, it will be done to him: fracture for fracture, *eye for eye, tooth for tooth*. As he has caused a disfigurement against a human being, thus it will be caused to him (Lev 24:19-20).

> You will not look compassionately (at the false witness): life for life, *eye for eye, tooth for tooth*, hand for hand, foot for foot (Deut 19:21; author's translation).

To this law and its application in his time Jesus responded with the new righteousness of the Kingdom of God and the early church stressed this teaching as well:

> You have heard that it was said, '*Eye for eye*' and '*Tooth for tooth*.' But I say to you, do not retaliate against wickedness[40] (Matt 5:38-39).

Do not pay back evil for evil. . . . Do not avenge yourselves, beloved, but release your anger, as it is written, 'Vengeance is mine. I will pay it back,' says the Lord (Rom 12:17,19).

Let no one pay back evil for evil (1 Thess 5:15).

(You should) not be paying back evil for evil or slander for slander (1 Pet 3:9; author's translation).

The *lex talionis* had wide appeal in the Judaism contemporaneous with Jesus. Scholars often maintain that it was given originally to put a control on the custom of the blood feud which exacted excessive vengeance for a crime. The law of talion said one could exact only so much vengeance and no more. Thus it was intended to put a humane brake on unbridled revenge, and one could say that it was a concession to the hardness of hearts in that culture and at that time. In addition, ancient law codes outside of Israel could exact brutal tortures as penalties and could even require multiple punishments. For example, according to one ancient near eastern law code, if one stole a sheep, he would suffer 100 stripes, have his hair torn out, do a month's hard labor, and pay back the sheep. The *lex talionis* was a brake on both the blood feud and excessive punishment and in the harsh culture in which it was given, it was humane.[41]

Whether the law was literally applied in a Jewish court in Jesus' time is debatable.[42] Two texts from the Second Temple Period, Jubilees (second century B.C.) and *Liber Antiquitatum Biblicarum* (first century A.D.) refer to this concept as something God will do to the offender but not as a legal action. Philo of Alexandria (first century A.D.) berated those officials who failed in a court of law to enforce the strict "eye for eye" punishments. Thus, obviously, at least some Jews were not interpreting and enforcing the law of talion literally. Josephus (first century A.D.) reports that one could often pay a fine instead of rendering the strict "eye for eye." As the rabbis looked back on the first century, they remembered that only the Sadducees and their ideological cousins, the Boethusians, demanded a literal enforcement of the *lex talionis*. They evidently thought that their intellectual predecessors, the Pharisees, did not insist on the strict interpretation of the law of retaliation.[43] Thus it appears that the law of the *lex talionis* was by Jesus' time being softened.

Alongside this legal trend to soften the law of talion was another trend, that also began in the Old Testament, to control revenge. Several texts counsel against retaliation (Lev 19:18; Deut

32:35; Prov 20:22; 24:29) in the sense that one pays back exactly what has been perpetrated on oneself. Rather, these texts urge the victim to let God avenge them. He will in his own time give justice. Our task is rather to love our neighbor as our selves. Jewish texts from the Second Temple Period and the rabbinic period also echo this teaching.[44]

Clearly Jesus was teaching from these lines of tradition in Matthew 5:38-39. His disciples must not seek revenge, must not retaliate, and must not justify revenge in any way based on the *lex talionis*. Jesus calls his followers to the righteousness of the kingdom of God, which includes peacefulness and love, even with respect to the enemy.[45] Paying someone back in the way that he/she has harmed you, is not part of Jesus' kingdom ethic. Such a teaching seems to me to exclude any justification of the death penalty based on retribution.

Proponents of the death penalty are quick to reply that Jesus was only speaking of interpersonal relationships and not in terms of civil government.[46] These are instructions for individual behavior not for society at large, it is maintained. Thus we should not seek to kill a murderer ourselves but let the civil government do it. To this I would reply in two ways: First, it may be true that Jesus was speaking primarily about personal relationships, but this observation simplistically ignores further questions. Would Jesus have differentiated so drastically in his conclusions regarding personal behavior and civil government? If his disciples are called from retaliation personally, how could they support the *lex talionis* civilly? If Jesus taught against retaliation, how does this affect the Christian's use of the retribution argument as a justification for capital punishment? I do not see how Christians can claim to abandon retribution individually then bring it in through the back door under the cover of civil government.

Second, not all scholars agree that these instructions are intended for individual or one-on-one relationships. Some scholars[47] argue that these teachings are addressed to the Christian community or community of disciples and thus are about social relationships beyond one's private behavior. If that is so—and I believe we should at least consider this interpretation—then there would be wider political implications. A quick and easy dismissal of this text by proponents of capital punishment is no longer possible.

Christian proponents of the death penalty seem increasingly to cite retribution as the favored argument.[48] By retribution some mean that we should punish people with death because they deserve it. They have it coming to them. Offenders should have to suffer the kind of harm that they have caused others, according to this view (although they usually only apply this rule to murderers). Others define retribution as balancing the scales. When a crime is committed, the equilibrium of society is upset and needs to be rebalanced by punishment of the criminal. This view emphasizes respect for the victim.[49] A human life has been harmed and out of respect for that life we must punish the offender. The second definition of retribution need not, however, involve capital punishment. The first definition, on the other hand, would require the death penalty and is tantamount to revenge.

It is not so much that Jesus' teaching on retaliation proves that Jesus abrogated capital punishment from civil law as that it creates a spiritual and theological climate in which capital punishment cannot easily survive. How can I, a disciple of the Jesus who required that his disciples not retaliate with like for like, demand that life be paid for life? Rather, a different rationale for punishment is necessary for the Christian. We punish murderers not to seek life for life (retaliation) but to protect others, to rehabilitate criminals, and perhaps to balance the scales of justice in society (the second definition of retribution). Thus life in prison is the proper Christian punishment for murderers.

> A different rationale for punishment is necessary for the Christian.

Early Christian Views of Capital Punishment

Christians for the first three centuries were guided by three overriding ethical considerations. They refrained from behavior that involved: 1) sexual immorality, 2) idolatry, 3) and the devaluing of human life. Thus Lactantius (A.D. 300 in Asia Minor) wrote that Christians should not kill at all, neither in war nor even by accusing someone of a capital crime in a court of law (*Divinae Institutiiones* 6.20). The *Apostolic Traditions* attributed to Hippolytus of Rome (c. A.D. 200) state that if a soldier becomes a Christian, he may remain in the army but must be taught not to execute people and must not take the oath. Theophilus of Antioch (A.D. 177 in Athens), Minucius Felix of Rome (A.D. 210), Tertullian of Carthage (A.D. 200), and Cyprian of Carthage (A.D. 250) wrote that Christians were forbidden even to witness gladiatorial contests where people might be killed by combat or by execution (*ad Autoc* 3.15; *Leg* 35; *Octavius* 37; *de Spect* 11, 19; *Ep* I.7). Hippolytus, again in the *Apostolic Traditions*, declared that no magistrate of a city who wears the purple might be received for baptism. Canon 56 of the Council of Elvira (held in Spain in A.D. 306) forbade a Christian to hold the office of the city magistrate. The apparent reason for the Christian's refusal to hold public office was given by Tertullian. He stated that Christians could hold public office only if they would have nothing to do with sacrifices, giving public shows, taking oaths, passing judgments on people, or giving penalties (*de Idol* 17). The point was that it was impossible to hold public office and refrain from these things. One of the reasons, then, for Christian hesitance in seeking public office was the distaste for punishing wrongdoers. Christians repudiated retaliation and were so respectful of human life that they would not even watch someone being put to death.[50]

Of course we could cite exceptions to these opinions. There were, for example, Christians in the army, even though the church frowned on it. Surely also some Christians held public office anyway even though Christian leaders taught against it. But the point is that overwhelmingly the church for the first three hundred years had a profoundly sensitive respect for human life, even the life of a criminal. Every life had value to God and thus should not be taken away.

> The church for the first three hundred years had a profoundly sensitive respect for human life, even the life of a criminal.

Hermeneutical Considerations

The discussion of capital punishment does not turn on exegetical questions alone. There are also hermeneutical questions.[51] Hermeneutics has to do with the big picture. It asks how we conceive of biblical revelation. Clearly, those who find justification for capital punishment are reading the Bible and understanding biblical revelation in a different way from those who think the Bible leads us away from capital punishment. Christians who seek to support the death penalty from the Bible tend to regard the Bible as a source of timeless rules. The Bible is "flat" in that what is in Genesis is of equal importance to what is in Matthew. Thus, whatever was commanded of Noah after the flood is timeless and binding on us and on our society.[52]

On the other hand, believers who conclude, based also on Bible study, that they should oppose capital punishment, tend to regard the Bible as a story of God's gradual disclosure of his will. This disclosure is only possible in dialogue with particular cultural and historical situations. Further, interpreters with this understanding think of God as speaking both understandably (i.e., to the culture or contextualized) and counterculturally (in opposition to and transcending their culture). For example, the *lex talionis* was understandable in that it still allowed for vengeance in a harsh and theologically immature age. It was countercultural in that the law put a halt to the unbridled blood feud and multiple punishments. This approach to revelation and the Bible sees the *lex talionis* as only one phase in the process of teaching that human beings should forgo vengeance both personally and collectively (as government).

In this respect the *lex talionis* may be compared to the divorce law of Deuteronomy 24. It was a humane law in its day, both understandable (since it allowed divorce for any reason) and countercultural (since it protected women with a document of divorce). But Jesus said that this was only a concession, needed temporarily because of the hardness of their hearts (Matt 19:8). We should think of capital punishment in the Old Testament in a similar way.[53]

Conclusion: Why I Oppose Capital Punishment

We must refrain from emotional arguments here. Both sides can tell stories that rightly move us. Those in favor of capital punishment can narrate stories of brutal murders that justifiably sicken and anger us. To murder someone is a terrible thing; I do not say that murderers are good persons. On the other hand, those opposed to capital punishment can tell heart wrenching tales of persons executed that later were proven innocent or of persons executed that had been converted to Christ. In making ethical decisions, however, we must ask what is right, not what arouses our emotions.

> In making ethical decisions we must ask what is right, not what arouses our emotions.

My reasons for opposing capital punishment are as follows:

1. Texts cited to support the Christian's advocacy of capital punishment do not, when weighed, support it. The two main pillars of the Christian argument for capital punishment are

Genesis 9:6 and Romans 13:1-7. At best one must draw an inference from these texts that Christians should support capital
punishment. The two texts actually say nothing, however, about
the civil employment of the death penalty and how it should be
enforced, decided, and carried out. But should we be willing to
kill people based on an inference? What if we are not so clever
after all and have been misinterpreting these texts? We have
tried to demonstrate above that this inference is invalid. Taken in
their literary and historical contexts, these two texts do not
speak about capital punishment at all, in my opinion.

2. Every human life has value because God is the creator and all
humans are created in the image of God. God the creator is the
Lord of life. This principle means that one should never take a
human life unless the taking of it is necessary in the immediate
protection of another life.[54] But in capital punishment, one takes
a person who is helpless, who is not at the time threatening
anyone, and kills him/her in a planned execution. One takes a
life when it is unnecessary to do so. It is not that the life of the
murderer is worthy; it is that the one who made him in his
image is worthy.[55] It is not that we have more sympathy for the
murderer than the victim; it is that we value God's creation even
when it is ugly and sinful because God made it. In the Old
Testament culture there were no prisons. Thus one must either
execute a murderer or let him go.
In our culture that is not the case;
we can incarcerate a person for
life. Executing a restrained person
is unnecessary. In his Nobel
Peace Prize acceptance speech in
2002, former President Jimmy

> *It is not that the life of the
> murderer is worthy; it is
> that the one who made him
> in his image is worthy.*

Carter declared: "War may sometimes be a necessary evil. But
no matter how necessary, it is always evil." I think I can paraphrase that idea with respect to this topic. To take a human life
is evil. Sometimes it is a necessary evil but it is always evil. We
should never do it unless there is no other alternative.

3. The Christian's advocacy of capital punishment is not consistent
with Jesus' ethic of the Kingdom of God. His disciples must
refuse retaliation and must love their enemies. They must base
their ethical behavior not on the common sentiment of their

society but on their Lord's teachings of forgiveness. Execution cannot find a place in such ethical thinking. Retribution must not be the Christian's purpose for punishment. And if retribution as a basis for punishment is abandoned, so must the death penalty be abandoned. Punishment must be given both to protect others from harm and in the hope of rehabilitation. Christians do not give up on people and consider them hopeless causes. Putting a person to death means that society has given up on him/her.[56] Thus life in prison is the best penalty for murderers.

4. The early church demonstrated a strong sensitivity for the worth of each human life. They generally forbade Christians to enter the military, to participate in (even to watch) gladiatorial games, and to serve as a magistrate (who may have to order executions). These prohibitions were all based on the early Christian valuing of each human being. Their sensitivity to human life may not necessarily prove that Jesus would have maintained the same thing but at least it should give us pause in our eagerness to advocate capital punishment. They were closer in time to the historical Jesus and the apostles than we are.

What I Want

It is customary for those who write in support of capital punishment to ask the reader for action. They exhort their followers to educate society regarding the importance of maintaining capital punishment and urge them to vote only for proponents of the death penalty.[57] I wish to offer exhortations for the opposite goal. I want Christians to accept the task of instructing our society about the value of every human life—from the moment of conception to the comatose state of an ill, elderly person—even the life of one who has done a despicable thing.

> We must never forget about the terrible pain and loss of the victims' families.

Christians should vote for those who are consistently pro-life, both with respect to abortions and with respect to capital punishment. And of course, Christians should pray for and show support for families of those murdered. We must never forget about the terrible pain and loss of the victims' families.[58]

Is capital punishment an instrument of justice or a tool of vengeance? In my view Christians should answer that it is the latter.

We gain nothing by executing persons; as a society we lose since persons who kill others also change themselves. We participate in a culture of killing and seek to justify it by our religious faith. Such faith would have been quite incompatible with that of most Christians for the first three hundred years of church history.

Notes

[1]M.L. Stephens, "Instrument of Justice or Tool of Vengeance?" *Christian Social Action* 3 (1990) 10-13.

[2]P. Wogaman, "The Death Penalty," *Christian Social Action* 9 (1996) 16. J.D. Charles, "Crime, the Christian and Capital Justice," *Journal of the Evangelical Theological Society* 38 (1995) 429-441, gives a Gallup Poll figure of 76% in favor of capital punishment. According to C. Fennelly, 84% of Americans favor the death penalty under certain circumstances ["To Die For," *Sojourners* 27 (1998) 14-25].

[3]J. Gittings, "Churches and Capital Punishment," *Christianity and Crisis* 50 (1990) 12-13; J.D. Charles, "Crime," 429-441; Editorial, "The Lesson of Karla Faye Tucker," *Christianity Today* 42 (1998) 15-16.

[4]See Fennelly, "To Die For," 14; and V.S. Owens, "Karla Faye's Final Stop," *Christianity Today* 42 (1998) 45-48.

[5]*U.S. Department of Justice Bureau of Justice Statistics: Capital Punishment Statistics* www.ojp.usdoj.gov/bjs/cp.htm (as of Nov. 2003). The number executed in 2001 was 66. The government source did not give the details for that year. For statistics on capital punishment from 1930-1980 see H.A. Bedau, *The Death Penalty in America* (New York: Oxford University Press, 1982) 25. In those 50 years 3,862 persons were executed in the United States. The most executions in one year took place in 1935 when 199 persons were put to death. From 1968 to 1976 there were no executions. The one estimating the number of mentally retarded inmates is Stephens, "Instrument," 11. For executions in the U.S. from 1608 see: "Executions in the U.S. 1608–1987: The Espy File," http://deathpenaltyinfo.org/article.php?scid=8&did=269 (as of Nov. 2003), from which the graph (opposite) is obtained.

[6]Bedau, *Death Penalty*, 33-34.

[7]See J. Olen and V. Barry, *Applying Ethics* (Belmont, CA: Wadsworth, 1989) 252-253; Charles, "Crime, 432; idem. "Sentiment as Social Justice," *Christian Research Journal* 17 (1994) 16-23; R. Holzer, "Punishing Evildoers with the Sword: Further Discussion?" *Word and World* 16 (1996) 60-71; A. Williams, "Christian Ethics and Capital Punishment: A Reflection," *The Journal of Religious Thought* 49 (1992) 59-77; M.R. LaChat, "Christian Ethics and Capital Punishment," *Journal of Theology* 102 (1998) 71-87; A. Campbell, "Is Capital Punishment Sanctioned by Divine Authority?" (private publication).

[8]See Olen and Barry, *Applying Ethics*, 248: "Currently, the consensus among social scientists is that no statistical studies on the deterrent effect of capital punishment yield a conclusive answer." Compare also J.H. Yoder in *The Death Penalty Debate*, H.W. House and J.H. Yoder (Dallas: Word, 1991) 115; G. Hanks, *Capital Punishment and the Bible* (Scottdale, PA: Herald Press, 2002) 15.

[9]See Yoder in *Debate*, 115.

[10]LaChat, "Christian Ethics," 84; A. Williams, "Christian Ethics," 63. Stephens, "Instrument," 12-13, estimates that it takes around $7.3 million to execute someone in New York and $4.5 million to execute someone in California.

[11]Olen and Barry, *Applying Ethics*, 250-251; LaChat, "Christian Ethics," 85; Williams, "Christian Ethics," 63-64. As Williams points out, race of the victim in a murder case also has an effect on the death penalty. A study on the death penalty in the state of Georgia indicated that when a white person was murdered, 11% of the time the convicted killer was

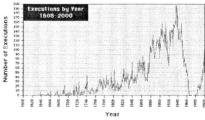

(Source: "Executions in the U.S. 1608-1987: The Espy File," with recent years added by DPIC)

given the death penalty. When a black person was murdered, 1% of the convicted killers were given the death penalty. For a report on the recent discovery of mistakes in death penalty cases see Jim Dwyer and Jodi Wilgoren, "System Jolted by Innocents," *Lexington Herald Leader* (April 21, 2002).

[12] The four categories are suggested by Hanks, *Capital Punishment*, 54-63. The list is a composite based on Stassen, "Biblical Teaching," *Review and Expositor* 93 (1996) 485-496; L.R. Bailey, *Capital Punishment: What the Bible Says* (Nashville: Abingdon, 1987) 19-22; and J. Cottrell, *Tough Questions—Biblical Answers* (Joplin: College Press, 1986) 56.

[13] Cottrell, *Tough Questions*, 56; Bailey, *Capital Punishment*, 31-32.

[14] B.W. Ballard, "The Death Penalty: God's Timeless Standard for the Nations," *Journal of the Evangelical Theological Society* 43 (2000) 471-487, maintains that he can demonstrate that Scripture requires the death penalty for all time and in every culture for seven crimes: incest, adultery, murder, homosexual acts, bestiality, cursing a parent, and being a sorcerer. He wants the death penalty in our society for each of these crimes. Bailey, *Capital Punishment*, 41, hints at a wider application than murder for the death penalty.

[15] Ballard, "Death Penalty," 472; V.J. Vellenga, "Is Capital Punishment Wrong?" in *Capital Punishment*, ed. by Stassen, 132; W.H. Baker, *On Capital Punishment* (Chicago: Moody, 1985) 30; J.D. Charles, "Sentiment as Social Justice," *Christian Research Journal* 17 (1994) 16-23.

[16] Hanks, *Capital Punishment*, 47; Yoder, *Debate*, 120; Marshal, *Beyond Retribution*, 216.

[17] שֹׁפֵךְ דַּם הָאָדָם – בָּאָדָם דָּמוֹ יִשָּׁפֵךְ. See J.H. Sailhamer, "Genesis," *Expositor's Bible Commentary* (Grand Rapids: Zondervan, 1990) II:94; C.A. Simpson, "Exegesis of Genesis," in *Interpreter's Bible*, ed. D.A. Buttrick (New York: Abingdon, 1952) 1:550; G. von Rad, *Genesis* (Philadelphia: Westminster, 1972) 132; N. Sarna, *Genesis* (Philadelphia: Jewish Publication Society, 1989) 61; H. Gunkel, *Genesis* (Macon, GA: Mercer University Press, 1997) 149. The saying is "masterfully pregnant both in form . . . and content" (von Rad, *Genesis*, 132).

[18] As Yoder observes, if governments followed Genesis 9:6 as a mandate for capital punishment, there would be no exceptions for minor killers, mentally ill killers, or even unin-

tentional killers. All would have to be put to death since they caused a human death. See Yoder, *Debate*, 127.

[19] Marshal, *Beyond Retribution*, 320; R. Westbrook, "Punishments and Crimes," in *Anchor Bible Dictionary*, ed. by D.N. Freedman (New York: Doubleday, 1992) V:546-556, esp. 551. Westbrook notes that the same ideology can be found in Hittite and Assyrian documents. Thus homicide was believed in the ancient near east to pollute the land. Bailey (*Capital Punishment*, 32) also points out this feature even though he favors use of the death penalty.

[20] See Marshal, *Beyond Retribution*, 208; La Chat, "Christian Ethics," 74. The translation is my own.

[21] The Mishnah existed for centuries as oral tradition and was finally written down around AD 200. Although some of its traditions are from the first century AD, most are from the second century AD.

[22] Thus if one sees a man with a sword pursuing someone into a building and later the man emerges with blood on his sword and a dead body is found inside, the man with the sword could still not be convicted since no one actually saw the crime. This story is in b. Sanhedrin 37b. See A. Steinsaltz, *The Essential Talmud* (London: Jason Aronson, 1976) 168; G.F. Moore, *Judaism* (Cambridge: Harvard, 1962) II:184.

[23] Rabbi Yohannan ben Zakkai allegedly dismissed a witness after questioning him about fig stems (b. Sanhedrin 41a). The rabbis made it a practice to place hurdles in front of capital punishment (b. Sanhedrin 81b). See G.J. Blidstein, "Capital Punishment: The Classic Jewish Discussion," in *Capital Punishment*, ed. by Stassen, 107-118.

[24] The word translated "cruel" is the Hebrew word: חוֹבְלָנִית (*ḥôblānîth*). M. Jastrow [*Dictionary of the Targumim, the Talmud Babli and Yerushalmi, and the Midrashic Literature* (New York: Judaica, 1975) I, 429] translates the word "tyrannical." H. Danby [*The Mishnah* (Oxford: Oxford University, 1933) 403] translates the word "destructive." J. Neusner [*The Mishnah* (New Haven: Yale University, 1988) 612] translates the word "murderous."

[25] The rules for the application of the death penalty are found in m. Sanhedrin. See also Moore, *Judaism* II, 184-187; Steinsaltz, *Essential Talmud*, 167-169; Blidstein, "Capital Punish-

ment," 107-118; L.I. Rabbinowitz, "Capital Punishment," *Encyclopedia Judaica* V:141-147; Hanks, *Capital Punishment*, 79-83.

[26]Those advocating capital punishment cite the following New Testament texts as proof that the New Testament does not teach against it: Matt 5:21-22; John 19:10-11; Acts 25:10. See Cottrell, *Tough Questions*, 61; Baker, *On Capital Punishment*, 49-62; and House, *Debate*, 63-66. Those who oppose capital punishment find its rejection in the following texts: John 7:53-8:11, Matt 5:33-38, Rom 12:19. See Stassen, "Biblical Teaching," 488-490; Williams, "Christian Ethics," 67; Marshall, *Beyond Retribution*, 230; N.P. Dake, "Who Deserves to Live? Who Deserves to Die? Reflections on Capital Punishment," in *Capital Punishment*, ed. by Stassen, 162.

[27]Cottrell, *Tough Questions*, 57.

[28]Ibid., 57, 61; Baker, *On Capital Punishment*, 69; House, *Debate*, 67; Charles, "Crime," 436.

[29]M. Borg, "A New Context for Romans XIII." *New Testament Studies* 19 (1972-1973) 205-281; O. Michel, *Der Brief an die Roemer* (Goettingen: Vandenhoeck und Ruprecht, 1966) 317. Michel suggests it was either "Jewish unrest" or early Christian "enthusiasm" (see next note).

[30]Michel, *Brief an die Roemer*, 314-315.

[31]See J. Friedrich, W. Poehlmann, and P. Stuhlmacher, "Zur historischen situation und Intention von Roem 13, 1-7," *Zeitschrift für Theologie und Kirche* 7, 131-166; J.A. Fitzmyer, *Romans* (New York: Doubleday, 1993) 35f, 662; P. Stuhlmacher, *Der Brief an die Roemer*, 179; N. Elliott, "Romans 13:1-7 in the Context of Imperial Propaganda," in *Paul and Empire*, ed. by R.A. Horsley (Harrisburg, PA: Trinity Press, 1997) 184-204.

[32]Friedrich et al., "Zur historischen Situation," cite Philo *Special Laws* II.92-95, III.159-163. Fitzmyer, *Romans*, and Stuhlmacher, *Der Brief*, cite Tacitus *Annals* 13.50-51; Suetonius *Nero* 10. Philo describes greedy tax collectors in Egypt. Tacitus and Suetonius narrate Nero's growing concern over complaints about taxation.

[33]Baker, *On Capital Punishment*, 69, cites M. Vincent, *Word Studies in the New Testament* (Grand Rapids: Eerdmans, 1946; 1887) III:164. Vincent's nineteenth-century study of Greek words obviously did not have the benefit of recent lexical information. This seems also to be the understanding of Rom 13:4 by C.K. Barrett, *The Epistle to the Romans* (New York:

Harper and Row, 1957) 247, and W. Sanday and A.C. Headlam, *The Epistle to the Romans* (Edinburgh: T. & T. Clark, 1902) 367-368.

[34]The *ius* (or *potestas*) *gladii* meant: "The right to try and punish capital crimes, delegated by the emperor to individual provincial governors." See P.G.W. Glare, ed., *Oxford Latin Dictionary* (Oxford: Clarendon, 1982) 765. See *CIL* 8.2582; and Ulpian, *Digest* 1.18.6.8; 2.1.3; Tacitus *Histories* 3.68; Dio Cassius 42.27.

[35]F.D. Danker, *A Greek-English Lexicon of the New Testament* (Chicago: University of Chicago, 2000) 662; W. Michaelis, "μαχαιρα," in G. Kittel et al., eds., *Theological Dictionary of the New Testament* (Grand Rapids: Eerdmans, 1967) 524-527.

[36]Friedrich et al., "Zur historischen Situation," 142-143. The Greek equivalent to *ius gladii* according to these authors was ξιφος φορειν. The authors cite several classical works such as Dio Cassius, Philostratus, and Josephus as well as a Mishnaic text that has borrowed the term into Hebrew. C.E.B. Cranfield (*The Epistle to the Romans* [Edinburgh: T. & T. Clark, 1979] II:667) agrees that Rom 13:4 does not refer to the *ius gladii* but on a different basis. J.D.G. Dunn (*Romans* [Dallas: Word, 1988] II:764) agrees with Cranfield but allows, unlike Cranfield, that Paul could still be referring to capital punishment in this verse.

[37]Friedrich et al., "Zur historischen Situation," 144. The authors cite a series of papyri from Egypt to demonstrate that μαχαιροφοροι "dagger carriers" (an expression similar to Rom 13:4) were police and not executioners.

[38]Marshall, *Beyond Retribution*, 231; Stassen, "Biblical Teaching," 488; Hanks, *Capital Punishment*, 152-156.

[39]See, e.g., L. Morris, *The Gospel according to John* (Grand Rapids: Eerdmans, 1995) 778: "The textual evidence makes it impossible to hold that this section is an authentic part of the Gospel." B.M. Metzger, *A Textual Commentary on the Greek New Testament* (London: United Bible Society, 1971) 219: "The evidence for the non-Johannine origin of the pericope of the adulteress is overwhelming." See also G.R. Beasley-Murray, *John* (Nashville: Thomas Nelson, 1999) 143-144; R.E. Brown, *The Gospel according to John* (New York: Doubleday, 1966) I:335-336.

[40]I prefer the translation "retaliate" to the translation "resist" for the Greek αντιστηναι

as H.D. Betz, *The Sermon on the Mount* (Minneapolis: Fortress, 1995) 280, translates. Resisting or opposing evil is of course what Jesus' disciples should do, but taking vengeance is another matter. For other interpretations see D.J. Weaver, "Transforming Nonresistance: From *Lex Talionis* to 'Do Not Resist the Evil One,'" in *The Love of Enemy and Nonretaliation in the New Testament*, ed. by W.M. Swartley (Louisville, KY: Westminster/ John Knox, 1992) 33. She lists also: Do not engage in rebellion and do not testify in court against an evildoer as possible interpretations of this expression. Likewise Weaver correctly indicates that the word I have translated "wickedness" (Gk: τω πονηρω) could be understood in the masculine gender as either a human assailant or as Satan himself; or in the neuter (as I have understood it) to mean "that which is wicked" (33-34).

[41]See G.A. McHugh, *Christian Faith and Criminal Justice* (New York: Paulist Press, 1978) 88-89; Yoder, *Debate*, 124-136; Hanks, *Capital Punishment*, 36-41; Stassen, "Biblical Teaching," 486. For the blood avenger in ancient Israelite culture see: Num 35:12,24,27; Josh 20:3,5. For excess in the blood feud see Gen 4:24, the boastful song of Lamech. On excessive and multiple punishments in ancient near eastern law codes see N. Sarna, *Exploring Exodus* (New York: Schocken, 1986) 176-178.

[42]For much of the following see W.D. Davies and D.C. Allison, *The Gospel according to Matthew* (Edinburgh: T. & T. Clark, 1988) I:540-543; and Betz, *The Sermon on the Mount*, 277-280.

[43]Jubilees 4:31-32; *Liber Antiquitatum Biblicarum* 44:10; Josephus, *Antiquities* 4.280; m. Makkot 1:6; Megilat Taanit 7:3; Philo, *Special Laws* 3.181-204.

[44]1QS 10:18-19; b. Shabbath 88b.

[45]See R.B. Hays, *The Moral Vision of the New Testament* (San Francisco: Harper Sanfrancisco, 1996) 319-325.

[46]Cottrell, *Tough Questions*, 60-61; Baker, *On Capital Punishment*, 51. Cf. Betz, *The Sermon on the Mount*, 278; Davies and Allison, *Gospel of Matthew*, I:542; D.A. Hagner, *Matthew 1-13* (Dallas: Word, 1993) 131.

[47]See Hays, *Moral Vision*, 319-325; and L. Schottroff, "Non-Violence and the Love of One's Enemies," in *Essays on the Love Commandment*, ed. by Schottroff et al. (Philadelphia: Fortress, 1978) 26.

[48]Cottrell, *Tough Questions*, 56-57; Baker, *On Capital Punishment*, 79. Baker states that the *lex talionis* is simply a literal application of retribution and that this is a universal divine principle. Cottrell states that the purpose for punishment of any kind is because the criminal deserves it as retribution. "The essence of justice is to see that each one gets what he deserves. . . ." See also Charles, "Sentiment as Social Justice," 16-23.

[49]See Olen and Barry, *Applying Ethics*, 245.

[50]See C.J. Cadoux, *The Early Church and the World* (Edinburgh: T. & T. Clark, 1925) 225-226. On the early church and the valuing of human life see D.A. Fiensy, "What Would You Do for a Living?" in *Handbook of Early Christianity: Social Science Approaches*, ed. by T. Blasi, J. Duhaime, and P.-A. Turcotte (New York: AltaMira, 2002) 555-574.

[51]Marshall, *Beyond Retribution*, 201, lists five considerations upon which Christians should reflect regarding capital punishment: exegetical (What is the meaning of Gen 9, John 8, and Rom 13?), hermeneutical (Is the Old Testament superseded by the New Testament?), theological (Is God a law-giver or a redeemer?), pragmatic (Is capital punishment beneficial to society?), philosophical (What is the nature of justice?).

[52]Baker, *On Capital Punishment*, 51, affirms that the *lex talionis* is a valid "principle of justice" which Jesus did not abrogate. Cottrell, *Tough Questions*, 57, maintains that the biblical rationale for punishment is retribution which is the principle in both the *lex talionis* and Rom 13:4. Charles, "Crime," 437, charges that Christians who use Matthew 5 to justify opposition to capital punishment undermine "God's eternal ethical standards." Ballard, "The Death Penalty," 471, argues that there is a transhistorical standard of right to which God holds every person. He then lists seven crimes for which God has and always will demand the death penalty (471-487).

[53]We could also cite as an example the issue of slavery. Slavery laws in the Old Testament and later slavery parenesis in the New Testament allowed for the institution to continue but went a long way toward protecting the life and worth of the individual. But would any Christian today argue that the institution of slavery should still be in existence in our society?

[54]See S.M. Ogden, "Theological Perspectives on Punishment," *Perkins School of Theology Journal* 39 (1986) 20-24. Ogden affirms that "You shall not kill" can only mean: "You shall control or minimize killing, killing only when and where failing to do so would result in an even greater violation of this fundamental principle" (22). Compare too the view of John Paul II who maintains that we should not practice the death penalty except in cases where it is absolutely necessary to defend society. In modern society such cases, maintains John Paul II, are very rare or maybe nonexistent. [See P. Black, "Do Circumstances Ever Justify Capital Punishment?" *Theological Studies* 60 (1999) 338-345, and T.R. Rourke, "The Death Penalty in Light of the Ontology of the Person: The Significance of *Evangelium Vitae*," *Communio* 25 (1998) 397-413.] I presume John Paul II means cases such as that cited above under public policy arguments in favor of capital punishment, number 4.

[55]Aquinas seems to have overlooked this point in his discussion of capital punishment. He maintained that the death penalty was acceptable because those who deviate from the rational order lose their human worthiness. To kill a person who retains his worthiness is intrinsically evil, but to kill a sinner is like killing an animal. An evil man, Aristotle said, is worse than an animal. See Black, "Circumstances," 339. But I would respond that we are worthy as human beings because God made us not because we are good persons.

[56]J.B.R. Gaie, "The Christian View on Capital Punishment," *AFER* 38 (1996) 362-375. Gaie's argument that execution is about the same as murder is a bit overreaching, however: The murderer feels aggrieved and therefore kills. Society feels aggrieved (with the murderer) and therefore kills.

[57]Charles, "Crime," 441, writes: "In keeping with its earthly mandate, the church is to instruct the state in matters of social justice." Ballard, "The Death Penalty," 486, wants those who believe in the Bible to support new laws that would facilitate the just administration of the death penalty. Williams, "Christian Ethics," 71, urges religious communities to help develop rules and models to approach capital punishment. Finally, Alexander Campbell, "Is Capital Punishment Sanctioned?" called on every patriot, philanthropist and Christian to use their influence in the public arena in support of capital punishment.

[58]M.W. Olson's essay for this reason is a disappointment. He urges support for the families of those executed but not for the families of murder victims. See Olson, "Practical Actions against Capital Punishment," *The Other Side* 33 (1997) 38-39.

Bibliography

Works in favor of Capital Punishment:

Bailey, L.R. *Capital Punishment: What the Bible Says*. Nashville: Abingdon, 1987.

The reflections, mostly from the Old Testament, by an Old Testament scholar.

Baker, W.H. *On Capital Punishment*. Chicago: Moody, 1985.

A solid assessment of the arguments for and against capital punishment from church history and the Bible.

Works opposed to Capital Punishment:

Hanks, G.C. *Capital Punishment and the Bible*. Scottdale, PA: Herald Press, 2002.

A good collection of arguments both for and against capital punishment by a self-confessed nontheologian.

Marshall, C.D. *Beyond Retribution*. Grand Rapids: Eerdmans, 2001.

The author places his discussion of capital punishment within a broader context of the Christian view of punishment.

Debates:

House, H.W., and J.H. Yoder. *The Death Penalty Debate*. Dallas: Word, 1991.

A debate between an evangelical scholar and a very influential Mennonite theologian.

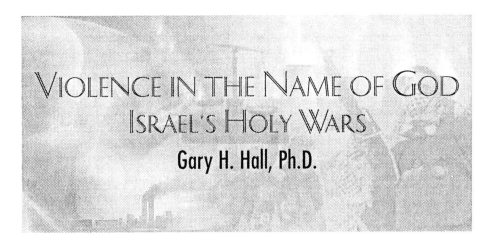

VIOLENCE IN THE NAME OF GOD
ISRAEL'S HOLY WARS
Gary H. Hall, Ph.D.

The Problem

Violence and war present a serious moral problem from almost any cultural or religious perspective. The problem becomes even more serious when the violence receives divine sanction. The fact that the Old Testament (OT) is full of war and presents God as commanding war presents a profound moral problem for the Christian.

War seems to be at the heart of the OT conceptualization of God. We are told as early as Exodus 15:3: "The LORD is a warrior; the LORD is his name."[1] When Israel marched through the wilderness following the Ark of the Covenant, they set out with a battle cry, "Rise up, O LORD! May your enemies be scattered; may your foes flee before you" (Num 10:35). Numbers 21:14 refers to the Book of the Wars of the LORD. Before attacking Jericho, Joshua met a warrior who apparently was God himself (Josh 5:13-15). Psalm 24:8 celebrates the God of Israel as the King of glory: "Who is this King of glory? The LORD strong and mighty, the LORD mighty in battle."

> The fact that the OT is full of war and presents God as commanding war presents a profound moral problem for the Christian.

It is easy to find texts that tell of Israel's destroying their enemies in battle, apparently at the command of God. Sihon, his army, and all women and children were destroyed (Deut 3:34). All of Jericho was to be destroyed (Josh 6:17) as well as Ai (Josh 8:26) and the southern and northern regions of Palestine (Josh 10:40; 11:12). Even the tribe of Benjamin within Israel met destruction at the command of the Lord (Judg 20:18). Samuel in God's name ordered Saul to kill all the Amalekites (1 Sam 15).

Furthermore, texts that speak of the destruction of enemies use a Hebrew word (ḥērem, חֵרֶם) that seems to mean that the killing took place because the enemy was in some way given over to God. Numbers 21:1-3; Deuteronomy 7:1-7; Joshua 7:12; 11:11; and other texts speak of Israel totally destroying men, women, and children because they are "devoted" to God.[2] Even in the directions for warfare in Deuteronomy, which on the whole suggest limits to warfare, enemies nearby are to be totally destroyed (Deut 20:16-17). Add to this the almost constant series of wars and battles in the books of Samuel and Kings and the portrait becomes even more disquieting.[3]

This picture is disturbing to Christians and non-Christians alike. We could perhaps understand if enemy armies were targeted for destruction, but when women and children are indiscriminately slaughtered we lose respect for a God who would command this. Many skeptics and atheists use the texts listed above as proof that the biblical God is not admirable but revolting. This attitude is best expressed in a famous passage in Fyodor Dostoyevsky's *The Brothers Karamazov*. Ivan the atheist protests, "I say nothing of the sufferings of grown-up people, they have eaten the apple . . . and the devil take them all! But these little ones!"[4] Furthermore, in the early twenty-first century, the phrase Holy War has become not just an idea, but an issue of painful relevance.[5]

This picture of the OT God stands in sharp contrast to the God revealed in the New Testament (NT). At least it seems so on the surface. Christians are taught that God is love and that the Christian should love one's enemies. The church is not a political entity but crosses all political and national boundaries. To continue to hold to a belief that God both commands and participates in warfare seems like ancient and unchristian ideology.

> To continue to hold to a belief that God both commands and participates in warfare seems like ancient and unchristian ideology.

Therefore, the modern Christian is faced with a dilemma. On the one hand the OT is a part of the Christian canon and is considered revelation by the church. Yet it presents what seems to be an unacceptable view of God. On the other hand, historically, Christians have used the OT as a basis to argue for Christian participation in war, whether it be something like the Crusades, the early Puritan battles with Indians,[6] or modern just-war theory.[7]

Possible Solutions

The problems outlined above are not new and several solutions have been offered over the centuries. (1) Many preachers and Bible teachers ignore these difficult texts. They prefer texts that are uplifting and positive. Difficult texts are best left for the scholars. However, this end run does not appeal to the thoughtful Christian. (2) Some Christians, including scholars and preachers, spiritualize the texts. The passages may have had relevance in the ancient context but now they speak to us about Christian spiritual warfare and provide guidance on how Christians are to face the evil power of Satan.[8] (3) Others view the OT as pre-Christian or sub-Christian in its morality on war and not a guide for Christians.[9] Similarly some scholars think the OT reflects ancient, primitive thinking.[10] (4) Other scholars dehistoricize the texts. Holy War was a later ideology or rhetoric read back into OT texts and was never actually practiced.[11] These last two positions do not remove the problem, for the texts are still part of the OT canon and need explanation, and the OT authors convey the impression that the events really happened. The above suggested solutions, often supported coherently by serious students of the Bible, are all deficient in some way and unacceptable. There should be a better solution.

Toward an Understanding of Holy War

A resolution of the vexing problem of God as Warrior and Holy War in the OT must start with some basic observations about the big picture. We must always keep in mind that the OT is a complex book grounded in the nature and character of a complex, sovereign Creator God of the universe. We must be willing to admit that some things are difficult to understand and that full understanding on some aspects of the character of God may await the full revelation of God in eternity. Humility before the biblical text is a necessary starting point.

> *In order to get the correct answer we must be sure we are asking the right question.*

In order to get the correct answer we must be sure we are asking the right question. The correct question is not, how could a good

263

God command war and destruction? The correct question is, does the viewpoint of the texts on holy war contradict the biblical understanding of God or is it consistent with the concept of a just and holy creator God?

The following nine observations are offered as an effort to provide a comprehensive approach that considers several complex issues.

1. It is an important teaching of the OT that the Creator God chose to act in human history. He was not the distant God of the deist but an immanent God both concerned about his creation and active in human life. The history of Israel in which God was active was not a mythical story or a suprahistory but was lived out in the real world as we know it.[12] From the beginning God "walked" with Adam and Eve (Genesis 2–3). He called Abraham to leave his family and country (Gen 12:1) and blessed his descendants. His most profound action for Israel was leading the nation out of slavery in Egypt to live in Canaan.

This important aspect of his character necessarily involved him in paradox and mystery. In order to act in human history he chose to act through humans to achieve his purposes. This meant a deliberate limitation of his power and holiness. This world is a world of sin and if God is going to be involved, he will have to be involved in what goes on in the world. He can only work in and through the lives of sinful and violent people. He must act in the world as it is. If he could only act through sinless people and nations, he would not be able to act at all. Consequently his purposes will be accomplished through limited means.

There are further limitations dictated by the fact that God's actions are described in human language, which limits the way the Bible can talk about God. Therefore, the language about God as a "Warrior" is metaphorical but it implies important truth about the nature of God and his redemptive work. It is not an abstraction but conveys his involvement in human life. It indicates that he will judge sin and violence by means of violence, but will also employ the same to redeem sinners (see below). It is primarily a demonstration of God's will and activity, not a revelation of his moral being.[13]

> God's actions are described in human language, which limits the way the Bible can talk about God.

Paradoxically this dramatic metaphor of God's involvement in human history has a positive end in view. It is an image of hope. The language "contains within it the seeds of hope for modern man. That hope is for the presence and participation of God in our own evil world, a world which might seem by definition to exclude even the possibility of knowing and experiencing God."[14]

2. The paradox is deepened by the election of Israel as the people of God and as a manifestation of the Kingdom of God on earth. The Kingdom in the OT was identified with the Israelite state and that has many implications. States are human organizations that have limited power, reflect particular ethnic and cultural values, and are involved in war and violence to establish themselves and to survive. The ancient Near East was an era of almost continuous warfare. For a state to emerge and survive it first had to be involved in offensive warfare to estab-

> *The ancient Near East was an era of almost continuous warfare. God's involvement in the life of Israel meant involvement in warfare.*

lish itself, then in defensive warfare to maintain its existence. Ancient Israel was no different.[15] Therefore, God's involvement in the life of Israel meant involvement in warfare.

3. We must investigate the Holy War concept in the OT carefully. The concept is not at the periphery of OT teaching but near the center. God as the Divine Warrior is a major theme not only in the OT but in the NT as well.[16] There are many facets to the concept.

God was the commander in chief of the armies of Israel (Josh 5:13-15). God is often referred to as the Lord of the armies or hosts (*ṣᵉvā'ôth*, צְבָאוֹת]) which refers to both Israelite armies and angelic armies (1 Sam 1:11; 17:45; 1 Kgs 18:15; Ps 24:10; Isa 1:9; 6:3; Jer 10:16; Micah 4:4; Zech 16:14; Mal 1:4).[17] Whenever the phrase was used, it invoked the image of the Divine Warrior and all its implications. The Lord as commander was present in the Ark of the Covenant and was at the head of the Israelites marching through the wilderness (Num 10:35). This presented the nation as the army of God with the Divine Warrior marching at the head. Thus the Ark led the way in the marches around Jericho (Josh 6:6,8,12). Israel would often take it into battle, even against God's wishes (1 Samuel 4–5).

Furthermore, God was the covenant God and divine King who promised victory over the enemies (Deut 28:7) and who used various methods to win: miracle (crossing of the Red Sea, Exodus 14), cooperation of nature (Josh 10:11, hailstones), the heavenly army (2 Sam 5:24), and even the Israelite troops (but not too many: Gideon, Judges 6–7). In all these instances, except the last, it could be argued that Israel's army had little to do in the battles but obey God. Even in the last case Israel was not to muster too large an army because then God might not get the credit. The principle is exemplified by David who fought by himself but credited the Lord with the victory, for God handed Goliath over to him (1 Sam 17:45-47). Millard Lind has argued that all OT war was a unilateral action by God in which Israel's basic responsibility was faith. According to Lind, if Israel took an active part, it was because she was disobedient to the Lord.[18]

Several have argued that Holy War is not the best term to use to reflect the situation in the OT.[19] Holy War is a term that originated in Islamic *jihad* and suggests making converts or coercing compliance by the sword. Neither the term nor the Islamic concept occurs in the OT. Gerhard von Rad apparently was the first to apply Holy War to the OT.[20] The OT itself speaks of Yahweh's going to war, not of Israel's conducting Holy War on his behalf. If Israel was involved in war it was in cooperation with Yahweh. Therefore, Yahweh War is a more fitting term. Von Rad tried to circumscribe Holy War with eleven elements.[21] However, his list was a composite from several texts. There were perhaps only three or four main elements

> The OT itself speaks of Yahweh's going to war, not of Israel's conducting Holy War on his behalf.

that characterized Yahweh War.[22] First, God commanded it (Joshua 6, Jericho; Josh 8:8, Ai; and other cities and land, Josh 10:40; 11:12,15,20,23). Second, it had a sacral nature. Before Israel attacked Jericho they circumcised the males and observed the Passover (Joshua 5). The practice of the "ban, devotion" (see below) also suggested the sacral character. Everything was given to God. Thus ". . . battle is portrayed as an act of worship."[23] The involvement of the Ark of the Covenant suggested its covenantal character. Third, Yahweh caused fear in the hearts of the enemies (Josh 5:1; 10:1-2) and used nature and miracle to achieve victory. Israel's role was to trust in the Lord and not be afraid (Josh 8:1; 10:8; 11:6). Fearful men were exempt from the battle (Judg 7:4; Deut 20:1,8). Finally, Yahweh War was a way for God to express, and Israel to experience, his sole sovereignty and kingship over Israel.[24] Those who violated this trust came under the sanction of the devoted thing

(Joshua 7, Achan and his family). If the above characteristics marked Yahweh War then not all war in the OT was Yahweh War. After Israel created the state and established dynastic rule, she established an army (despite Samuel's warning, 1 Sam 8:11-12). By Solomon's time the transformation to an independent state and standing army was complete. War was initiated for a variety of reasons. Some were directed by God (1 Kgs 20:13-28) and some were not (1 Kings 22). Yahweh gave laws to Israel for conducting war that were basically humane (Deuteronomy 20). Israel was to offer peace first. They were to go to war only if the offer was not accepted. Was it for this reason that Israel's kings had earned a reputation for leniency (1 Kgs 20:31)?

4. Understanding fully the concept of *ḥērem* (חֵרֶם), "devote, destroy" will also help clarify the issues. The notion is a complex one. Part of the problem is finding an English word or phrase that conveys the concept.[25] "Devoted, ban, totally destroy, completely destroy, annihilate, devoted thing, curse" and other words have been used.[26] Lilley begins his study with the observation that a military meaning is not necessary or primary.[27]

A nonmilitary use is evident in several texts. In Leviticus 27:20-29 a distinction is made between dedicating something or someone to God and devoting it. That which is dedicated can be redeemed, that which is devoted cannot. If property is devoted, it remains in possession of the priests (Num 18:14; Ezra 10:8). Devoted people however lost their life. Exodus 22:20 prescribes death for an idolater, and Deuteronomy 13:12ff. prescribes death for the entire community involved in idolatry. The latter situation includes the destruction of property also. In military situations the word has a variety of implications, depending on the context. Israel's defeat of Sihon and Og in the Transjordan in Deuteronomy 2:34 and 3:6 are described by *ḥērem*. In the context it seems to have the meaning of "destroy." The word is first applied to the Canaanites in Deuteronomy 7:2. The words "devote" (*ḥērem*) and "destroy, devour" (אָכַל, *'ākal*, v. 16) are used together, the latter verb adding to the meaning of the former. Further implications of devoting are spelled out (7:3-7). Israel is to make no covenant, show no mercy, and permit no intermarriage with the Canaanites. All implements of idolatry are to be smashed, cut down, and burned. In Deuteronomy 20:17 *ḥērem* is used to explain the phrase "do not leave anything alive that breathes" in verse 16.[28] In Joshua the noun is used of Jericho in 6:17,18, and the verb in 6:21.[29] The treasure was not to be destroyed but put in the Lord's treasury (6:19). The story of Achan in Joshua 7 shows the consequences of taking a devoted thing, in this case treasure, for personal use.[30] At Ai Israel put the people to the sword but carried off the livestock and plunder (Josh 8:24-27). So Jericho seems to be a special case as the firstfruit of the conquest. The people could take nothing for themselves. The case of the Amalekites in 1 Samuel 15 is a similar special case, for the Amalekites had a long history of plundering Israel (15:2; Exod 17:8-16; Deut 25:17-19) when they had the chance. In this case, as in Jericho, both people and plunder were to be destroyed. Lilley concludes that *ḥērem* referred to an "irrevocable renunciation of any interest in the object 'devoted.'"[31] When applied to persons, it meant enslavement or treaties were forbidden, so that "destroy" is a semantic equivalent. However, this was not the usual war policy as Deuteronomy 20 makes clear. Booty was usually made available to the people, Jericho and the Amalekites being exceptions. Application of the principle did not make the war holy, but it did introduce a "theological dimension which forbade taking booty, or prisoners, or both, according to the instructions given in the particular case."[32]

However, this refined understanding still does not explain the practice of *ḥērem*. Why would God apply the concept to the Canaanites and Amalekites? Niditch has suggested that it was intended to reduce lust for war by removing the possibility of the common spoils of ancient warfare, human slaves and wealth.[33] It may have also been a disincentive for war, for human slaves were a main source of armies in the ancient world.[34]

But, there is more to the concept, for it was a part of the larger picture of Israel's conquest of the Canaanites and settlement in the land. Two major reasons for *ḥērem* must be considered: the purity of Israel and judgment on the nations.

First of all, Israel was God's witness in the world, and she was to reflect his character as a holy God by being a holy people (Lev 11:44; 19:1; 20:7,26, etc.). She was to bear witness to what God originally intended for his people, living an ordered life in an ordered world. This could not happen if she was influenced by foreign culture and idolatry. Therefore, Israel needed a sacred space, a secure land in which she could live under the covenant. There was also a cosmic dimension to this struggle, for God was fighting the gods of the nations. But the cosmic battle was being fought on the earthly level against the forces of evil displayed in the Canaanite culture and religion. "In other words, holy war is a spiritual battle fought out on the historical plane; it is an event in the arena of history that possesses cosmic, spiritual significance."[35] To secure this sacred place Israel had to destroy the Canaanites and their idolatry so that she could rightly worship Yahweh as the only, true God. The *ḥērem* enabled Israel to achieve a world ordered by God by destroying the disordered, chaotic world of the Canaanite civilization. By this Israel was able to introduce the created order into the land. "In a world of chaos and disorder, Israel was to bear witness through its worship and daily routines to the divine intent for a good and ordered creation."[36] The most important part of the book of Joshua is the second half which details the parceling out of the land to the Israelite tribes (chapters 13–22). Every family had its portion of land to bear witness to God's intent for creation. Land and wealth were not to be the possession of a powerful few. This stood in direct opposition to the Canaanite system of city-states which concentrated power in a few, promoted a caste system, and practiced a religion that was used as a tool for oppression.

In this sacred space Israel could experience the sovereign rule of God in real terms in time and space. God was king, judge, and warrior. He was totally in charge of Israel's life and she could recognize in the various aspects of her existence that God was at work, even in defending her.[37]

The second major reason for the *ḥērem* was its role in God's judgment on the Canaanites.[38] When God promised the land to Abraham in Genesis 15 he spoke of a delay of the promise because "the sin of the Amorites has not yet reached its full measure" (Gen 15:16). By this he implied that he was willing to wait on the inhabitants of Canaan. Perhaps they would yet turn from their sin. If they did not, he would bring judgment on them, but he was not ready to do so. Therefore, when in Deuteronomy 7 the command was given to Israel to drive out the seven nations in Canaan and destroy their idolatry, we are to understand that now the sin of the Amorites had reached its full measure. Their society had become totally corrupt and had defiled the land. The land was ready, to use Leviticus's colorful phrase, "to vomit them out" (Lev 18:24–25; 20:22). Details of the vile nature of Canaanite religion are abundantly clear from the discovery of major literary texts in the twentieth century.[39] Its main features were child sacrifice, sacred prostitution, fertility cult, divination, and a cult for the dead. Some elements of this culture were reflected in Leviticus 18:1-24,27. Now was the time for judgment on their corrupt religion and society, and Israel would serve as God's instrument of that judgment (Deut 9:4-5).[40] But even then it was God's action, for he would "drive out" before them the many nations and "deliver" them into Israel's hands (Deut 7:1-2,22-23). In the process Israel was to destroy the people, their idols, and their wealth. But Israel was not to think of herself as more virtuous than the Canaanites or as God's avenging angel (Deut 9:6). They were little better for they were a stiff-necked people.

What was at stake was God's justice: would he execute righteous judgment on evil or not? The answer is yes. Abraham knew that the Judge of the whole earth would do right (Gen 18:25). Christians do not object to the idea of God's eschatological judgment on the wicked or his providential verdict on sin. Therefore, there should be no objection to the fact that in this case at least God's eschatological judgment had entered into the present. For the Canaanites this judgment meant death, but for Israel it meant redemption and safety in the land. But much more was at stake than this. What was at stake was God's intended redemption of his whole creation. "The goal was for a people to be formed who would bear witness to that intent by dwelling in the land in a way different from that of the Canaanites."[41]

The judgment on the Canaanites was a one-time event. God's command for aggressive war was not a mandate but an exception. The rules of warfare in Deuteronomy 20 were quite specific. Only Canaanites, that is, those who lived in the land, were to be totally destroyed. No other nation was to be treated as they were. Israel was "not to expect that even God would call on them again for this strange work of judgment."[42]

> God's command for aggressive war was not a mandate but an exception.

We must also point out that behind every divine pronouncement of judgment is an "if." If a nation would turn from the evil and repent, God would relent and not bring on it the threatened harm (Jer 18:7-10). So the Canaanites had centuries to turn to God. Furthermore, Rahab made clear that they had recently heard of God's work through Israel (Josh 2:9-14). She responded in faith and was spared. We can assume the same option was available to all Canaanites.[43]

Some object to God using human agents like Israelites to carry out his judgment. The OT makes it clear that God does the same to Israel. He used both Assyria (Isaiah 10) and Babylon (Jeremiah 21) as instruments of judgment and destruction against Israel and Judah. The theology of God's retributive justice in the OT is that he

> *The theology of God's retributive justice in the OT is that he uses Israel as an instrument to exercise judgment on the nations, and he uses the nations to exercise judgment on Israel.*

uses Israel as an instrument to exercise judgment on the nations, and he uses the nations to exercise judgment on Israel. If one objects to the former, he should object to the latter.

The above explanation is fundamental to understanding Yahweh War and should meet many objections. But perhaps it still does not resolve totally the issue of the children dying. Adult Canaanites had made their choice, but the children seem to be innocent victims. To come to a better understanding we need to probe deeper into the ancient world. Their mind-set and anthropology were much different than our modern one. In the ancient world the community or family was the most important social group. Individuals were not important by themselves but only as part of a larger group. The fortunes of the group took precedence over the

> *In the ancient world the community or family was the most important social group.*

individual. This "corporate personality" idea[44] or better "corporate solidarity" meant that the whole group could be treated as a single individual (1 Sam 5:1-11; the whole people of Ekron are referred in the singular). Also a single representative person could embody the whole group (the Suffering Servant in Isaiah 53). A combination of both is also found, where an individual embodies the group and the group is treated like an individual. The case of Achan in Joshua 7 is an example of this perspective. The sin of one affected the entire extended family. It also meant that an "innocent" individual as a part of a wicked group would suffer with the group. Some examples can be found in the death of the wives and children of Korah, Dathan, and Abiram because of the latter's sin (Numbers 16), the condemnation of Israel because of Saul's violation of a treaty with the Gibeonites (2 Samuel 21), and judgment on a whole city for lack of a few righteous people (Genesis 18–19).[45] Moderns may find this concept difficult to understand, but one can ask whether modern, western radical individualism has made things better or worse for "innocent" children and others.[46]

On the other hand, there was a positive side to this concept. God was willing to treat a larger group with grace for the sake of a few members in it. He was willing to spare wicked Sodom for as few as ten righteous (Gen 18:32) or the whole city of Jerusalem for the sake of one (Jer 5:1). He blessed Judah for David's sake (2 Kgs 8:18; 19:34) and the house of Obed-Edom for the sake of the Ark (2 Sam 6:11 ff).[47]

5. To fully understand the *ḥērem* principle we must recognize that God was willing to apply it to Israel as well. If Israel rebelled against God, he would turn his devastating judgments on her and destroy her. Thus he warned Israel as early as Deuteronomy 28:25-26 that if they disobeyed they would be defeated by their enemies. This was a direct reversal of the promise of Deuteronomy 28:7. Israel's attack on Ai under Joshua failed for this reason. Israel had sinned through Achan's disobedience (Josh 7:10-12), and the whole nation suffered. Near the end of Israel's history the prophet Jeremiah made this point abundantly clear. "I myself will fight against you with an outstretched hand and a mighty arm in anger and fury and great wrath" (Jer 21:5). Jeremiah uses the word *ḥērem* in 25:9 against Israel. God will use his "servant Nebuchadnezzar king of Babylon" to come up against the land and completely destroy (*ḥērem*) it. Jeremiah later lamented that God had become Israel's enemy (Lam 2:5). The historian(s) who wrote 1 and 2 Kings emphasized this point also.[48] From this we learn of God's absolute justice. The *ḥērem* is not something that was used only to favor Israel; it represented God's judgment against any sinful people, including his elect.

6. The metaphor of God as the Divine Warrior is not limited to one portion of the OT. Longman and others have shown that it is a prominent theme throughout the whole OT.[49] An important part of this theme is its future orientation. God as Divine Warrior would be the future deliverer of Israel. God provided a picture of the future to the prophets that included his appearance to fight on behalf of his people. He would intervene to free them from oppression and injustice and establish them anew in the land. The theme appears especially vivid in Daniel and Zechariah. Daniel had a vision of "one like a son of man" who was given power and authority, everlasting dominion that would never pass away, and a kingdom that would

272

never be destroyed (Dan 7:13-14). These are strong military terms. Zechariah saw the Day of the Lord coming when the Lord would fight against the nations and would establish himself as king over all the nations (Zech 14:3-9). This is how the OT ends.

7. We need to recognize that the texts on Yahweh War and Divine Warrior are not the only texts in the OT that address the issue of war. There are a group of texts that call the people to trust in God and renounce trust in wealth or military might. "Some trust in chariots and some in horses, but we trust in the name of the LORD our God" (Ps 20:7; compare Ps 33:16-17). Among the sins that Isaiah condemns are the accumulation of horses and chariots (Isa 2:6; 22:8-11). Second Chronicles 20 relates the account of Jehoshaphat's war with the Moabites and Ammonites. Jehoshaphat responded to their attack with a prayer to God. He was assured by a prophet not to fear but trust in God. When the Israelite army went to the battle, led by singers praising God, they found that the attackers had turned on each other and destroyed their armies.

Further, the OT has a vision of God ending all war and bringing peace.[50] Isaiah looks to the future when peace will break out and all nations will come to Jerusalem to learn of the Lord (Isa 2:1-5). He also anticipates the time when God will anoint a descendant of David with his Spirit and peace will ensue (Isaiah 11). From these texts we learn that Israel could live in the world by trusting in God not military prowess. Peace would come by the hand of God, not through her superiority.

> The OT has a vision of God ending all war and bringing peace.

8. As Christians we must acknowledge that the theme of God as Warrior is not confined to the OT. God or Jesus as Warrior appears throughout the NT as well.[51] In the Gospels the theme is noticeable in the conflict between Jesus and demonic powers, and in the theme of the coming Son of man on the clouds which goes back to Daniel 7.

John the Baptist was the forerunner to Jesus. As the new Elijah in the wilderness he prepared the way for Jesus. He announced the coming of the Messiah in terms reminiscent of warfare. The Messiah was more powerful than John and would winnow and thresh and burn up the chaff (Matt 3:11-12). Matthew understood that the early life of Jesus recapitulated the exodus of Israel out of Egypt into the wilderness (Matt 2:15; 4:1). The Messiah of God was both Israel and the Divine Warrior of the OT wrapped into one. His conflict in the wilderness with Satan himself introduced the cosmic dimension of Jesus' ministry at the very beginning.

The cosmic and spiritual aspects of Jesus' warfare are abundantly attested in the Gospels with the numerous conflicts with demonic forces. Jesus began preaching repentance for the Kingdom was near (Mark 1:15), an eschatological announcement that the rule of the Divine Warrior of the OT was near. In the Nazareth synagogue he read from Isaiah 61 (Luke 4:17-21), invoking an image of the victory of God over the powers of evil. Chased out of Nazareth, Jesus went to Capernaum and was immediately confronted with a demon-possessed man. This was a challenge to his authority by the ruler of this world. The demon recognized that Jesus had come to destroy him (Luke 4:34). The cosmic battle was engaged. This conflict continued throughout Jesus' ministry.[52]

Jesus' use of the son of man imagery from Daniel reflects a conscious decision to identify with that militaristic figure (Matt 24:29-31; Mark 13:24-27; 14:62; Luke 21:25-28). His coming on the clouds will be accompanied by cosmic alterations. These alterations are associated in the OT with God coming in the future to totally destroy (ḥērem) the nations (Isa 34:2; 13:10), bringing his warriors against them in judgment (Joel 3:9-16). Jesus will come with "power and great glory. And he will send his angels with a loud trumpet call . . ." (Matt 24:30-31). The language is that of military conquest. The trumpet call is a call to battle, reminiscent of the Israelite trumpets used in the conquest of Jericho.

Paul can look back at the life, death, and resurrection of Jesus and use military language to describe the outcome. Thus Jesus "disarmed the powers and authorities" and "made a public spectacle of them" (Col 2:15). This is clear war language. Paul also cites an OT divine warrior hymn (Psalm 68) in Ephesians 4:8, "When he ascended on high, he led captives in his train and gave gifts to men."[53] For Paul, Jesus the Messiah is also the triumphant warrior who defeats the cosmic forces of evil and leads his people to freedom.

9. The transference of warrior imagery to Jesus demonstrates how the NT transforms the metaphor. In Jesus, the Warrior becomes the crucified God. God in Jesus receives the brunt of evil and violence. Israel was established by the use of violence, but the new kingdom

> In Jesus, the Warrior becomes the crucified God.

is established through Jesus Christ when he receives violence. This marks the transformation of the Kingdom into a spiritual reality. The new kingdom is not of this world (John 18:36). Its members do not fight with physical implements of human foes but with spiritual weapons for a spiritual battle (Eph 6:10-18; 2 Cor 10:3-4; 1 Thess 5:8; 2 Tim 2:3-4). For Paul, the Christian is not exempt from war or conflict, but the battle has shifted from the physical to the spiritual plane. In one respect the church is in the same situation as ancient Israel. She has to fight for her existence and is constantly under attack.

> For Paul, the Christian is not exempt from war or conflict, but the battle has shifted from the physical to the spiritual plane.

Likewise, when Paul spoke of the future return of the Messiah, he did so in warrior terminology. The Lord will be "revealed from heaven in blazing fire with his powerful angels" (2 Thess 1:7). These angels are his "holy ones" (1 Thess 3:13). They are certainly the heavenly hosts, the army of the Lord of the OT. Finally, when Jesus triumphs over all his foes, he will hand the kingdom over to God the father. "Then the end will come, when he hands over the kingdom to God the Father after he has destroyed all dominion, authority and power. For he must reign until he has put all his enemies under his feet. The last enemy to be destroyed is death" (1 Cor 15:24-26). This passage is replete with military language.

In the NT the most vivid battle language is reserved for the book of Revelation which describes the final cosmic battle between Jesus Christ and Satan and his armies. The imagery begins in the first chapter with the description of "someone like a son of man" who has a sword coming out of his mouth (1:12-16). John also sees a lamb that was slain (5:6), a clear reference to the crucified Christ. This lamb becomes a figure of strength and warfare. The conflict between God and Satan takes place on earth and in the heavens. The most explicit language is used in Revelation 19:11-21. The passage is full of allusions to Isaiah, Ezekiel, and the Psalms. The rider on a white horse has a sword in his mouth (Isa 11:4; 49:2). His garments are red from the blood of the winepress that has been trodden in wrath (Isa 63:1-3). He will rule with an iron scepter (Ps 2:9) over the conquered nations. When the beast gathers to make war against him, the beast is captured and thrown into the fiery lake. The birds gorge themselves on the remains of the slain army (Ezek 39:17-20;

Isa 34:1-7). This vivid language that describes the victory of the Divine Warrior lamb surpasses anything we find in the OT. As in the OT this Warrior even fights against God's people, the church, when it rebels (Rev 2:16).

We find throughout the Bible the image of God as Warrior. In the OT, God fights against enemies of flesh and blood. In the NT, Jesus leads the church in battle against spiritual forces of evil. These battles anticipate the final war that takes place at the end of time. Therefore the portrayal of God as a Warrior engaged in "holy" war is not confined to only one part of the Christian canon. God's desire to defeat evil to carry out his redemptive plan is the key theme of the Bible. God has recruited his people, Israel and the church, in this battle. His victory, which certainly has and will involve violence, is crucial to our future hope. Is the violence done in the name of the Lord in the book of Revelation any different than that done in Joshua? Perhaps not, though Christians and others seem to be more comfortable with a judging God who destroys men, women, and children in the future rather than in the past. Or maybe we are always looking beyond the war in Revelation to the beautiful picture of the new heaven and earth.

Summary

We have tried to present in this essay the holistic understanding of the problem of divinely directed violence in the OT. The foundational principle is that God has been at work from the beginning of the world to redeem his creation. We observed that the Creator God chose to work actively in this world through the Israelite state. This necessarily involved him in real history and limited many of his actions to human agency. By creating and sustaining Israel, God became known as the Divine Warrior, a metaphor used throughout both the OT and the NT. In this guise God fought for Israel and against her enemies. But this was not Holy War, that is, not war for conversion or coercion. The wars he fought for Israel had a narrow limit. God led in establishing Israel in the Promised Land. This kind of war, best called Yahweh War, had two purposes: to create a sacred space in which Israel could bear witness to his holiness, and to execute judgment on the vile sins of the Canaanites, a judgment that had been delayed for centuries. There were also cosmic dimensions to this war. But because God is a just God, he also applied

Yahweh War against Israel as a judgment when she rebelled against the covenant. We also discovered that wars of conquest and defense are only part of the OT picture. There is also a call in the OT to abandon instruments of war, trust in God, and await his bringing peace to all nations. We also learned that as Christians we must acknowledge that Jesus is presented as a Divine Warrior in the NT. He was in a cosmic battle with the forces of Satan from the beginning of his ministry and Revelation depicts his final victory. As Christians we are called to participate in this cosmic and spiritual battle by putting on the armor of a soldier.

By these observations we have tried to show that the "ethical" dilemma of the killing of "innocents" in the OT is understandable in the large picture. God is the just Judge who will do right and eventually will right every wrong and bring judgment on the wicked. The fact that his eschatological judgment broke into human history from time to time in the OT should be understandable and not an occasion for attacks on the ethics of the OT.

Some will probably not be satisfied with our explanation, but hopefully the contributions of this study will be helpful to the thoughtful questioner.

Concluding Observations

Jeph Holloway asks two important questions for the dilemma of war in the OT: Whose dilemma? Which holy war?[54] The context in which we evaluate the violence in the OT is our modern one in which the question is "How could a God of love sanction killing in war?" There is a tone of moral superiority and condescension to this question. The tone of the question suggests that the OT represents a primitive perspective, but we moderns are more advanced in our thinking. However, the situation in the OT can be evaluated from other contexts. Some people find what God did for Israel in the Exodus and in the subsequent conquest of the land very liberating. Here is a God who cares for the oppressed and poor and works in real history to free them.[55] From a different perspective, for many Muslims, Holy War is not a problem but is carried out in obedience to God.

For the ancient Israelite and the modern Muslim there is no distinction between church and state, religious activity and political action. All of life was and is a whole piece, and faith cannot be separated from activities in any sphere. Our modern worldview, that it is crucial to have a secular state totally separated from religion, is a product of the Enlightenment. The sixteenth- and seventeenth-century Enlightenment's agenda was to separate society from religion, especially Christianity, by denying God and belief in immortality. This was accomplished by first destroying confidence in the Bible, then making God irrelevant through science, then pushing religious discourse out of the public square.[56] In our culture, religious belief is supposed to be an entirely private matter and has no place in public discourse. Therefore, it is difficult for the modern mind to understand how the sacred and secular can be unified.[57]

It is also difficult for the modern mind to understand that some may think the development of a purely secular culture is a monstrosity and utterly reprehensible, that a culture devoid of transcendence and purpose is dangerous. The development of nations and cultures in the twentieth century based on the secular vision lends support to those who view such a vision as dangerous. The twentieth century, the era of the triumph of the secular state, saw more wars and more slaughter of humans in the name of the state than in all the previous centuries of human history. The estimates vary, but one puts the number killed in war in the twentieth century in excess of 100 million.[58] Add to this the 100 million citizens who were killed by communist states.[59] Add also the millions of babies killed in abortions. This slaughter is unprecedented in human history. In light of this, the few hundred or thousand killed by Joshua's army pale to insignificance. As Holloway observes, this "is a reminder that we have found plenty of nonreligious causes for which we are willing to kill."[60] It seems clear that a society that considers the state to be god is exceedingly more dangerous than a society grounded in belief in a transcendent God.

> It seems clear that a society that considers the state to be god is exceedingly more dangerous than a society grounded in belief in a transcendent God.

The secular state also fails to recognize the importance of religious faith for many people. It cannot understand that people would be willing to die for their beliefs. Many missteps have been made and will continue to be made in various areas of the world, such as the Middle East, until this is understood. "Religion as a matter of life and death? Hardly. National interest, economic systems, ideology, cheap oil—now those are matters worth dying for, even killing for. But not religion."[61]

Does this mean then that Christians should campaign for the reintroduction of the holy war concept into public life? No. Holy war or Yahweh War was one facet in the history of redemption. Yahweh War was crucial to the establishment and survival of Israel as the kingdom of God in the OT. That situation is unrepeatable. Yet the NT understands the Warrior God is still at work and that God's people are still involved in the cosmic struggle with evil. The weapon given to the Christian to combat this evil is the gospel, the message of the cross. The message of the crucified God is the

> The message of the crucified God is the means the church is to use to combat evil and introduce peace.

means the church is to use to combat evil and introduce peace. In many settings this may seem as foolish as Joshua and Israel marching around Jericho for seven days. But it is the means God has chosen to win the war.

How do we then handle the ethical dilemma? To ask "why" is usually the wrong question. The question we should ask is, for what end, for what purpose?[62] God has chosen to work in human history and we may not know the why of what he does. But we can often understand the purpose. Yahweh War in the OT had a clear purpose. It was working to the end of bringing redemption to the whole world.[63] As Christians we reap the benefits of this divine plan. Because we are convinced that the God who worked out this plan is compassionate to save, we can be assured that he deals just-

> To ask "why" is usually the wrong question. The question we should ask is, for what end, for what purpose?

ly with all people, even the "innocent ones" who may suffer along the way. From the larger biblical perspective there are some things worse than death. Israel was called to live by faith and trust in the Divine Warrior without fear. So are we: "But take heart! I have conquered the world" (John 16:33b, NRSV).[64]

Notes

[1]Quotes are from the NIV unless otherwise indicated.

[2]See further in chapter for a discussion of the meaning of this word.

[3]The Hebrew word for "war, battle," מִלְחָמָה, occurs 319 times in the OT.

[4]Dostoyevsky's Ivan Karamazov is thought by many to give one of the most cogent and

profound critiques of the problem of evil in all of world literature. His case is passionately made from real-life examples of horrible treatment of innocent children by parents and others. With this he intended to refute the standard free-will argument as the above brief quote shows. Adults, by their choices, earned suffering and punishment, but not children. See the excellent analysis by Ralph C. Wood, "Ivan Karamazov's Mistake," *First Things* 128 (December 2002) 29-36.

[5]"But it remains true that there is no way of attributing mass carnage and vindictive slaughter to a God worth believing in. Even the fiercest believer among us must, I think, admit that these operations were the work of human beings who had wrongly convinced themselves that God was on their side." Thomas Cahill, *The Gifts of the Jews: How a Tribe of Desert Nomads Changed the Way Everyone Thinks and Feels* (New York: Doubleday, 1998) 246.

[6]Susan Niditch, *War in the Hebrew Bible* (New York: Oxford University, 1993) 3-4. Niditch summarizes a sermon by Cotton Mather in which he sees the Puritans as ancient Israel and the Indians as Canaanites to be driven out. This line of reasoning has been common in the history of the church.

[7]Derek Kidner, "OT Perspectives on War," *The Evangelical Quarterly* 62/2 (1985) 108-111; Arthur Holmes, "The Just War," in *War: Four Views*, ed. by Robert G. Clouse (Downers Grove, IL: InterVarsity, 1981) 115-135; Peter C. Craigie, *The Problem of War in the Old Testament* (Grand Rapids: Eerdmans, 1978) cites research that shows that among Christians the more orthodox they are the more militaristic (14-15).

[8]H.A. Ironside, *Addresses on the Book of Joshua* (Neptune, NJ: Loizeaux Brothers, 1950) 68.

[9]Willard M. Swartley, *Slavery, Sabbath, War and Women* (Scottdale, PA: Herald Press, 1983) 118, referring to a document published by the peace churches and the International Fellowship of Reconciliation; John Bright, *The Authority of the Old Testament* (Nashville: Abingdon, 1967) 245; Myron Augsburger as quoted in Swartley, *Slavery*, 140.

[10]Jeph Holloway, "The Ethical Dilemma of Holy War," *SWJT* 41 (1998): 45, referring to an article by Norman Gottwald.

[11]Moshe Weinfeld, *Deuteronomy 1–11* (New York: Doubleday, 1991) 365; N. Gottwald,

"Holy War," *IDBS* 942; N. Lohfink, "חרם, haram," *TDOT* 5:193-198. Craigie remarks that the last two views contradict each other. The former sees the concept as early and primitive and the latter as late and idealistic. A conservative variant is that holy war and especially the *ḥērem* was a policy that was never implemented. See Eugene Merrill, *Deuteronomy* (Nashville: Broadman and Holman, 1994) 180. Support can be found by comparing Deut 7:2 with verses 3-4 and 22. See also Josh 10:20 which says the mentioned cities were totally destroyed but some escaped. Compare Josh 10:36-39 with 15:13-17 which recounts that the same conquered cities had to be retaken.

[12]Patrick D. Miller Jr., "God the Warrior," *Interpretation* 19 (1964) 44.

[13]Craigie, *War*, 42; Walther Eichrodt, *Theology of the Old Testament*, 2 vols. (Philadelphia: Westminster Press, 1961) 1:228-229.

[14]Craigie, *War*, 97. See also Holloway, "Ethical Dilemma," 53-55.

[15]Craigie, *War*, 65-74.

[16]Tremper Longman III and Daniel G. Reid, *God Is a Warrior* (Grand Rapids: Zondervan, 1995); idem., "Divine Warrior," *Dictionary of Biblical Imagery*, 210-213; Miller, "God the Warrior," 41. For the NT theme see points 8 and 9.

[17]Miller, "God the Warrior," 39; the phrase occurs nearly 250 times in the OT, often in the prophets.

[18]Millard Lind, *Yahweh Is a Warrior: The Theology of Warfare in Ancient Israel* (Scottdale, PA: Herald Press, 1980) 171.

[19]Craigie, *War*, 49-50.

[20]Gerhard von Rad, *Holy War in Ancient Israel*, trans. and ed. by Marva J. Dawn and John H. Yoder (Grand Rapids: Eerdmans, 1991). The original was published in German in 1958. His schematization is now widely questioned; Gottwald, "Holy War," 942-943.

[21]Von Rad, *Holy War*, 41-51.

[22]Holloway, "Ethical Dilemma," 49-52; Tremper Longman, "לחם," *NIDOTTE* 2:785-789.

[23]Longman and Reid, "Divine Warrior," 34.

[24]Holloway, "Ethical Dilemma," 52.

[25]J.P.U. Lilley, "Understanding the *Ḥerem*," *TB* 44/1 (1993) 169-177; Lohfink, "חרם," 181-185.

[26]The Greek translators used mostly two words, *anathema* and *olethron*. The former is familiar from the English. The latter word means "destroy." The NIV most often translates *ḥērem* as "totally or completely destroyed, devoted things or devoted" which it then footnotes with this explanatory sentence, "The Hebrew term refers to the irrevocable giving over of things or persons to the LORD, often by totally destroying them." See for example Num 18:14. The verb occurs 51 times and the noun 29 times in the Hebrew Bible, mostly in narrative texts.

[27]Lilley, "Understanding," 173.

[28]Ibid., 174.

[29]The NIV "They devoted . . . and destroyed. . . ." translates one word, the verb form of *ḥērem*.

[30]*Ḥērem* occurs in 7:1,11,12,13, and 15.

[31]Lilley, "Understanding," 176.

[32]Ibid., 177.

[33]Niditch, *War*, 35.

[34]Holloway, "The Ethical Dilemma," 56, quoting John Yoder.

[35]Ibid., 57.

[36]Ibid., 58.

[37]Miller, "God the Warrior," 44.

[38]J.P.U. Lilley, "The Judgment of God: The Problem of the Canaanites," *Themelios* 22 (1997) 3-12.

[39]See for example Michael Coogan, *Stories from Ancient Canaan* (Philadelphia: Westminster, 1978); Helmer Ringgren, *Religions of the Ancient Near East* (Philadelphia: Westminster, 1973) 27-54; John Day, "Canaan, Religion of," *ABD* 1:832-837. "These heathen practices were not only degrading and seductive, they were often backed by ruthless power," according to John W. Wenham (*The Goodness of God* [Downers Grove, IL: InterVarsity, 1974] 127). See pages 125-128 for a helpful description of the situation Israel faced. Jezebel's actions in 1 Kings 18 and 19 are an example of the ruthless power at work.

[40]Craigie, *War*, 74.

[41]Holloway, "The Ethical Dilemma," 61.

[42]William Brenton Greene, "The Ethics of the Old Testament," in *Classical Evangelical Essays*, ed. by Walter Kaiser (Grand Rapids: Baker, 1972) 222.

[43]Walter Kaiser, *Toward Old Testament Ethics* (Grand Rapids: Zondervan, 1983) 368.

[44]Coined by H. Wheeler Robinson, *The Christian Doctrine of Man* (Edinburgh: T. & T. Clark, 1911) 8; idem., *Corporate Personality in Ancient Israel* (Philadelphia: Fortress, 1964). Robinson has been criticized for lack of clarity and relying on an illegitimate anthropological theory. Therefore, "corporate solidarity" is a better term. See John Rogerson, *Anthropology and the Old Testament* (Atlanta: John Knox, 1978) 55-59; Kaiser, *Ethics*, 67-70.

[45]Kaiser, *Ethics*, 69-70.

[46]This point will be discussed further later in this chapter.

[47]Kaiser, *Ethics*, 70.

[48]Lind, *Yahweh Is a Warrior*, 173.

[49]Longman and Reid, *God Is a Warrior*, 13-88; "Divine Warrior," *DBI*, 210-213.

[50]Kidner, "OT Perspectives," 113-114.

[51]Longman and Reid, *God Is a Warrior*, 91-192.

[52]See ibid., 91-118 for details.

[53]This is a quote of Ps 68:18. Psalm 68:17 refers to the chariots of God, and verse 21 speaks of God's crushing the heads of his enemies. Therefore Paul's quote is laden with warrior images in its original context.

[54]Holloway, "The Ethical Dilemma," 63.

[55]Several Liberation Theologies are built on this premise. Violence in the service of liberation from injustice is acceptable and approved by both the OT and the NT. See for example Charles Bayer, *A Guide to Liberation Theology for Middle-class Congregations* (St. Louis: CBP Press, 1986); and James Cone, *Speaking the Truth* (Grand Rapids: Eerdmans, 1986).

[56]See the excellent analysis in Benjamin Wiker, *Moral Darwinism* (Downers Grove, IL: InterVarsity, 2002).

[57]One cannot imagine Ps 149:6 reflecting a modern attitude: "Let the high praises of God be in their throats and two-edged swords in their hands. . . ."

[58]Holloway, "The Ethical Dilemma," 65.

[59]See Vincent Carroll and David Shiflett, *Christianity on Trial: Arguments against Anti-religious Bigotry* (San Francisco: Encounter Books, 2002) 109.

[60]Holloway, "The Ethical Dilemma," 65; Craigie, *War*, 38, note 10, "But in the matter of war, mankind has not clearly progressed, and may indeed have regressed from the standards of the biblical period."

281

[61]Ibid.

[62]See Helmut Thielicke, *Christ and the Meaning of Life*, ed. and trans. by John Doberstein (New York: Harper and Row, 1962) 14-15.

[63]John Wood, *Perspectives on War in the Bible* (Macon, GA: Mercer University Press, 1998) chapter 5.

[64]My sincere appreciation is extended to Mark Mangano, Walt Zorn, and John Castelein, my colleagues at Lincoln Christian College and Seminary, who read drafts of this essay and made many valuable comments.

Bibliography

Clouse, Robert G., ed. *War: Four Views.* Downers Grove, IL: Inter-Varsity, 1981.

This is a collection of essays presenting four evangelical Christian perspectives on war. Pacifism, passive resistance, just war, and preemptive offensive war are the views presented. Each essay by a proponent of one view is responded to by the other three authors. Although no one directly deals with holy war in the Old Testament, the book affords one an opportunity to see the various ways Bible-believing Christians interpret the biblical texts.

Cowles, C.S., et al. *Show Them No Mercy: Four Views on God and Canaanite Genocide.* Grand Rapids: Zondervan 1981.

A very helpful overview by four evangelical scholars on how to understand the *ḥērem* concept in the OT. The four views are: radical discontinuity, moderate discontinuity, eschatalogical continuity, and spiritual continuity.

Craigie, Peter C. *The Problem of War in the Old Testament.* Grand Rapids: Eerdmans, 1978.

This is a foundational introduction to the issue of war in the Old Testament. Craigie poses the problem as threefold: the problem of God, the problem of revelation, and the problem of ethics. It is a given that we must retain the whole Bible, and a fact that the Old Testament has been used throughout church history to support war. Craigie offers reflections on topics from biblical texts to the nature of the state, and war and the state. He concludes that we need to explain rather than defend Old Testament war texts. We also must not ignore those texts but teach from them. He suggests that perhaps we have to hold to the paradox that both the just war theory and Christian pacifism are valid conclusions from the Bible. That is part of the tension of being in the world but not of it.

"Divine Warrior," *Dictionary of Biblical Imagery,* 210-213. Downers Grove, IL: InterVarsity, 1998.

This article is a very helpful survey of the basic biblical texts from both the Old and New Testament. If a person has time to study only one resource this should be it.

Holloway, Jeph. "The Ethical Dilemma of Holy War." *Southwestern Journal of Theology* 41 (1998) 44-69.

Holloway's essay is directly relevant to the topic of my chapter in this book. It is an excellent survey of the texts and issues with some provocative conclusions. I am indebted to him for many thought-provoking observations.

Lind, Millard C. *Yahweh Is a Warrior.* Scottdale, PA: Herald Press, 1980.

Lind, a Mennonite, writes from the perspective of the traditional "Peace" churches. This is a study of the major texts on war and warfare in the Old Testament. Lind differs from Craigie in that he studies only the biblical texts. He begins with warfare in the patriarchal period and continues through the Old Testament to the theology of the historian who edited the history books. The exodus event provided the paradigm for the concept of Yahweh as King over Israel. The ancient theology of warfare was obedience to God and trust in his miracles. Israel was not expected to do anything but obey. Any time the leaders or kings took action on their own they were being disobedient.

Longman, Tremper III, and Daniel G. Reid. *God Is a Warrior.* Grand Rapids: Zondervan, 1995.

Longman and Reid trace the theme of God as warrior through the whole Bible. Longman, who writes the Old Testament half, includes chapters on the Day of the Lord, God's battle against chaos, and warfare in other ancient Near Eastern countries. Reid's half on God as warrior in the New Testament will perhaps be the most enlightening to the Bible student. This aspect of the theme is not generally acknowledged or well-known. This brings a helpful dimension to the study.

Niditch, Susan. *War in the Hebrew Bible: A Study in the Ethics of Violence.* New York: Oxford University Press, 1993.

Niditch represents the critical approach to the Old Testament. She finds seven different and conflicting approaches to war in the Old Testament. She finds the ban or *ḥērem* principle originating in the early belief that God desired human sacrifice. Among the ideologies she finds those of Tricksterism and Expediency. She offers little in the way of applying the texts, and her analysis will probably not be satisfying to the evangelical Christian.

Swartley, Willard M. *Slavery, Sabbath, War and Women: Case Issues in Biblical Interpretation.* Scottdale, PA: Herald Press, 1983.

This is a book that intends to prompt Christians to think deeply about hermeneutics by offering four topics that have prompted conflicting Interpretations among Christians. The discussions are succinct and packed full. The section on war compares just war theorists and pacifists. His concluding discussion of some main issues in interpretation is insightful.

Wood, John A. *Perspectives on War in the Bible.* Macon, GA: Mercer University Press, 1998.

Wood finds several different traditions about war in the OT, some of them conflict with each other, some are complementary. There are also traditions about peace. God as Divine Warrior is an important biblical metaphor that conveys important truth, but today we would do well to concentrate on more apt metaphors like God as Father. We need to analyze both the motives and consequences of war in the Bible. Both just war and pacifist traditions can be supported by the Bible, and they belong to the same family. Therefore, the Bible can be used to mold attitudes and convictions about warfare that will contradict the current addiction to violence and warfare.

Abbreviations

ABD – *Anchor Bible Dictionary*
DBI – *Dictionary of Biblical Imagery*
IDBS – *Interpreters Dictionary of the Bible Supplement*
NIDOTTE – *New International Dictionary of Old Testament Theology and Exegesis*
SWJT – *Southwestern Journal of Theology*
TB – *Tyndale Bulletin*
TDOT – *Theological Dictionary of the Old Testament*

THE NONVIOLENT REIGN OF GOD[1]

Lee C. Camp, Ph.D.

Scripture as Story

In my teaching and preaching, and in my suggesting that Christians ought to take Jesus' nonviolence seriously, it is not uncommon for numerous objections to be raised. "But Jesus didn't tell the centurion to quit his job," and "But Jesus wasn't very pacifist when he cleansed the temple," and "God used war in the Old Testament." That these questions get raised so quickly indicates that the questioner is starting at the wrong place: namely, without an appreciation of the overarching story of Scripture.

It is conventional wisdom that Scripture should not be "taken out of context." That is, one must appropriate, say, a verse of Scripture with respect to the larger context of its paragraph, or its book. This assumes, of course, that a verse or chapter should not be wrenched out of the entire context of Scripture as a whole: in other words, to make sense of or appropriate a particular part of Scripture, we must place it in the context of the whole of the canon. But it is precisely the *whole* that appears to too often get overlooked. As a rabbi who had been invited to our campus to speak to a Bible class remarked afterwards, "The students here know a whole lot about a very little of Scripture."

Without this wholeness, we cannot properly understand the relation of the church to the world, or the relation of the church to the world's wars. The proof-texting that often characterizes debates over Christian involvement in warfare fails, too often, to take account of Scripture *as a whole*. Taken as a whole, Scripture is *not* a reposito-

> The proof-texting that often characterizes debates over Christian involvement in warfare fails, too often, to take account of Scripture as a whole.

ry of commands or legal proscriptions (though there are, clearly, numerous commands and legal codes preserved in Scripture). Taken as a whole, neither is Scripture a collection of rules about how to conduct worship or liturgy (though again, there is such material in Scripture). Taken as a whole, Scripture is *not* a collection of stories each of which has a nice little concluding moral, say something akin to William Bennett's *Book of Virtues* (though again, there are, apparently such stories embedded here and there in Scripture). Instead of these things, taken as a whole, Scripture provides us with an overarching grand narrative, a story which we take to be the truest representation of the meaning of all of human history.

In brief, that *wholeness* might be briefly described this way: God created a good creation. The Hebrew word *shalom* proves useful in describing the nature of that good creation: not just a "peace" that is the absence of conflict or killing, but a positive harmony, wholeness, abundance, and plenty, in which God and humankind shared deep fellowship, in which the human was intended to "image" the character and concerns of the Creator for the creation. Nonetheless, in response to God's act of creation, the human rebelled against the rightful sovereignty of God, rejected the offer of relationship, and struck out on his own, loving neither God nor neighbor.

As a result of this rebellion, the *shalom* of God's creation gets shattered by lust, greed, violence, and murder. And with the Fall comes death, the epitome of the consequences and meaning of rebellion. But the Creator God is also the God of Redemption, refusing to leave the creation to its own demise; so God seeks first to redeem the human race through Noah, and subsequently enters into a covenant relationship with Abram, promising the patriarch that "in you all the families of the earth shall be blessed" (12:3). We might simplistically characterize the remainder of the canon as the story of God working in the midst of human history to redeem the rebellious creation back to its original intention.

Violence and the Fall,
Nonviolence and Our Redemption

Violence plays a particularly prominent role throughout the story of Scripture. As the Hebrew Scriptures recount the work of the Creator, violence is *not* part and parcel of God's creation (as is true, for example, in the Babylonian creation myths). Instead, violence comes in the wake of the humans' sin, in the wake of human rebellion.[2] So Genesis relates Cain's murder of his brother Abel as the first significant story following humankind's expulsion from the garden. Violence and homicide are depicted as the immediate consequence of the Fall, and the account falls off into a descending spiral of tit-for-tat "justice"—if anyone

> Violence and homicide are depicted as the immediate consequence of the Fall, and the account falls off into a descending spiral of tit-for-tat "justice."

kills Cain, his death will be avenged seven times. Then Lamech kills "a young man for striking me" (4:23). (We might note in passing here that the *lex talionis*, "an eye for an eye and a tooth for a tooth," stands as a great improvement upon ancient near-eastern standards of "justice" which looked like Lamech's disproportionately harsh response.) Lamech then proclaims that if anyone kills him, he will be avenged seventy-seven times (4:24).

Given this violent start to the narrative of fallen human history, the narrative soon recounts that God expresses sorrow for having created humankind at all because "the earth was corrupt in God's sight, and the earth was filled with violence. . . . And God said to Noah, 'I have determined to make an end of all flesh, for the earth is filled with violence because of them; now I am going to destroy them along with the earth'" (6:11,13). Thus God starts afresh with the Noahic flood because of the violence and injustice of humankind. But this obviously does not remove violence from human history, for it is not long before the covenant people are themselves trapped in slavery, ensnared in the violence and injustice of Egypt in which the people of God are treated like mere chattel. After God's powerful liberation from Egypt, Israel gets called to live as a communal alternative to the nations round about them. The Sabbath law, for example, stands as a powerful illustration of the manner in which the covenant laws were to represent the identity and history of Israel:

they are not to live according to the ethic of Egyptian slavery, in which humans were treated as mere resources, mere cogs in the wheel of the Egyptian economy that demanded ever greater "productivity." Instead, the people of God were to live according to the good news of *rest*. Yes, labor six days, but remember that you do not survive and you are not sustained by your labor, but by God. You are to rest, and allow others to rest. "Remember that you were a slave in the land of Egypt, and the Lord your God brought you out from there . . . therefore the Lord your God commanded you to keep the sabbath day" (Deut 5:15).

The Law, in other words, prescribes the Way of life of an alternative community, exhibiting to the nations round about them the good life with which God had graced them. In a world of oppression and injustice, the people of God were to be a people of righteousness and justice. Precisely in response to the failure of the covenant people to embody God's desire for justice and mercy, the prophets came bearing the "word of the Lord," calling Israel back to her covenant commitments. They foresaw and anticipated a day in which the righteous judgment of God would come, in which God's purposes would be fully established. They anticipated a coming Reign of God in which the violence of the fallen world will be undone, oppression defeated, and injustice overthrown. This renewal of God's creation will result from all people knowing and receiving the "knowledge of God," an intimate relationship with God and participation in God's will. In poetic imagery, the eighth-century B.C. prophet Isaiah described God's Reign this way:

> The wolf shall live with the lamb,
>   the leopard shall lie down with the kid,
> the calf and the lion and the fatling together,
>   and a little child shall lead them.
> The cow and the bear shall graze,
>   their young shall lie down together;
>   and the lion shall eat straw like the ox.
> The nursing child shall play over the hole of the asp,
>   and the weaned child shall put its hand on the adder's den.
> They will not hurt or destroy
>   on all my holy mountain;
> for the earth will be full of the knowledge of the Lord
>   as the waters cover the sea (Isa 11:6-9).

Using language also employed by Isaiah, his contemporary Micah proclaimed:

> In days to come
>   the mountain of the LORD's house
> shall be established as the highest of the mountains,
>   and shall be raised up above the hills.
> Peoples shall stream to it,
>   and many nations shall come and say:
> "Come, let us go up to the mountain of the LORD,
>   to the house of the God of Jacob;
> that he may teach us his ways
>   and that we may walk in his paths."
> For out of Zion shall go forth instruction,
>   and the word of the LORD from Jerusalem.
> He shall judge between many peoples,
>   and shall arbitrate between strong nations far away;
> they shall beat their swords into plowshares,
>   and their spears into pruning hooks;
> nation shall not lift up sword against nation,
>   neither shall they learn war any more;
> but they shall all sit under their own vines and under
>   their own fig trees,
>   and no one shall make them afraid;
> for the mouth of the LORD of hosts has spoken
>   (Micah 4:1-4).

Though we might point to other numerous passages of interest to our topic here—noting that the prophets decry a reliance upon force and military might, that they regularly denounce the violence and abuse of warfare, and that they call the people of God to depend upon God's deliverance[3]—the most important point for consideration here is something different. It is this: they long for the coming Day of the Lord, in which the nations will put away their war-making, and the peaceful Reign of God will be established in the midst of human history. In place of the dissipation of war and the extravagant waste of militarism will come a new way, in which all peoples will seek "the knowledge of the Lord" and "learn war no more." Instead of want and hunger, everyone will have "their own vine" and sit "under their own fig tree." Thus the prophets describe this reality: the primeval *shalom* that marked God's good creation will be redeemed, will reenter human history in a powerful way. Warfare—

> Warfare—in and of itself—is symptomatic of rebellion against God's purposes.

in and of itself—is symptomatic of rebellion against God's purposes. Thus, when God acts to redeem the rebellious creation, warfare would be unlearned. Isaiah thus depicts the "knowledge of God" as mutually exclusive with war-making. When all peoples surrender themselves to the will of God, they no longer spend themselves in learning the art of war (see also Isa 2:2-4; 9:1-7).

When Jesus comes upon the scene, he does so precisely declaring the coming near of the Reign of God. "Repent, the Kingdom of Heaven is at hand," we are told Jesus preached (Matt 3:2; 4:17; Mark 1:15; cf. Mark 6:12; Luke 4:43; 8:1; 9:2,11,60; 10:9, etc.). Thus Jesus teaches his disciples to pray for the coming of the Kingdom, which Jesus implicitly defines as "God's will being done on earth, as it is in heaven" (Matt 6:10). "Kingdom" language confuses us if we think territorially. In geopolitics, there exist discrete kingdoms and nation-states whose boundaries are defined geographically. But in Scripture, the whole creation belongs to God the Creator—though the human inhabitants have rebelled against God's rightful reign. Thus the coming of the Kingdom is the restoration of God's rightful reign over God's Creation; in the Kingdom God's original intent, the "image of God," is restored to us (cf. Col 3:10). The "Kingdom" is not merely a new religious group, a group of folks finally "doing church right." Nor

> The Kingdom is the Rightful, Peaceable Reign of God over God's creation.

is the Kingdom to be equated with "going to heaven." Instead, the Kingdom is the Rightful, Peaceable Reign of God over God's creation.

How seldom we hear the message of the Kingdom of God from our pulpits, when this, according to the New Testament, is precisely *the* content of the Good News. The long-awaited Reign of God's Redemptive purposes has broken into human history, making all things new. The fallen creation is beginning to experience renewal; the Rule of righteousness, peace, justice, and mercy has begun.

God's Way of Making Peace

Perhaps to this point in the discussion, few will find much over which to object. "Yes, of course Christians desire peace, of course Christians are opposed to injustice and oppression, of course we do not want war, and of course we, along with the prophets, await the day in which swords will be beaten into plowshares. But that's all beside the point. The question is, *how* should we Christians contribute to a world of peace? How are we going to help address the real problems of injustice, oppression, and violence in the world?"

Before addressing precisely this question, we should note that the scriptural storytelling above makes it plain that the story of redemption *is* concerned with this-worldly issues of injustice, oppression, and violence. All forms of hatred, animosity, alienation, and estrangement portray the rebellious, fallen creation; and redemption is concerned to undo the forces of rebellion. Paul thus longed for the complete redemption not only of our bodies, but of the entire created realm (Rom 8:19-23). The Gospel is thus not a message merely concerned with "spiritual" realities, but with *all* reality, all human existence, with every sphere and facet of God's creation.

> The Gospel is thus not a message merely concerned with "spiritual" realities, but with all reality, all human existence, with every sphere and facet of God's creation.

Thus when we ask the question of "how," of the *means* and *methods* we are to employ in responding to injustice and violence, surely the means employed by the God revealed in Jesus Christ are most important to us. If we truly seek the end (that is, the goal) of the Reign of God—of peace, of reconciliation, of righteousness—then surely we are beholden to those methods employed by God in precisely this pursuit.

But this gets the cart before the horse. First we must address this: what means *has* God used in order to effect reconciliation or redemption? On this question, the New Testament with great consistency answers this way: in the cross. *Reconciliation* between estranged and alienated parties is effected through Jesus' crucifixion, through Jesus' absorption of hostility and sin, through taking on the stripes of punishment and shame. "Reconciliation" becomes the word Paul used to describe his very ministry—a "ministry of reconciliation" (2 Cor 5:18)—and he makes it plain to the Corinthians that that reconciliation comes through the "foolishness of the cross" (1 Cor 1:18-25). Or to the Colossians, the work of Christ is described this way: "in him all the fullness of God was pleased to dwell, and through him God was pleased to reconcile to himself all things, whether on earth or in heaven, *by making peace through the blood of his cross*" (Col 1:19,20, emphasis added).

291

If in Jesus' cross, God was reconciling all things to himself, then we should not be surprised that Paul emphasizes one very concrete, specific implication of this reconciliation. Given that God, in Christ, is reconciling all things, then all those things that alienate and estrange *peoples* from *one another* are also broken down in Christ. Thus Paul emphasizes that in the cross, God broke down that very powerful socioreligious force of alienation between Jews and Gentiles.[4] This is not merely a *religious* assertion; it is a *sociopolitical* assertion. The hostility between those who were counted "God's people" and those who were counted "not God's people" had been brought into a "new humanity," a new creation.

> But now in Christ Jesus you who once were far off have been brought near by the blood of Christ. For he is our peace; in his flesh he has made both groups into one and has broken down the dividing wall, that is, the hostility between us. . . . that he might create in himself one new humanity in place of the two, thus making peace, and might reconcile both groups to God in one body *through the cross*, thus putting to death that hostility through it. *So he came and proclaimed peace* to you who were far off and peace to those who were near . . . (Eph 2:13-18, emphasis added).

Indeed, for Paul, Christian baptism is itself a calling to participate in this new order in which the old hostilities and categories for disaffection are set aside: "As many of you as were baptized into Christ have clothed yourselves with Christ. There is no longer Jew or Greek, there is no longer slave or free, there is no longer male and female; for all of you are one in Christ Jesus" (Gal 3:27-28).

Rather than buying into a model of Kingship desired by many of Jesus' contemporaries, he heralded an alternative approach to kingship. As John Yoder put it, "The alternative to how kings rule the world is not 'spirituality' but servanthood."[5] Jesus' disciples and hearers were not wrong to expect a *kingdom*—that is, a New Order that has a distinct identity in the here-and-now, in the midst of human history. They were wrong on their understanding of the *method* of that Kingdom. While many desired it to be a Davidic kingdom of power and might,

> *Rather than buying into a model of Kingship desired by many of Jesus' contemporaries, he heralded an alternative approach to kingship.*

Jesus came proclaiming a peace unattainable through those means. He came proclaiming a peace attainable only through the way of a suffering Lamb, who yields, submits, serves. His peace comes not through imposition, coercion, or force, but through offering, persuading, and sharing. Jesus is the one who "though he was rich, yet for your sakes he became poor" (2 Cor 8:9). Rather than holding onto might, power, and security, it was relinquished in order to effect reconciliation; rather than asserting his muscle and power, he divested himself of divine prerogative:

> who, though he was in the form of God,
>   did not regard equality with God
>   as something to be exploited,
> but emptied himself,
>   taking the form of a slave,
>   being born in human likeness.
> And being found in human form,
>   he humbled himself
>   and became *obedient to the point of death*—
> even death on a cross (Phil 2:5-8, italics added).

Such scriptural examples could be multiplied: but again and again, consistently throughout the New Testament, we are taught that Jesus' Messiahship was authenticated and characterized by his suffering, his willingness to take on himself injustice, hatred, and the consequences of sin. He traveled the way of the cross, willingly suffered in love, and died in response to human rebellion. This is, indeed, the very message of the word of Christ.

What does this have to do with Christians waging (or not waging) warfare? Precisely this: that disciples are also, throughout Scripture, always called to take up the way of the cross, to follow in the way of Jesus. So Jesus' cross is not to be borne by Jesus alone, but by all his followers. In the context of the passages just discussed, the way of Christ is also set forward as the way of Jesus' disciples. So Paul prefaces the hymn of praise to the Christ who "did not regard equality with God as something to be exploited," this one who "became obedient to the point of death," with this admonition: "Let the same mind be in you that was in Christ Jesus" (Phil 2:5).

> So Jesus' cross is not to be borne by Jesus alone, but by all his followers.

Similarly, consider the passage from Ephesians (2:13-18) in which Paul extols Jesus for effecting reconciliation and peace through the cross. As a consequence of Christ's reconciling work, we are "taught to put away your former way of life, your old self, corrupt and deluded by its lusts, and to be renewed in the spirit of your minds, and to clothe yourselves with the new self"—and note the manner in which this reconciling work is intended to return us to God's original intentions—"created according to the likeness of God in true righteousness and holiness" (Eph 4:22-24). What does this look like? Paul gives plenty of particulars, but of most importance here is the calling to emulate the suffering love of Christ:

> Put away from you all bitterness and wrath and anger and wrangling and slander, together with all malice, and be kind to one another, tenderhearted, forgiving one another, as God in Christ has forgiven you. Therefore be imitators of God, as beloved children, and live in love, as Christ loved us and gave himself up for us, a fragrant offering and sacrifice to God (Eph 4:31–5:2).

In numerous other contexts, the cross serves as the model for Christian ethics. To the Corinthians, suing one another in order to avoid being defrauded, Paul commanded: "why not rather be wronged? Why not rather be defrauded? But you yourselves wrong and defraud—and believers at that" (1 Cor 6:7f.). Or to the Romans:

> Bless those who persecute you; bless and do not curse them.
> . . . Do not repay anyone evil for evil, but take thought for what is noble in the sight of all. . . . Beloved, never avenge yourselves, but leave room for the wrath of God. . . . No, 'if your enemies are hungry, feed them; if they are thirsty, give them something to drink; for by doing this you will heap burning coals on their heads.' (Rom 12:14-21; cf. almost identical language in 1 Thess 5:15).

Such admonition to the Romans flows from what Paul had already said about awaiting and participating in God's redemptive work: we are "heirs of God and joint heirs with Christ—if, in fact, we suffer with him so that we may also be glorified with him" (8:17).

Or from 1 Peter:

> But if you endure when you do right and suffer for it, you have God's approval. For to this you have been called,

because Christ also suffered for you, leaving you an example, so that you should follow in his steps.

'He committed no sin,
  and no deceit was found in his mouth.'

When he was abused, he did not return abuse; when he suffered, he did not threaten; but he entrusted himself to the one who judges justly. He himself bore our sins in his body on the cross. . . . Do not repay evil for evil or abuse for abuse; but, on the contrary, repay with a blessing. It is for this that you were called—that you might inherit a blessing (1 Pet 2:20-24; 3:9).

Such logic simply reflects the ethic of the Kingdom proclaimed in Jesus' Sermon on the Mount. As noted above, many of Jesus' contemporaries longed for a King who would make war on their enemies, specifically the oppressive and unjust rule of the Roman empire. Precisely *in that context* does Jesus advocate a different ethic:[6]

But I say to you, Love your enemies and pray for those who persecute you, so that you may be children of your Father in heaven; for he makes his sun rise on the evil and on the good, and sends rain on the righteous and on the unrighteous. For if you love those who love you, what reward do you have? Do not even the tax collectors do the same? And if you greet only your brothers and sisters, what more are you doing than others? Do not even the Gentiles do the same?" (Matt 5:44-47).

Why should we love our enemies, rather than seek their destruction? Because this is the way God loves. Jesus requires that we always see in the other their common humanity, their need—along with our need—for the gracious, compassionate mercy of God. Jesus here undercuts our tendency to see in the "enemy" an embodiment of evil. Jesus will not let us demonize peoples or nations as an "axis of evil," but instead calls us to see in the alleged enemy one who, like us, needs the transformative grace of God.

> *Jesus will not let us demonize peoples or nations as an "axis of evil," but instead calls us to see in the alleged enemy one who, like us, needs the transformative grace of God.*

The point is simply this: a "disciple" is not merely someone who likes Jesus, honors Jesus with praise songs, or wears a WWJD bracelet. A *disciple* is someone who follows Jesus, who seeks to embody Christ's intentions in every facet of their lives. The way of Christ is not something to be compartmentalized, whether it be a Sunday morning compartmentalization, or a political compartmentalization. The way of Christ is not to be restricted to the arena of "personal relationships" or "the attitudes of one's heart." Instead, the work, person, and way of Jesus is the revelation of the Kingdom Come. If we claim him as Lord, then we seek to bring every sphere, realm, and arena of our lives under his Lordship, submitted to the rightful, Peaceable Reign of God—even when, especially when, others hate us.

> Making war simply does not, cannot, bear witness to the Peaceable Reign of God revealed in a Suffering Messiah.

Making war simply does not, cannot, bear witness to the Peaceable Reign of God revealed in a Suffering Messiah.

The Church and the Kingdom

The church lives and exists as a community bearing witness, in word and deed, to the reality of the Reign of God. The church should be nonviolent because we believe that God has inaugurated the Kingdom of Peace. We believe—we have faith, we trust, we live by and stake our lives on—the reality of God's Kingdom. The Kingdom of God has not yet been fully established,[7] but it *is* already begun, and it is the Rule to which we are to orient, conduct, and live our lives.

> The church should be nonviolent because we believe that God has inaugurated the Kingdom of Peace.

It is this one contention that is the heart of a biblical pacifism: the Good News of the Peaceable Kingdom of God. Some stereotype pacifism as a rule-based ethic, or a legalistic interpretation of Jesus' command to "turn the other cheek." But a biblical pacifism finds its basis not in any one rule or command (though there are plenty such commands that support the argument being made here). As Walter Wink has put it, "Nonviolence is not a matter of legalism but of discipleship. It is the way God has chosen to overthrow evil in the world."[8] Thus

> "Nonviolence is not a matter of legalism but of discipleship. It is the way God has chosen to overthrow evil in the world."

pacifism flows very simply from the Gospel of the Peaceable Kingdom: we are to seek, in all things, to bear witness to the reconciliation, peace-making, and forgiveness made available in God's New Order. We are to seek, in all things, to show to the world the unfathomable measure of God's grace, love, and mercy. War-making, *even as a last resort*, does not do this. We are to seek, in all things, to demonstrate by word and deed the New Creation which has begun in Christ.[9] War-making, instead, is an ongoing participation in the very violence (whether "defensive" or "offensive") that the Reign of God is intended to overcome.

But some may object that since we still live "between the times," that we should not be expected to live as if the Kingdom is fully here.[10] One cannot "love his enemies" until the kingdom comes in its fullness; one cannot "turn the other cheek" when there are people out there that will kill you; one cannot be nonviolent when the world continues to live in violence. Such questions cut to the heart of "ecclesiology"—how are we to understand the identity, purpose, nature, and function of "church"? Too often our debates focus upon "religious" questions: that is, we sometimes argue and bicker over how to "do church right."

> The task of the church is to be a body of people exhibiting to the world the kind of life God created the world to enjoy.

But if we take Paul, or Jesus, seriously, settling such questions is *not* the primary task of the church. The task of the church is to be a body of people exhibiting to the world the kind of life God created the world to enjoy. In the language of the letter to the Ephesians, it is "through the church [that] the wisdom of God in its rich variety might now be made known to the rulers and authorities in the heavenly places" (3:10).

The radical significance of this ecclesiology is perhaps best highlighted by contrast to competing ecclesiologies: The church is not a community that, like a pharmacist, dispenses whatever it is one needs in order to "be saved" and thus "go to heaven" when one dies. Such a model is seen in those who emphasize "church" as a body that rightly dispenses sacraments or religious practices or church services, always with the fear that if one does not do so, one may forfeit his opportunity to "go to heaven." Others object, however: the church must not be grounded in works-righteousness, but in "right doctrine," such as salvation by grace through faith alone;

rightly receiving that doctrine, we may receive "salvation" and thence "go to heaven." But we might actually say that both of these models are "legalistic," in the sense that they are concerned with pleasing God, keeping God's rules or God's stipulations, or receiving God's gift so that they might not go to hell, and instead, go to heaven. Both picture the primary role of the church as the dispenser of the ticket one needs to have punched.

But neither of these models is particularly helpful in getting at a more biblical ecclesiology: the church is, in Paul's favorite metaphor, the "body of Christ" (see Rom 12:4,5; 1 Cor 10:17; 11:29; 12:12-27; Eph 1:22-23; 3:5-6; 4:4,12,16; 5:23,29,30; Col 1:18,24; 2:18,19; 3:15). The church continues the work Jesus began. We are called to demonstrate to the world what God created it to be. Similarly, Jesus taught his disciples to be "salt" and "light." If we refuse our role to be salt, then the world will continue in its festering, its rotting; if we refuse to be light, then the world will continue to stumble about in the darkness, wounded and wounding. Similarly does the ecclesiology developed in Luke-Acts have it: what Luke depicts Jesus doing in his ministry, Acts depicts the church doing in its ministry.

Our task, then, is simply to *be the church*. We offer to the world a positive, constructive alternative to the war-making, hate-mongering, and demonizing that characterizes rebellious human history. Thus numerous historians and theologians have documented that the early church fathers, until the time of Constantine in the fourth century, all rejected the legitimacy of Christians participating in warfare.[11] This rejection was due not only to danger of participation in idolatry by participation in the Roman military, but also to the fact that, to use our language, they deemed war-making, in itself, immoral. They could not

> The early church fathers, until the time of Constantine in the fourth century, all rejected the legitimacy of Christians participating in warfare.

square the Christian profession with the profession of war-making; they could not square the love to which Jesus called us with the killing of one's enemies. So Tertullian queried, "If we are enjoined to love our enemies, whom have we to hate? If injured we are forbidden to retaliate. Who then can suffer injury at our hands?" Or Clement of Alexandria, to unbelievers, proclaimed: "If you enroll as one of God's people, heaven is your country and God your lawgiver.

And what are his laws? . . . Thou shalt not kill . . . . Thou shalt love thy neighbor as thyself. To him that strikes thee on the one cheek, turn also the other." Or Cyprian: "And what more—that you should not curse; that you should not seek again your goods when taken from you; when buffeted you should turn the other cheek; and forgive not seven times but seventy times seven . . . That you should love your enemies and pray for your adversaries and persecutors?" Similarly Tertullian acclaimed as the "principal precept" of the disciple the command to love our enemies, just as Dionysius of Alexandria said, "Love is ever on the alert to do good even to him who is unwilling to receive it." And Justin asked, "If you love merely those that love you, what do you that is *new*?"[12]

Obviously, such a stance creates significant tension with a world caught up in not only the legitimacy, but the nobility and necessity, of war-making. At least some of the early Christians found that their discipleship created such tensions. Of interest, the ongoing reality of warfare in the midst of human history was used by some critics of the early church to argue that Christians ought not profess belief in Jesus as the Messiah—he could not have been the Messiah, because if he was (so the prophets say), then the nations would have beaten their swords into plowshares, and there would be war no more. But each of the early church fathers Justin, Tertullian, Irenaeus, and Origen basically responded similarly: yes, the Messiah of peace *has* come, because *the church*, even now, comprises people of all nations who have put away their swords, put away their war-making, and constitute the new order given in Jesus Christ.[13]

Objections

"That's Just Not Realistic"

The ecclesiology—both of the New Testament and the early church fathers—stands in opposition to an ecclesiology which suggests that the teaching of Jesus is a "personal" ethic, while some other rules or standards are used in the "public" sphere. Protestant Reformer Martin Luther popularized this latter ecclesiology in suggesting that the Sermon on the Mount does not provide us any direction for how we are to act in the realm of government or politics; instead, it gives us direction in the areas of our personal lives and our attitudes. Similarly have many in the twentieth-century Stone-Campbell movement interpreted Jesus' teachings. For example, Foy E. Wallace, one of the major characters that helped move Churches of Christ away from its earlier sympathies and commitments to pacifism, asserted that "the Christian's obligations exist in two realms—the civil and the spiritual."[14] This distinction sets Jesus' teaching to one side, rather than upholding Jesus' teaching as authoritative in every realm; one ought not, it is claimed, take Jesus seriously as an ethic in the "real world" in which there remains sin, rebellion, and violence.

Often this objection—"that's just not realistic"—simply appeals to a gut-level emotion, asserting that the Christian proponent of nonviolence could not "really" expect someone to take his viewpoint seriously. "Plain ol' common-sense shows us that" and "there are some people you just can't reason with." But this kind of objection simply fails to take Jesus seriously. Such arguments fail to take into account the theological undergirding of Christian nonviolence: namely, that God's Kingdom has come, Jesus has shown us how to participate in it, and we have been called to follow him in his lead. Because it's a Kingdom—a real, sociopolitical entity—and not merely a "religion," then we must take Jesus' way seriously, right here in the midst of human history. If someone wants to argue, from a Christian perspective, for the legitimacy of the use of violence, then they must make that argument with Jesus as their authority—rather than ignoring him.

> Because it's a Kingdom—a real, sociopolitical entity—and not merely a "religion," then we must take Jesus' way seriously, right here in the midst of human history.

But it is precisely ignoring Jesus that so often happens when it comes to talk of warfare. Out of such a fabric did Reinhold Niebuhr argue in his classic essay, "Why the Christian Church is Not Pacifist."[15] Jesus' way always stands over us, making us realize our failings and sins, making us realize our pride and selfish ambition. Jesus' teaching is thus useful in making us realize our need for God's gracious forgiveness. But Jesus' way, Niebuhr contended, cannot be taken seriously if we want to make a real contribution to human history. We shall have to compromise, seeking to implement justice (equity, returning like-for-like) rather than love (returning good for evil). Violence, then, is thought to be to some measure redemptive, to the point of limiting violence and bloodshed and providing a means to attain justice. Violence is seen as the way to restrain chaos, a way to check the loss of innocent life, a last resort in a fallen and violent world.

There are numerous difficulties with such a view: first, such "realists" ought not assume that their politic is more 'realistic' than the Christian Gospel. The Gospel proclaims that it is possible, in the very midst of fallen, rebellious human history, to love as God loves, empowered by God's Holy Spirit. This is not some assertion of moral perfectionism, but is the meaning of our most orthodox claims about Jesus: in his humanity, he demonstrated for all humankind what we were made to be, and what we can be, through God's power. We must not forget that Jesus, though fully divine, was also fully human; and his way is the way we are called to be.

For the Christian, what is *most real* is the rule of Jesus as Lord over the cosmos. The proclamation "Jesus is Lord" is not merely wishful thinking; the Christian confession that "Jesus is Lord," is, instead, a statement about the very nature of reality, about what has come to pass by virtue of Jesus' resurrection from the dead. Christian pacifism is rooted not in "idealism," but in the conviction that Jesus is ruling over the cosmos. In other words, one contradicts oneself when one says "Jesus is Lord" and then says that one should kill one's enemies. These two claims cannot stand side-by-side, for

> Christian pacifism is rooted not in "idealism," but in the conviction that Jesus is ruling over the cosmos.

the Lordship of Jesus calls us to another way to deal with enemies. To put it in Paul's language (Rom 12:20), if the enemy is hungry, we feed him, not starve him; if the enemy is thirsty, we give him drink, not destroy his infrastructure. Jesus is Lord, or he is not.

What is most *real*, then, is the present and still-coming Kingdom of God. The "realist," on the other hand, would have the statesman, Christian or not, make use of consequentialist reasoning to make the best possible approximation of what pressure to apply to bring about a balance of geopolitical forces to maintain "order." But the disciple of Jesus cannot but simply proclaim such consequentialist discounting of the teaching of Jesus as unfaithfulness: our task is not to maintain a balance of power among the nation-states that refuse to submit to the Lordship of Christ. Our task, first and foremost, is to walk in faithfulness to the ways of Jesus. Our task, first and foremost, is to be the church, not maintain the empire.

If we accept this Gospel—that God is Sovereign, that God is in control, that God will bring about God's Kingdom purposes, and that it is not our task to "make things turn out right," that it is not our task to be "in control" or "in charge"—then innumerable conclusions immediately follow in its wake. So many of the "what if" questions, so many of the horrible dilemmas placed before the proponent of Christian nonviolence, immediately become irrelevant (or at least assessed on an entirely different plane) once this one element of the Gospel is received. The Kingdom has come, and our task is to walk in obedience to the ways of the Kingdom. This type of obedience is what the New Testament means by *faith* (see Hebrews 11, e.g.). As a corollary, we may conclude that try-ing to run the world using the ethic of the kingdoms of this rebellious world is not an act of faith, but an act of unbelief.

> *Trying to run the world using the ethic of the kingdoms of this rebellious world is not an act of faith, but an act of unbelief.*

"Realism" ultimately makes Jesus out to be a naïve, utopian idealist, unaware of the way in which the world "really works." "You can only love those who love you," the realist seems to say. But Jesus explicitly rejects such: if you only love those who love you, so what? Even the pagans do that (Matt 5:46-48). Everyone can respond with affection when they are treated with affection. Jesus' point is pre-cisely that we must *love* when we are *not* treated with love. A "Christian realist," it would appear then, does not prioritize *Christian theology*, but an insufficient *anthropology*: a theory about the nature of self-seeking social and political systems. Missing is any aware-ness of the historical reality of the Kingdom of God, as well as any doctrine of redemption. The theology of the Kingdom is trumped with an anthropology that does not believe that the Power that raised Jesus from the dead might really be at work *now* to redeem apparently hopeless situations (contrast, e.g., the latter portions of both Ephesians 1 and 3).

"But Warfare on Behalf of the Innocent Is 'Love of Neighbor'"

Is not a willingness to stop an attacker from harming one's neighbor an act of Christian love? And if so, could warfare not be, similarly, an act of Christian love, if done in defense of an innocent party?[16] Warfare, such logic argues, should be a last resort that is employed only when peaceful means have been first tried and found ineffective. In such a case, so the reasoning continues, war is then a positive good, exemplifying love—acting positively on behalf of the defenseless or innocent.

This type of logic, when fully played out, gives rise to one version of the "Just War Tradition." The JWT claims that under certain circumstances warfare is a legitimate action. Typically, the JWT has two sets of criteria: *jus ad bellum* (the criteria or rules for when it is legitimate to go to war, or when may one justifiably start a war) and *jus in bello* (the criteria of rules for what is legitimate to do *in* a war, or what *means* are legitimate to use in warfare). The various lists of criteria have grown and developed somewhat in the Christian tradition (and in the logic of western and international law), but a typical list may look like this:[17]

Ius ad Bellum
- The war must be fought or declared by a legitimate authority (e.g., a king, a president, a prime minister, a congress).
- The war must be fought for a just cause. This excludes fighting a war for national self-interest, for honor, for trifles. The war must respond to an actual offense or attack, and that attack must not have been provoked.
- The war must be fought with the right "intention," in that the war must intend peace.
- The war must be fought with the right "intention," in the subjective sense, in that it should not be waged out of vengeance or hatred.
- War must be a last resort. All possible peaceful means should be exhausted. Some suggest that this means efforts to waging peace nonviolently should be expended equivalent to the efforts and resources invested in waging war.
- A war should be fought only if there is probability of success.

Ius in Bello
- The means employed must be necessary, or indispensable, to the desired end.
- The means employed, and the entire response of the war, must be proportional. That is, the damage done must not be greater than the harm the war seeks to prevent.
- The means employed must protect the "immunity of the innocent." That is, civilians and noncombatants are not legitimate targets.
- The means employed must respect international law.

Such criteria began to arise in the Christian tradition beginning in the fourth century A.D. Prior to the fourth century, as noted previously, all extant Christian writings oppose Christians killing in warfare. But along with the rise of the legalization of Christianity—and ultimately the move in which Christianity became the *only* legal religion in the empire—the church developed the JWT. (This development is significant: the JWT is *not* a system simply derived from the New Testament, but arose in a new historical context. This observation does not, simply on its own, make such a historical development illegitimate. But many overlook the fact that the JWT *is* a historical development within the Christian tradition—it is *not* a moral system simply derived from *either* the OT or the NT. Ethicists often classify the wars of the Old Testament as "Holy Wars," in which God calls a particular leader to lead the people into war, and no restraints upon means are observed. This is categorically different from the JWT, in which the use of these supposedly objective criteria, apart from any revelation from God, determines the legitimacy of participating in the war.)

The primary difficulty with the JWT is the same as that of "realism"—it fails to take seriously the way of Christ. The New Testament consistently, as already argued above, appeals to Jesus' life and giving of his own life as the example of "love" we are to emulate. The extravagant love to which we are called is giving *unmerited, undeserved* love to those who most desperately need it. It may cost our life, and it may cost the lives of dear ones around us.

Other versions of the JWT[18] will often suggest that nonviolence is an ideal which should generally be upheld; but as a *last resort* one may make an exception to that norm.

> The Christian community is called to live as a community not afraid of death.

But this move sets aside the call to faithfulness that pervades both Old and New Testaments alike. We are called to follow one who obeyed even unto death; and we proclaim as Lord one who was raised victorious from the grave. We serve one who, according to the Hebrews writer, came so that "he might destroy the one who has the power of death, that is, the devil, and free those who all their lives were held in slavery by the fear of death" (2:14-15). If this be true, then we are freed to declare with the Hebrews writer, as he employs a perennial theme of the psalmists and prophets alike, "I will put my trust in him" (Heb 2:13).

That is, the Christian community is called to live as a community not afraid of death. The church might learn a great deal from the armed services: that we must train ourselves to be willing to die, to lay down our lives for a cause greater than our own selves. But the method of the Christian army, the soldiers of Christ, is not the way of the sword, but the way of love and service. *Even if* things look really bad, *even if* things are very unjust, *even if* terrorists strike innocent civilians, the church is not invested in preserving kingdoms of this world, but in bearing witness to the Kingdom of God; and that Kingdom does not come with MI Abrams tanks and cruise missiles, but with the cross. Furthermore, Christian soldiers have an ace up their sleeves not possessed by the nation-states and their armies. We know the Easter secret: that on the other side of the cross lies the celebration and vindication of resurrection.

Nonetheless, in spite of its flawed basis, we may still learn a great deal from the Just War tradition, and I suggest (as many others have before me) that we should encourage Christians who refuse to accept pacifism as a legitimate Christian ethic, to take the JWT all the more seriously. In my experience, most do *not* take it seriously. Few of my students have ever heard sermons on the criteria of the tradition, and do not understand the very stringent moral demands required of "Just War Christians."

Innumerable instances can be accounted in which the tradition is simply set aside, or used as rationalization. Often the *rhetoric* gets employed, making the populace *feel* as if the war is "justified," but underneath the rhetoric lies some other form of reasoning, that refuses to take the logic of the tradition seriously. Whether starting a war preemptively because of the fear that a middle-eastern dictator might fuel terrorism, or bombing civilian populations during WWII, or napalming children in the Vietnam era, or holding to the policy of Mutually Assured Destruction by means of nuclear weapons during the Cold War—all such actions and policies have been embraced by Christians who allegedly hold to the justifiable nature of some wars. But all such acts of war-making are clearly deemed immoral by the JWT.[19]

In other words, the JWT, if taken seriously, requires very serious moral commitments and training. Significantly, the JWT calls believers to *selective* conscientious objection. That is, in theory, the system would call a believer, with the help of his or her Christian community, to make judgments about the legitimacy of *particular* wars and then refuse to fight in whatever particular wars are deemed unjustified. But such a stance is *not* legally protected in the United States, while a more general stance of conscientious objection to warfare in all circumstances is protected as a right of U.S. citizens. Thus a JWT stance is a costly one, and one to be taken seriously, and will require serious training of Christians who do choose to participate in the military. Further, it requires *critique* of governmental claims, such as testing the evidence a president, king, or prime-minister provides for a justifiable cause.

In addition, the JWT clearly rules out nationalistic flag-waving and knee-jerk patriotism, like "if you don't love it, leave it." It sounds trite, but the logic of the Just War Tradition, if taken seriously, requires that we "kill with a tear in our eye," for warfare is always looked upon within the system as a very tragic "necessity," and is therefore never a cause for celebration, bravado, or the rhetoric of "blood, guts, and country." Thus in the middle ages, warriors who participated in a war deemed justifiable were required to do penance upon their return from the battlefield[20]—a far cry from ticker-tape parades that celebrate western power and dominance upon the return of their warriors from the battlefield. That the modern practices of warfare seem so remote from the original intention and serious practice of the Just War Tradition might indicate something troubling: that there are other values, commitments, or gods at work in our midst, rather than a serious engagement with the Just War Tradition.

Most Christians claim to be "Just War" Christians. This is a twofold problem. First, the Just War Tradition is not biblical. Second, speaking practically, most Christians haven't the foggiest notion of what it *means* or *requires* to be a "Just War" Christian. The claim to be a "Just War" Christian turns out, often, to be mere rhetoric; instead, the Christian populace often turns out to be nationalistic, growing indignant when anyone questions the government or its leaders or its agendas. Often conservative Christians, in particular, fall prey to a flabby piety which suggests we ought not question a president who apparently prays on a regular basis. "I can't help but trust him," many suggest. But a true Just War adherent knows that questioning governmental leaders is part and parcel

> A true Just War adherent knows that questioning governmental leaders is part and parcel of what it means to be a Just War Christian.

of what it means to be a Just War Christian. And a true Just War Christian knows that many wars, and the way they are fought, are not deemed appropriate by the Just War tradition. Just War Christians thus have a hefty responsibility upon them to take their moral rhetoric seriously, rather than allowing it to serve merely as rationalization for whatever the government tells the Christian church to do.

"What Would You Do If . . ."

"So what would you do if someone threatened your family or your wife? So you're saying you'd just stand there and let them do whatever they want?" Of course not. Such a question proceeds from the false understanding that pacifism is to be equated with passivism (as discussed below). The more appropriate question, instead, is this: how can we intervene in such a way that bears witness to the Lordship of Christ? The "what would you do if" question generally assumes that violence is the only way to respond to such a crisis. It also assumes that if you engage the assailant with violence, you will have greater chance of victory and be able to overcome him, and assumes that a nonviolent response would have little to no chance of victory. All these assumptions can be questioned.[21] In addition, the apparent commonsensical answer to the "what would you do if" question derives from the emotional strings attached. Whether this is a legitimate way to carry out ethical discourse is also highly suspect. Jesus' point—much to our disliking—was that he expects us to do for enemies what we would normally do for family (Matt 5:46f.).

This way of making an ethical argument is also questionable because it begins with a tragic dilemma, and then seeks to generalize to a universal ethical theory. That is, through use of an emotionally charged example, the opponent attempts to force the pacifist to concede that there may be some situations in which he or she would grant the use of violence—and then from that exception, a principle of self-defense is derived. From that principle, further, is derived justification for the JWT.

But even if one does grant the right of personal self-defense (which I would not), warfare remains a very different matter. Warfare is typically fought upon nationalistic lines, in which one kills not because one has been personally threatened by a clear assailant on the other side, but because one has been convinced by one's government that one should kill the other. Further, warfare leads to the death of innocents (which military parlance refers to as "collateral damage"). In any case, a more biblical way to proceed is to begin with a theological understanding of what kind of people we are supposed to *be*, and then seek to be faithful to that vision even in the midst of difficult dilemmas or circumstances. If we begin with our identity as a certain kind of people (namely, to be a "cruciform" people, to be people of God's Kingdom), and then ask questions about dilemmas, we might generate some possible creative responses that would never occur to us otherwise. For example, I know of a family whose home—while all the family was present—was invaded by armed robbers. The mother, incensed that people would dare violate her home and family in such a way, told me that there came from deep within her a voice which she did not know she had, and that from the depths of her being she began to rebuke the men in the name of Jesus, demanding that they immediately leave her home. The men were so frightened that they threw up their arms, shot their guns into the wall, and ran from the house. Once one begins to investigate such matters, one finds all sorts of similar stories.[22]

> *If we begin with our identity as a certain kind of people and then ask questions about dilemmas, we might generate some possible creative responses that would never occur to us otherwise.*

"But Jesus Didn't Tell the Centurion to Quit His Job"

One might find innumerable "negative proof-texts" to argue against pacifism. For example, some object that "the centurion in Acts 10 was not told to quit his job." But a few observations about this text could be equally applied to other such proof-texts. First, arguments from silence are simply not legitimate arguments.[23]

Second, in fact, there is another, larger theological theme in this passage, which is the concern of Luke, the writer of Acts—namely, that the division between peoples (in this case, that division between Jews and Gentiles) had been abolished. This abolition of the hostility between Jew and Gentile is a major theme throughout Acts, and thus Luke relates the story of Cornelius. And this very theme itself has great bearing upon the subject matter at hand, as already noted: in the New Testament, all of the divisions that are used to alienate and estrange peoples from one another are broken down in baptism (see Gal 3:27-29). But warfare since the sixteenth century has typically been fought upon nationalistic lines: that is, German Christians are told by their government to kill the French Christians who have been told by their government to kill the German Christians. Both sides believe their cause is "just," and thus kill fellow baptized believers in the name of "justice," "civilization," "liberty," or "freedom." So Christians kill Christians (and Christians kill their enemies, whom they are to love) in the name of values that are of lesser importance than the Kingdom of God.

So What?

In a campus dialog regarding Christian involvement in war-making, one student stridently protested, "The problem with all the pacifists is that they give no possible solutions. All they say is 'war is not the answer,' and when asked, 'what is the answer?' they respond by saying 'war is not the answer.'" Whether this is true of "all the pacifists," or lots of pacifists, I cannot say. But it is most certainly untrue of a biblical advocacy of nonviolence. Nonetheless, care must be taken in answering the "what should we do" question, for often lurking underneath this question is the assumption that we must make things turn out right, that we must "do something that works." But the tragedy of the crucifixion assures us that it may be the case that there is no short-term solution that "works," if by "works" we mean defeating the "bad guys."

The right theological or biblical answer to the "what should we do" question is this simple: *be the church*. That is, be a faithful church, actively bearing witness to the Reign of God. This one answer gives rise to an innumerable host of possible responses, and the particular shape of any one particular response at a particular time will surely be dependent upon the context, dependent upon the calling of God upon an individual or local church body, and dependent upon the gifts that God pours out in that place and time.

This should make it plain, but it should be said anyway, that "nonviolence" does not mean *passivity*. "Pacifism" ought not mean "passivism." Christians must not be *passive* in the face of evil and injustice; instead, we

> "Pacifism" ought not mean "passivism."

seek peaceful, nonviolent resolutions to conflict. (But again, we should not cede the legitimacy of violence, even as a "last resort.") Jesus' own example shows that his way is not some naïve "niceness." Many point to Jesus' cleansing the temple with a whip as if this case settles the question once-and-for-all that Jesus could not have possibly been advocating nonviolence. Quite to the contrary, all this shows is that Jesus was not advocating *passivity*. He was willing to make a scene in order to question the offensive and complacent practices that everyone accepted as quite normal. His action in the temple was all very un-Messianic—his actions proclaimed in no uncertain terms that he would not accept the prevailing social and religious and cultural norms, but was bringing about a fundamentally different order. Burning a flag might be the closest cultural analog we have to the type of offense Jesus here engendered.

The gospel *does* call us to bear witness against injustice, oppression, and violence. And our methods are truth-telling, forgiveness of offenses, and nonviolent reconciliation. Rather than Lamech's ethic, of killing seventy-seven for one, we adopt Jesus' ethic of forgiving seventy-seven times. This entails the hard work of reconciliation, speaking truth to power, and overcoming our fear of the consequences.

> The gospel does call us to bear witness against injustice, oppression, and violence.

But what does such language mean at the level of "political engagement"? It may mean joining Christian Peacemaker Teams, as they practice the theological art of nonviolently "getting in the way" in situations of conflict, like that in Palestine. It may mean finding ways to minister to the desperately poor in Palestine or Pakistan or Afghanistan, in order to communicate the love of Christ. It may mean feeding the homeless in our cities. It may mean finding ways to get antibiotics to sick children in Iraq (against international law, and against the sanctions that have led in the last 12 years to the deaths of 750,000 Iraqi children aged five and under). It may mean telling Christians that they ought not join the military. It may mean that we repent of making July Fourth (a day in which the U.S. colonies violated the explicit teaching of Romans 13) a wannabe American Christian holiday. It may mean some churches get serious about having people in their pews that don't look just like them, whether racially or economically. It may mean that we not only speak up on behalf of the poor and disenfranchised, but find concrete measures to share our surfeit of goods. It may mean being a whistle-blower in a corporate America that often seeks the good only of its own bottom line, sometimes at great expense to the helpless and ignorant. It may mean demonstrating against war-making, or protesting the obscene waste of resources poured out in our idolatrous worship of military might. It may mean nonviolent civil disobedience. It may mean that when dealing with despotic rulers, we take more seriously the method of a Gandhi, who encouraged Christians to take their Jesus more seriously, and thereby freed India from harsh British rule. Or closer to home, we might teach our Sunday School classes about Martin Luther King, Jr., first and foremost a preacher of the gospel, who made great strides in overcoming the systematic oppression of African-Americans in the United States, precisely because he took seriously Jesus' command to love enemies.

Whatever the particulars, it ultimately *does* mean a willingness to be killed while we, as sheep following our shepherd, proclaim God's love and mercy to a world that continues in its rebellion, that continues to prefer merit over grace, retaliation over forgiveness, punishment over reconciliation, and war over mercy. In any case, it should be clear that a call to nonviolence does

> A call to nonviolence does not mean a call to do nothing.

not mean a call to do nothing. (We may need, of course, the grace to know those times when it *is* appropriate to do nothing; but a call to nonviolence is not to be simply equated with doing nothing.) And we should not think that such a call means a naïve endorsement of a stupid social strategy that will "never work." For there are cases, and plenty of them, when nonviolent responses "worked" (again, when by our use of the word "worked" we mean accomplishing a short-term goal of avoiding oppression or injustice or killing). Besides Gandhi and King, already mentioned, innumerable other examples could be cited, whether under the Nazis, or Apartheid in South Africa, or the overthrow of the Marcos dictatorship in the Philippines.[24]

We might also ask "what should we do" with regard to the particular shape and vocabulary of our church assemblies. American churches must make every effort to clearly communicate that their citizenship is first and foremost in the kingdom of God, and that we therefore have a more binding relationship and commitment to Iraqi believers, or French believers, or German believers, than to American unbelievers. We might seriously question the appropriateness of our allegiance to U.S. flags in worship assemblies (or anywhere else, for that matter), for the appearance of the Kingdom of God undoubtedly undercuts the (sometimes implicit, sometimes explicit) assumption that America and Christianity go hand in hand. America is no Israel, and is not God's hope for the world; the *church* is supposed to be the community that offers God's hope to the world. As disciples of Jesus we participate in the one social entity that transcends all national identity; being the body of Christ, we must always loudly proclaim, is our first and unquestionably prioritized form of identity.

In this vein, our public worship assemblies should be careful in the use of the words "our" and "we." Our use of these words betray our most basic conception of our fundamental identity. If we pray,

> *Our public worship assemblies should be careful in the use of the words "our" and "we."*

for example, that the Lord will "keep our troops safe," who else is the "our" but the United States? Do we not deny the unity granted all God's people in baptism by such statements—for seldom are such prayers accompanied by prayers for the safety of the troops of the supposed enemy, or the civilian populations of the supposed enemy. Do not such prayers overlook the fact that U.S. troops might be engaged in killing Christians who happen to live within the confines of some other set of arbitrary geographical boundaries?

Of utmost importance, our churches must be schools of peace-making and reconciliation. Given that our ministry is one of recon-ciliation, we must learn—as church bodies—to get along with one another, to bear with one another, to put up with one another, even when we don't like each other. We must learn to bear differences, disagreements, and arguments in a way that does not betray the unity given us in Christ. What else is war-making but the systemat-ic extension of difference and argument, dealt with by weapons of the flesh? And if we cannot be reconciled to the brother or sister whom we can see, how can we expect, in the midst of a hate-filled world, to bear witness to that love that loves even unto death?

All such peacemaking, all such ministry of reconciliation is not possible, of course, unless we as individuals are seeking the trans-formative power of God to overcome the violence and hatred in our own hearts. A call to nonviolence must begin with my willingness to submit myself to the authority and accountability of fellow believers who are also seeking first the peaceable Kingdom of God. Without the power of God's Spirit renewing my self, my heart, my mind, I cannot possibly walk in the way of Christ. The spirit may be willing, but the flesh is weak. But with God, all things are possible.

Notes

[1]Some paragraphs of this essay are taken from "Why the Christian Church Ought to Be Pacifist," *Leaven: A Journal of Christian Ministry* 10 no. 2 (Second Qtr, 2002) 79-84; and "The Case for Christian Non-Violence," *New Wineskins* (January/February 2002) 25, 27. Grateful recognition is given to Stuart Love, editor of *Leaven*, and to Greg Taylor, editor of *Wineskins*, for their permission to use some of that material here. I would also like to express my thanks to Allison Barney, Sam Braddock, and Lee Edwards, each of whom provided very helpful feedback on an earlier version of this essay.

[2]The contrast between the Genesis account and the Babylonian creation account is instructive here. The Babylonian account characterizes violence as existing as a part of the very warp and woof of the universe, in which the forces of good and evil are pitted against one another in a violent struggle, each seeking to destroy the other. In fact, the creation of the world is an act of violence in the Babylonian account, and the humans are created, in effect, as cheap slave labor. In the Hebrew account, on the other hand, violence enters the story only as a result of the Fall, and the creation is depicted as a result of the Creator's desire for fellowship and communion. Violence truly "violates" the *shalom* of God's creation, and is a parasite off of God's created goodness, rather than being inherent to it.

[3]See the very helpful and extended discussion of this in Abraham Heschel's work, *The Prophets* (New York: Perennial Classics, 2001) especially part I, chapter 9, "History."

[4]Not only is this a concern in Pauline writings. This is a major concern of the book of Acts.

[5]John Howard Yoder, *The Politics of Jesus: Vicit Agnus Noster*, 2nd ed. (Grand Rapids: Eerdmans, 1994) 39.

[6]For a very helpful discussion of the "love of enemies" ethic of Jesus, contrasted with Greco-Roman codes, see Marius Reiser, "Love of Enemies in the Context of Antiquity," *New Testament Studies* 47 (Oct. 2001) 411-427.

[7]There is much to be said here, of course, that cannot be covered. The eschatology of Paul, in particular, is one of a "now but not yet" perspective. It has been established, but its full consummation awaits in the future, upon the appearance of Christ.

[8]Walter Wink, *Engaging the Powers: Discernment and Resistance in a World of Domination* (Minneapolis: Fortress Press, 1992) 217.

[9]So Lisa Sowle Cahill, *Love Your Enemies: Discipleship, Pacifism, and Just War Theory* (Minneapolis: Fortress, 1994) 13, notes that it is actually the just-war tradition which is a more rule-based approach, instead of pacifism. Instead of starting with a rule against the use of violence, biblical pacifism gives rise to a viewpoint in which "disciples ask after a way of life consistent with incorporation into Christ." Or, p. 19: "The Christian just war tradition has been built on the premise that the present world so entangles the disciple in conflict and 'brokenness' that gospel fidelity requires compromise action. Christian pacifism is premised instead on the accessibility of the kingdom life now and the reality of a community in which the kingdom already begins."

[10]There are numerous places such a contention is made. For a recent example in the Stone-Campbell movement, see Rubel Shelly, "Just War: Quandary of Christian Conscience," *New Wineskins* (Jan/Feb 2002) 24, 26. Rubel is a friend and brother, but I think him quite wrong on this score.

[11]See, as one example, the classic work of Roland Bainton, *Christian Attitudes toward War and Peace: A Historical Survey and Critical Reevaluation* (New York, Abingdon Press, 1960), chap. 5. Bainton treats with much more nuance the variety of ways pacifism got articulated in the early church, and some of the competing interpretations of modern interlocutors.

[12]All cited in Bainton, *Christian Attitudes*, 77.

[13]See the discussion in John Driver, *How Christians Made Peace with War: Early Christian Understandings of War* (Scottdale, PA: Herald Press, 1988) 20-22. Justin, e.g., says: "We who were filled with war, and mutual slaughter, and every wickedness, have each through the whole earth changed our warlike weapons—our swords into ploughshares, and our spears into implements of tillage—and we cultivate piety, righteousness, philanthropy, faith, and hope, which we have from the Father Himself through Him who was crucified" (*Dialog with Trypho*, in *ANF*, vol. 1, chap. 110).

[14]On Martin Luther, see particularly *The Sermon on the Mount*, excerpted in O. O'Donovan

313

and J.L. O'Donovan, *From Irenaeus to Grotius* (Grand Rapids: Eerdmans, 1999) 599. It was also used by Foy E. Wallace, *The Sermon on the Mount and the Civil State* (Nashville: Foy E. Wallace Jr. Publications, 1967) 110.

[15]In Robert McAfee Brown, ed., *The Essential Reinhold Niebuhr: Selected Essays and Addresses* (New Haven: Yale University Press, 1986) 102-119.

[16]This line of reasoning is developed with regard to the Just War tradition by the well-known Protestant theologian Paul Ramsey. See, for example, "The Case for Making 'Just War' Possible," in Ramsey, *The Just War: Force and Political Responsibility* (New York: University Press of America) 148ff.

[17]This list is typical of many discussions of the JWT. For history on the development of this tradition, see the work of both Bainton and Cahill. For another critical but serious assessment of the JWT, see John Yoder, *When War is Unjust: Being Honest in Just War Thinking* (Minneapolis: Augsburg, 1984).

[18]The work of James Childress, e.g., supports this construal of the JWT; the work of Paul Ramsey, on the other hand, sees war-making not so much an exception to an otherwise accepted norm, but as a positive out-working of love of neighbor.

[19]An example of this has occurred during my writing this essay. The U.S. government, under the George W. Bush administration, appears readying itself for war with Iraq. In his State of the Union address at the beginning of 2003, Mr. Bush (a self-proclaimed Christian) suggested that we would preemptively attack Iraq, even if we do not have the support of other nations to do so. The National Council of Churches and the U.S. Conference of Catholic Bishops—both organizations that hold to the JWT—have made clear that this is immoral, and not an acceptable use of the "just cause" criterion of the tradition. Nonetheless, later in his speech, Mr. Bush claimed that we would be fighting with a "just cause."

[20]Bainton, *Christian Attitudes*, 109, notes that during the middle ages, the clergy were not allowed to participate in shedding the blood of others; they should rather be prepared to imitate Christ, laying down their own lives rather than taking the lives of others, given that they administer the sacraments. But even for the laity, for whom warfare was seen as permissible under just war constraints, penance was required. After the Norman conquest, for example, "a council at Winchester in 1076 enacted that he who had killed a man should do penance for a year. He who did not know whether his wounded assailant had died should do penance for forty days. He who did not know how many he had killed should do penance one day a week throughout his life. All archers should do penance thrice for the space of forty days."

[21]For a more thorough and systematic treatment of these issues, see John Howard Yoder, *What Would You Do? A Serious Answer to a Standard Question* (Scottdale, PA: Herald Press, 1983); and also Wink, *Engaging the Powers*, chapter 12.

[22]Walter Wink, *Engaging the Powers*, 233, relates the following account: "William Jennings Bryan once visited Tolstoy and pressed him with the perennial problem of what to do if a criminal is about to kill a child. Tolstoy responded that, having lived seventy-five years, he had never, except in discussions, 'encountered that fantastic brigand, who, before my eyes desired to kill or violate a child, but that perpetually I did and do see not one but millions of brigands using violence toward children and women and men and old people and all the labourers in the name of the recognized right of violence over one's fellows. When I said this my kind interlocutor, with his naturally quick perception, not giving me time to finish, laughed, and recognized that my argument was satisfactory.' There is considerable irony in the presumed compassion of the interlocutor who is so concerned about the potential rape of a single grandmother, when the same questioner accepts war, where the rape of grandmothers, wives, daughters, and children is so routine that many soldiers have regarded it as one of the perquisites of warfare."

[23]On the centurion example in particular, there is a common reply from some interpreters of the early church record that military service in the Roman empire, particularly during peacetime, was more akin to police service today, which, in the run-of-the-mill service, has little to do with violence anyway. Instead, police service is much more concerned with issues of public civil service.

[24]See Wink, *Engaging the Powers*, chapter 13. See also the PBS documentary, *A Force More Powerful* for discussion of numerous nonviolent protests and movements.

Bibliography

Bainton, Roland. *Christian Attitudes toward War and Peace: A Historical Survey and Critical Re-evaluation.* New York, Abingdon Press, 1960.

This older book remains a classic survey of the development of various ways of thinking about warfare in the Christian tradition. For newcomers to the questions surrounding Christians, war, and peace, it is a very helpful work.

Casey, Michael. "From Religious Outsiders to Insiders: The Rise and Fall of Pacifism in the Churches of Christ." *Journal of Church and State* 44/3 (Summer 2002) 455-475.

In Churches of Christ, Casey has done the greatest amount of historical research on pacifism in the Stone-Campbell movement. He has numerous articles and works on this subject. This particular article provides a helpful overview.

Hauerwas, Stanley. *The Hauerwas Reader.* Durham, NC: Duke University Press, 2002.

Hauerwas is perhaps the best-known Christian pacifist theologian in the United States. In the *Reader*, essay six, "Jesus and the Social Embodiment of the Peaceable Kingdom" is particularly helpful. The *Reader* presents much of Hauerwas's theological work, some (much?) of which is not very accessible to "lay" readers. For a more popular telling of his viewpoint, see his book *Resident Aliens*, co-authored with William Willimon.

Hays, Richard B. *The Moral Vision of the New Testament: Community, Cross, New Creation: A Contemporary Introduction to New Testament Ethics.* San Francisco: HarperSanFrancisco, 1996.

Hays's work sets forward hermeneutical considerations for how we are to garner ethical guidance from the New Testament, using three concepts as central to reading and appropriating its authority: cross, community, and new creation. In the last part of the book, he deals with a number of concrete issues, one of which is Jesus' teachings on nonviolence.

Jordan, Clarence. *The Substance of Faith and Other Cotton Patch Sermons.* Ed. by Dallas Lee. New York: Association Press, 1972.

A folksy, fun-to-read collection of some of the work of Clarence Jordan, founder of Koinonia Farm, an interracial, pacifist community, which began in the midst of the racially segregated

South. Jordan speaks of the God Movement (his vernacular for the "Kingdom of God"), a sociopolitical alternative that transcends the racist and nationalistic boundaries that separate peoples; in the God Movement, we are called to love of enemy and the work of reconciliation.

Wink, Walter. *Engaging the Powers: Discernment and Resistance in a World of Domination.* Minneapolis: Fortress Press, 1992.

The third and final volume in his trilogy on "the powers," Wink develops a biblical theology in which he understands the notion of "authorities" and "powers" in Pauline theology as representative of sociopolitical forces that enslave humankind rather than serve it as God intended. God's redemptive purposes—to restore the powers to their rightful place of service, and to free humankind from all forms of domination and oppression—is revealed in the nonviolence of Jesus, a method we are called to employ as disciples of Jesus.

Yoder, John Howard. *The Politics of Jesus: Vicit Agnus Noster.* 2nd ed. Grand Rapids: Eerdmans, 1994.

In Yoder's classic treatment of many of these questions, he argues (integrating both biblical scholarship and systematic theology) that Jesus and the New Testament *do* intend to communicate a social and political ethic. Jesus' teachings regarding servanthood (rather than seeking power), forgiveness (rather than retaliation), nonviolence (rather than war-making), and sharing (rather than accumulation or merely tithing) are to be taken seriously as an alternative sociopolitical ethic by the Christian community.

THE FAMILY AND
ETHICAL CHOICES

In This Section

Leonard Knight
Divorce and Remarriage

John Mark Hicks
Homosexuality and the Biblical Witness

Gregory Linton
Sexual Ethics in the New Testament

DIVORCE AND REMARRIAGE
A STUDY OF THE ETHICAL IMPLICATIONS
Leonard Knight, Ph.D.

God's Original Intention

Has the wrong question been asked? Jesus' question to the Pharisees when they approach him about the meaning of Deuteronomy 24:1-4[1] as it applies to divorce is, "Haven't you read . . ." (Matt 19:4). His response indicates that they have misunderstood the intent of God. Stassen and Gushee suggest that scholars and churches have historically focused on the wrong questions. Like the Pharisees, we have all asked the "permissibility questions."[2]

> Has the wrong question been asked? Like the Pharisees, we have all asked the "permissibility questions."

Soon after I had completed my doctoral training in marriage and family counseling, I returned to my childhood home to visit my parents. My father, who had been an elder in our congregation since I was a teenager, asked me if I would accompany him to the Saturday morning breakfast meeting that the elders held each month. I was very honored but a little hesitant, for as far as I knew, members of the congregation were not often invited to participate in this event. It was a joy for me to be there, for these were the men who had been my spiritual mentors since childhood. I loved and admired each of them. We had our breakfast, shared rich fellowship, and I quietly observed as they discussed some practical issues regarding the church. Then one of the elders turned to me and began explaining that they were struggling with a particular situation in the church. A man who had grown up in the congregation had divorced his wife for what the elders believed was an unbiblical reason. He was now expressing his intent to remarry. The elders struggled with whether the church could continue to fellowship with him since he would now be "living in adultery." They were asking for my thoughts regarding this situation. I was astounded and sat there considering how I should answer.

Stassen and Gushee state that those who have guided our religious communities have wrestled with ". . . rules and exceptions rather than the character of God, scriptural principles that reflect that character, real human situations that reflect our bondage to sin, and transformative practices."[3] The emphasis of this study will be on the meaning of marriage as a blessing intended by God for the good of his creation. Although the relevant passages on marriage and divorce will be considered, the intent is not to focus solely on a legal interpretation of what may be "permissible" in those crushing situations where a divorce is about to or has taken place. Rather, it is to focus on marriage and how the church may assist all of us in learning how to have richer and more meaningful relationships as husbands and wives.

As a beginning marriage and family therapist twenty-five years ago, I was amazed by the assertion of couples or individuals coming for counseling that they no longer loved their mates. How could people who had stood with each other before their families, their communities, and God and stated their devotion to one another now insist that the commitment that they had once made was no longer meaningful or binding? Over the years, I have come to recognize that my clients are telling the truth. The love, dedication, and commitment with which they had once bound themselves to one another has died. When I began to investigate the reasons, I discovered that at some point in their relationship, my clients had ceased doing those things that made them want to be together in the first place. They had stopped working at their relationship, stopped reaching out to one another, and stopped placing the highest priority on the other person and on their relationship together. Very often, they had slowly drifted apart into private lives, private hopes and goals, and private perspectives. In most cases, there had been no abuse, no adultery, no desertion, and no cruelty except the cruelty that comes with selfishness and rejection.[4]

Both in the example of God "at the beginning" (Matt 19:4;

Mark 10:6) and in his relationship to Israel and Judah, as referenced in Hosea and other of the prophets, it is God's intention to resist divorce as the outcome to marriage. It was he who tenderly joined the man and the woman in marriage. The text of Genesis 2:20b-24 is the reiteration of a question of which the narrative is the answer. The question is this:

> "Why are the sexes so powerfully drawn towards each other? Whence comes this love strong as death (Song of Solomon 8:6) and stronger than the ties to one's own parents, whence this inner clinging to each other, this drive toward each other which does not rest until it again becomes one flesh in the child?"[5]

Thus, the author indicates that it is because of the specific creation of the woman as one who is a "helper suitable for him"[6] (Gen 2:18,20) that the man recognizes and identifies with her. She is one who is both similar to him and supplements him. She is uniquely suited to his need and thus is "bone of my bones and flesh of my flesh" (Gen 2:23). This emphasizes the truth deriving from God's creative action that she is the only true reflection of the man in creation and yet she also fills up what is missing in him.[7]

To speak of the woman as bone of the man's bone and flesh of his flesh indicates a mutuality of relationship. It may even have reflected an ancient Jewish covenantal formula that speaks of "commonality of concern, loyalty, and responsibility."[8] The formula emphasizes a meaningful interpersonal relationship rooted in an oath of solidarity to which both the man and the woman commit themselves.

The Marital Metaphor

Marriage is the most powerful metaphor for meaningful relationships found in Scripture. It is the analogy used to describe God's relationship to his people as well as the social, cultural, and legal description of the most intimate relationship that a man and woman can ever have. The identification of the man and woman as "one flesh" (Gen 2:24) emphasizes the phenomenon of marriage which "shapes both partners so that they are congruous to each other."[9] It is this life-long commitment of one man to one woman in marriage that Jesus

> *Marriage is the most powerful metaphor for meaningful relationships found in Scripture.*

says was the original intention of God in creation (Matt 19:4-6; Mark 10:6-9).[10]

The ideal for the marital relationship as it is conceived in Scripture is acted out in the covenant intent for God and his people.

> The ideal for the marital relationship as it is conceived in Scripture is acted out in the covenant intent for God and his people.

"The Rabbis eulogized the conclusion of the covenant at Sinai as the marriage between Yahweh and his people. The Torah is the marriage contract, Moses is the one who leads the Bride and Yahweh meets Israel in the same way as the Bridegroom his bride."[11] The event itself was alluded to often in the writings of the prophets.[12] Hosea reminds God's people of their covenant contract in language that is reminiscent of the sexual consummation of the marriage. He says: "I am the LORD your God from the land of Egypt. . . . It was I who *knew* you in the wilderness, in the land of drought" (Hos 13:4,5; emphasis added).

The content of Hosea's message is revealed in the conceptual phrases embedded in his language.[13] Hubbard suggests that the concept of the "knowledge of God" (Hos 2:19-20) emphasizes intimate, interpersonal knowledge and relationship that results in a commitment that is lifelong.[14] The knowledge of God is implied in the concept of "covenant love" or *ḥesed*. Stassen and Gushee define the covenant concept as: ". . . a sacred, God-witnessed, public, mutually binding, irrevocable relationship between two parties who willingly promise and undertake to live by its terms."[15] Wherever *bᵊrîth* (covenant) governs the relationships of people in marriage, family, or community, then the normal kinds of conduct expected of individuals is called *ḥesed* or covenant-love.[16] The expected result of the *bᵊrîth* is mutual commitment, love, and service.[17]

Repentance is the third key to understanding Hosea's message. In chapter two, he defines repentance simply as returning to God, which is the essence of the concept of reconciliation (Hos 2:7; cf. Rom 5:6-11; 2 Cor 5:17-21). Only awakening to the truth about God and his grace can make such a return possible. Israel's repentance is brought about by the misery of the nation, a new understanding of the gracious love of God, and the felt guilt in turning from him. Thus, Smith says: "To Hosea, repentance is no mere change in the direction of one's life. It is a turning back upon one's self, a retracing of one's footsteps, a confession and acknowledgement of what one has abandoned."[18]

In Hosea, God reveals himself as the partner who loves his people deeply and is willing that they should be reconciled to himself (Hos 2:16-20). Rowley writes:

> . . . the wife whom Hosea deeply loved was unfaithful to him . . . her infidelity brought him intense anguish yet without destroying his love, so that he found God approaching him through his agony to illumine his mind with an understanding of the depth of the divine love for Israel that is unsurpassed in the Old Testament.[19]

Because of this very personal realization, the prophet could witness to Israel of the Lord's steadfast, undying, patient love. Hosea came to understand God's feeling in relationship to his people and his reluctance to completely abandon them even in the light of their faithlessness. Snaith interprets Hosea's thought in this manner:

> But through the troubles which beat against and broke the marital covenant between Jehovah and Israel, there was one fact that never changed. This was God's sure love for Israel. Because of this unswerving love, the Covenant can never be finally and completely broken. It takes two to make a covenant and also takes two to break it. Israel may have rejected God, but God has not rejected Israel.[20]

Because of this great, redemptive love, Yahweh continually calls his bride back to himself in order to effect a reconciliation. This reconciliation leads to the establishment of a new covenant based on mutual and compassionate love, faithfulness, and forgiveness. Thus, the marital metaphor implicitly carries with it the suggestion of repentance, forgiveness, and the renewal of the covenant relationship.[21]

The concept of faithfulness in the marital metaphor is central to the understanding of God's assertion, "I hate divorce" (Mal 2:16). The faithless (*bāgad*) behavior of individuals and society identified by Malachi is used to illustrate faithlessness toward God. The language of faithlessness is

> Thus, the marital metaphor implicitly carries with it the suggestion of repentance, forgiveness, and the renewal of the covenant relationship.

". . . used when the OT writer wants to say that a man does not honor an agreement, or commits adultery, or breaks a covenant or some other ordinance given by God."[22] In Malachi 2:10-16, Judah is indicted by God for having "broken faith" or dealt "treacherously" by violating vows she has made. The entire passage is developed around the concept of God's call to be faithful to one's covenant promises. The married couple are joined by God through the creation event in which they are designed specifically for each other. They bind themselves in marital promises, and God is portrayed as one who witnesses their promises (Mal 2:14), exhorts them to be faithful to each other (Mal 2:15), and is deeply angered when those promises are broken (Mal 2:16).[23]

Divorce in Jewish Practices

Instone-Brewer points out that rabbinic Judaism identified four justifications for divorce. "The rabbis agreed that the grounds for divorce were childlessness, material neglect, emotional neglect, and unfaithfulness."[24] The first justification grew out of the rabbinic interpretation of the creation account. In Genesis 1:28 the first couple is commanded to "be fruitful and increase in number." All Jews were expected to honor this command by marrying and having children. However, the burden for having children fell on women, and it was they who bore the social rejection of barrenness (cf. Gen 16:1-2; 1 Sam 1:1-8; Luke 1:5-7). By New Testament times, the schools of Hillel and Shammai had debated the purpose of marriage and concluded that it was essentially for the goal of having children. Thus, childlessness had become a reason for divorcing although it was not required that the couple divorce if they had no children (cf. Luke 1:5-7).[25]

Marital unfaithfulness or adultery as a ground for divorce derived from the seventh of the ten commandments (Exod 20:14) and the declaration in Leviticus 20:10 that this was a capital offense. Adultery was very difficult to prove since it required two witnesses.[26] Additionally, as demonstrated in the case of David and Bathsheba, the death penalty was not necessarily enforced (2 Samuel 11 & 12). Rabbi Tigay stated, "Whether the severe provisions of the law were actually carried out in biblical times cannot be ascertained. . . . Evidence for prosecution of adultery is scant in the Bible."[27] Even divorce was not compulsory for unfaithfulness. However, it was assumed that a man would want to divorce an adulterous wife in order that he might keep her *ketubah* or dowry. Even if a man only suspected but could not prove infidelity, he was encouraged to divorce his wife or betrothed because of the social stigma attached to her sin. A husband would usually pursue this course of action even though he would lose the *ketubah* (cf. Matt 1:18-25).

As suggested by the language in the rabbinic discussions, usually only the man had the right of divorce. Because of the acceptance of polygamy as a cultural norm prior to the first century, the husband did not have to promise faithfulness in the marital contract. A man could not commit adultery against his own wife. If he committed adultery, it was an offense against another woman's husband and against their marriage, as in the case of David and Bathsheba's sin against Uriah the Hittite (2 Sam. 11:1-5).[28]

The concepts of emotional and material neglect as grounds for divorce developed from the rabbinic interpretation of Exodus 21:10-11. This passage is found in a context dealing with the rights and responsibilities of masters and slaves. The specific text deals with the experience of the female slave or *amah* who is also the concubine of her master. It provides a protection for the female concubine when the master takes another wife.[29]

Exodus 21:10 states that the master must continue to provide the slave woman's "food, clothing, and marital rights" as he had done before. The meaning of these three ideas in Hebrew is difficult. The explanation of marital rights as understood in the rabbinic theology of first-century Judaism is suggested by the Apostle Paul in his references to the sexual or conjugal rights of a marriage partner in 1 Corinthians 7:3-5. The assumption in Hebrew society is that if an individual is capable of sexual relations, then he or she will find an outlet for the sexual drive. Thus, if the master/husband cannot fulfill his responsibilities, he is to release her (Exod 21:11). As in Deuteronomy 24:1-4, this will allow her to find another husband and thus protect her and the community from the stain of sin.[30]

Divorce, a Consequence of the Fall

When Jesus points his questioners to the original intention of God "at the beginning" (Matt 19:4; Mark 10:6), he is appealing to the example of God as a model. The force of this argument is reflected in its use in the Hillel-Shammai debate over the meaning of Genesis 1:28, "be fruitful and increase in number." The School of Shammai used the example of Moses (Exod 18:2-3) to argue that two children were enough. But the School of Hillel won the debate when they said that it must be at least one male and one female because of the example of God in creation, a more significant example than that of Moses.[31]

Jesus' identification of marriage with the divine plan "at the beginning" indicates that the meaning of the married relationship is defined by God before the Fall. In the earliest history of humanity, there is no divorce. It is not part of God's original plan but appears first because of human "hardness of heart" (Matt 19:8; Mark 10:5). Later, it is legalized on limited grounds as an accommodation or allowance to protect the defense-less wife and to keep the community from sponsoring evil (Exod 21:10-11; Deut 24:1-4).[32]

> In the earliest history of humanity, there is no divorce.

In the account of the Fall, both the man and the woman sin, yet neither one accepts the responsibility for his or her behavior. Each finds another to blame. The woman blames the serpent who lied to her and undermined her faith in God. The man blames God for giving him the woman in the first place and then blames the woman for leading him into sin. Their sin and their unwillingness to accept responsibility, repent, and seek forgiveness changes the existential nature of their relationship with God and with each other. Their sin has exposed their nakedness, and God mercifully and generously covers them. But their sin has produced other significant losses. The woman's consequences are that she, removed from the protection of God, shall now experience birthing in pain. Their sin will also result in the woman experiencing subordination to the man, and his headship over her will be experienced as trouble and anguish rather than as joy and blessing. Continuing selfishness and sin will create conflict and loss for both of them. The man will also suffer because the environment will now become his enemy and he will have to wrestle his livelihood from the earth. Finally, the man and woman are expelled from the presence of God to prevent them from compounding their original sin by eating of the tree of life and living forever (Gen 3:1-24).[33]

Divorce as a societal phenomena is an outcome to be expected when humanity asserts its independence from God. The temptation of Adam and Eve was focused on their selfish desire to be free of God and even to challenge God in his divinity (Gen 3:4-5). Crabb notes: "Selfishness, self-centeredness, and self-indulgence have their roots, not in longings of our soul, but rather in our arrogant determination to act independently of God in the pursuit of satisfaction."[34] Marriage requires a willingness to give priority to the needs, goals, hopes, and fears of another. Often it is the unwillingness

of people in their self-centeredness to continue working at their relationship that leads to its dissolution.

Is It Lawful?

Jesus' teaching regarding divorce is found in Matthew 5:31-32; 19:3-9; Mark 10:2-12; and Luke 16:18. A composite of the four passages suggests that a man who divorces his wife except for the reason of sexual immorality is in violation of the law. It is important to recognize that when the Pharisees ask, "Is it lawful for a man to divorce his wife for any and every reason?" (Matt 19:3), they are asking for an interpretation of the Torah statements found in Deuteronomy 24:1-4. More specifically, they are inviting Jesus to choose between the positions taken by the Schools of Hillel and Shammai. Matthew's and Mark's comments also suggest that the intent of the Pharisees is to entrap Jesus in a discussion that had political, cultural, and social overtones.[35]

Instone-Brewer identifies six implications of Jesus' teaching in these passages:

1. Monogamy is the original intention of God and thus a person can only be married to one other individual at a time.
2. Marriage was intended to last for the lifetimes of the two people who bound themselves to one another. It is against God's will to do anything that will result in the dissolution of that marriage.
3. Divorce is never required even in the case of adultery.
4. Divorce may be allowed only in those situations where there is a stubborn refusal to discontinue one's ongoing sexual immorality.
5. Marriage is not a requirement, and thus childlessness is not a ground for divorce.
6. Divorce for "any and every reason" is not acceptable, and those who remarry following such a divorce will be committing adultery.[36]

Central to the question raised by the Pharisees is the meaning of the Hebrew phrase, *'ervath dābār* in Deuteronomy 24:1. It has been variously translated as "some deficiency,"[37] "something indecent,"[38] and "indecency of a matter/nakedness of a matter."[39] The School of Hillel explained the text with the phrase, "thing of unseemliness," emphasizing the term *dābār* (thing or matter) and seeing in the construction a reference to two categories of justification for divorce: first, adultery, and second, all other possible failures of the wife.[40] They concluded that *'ervath dābār* meant anything that could discomfit or inconvenience the husband.[41] The second-century Rabbi Akiba stated that divorce was justified even if a husband was more attracted to some other woman.[42]

The School of Shammai disagreed and translated the awkward construction in Deuteronomy 24:1 as "a matter of indecency." They understood the language to refer to unchastity which was interpreted as immoral sexual behavior on the part of the wife, particularly adultery.[43]

Jews in the time of Jesus and ever since have taken the position that the School of Hillel had correctly parsed the meaning of this phrase. Thus, a man could divorce his wife for any behaviors or mannerisms that he found to be obnoxious or otherwise unacceptable and not just because she had been sexually unfaithful.[44]

A review of the uses of *"'ervāh"* in the Old Testament indicates that it is primarily translated as "nakedness" where it describes a situation involving exposure of the body and/or sexual relations.[45] Leviticus 18 is entirely given over to a discussion of unlawful sexual behavior and in the twenty plus occurrences of *'ervāh*, it is translated each time by the New International Version as having sexual relations. The verbal form of *'ervāh (ārāh)* has the general sense of "to be naked" or "to make naked [or] strip bare" with reference to sexual offenses. In the Hebrew intensive-reflexive, it is translated to "expose oneself, make oneself naked, [or] spreading oneself."[46] In Leviticus 20:19, it is a euphemism for unlawful sexual behavior: "Do not have sexual relations (*ārāh*). . . ," or, literally "expose your aunt's nakedness."

Based on a word study of *'ervāh* as it is generally used in the Old Testament, it would appear that Moses in Deuteronomy 24:1 is allowing divorce only for sexual unfaithfulness and not "for any and every reason." The School of Shammai appears to be correct in its interpretation of Moses' language although it is uncertain that they really understood Moses' intent in this legislation. However, despite this interpretation, Shammaite teaching did not hold that sexual immorality was the only ground for divorce. They also permitted divorce for childlessness, material neglect, and emotional neglect.[47]

Jesus' assertion that divorce was not part of God's original plan causes the Pharisees to protest, "Why then did Moses command [ἐνετείλατο][48] that a man give his wife a certificate of divorce and send her away?" (Matt 19:7-8). When comparing the Matthew and Markan accounts of this discussion, a discrepancy appears in the textual record because in Mark, Jesus questions the Pharisees by asking, "What did Moses command you?" They respond, "Moses permitted (ἐπέτρεψεν) a man to write a certificate of divorce and send her away" (Mark 10:3-4). There is a significant difference between *entellomai* (command/order concerning something)[49] and *epitrepō* (allow/permit someone).[50]

Similar to rabbinic literature, the Gospel writers often compress the dialogue involved in discussions during various encounters in Jesus' ministry and parallel accounts will retain some details while leaving out others.[51] The process of abbreviating a particular teaching was influenced by the manner in which that teaching was to be delivered and the audience to whom the Gospel writer is addressing the text. Matthew has prepared a syllabus of Jesus' teachings that he is delivering to a Jewish audience, much like a rabbi in the synagogue. It is organized around five major themes and this influences the organization and content of the text. Chouinard observes: "Matthew's compositional scheme greatly facilitated learning by providing the listener (or reader) with a coherent and orderly presentation that aided comprehension and memorization."[52] By contrast, Mark is recording the preaching of sermons in which the oral material that Jesus delivered in the presence of his disciples is being rehearsed in story and instruction for a Gentile audience that does not understand the Hebrew roots of Jesus' teaching.[53]

The purpose of compressing these accounts is to enable the reader to retain in memory highly significant information that was originally delivered orally. When considering the marriage/divorce/remarriage discussion found in Matthew's and Mark's Gospels, it is instructive to realize that these two writers are reflecting different points in the dialogue when the terms "command" and "permit" are introduced. Integrating Matthew 19:7-8 and Mark 10:2-5 provides a more complete account of the debate at this point and would appear like this:

1. Jesus announces that divorce was not part of God's original intention for marriage.
2. The Pharisees dissent by saying: "Why then did Moses *command* that a man give his wife a certificate of divorce and send her away?" (Matt 19:7).
3. Jesus challenges their assertion: "What did Moses *command* you?" (Mark 10:3).
4. The Pharisees indicate they have made an overstatement by admitting: "Moses *permitted* a man to write a certificate of divorce . . ." (Mark 10:4).
5. Jesus acknowledges the rephrasing of their position: "Moses *permitted* you to divorce your wives because your hearts were hard" (Matt 19:8a; Mark 10:5).
6. Jesus reiterates, "But it was not this way from the beginning" (Matt 19:8b; Mark 10:6-7.[54]

In his concluding statement (Matt 19:8), Jesus uses the Greek perfect tense and his statement is translated, "it has not been so" with reference to the practice of divorcing a wife for "any and every reason." This is the emphatic method in Greek of presenting a fact or condition. "It is the strong way of saying that a thing *is*."[55] The force of this tense in Matthew 19:8 is to suggest that something was not so in the beginning and has not been so right up to the present.[56] The reference is to the Pharisee's original question, and thus Jesus is saying emphatically that it has never been acceptable under the Law of Moses for a man to divorce his wife for "any reason at all." Although Moses permitted divorce, this was a concession to their unwillingness to abide by God's original plan for marriage.[57]

Jesus' statement regarding "hardheartedness" provides an insight into the social situation inherent in Deuteronomy 24:1-4. The meaning of this phrase has been debated. It has been defined as "stubbornness"[58] or a "moral and spiritual petrification."[59] The implication of the text is that the ruthless behavior of the men seeking divorce reflects a deep selfishness and self-centeredness. They can no longer identify with the "wife of their youth" (Mal 2:14) at any level. They have forgotten all of the reasons why they originally wanted to be with this woman. Thus, they want to be rid of her and must have their own way no matter what it costs anyone else, including the wife, their children, their families, or the community. The language used to describe the process of divorcing is illuminating. They are spoken of as "cutting off," "driving out," "put[ting] her away," or "put[ting] her out."[60] Their unwillingness to forgive is in stark contrast to God's actions with his unfaithful bride, Israel, in the metaphor of Hosea's marriage. The lack of a forgiving attitude may in fact be the core of "hardheartedness" in this context and a greater sin than divorce (Matt 6:14-15; 18:35).

The "hardness of heart" which has resulted in divorce becoming a significant issue in Hebrew society has led to a concession that is not part of the original plan of God. Moses is not commanding divorce for sexual immorality. He is dealing with a situation in which a man is unwilling to forgive and accept back his unfaithful wife, but also unwilling to release her to become the wife of another. He wants to remain her master but will no longer be her husband. The wife in this case is forced to remain in a deeply humiliating position. This creates the likelihood that she will choose to participate in sexual immorality again, making her a real threat to the sanctity of the community. Thus, God through Moses provides two possibilities for husbands. They can choose to be fully reconciled to their wives which would reflect both God's behavior and his original intention. But if they will not reconcile with her, they must give her a *get* (certificate of divorce)[61] and allow her to go and become the wife of another (Deut 24:2).[62] Instone-Brewer states:

> The purpose of the divorce certificate was to allow an abandoned woman to remarry. It was an abrogation by the man of his rights as her husband to reclaim her after abandoning her. He had to give her this certificate before he sent her from his house. If she exercised this right and remarried, his right to her was then irrevocably lost.
>
> The divorce certificate was therefore both a disincentive to divorce as well as a benefit to a divorced woman. Without the law of the certificate of divorce, a man could simply dismiss his wife from the house and then change his mind on a future occasion. The certificate made this dismissal a more significant event and gave the woman legal rights.[63]

Except for Πορνεία

Jesus' identifies three consequences of an invalid divorce in his response to the insistence of the Pharisees that divorce is acceptable "for any and every reason":

1. The man who divorces his wife causes her to commit adultery when she marries again (Matt 5:32).

2. The man who marries an unlawfully divorced woman will be committing adultery against her existing marriage with her lawful mate (Matt 5:32; Luke 16:18).

3. The man who divorces his wife commits adultery against her when he marries again (Matt 19:9; Mark 10:11; Luke 16:18).[64]

To understand the meaning of these statements, it is necessary to recognize that marriage was the status quo in Jewish culture. The Pharisees regarded marriage as necessary for those who would honor God. To fail to marry and have children was a denigration of the image of God. Thus, the expectation of remarriage was inherent in the discussion of divorce. It is a foregone conclusion in the minds of Jesus' audience that anyone who divorced would remarry, and Jesus does not suggest otherwise. Indeed, the right of remarriage is assumed in Deuteronomy 24:2. The essential part of a Jewish bill of divorcement was the statement, "You are free to marry any man."[65] In fact, Jesus' statement in Matthew 5:32 (". . . anyone who divorces his wife except for marital unfaithfulness, *causes* [literally, makes] her to become an adulteress . . .") only makes sense when one assumes that she will exercise her right to remarry.

> *Marriage was the status quo in Jewish culture.*

In Matthew 5:32 and 19:9, an exception clause is included in Jesus' statements about divorce and adultery. He says that remarriage after a divorce is adultery except in the situation where the divorce occurred because of *porneia* or sexual immorality. The transliteration into English of this term as "fornication" results in a loss of meaning compared to the cultural contexts of Judaism reflected in both the Old and New Testaments. The cognate form of the word πορνη references a prostitute, whether a man or a woman, and is a general term for a sexually immoral lifestyle. The Hebrew term which is translated *porneia* refers to prostitution (Gen 38:24; Ezek 23:11,29) and harlots (Nahum 3:4). *Porneia* is used similarly in the New Testament where it refers to a number of unlawful sexual acts such as incest (1 Cor 5:1), prostitution (Matt 21:31-32; Luke 15:30; 1 Cor 6:13-18), and sexual immorality in general (Mark 7:21-22; Matt 15:19; 1 Cor 6:9-11; 7:2). In both the Old and the New Testaments, these terms are also used as analogies for spiritual unfaithfulness (Hos 4:11, Rev 17:1-5,15-16).[66]

The meaning of *'ervāh* (Deut 24:1) as sexual promiscuity parallels the idea of *porneia* (Matt 5:32; 19:9). Jesus' use of the word *porneia* seems intentional, and although many have chosen to translate *porneia* with the word "adultery" in the Matthew passages, the Greek for "adultery" (*moicheia*) cannot be equated with *porneia* (Mark 7:21-22//Matt 15:19; 1 Cor 6:9; Heb 13:4). Adultery (*moicheia*) specifies a single act of sexual unfaithfulness whether that act is repeated or not. As a sin, adultery is committed against the marriage of another person. Notice the phrase "against her" in Mark 10:11. The behavior of her husband is a violation of her exclusive rights within the covenant relationship of the marriage. By contrast, *porneia* describes an immoral course of life. It involves a broader context of sexual sin much like *'ervāh*. Thus, Jesus' use of *porneia* instead of "adultery" when describing the behavior that would destroy the covenant relationship raises the question as to whether he ever considered a single act of unfaithfulness as grounds for divorce. In this sense, the Matthew 5:32 and 19:9 passages parallel Mark 10:11 and Luke 16:18 which do not list any exception to the statement that when one divorces and marries another, he or she will be committing adultery.[67]

Porneia and its Hebrew counterpart (זְנוּנִים) describe unfaithfulness whether sexual or spiritual (Hos 1:2; 2:6; 4:11-12; 5:4; Rev 17:1-5,15-16). This unfaithfulness is so inimical to the marriage relationship that it makes it impossible for the relationship to continue. It was through Israel's failure to maintain the covenant (Hos 5:7; 6:4-10)[68] that she became the party responsible for the dysfunctional relationship between herself and her Lord. However, in using the marital analogy, Hosea's message focused on the deep and constant love that Yahweh brought to his bride. Even in describing Israel as an adulterous wife and comparing her with a prostitute, he emphasizes the dramatic nature of this love, for God wants to draw Israel back to himself.

Here, one encounters principles in the marital fellowship of God with Israel that are analogous to the marital bond of any man and woman. The lovingkindness and forgiveness with which the Lord approached Israel and the need for repentance, confession, and responsible action on

> The way in which the Lord approached Israel and the need for their response reflect dynamics that are necessary to the proper functioning of any marriage.

the part of Israel reflect dynamics that are necessary to the proper functioning of any marriage.

Marriage and Divorce in the Apostolic Teaching

The deliberate arrangement of the Matthean Gospel in a format that emphasizes Jesus' five great discourses influences the interpretation of those texts which center on each of the discourses. In Matthew 16:21–20:34, Jesus discusses with his disciples and others the meaning of his messianic mission for those who will be faithful to the call of God.[69] Matthew 18, the fourth discourse, begins with a question about what it means to be great in the Kingdom of God. Jesus' initial response is to challenge the disciples' socio/cultural understanding of greatness by telling them that the protection of the defenseless is what defines those who belong to God.[70] This response is reflected in his confrontation with the Pharisees in Matthew 19 when he points them back to the original intention of God and asks them why they do not understand what God has done and said (Matt 19:4-6). In Matthew 19, he goes on to say that it was because of their "hardness of heart" that they were so willing to dismiss those who were dependent on them for protection, kindness, and care. In this sense, Matthew 19 becomes an explicit example of the meaning of Jesus' teaching in Matthew 18.

The text of Matthew 18 states three great principles that will describe those who belong to the Kingdom of God. First, as suggested above, the stories of the children and the sheep emphasize a spirit of humility in which one welcomes those who are in need of protection and recognizes that they are of ultimate importance to God.[71] Second, Jesus emphasizes the importance of seeking reconciliation in those situations where a broken relationship has developed. The responsibility lies with the one who feels offended. He is directed to seek out the other person and engage in a conversation which is intended to resolve the conflict. If this initial step fails, the believer is counseled first to involve two others who might act as mediators. Should this also fail, the church should be requested to intervene. Only if the individual out of hardness of heart stubbornly refuses to resolve the matter, is the church to separate itself from him. To this guidance, Jesus appends the teaching that God is deeply interested in the interpersonal difficulties experienced by his children and wants to use his power to help them resolve these matters (cf. Mal

3:16).[72] Finally, Jesus addresses Peter's question in which he seeks to justify himself by going beyond the common rabbinic guidance about forgiveness and suggesting that one should forgive his brother at least seven times.[73] Jesus says that even seven times is not enough. One should be willing to forgive as many as "seventy-seven times." He tells a parable which demonstrates the difference between God's response to an individual's failures and the response often considered appropriate. One servant who cannot repay an extraordinary debt is forgiven the entire debt upon his plea for mercy. The same servant finds a fellow servant who owes a very small amount, cannot pay, and asks for more time. Having forgotten the grace he has just experienced, the first servant has his fellow servant thrown into prison. Hearing of this, the outraged king condemns the unforgiving servant to be punished until he can pay back all that he owes. The discourse is concluded with Jesus' statement: "This is how my heavenly Father will treat each of you unless you forgive your brother from your heart" (Matt 18:35).

Each of these principles has implications for Jesus' teaching on marriage and divorce at the beginning of Matthew 19. He calls for protection of the defenseless, serious efforts at reconciliation, and willingness to forgive. This flatly contradicts the Pharisee's teaching that one could easily discard an inconvenient marriage. Osborne states:

> It is thus no coincidence that in Matthew Jesus' teaching on marital commitment directly follows his teaching on forgiveness (18:21-35), just as in Mark it follows a discussion of sinning against a "little one" (Mk 9:42-50; compare Mt 18:7-9). The more intimate the relationship, the deeper the wounds of interpersonal friction sear; marriage without forgiveness and reconciliation would be difficult.[74]

> "It is no coincidence that in Matthew Jesus' teaching on marital commitment directly follows his teaching on forgiveness."

In addition, where divorce has taken place, these principles suggest that the church needs to approach those involved with a gracious attitude that reflects the forgiving spirit of the Father.

The apostolic guidance of Paul and Peter regarding marriage emphasize the importance of the example of Jesus in his relationship to the church and the implications of submitting to the reign of God in our marital relationships. In Ephesians 5:21-31, Paul introduces the section

> The apostolic guidance regarding marriage emphasizes the importance of the example of Jesus in his relationship to the church.

with the command: "Be subject to one another out of reverence to Christ" (Eph 5:21). According to Arndt and Gingrich, this verb, *hupotassō*, as it is used here, signifies "submission in the sense of voluntary yielding in love."[75] Paul's object for entering such a command into the thought of this particular logion seems to be to guard against the possibility that one Christian would unjustly mistreat another. Rather, a Christian should always be ready to place the interests of fellow Christians above his or her own (cf. Phil 2:3-4).

Paul follows up the general instructions that set the tone for this text with specific comments concerning the relationship of men and women in marriage. The wife is to choose to submit to her husband out of love and respect for him and also in honor of her Lord. However, this is not to be a one-sided domination, for the husband is exhorted to love her sacrificially, following the example of Christ.[76] Peter also believes the wife should reflect a deep and abiding respect for her husband. Her behavior is not only intended to honor her husband but also to honor Christ and thus convince

> The wife is to choose to submit to her husband out of love and respect for him and also in honor of her Lord.

unbelievers regarding the truth. Husbands are to be considerate of their wives, reflecting an awareness of the wife's needs and her status as a joint heir in the Kingdom of God. Peter's comments to husbands are concluded with the sober reminder that a husband's failure to treat his wife with respect and honor will negatively impact his spiritual relationship with God (1 Pet 3:1-7).[77]

> Husbands are to be considerate of their wives, reflecting an awareness of the wife's needs and her status as a joint heir in the Kingdom of God.

The command of Paul to men is: "Husbands, love your wives, even as Christ loved the church" (Eph 5:25). The quality of that love is defined by the uniquely biblical concept of love bound up in the Greek word, *agapē*. As Thielicke writes:

. . . now that the headship of the husband is to be understood in analogy with Christ we perceive a new and unprecedented

tone: husbands should love their wives as Christ loved us all—
men and women (5:25). And here "love" is to be understood
not in the sense of *eros* but of *agape*. This is the new note which
appears nowhere else in late antiquity. What *agape* means here
is made amply clear in statements that follow (5:25ff.) in reference to the service of Christ to his Church. *The respect the
woman should show toward the husband therefore has its corre-
spondence in the sustaining love the husband bears toward her.*[78]

In designating the love of Christ as a model for the husband, Paul
sets forward the self-giving love that distinguishes God who cares
regardless of the value of the object of his care (cf. Rom 5:6-8).
Nygren identifies four aspects of the divine love that define the husband's response to his wife's needs. They are:

1. *Agapē* reflects the very character of the one who is doing the
   loving.
2. *Agapē* is not based on the value of the other person or what
   that person can give in response to what is given.
3. *Agapē* is creative and thus encourages worth and meaning in
   the one loved. It imparts value by loving.
4. *Agapē* creates relationship where none existed before and
   repairs broken relationships. This happens first with God and
   then with others.[79]

In binding this form of love on husbands, Paul indicates that the husband approaches his wife with more than simple affection or attraction based on her value as a person. Rather, he is to exercise an
active and concerned love that reaches out to meet her needs. His
wife then becomes the most important priority in his life, after God,
for she now takes the place of himself in the hierarchy of his personal love and fellowship. He comes to serve her as he would himself by recognizing her needs and desires as he would his own. More
than this, he loves her so much that he is willing to sacrifice himself
in order to enhance and fulfill her.

The model of Christ's love sheds light on the purpose of his
sacrificial act that leads to the sanctification of the believer. Sacrifice
is not an end in itself but a means to create and establish the life of
the church. Ephesians 5:26-27 lists three reasons for Christ's death,
and Westcott orders them in this way: (1) to sanctify the church,
(2) to present the church to himself in splendor, so (3) that it may
continue to be holy, and without spot or wrinkle.[80]

These statements correspond to Jewish marriage customs in that the bride is prepared and then presented to her husband. She then continues with him in marital fellowship to the end of their life together. As it is in the relationship of Christ to the church, so it is in the relationship of the husband to the wife. When the bride is accepted, she is placed in a position of honor next to her bridegroom.[81]

The last phrase of Paul's thought in Ephesians 5:28 identifies a unity that is described in terms of caring for one's body. He is making a literal inference from Genesis 2:24 which identifies God's original intention that a man and woman should become one flesh in marriage. Based on this inference, Paul identifies the man's love for the woman as self-love. It is his contention that a man should exercise a concern for his wife equivalent to that which he exercises not only in consideration of his own body, but of his whole person. In support of this understanding, Abbott states, such love "leads him to regard her welfare as his own and to feel all that concerns her as if it concerned himself."[82]

In Ephesians 5:31, the Apostle quotes Genesis 2:24, "For this reason a man will leave his father and mother and be united to his wife, and they will become one flesh." In a patriarchal culture, it would be expected that a wife would join her husband's family. Instead, the Genesis text emphasizes that a man leaves his family and joins himself to her (not even to her family). The writer is ruling out all possible depreciation of the woman and even emphasizing her great worth by saying that the husband loves her so much that he is willing to sever the closest of family ties in order to ally himself with her. It is then that both experience a love that draws them into the reality of being "one flesh."

This experience of being "one flesh," which Paul calls a "great mystery," is God's will for the marital relationship. Christ and the church are the complete realization of this union. The man and woman who covenant together as man and wife are encouraged to strive after this type of unity in order that they might be "one flesh" as God intended them to be. They will each attempt to be an integral part of the other's life. Their sharing together, interdependence, and inner-relatedness will reflect those qualities within the context of Christ's relation with the covenant people. As the church exists as the real and tangible body of Christ, so the union of a man and woman in marriage is so complete that they may be spoken of as "one flesh."[83]

The Apostle Paul also addresses questions of conflict and divorce in the marital relationship. In 1 Corinthians 7, he is writing to a community of Christians who reflect both Jewish and Gentile cultural roots. These Christians have been immersed in a society that is defined by Roman and Greek philosophy and pagan religion. As they attempt to have meaningful, Christian interpersonal relationships, they must confront ascetic and hedonistic philosophical models found in their popular culture. Chapter seven begins with a current ascetic slogan, phrased as a question that sets the tone for the issues to be dealt with. The query is framed with the words: "It is good for a man not to marry" (1 Cor 7:1) which literally means that it is good for a man not to have sexual relations with a woman.[84] The apostle's response to the marital issues raised in this chapter reflects both his understanding of the teaching of Jesus and the influence of his training in the Old Testament.

Central to Paul's approach is an emphasis on the moral needs of his readers. His answers to the questions that have been posed to him suggest a Jewish cultural concern about the need to protect the community of believers from sexual immorality (cf. 1 Cor 5:1-5).[85] He counsels that a man should be married rather than succumb to sexual temptation (1 Cor 7:8-9). According to Paul, the answer to the temptations implicit in a hedonistic society is that each person should have his or her own spouse, and that both partners should be dedicated physically as well as spiritually and socially to each other.

He is concerned about the ascetic suggestion that married couples should separate and thus avoid the influence of the flesh on their spiritual lives. For Paul, the proper expression of sexual relations is in the context of marriage. A choice to permanently abstain from sexual relations deprives the other partner of his or her natural, marital rights and may result in temptation to sin (1 Cor 7:1-7).

The Apostle references the teaching of Jesus as the ground for understanding that divorce is not an appropriate choice for the Christian. He tells the reader that the Lord commanded that spouses were not to separate, and if they did, they must remain either unmarried or be reconciled to their mates. Paul appends a directive to Jesus' command about divorce that speaks directly to the marital situation of some of the Christians in Corinth. He says that they should not divorce on the basis that their mates might be non-Christians. On the contrary, if the mate is willing to remain with them, they should continue in that marriage. Like Peter (1 Pet 3:1-7), Paul suggests that truly Christian attitudes and behavior may be the witness needed to convince the unbelieving mate of the truth of the gospel.[86]

Paul addresses one issue that is not dealt with in the Gospel accounts. This has to do with the marriage of a believer to an unbeliever. The context suggests that the marriage already existed when one of them became a Christian. The other is unwilling to remain in the marriage if the Christian mate will not give up his or her commitment to Christ. The unbelieving mate then abandons the marriage.

Although the Apostle says that he does not have a specific command from the Lord, he does give guidance based on his authority as an Apostle (1 Cor 7:40). He applies two principles. First, when he says that the believer is "not bound" (1 Cor 7:15), the Apostle implies that faith in Christ must supersede the marriage relationship if one's mate is unwilling to stay. Second, the Old Testament principle of the protection of the defenseless (Exod 21:10-11) is implied in his advice because the unbelieving spouse will now fail to fulfill both the material and the emotional the needs of his or her mate.[87]

When the Apostle says that the believer is not "bound" to an unbeliever who deserts him or her, he is indicating that the believer is free to divorce and to remarry. In the Greco-Roman and the Jewish cultural contexts as in our own social milieu, it was expected that people would remarry following the dissolution of an earlier marriage. The Christians of the first century would not have understood the assertion that there could be no remarriage. Like Jesus, Paul does not suggest otherwise.[88]

> The Christians of the first century would not have understood the assertion that there could be no remarriage.

Like Jesus, Paul also indicates that the single life can be an appropriate choice for a Christian (see Matt 19:10-12). This is true because a married person must focus on the needs of his or her mate whereas the single person can place a greater emphasis on serving in the Kingdom of God.[89] This is not a call to a celibate pastoral system (cf. 1 Tim 4:1-3) but an acknowledgment of the kind of commitment and dedication that it takes to sustain a successful marriage relationship. Paul also recognizes, as does Jesus, that the choice to be single is one that carries with it personal challenges and that not everyone has the spiritual strength to remain pure as a single person.

The Importance of Marriage

The positive implications of God's plan for his creation are demonstrated in the experience of the fifty percent of American marriages that do not end up in divorce. A project in the social sciences which summarized the findings of a large body of scientific research on the importance of marriage as a social institution highlighted the following conclusion: "Marriage is an important social good, associated with an impressively broad array of positive outcomes for children and adults alike."[90] The data suggests that marriage contributes to the stability, health, and sense of fulfillment for family members where marriages remain intact. As a rule, these families are better off economically than families guided by a single adult. Children raised in families with parents who have stayed together tend to do better in school, are more emotionally stable, and are less likely to be involved in substance abuse or crime.[91]

For Christians, one of the social implications of the teaching of Jesus and the New Testament writers has to do with a change in status for women. Jesus was unusual as a rabbi who accepted women among his followers, was concerned about their needs, and even referenced their life experiences in his teaching. The passages on marriage and divorce in the Gospels reflect Jesus' concern for the difficulty that women experience at the hands of "hardhearted" men. His teaching places men and women on equal footing in regard to responsibility for the marriage relationship and provides women with equal access to the justice that the community should provide for all people. The presence of the Kingdom in the person of Jesus reintroduces an ethic into human relationships that was part of the original plan of God for his people. The Apostle Paul suggests in his

> *The presence of the Kingdom in the person of Jesus reintroduces an ethic into human relationships that was part of the original plan of God for his people.*

writing that the greater responsibility for the success of the marriage relationship belongs to the husband. Thus, the husband's role is to mirror that of God and Jesus as they sacrifice themselves in order to purify and sanctify the people of God. Peter says that women are heirs together with men in the Kingdom of God (1 Pet. 3:7), and Paul states that there are to be no barriers between different groups, including men and women, because "all are one in Christ Jesus" (Gal 3:28).

An extensive review of research data entitled "Does Divorce Make People Happy?" listed the following findings:

- Unhappily married adults who divorced or separated were no happier, on average, than unhappily married adults who stayed married.
- Divorce did not reduce symptoms of depression for unhappily married adults or raise their self-esteem, or increase their sense of mastery, on average compared to unhappy spouses who stayed married.
- The vast majority of divorces (74%) happened to adults who had been happily married five years previously.
- Unhappy marriages were less common than unhappy spouses.
- Staying married did not typically trap unhappy spouses in violent relationships. No violence was reported in the relationships of 86% of unhappily married adults (including 77% of unhappy spouses who later divorced or separated). No violence existed five years later in the marriages of 93% of unhappy spouses who avoided divorce.
- Two out of three unhappily married adults who avoided divorce or separation ended up happily married five years later.
- Many currently happily married spouses have had extended periods of marital unhappiness, often for quite serious reasons, including alcoholism, infidelity, verbal abuse, emotional neglect, depression, illness, and work reversals.[92]

The study concluded with this general observation:

While these averages likely conceal important individual variations that require more research, in a careful analysis of nationally representative data with extensive measures of psychological well-being, we could find no evidence that divorce or separation typically made adults happier than staying in an unhappy marriage.[93]

Although growing up in dysfunctional families leaves emotional scars on children, the research seems to indicate that only in those families which are extremely disorganized is a child better off if his parents divorce. In 1971, Judith Wallerstein began a twenty-five year, longitudinal study in which she followed the life experiences of 131 children whose parents divorced. Her results parallel those of other major studies on the impact of divorce on children. She found that children of divorce are more likely to have delayed emotional and social development and find it much more difficult to develop meaningful, long-term relationships with others, particularly persons of the other gender, and are more likely to divorce than children from intact families.[94]

The impact of divorce on the lives of individuals and society and the evidence for the social value of marital relationships emphasize the importance of the divine plan for human relationships. God's plan for marriage and families reflects the deepest needs of those created in his image. Stassen and Gushee comment that the heart of Jesus' teaching on marriage and divorce is *"What God has joined together, keep together! Go and be reconciled!"*[95]

Ethical Implications of Divorce and Remarriage Decisions

The "Is it lawful . . . ?" question with which the Pharisees approached Jesus to test him (Matt 19:3; Mark 10:2) parallels the "What if . . . ?" question that Christians often ask as they struggle to understand what is allowed in Scripture. Too often, the biblical texts are treated as if they were case law. The difficulty is that the Bible does not speak directly to every possible ethical or

> *Too often, the biblical texts are treated as if they were case law.*

moral issue. Rather, it identifies principles that provide guidance, and with faith and confidence in God, we ". . . continue to work out [our] salvation with fear and trembling, for it is God who works in [us] to will and to act according to his good purpose" (Phil 2:12-13). In a spirit of trust in the grace and mercy of God and in submission to his will, we can be guided by the Holy Spirit to apply the principles found in Scripture to real life events.

Jesus clearly teaches that the marital relationship of one man to one woman was intended to last for the lifetimes of the marital partners. This was God's original intention and it has not changed. Faithfulness, loving-kindness, and repentance/forgiveness are to

> Both the OT and NT writers used the metaphor of marriage to describe God's relationship to his people.

mark this relationship. Both the Old and New Testament writers used the metaphor of marriage to describe God's relationship to his people. In Hosea, the unfaithfulness of Israel is met with the faithfulness of God. He does not want to be separated from his people and thus takes every opportunity to reconcile his people to himself. The Apostle Paul uses the model of Jesus' relationship to the church to teach the husband how to love the wife and how to become a helper suitable to her.

In only two situations addressed in Scripture, sexual immorality (Matt 5:32; 19:9) and desertion (1 Cor 7:15), is divorce and subsequent remarriage specifically allowed. In both cases, the text encourages the Christian to seek every opportunity to avoid divorce. The New Testament priority is on helping couples to have successful marriages. Stein comments: "In light of this [these texts], it is difficult to counsel a Christian that divorce is an option for them. Clearly the burden of proof weighs heavily on anyone considering divorce, for God hates divorce. Divorce is never good, for it witnesses to a failure of the divine purpose. Yet there may be occasions when divorce is the lesser evil."[96] From Matthew 18, we learn that God wants Christian couples to seek every avenue for reconciliation and that there should be repentance and forgiveness on the part of both.

Jesus' primary purpose in responding to the Pharisees in Matthew 19, and Mark 10 is to emphasize that divorce is not part of the divine plan. It is a concession to the sin that defines the lives of men and women. In most marital breakdowns there are no innocent parties.[97] Echols states: "Most generally

> In most marital breakdowns there are no innocent parties.

both parties must share the blame for the collapse of marriage and, not infrequently, the real source of the problem is in the failure of the *innocent* party to fulfill his (her) marital obligations."[98] Many marriages that end in divorce have deteriorated over time through the failure of the spouses to work at their relationship. John Gottman identifies six indicators that a relationship may be heading for divorce. He comments with regard to the sixth sign:

> When a relationship gets subsumed in negativity, it's not only the couple's present and future life together that are put

at risk. Their past is in danger, too. When I interview couples, I usually ask about the history of their marriage. I have found over and over that couples who are deeply entrenched in a negative view of their spouse and their marriage often rewrite their past.[99]

The exception to the conclusion of "no innocent party" may be those situations involving abusive relationships. Paul Hegstrom reports that the person to whom a woman who is being abused is most likely to report her situation is her minister. He goes on to say that in seventy percent of those situations, the minister counsels the wife to return to her home and to be a better wife to her husband.[100] This procedure fails to recognize the meaning of abuse by assuming that the victim has some power over the situation. The phenomenon of abuse describes the needs of the abuser. Very often abusers have lived in a family system where abuse was experienced. As a learned behavior for solving problems, abuse usually appears in those settings where the abuser's tolerance for stress is exceeded and he expresses his sense of powerlessness by attacking those closest to him. Ray Anderson states, "The typical pattern in abusive incidents is one in which the need to control is strongly present, coupled with perceptions of self-inadequacy."[101]

In these circumstances, the principle that applies derives from Jesus' fourth discourse. In Matthew 18, the protection of the defenseless person is described as the duty of those who belong to the Kingdom of God. It is a reflection of the Old Testament model in which the people of God were commanded and expected to "loose the chains of injustice . . . set the oppressed free . . . share your food with the hungry . . . provide the poor with shelter, and when you see the naked, to clothe him. . . ." (Isa 58:6-12). In all circumstances where domestic abuse is identified and especially in those situations involving children, it is incumbent on the part of ministers, family members, or friends to take action to protect the victims from injury, either physical or emotional by removing them from the primary setting where abuse is likely to occur, usually the home. Then church leaders need to make every effort to help the abuser and the abused to heal. Through spiritual guidance and therapy both need to be empowered with new skills and understandings that will prevent the reoccurrence of abuse. If, however, the abuser is unwilling to work at changing and continues to pose a significant danger physically

> *When divorce is allowed on biblical grounds, then remarriage is also allowed.*

and emotionally to his spouse or children, then the principle of protection of the innocent would allow the separation to become permanent by means of divorce. When divorce is allowed on biblical grounds, then remarriage is also allowed. Moses specifically notes that the woman "becomes the wife of another" (Deut 24:1-4). In the social and cultural context of first-century Judaism as well as Roman and Greek societies, it was accepted that one who divorces is allowed to remarry and as noted above, neither Jesus nor Paul indicate that this was unacceptable to God (cf. Matt 19:3-10; Mark 10:2-9; 1 Cor 7:1-40).

An important question with regard to Jesus' exception clause (Matt 5:32; 19:9) is, when does an unbiblical divorce cease to be adultery? Is there a point at which people are free from an earlier marriage, can be forgiven of past sins, and can truly move on with their lives both spiritually and socially? The answer to that question derives from the meaning of the term adultery (*moicheia*). Jesus clearly teaches that all subsequent marital relationships after a divorce on any other ground than *porneia* involve adultery. Adultery is a violation of the marital covenant. If that covenant ceases to exist, then there can be no adultery. Thus, the Apostle Paul states that when a woman's husband dies, she is released from that relationship and can marry another (Rom 7:2-3; 1 Cor 7:39). This applies to a divorce-remarriage situation when one or both partners cease to recognize the first marriage, will not consider reconciliation, and reorient their lives around a new relationship. When that first marriage truly ceases to exist for one person so that there is absolutely no hope of reconstituting it, then it ceases to exist for the other one as well.

> *For there to be a marital covenant, it must exist for both people.*

For there to be a marital covenant, it must exist for both people. At this point, whatever sins are being committed, they are not by definition adultery. In addition, repentance of sin committed during the failure of a marriage leads to forgiveness by God in the same sense that God forgives any other sin that is repented.

Though remarriage may be allowed in certain circumstances, it does not always mean that this is the best choice. When asked whether I would work with a Christian couple who were considering remarriage, I asked them to consider what they really believed about the scriptural teachings on divorce and remarriage. It is critically important for people not to violate their own consciences regarding this matter. In addition, I asked them if they could explain why their first marriages had failed and if they had made the changes necessary so

> *Though remarriage may be allowed in certain circumstances, it does not always mean that this is the best choice.*

that it would not affect the new marriage they were contemplating. H. Norman Wright states:

> It is essential that divorced people complete a divorce recovery program before moving into a new marriage. I've also found it helpful for the divorcee's future partner who has never been married to go through the recovery program as well because it gives the person a greater understanding of what their future partner has experienced.[102]

Those who have suffered through a divorce involving sexual unfaithfulness, abuse, or abandonment may experience the symptoms of trauma for a long time. Healing past hurts as much as is possible is an important goal before initiating a new relationship.

> *Healing past hurts as much as is possible is an important goal before initiating a new relationship.*

Twenty-five years ago when my elders asked me what they should do about the Christian man who was entering into what they believed was an unscriptural marriage, I said to them, "During my growing up, you never provided us with any teaching about the meaning of marriage and how to have successful marital relationships. There were no classes, no programs, and no counseling to prepare us to deal with the challenges that we would encounter in our marriages. Since you have not provided us with the spiritual leadership that we needed, I do not believe that you can now judge us when we fail."

Today I would go on to say that the role of the Christian community in promoting healthy marriages should include an emphasis on the positive value and meaning of marriage. It is important to prepare people with the skills to make marriages work. Courses for young adults, premarital counseling, mentoring by more mature individuals and couples, marriage and family enrichment training sessions and activities, divorce recovery programs, and the avail-

> *It is important to prepare people with the skills to make marriages work.*

ability of marital and family counseling are a means by which the church can support its system of marriages and families. Men need to be taught how to respect, honor, and love the women that come into their lives, as well as how to successfully provide servant-leadership as husbands and fathers. In those situations where domestic abuse develops, the religious leadership needs to take an active role in protecting those in need and support every possibility of changing the behavior that is going on in that home. Finally, in those tragic circumstances where people have divorced, the church can fulfill a redemptive role through an attitude of unconditional acceptance that encourages repentance, forgiveness, and reconciliation within the context of the Kingdom of God.

Notes

[1] Scriptural references are taken from the New International Version (NIV) unless otherwise specified.

[2] Glenn H. Stassen and David P. Gushee, *Kingdom Ethics: Following Jesus in Contemporary Context* (Downers Grove, IL: InterVarsity, 2003) 273.

[3] Ibid., 272-273.

[4] Ibid., 271; see also H. Wayne House, ed., *Divorce and Remarriage: Four Christian Views* (Downers Grove, IL: InterVarsity, 1990) 216.

[5] Gerhard von Rad, *Genesis* (Philadelphia: Westminster Press, 1972) 84.

[6] עֵזֶר כְּנֶגְדּוֹ (*'ēzer kᵉnegdô*) Hebrew references are taken from *Biblia Hebraica Stuttgartensia* (Stuttgart: Deutsche Bibelgesellschaft, 1990).

[7] Von Rad, *Genesis*, 82; see also David Instone-Brewer, *Divorce and Remarriage in the Bible* (Grand Rapids: Eerdmans, 2002) 140-141.

[8] W. Brueggeman, "Of the Same Flesh and Bone (GN 2,23a)," *Catholic Biblical Quarterly*, XXXII (October 1970) 540-542.

[9] Paul K. Jewett, *Man as Male and Female* (Grand Rapids: Eerdmans, 1975) 140.

[10] Instone-Brewer, *Divorce and Remarriage*, 136-141, 178-180; see also Stassen and Gushee, *Kingdom Ethics*, 276.

[11] S. Hanson, *The Unity of the Church of the New Testament* (Sweden: Upsala Press, 1946) 139.

[12] Instone-Brewer, *Divorce and Remarriage*, 39-58.

[13] (1) דַּעַת אֱלֹהִים (*da'ath 'ĕlōhîm* or "the knowledge of God"); (2) חֶסֶד (*ḥesed* or "the covenant love"); and (3) שׁוּבָה (*šûbāh* or repentance).

[14] David A. Hubbard, *Knowledge of God in Hosea*, unpublished Master's thesis (Pasadena, CA: Fuller Theological Seminary, 1954) 38; see also, Francis Brown, S.R. Driver, and C.A. Briggs, *Hebrew and English Lexicon of the Old Testament* (Oxford University Press, 1972) 394.

[15] Stassen and Gushee, *Kingdom Ethics*, 276.

[16] Walther Eichrodt, *Theology of the Old Testament* (Philadelphia: Westminster Press, 1960) 232-233.

[17] N. Glueck, *Ḥesed in the Bible* (Cincinnati: Hebrew Union College Press, 1967) 57; in Hosea, *ḥesed* is a lofty concept, highly refined in the heart of the prophet. It is no longer conduct corresponding to a reciprocal relationship within a narrow circle, but the proper conduct of all men to one another. On the one hand, mankind is regarded as one large family, and on the other, as children of one heavenly father. The word *ḥesed* signifies man's readiness for mutual aid, stemming from pure love of humanity; it is the realization of the "generally valid divine commandment of humaneness." *Ḥesed* does not reside in the punctilious offering of sacrifices or external

religiosity, but in ethical and religious behavior and the devoted fulfillment of the divinely ordained ethical commandments. In this respect, *ḥesed* as humane conduct is not different from the *ḥesed* of men toward God. True religious motivation is discernible from ethical deeds.

[18]Elliott N. Dorff, "The Elements of Forgiveness: A Jewish Approach," in *Dimensions of Forgiveness: Psychological Research & Theological Perspectives*, ed. by Everett L. Worthington (Philadelphia: Templeton Foundation Press, 1998) 29-58. Dorff describes the concept of *teshuvah*, repentance or "return" in Jewish theology and practice and compares it to a Christian view of repentance. See also G.A. Smith, *The Expositor's Bible: The Minor Prophets* (New York: A.C. Armstrong and Son, 1903) 335-338.

[19]H.H. Rowley, *The Faith of Israel* (Philadelphia: Westminster Press, 1950) 34.

[20]N.H. Snaith, *Distinctive Ideas of the Old Testament* (London: Epworth Press, 1950) 111.

[21]Eric F. Evenhuis, *Marital Reconciliation under the Analogy of Christ and His Church.* unpublished Doctoral diss. (Pasadena, CA: Fuller Theological Seminary, 1974) 34-35.

[22]Erlandsson, "*Baghadh*," (בָּגַד) in *Theological Dictionary of the Old Testament*, ed. by Johannes G. Botterweck, Helmer Ringgren, and Heinz-Joseph Fabry (Grand Rapids: Eerdmans, 1974) 1:470.

[23]Instone-Brewer, *Divorce and Remarriage*, 54-58, 141.

[24]Ibid., 85.

[25]Ibid., 91-93.

[26]Isidore Epstein, ed., Gittin *in the Babylonian Talmud*, trans. by Maurice Simon (London: Soncino Press, 1936) 88b-89a, 90a.

[27]Jeffrey H. Tigay, "Adultery," in *Encyclopedia Judaica* (Jerusalem: Encyclopedia Judaica Jerusalem, 1996) 2:314.

[28]Instone-Brewer, *Divorce and Remarriage*, 94-96.

[29]Brevard S. Childs, *The Book of Exodus* (Philadelphia: Westminster Press, 1974), 467-469.

[30]Instone-Brewer, *Divorce and Remarriage*, 99-102. The interpretive process by which this reference to the rights of the slave woman became the standard for allowing divorce for emotional or material neglect is called *qol vahomer*. It involves arguing from the least important to the more important. In the Western-European/American philosophical tradition, it would be framed as "If A is true, then surely B is also true." Thus, if the slave woman has these rights, then the free wife must also have the same rights. If the wife should have these expectations of her marriage, then surely the husband must also be allowed the same expectations. However, the exegetical process is less important than the recognition that the ethical and moral intent of the law was to provide a protection for the individual who is defenseless and for the community that might be coopted into sin by its failure to recognize the needs of its citizens.

[31]Ibid., 139.

[32]Charles R. Eerdman, *An Exposition of the Bible: Gospel of Matthew* (Philadelphia: Westminster Press, 1929) 153. See also Everett Ferguson, *The Gospel according to Matthew Part II, 13:53-28:20*, The Living Word Commentary (Austin, TX: Sweet, 1976) 66; Larry Chouinard, *Matthew*, The College Press NIV Commentary (Joplin, MO: College Press, 1997) 338.

[33]Helmut Thielicke, *The Ethics of Sex* (New York: Harper and Row, 1964) 8; see also Jewett, *Man as Male and Female*, 123-126.

[34]Lawrence J. Crabbe, *Understanding People* (Grand Rapids: Zondervan, 1987) 108.

[35]Eldred Echols, *Divorce and Remarriage: A Continuing Study* (Arlington, TX: North Davis Church of Christ—Unto the Uttermost Part, n.d.) 3-5; see also Instone-Brewer, *Divorce and Remarriage*, 155 and 160.

[36]Instone-Brewer, *Divorce and Remarriage*, 178.

[37]"עֶרְוַת דָּבָר (*ervat davar*)," *The Interlinear Hebrew/Greek English Bible*, ed. and trans. by Jay Green (Wilmington, DE: Associated Publishers and Authors, 1976) 1:523.

[38]Deut 24:1, NIV.

[39]Instone-Brewer, *Divorce and Remarriage*, 111.

[40]Ibid.

[41]Epstein, *Gittin*, 89b-90a, fns 6 & 7.

[42]Ibid., 89b-90a & 90a. "Beth Hillel, however says: [that he may divorce her] even if she has merely spoilt his food, since it says, because he hath found some unseemly thing in her. Rabbi Akiba says: [He may divorce her] even if he finds another woman more beautiful than she is, as it says, it cometh to pass, if she find no favour in his eyes."

[43]Ferguson, *Matthew Part II*, 13:53–28:20, 65. See also Instone-Brewer, *Divorce and Remarriage*, 111-112.

[44]Ben Zion Schereschewsky, "Divorce," in *Encyclopedia Judaica*, 6:123-124. "Bet Hillel was clearly correct in its interpretation of *'ervat davar* (Deut. 24:1) as any kind of obnoxious behavior or mannerisms, and in concluding that a man was not restricted to grounds of sexual offense in seeking to divorce his wife (Git. 90a; Deut. 23:15)."

[45]Brown, Driver, and Briggs, "עֶרְוַת דְּבָר," *Hebrew and English Lexicon of the Old Testament*, 789, "nakedness of a thing, i.e., prob. *indecency, improper behavior* Dt 23:15, 24:1. . . ."; see also Echols, *Divorce and Remarriage*, 6.

[46]עָרָה, *arah*, in the *Enhanced Strong's Lexicon* (Oak Harbor, WA: Logos Research Systems, 1995).

[47]Instone-Brewer, *Divorce and Remarriage*, 111-112, 163.

[48]Greek references are taken from Kurt Aland, Matthew Black, Carlo M. Martini, Bruce M. Metzger, and Allen Wikgren, *The Greek New Testament* (Stuttgart: Deutsche Bibelgesellschaft, 1983).

[49]William F. Arndt and F. Wilbur Gingrich, *A Greek-English Lexicon of the New Testament* (Chicago: University of Chicago, 1957) 268.

[50]Ibid., 303.

[51]Instone-Brewer, *Divorce and Remarriage*, 162, "Rulings were therefore abbreviated down to their absolute minimum and were arranged in balanced phrases that were easy to remember. Anything that was implicit or obvious was omitted for the sake of brevity. This often makes individual rulings difficult to understand outside the context of the debate that prompted them."

[52]Chouinard, *Matthew*, 23.

[53]Instone-Brewer, *Divorce and Remarriage*, 173.

[54]Echols, *Divorce and Remarriage*, 7-9.

[55]H.E. Dana and Julius R. Mantey, *A Manual Grammar of the Greek New Testament* (Toronto: Macmillan, 1955) 202; οὐ γέγονεν οὕτως, This use of the tense is referred to as the "perfect of existing state" or "intensive perfect." Dana and Mantey state: "When special attention is thus directed to the results of the action, stress upon the existing fact is intensified."

[56]W.D. Davies, *Matthew*, The International Critical Commentary (Edinburgh: T & T Clark, 1997) 15; Davies recognizes the impact of this construction as indicating that priority in time ("in the beginning") reflects priority in God's will.

[57]Echols, *Divorce and Remarriage*, 8-9. See also, Ferguson, *Matthew Part II*, 66.

[58]Instone-Brewer, *Divorce and Remarriage*, 144. See also William Hendriksen, *Exposition of the Gospel according to Matthew*, New Testament Commentary (Grand Rapids: Baker, 1973).

[59]Davies, *Matthew*, 14.

[60]Epstein, *Gittin*, 37 (fn 6), 65b, 90b.

[61]Ibid., 65b. See also Instone-Brewer, *Divorce and Remarriage*, 113. Schereschewsky, *Encyclopedia Judaica*, 6:123, refers to it as a *sefer keritut* ("bill of divorce").

[62]Echols, *Divorce and Remarriage*, 12-13.

[63]Instone-Brewer, *Divorce and Remarriage*, 32-33. See also Stassen and Gushee, *Kingdom Ethics*, 278.

[64]Echols, *Divorce and Remarriage*, 2, 16. See also Stassen and Gushee, *Kingdom Ethics*, 279-281.

[65]Instone-Brewer, *Divorce and Remarriage*, 30-32. See also Epstein, *Gittin*, 9.3; Echols, *Divorce and Remarriage*, 14-15; and R.H. Stein, "Divorce," *Dictionary of Jesus and the Gospels*, ed. by Joel Green, Scot McKnight, and I. Howard Marshall (Downers Grove, IL: Inter-Varsity, 1992) 195-196.

[66]Arndt and Gingrich, *Greek-English Lexicon*, 699-700. See also F. Hauck and Siegfried Shultz, "πόρνη, πορνεία," *Theological Dictionary of the New Testament*, ed. by Gerhard Kittel, trans. by Geoffrey W. Bromiley (Grand Rapids: Eerdmans, 1964) 584-585, 590-595; Stein, "Divorce," *Dictionary*, 195.

[67]F. Hauck, μοιχεία, 730. See also Stein, "Divorce," *Dictionary*, 195; and, Echols, *Divorce and Remarriage*, 2-3, 16-17.

[68]S. Erlandsson, *"Baghadh,"* 1:470-473, esp. 472.

[69]Chouinard, *Matthew*, 26.

[70]W.C. Allen, *St. Matthew*, The International Critical Commentary (Edinburgh: T. & T. Clark, 1907) 194. See also Chouinard, *Matthew*, 322-323.

[71]Allen, *St. Matthew*, 196-197. See also Chouinard, *Matthew*, 324-325.

[72]Allen, *St. Matthew*, 197-199. See also Chouinard, *Matthew*, 327-329.

[73]Chouinard, *Matthew*, 331, fn 11, reference to a rabbinic limitation to three as the necessary number of times that forgiveness is called for when sinned against.

[74]Grant R. Osborne, *Matthew*, The IVP New Testament Commentary Series (Downers Grove, IL: InterVarsity, 1997) 294.

[75]Arndt and Gingrich, "ὑποτάσσω," in *Greek-English Lexicon*, 855.

[76]Thielicke, *Ethics of Sex*, 11-12.

[77]Charles Bigg, *St. Peter and St. Jude*, The International Critical Commentary (Edinburgh: T. & T. Clark, 1901) 150-156.

[78]Thielicke, *Ethics of Sex*, 12-13.

[79]Anders Nygren, *Agape and Eros* (New York: Harper and Row, 1969) 75-81.

[80]B.F. Westcott, *St. Paul's Epistle to the Ephesians* (Grand Rapids: Eerdmans, 1950) 84.

[81]J.P. Sampley, *And the Two Shall Become One Flesh: A Study of Traditions in Ephesians 5:21-33* (Cambridge: The University Press, 1971) 135.

[82]T.K. Abbott, *Ephesians and Colossians*, The International Critical Commentary (Edinburgh: T. & T. Clark, 1964) 171.

[83]Westcott, *Ephesians*, 84-85.

[84]Ben Witherington, *Conflict and Community in Corinth: A Socio-Rhetorical Commentary on 1 and 2 Corinthians* (Grand Rapids: Eerdmans, 1995) 174-176.

[85]Hauck, "μοιχεία," 734. See also Hauck and Shultz, "πόρνη," 593; Stein, "Divorce," *Dictionary*, 198.

[86]Witherington, *Conflict*, 178.

[87]Ibid., 177-178. See also, Instone-Brewer, *Divorce and Remarriage*, 189-201, 204.

[88]Instone-Brewer, *Divorce and Remarriage*, 201-204. See also Stein, "Divorce," *Dictionary*, 193-194; Craig S. Keener, . . . *And Marries Another: Divorce and Remarriage in the Teaching*

of the New Testament (Peabody, MA: Hendrickson, 1991) 61-65.

[89]Witherington, *Conflict*, 179-180.

[90]Norval Glenn, Steven Nock, and Linda Waite, eds., *Why Marriage Matters: Twenty-one Conclusions from the Social Sciences* (New York: Institute for American Values, 2002) 6.

[91]Ibid., 7-18.

[92]Linda J. Waite, Don Browning, William J. Doherty, et. al., *Does Divorce Make People Happy? Findings from a Study of Unhappy Marriages.* (New York: Institute for American Values, 2002) 1-42.

[93]Ibid., 6.

[94]Judith Wallerstein, Julia Lewis, Sandra Blakeslee, *The Unexpected Legacy of Divorce: A 25 Year Landmark Study* (New York: Hyperion, 2000) xxi-38, 87-158.

[95]Stassen and Gushee, *Kingdom Ethics*, 289. See also, Stassen and Gushee, 289 for a list of implications of a commitment to Jesus' teaching on the priority of marriage.

[96]Stein, "Divorce," *Dictionary*, 198.

[97]Echols, *Divorce and Remarriage*, 17-18.

[98]Ibid., 18.

[99]John M. Gottman, *The Seven Principles for Making Marriage Work* (New York: Three Rivers Press, 1999) ch. 2, quote from page 42. See also John Gottman, *Why Marriages Succeed or Fail* (New York: Simon and Schuster, 1994) for a review of his extensive research on marriage.

[100]Paul Hegstrom. "The Bible and Domestic Abuse," Conference presentation at the Regional Meeting of the American Association of Christian Counselors (Cincinnati, October 11, 2002).

[101]Ray S. Anderson, *Self-Care: A Theology of Personal Empowerment and Spiritual Healing* (Wheaton, IL: Victor Books, 1995) 130.

[102]H. Norman Wright, *The Premarital Counseling Handbook* (Chicago: Moody Press, 1992) 257.

Bibliography

Gottman, John M. *Why Marriages Succeed or Fail.* New York: Simon and Schuster, 1994.

Dr. Gottman discusses the implications of his intensive psychobiological research with more than 2,000 couples. He says that when the ratio of positive to negative interactions between mates drops below five to one, then the marriage will begin to break down. He identifies four common behaviors that are significant to the deterioration of a marriage: criticism, contempt, defensiveness, and stonewalling. In this text and in his later book (*The Seven Principles for Making Marriage Work.* New York: The Three Rivers Press, 1999) he provides extensive exercises that can be used with individual couples and in groups for strengthening marriage relationships.

Instone-Brewer, David. *Divorce and Remarriage in the Bible: The Social and Literary Context.* Grand Rapids: Eerdmans, 2002.

Beginning with the cultural and social history of the development of the marriage contract in the ancient Near East, Instone-Brewer traces the legal and theological processes that governed marriage and divorce through the Pentateuch, the Prophets, the intertestamental period, and the rabbinic teaching to the time of Jesus. He evaluates the teaching of Jesus and the Apostle Paul in the context of its cultural, linguistic, and historical referents. He also briefly reviews the position of the Christian community on marriage and divorce throughout church history. Finally, he provides the reader with pastoral suggestions. It is a very detailed study and yet very readable.

Stassen, Glen H., and David P. Gushee. *Kingdom Ethics: Following Jesus in Contemporary Context.* Downers Grove, IL: InterVarsity, 2003.

Stassen and Gushee identify a rubric that they describe as traditional piety, mechanisms of bondage, and transforming initiatives that is based on the model of Jesus' teaching found in the Sermon on the Mount. They evaluate scriptural, historical, and cultural issues associated with each ethical question and conclude with principles for guiding the reader in ethical decision-making. In addition to marriage and divorce, they address the ethical issues involved in topics such as war, capital punishment, biotechnology, sexuality, race relations, and the environment.

Wallerstein, Judith S., Julia M. Lewis, and Sandra Blakeslee. *The Unexpected Legacy of Divorce: A 25 Year Landmark Study.* New York: Hyperion, 2000.

Wallerstein, Lewis, and Blakeslee wrap the evidence regarding the negative impact of divorce in the stories of the children now adults that they have been following for twenty-five years. Wallerstein concludes that two long-held beliefs about the effects of divorce are in fact myths: (1) if parents are happier, then the children will be happier; and (2) divorce is a temporary crisis that exerts the most harmful effects on parents and children at the time of the dissolution of the marriage. The results of her research suggest that the parent's divorce continues to affect the lives of children at least into young adulthood.

Worthington, Everett L. Jr., ed. *Dimensions of Forgiveness: Psychological Research and Theological Perspectives.* Philadelphia: Templeton Foundation Press, 1998.

Dimensions of Forgiveness is a series of essays reflecting theological backgrounds, psychological research, and counseling perspectives on forgiveness as an aspect of human interpersonal relationships. Lewis Smedes' book, *Forgive and Forget: Healing the Hurts We Don't Deserve*, is identified as an inspiration for the seminar discussions that led to the publication of this set of essays. An important related text which also reviews the extensive scientific research on forgiveness and the implications for interventions in working with situations of unforgiveness is *Forgiveness: Theory, Research and Practice* by Michael E. McCullough, Kenneth I. Pargament, and Carl E. Thoresen.

HOMOSEXUALITY AND THE BIBLICAL WITNESS

John Mark Hicks, Ph.D.

During the last thirty-five years of the twentieth century American culture increasingly accepted homosexuality as an alternative lifestyle. Whether due to a proactive Gay agenda, the cultural presence of the lifestyle in American art and media, or a more tolerant legal perspective in the light of social justice, Americans are now equally divided about whether "homosexuality should be considered an acceptable lifestyle alternative." According to a Barna organization survey, 45% of Americans affirm this statement, while 46% deny it, and 9% are uncertain.[1]

However, the language is ambiguous. What does "acceptable" mean? If it means "acceptable" in the sense that society should not oppress or discriminate against it, then it is a legal or civil judgment. But if "acceptable" means that it is an ethically viable alternative, then it is a moral judgment. Many, including myself, might grant the former, but not the latter. There is a difference between defending the legal rights of homosexuals due to their personhood and defending the moral rectitude of that lifestyle. There are many activities and lifestyles that are legal, but not, according to the Christian ethic, moral (e.g., adultery, cohabitation without marriage, etc.).

> There is a difference between defending the legal rights of homosexuals due to their personhood and defending the moral rectitude of that lifestyle.

Due to this distinction, Christian ethicists face at least two fundamental questions. First, ought homosexual persons receive equal and fair treatment as persons in both legal and personal relation-

354

ships? Second, ought Christians regard homosexual behavior as ethical? The first question is a matter of social justice, but the second concerns sexual ethics. As Christians we can, and should, defend the legal and civil rights of homosexual persons because every person, as a creation loved by God, deserves to be treated with dignity, but this does not mean that we thereby sanction their lifestyle as an ethical alternative within the Christian understanding of sexuality.

While both questions deserve sustained treatment, this chapter addresses the sexual issue rather than social justice. The quest for justice in society for all persons is a broader question than the more narrow concern of whether ethical sexuality includes homosexual behavior.

Most Christian ethicists regard a promiscuous lifestyle—multiple partners—as immoral for not only homosexuals but also heterosexuals. They condemn any uncommitted and/or merely self-serving sexual relationship as unethical. They certainly condemn any violent sexual activity (rape) or underage relationships (e.g., pederasty or heterosexual relations with a minor). Sexual activity, according to traditional Christian ethics, is blessed and ordained by God only in a monogamous, loving, committed relationship (e.g., marriage).

> *The primary discussion among Christian ethicists is whether a monogamous, loving relationship between two homosexual persons in a "gay marriage" is morally acceptable.*

The primary discussion among Christian ethicists is whether a monogamous, loving relationship between two homosexual persons in a "gay marriage" is morally acceptable. This is the focus of this chapter.

The Hermeneutical Crux

In 1967 the prominent theologian Norman Pittenger published a book entitled *Time for Consent*.[2] He affirmed the ethical character of homosexual unions and others supported his argument, including evangelical authors such as Scanzoni and Mollenkott.[3] Pittenger identified six qualities that give homosexual relations—and all human sexual relationships—ethical value: commitment, mutuality, tenderness, faithfulness, hopefulness, and a desire for union. According to this line of reasoning, when these are present, human relationships are divinely sanctioned as the highest expression of human love, whether they are heterosexual or homosexual. Gender is immaterial as long as the love expressed between two people is expressive of the divine love that embodies these defined qualities. Whether heterosexual or homosexual, the most important dimension of the sexual relationship is love.

Another important aspect, according to advocates of homosexual unions, is that God intends that each of us find and celebrate our true natures, and he intends that we have the freedom to express our sexuality because sexuality is integral to our natures. God values committed relationships of love. If our "true nature" (orientation) is homosexual, then God gives us the freedom to express our true nature in a committed relationship because it manifests love through our sexuality. This is true because what God values is a loving, committed relationship, and whether it is homosexual or heterosexual is ultimately inconsequential as long as it is true to one's own personal orientation. Committed homosexual relationships, then, are an expression of God's ideal of loving communion between human beings.

This perspective is a problem for those who believe that Scripture bears witness to God's desire for human beings. While only 53% of Americans agree that the Bible condemns homosexuality (27% disagree and 20% are uncertain),[4] the uniform witness of Scripture, as traditionally interpreted, is that homosexual behavior is aberrant, forbidden, and unnatural. This creates two hermeneutical questions. First, is the traditional understanding of Scripture correct? Second, if it is correct, are there hermeneutical or theological reasons why Scripture's understanding is more part of its ancient cultural setting than it is God's intent for humanity?

The first question centers on the interpretation of specific texts in Scripture. What does the Bible say about homosexuality? Is the condemnation of homosexual acts in Leviticus 18 and 20 more about idolatry than sexuality? Is the condemnation of homosexual relationships in Romans 1 more about pederasty than loving homosexual unions? Contemporary scholarship is embroiled in an exegetical contest between traditional and revisionist readings of these biblical texts. I will engage this discussion in the section entitled "Biblical Texts." I will conclude that the traditional readings—for the most part—are correct, and that the revisionist attempts to circumvent the biblical condemnation of homosexual behavior are mistaken.

The second question seeks to understand why Scripture condemns homosexual behavior. If the first question is "What does the

Bible say?" the second question is "Why does the Bible say it?" There is a theological struggle between those who believe the condemnation is rooted in God's intent in creation and those who believe the condemnation is

rooted in the limited exposure of biblical writers to homosexuals (e.g., they were not aware of loving homosexual unions), or in their limited understanding of homosexuality (e.g., they did not know about the genetic roots of homosexuality or the distinction between natural homosexual orientation and heterosexuals who commit homosexual acts against their own nature), or was culturally accommodative to consensus opinions within their social contexts (e.g., Jewish polemics against pagan homosexuality).[5] I will engage this discussion in the section entitled "The Christian Story." I will argue that the biblical condemnation of homosexual behavior is rooted in God's intent for humanity as expressed in his creative act.

Yet, some ethicists believe the biblical picture is ultimately irrelevant or transcended by the larger vision of God's love and his desire for loving human relationships. Pittenger, for example, believes that the principles embedded in the Christian story move us to sanction homosexual unions because they embody a loving communion that reflects God's own love. In addition, Luke Timothy Johnson argues that the fruit of the Spirit in the lives of monogamous homosexual couples is evidence that God has transcended the limitations enjoined in Scripture. Evidence of holiness or "Christian experience" demands their inclusion in the fellowship of the church. By God's acts in the lives of homosexuals, he has demonstrated that he has accepted their lifestyle in much the same way that he demonstrated his acceptance of uncircumcised Gentiles in Acts 15. Whereas once God excluded uncircumcised Gentiles from his redeemed people, the Jews, but then transcended his own limitations, so now God includes those who were once excluded. Consequently, the church should recognize this new work of God and accept homosexual unions just as it accepts heterosexual unions.[6]

This hermeneutical move exalts experience over the story in Scripture. Instead of receiving and embodying a story, it creates a new story out of the fabric of human experience. It judges relationships as loving and fruitful through the lens of a different story. Yet, the values it uses to judge whether a relationship is "loving" and "fruitful" are rooted in the story of Scripture and the person of Jesus.

It accepts the values of Scripture (e.g., love), but it does not accept the matrix in which those values are articulated (e.g., creation and sexual ethics). It rejects the biblical story while accepting its values.

> To exalt experience over the story in Scripture is to create humanity in its own image.

In other words, it applies biblical values within a new story and thus fashions human relationships in the image of experience rather than in the image of the God of the biblical story. To exalt experience over the story in Scripture is to create humanity in its own image. Scripture is our hermeneutical lens—our metanarrative—for understanding God's intent for us. If the church is to sanction homosexual unions, its rationale must be rooted in Christian experience that is interpreted and shaped by the biblical story.

Biblical Texts

Scripture condemns homosexual behavior—at least this has been the consensus Christian understanding for over nineteen centuries. Only in the late twentieth century did a thoroughgoing revisionist understanding of the biblical texts emerge with any strength.

Revisionist interpretations tend to limit the application of the texts that apparently condemn homosexual behavior. They limit them to homosexual idolatrous practices, or to pederasty, or to condemnations of those with a heterosexual orientation who

> Revisionist interpretations tend to limit the application of the texts that apparently condemn homosexual behavior.

engage in homosexual behavior. Some, though few, argue that there is a sanctioned homosexual relationship within Scripture, that is, Jonathan and David.[7] Others apply a strong Christomonistic hermeneutic, that is, they ask: "Where did Jesus condemn homosexual unions?" If Jesus, who is the only legitimate interpreter of God's values, did not condemn them, then they must be acceptable.

This section surveys the biblical texts about homosexual behavior in the context of this traditional versus revisionist discussion. What do the texts actually say and what do they mean for us?

Old Testament

Genesis 9:20-27. When Noah was drunk and was lying "uncovered" in his tent, Ham—one of Noah's sons—"saw his father's

nakedness." As a result of his action, Ham's descendants, especially Canaan, were cursed. The severity of the curse indicates that this
is more than mere voyeurism. The language is best understood as
sexual relations. To "see (or uncover) the nakedness of another" is a
euphemism for sexual intercourse (cf. Lev 20:17; cf. 18:6-18;
20:11,7-21). In other words, Ham's sin was the homosexual rape of
his father. This, however, was not a matter of sexual lust but was
part of the Ancient Near Eastern practice of one man emasculating
and disgracing another. Thus, "by raping his father and alerting his
brothers to the act, Ham hoped to usurp the authority of his father
and elder brothers, establishing his right to succeed his father as
patriarch."[8] While the domination by one male over another through
homosexual rape was an accepted practice in the Ancient Near East
as a means of establishing authority, it is condemned here in the
most severe way through the curse on Canaan.[9]

Genesis 18–19 (19:4-8). The Sodom and Gomorrah narrative is
probably the most well-known story about homosexuality in the
Bible. Indeed, the term "sodomite" derives from this story. The narrative has been used to prove too much, but at the same time it has
been too easily dismissed.

On the one hand, the dominant narrative intent is to contrast
the hospitality Abraham showed to the angelic guests in Genesis 18
with the inhospitable reception they received from the men of Sodom
in Genesis 19. Though Lot received them hospitably, males in the
town approached them sexually. The men wanted to "have sex with
them" (literally, "to know" them; cf. Gen 4:1,17,25; 19:8; 24:16;
38:26). They wanted to dominate and emasculate the visitors
through a homosexual gang rape, which is the opposite of hospitality in the Ancient Near East.[10] As a consequence, but also for other
reasons (including luxurious living and mistreatment of the poor, cf.
Ezek 16:49-50), Sodom is destroyed by fire.

On the other hand, the presence of homosexual activity signals
the depth of the inhospitality. Though Ezekiel does not attribute the
destruction of Sodom solely to homosexuality, he does say, "they did
detestable things before me" (Ezek 16:50; literally, "they committed
an abomination before me"). To "commit an abomination" (cf. Ezek
18:12) is probably an allusion to sexual sin (cf. Lev 18:24-30,
describing Lev 18:6-23), but the only sexual sin that is singled out
specifically as an "abomination" is homosexual behavior (Lev
18:22). In addition, Jude 7 literally reads that they "went after dif-

ferent flesh" (*sarkos heteras*). While this might possibly refer to the "flesh" of angels, the men of Sodom were not aware that they were angels, and Jude portrays their actions as a negative example. Was his audience tempted to have sex with angels? Thus, the sin of Sodom was not merely social injustice, nor even homosexual rape, but the sin of Sodom was also its homosexual behavior.

Judges 19–20 (19:22-24). Like the Sodom and Gomorrah narrative, the primary motif is hospitality. While the traveling Levite received hospitality in Bethlehem, he was treated with inhospitality in the Benjamite city of Gibeah. When someone finally showed him some hospitality, "some of the wicked men of the city" demanded sex with the visitor (Judges 19:22; literally, "that we may know him"). Again, this probably reflected the desire to dominate a stranger. The ultimate effect of this was the near annihilation of the Benjamites by the rest of Israel.

Each of the above stories is about homosexual rape. We should not condemn homosexual behavior simply because these stories condemn homosexual rape any more than we should condemn heterosexual behavior because Judges 19:25-30 condemns heterosexual rape. Nevertheless, each of these stories has a common thread— the ultimate act of inhospitality was a homosexual act. The evil of society was epitomized by homosexual rape.[11] It was a powerful image of degradation and humiliation—the reverse of what was expected of one who was shaped by God's intent for humanity (cf. Job 31:31, which may be allusion to these stories [NRSV]: "O that we might be sated with his flesh!").

Deuteronomy 23:17-18; 1 Kings 14:24; 15:12; 22:46; 2 Kings 23:7; Job 36:14. These texts all refer to male cult (temple) prostitutes, whether among the Canaanites or in Israel. This was the most accepted form of homosexual behavior in the Ancient Near East. Thus, the Hebrew Scriptures at this point are countercultural, that is, they reject an accepted cultural practice. The Hebrew word that describes this occupation literally means "dog" (see NIV footnote). John in Revelation may allude to Deuteronomy 23:18 in his description of "dogs" that are outside the New Jerusalem (22:15) and the "abominable" ("vile" in NIV) who will experience the second death (21:8). According to Gagnon, "dogs" may refer specifically to male cult prostitutes but the "abominable" reminds us of the Leviticus texts where homosexual behavior is described in the same language.[12] The reason for the rejection of male cult prostitutes is not simply idolatry or prostitution but also because it is homosexual in character.

Leviticus 18:22 and 20:13. Sexual ethics is a prominent part of the Holiness Code of Israel (Leviticus 18–20). This legal material covers the same sexual ground twice (Lev 18:6-23; Lev 20:10-20). Embedded in these series of prohibitions are two verses about homosexual behavior: "Do not lie with a man as one lies with a woman; that is detestable" (18:22), and "If a man lies with a man as one lies with a woman, both of them have done what is detestable" (20:13a). The death penalty is prescribed for this sexual offense (20:13b). Consequently, the seriousness of this violation is underscored in several ways: (1) it is called an abomination; (2) the death penalty is prescribed; and (3) it appears in the same context as adultery (18:20; 20:10), bestiality (18:23; 20:15), incest (18:6-17; 20:13,17,19), and child sacrifice (18:21; 20:2-5).

Revisionist interpretations vary. Some dismiss it because it is part of the Old Testament, but one cannot equally dismiss child sacrifice because it is only condemned in the Hebrew Scriptures. More significantly, some believe that this text is related only to male prostitutes in pagan temples. The Holiness Code is set against the backdrop of Canaanite idolatrous practices (Lev 18:2-5,24; 20:23). But while the general context of the Torah itself and Leviticus 18–20 in particular is to distinguish Israel from other nations, there is no direct connection between homosexual behavior and idolatry in the text. While Leviticus 18:22 is followed by a prohibition against idolatry, the injunction against homosexual behavior in Leviticus 20:13 is stated between prohibitions against adultery, incest, and bestiality. To ban homosexual behavior included the banning of male cult prostitutes, but if this was the specific intent of Leviticus 18–20, then the Torah could have used a word that specifically refers to that practice (as in Deut 23:17-18).

But not all sexual sins described in Leviticus 18–20, so a counterargument runs, are regarded as such today. For example, Leviticus 18:19 and 20:18 forbid heterosexual relations during menstruation. However, several particulars distinguish this prohibition from others (including adultery, incest, etc.). The penalty for sexual sin is death, but the penalty for menstrual sex is exclusion from the people of God in terms of ritual purity ("cut off from their people," Leviticus 20:18). Whereas homosexual relations are described as an "abomination," menstrual sex is only described as "uncleanness" (Lev 18:19). Consequently, menstrual sex is a violation of ritual purity due to contact with blood (cf. the importance of blood in Leviticus 17) and does not fall into the same category as incest, homosexual relations, and adultery. Leviticus itself draws the distinction between all the sexual sins listed in the Holiness Code and the uncleanness of menstrual sex. Since the distinction between clean and unclean no longer obtains in the light of the teaching of Jesus (cf. Mark 7:1-23), we may regard this prohibition against menstrual sex as inapplicable to the Christian community.

Yet some argue that the Levitical proscription does not take into account the difference between homosexual behavior and homosexual orientation. What Leviticus condemns, so the argument runs, is heterosexually oriented males treating other males as women. But this reads a modern distinction into an ancient text. Whether or not biblical writers were aware of such distinctions, the text condemns the behavior without regard to origin, motive, or context. The behavior is condemned—just as it is with adultery—regardless of the circumstance.

New Testament

The Silence of Jesus. "What did Jesus say about homosexuality?" I once heard a gay preacher ask. "Nothing!" She concluded that silence means sanction. This trumps all other data in Scripture, according to the argument. The personal ministry and teaching of Jesus is the primary hermeneutical lens for ethics. If Jesus does not condemn homosexual behavior, then no one should.

But this assumes that Jesus spoke to every ethical concern imaginable and that those he did not address (including, for example, bribery or bestiality) he sanctioned. There may be other reasons for silence than approval. For example, perhaps there was no occasion to address the question of homosexual behavior. He never encountered a question about it or a person involved in it. Jesus' silence, however, is not total. On the contrary, Jesus is committed to the creation story that focuses on the complementary relationship between male and female in sexual union. Jesus appeals to God's creative act in order to ground the legitimacy of marriage and the illegitimacy of divorce (Mark 10:1-12; Matt 19:4-9). Marriage, for Jesus, is heterosexual in nature by virtue of God's creative intent and condemns sexual sin that violates marriage's sanctity (cf. Mark 7:21).

Romans 1:18-32 (1:26-27). This is perhaps the most important text in the biblical discussion of homosexuality. It is certainly the most extended discussion in Scripture, though it only consists of two verses that explicitly comment on homosexual relations. Yet, the context of this comment is what gives it significant weight. Consequently, it is a central point of discussion in the debate between traditional and revisionist understandings of homosexuality.[13]

Romans 1:18–3:29 climaxes with the resounding judgment that "all have sinned" (3:23) and that God has provided mercy for sinners through faith in Jesus (3:24). Paul develops the case for human depravity by rehearsing the moral history of both Jews and Gentiles. The Jews knew the law but broke it (2:23). The Gentiles knew God but suppressed the truth (1:18-20). Both are sinners and thus deserve God's wrath; they deserve spiritual death (1:18,32; 3:5). Yet, God in his mercy provided Jesus as an atoning sacrifice "who would turn aside his wrath" (3:25, NIV footnote).

In Paul's moral history of the pagan world he notes how they "exchanged" the glory of God for idolatry (1:23), how they "exchanged" the truth for a lie (1:25), and how they "exchanged natural relations for unnatural" (1:26). In response, God "gave them over" to "sexual impurity for the degrading of their bodies with one another" (1:24), and "gave them over to shameful lusts" (1:26), and "gave them over to a depraved mind" (1:28). Paul portrays a degenerative moral dynamic. As people suppressed the truth and exchanged God's story for their own, God permitted the full release of their desires. The pagan world underwent a degenerative spiral away from God and his intent for humanity (1:29-32).

Idolatry is at the foundation of this moral degeneration, but part of the process—as one of Paul's primary examples—is homosexual relations. This does not mean that all pagans were homosexuals but rather that the prominence of homosexuality was a primary evidence of the degenerative character of pagan culture. But we must not think that somehow, then, homosexuality is the epitome of sin because Paul balances the moral degeneration of the pagan world with the moral hypocrisy of the Jewish world (a hypocrisy which is part of the Christian world as well). Both Jew and Gentile, both hypocrite and homosexual, have sinned

> *Paul balances the moral degeneration of the pagan world with the moral hypocrisy of the Jewish world (a hypocrisy which is part of the Christian world as well).*

before God. If anything, it seems that Paul would say that those who had the oracles of God and the promises of the covenant should have known better and consequently their moral responsibility is greater.

Nevertheless, Paul does use homosexuality as evidence of human depravity. But what does Paul mean by Romans 1:26-27? Some believe that Paul only has pederasty in mind, that is, young male prostitutes or the relationship between a young boy and older adult. However, Paul does not describe this relationship as between young and old, but between men or males (*arsenes en arsesin*). Also, Paul—and only here in Scripture—specifically condemns lesbian relationships that did not have the pagan sanction of pederasty. It is not simply a male problem, but also a female one.

Some believe that Paul only describes homosexual relations as ritual or cultic "impurity" (1:24) or "uncleanness." In other words, Paul simply means that pagans participated in ritually impure acts that are condemned by Leviticus but these are not immoral actions. But this obscures the whole context of moral degeneration and Paul's conclusion that "all have sinned." In fact, Paul uses the term "impurity" (*akatharsian*) in connection with sexual immorality in 1 Thessalonians 4:6-7 and in different "vice" lists (cf. 2 Cor 12:21; Gal 5:19; Col 3:5; Eph 4:19; 5:3).

Some believe that Paul only addresses homosexual practices within idolatrous contexts. Idolatry, according to Paul, led to homosexual behavior. However, Paul does not locate homosexual behavior in the pagan cult, though it was present there. Rather, his appeal is broader. Idolatry gave occasion to homosexual behavior as the truth of God was exchanged for a lie. The lie sanctioned homosexual acts. David Greenberg has shown that polytheistic societies have given sacramental significance to homosexual acts while societies that envision God as transcendent and monotheistic reject homosexual behavior. This is rooted in the identification of polytheistic deities with creatures so that they are gendered whereas transcendent deities have no gender.[14]

Some believe that Paul is addressing "perverts" rather than "inverts." In other words, Paul is describing those who are heterosexual in orientation but nevertheless engage in homosexual acts against their "nature." Accordingly, Paul makes no comment on "inverts"—those who are homosexual in orientation and act according to their "nature." However, Paul is not describing a particular person's own nature. Rather, he claims that they exchange "*the* natural" (*tēn phusikēn*) for what is against nature (*para phusin*). Paul roots his moral judgment in what is "natural." Yet it is not what is natural to a particular person but what is nature itself.

The critical question is what Paul means by "nature." Some believe it merely refers to social convention (as it probably does in 1 Cor 11:14). Others believe that Paul has bought into a Stoic notion of defined natures. However, these perspectives overlook how Paul's language is linked to God's act in creation. Romans 1:19-20 appeals to God's act as evidence of his transcendent character. The exchange of the "glory of the immortal God for images made to look like mortal man and birds and animals and reptiles" reflects the language of Genesis 1 where God created humanity in his image and therefore there are no other images needed. When humanity turns stone and gold into images of God—whether those images are humanoid or animals—it is a denial of creation. Further, Paul's language to describe gender is the language of Genesis 1:27. Paul does not use the normal words for man and woman (*anēr* and *gunē*), but the creation language of male and female (*arsen* and *thēlus*). Consequently, for Paul, what is "natural" is what God created and whatever is "unnatural" is a "perversion" (1:27), including homosexual behavior as a primary example of what is "unnatural."

1 Corinthians 6:9; 1 Timothy 1:10. These two texts are part of "vice lists" in Paul's letters, which include such sins as greed or theft, adultery, and idolatry. The Greek term (*arsenokoitai*) translated "homosexual offenders" (NIV) in Corinthians is the same word that is translated "perverts" (NIV) in Timothy. In 1 Corinthians, Paul also includes an additional term that is translated "male prostitutes" (*malakoi*). The translation of both terms is disputed.

Arsenokoitai, derived from *arsenos* (meaning male) and *koite* (meaning bed), first appears in Greek literature in Paul's letters. David F. Wright argues that the word was coined by Hellenistic Jews, of whom Paul was one, from the conflation of the Greek translation (LXX) of Leviticus 18:22 and 20:13.[15]

> Leviticus 18:22, *kai meta **arsenos** ou koimethese **koiten** gunaikeian*
> And with a male do not lie coitally as with a woman
>
> Leviticus 20:13, *kai hosan koimethe meta **arsenos koiten** gunaikos*
> And whoever lies with a man coitally as with a woman

The derivation from Leviticus accounts for the fact that this word does not occur in Greco-Roman literature. The word only makes sense in the context of the Greek translation of the Jewish Torah. It parallels the Hebrew phrase "lying with a male" (*miskab zakur*) and is thus synonymous with homosexual behavior, no matter what the age or role of either male. It condemns the behavior, not the motive or age of the participant. Paul does not limit this term to pederasty, and if he had intended to limit the vice to such he would have used the Greek term *paiderastēs*. In addition, the connection to the prohibitions in the Torah are underscored by Paul's list in 1 Timothy 1:10 where it follows the general outline of the Ten Commandments: the first four ("unholy and irreligious"), the fifth ("kill their fathers and mothers"), the sixth ("murderers"), the seventh ("adulterers and perverts"), the eighth ("slave traders"), and the ninth ("liars and perjurers"). The prohibition against homosexual behavior is rooted in the Torah, and Paul continues the prohibition with his "vice" lists.

Malakoi literally means "soft ones." While some particularize this to mean "male prostitutes" (NIV) in the sense of young callboys, others broaden it to "effeminate" (one who assumes feminine characteristics). The meaning probably lies somewhere between these extremes. Since *malakoi* is sandwiched between adulterers and *arsenokoitai*, it has a predominantly sexual implication. Most likely, the term refers to the effeminate or passive partners in a homosexual relationship, inclusive of young boys who play the passive role with older men.[16]

Summary

Is this a marginal topic in Scripture? Is homosexuality, as a matter of biblical sexual ethics, peripheral to biblical theology? Actually, the witness of Scripture is consistent and uniform. There is no hint in Scripture that homosexual unions are sanctioned and every reference to homosexual behavior—in whatever form—is condemned. The limited number of texts does not undermine the seriousness of the ethic for two reasons. First, the texts in which homosexuality is condemned are explicitly ethical in character and positioned alongside other weighty sins. Indeed, its appearance in two vice lists (1 Corinthians 6 and 1 Timothy 1), as a primary

> There is no hint in Scripture that homosexual unions are sanctioned and every reference to homosexual behavior—in whatever form—is condemned.

example of fallenness in Romans 1, and as part of the sexual Holiness Code of Leviticus 18 and 20 demonstrates the weighted character of the witness present in Scripture. Second, the occasionality of Scripture means the topic is addressed as the occasion demands, that is, when it is necessary to speak to the issue due to circumstances. Notice, for example, how little is said about certain other kinds of sexual sin within Scripture (e.g., bestiality or incest). They are condemned but rarely discussed because there was no occasion or need for their thorough discussion.

More importantly, however, is what Richard B. Hays calls the "symbolic world" of Scripture.[17] The reason homosexual behavior is condemned is not because it is part of the cultural milieu of Hellenistic Judaism, but because it stands in conflict with the "symbolic world" of created heterosex-

> *The theological rationale for the inclusion of homosexual behavior in Christianity's vice lists is its commitment to the story of God in creation.*

uality. In other words, the theological rationale for the inclusion of homosexual behavior in Christianity's vice lists is its commitment to the story of God in creation.

The Christian Story

As Christians, we are committed to the biblical story of God as it is given to us in Scripture. The story is important because it molds our character, and ethical decisions, especially sexual ones, arise out of our character. The story must shape us so that our decisions flow from our identity in the image of God rather than from the immediacy of the moment. Conviction and commitment to the story of God are the fundamental barriers to sexual misconduct.

> *Conviction and commitment to the story of God are the fundamental barriers to sexual misconduct.*

God created humanity as male and female, and he created them in his own image. He created them as family who would image the divine family. God said, "Let us make [humanity] in our image, in our likeness, and let them rule over the fish . . ." (Gen 1:26). Humankind is created in the image of God as male and female. The divine community created a human community. Even before the foundation of the world, the Father loved the Son and the Son loved the Father (John 17:24). They, along with the Spirit of God (Gen 1:2), existed as a divine community of holy love. Humanity, as male and female, mirrors the nature of God. The story of Scripture begins with the divine community creating a human community to image the holy love of God in communal relationship.[18]

God created out of his overflowing, self-giving love. Just as God created humanity to share his loving community, so husbands and wives create children to share their loving community. Sexual intercourse involves the implicit commitment of two partners to receive and be responsible for new life. Procreation itself, then, images the creative work of God. Sexuality, of course, is at the heart of this communal relationship that produces children. The sexual experience expresses the oneness of male and female in community. We become "one flesh" (Genesis 2:24). That oneness images the oneness of God's fellowship and love. Our sexuality images God, and so our sexuality must reflect the nature of God. Sex is intended for a communion born out of commitment and intimacy that images the self-giving love of God's community.

> Our sexuality images God, and so our sexuality must reflect the nature of God.

Homosexuality is a perversion of the divine intent for intimacy that mirrors his own intimacy. Sexuality belongs to the creative act of God that intended marriage to proceed along sexual lines, male and female, because through the communion and procreation of that sexuality God's community is mirrored in human relationships. Homosexuality circumvents the creative intent of God for sexuality. God created male and female with sufficient differences and similarities that they provide the basis for bonding in family. Sexuality expresses God's intent for human bonding. It is the means by which male and female consummate and celebrate their marriage union. Sex is the ultimate bonding act. As such, it reflects the loving fellowship of God. The community of God is imaged through the loving fellowship of husband and wife.

> The community of God is imaged through the loving fellowship of husband and wife.

Our identity as sexual beings drives us to bond with other humans. The dynamic of bonding is the basic purpose of our existence as sexual beings.[19] The creative intent of God for us as sexual beings is family. The sexual impulse drives a person beyond their own self to seek bonding (communion) with others. The void in Adam's loneliness was sexually based. God created Eve to fill the loneliness of Adam's heart (Gen 2:18). Without the sexual other, we are incomplete and the bonding drive will be channeled in other directions. Homosexuality is dysfunctional because it seeks human bonding in a direction other than what God intended. Adam's solitariness could not have been overcome by the presence of another male.

Family (male-female marriage with children) is the place of human bonding where husband and wife are "one flesh" and produce "godly children" (Mal 2:14-15) in a context where children receive an identity and share in a loving story. Family provides the loving environment where children learn to love by being loved, just as we learned to love God by his loving us in Jesus Christ. This loving fellowship of family is the foundation of social stability. Confusion in sexual ethics tends to destabilize society and render it inhospitable (e.g., Genesis 19 and Judges 19). The diversity of sexual ethics destabilizes culture and ultimately undermines community.

> The diversity of sexual ethics destabilizes culture and ultimately undermines community.

The "male-female" polarity is essential to the doctrine of creation and sexuality. While there are many differences between male and female, the primary distinction is sexual and this is biological, rooted in creation. The relationship between them is essential to the full realization of human potential. Humanity exists, not as an abstract, but as male and female. The male-female relationship, then, is the fundamental norm for all other human relationships. The image of God involves both male and female as the ordered reality of creation. On the basis of this reasoning, Karl Barth concluded that homosexuality is not only a violation of the created order, but is also idolatrous in that it seeks self-fulfillment and self-sufficiency in one's own gender rather than in God's gift of the other gender. In seeking a substitute for the rejected partner one actually worships one's own sex.[20]

Thus, the biological complementarity of male and female reflects the divine act of creation. The argument for a heterosexual norm, however, is not merely biological (male/female genitalia are complementary). Rather, it is rooted in the divine intent of creation. Homosexuality, then, subverts the divine intent in creation in at least three ways. *First*, it undermines the divine intent for human bonding in a way that mirrors the intimacy of the divine community. Humanity was created as a duality and that duality is the mechanism of human bonding. *Second*, it circumvents the fullness of God's intention for sex by undermining one of its significant purposes. Procreation, while not the only purpose of sex, is a fundamental function of sex. Males and females participate in the creative work of God through procreation as they fulfill God's mandate to fill the earth. *Third*, the homosexual act and relationship does not fully image God because God created the relationship between male and female as his image. To pursue sexuality solely in the context of one's own sex is to pursue the image of God in a deficient way. It cannot fully embody God's intent for sexuality.[21] The divine act of creating humanity as male and female, then, grounds the normative ethical value of heterosexuality.

> *Humanity was created as a duality and that duality is the mechanism of human bonding.*

But if this is the normative creation value, why do so many experience a homosexual orientation that is seemingly beyond their choice and feels so "natural"? "Many," of course, is a relative term. The most recent study concluded that only 1-4% of males and 1-2% of females practice exclusive homosexuality.[22] Yet this "feels natural," and some have suggested that the causes are genetic. In other words, they were born gay.

While I do not have time to discuss the different scientific perspectives on this issue, others have.[23] There is no reliable, scientific evidence of a "gay gene" or a kind of inborn determinism. Most studies suggest that there may be some predisposition to homosexual behavior that is nurtured through various circumstances, but there is no genetic necessity for homosexual choices. Nevertheless, homosexual persons often feel that they had no choice or they have no conscious memory of making a choice. We should grant this feeling rather than dispute it. However, this does not render their behavior ethical.

Everyone experiences a predisposition to evil, but not necessarily the same particular forms of evil. Indeed, Christians affirm that humanity shares a depraved nature, a fallen predisposition to sin. We are born into a fallen world with fallen bodies. In a fallen world it is "natural" that sin would feel natural. Alcoholism is a "natural" predisposition. Pederasty was "natural" in the ancient Greek world. Male prostitution was "natural" in the Ancient Near East. What is "natural" to fallen humanity is not necessarily ethical.

Rather, the biblical story articulates a vision of what is "natural" that is rooted in the divine act of creation rather than in fallenness. We were created to image God and live as male and female in sexual communion, which

> *What is "natural" to fallen humanity is not necessarily ethical.*

is true humanity. When we fail to image God in this way (just as when we fail to image God in other ways), we lose something. It scars our humanity and hinders God's goal of intimacy and community.

Life in the Church

The church is a maligned institution in the history of western civilization. It deserves much of the criticism it has received. Instead of serving the world with grace and love, it has often been the locus of institutional intolerance, hate, and prejudice. This has been particularly true of the church's relationship to homosexual persons. So-called Christian people have been known to protest social justice for homosexuals with signs such as "God hates Homos!" In such instances the church becomes homophobic and subtly encourages hostility towards homosexuals.

But this hostility is not what the church is intended to represent. Rather, the church is the presence of Christ in the world through the Spirit. The church is the Spirit-filled people of God who represent Christ before the world. Just as the Father sent his Son as his presence in the world, so Christ has sent us. The church follows Christ into the world as light and salt. The church fulfills the ministry of Christ. And the ministry of Christ was to reach out to the outsider, the sinner, and the disenfranchised in order to invite them into the kingdom of God. The ministry of Christ is the ministry of the church; it is the instrument of God's redemptive presence in the world.

At the same time, the church is the manifestation of God's kingdom on the earth. It participates in the new order of humanity. It no longer participates and shares in the fallenness of the old world. The church is a holy community called to reflect the glory of God in the fallen world; a light that shines in the darkness but does not participate in the darkness. Thus, it can neither sanction nor tolerate evil in its midst. Since homosexual behavior is an expression of the fallenness of the world, the church can neither sanction nor tolerate it within its holy fellowship.

On one hand, the church invites homosexuals into the kingdom of God, but it calls homosexuals to a new order of living. The

> On one hand, the church
> invites homosexuals into
> the kingdom of God, but
> it calls homosexuals to a
> new order of living.

church seeks to minister to homosexuals, but it cannot sanction homosexual
behavior. Of course, this is not only true
of homosexuals, but it is true for all of us
since we all participate in fallenness.
Whether it is adultery, murder, theft,
slander, greed, or lying, the church seeks
to minister to fallen people without
sanctioning or participating in their fallenness. And yet the church is
composed of fallen people who yearn for the fullness of the new
order in their lives and seek the transformation of their fallenness
into the image of Christ—to be like Christ.

First Corinthians 5–6 provides a model for the church. The
context is charged with the problem of sexuality. In 1 Corinthians 5
Paul addresses an incestuous situation in the church and in 1 Corinthians 6 reminds the church that how they act as sexual beings is
important to God. Paul commands the Corinthians to discipline the
incestuous man who refuses to repent. They are to "hand this man
over to Satan" as a last ditch effort to awaken his faith and renew his
life (1 Cor 5:5). But even if the redemptive purpose is not effective,
the church must exclude this man from their community because his
influence will infect the whole community. A little leaven will leaven
the whole lump.

In 1 Corinthians 6:12-20 Paul rebukes those Corinthians who
continued to visit prostitutes. Since they are the body of Christ and
the Holy Spirit dwells in them, how can they unite Christ and his
Spirit with a prostitute? Sexual ethics, for Paul, is shaped by our
identity in Christ. Our bodies do not belong to us any longer. They
belong to Christ. He has bought us, his Spirit dwells within us, and
our bodies are members of his body. How we behave sexually is no
longer our autonomous right. Rather, we submit our sexuality to the
one who bought us.

Between the discussion of the incestuous man and the visita-
tion of prostitutes, Paul asks the question: "Do you not know that the
wicked will not inherit the kingdom of God?" (1 Cor 6:9). At the head
of his list of wicked are: sexually immoral, idolaters, adulterers,
"male prostitutes," and "homosexual offenders." But he also
includes the greedy, drunkards, slanderers, and swindlers. The

emphasis in the context is on sexual sin, but this is not an exclusive interest. Sin condemns, whether it is adultery, homosexual acts, or greed. All who persist in such and rebel against God's values are excluded from the kingdom, and thus from the church.

> Sin condemns, whether it is adultery, homosexual acts, or greed.

How, then, does the church relate to a homosexual person in the light of 1 Corinthians 5–6? One the one hand, it should accept those who struggle against their homosexual orientation. On the other hand, it should discipline those who rebelliously practice a homosexual lifestyle just as it should discipline those who persist in other expressions of fallenness (e.g., greed, drunkenness, thievery, etc.). In other words, the church ought to lovingly receive those who struggle with a homosexual orientation, but it ought to discipline those who participate in homosexual behavior. Nevertheless, the disposition of the church to all homosexuals ought to be loving, faithful, and hopeful.

> The church ought to lovingly receive those who struggle with a homosexual orientation, but it ought to discipline those who participate in homosexual behavior.

A homosexual orientation—as a participation in fallenness—does not exclude one from the fellowship of the church any more than other kinds of orientations to fallenness (e.g., alcoholism, addictions of various kinds) exclude people from that fellowship. Every Christian struggles with his or her fallen orientations. We all have the same fundamental problem—we are fallen. Because of the Fall the disposition toward sin is a human problem, and Christians are not immune. Though we neither share the same orientations to particular sins nor the same depth of attraction to particular sins, we are all in the process of being transformed into the image of Christ, and we are at different places in that process. As long as people seek transformation and acknowledge their struggle, the church should be a safe place for the struggle against fallen orientations, including a homosexual orientation.

According to Paul, practicing homosexuals are excluded from the kingdom of God (along with the greedy, drunkards, thieves, adulterers, etc.). They will not inherit the kingdom of God and thus cannot participate in the church that is the present manifestation of that kingdom. The holy community cannot tolerate habitual, rebellious,

> As Paul said, it is not our business "to judge those outside the church," but it is important to "judge those inside."

and impenitent homosexual behavior. Just as Paul demanded that the Corinthians discipline the incestuous man, the church must also exclude from the church those believers who imitate his arrogant rebellion. The church cannot tolerate people who willfully and rebelliously continue to practice their homosexual orientation. As Paul said, it is not our business "to judge those outside the church," but it is important to "judge those inside" and exclude every rebellious sinner—no matter which sin—from God's holy community (1 Cor 5:12-13).

Conclusion: Theological Perspectives

In the light of creation, heterosexuality is the divine intent and thus the moral norm. God created what he wanted. He created what imaged him—he created unity in diversity. Male and female is the diversity of humanity united in one community. Sexuality is the primary witness to this diversity, and sexual union is the primary means of unity. As male and female unite sexually in marriage, they bear witness to the unity and equality of humanity. They thus image the unity and diversity of God where the intimacy of the Father, Son, and Spirit exhibits a unity within diversity. To use sexuality for an intimacy that violates this unity is to deflect the image of God and deny the diversity. Homosexual union is idolatry because it adulterates

> As male and female unite sexually in marriage, they bear witness to the unity and equality of humanity.

the image God created of himself and substitutes homosexuality for the duality God created.

In the light of the Fall, homosexuality participates in fallenness. Homosexuality is an exchange of God's creative intent for human self-interests. Homosexuality is the love of one's own sex and the rejection of divinely created duality (diversity). Homosexuality, as an orientation, is a fallen condition, but fallenness is something in which all humans participate though with varying orientations and degrees. Homosexuality, like other sins, is an expression of the deeper problem of fallenness that we all share. Fallenness feels natural, so it should not surprise us that a homosexual orientation feels natural to some.

In the light of God's redemption, the church should orient itself toward homosexual persons in faith, hope, and love. We call homosexuals to the acceptance of God's Lordship and submit to his intentions for human life through faith. In consequence, those who experience a homosexual orientation should struggle against that fallen predisposition in their natures (whether acquired or inborn). The church is called to share this struggle through communal support, compassionate listening, clearly defined expectations, humble accountability, and patient dialogue (cf. Gal 5:1-2). The church, too, must submit to God's Lordship as it receives, counsels, and fellowships those who struggle with an orientation they did not choose. As they struggle to resist what seems so natural to them, the church must resist condemnation and self-righteous arrogance.

We call homosexuals to hope through trusting in God's transforming power. Fallenness is deeply embedded in the human psyche and nature. Consequently the struggle is real, as everyone who struggles with any dimension of sin and fallenness understands. We struggle with some dimensions of fallenness our whole lives. However, God is at work in us through his Spirit to transform us into

> *We call homosexuals to hope through trusting in God's transforming power.*

his image. There is hope for homosexuals, just as there is hope for all of us. Our hope is God's transforming work whereby he renews life and gives strength in our struggle. As the lives of many people who have experienced transformation testify, including those who have experienced deliverance from the fallenness of a homosexual orientation and/or behavior, God can give his people victory over sin in their lives. The church bears witness to the hope of transformation and offers that hope to everyone who is burdened with fallenness. Thus, Paul affirms that some of the Corinthians were engaged in homosexual practices (1 Cor 6:9), but they have now been washed, justified, and sanctified in the name of Jesus and in the Spirit (1 Cor 6:11).

We call the church to love their homosexual neighbors. The church must demonstrate *agape* toward homosexuals. God is our model—he loved us before we loved him, and even while we were yet his enemies, God demonstrated his love toward us in that Christ died for us. Our practice of this example of love must be proactive; it seeks friendships with our homosexual neighbors. It treats our homosexual neighbors with equity, justice, and compassion. It does not fear them or discriminate against them but rather invites them into friendship and calls them to faith and hope in love. Love means that we seek social justice for our homosexual neighbors but that we also call them to experience the transforming grace of God through faith and hope.

Notes

[1]Available at **http://www.barna.org/cgi-bin/ PageCategory.asp?CategoryID=2**. A good survey of views among professing Christians is found in Larry Holben, *What Christians Think about Homosexuality: Six Representative Viewpoints* (Richland Hills, TX: D. & F. Scott, 1999).

[2]Norman Pittenger, *Time for Consent: A Christian's Approach to Homosexuality* (London: SCM Press, 1967; 3rd. ed., 1976).

[3]Letha Scanzoni and Virginia R. Mollenkott, *Is the Homosexual My Neighbor? Another Christian View* (San Francisco: Harper & Row, 1978; 3rd ed., 1994).

[4]Barna survey available at **http://www.barna. org/cgi-in/PagePressRelease.asp?PressRelease ID=122&Reference=F.**

[5]See the essays edited by David L. Balch, *Homosexuality, Science, and the "Plain Sense" of Scripture* (Grand Rapids: Eerdmans, 2000); and Jeffrey S. Siker, *Homosexuality in the Church: Both Sides of the Debate* (Louisville, KY: Westminster John Knox, 1994).

[6]Luke Timothy Johnson, *Scripture & Discernment: Decision Making in the Church* (Nashville: Abingdon, 1996) 144-148.

[7]Robert A.J. Gagnon, *The Bible and Homosexual Practice: Texts and Hermeneutics* (Nashville: Abingdon, 2001) 146-154, effectively responds to this possible example.

[8]Ibid., 66-67.

[9]Donald J. Wold, *Out of Order: Homosexuality in the Bible and the Ancient Near East* (Grand Rapids: Baker, 1998) 48, quotes a Mesopotamia legal text: "If a man has intercourse with the hindquarters of his equal (male), that man will be foremost among his brothers and colleagues." On homosexuality in the ancient world, see Martti Nissinen, *Homoeroticism in the Biblical World: A Historical Perspective* (Philadelphia: Fortress, 1998); and James B. DeYoung, *Homosexuality: Contemporary Claims Examined in the Light of the Bible and Classical*

Jewish, Greek, and Roman Literature and Law (Grand Rapids: Kregel, 2000).

[10]Kenneth Dover, *Greek Homosexuality*, 2nd ed. (Cambridge: Harvard University Press, 1989) 105, writes: "human societies at many times and in many regions have subjected strangers, newcomers and trespassers to homosexual anal violation as a way of reminding them of their subordinate status." Further, a Middle Assyrian law describes the effect of homosexual penetration as "masculinity . . . transformed into femininity" (Gagnon, *Bible*, 75).

[11]See S. Niditch, "The 'Sodomite' Theme in Judges 19-20: Family, Community and Social Disintegration," *Catholic Biblical Quarterly* 44 (1982) 357-369.

[12]Gagnon, *Bible*, 105.

[13]Given current revisionist approaches, the best discussion of this text is by Richard B. Hays, "Relations Natural and Unnatural: A Response to John Boswell's Exegesis of Romans 1," *Journal of Religious Ethics* 14 (1986) 184-215.

[14]David F. Greenberg, *The Construction of Homosexuality* (Chicago: University of Chicago Press, 1988) 182-183.

[15]David F. Wright, "Homosexuals or Prostitutes? The Meaning of *Arsenokoitai* (1 Cor. 6:9; 1 Tim. 1:10)," *Vigiliae Christianae* 38 (1984) 125-153.

[16]See Gagnon, *Bible*, 306-312.

[17]Richard B. Hays, *The Moral Vision of the New Testament: A Contemporary Introduction to New Testament Ethics* (San Francisco: Harper, 1996).

[18]See Stanley J. Grenz, *Sexual Ethics: A Biblical Perspective* (Dallas: Word, 1990) 31-37, for an extended theological discussion of this point.

[19]I am indebted to Grenz, *Sexual Ethics*, 19ff., for much of this material. See also

Donald M. Joy, *Bonding: Relationships in the Image of God* (Waco, TX: Word, 1985).

[20]Karl Barth, *Church Dogmatics* (Edinburgh: T. & T. Clark, 1961) III/4, 116-239, esp. 166ff.

[21]Stanley J. Grenz, *Welcoming but Not Affirming: An Evangelical Response to Homosexuality* (Louisville, KY: Westminster John Knox, 1998) 109-115.

[22]Robert T. Michael et al., *Sex in America: A Definitive Survey* (Boston: Little, Brown, & Co., 1994) 172-174.

[23]See Gagnon, *Bible*, 395-432.

Bibliography

Marital Heterosexuality Only

Gagnon, Robert A.J. *The Bible and Homosexual Practice: Texts and Hermeneutics.* Nashville: Abingdon, 2001.

The best single volume on the exegetical and biblical dimensions of homosexuality, it is the most comprehensive scholarly work available. It also tackles the problem of whether homosexual persons can change and whether the orientation is genetic. This book is not for the novice. See his web site at **www.robgagnon.net**.

Grenz, Stanley J. *Welcoming but Not Affirming: An Evangelical Response to Homosexuality.* Louisville, KY: Westminster John Knox, 1998.

Excellent exploration of the theological issues involved in the discussion, including the relationship of the church to homosexual persons.

Schmidt, Thomas E. *Straight and Narrow? Compassion and Clarity in the Homosexuality Debate.* Downers Grove, IL: InterVarsity, 1995.

A compassionate but strong argument in favor of a traditional position. Though informed and judicious, it is easily accessible to all readers.

Webb, William J. *Slaves, Women and Homosexuals: Exploring the Hermeneutics of Cultural Analysis.* Downers Grove, IL: InterVarsity, 2001.

Excellent argument that homosexuality does not share the same hermeneutical ground as the discussion of slavery or gender. One cannot lump the homosexual discussion together with the gender discussion as if they share the same theological rationale.

Web Resource: Exodus International. North America. http://www.exodusnorthamerica.org.

This organization assists those who are struggling with a homosexual orientation. It provides many resources for the discussion of homosexuality in both ancient and contemporary contexts.

Covenant and Equal-Partner Homosexuality

Countryman, L. William. *Dirt, Greed, and Sex: Sexual Ethics in the New Testament and Their Implications for Today*. Philadelphia: Fortress, 1988.

A contemporary theological argument for homosexual unions in the context of New Testament sexual ethics.

Scanzoni, Letha D., and Virginia R. Mollenkott. *Is the Homosexual My Neighbor? A Positive Christian Response*. Rev. ed. San Francisco: HarperCollins, 1994.

An evangelical argument for homosexual unions.

Wink, Walter, ed. *Homosexuality and Christian Faith: Questions of Conscience for the Churches*. Minneapolis: Fortress, 1999.

A collection of essays that promote revisionist understandings of biblical texts. Wink favors a view that admits Scripture prohibits homosexual unions but moderns can judge it ethical due to experience, scientific knowledge, and social justice (see his brief pamphlet available at http://www.bridges-across.org/ba/wink.htm).

Web Resource: Evangelicals Concerned Western Region. http://www.ecwr.org.

This organization promotes an evangelical theology that sanctions homosexual unions. It provides many resources for exploration as well as information about worshiping communities that accept homosexual couples.

Sexual Ethics in the New Testament

Gregory L. Linton, Ph.D.

Perhaps no other ethical issue is as personal in its implications and universal in its relevance as the issue of sexual ethics. Many people will never have to confront personally some of the ethical issues discussed in this volume, but, as Lisa Sowle Cahill observed, "all people at least some of the time are unsure how to understand their sexuality and how to behave sexually in ways that are morally praiseworthy rather than reprehensible."[1] Sin has so distorted human sexuality that all people struggle with appropriate ways to fulfill and express their sexual desires. The consequences of their decisions can dramatically affect their physical health, emotional stability, relational security, and spiritual maturity. Therefore, the conclusions that people reach concerning proper sexual behavior can either enhance or damage their well-being in the physical, spiritual, emotional, and relational spheres of life.

Despite the importance of sexual ethics, the New Testament says astonishingly little about it. On the one hand, as Raymond F. Collins notes, "all but six of the books of the New Testament have something to say that is pertinent to sexual ethics."[2] On the other hand, many of the references contain just a word or two about sex. Most of the explicit teaching on sexual ethics is concentrated in 1 Corinthians 5–7. Lewis B. Smedes concludes: "The writers of the Bible did not make sexuality a major theme. They had more urgent matters on their minds: they were responding to the great acts of God for human salvation. They were not divinely inspired to theorize about sex."[3] The apparent reticence of the New Testament writers on the subject may reflect a sense of propriety and tactfulness about the subject. Also, the lack of attention to sexual issues may indicate that the early Christians were not confused about these matters.

Despite the lack of lengthy discourse on sexual ethics, the teaching of the New Testament does provide clear boundaries for sexual expression. This essay will describe first the norm of sexual behavior, then deviations from that norm, and finally sexual issues that the New Testament does not address. New Testament sexual ethics will be compared with the sexual ethics of Judaism, the Greco-Roman world, and contemporary American culture.

> Despite the lack of lengthy discourse on sexual ethics, the teaching of the New Testament does provide clear boundaries for sexual expression.

The Norm of Heterosexual Monogamy

In ancient Rome, two citizens married when they had the consent of the *paterfamilias* and lived together with the intention of being married. Older members of the family arranged these matches, but sometimes the partners might have had some say in the decision. The wedding festivities probably began in the bride's home and then proceeded to the groom's home where a religious rite signified her acceptance into the new home. The bride's family would provide a dowry of property and cash, which the groom would return if the marriage ended by death or divorce. The purpose of Roman marriage was the production of legitimate children, but companionship and love were also important components.[4] Divorce was simply a matter of either or both parties expressing a desire to end the marriage. Consequently, divorce was a widespread phenomenon.

A woman who lived with a man without being married to him was called a "concubine." Such arrangements occurred when the man's higher social status prevented marriage. Typically, concubines were freed female slaves. They were expected not to have children, but if they did, the children bore the mother's name and could not inherit from the father. Married men could not have a concubine, and a man could not have two concubines at once.[5]

Jewish marriage involved payment of a *mōhar*, or bride-price, to the person in authority over the woman, the drawing up of a contract that specified the contents of the bride's dowry, and the conditions for dissolution of the marriage. The married couple usually moved in with the groom's parents. Divorce occurred simply by declaration of either spouse. Adultery by the wife led directly to divorce, but extramarital intercourse by the husband was not explicitly prohibited. Evidence suggests that Jewish women occasionally divorced their husbands. The Mishnah later allowed only husbands the right to divorce, but a wife could request the courts to require her husband to grant her a divorce.[6]

Judaism promoted a positive view of the role of sex in marriage. The wife had a fundamental right to have her sexual needs satisfied. Later Jewish regulations show that a wife could ask the local council to request a divorce from her husband if he had abstained from intercourse for more than one or two weeks (*m. Ketub.* 5:6). Other positive views of sex within marriage can be found in the Song of Songs; Proverbs 5:18-19; and Sirach 16:17-18. However, Jewish writings such as Philo, Tobit, and Pseudo-Phocylides warn against using one's wife merely to satisfy one's lust.[7]

The New Testament allows sexual expression only within a marriage relationship between one man and one woman. Jesus himself promoted this norm in answer to a question about the lawfulness of divorce (Matt 19:3-6). In verse 4, he quotes Genesis 1:27: "Have you not read that the one who made them at the beginning 'made them male and female.'" In verse 5, he quotes Genesis 2:24: "For this reason a man shall leave his father and mother and be joined to his wife, and the two shall become one flesh." In verse 6, he draws the appropriate conclusion: "So they are no longer two, but one flesh. Therefore what God has joined together, let no one separate." Joining together and becoming one flesh suggest that the sexual act finalizes the marriage covenant and binds the lives of the spouses together in a physical and spiritual union.

Jesus taught that marriage is to be exclusive and permanent. In verse 8, he explains that Moses' instruction about divorce in Deuteronomy 24:1 was a realistic concession to the sinfulness of people but that it did not reflect God's intention for marriage. In verse 9, he equates remarrying after divorce with adultery. In God's eyes, marriage is a permanent covenant that is ended only by death. Once one has entered that covenant, to

> Jesus taught that marriage is to be exclusive and permanent.

marry or have sexual relations with someone else is adultery in God's eyes. According to Jewish law, adultery always involved another man's wife, but Jesus expanded the definition of adultery to include any woman, whether married or not. He also expanded the definition of adultery to include married men as well as married women who were unfaithful.[8]

The only condition that would allow divorce is *porneia* ("unchastity") on the part of the wife. This vague term could refer to four possible situations: 1) The man discovers on the wedding night that his wife is not a virgin,[9] 2) the man discovers that he and his wife share a close blood relationship that would be considered incest,[10] 3) a husband discovers that his wife was a prostitute in her former life,[11] or 4) the man discovers that his wife has committed adultery.[12] The last interpretation is supported by the fact that the righteous Joseph considered divorcing Mary in Matthew 1:18-25 because he presumed she was unfaithful. Also, Jeremiah 3:1-10 depicts God giving Israel a bill of divorce for adultery. Roman law required a man to divorce his wife if he discovered that she had committed adultery. In contrast, Jesus permits divorce but does not command it. After the time of Christ, Jewish husbands were required to divorce adulterous wives, and the Church Fathers also taught that adultery required separation.[13]

Stanley J. Grenz concludes from Jesus' teaching: "He asserts that according to the design of the Creator marriage consists of the monogamous union of a male and female in a lifelong commitment to one another which is to be characterized by fidelity."[14] Jesus presents marriage as the joining of a *man* and a *woman*. Also, he envisions only *one* man and *one* woman joining together in marriage.[15] In addition, the husband and wife join together and become one flesh only after a decisive departure from the family of origin in order to establish a new household. This public act suggests the need for a wedding ceremony. In this concise teaching, Jesus excludes the following sexual practices from the acceptable norm: homosexuality, polygamy, premarital sex, adultery, and divorce.

Paul echoes Jesus' teaching on marriage when he addresses the problem of prostitution in 1 Corinthians 6:12-20. Influenced by Hellenistic dualism of the body and the spirit, some believers in Corinth thought that freedom in Christ implied that what one does with the body does not matter to God. Therefore, they were free to engage in sexual relations with prostitutes.[16] Paul responds by applying Genesis 2:24 to the situation: "Do you not know that your bodies are members of Christ? Should I therefore take the members of Christ and make them members of a prostitute? Never! Do you not know that whoever is united to a prostitute becomes one body with her? For it is said, 'The two shall be one flesh'" (1 Cor 6:15-16). Genesis 2:24 shows that sex unites a man and a woman in a physical and spiritual bond, but such a union should take place only between a man and a woman who enter the commitment of marriage. Since Paul uses the term *porneia* ("fornication") instead of *moicheia* ("adultery"), these men may have been young, unmarried men who enjoyed the sexual favors of prostitutes in the context of banquets.[17]

Paul deals directly with the sexuality of marriage in 1 Corinthians 7:1-9. He responds to a statement made by the Corinthians in a letter to Paul: "It is well for a man not to touch a woman" (1 Cor 7:1). In contrast to those libertines of chapter 6, other Corinthians were promoting sexual abstinence between husbands and wives as an expression of their freedom in Christ.[18] This ethic may reflect the common Hellenistic view that the body was evil. Other religions and philosophies promoted such ascetic practices as expressions of freedom from physical desires.[19]

Paul responds by warning that such a practice can promote acts of *porneia*. Sexually deprived husbands may seek satisfaction with prostitutes, accepted behavior for men in the Greco-Roman world. To avoid this problem, husbands and wives "should have" one another, which is a euphemism for sexual relations (7:2).[20] Paul's instruction restricts sexual relations to one's spouse.

Husbands and wives should freely provide their spouses with their "conjugal rights" (7:3). The Greek word *opheilēn* suggests that it is a duty and obligation to provide the spouse with sexual relations. To support this instruction, Paul expands on the meaning of Genesis 2:24: "For the wife does not have authority over her own body, but the husband does; likewise, the husband does not have authority over his own body, but the wife does" (7:4). Because they are one flesh, their bodies do not belong to themselves but to their spouses. The closest parallels to this ideal of mutual and equal privilege and responsibility are found in Stoicism.[21]

Because of the duties of the spouses to each other, they should engage in free and frequent sexual intimacy: "Do not deprive one another" (7:5). They are not to take away what rightfully belongs to the other.[22] Richard J. Foster draws out the possible implications of this teaching: "Those who try to limit sex to procreation are simply ignoring the Bible. Scripture enthusiastically affirms sex within the bonds of marriage. Frequency of sex and variations of sexual technique simply are not moral issues, except in the sense of consideration for one another. In other words, married couples are free in the Lord to do whatever is mutually satisfying and contributes to the relationship."[23]

The only concession Paul allows is to devote oneself to prayer by mutual consent, but abstinence should last briefly in order to avoid giving Satan the opportunity to lead one astray. In Paul's view, Satan wants people to engage in *porneia*, but God wants a man and a woman to enjoy sexual intimacy within the bond of marriage. Nowhere in this discussion of marriage does Paul suggest that sex is intended solely for procreation. Paul's teaching also does not support Augustine's notion that every sex act is tainted by evil.[24]

Paul goes on to explain that marriage is the only relationship within which one should enjoy sexual intimacy. He expresses the desire that all had the gift of celibacy as he himself did, but God does not give that gift to everyone (7:7).[25] He encourages widows and widowers to remain unmarried as he was (7:8).[26] This suggestion, however, does not apply to everyone: "But if they are not practicing self-control, they should marry. For it is better to marry than to be aflame with passion" (7:9). As 7:5 also indicates, self-control is the quality or virtue that enables one to resist *porneia*.[27] To lack self-control is, as the Greek literally says, "to burn."[28] Paul could have recommended satisfying one's sexual desires by uniting with a prostitute or slave or by engaging in pederasty with a young boy, which were acceptable practices in the Greco-Roman world. But in Paul's ethic, the only acceptable expression of one's sexual desires is within marriage. In effect, Paul prohibits all sexual relations outside of marriage.

Paul expresses this same ethic later in chapter 7. In verse 25, Paul addresses engaged couples who questioned whether they should remain unmarried. Paul uses the term *parthenos* ("virgin"), which could refer to unmarried men or women.[29] The term implies that Christian men and women who were not married have not engaged in sexual relations. Paul prefers that they remain unmarried so that they can avoid the distractions of marriage and devote themselves to the Lord's work in the short time that remains (7:25-35). However, to marry is not a sin (7:28).

If the sexual desires of the engaged man are too strong to maintain celibacy, the only alternative is to marry (7:36).[30] This is the proper remedy for "not behaving properly toward his fiancée," a phrase that had sexual connotations in the ancient world.[31] This phrase may imply that he is tempted to engage in sexual relations before the marriage is officially completed. Alternatively, it may mean that he is bringing shame on the other person by backing out on the commitment he (or his family) had made. The man who is able to keep his sexual desires under control is free not to marry (7:37). Paul's instructions again reveal that believers have two options for sexual behavior: celibacy outside of marriage or sexual relations between one man and one woman within marriage.

This same sexual ethic is implied in the controversial phrase "married only once," which occurs in 1 Timothy 3:2 with reference to bishops, in 1 Timothy 3:12 with reference to deacons, and in 1 Timothy 5:9 with reference to widows. The Greek phrase *mias gunaikos andra* literally means "one-woman man." The phrase used for widows is "one-man woman." This phrase may rule out one or more of the following behaviors: premarital sex, adultery, polygamy, remarriage after the death of a spouse, and remarriage after divorce. Whatever its specific reference, it is consistent with Jesus' and Paul's sexual ethic of heterosexual monogamy.

This ethic occurs again in the instruction not to put younger widows on "the list" to be cared for by the church along with the older widows (1 Tim 5:9-16). The reason is that "when their sensual desires alienate them from Christ, they want to marry" (5:11). Their desire for marriage may overcome their devotion to Christ and may cause them to marry someone who is not a Christian. Again, the only appropriate outlet for their sensual desires is marriage.

Both Jesus and Paul taught that the ethical norm for sexuality is heterosexual monogamy. Cahill concludes from her examination of biblical teaching: "Perspectives on sexuality in both Testaments favor the institutionalization of sexuality in heterosexual, monogamous, permanent, and procreative marriage that furthers the cohesiveness and continuity of family, church, and body politic, and that respects and nurtures the affective commitments to which spouses give sexual expression." Smedes draws the same conclusion: "The sexuality of every person is meant to move him [sic] toward a heterosexual union of committed love."[32] Sexual relations should occur only between one man and one woman who have bound themselves together in the life-

> Both Jesus and Paul taught that the ethical norm for sexuality is heterosexual monogamy.

long covenant of marriage. The New Testament offers warnings to avoid deviations from that norm.

Deviations from the Norm

In the New Testament, the most frequent term for deviations from heterosexual monogamy is *porneia*, a term that "connoted any and all forms of sexual misconduct."[33] The word came from *porne*, the word for "prostitute." The related word *pornos* is one who commits *porneia*. According to H. Reisser, "the word-group can describe various extra-marital sexual modes of behavior insofar as they deviate from accepted social and religious norms (e.g., homosexuality, promiscuity, paedophilia, and especially prostitution)."[34] It is usually translated as either "sexual immorality" or "fornication." The word can refer to adultery, although the Greek word *moicheia* is the specific term for adultery. It can also refer to incest and was used figuratively for idolatry.[35] The following survey of sexual deviations will focus on three types of sexual immorality that affect many people: premarital sex, adultery, and lust.

Fornication

Old Testament Texts: Old Testament regulations protected female virginity so that the man who married could be certain that his children belonged to him. Deuteronomy 22:13-21 prescribes the penalty of death by stoning if a woman was discovered on her wedding night not to be a virgin. A man who slept with a woman to whom he was not engaged was required to pay the dowry to her father and marry her (Deut 22:28-29). If a man violated the rights of a fellow Israelite by sleeping with his betrothed, he was to be stoned to death. If the act was committed in the city, the woman would also be stoned to death because she did not call for help (Deut 22:23-27).[36] Leo G. Perdue notes that, in spite of these laws, "it is clear that prostitution was widespread (e.g., Genesis 38), adultery frequent, and thus the laws were often ignored or not enforced."[37]

Jewish writers assumed that Gentiles routinely engaged in sexual immorality.[38] In contrast, John J. Collins observes that "Judaism was distinguished in the ancient world for the strictness of its sexual morality. Josephus declares emphatically that 'the Law recognizes no sexual connexions, except the natural union of man and wife, and that only for the procreation of children' (*Ap.* 2.199)."[39]

Roman Law: Romans expected women to remain chaste before marriage, but they permitted young men to engage in sex. Augustus's legislation required men to be punished as criminals for committing fornication (*stuprum*) with single women.[40] The regulation probably applied to "respectable" unmarried women, and the punishment was exile. Single men, on the other hand, could engage in sexual relations before marriage, as Paul Veyne describes: "Puberty and sexual initiation were synonymous for boys, while the virginity of young girls remained sacrosanct. . . . For five or ten years young men chased prostitutes or lived with mistresses."[41] Boys could have intercourse with slaves and prostitutes before they were married. When they donned the *toga virilis* at age eighteen, they could recline at banquets and enjoy the sexual services of prostitutes who provided the entertainment after dinner.[42]

New Testament Texts: No New Testament writer offers a lengthy or detailed discourse on the need to avoid sexual intercourse before marriage. James B. Nelson observed that "if the Old Testament is specific about the sexual violation of property rights and about idolatrous and cultic intercourse, and if the New Testament is specific about prostitution, adultery, and incest, neither gives highly concrete guidance on premarital sex."[43] Perhaps New Testament writers assumed that their readers accepted this ethical standard, so they did not argue for it.

A. Terminology: The English word "fornication" can refer to illegitimate sexual activity in general or, more specifically, to sexual relations between unmarried people. Translators sometimes use this word to translate *porneia* in the New Testament. In an influential article, Bruce J. Malina argued that *porneia* referred to sexual conduct outlawed by the Torah. Since the Torah did not prohibit sex between unmarried men and women, he concluded that the term could not refer to premarital sex. In a persuasive rebuttal, Joseph Jensen revealed the weaknesses of Malina's arguments and concluded that "there is no basis for denying that the New Testament could use *porneia* to designate simple fornication."[44]

Two other general Greek terms can also have this more specific meaning. *Akatharsia* is usually translated "impurity." Originally it was a cultic term that referred to being under the influence of evil and demonic powers, but it came to refer to moral deficiency such as sexual immorality.[45] *Aselgeia* is translated "licentiousness."

R.F. Collins explains the term: "Etymologically the term suggests wanton, outrageous, or brutal behavior. In the New Testament, and especially in its catalogues of vices, the word means debauchery, voluptuousness, or sexual excess."[46] Like *porneia*, these terms describe sexual immorality in general but in some contexts can refer specifically to sexual intercourse before marriage.

These three terms appear in the various vice lists of the New Testament. R.F. Collins notes: "All but five of the New Testament's twenty-two catalogues of vices list one or another sexual vice." He also observes that *porneia* occurs in twelve of the twenty-two lists, the only term that occurs in a majority of the lists (Matt 15:19; Mark 7:21; 1 Cor 5:10,11; 6:9; 2 Cor 12:21; Gal 5:19; Eph 5:3,5; Col 3:5; 1 Tim 1:10; Rev 9:21; 21:8; 22:15).[47] The term is also listed first in seven of the lists. Since the specific term for "adultery" (*moicheia*) is sometimes used in the same list with these three terms, they may refer more specifically to premarital sex (Mark 7:21-22; Matt 15:19; 1 Cor 6:9).

> "All but five of the New Testament's twenty-two catalogues of vices list one or another sexual vice."

A less common term for sexual immorality occurs in Romans 13:13, which contains a list of behaviors that do not characterize those who live honorably "as in the day." *Koitais*, usually translated "debauchery," is the plural form of the Greek word for the marriage bed (which occurs in Luke 11:7 and Heb 13:4). According to R.F. Collins, "the term is used in a metaphorical sense to connote some sort of violation or defilement of the marriage bed." He suggests that it "consists of adultery and other forms of sexually immoral conduct that are harmful to a marriage relationship."[48] *Aselgeia* is listed after this term, which indicates that it refers to a variety of sexual immorality other than adultery.

B. First Timothy 1:9-10: This passage of Scripture illustrates the uncertainty of interpreters about the meaning of these terms. Among those who need the guidance of the law are the *pornois*, which is translated as "fornicators" in the NRSV, "immoral men" in the NASB, and "adulterers" in the NIV. These differences reveal the difficulty of pinning down the specific meaning of the term when the context provides little direction.

C. Jude and Revelation: Both of these New Testament books warn of the spiritual danger of *porneia*. Jude 7 uses a participle form of *porneia, ekporneusasai,* to describe the actions of the residents of Sodom and Gomorrah. The Revelation of John also uses "fornication" and "fornicators" to describe activities of pagans that God will judge (9:21; 21:8; 22:15). The term is often associated with idol worship in the Bible.

D. First Thessalonians 4:3-8: The term *porneia* also appears in 1 Thessalonians 4:3-8. In verse 3, Paul identifies abstaining from fornication with sanctification and the will of God. This connection between religious practice and moral behavior distinguishes Christianity from paganism.[49]

Verse 4 redefines the phrase "abstain from fornication": "that each one of you know how to control your own body in holiness and honor." The Greek phrase literally says "acquire his own vessel." Translators have offered three different metaphorical meanings for *skeuos* ("vessel"): wife, body, or male sexual organ. The latter two options require understanding the verb *ktasthai* to mean "gain control over," a meaning it does not appear to have in Greek literature. The advantage of the translation "wife" is that it fits the normal meaning of the verb. "Vessel" also has this meaning in rabbinic literature and perhaps in 1 Peter 3:7.[50] This translation also agrees with similar statements of Paul in 1 Corinthians 7:9,36: It is better to marry than to be tempted to engage in sexual immorality.[51] If this translation is correct, then *porneia* here must refer to premarital sexual activity. The only option apart from acquiring a wife is to practice self-control and abstain from sexual activity.

In verse 5, Paul contrasts the sexual behavior of Christians with that of Gentiles, a comment that reflects the influence of traditional Jewish attitudes.[52] The characteristic attitude of Gentiles is "lustful passion." To acquire a wife without involving lustful passion may seem strange until one realizes that Gentiles sometimes used their wives to satisfy their sexual desires in abusive ways. In the Greco-Roman world, a newly married man would violently force sexual relations on his bride on their wedding night: "The wedding night took the form of a legal rape from which the woman emerged 'offended with her husband' (who, accustomed to using his slave women as he pleased, found it difficult to distinguish between raping a woman and taking the initiative in sexual relations)."[53] By contrast, a Christian man is not to use his wife in a violent and impersonal way for his own gratification.[54]

Verse 6 also contains an ambiguous phrase: "that no one wrong or exploit a brother or sister in this matter."[55] This is the only occurrence in the New Testament of the verb *hyperbainein*, which means "to wrong," "to overstep," "to transgress." Among New Testament writers, only Paul uses the second verb *pleonektein*, which means "to take advantage of." "In this matter" refers back to the issue of sexual immorality. Paul prohibits a Christian man from violating the rights of another man by having sexual relations with his wife.[56] Rather than commit adultery with another man's wife, a man should acquire his own wife to satisfy his desires. Although this phrase refers primarily to adultery, it could also refer to fornication since having sexual relations with an unmarried woman would make her unsuitable for marriage by someone else. Such an act might wrong a brother who would later want to marry that woman, or it might wrong a father who would not be able to find a husband for his daughter. The warrant for this command is that "the Lord is an avenger in all these things" (4:6).

Verse 7 contrasts impurity and holiness. The appearance of *akatharsia* here supports identifying it as sexual immorality in other passages where it appears. In verse 8, Paul reminds them that these ethical standards are not his opinions or ideas but that they are based on the authority of "God, who also gives his Holy Spirit to you."

E. First Corinthians 5:9-11: Paul uses the noun *pornos* three times in this Scripture to refer to the person who commits *porneia*. The word originally meant someone who used the services of prostitutes, but English translations translate the term as "sexually immoral people" or "immoral people." Although the use of *porneia* in 5:1 refers to incest, the use of *pornos* in verses 9-11 probably includes more than incestuous people. The word here encompasses all the varieties of sexual immorality. He instructs the readers not to even eat with a brother who is a *pornos*.

F. First Corinthians 6:12-20: Paul here addresses believers who were engaging in sexual relations with prostitutes. He notes that "the body is meant not for fornication but for the Lord, and the Lord for the body" (6:13). Paul offers a number of warrants for not having sex with prostitutes. First, since God will raise the body from the dead, it should be dedicated to the Lord and not to fornication (6:14). Second, the bodies of believers are united with Christ; therefore, they should not unite their bodies with unholy persons (6:15). Third, sexual sin is a sin "against the body," unlike sins that are "outside the body" (6:18).[57] Since sexual intercourse results in a physical and spiritual union of two bodies, sexual relations outside of marriage involves the whole person in sin. Fourth, the Holy Spirit dwells in the body; therefore, one should not use the body for unholy behavior (6:19). Fifth, the body belongs to God, who sacrificed his Son to redeem the body from sin (6:20). For all these reasons, Paul commands: "Shun fornication!" In Greco-Roman culture, both unmarried and married men could have sex with prostitutes without shame, so "fornication" here could include both premarital sex and adultery.

Paul's view of sex challenges the contemporary view that sex is a mere biological function that has no deeper moral or spiritual meaning. Like people in the Greco-Roman world, many people today view the urge for sex simply as an itch that must be

> *Paul's view of sex challenges the contemporary view that sex is a mere biological function that has no deeper moral or spiritual meaning.*

scratched. This view results from a dualism of body and spirit that says that what one does with one's body has no effect deeper than the physical.[58] Grenz responds thus to the modern dualistic view:

> But to assert that the sex act is purely recreational and totally devoid of meaning is to deny our embodied existence, our fundamental sexuality. It is to suggest that sexual intercourse is an act which our bodies engage in apart from our real selves. . . . The sex act is not merely a function of the body. It is an act of our whole selves as sexual beings. As a result, it carries meaning whenever it is practiced.[59]

In contrast to the contemporary view of meaningless sex, Smedes eloquently draws out the implications of Paul's teaching:

> Nobody can really do what the prostitute and her customer try: nobody can go to bed with someone and leave his soul parked outside. This is why a lot more is involved in sexual intercourse than the celebrated "joys of sex." The persons are involved because, creatively or destructively, the soul is in the act. The physical side of sexual intercourse is a sign of what ought to happen on the inside. It is the final physical intimacy. Two bodies are never closer: penetration has the mystique of union, and the orgasmic finale is the exploding

climax of one person's abandonment to another, the most fierce and yet most sensitive experience of trust.[60]

> One should not conclude from Paul's teaching that sexual intercourse automatically unites the two people in a permanent union in God's eyes.

One should not conclude from Paul's teaching that sexual intercourse automatically unites the two people in a permanent union in God's eyes. Marriage results from a public declaration of a covenant between the two people.[61] Paul's point is that sexual intercourse should not occur apart from the context of that covenant.

G. First Corinthians 7: Paul's instructions on marriage in 1 Corinthians 7 provide the clearest indication that he considered celibacy the only alternative to marriage. Verse 36, for example, says that engaged people who cannot control their passions should marry. Engaging in sexual relations without being married is not an option. In this chapter, Paul does not argue for the need to practice celibacy outside of marriage; rather, he assumes that the readers will recognize the need for this. Paul probably taught this ethic to his converts when he was with them, so he felt no need to persuade them of its necessity.

H. Matthew 19:11-12: These teachings of Paul are consistent with Jesus' teaching in Matthew 19:11-12. After he declared the permanence of marriage, his disciples sarcastically responded to his exaltation of monogamy by exalting celibacy.[62] If marriage is a lifetime commitment, they conclude that it would be better not to marry. Jesus responds by noting that "there are eunuchs who have made themselves eunuchs for the sake of the kingdom of heaven" (19:12). Some men voluntarily choose to abstain from marriage and sexual relations in order to devote themselves to the kingdom of heaven. Jesus, John the Baptist, and Paul are examples of such men.[63] Jesus' teaching indicates that the only alternative to marriage is celibacy. His words, however, do not exalt either marriage or celibacy over the other, in contrast to both Roman Catholicism (which exalted celibacy) and Protestantism (which exalted marriage).

Although the New Testament does not contain much instruction dealing with sex before marriage, it consistently assumes that Christians have sex only with a married partner. Sexual intercourse by unmarried people is wrong "because it violates the inner reality of the act; it is wrong because unmarried people thereby engage in a life-uniting act without a life-uniting intent."[64] According to Grenz, sexual intercourse before marriage violates three intentions of sex within marriage: "a recalling of their commitment to one another," "expression of the desire to please each other in all areas of their relationship," and expression of the willingness to welcome new life that may result from their union.[65]

Premarital Sex in American Society: Since the sexual revolution of the 1960s, contemporary American culture has rejected this ethic. Smedes observes that "the majority of American young people have adopted a new standard for the rightness of sexual intercourse: the standard is sincere affection."[66] The widespread acceptance of premarital sex is illustrated by the National Health and Social Life Survey (NHSLS), which found that only 19.7 percent of Americans agree that "premarital sex is always wrong." However, 60.8 percent agree that "premarital sex among teenagers is always wrong."[67]

This "morality of personal relationships" has resulted in the increasingly popular practice of cohabitation before marriage. The NHSLS found that only 36 percent of women born between 1963 and 1974 got married without living with their spouse first, compared to 93 percent of those born between 1933 and 1942.[68] According to the Current Population Survey, "in 2000, there were 3.8 million households that were classified as unmarried-partner households, representing 3.7 percent of all households in the United States."[69] Of these households, 41 percent included children under eighteen.[70] Between fifty percent and sixty percent of new marriages involve couples who lived together first, a dramatic increase from ten percent of those married between 1965 and 1974.[71]

Many couples think that living together before marriage will result in a stronger marriage. They see it as a trial run that will determine their compatibility before marriage.[72] Unfortunately, the facts do not support this theory. Studies have consistently shown some disturbing facts about cohabitation. First, seventy percent of cohabiting couples break up before marriage. Second, cohabiting couples who marry report more problems and less satisfaction with marriage than those who did not cohabit. Cohabiting couples often discover that the marriage relationship is far different from just living together. Third, married couples who cohabited before marriage have a much higher rate of divorce than those who did not cohabit.

Fourth, women in cohabiting relationships are twice as likely to suffer physical and sexual abuse as married women.[73] Based on this research, Judith K. Balswick and Jack O. Balswick conclude: "Contrary to predictions made in the 1970s, one's participation in pre-marital cohabitation does not mean one adjusts better to marriage. Even more important, evidence points to the contrary of this initial optimistic prediction."[74]

Cohabitation tends to be a better deal for young men, who can enjoy the sexual pleasures of marriage without the long-term commitment of marriage, than it is for women, who typically hope that it will result in marriage.[75] Smedes notes the disadvantages of cohabitation: "I suspect that open-ended cohabitation is an infantile solution because it grabs the goodies of life without the long-term responsibilities of life. It achieves instant closeness but avoids the tensions and conflicts that are built into a life-partnership that is achieved only by a love that is willing to struggle."[76]

Observing the New Testament ethic offers practical benefits. Grenz notes three advantages for partners who enter marriage without prior experience of intercourse. First, they do not carry with them the emotional and spiritual baggage of a previous sexual bond. Second, they do not experience the danger of comparison and competition with previous sexual partners. Third, they do not run the risk of long-term health consequences resulting from sexually transmitted diseases.[77]

Unfortunately, two recent trends in Western culture complicate the ability of singles to resist sexual temptation before marriage: the earlier onset of puberty and the delay of marriage. In the middle 1800s, girls reached menarche between ages fifteen and sixteen and married around that same age, but the onset of menarche has now dropped to around ages twelve and thirteen.[78] Recent census data show that in 2000 the median age of first marriage was 25.1 for women and 26.8 for men, a rise from 1970 when the median age was 20.8 for women and 23.2 for men.[79] Most singles now must wait more than ten years between their first sexual impulses and satisfaction of those feelings in marriage. To complicate matters even more, their physical urges are stimulated by sex-saturated media, unsupervised dating, and peer influence.[80]

These two trends mean that many people are unmarried during the age when their sexual desires are the strongest. In 2000, 84 percent of men and 73 percent of women aged 20 to 24 were never

married, an increase from 55 percent and
36 percent respectively in 1970. Of people aged 30 to 34, 30 percent of men and
22 percent of women were never married, an increase from 9 percent and 6
percent in 1970.[81]

> *These two trends mean that many people are unmarried during the age when their sexual desires are the strongest.*

One consequence of these trends is
that people have first sexual intercourse at a younger age. The average age of first intercourse is sixteen for boys and seventeen for girls.
More than a third of fifteen-year-old boys and 27 percent of fifteen-
year-old girls have had sexual intercourse. Also, a 1992 study found
that 43 percent of teenagers from ages fourteen to seventeen had
engaged in sexual intercourse at least once.[82]

Another consequence is that young people now have more sex
partners before they marry than those of older generations. The
NHSLS found that half of all Americans aged thirty to fifty have had
five or more partners, but only a third of Americans over fifty have
had five or more. At least four out of five Americans have had intercourse before leaving their teen years.[83] These facts support the conclusion of journalist David Whitman:

> Americans, at least tacitly, have all but given up on the
> notion that the appropriate premarital state is one of chasti-
> ty. The Bible may have warned that like the denizens of
> Sodom and Gomorrah, those who give 'themselves over to
> fornication' will suffer 'the vengeance of eternal fire.' Yet for
> most Americans, adult premarital sex has become the 'sin'
> they not only wink at but quietly endorse.[84]

Widespread acceptance of premarital sex was illustrated by a
U.S. News & World Report poll in 1997: "While most Americans—74
percent—have serious qualms about teens having sex before marriage, more than half believe it is not at all wrong, or wrong only
sometimes, for *adults* to have premarital sex." The same poll found
that "less than half of those under the age of 45 thought it was a
good idea for adults to remain virgins until they marry. And a majority of respondents agreed that having had a few sexual partners
makes it easier for a person to pick a compatible spouse."[85] Another
survey conducted in twenty-four countries found that 61 percent of
respondents agreed that premarital sex was not wrong; however,
only 7% approved of teenage sex.[86]

> Recent trends indicate a return to traditional sexual ethics among young people.

Recent trends indicate a return to traditional sexual ethics among young people. A recent Centers for Disease Control study found that the number of high-school students who say they have had sex dropped from fifty-four percent in 1991 to forty-six percent in 2001.[87] Teen pregnancy has also declined from 1991 to 2000.[88] These encouraging trends may result from fear of sexually transmitted diseases, fear of the consequences of premarital pregnancy, and sex education programs with an emphasis on abstinence.

Although the New Testament prohibits sexual intercourse before marriage, it does not address the question of what kinds of physical expressions are permissible before marriage. This silence causes ethicists to rely on other arguments to suggest the boundaries of proper behavior.[89]

Adultery

In the Roman Empire, adultery was "usually narrowly defined as sexual intercourse of a married woman with a man other than her husband."[90] Men were not held to the same standard unless they had sex with the wife of another man. They were not expected to limit sexual activity to marriage. Some Roman men engaged in sex with their slave women.[91]

Augustus was so concerned about the social consequences of marriage that he passed two blocks of legislation governing its practice: the *Lex Iulia* in 18 B.C. and the *Lex Papia Poppaea* in A.D. 9. His legislation required husbands to divorce adulterous wives. It also required men to be punished as criminals for committing adultery with married women. However, the law did not allow a wife to charge her husband with adultery. Although the evidence does not show that this legislation had any discernible effect on marital misbehavior, later emperors maintained the regulation. Many philosophers and writers condemned adultery and lamented its prevalence.[92]

The Jewish view of adultery is reflected in the prohibition of adultery in the Ten Commandments (Exod 20:14; Deut 5:18). The Old Testament calls it a "great sin" (Gen 20:9) and a "sin against God" (Gen 20:6; 39:9; Ps 51:6). Other Jewish writings also warned against adultery (Prov 6:34; Sir 23:16-21).

The Mosaic Law specified the death penalty as the punishment for both the man and the woman who commit adultery (Lev 20:10;

ronomy 22:23-24 prescribed stoning as the form
case of a man who commits adultery with anoth-
l. The Mishnah also prescribed stoning as the
n committed adultery with a betrothed woman.
ried out by binding them and throwing them into
:4). According to Genesis 38:24, Tamar, who had
.... Jnelah but had become pregnant by her father-in-
law Judah, was to be burned. Jews may not have enforced such
extreme penalties. Divorce was probably the usual response.[93]

L. William Countryman interprets the Old Testament prohibitions against adultery as reflecting a concern with property rights. If
a man had intercourse with a married woman, he would steal the
husband's right to legitimate offspring. He concludes, therefore, that
"adultery, in this context, referred purely and simply to a man's having intercourse with a married woman. The man's own marital status was irrelevant, for it was not a matter of violating his own vows
or implicit commitments of sexual fidelity, as in a modern marriage,
but rather of usurping some other man's property rights in his wife."
Like the Romans, Israelites had a double standard for adultery: "The
husband could commit adultery only by having intercourse with the
wife (or betrothed) of another man; if he had sexual relations with a
slave, a prostitute, a concubine, or a divorced or widowed woman,
this did not constitute adultery against his own marriage."[94]

The Greek word for "adultery" is *moicheia*, which is more specific than *porneia*. The term refers to the act of a married person who
has sexual relations with someone other than his or her spouse.
Some of the vice lists include both *porneia* and *moicheia* as behaviors
that can disqualify a person from the kingdom of God (Mark 7:20-
23; 1 Cor 6:9).

New Testament teaching requires both husbands and wives to
remain faithful to their vows. New Testament writers cite the commandment of Exodus 20:13 and Deuteronomy 5:17 six times (Matt
5:27; 19:18; Mark 10:19; Luke 18:20; Rom 13:9; Jas 2:11). F. Hauck
observes that "the apostolic message from the very outset made it
clear to the churches that the full marital fidelity of both spouses is
an unconditional divine command."[95]

Paul assumes that his hearers understand that adultery is a
sin. In Romans 13:9, he quotes several of the Ten Commandments as
summed up in the command to love, and he includes the command
against adultery in that list. As discussed above, 1 Thessalonians 4:6

may refer to committing adultery with the brother's wife. Paul does not define what he considers adultery, but G.F. Hawthorne speculates that "he would also have defined adultery as sexual intercourse between a married man with a woman other than his wife—quite contrary to the norms of sexual morality in the Roman world."[96]

Hebrews 13:4 explicitly warns against adultery: "Let marriage be held in honor by all, and let the marriage bed be kept undefiled; for God will judge fornicators and adulterers." The first two statements are parallel, the first stating the command positively and the second stating it negatively. Marriage is held in honor by not committing adultery. As Paul expressed in 1 Corinthians 6:9-10, people who commit sexual immorality cannot expect to enter the kingdom of God; instead, judgment awaits them. Other New Testament writers also condemned adultery (Jas 2:11; 1 Pet 2:14; Rev 2:20-23).

Americans generally agree with the New Testament prohibition of adultery. The NHSLS found that 76.7 percent of Americans agree that "extramarital sex is always wrong."[97] Another study conducted in twenty-four countries found that only 4 percent of respondents approved of extramarital sex.[98]

But does the behavior of people match their words? Although some unscientific surveys have created the impression that adultery is a widespread practice in American society, the NHSLS found that 94 percent of married people had one sex partner in the past year. In addition, the study found that "more than 80 percent of women and 65 to 85 percent of men of every age report that they had no partners other than their spouse while they were married." The researchers drew the following conclusion from their study: "Our study clearly shows that no matter how sexually active people are before and between marriages, no matter whether they lived with their sexual partners before marriage or whether they were virgins on their wedding day, marriage is such a powerful social institution that, essentially, married people are nearly all alike—they are faithful to their partners as long as the marriage is intact."[99]

> 94% of married people had one sex partner in the past year.

In opposition to some thinkers today who argue that sexual relations outside of marriage can actually benefit a marriage, Stanley J. Grenz notes three harmful effects of extramarital sex: 1) it devastates the self-worth of either or both partners, 2) it produces feelings of guilt, and 3) it undercuts trust and openness between the marital partners.[100] Also, adultery results in divorce 65 percent of the time.[101] The New Testament ethic on adultery provides practical benefits, which may explain its acceptance by most people.

Lust

Jewish writings contained prohibitions of lust. *Testaments of the Twelve Patriarchs* contains this statement on lust: "For the person with a mind that is pure with love does not look on a woman for the purpose of having sexual relations" (*T. Benj.* 8:2-3).[102] A Jewish midrash states: "Even the one who commits adultery with his eyes is called an adulterer" (*Lev. Rab.* 23). The Talmud also instructed that "whoever looks at a woman with (lustful) intention is counted as one who sleeps with her." Other rabbinic writings refer to committing adultery in the eye and in the heart.[103]

Moralistic pagans also warned against the dangers of lust. Stoics included "desire" (*epithymia*) and "pleasure" (*hēdonē*) among the four principal passions or emotions that destroyed a human being. These terms sometimes referred specifically to sexual desire.[104]

In the Sermon on the Mount, Jesus radicalized the commandment against adultery: "But I say to you that everyone who looks at a woman with lust has already committed adultery with her in his heart" (Matt 5:28). Based on the traditional understanding of adultery in Judaism, Jesus refers primarily to a man who desires sexual relations with a married woman. Jesus' extreme ethic points out the connection between lust and adultery. Extramarital affairs are often premeditated acts. By avoiding covetous thoughts of someone outside the marriage, one can avoid the act itself.[105] Foster notes the consequences of lust: "Lust produces bad sex, because it denies relationship. Lust turns the other person into an object, a thing, a nonperson. Jesus condemned lust because it cheapened sex, it made sex less than it was created to be. For Jesus, sex was too good, too high, too holy, to be thrown away by cheap thoughts."[106]

> By avoiding covetous thoughts of someone outside the marriage, one can avoid the act itself.

In Matthew 5:29, Jesus recommends taking extreme action to rid oneself of lust: "If your right eye causes you to sin, tear it out and throw it away; it is better for you to lose one of your members than for your whole body to be thrown into hell." Other versions of this saying are recorded in Mark 9:47 and Matthew 18:9. The eye causes one to stumble when a man looks at a woman in a way that reduces her to a means of his own gratification.

The Pastoral Epistles include passions and lusts among the vices to be shunned. Titus 3:3 describes pre-Christians as "slaves to various passions and pleasures," using the two terms that Stoics included among the four destructive emotions. Titus 2:12 includes "worldly passions" among those things that Christians have renounced. Second Timothy 3:4 includes "lovers of pleasure" (*philēdonoi*) in the description of those who do not love God. The women who are attracted to false teaching are "swayed by all kinds of desires" (2 Tim 3:6). Timothy is encouraged to "shun youthful passion" (2 Tim 2:22).

"Passion" or "lust" (*epithymia*) is connected with fornication and impurity in the vice list of Colossians 3:5 and with licentiousness in 1 Peter 4:3. This word is also used in Ephesians 4:22 to describe the former way of life, the old self, that is to be put away. Jude 16 describes false teachers as those who "indulge their own lusts." Second Peter 1:4 associates lust with the corruption of the world. According to this author, lust is one of the characteristics of false teachers and the unrighteous (2:10,18; 3:3). Second Peter 2:14 uses a descriptive phrase for lust: "eyes full of adultery."

The virtue that overcomes passions and desires is "self-control" (*enkrateia*), which can be defined as "human freedom from subjection to various desires, particularly for food, drink, sex, and conversation." Aristotle viewed self-control and licentiousness as opposites.[107] Older women are encouraged to instruct younger women to be self-controlled (*sophronas*) and chaste (*hagnas*) (Titus 2:5). Similarly, in Titus 2:12 self-control is one of the virtues contrasted with "worldly passion." Titus 2:6 also encourages young men to develop this quality. Self-control is also a characteristic of overseers (1 Tim 3:2; Titus 1:8).

The Silence of the New Testament on Sexual Issues

The New Testament does not directly address many issues of sexuality that concern people today. As Mark D. Jordan writes,

> The New Testament does not directly address many issues of sexuality that concern people today.

"Certainly there is no explicit discussion in the New Testament of a number of sexual practices that preoccupy modern moral theology."[108] Several reasons may explain this silence. First, some of these issues are more prevalent in our culture than in ancient culture. Second, these issues were not a problem with which the recipients of the New Testament writings struggled. Third, the writers may have assumed that their readers shared their perspectives on these issues.

For example, the New Testament does not directly address the practice of masturbation.[109] The principle of Matthew 5:28 on lust might apply to this issue. Since it seems impossible to masturbate without fantasizing about sex, this statement would prohibit masturbation. Others think that masturbation is an acceptable practice within certain limits.[110]

Child abuse is a prevalent concern in our culture, but the New Testament does not clearly address the issue. R.F. Collins has applied Mark 9:42 to this issue: "If any of you put a stumbling block before one of these little ones who believe in me, it would be better for you if a great millstone were hung around your neck and you were thrown into the sea." This statement occurs a few verses after Jesus took a little child in his arms and declared: "Whoever welcomes one such child in my name welcomes me, and whoever welcomes me welcomes not me but the one who sent me" (Mark 9:37). Based on parallels with rabbinic writings, Collins concludes: "To cause one of the little ones to stumble is to commit a sexual offense against a child." He believes that it reflects the typical Near Eastern abhorrence of pederasty, sexual relations between an adult male and a young boy.[111]

Pornography is a prominent concern among Christians today. The New Testament, however, never addresses the issue even though erotic art was common in the Greco-Roman world, as the excavations at Pompeii have revealed. Here again the general warning against lust in Matthew 5:28 can apply to this issue.[112]

More unusual forms of sexual deviance, often called paraphilia, also are not directly addressed in the New Testament. Paraphilia includes behaviors such as transvestitism, transsexualism, bestiality, fetishism, masochism, sadism, exhibitionism, voyeurism, and necrophilia. Other teachings on lust and homosexuality may apply indirectly to these issues.[113]

Conclusion

Comparison of the New Testament teaching on sex with the sexual ethics of the ancient world reveals both continuity and discontinuity. Countryman concludes:

The New Testament writers did not try to construct a new sexual ethic from the ground up. They took over the existing cultural patterns and refocused them, pushing some elements from the center to the periphery, altering the balance of powers allotted to various members of society, and, most important, relativizing the familiar life of this world by subordinating it to the reign of God.[114]

The majority of Americans today agree with the New Testament's prohibition of adultery but not the prohibitions of premarital sex and lust. R.F. Collins's observation based on his study of sexual ethics offers an appropriate conclusion to this study:

The dominant motif might well be that the disciple of Jesus is called to live with his or her sexuality in a way that is different from the way that others live with their sexuality. Those who have embraced the gospel of Jesus as adults might be able to contrast the way they live out their sexuality as disciples with their own previous sexual behavior. The sexual mores of the Christian are to be different from the rampant pursuit of sexual pleasure that often characterizes those who are not Christian.[115]

Notes

[1]Lisa Sowle Cahill, *Between the Sexes: Foundations for a Christian Ethics of Sexuality* (Philadelphia: Fortress, 1985) 1.

[2]Raymond F. Collins, *Sexual Ethics and the New Testament: Behaviors and Beliefs*, Companions to the New Testament (New York: Crossroad, 2000) 183.

[3]Lewis B. Smedes, *Sex for Christians: The Limits and Liberties of Sexual Living*, rev. ed. (Grand Rapids: Eerdmans, 1994) 11. Cahill would concur: "While I would judge that the biblical literature points toward heterosexual, monogamous, lifelong, and procreative marriage as the normative or ideal institutionalization of sexual activity, I would not say that the biblical texts represent preoccupation with, or indeed much interest in, the justification or exclusion of other sexual expressions" (*Between the Sexes*, 8).

[4]Suzanne Dixon, *The Roman Family* (Baltimore: Johns Hopkins University Press, 1992) 61-71.

[5]Dixon, *The Roman Family*, 93-94; Craig S. Keener, "Adultery, Divorce," *DNTB* 12; Paul Veyne, *The Roman Empire*, trans. by Arthur Goldhammer (Cambridge, MA: Belknap Press, 1987) 76-77.

[6]John J. Collins, "Marriage, Divorce, and Family in Second Temple Judaism," in *Families in Ancient Israel*, ed. by Leo G. Perdue et al., The Family, Religion, and Culture, ed. by Don S. Browning and Ian S. Evison (Louisville, KY: Westminster John Knox Press, 1997) 106-112, 115-121.

[7]R. Collins, *Sexual Ethics*, 120; J. Collins, "Marriage, Divorce," 136-137.

[8]W.D. Davies and Dale C. Allison, Jr., *A Critical and Exegetical Commentary on the Gospel according to Saint Matthew*, 3 vols., International Critical Commentary (Edinburgh: T. & T. Clark, 1988-1997) 3:16; Leon Morris, *The Gospel according to Matthew*, Pillar Commentary (Grand Rapids: Eerdmans, 1992) 122.

[9]L. William Countryman, *Dirt, Greed, and Sex: Sexual Ethics in the New Testament and Their Implications for Today* (Philadelphia: Fortress, 1988) 175.

[10]Cahill, *Between the Sexes*, 74; Robert A. Guelich, *The Sermon on the Mount: A Foundation for Understanding* (Waco, TX: Word, 1982) 204-209, 245.

[11]H. Reisser, "πορνεύω," *New International Dictionary of the New Testament*, 1:500.

[12]Davies and Allison, *Matthew*, 1:529-531.

[13]Ibid., 3:16.

[14]Stanley J. Grenz, *Sexual Ethics: An Evangelical Perspective* (Louisville, KY: Westminster John Knox Press, 1997) 57-58.

[15]Davies and Allison observe: "19.9 indirectly condemns polygamy. If it were permitted to have two wives at once, then it would not matter whether a first wife had been lawfully divorced or not before taking a second wife" (*Matthew*, 18).

[16]Raymond F. Collins denies that Corinthian Christians were actually using the services of prostitutes. He views this section as conventional rhetoric that used prostitution as an illustration of sexual immorality (*Sexual Ethics*, 113-114). However, it seems unlikely that Paul would have to argue so persuasively against the practice unless some Corinthians were actually participating in it. Since this was a widely accepted practice in the Greco-Roman world, Gentile converts may have found it difficult to give it up. Bruce W. Winter argues that the phrase "all things are lawful" refers to young men who reached lawful age when they could attend banquets and have sex with prostitutes (*After Paul Left Corinth: The Influence of Secular Ethics and Social Change* [Grand Rapids: Eerdmans, 2001] 88-92).

[17]Winter, *After Paul Left Corinth*, 91.

[18]"Touch" was a euphemism for sexual relations. "Man" and "woman" here probably refer to a husband and wife since Paul would agree that men and women outside of marriage should not engage in sexual relations. The translation of the New International Version ("not to marry") is inaccurate. The immediate issue concerns the practice of sexual abstinence within marriage, not the practice of marriage itself. See Winter, *After Paul Left Corinth*, 225-226.

[19]Gordon D. Fee believes it also resulted from a "spiritualized eschatology" on the part of some women who viewed marriage as belonging to this passing age to which they did not belong (*The First Epistle to the Corinthians*, The New International Commentary on the New Testament, ed. by F.F. Bruce [Grand Rapids: Eerdmans, 1987] 269-270).

[20]Ibid., 278-279; Winter, *After Paul Left Corinth*, 227-229.

[21]Carolyn Osiek and David L. Balch, *Families in the New Testament World: Households and House Churches*, The Family, Religion, and Culture, ed. by Don S. Browning and Ian S. Evison (Louisville, KY: Westminster John Knox Press, 1997) 115; Winter, *After Paul Left Corinth*, 229.

[22]Fee, *Corinthians*, 281.

[23]Richard J. Foster, *The Challenge of the Disciplined Life: Christian Reflections on Money, Sex & Power* (San Francisco: Harper & Row, 1985) 138-139.

[24]Mark D. Jordan, *The Ethics of Sex*, New Dimensions to Religious Ethics, ed. by Frank G. Kilpatrick and Susan Frank Parsons (Oxford: Blackwell, 2002) 109-114; Grenz, *Sexual Ethics*, 4-5, 18, 67-68, 91-92; James B. Nelson, *Embodiment: An Approach to Sexuality and Christian Theology* (Minneapolis: Augsburg, 1978) 53; Morton Kelsey and Barbara Kelsey, *Sacrament of Sexuality: The Spirituality and Psychology of Sex* (Rockport, MA: Element, 1986) 27-29, 109-110, 113. For Thomas Aquinas's development of Augustine's ideas, see Cahill, *Between the Sexes*, 105-122.

[25]Gordon Fee defines the gift of celibacy as "that singular gift of freedom from the desire or need of sexual fulfillment that made it possible for him to live without marriage in the first place" (*Corinthians*, 284).

[26]"The unmarried" (*tois agamois*) most likely refers to widowers since the Greek of that time did not use the masculine form of the word for "widows" (*kērais*). Also, Paul's term for the never-married was *parthenos* ("virgin"). By including himself among these people (the unmarried), Paul implies that he had been married and that his wife had died.

[27]Verse 5 uses the noun *akrasia*, which means "lack of self-control." Verse 9 uses the present-tense verb *enkrateuontai* preceded by the negative *ouk* to mean "they are not practicing self-control."

[28]Some interpreters have argued that *purousthai* refers to burning in judgment as the result of God's wrath (Michael Barré, "To

Marry or to Burn: *Purousthai* in 1 Cor. 7:9," *CBQ* 36 [1974] 193-202). Most interpreters rightly see it as a euphemism for uncontrollable sexual desire (Fee, *Corinthians*, 289).

[29]Other interpretations are that he is addressing fathers giving their daughters in marriage or that he is referring to "spiritual marriage" where a man and woman lived together without engaging in sexual relations. The interpretation followed here offers the fewest difficulties. See Fee, *Corinthians*, 325-327.

[30]When used for a man, *huperakmos* refers to his sexual passion (Winter, *After Paul Left Corinth*, 246-249). C.K. Barrett suggests the translation "over-sexed" (*A Commentary on the First Epistle to the Corinthians*, Harper's New Testament Commentaries, ed. by Henry Chadwick [Peabody, MA: Hendrickson, 1968] 182). Some think the word refers to the engaged woman who is passing her prime years.

[31]Winter, *After Paul Left Corinth*, 243-245.

[32]Cahill, *Between the Sexes*, 143; Smedes, *Sex for Christians*, 29.

[33]R. Collins, *Sexual Ethics*, 82.

[34]Reisser, "πορνεύω," 497.

[35]Joseph Jensen, "Does *Porneia* Mean Fornication? A Critique of Bruce Malina," *NovT* 20 (1978) 180; Reisser, "πορνεύω," 499.

[36]Smedes, *Sex for Christians*, 107-108.

[37]Leo G. Perdue, "The Israelite and Early Jewish Family: Summary and Conclusions," in *Families in Ancient Israel*, Leo G. Perdue et al., The Family, Religion, and Culture, ed. by Don S. Browning and Ian S. Evison (Louisville, KY: Westminster John Knox Press, 1997) 184. John J. Collins agrees that these penalties were not enforced ("Marriage, Divorce," 143).

[38]R. Collins, *Sexual Ethics*, 83 n. 36; Keener, "Adultery, Divorce," 10.

[39]J. Collins, "Marriage, Divorce," 135.

[40]Dixon, *The Roman Family*, 79.

[41]Veyne, *The Roman Empire*, 23.

[42]Winter, *After Paul Left Corinth*, 89-90.

[43]Nelson, *Embodiment*, 153.

[44]Bruce J. Malina, "Does *Porneia* Mean Fornication?" *NovT* 14 (1972) 10-17; Jensen, "Does *Porneia* Mean Fornication?" 179-180.

[45]R. Collins, *Sexual Ethics*, 83. Countryman attempts unconvincingly to interpret the term so that it refers to social greed, not to sexual impurity (*Dirt, Greed, and Sex*, 105-106).

[46]R. Collins, *Sexual Ethics*, 84.

[47]Ibid., 76, 80.

[48]Ibid., 85-86.

[49]Ibid., 102.

[50]Ibid., 103-104. For a defense of the view that the reference is to male genitals, see Charles A. Wanamaker, *The Epistles to the Thessalonians: A Commentary on the Greek Text*, NIGTC (Grand Rapids: Eerdmans, 1990) 152-153.

[51]Collins offers another argument against the translation "body": "The holistic anthropology of Judaism would not abide the notion of one's mind gaining control over one's body as if the body were simply the instrument of the *logos*" (*Sexual Ethics*, 108 n. 16).

[52]Ibid., 104.

[53]Veyne, *The Roman Empire*, 34.

[54]For a critical analysis of Luther's and Calvin's views on restricting lust within marriage, see Jordan, *The Ethics of Sex*, 118-124.

[55]The NRSV has added "or sister," but the likely focus of this verse is the behavior of men in particular.

[56]Collins, *Sexual Ethics*, 106.

[57]Some commentators think that Paul is quoting a Corinthian slogan that denied that what one did with the body affected one's spirit. He then refutes that slogan by stressing that fornication is actually a sin committed against the body. For an overview of interpretations of the phrase, see Bruce N. Fisk, "ΠΟΡΝΕΥΕΙΝ as Body Violation: The Unique Nature of Sexual Sin in 1 Corinthians 6.18," *NTS* 42 (1996) 540-558.

[58]Grenz, *Sexual Ethics*, 79-81, 112. Judith K. Balswick and Jack O. Balswick refer to this view as "permissiveness without affection," a view which has become increasingly accepted in the last thirty years (*Authentic Human Sexuality: An Integrated Christian Approach* [Downers Grove, IL: InterVarsity, 1999] 109).

[59]Grenz, *Sexual Ethics*, 217.

[60]Smedes, *Sex for Christians*, 112.

[61]Balswick and Balswick, *Authentic Human Sexuality*, 141-143; Smedes, *Sex for Christians*, 123-125; Grenz, *Sexual Ethics*, 72-77; John White, *Eros Defiled: The Christian and Sexual Sin* (Downers Grove, IL: InterVarsity, 1977) 64-66.

[62]Davies and Allison, *Matthew*, 19.

[63]Jordan observes that "we see in the New Testament no detailed representation of a

married believer. All of the central models for the faith are, when Christian readers encounter them, living the faith outside of marriage" (*The Ethics of Sex*, 50).

[64]Smedes, *Sex for Christians*, 110.

[65]Grenz, *Sexual Ethics*, 204-205.

[66]Smedes, *Sex for Christians*, 91. Balswick and Balswick note that "permissiveness with affection is the most practiced sexual standard when it comes to actual behavior" (*Authentic Human Sexuality*, 109).

[67]Michael et al., *Sex in America: A Definitive Survey* (New York: Warner Books, 1994) 234.

[68]Ibid., 97.

[69]Jason Fields and Lynne M. Casper, *America's Families and Living Arrangements: March 2000*, Current Population Reports, P20-537 (Washington, DC: U.S. Census Bureau, 2001) 12. The report notes that "these numbers may underrepresent the true number of cohabiting couples because only householders and their partners are tabulated (not all unmarried couples within the household), and respondents may be reluctant to classify themselves as such in a personal interview situation and may describe themselves as roommates, housemates, or friends not related to each other."

[70]Ibid., 13.

[71]Karen S. Peterson, "Living Together, Not Always Forever," *Lansing State Journal* (July 15, 2002); Douglas E. Rosenau and Erica S.N. Tan, "Single and Sexual: The Church's Neglected Dilemma," *Journal of Psychology and Theology* 30 (2002) 185.

[72]Balswick and Balswick, *Authentic Human Sexuality*, 130, 134-135; Fields and Casper, *America's Families*, 14.

[73]Balswick and Balswick, *Authentic Human Sexuality*, 131, 135-138; David Whitman, "Was It Good for Us?" *U.S News & World Report* (May 19, 1997) 60; David Popenoe and Barbara Dafoe Whitehead, "Should We Live Together? What Young Adults Need to Know about Cohabitation before Marriage," n.p. Online: http://www.marriage.rutgers.edu/shouldwe.htm.

[74]Balswick and Balswick, *Authentic Human Sexuality*, 138.

[75]Popenoe and Whitehead, "Should We Live Together?" n.p.

[76]Smedes, *Sex for Christians*, 120.

[77]Grenz, *Sexual Ethics*, 206-208.

[78]Balswick and Balswick, *Authentic Human Sexuality*, 107; Archibald D. Hart, *The Sexual Man: Masculinity without Guilt* (Dallas: Word, 1994) 42-45, 109-110.

[79]Fields and Casper, *America's Families*, 9.

[80]Grenz, *Sexual Ethics*, 201-203.

[81]Fields and Casper, *America's Families*, 9.

[82]Balswick and Balswick, *Authentic Human Sexuality*, 110; Kerby Anderson, "Teen Sexual Revolution," in *Marriage, Family, & Sexuality: Probing the Headlines That Impact Your Family*, ed. by Kerby Anderson (Grand Rapids: Kregel, 2000) 14, 21.

[83]Michael et al., *Sex in America*, 88-92.

[84]Whitman, "Was It Good," 58.

[85]Ibid., 58-60.

[86]Rosenau and Tan, "Single and Sexual," 185.

[87]Debra Rosenberg, "The Battle over Abstinence," *Newsweek* (December 9, 2002) 68.

[88]Lorraine Ali and Julie Scelfo, "Choosing Virginity," *Newsweek* (December 9, 2002) 66.

[89]Balswick and Balswick, *Authentic Human Sexuality*, 113-124; Foster, *Challenge*, 127-131; Grenz, *Sexual Ethics*, 211-212; Rosenau and Tan, "Single and Sexual," 190-192; Smedes, *Sex for Christians*, 114-115, 129-138.

[90]G.F. Hawthorne, "Marriage and Divorce, Adultery and Incest," *DPL*, 594.

[91]Jo-Ann Shelton, *As the Romans Did: A Sourcebook in Roman Social History*, 2nd ed. (New York: Oxford University Press, 1998) 54-55; F. Hauck, "μοιχεύω," *TDNT* 4:732; Keener, "Adultery, Divorce," 12; Winter, *After Paul Left Corinth*, 123-124.

[92]Dixon, *The Roman Family*, 79, 120-121; Keener, "Adultery, Divorce," 7-9.

[93]Elaine Adler Goodfriend, "Adultery," *ABD* 1:83-84; F. Hauck, "μοιχεύω," 4:731-732; Morris, *Matthew*, 121; Collins, "Marriage, Divorce," 140.

[94]Countryman, *Dirt, Greed, and Sex*, 157, 159. See also Collins, *Sexual Ethics*, 3-4.

[95]Hauck, "μοιχεύω," 734.

[96]Hawthorne, "Marriage and Divorce," 599.

[97]Michael et al., *Sex in America*, 234.

[98]Rosenau and Tan, "Single and Sexual," 185.

[99]Michael et al., *Sex in America*, 101, 105.

[100]Grenz, *Sexual Ethics*, 106. See also Balswick and Balswick, *Authentic Human Sexuality*, 170-172.

[101]Kerby Anderson, "Adultery," in *Marriage, Family, & Sexuality: Probing the Headlines That Impact Your Family*, ed. by Kerby Anderson (Grand Rapids: Kregel, 2000) 95-97.

[102]The *Testaments of the Twelve Patriarchs* may be a Christian revision of a Jewish writing, so many of its teachings reflect Jewish traditions. Separating Jewish from Christian traditions is a notorious problem for this writing. See John J. Collins, *Between Athens and Jerusalem: Jewish Identity in the Hellenistic Diaspora*, The Biblical Resources Series, ed. by Astrid B. Beck and David Noel Freedman, 2nd ed. (Grand Rapids: Eerdmans, 2000) 174-177.

[103]R. Collins, *Sexual Ethics*, 46, 72 n. 17.

[104]Ibid., 84.

[105]Balswick and Balswick, *Authentic Human Sexuality*, 169-170; Foster, *Challenge*, 103-104, 120-123; Nelson, *Embodiment*, 160-163; White, *Eros Defiled*, 92-96. For a discussion of men's struggles with sexual fantasies, see Hart, *The Sexual Man*, 57-67, 131-136, 141-146.

[106]Foster, *Challenge*, 9.

[107]R. Collins, *Sexual Ethics*, 182 n. 39, 158-159.

[108]Jordan, *The Ethics of Sex*, 44.

[109]Raymond Collins, however, has discerned a reference to it in Matthew 5:30: "And if your right hand causes you to sin, cut it off and throw it away; it is better for you to lose one of your members than for your whole body to go into hell." Since this occurs in the context of a discussion on lust, Collins believes that it refers to masturbation. He connects this verse with a rabbinic writing that prescribed the punishment for masturbation as having the hand cut off while placed on the offender's stomach. He interprets the reference to the foot in Mark 9:45 as a Hebraic euphemism for the male sex organ (Exod 4:25; Isa 6:2; Ruth 3:4,7,8,14) (*Sexual Ethics*, 46, 67). Countryman suggests that *malakos* in 1 Corinthians 6:9, which is translated "male prostitutes" in the NRSV, refers to masturbators or metaphorically to "the person so devoted to the pursuit of private pleasure as to be devoid of responsibility" (*Dirt, Greed, and Sex*, 202). This interpretation is consistent with his strained attempts to reinterpret the Bible's prohibitions of homosexuality.

[110]Balswick and Balswick, *Authentic Human Sexuality*, 244-249; Foster, *Challenge*, 123-127; Grenz, *Sexual Ethics*, 214-215; Hart, *The Sexual Man*, 117-120, 136-141; Jordan, *The Ethics of Sex*, 95-104; Michael et al., *Sex in America*, 158-168; Nelson, *Embodiment*, 168-173; Rosenau and Tan, "Single and Sexual," 190-191; Smedes, *Sexual Ethics*, 138-142, 218-221; White, *Eros Defiled*, 33-46.

[111]R. Collins, *Sexual Ethics*, 65-66. Since Luke 17:2 lacks the qualifier "who believes in me," Collins suggests that the saying originally referred to children and that the phrase was added when the saying was used as a general instruction for disciples (71 n. 8).

[112]For discussions of pornography, see Kerby Anderson, *Moral Dilemmas: Biblical Perspectives on Contemporary Ethical Issues*, Swindoll Leadership Library, ed. by Charles R. Swindoll (Dallas: Word, 1998) 143-154; Balswick and Balswick, *Authentic Human Sexuality*, 235-244; Foster, *Challenge*, 102-103; Hart, *The Sexual Man*, 85-100; Michael et al., *Sex in America*, 156-157; Nelson, *Embodiment*, 163-168; Smedes, *Sex for Christians*, 189-191.

[113]For discussions of these issues, see Foster, *Challenge*, 104-105; Nelson, *Embodiment*, 173-179; Smedes, *Sex for Christians*, 39-48.

[114]Countryman, *Dirt, Greed, and Sex*, 239.

[115]R. Collins, *Sexual Ethics*, 183.

Bibliography

Balswick, Judith K., and Jack O. Balswick. *Authentic Human Sexuality: An Integrated Christian Approach*. Downers Grove, IL: InterVarsity, 1999.

Comprehensive discussion of all aspects of human sexuality informed by psychology, sociology, and theology.

Collins, Raymond F. *Sexual Ethics and the New Testament: Behaviors and Belief*. Companions to the New Testament. New York: Crossroad, 2000.

Thorough exegetical treatment of New Testament texts that deal with sexuality. Contains little reflection on contemporary application to issues of sexuality in the contemporary world.

Foster, Richard J. *The Challenge of the Disciplined Life: Christian Reflections on Money, Sex & Power*. San Francisco: Harper & Row, 1985.

Simple but profound reflections on sexuality by one of the leading writers on Christian spirituality.

Grenz, Stanley J. *Sexual Ethics: An Evangelical Perspective*. Louisville, KY: Westminster John Knox Press, 1997.

Thorough, well-informed discussions of all aspects of human sexuality. Especially profound theological reflections of Christian marriage. Lacks extensive exegetical treatments of biblical passages.

Hart, Archibald D. *The Sexual Man: Masculinity without Guilt*. Dallas: Word, 1994.

Insightful study of the particular struggles of men with their sexuality.

Michael, Robert T., John H. Gagnon, Edward O. Laumann, and Gina Kolata. *Sex in America: A Definitive Survey*. New York: Warner Books, 1994.

Reports the results of the National Health and Social Life Survey, one of the most scientifically conducted surveys of sex practices ever conducted. Dispels many myths about American sexuality and provides a greater understanding of sexual attitudes and practices among Americans.

Smedes, Lewis B. *Sex for Christians: The Limits and Liberties of Sexual Living*. Rev. ed. Grand Rapids: Eerdmans, 1994.
Provocative, frank, and frequently profound discussion of all aspects of human sexuality. Contains limited interaction with the biblical texts.

Yarbrough, O. Larry. *Not Like the Gentiles: Marriage Rules in the Letters of Paul*. Society of Biblical Literature Series, no. 80. Atlanta: Society of Biblical Literature, 1985.
Comparison of Paul's marriage ethic with the ethics of Jews and Greco-Romans with special attention to 1 Thessalonians 4 and 1 Corinthians 7.

THE CHRISTIAN &
MEDICAL ETHICS

In This Section

Larry Chouinard, David Fiensy, & Gail Wise
Medical and Ethical Guidance on Abortion

David Musick
Biomedical Issues Facing the Church

Gregory Rutecki
To Care for the Dying Is to Affirm Life

Medical and Ethical Guidance on Abortion
Larry Chouinard, Ph.D.; David Fiensy, Ph.D.;
Gail Wise, Ed.D., MSN

A Personal Story

A 22-year-old college senior prepared to graduate from nursing school. As each day passed, she grew more excited about the prospect of returning to her hometown to work in the local hospital. There she could apply the new skills and ideas she had gleaned from the academic setting. The past four years had enlightened her not only in nursing theory but had also encouraged her to be more open-minded about many issues.

Two weeks before graduation she began feeling sick—perhaps she caught a virus from one of her patients. After not feeling well for several days, she went to the university student health service. While visiting the clinic, the physician suggested a pregnancy test. She agreed to the test, which to her dismay was positive. The look on her face revealed disbelief, frustration, and even anger. She had her career ahead of her—no time for rearing a child. She and her husband had been married for four years, in an extremely rocky marriage. They had talked about divorce numerous times and agreed that they did not want children because the marriage probably would not last.

The physician immediately offered the option of abortion. After she discussed this option with her husband, they both agreed this decision was best. Even after growing up in a stable Christian home, the nursing student's professors and others at the university had strongly influenced her by a radical feminist ideology. Their feminist mantra declared that women who espoused a pro-life stance did so because they depended on their sense of identity and worth coming from their roles as wives and mothers. Furthermore, *Roe v. Wade*, the Supreme Court ruling handed down in 1973 that legalized abortion on demand, made the process of obtaining an abortion legal and more accessible. She scheduled an appointment with a physician to terminate the pregnancy, but the physician informed her that the pregnancy had advanced too far for him to abort the fetus via the procedure he used. The abortionist readily scheduled an appointment for her with a physician in a larger city who performed abortions on women more advanced in their pregnancy.

Introduction

The questions surrounding the crisis faced by this young nursing student surface some real issues that often drive women to consider abortion. What kind of professional future could she have now facing the complications of motherhood? In the midst of a volatile marriage, is it in the best interest of the baby to be born to a couple possibly on the brink of divorce? What would be the consequences for the development of the baby to be raised by a single parent? Would this young mother be able to afford day care, and what possible impact might such arrangements have on the life of a newborn baby? When someone considers an abortion in the midst of an unplanned pregnancy they are in a particularly vulnerable state, often never seriously addressed by those who consider themselves pro-life.[1] On the other hand, the language of those who advocate pro-choice seems to offer a quick fix, sanitized by clinical terms to numb any maternal instincts and neutralize the gruesome details of abortion procedures. If the faith community is to speak in terms that provide ethical guidance to young women facing the crisis of an unwanted pregnancy, we must model a "countercultural ethos of respect for life" at every stage and in every context.[2] Only by modeling a commitment to the dignity and worth of every human life can we offer women in crisis a viable alternative to the short-term solution provided by the abortionist.

> *Only by modeling a commitment to the dignity and worth of every human life can we offer women in crisis a viable alternative to the short-term solution provided by the abortionist.*

It would seem that a consistent pro-choice position would favor a woman securing all the possible information she could about the new life growing within her. However, it appears that anyone who attempts to slow the rush to surgery, or calls for a pause for reflection and honest inquiry about the development of the unborn and possible alternatives to abortion, is labeled as having little compassion for the plight of a distressed woman. Information and alternative strategies would seem to be fundamental to making an informed and thoughtful "choice." This chapter is an attempt to encourage critical and thoughtful reflection on one of the most important issues of our time. Space forbids an attempt to critically analyze every argument for or against the legal or moral grounds that might justify or prohibit an abortion.

The issues are extremely complex, and unanimity seems dependent upon both religious values and the clarity of medical interpretations. Presently on the books in more than half the states is the recognition of the fetus as a separate person, possessing legal rights separate from the expectant mother.[3] In many instances the developing fetus has been extended the same rights afforded a breathing newborn child. Fetal surgery can now be performed within the womb to correct some abnormalities and save the life of the fetus. Drugs can be prescribed to address the medical needs of the unborn and assure their healthy prenatal development. But, as Kathleen Berger has noted, although more and more fetuses might benefit from such procedures, "the question arises as to whether expectant women should be legally required to go through such procedures—to experience pain and medical risk if doing so might save the life of a fetus." Berger raises some interesting legal and moral questions:

> ". . . should every pregnant woman be prohibited from smoking, required to eat nutritious foods, and forced to abstain from alcohol altogether? Is possible harm to a developing person sufficient to negate a developed person's right to privacy and self-determination? . . . [Should] violence by anyone toward a pregnant woman . . . be considered an attack on a child, even if the woman is unwilling to bring charges[?] . . . At what point is a mother fully responsible for her child—at conception, as some argue; at viability, as others believe; or weeks or even months *after* birth, as was the case in some traditional societies where newborn infanticide was acceptable?"[4]

Answers to these and other complicated issues surrounding abortion ultimately are determined by the value one places upon prenatal life. The two competing proposals (i.e., pro-choice and pro-life) are often more concerned to win the rhetorical debate than offer a balanced and sensitive response to women who find themselves in a crisis of an unwanted pregnancy. In this paper we intend to offer an alternative proposal that takes seriously both the woman in crisis and the value of unborn life. Finally, for the Christian, the biblical witness is crucial, both for what it says and does not say. We will examine abortion in the ancient world and what perspective the Bible brings to the discussion. While space forbids a detailed analysis, it is hoped that our reflections will provide a solid informative base to provide ethical guidance on this complex and important subject.

The Current Debate

Few subjects have proven to be as divisive and emotionally charged as the debate surrounding the abortion controversy. However, in recent years, it appears that the so-called debate has become a battle of slogans (e.g., "abortion is murder"; "women have a right to control their own body"), rather than a serious discussion of the issues associated with this complex subject. Positions have been staked out, and a passionate yet civil debate has all but ceased.[5]

> Positions have been staked out, and a passionate yet civil debate has all but ceased.

The failure to continue to dialogue on this issue has given rise to extremist's views and vitriolic sound bites that contribute little to bringing clarity and mutual understanding. On the one hand, some extremists have become so riveted upon saving the life of the unborn, they see nothing morally inconsistent with taking the life of a physician who performs abortions. They block the doors at abortion clinics and shout demeaning epithets at young women attempting to enter. Others have planted bombs in clinics to bring a halt to what is perceived as a modern holocaust directed at the most vulnerable of our society.

On the other hand, extreme views within the pro-choice camp seem to be only interested in the easy availability of abortions, with little regard for the life of the unborn regardless of the level of development. All efforts to restrict or regulate abortion availability are seen as largely male intrusion on women's right to control their own destinies through procreative choice. However, their claim of a compassionate regard for the well-being of women rings hollow with the rise of power and big money associated with the abortion clinic. Since abortion is the only medical procedure in the United States not regulated by the medical com-

> *All efforts to restrict or regulate abortion availability are seen as largely male intrusion on women's right to control their own destinies through procreative choice.*

munity, it is to the advantage of the lucrative clinics to insist that a woman not be legally forced to sacrifice her "rights" for the welfare of the unborn. As noted by Bevere: "For a movement that claims to be on the side of the marginalized, it is in reality quite bourgeois and status quo."[6]

For the most part, the values at stake have largely been articulated in terms of the "rights of the unborn" versus the "rights of the woman to have reproductive choice and control in procreation." We shall return subsequently to examine the prevailing assumption that the debate is best framed in terms of conflicting "rights." First, however, we will attempt to bring clarity to the discussion by defining key terms and concepts related to the subject.

Partisans on both sides of the abortion debate conceptualize or describe terms or procedures in very different ways. On the one side

> *Partisans on both sides of the abortion debate conceptualize or describe terms or procedures in very different ways.*

abortion is defined and the procedures used are described in the most innocuous manner so as not to offend human sensibilities. But others articulate and conceptualize their position in the most extreme either-or terms, using highly emotional graphics and inflammatory rhetoric. As has been noted, the debate is polarized by two very different ways of conceptualizing the status and worth of prenatal life:

> To one side, the developing fetus is a cuddly, unborn baby, and abortion is murder. To the other, the developing fetus is amorphous tissue, a product of conception, and abortion is a safe medical procedure. Political activists often use heavily emotive words and so obscure finer, yet important distinctions in their rush to gain the rhetorical advantage.[7]

Even the definition of abortion accents the highly charged differences between the diverging groups. Pro-choice advocates are content to define abortion in terms found in most medical dictionar-

> Even the definition of abortion accents the highly charged differences between the diverging groups.

ies and health care textbooks, which define abortion in the broadest medical and scientific terms. Typically, health care literature simply defines abortion as the ending of pregnancy before the viability of the fetus.[8] Moore and Persaud discuss viability in the following manner:

> There is no sharp limit of development, age, or weight at which a fetus automatically becomes viable or beyond which survival is assured, but experience has shown that it is rare for a baby to survive whose weight is less than 500 gm. Or whose fertilization age is less than 22 weeks. Even fetuses born between 26 and 28 weeks have difficulty surviving, mainly because the respiratory system and the central nervous system are not completely differentiated. The term *abortion* refers to all pregnancies that terminate before the period of viability.[9]

Such language is obviously neutral with respect to the nature of the aborted fetus, and the medical justification that might warrant an abortion. Older health care texts tended to describe *therapeutic abortions* as those performed before viability due to endangerment of the life or health of the mother, the prevention of the birth of a deformed child, or in cases involving rape or incest. Although terminology such as "elective abortion" or "abortion on demand" are seldom used in health care textbooks, many texts no longer describe the procedure in terms of any medical justification, but have acquiesced to the legal ruling that recently justified abortion as a basic "right" of a pregnant women. That "right" is now recognized as an option that can be exercised anytime during gestation.[10]

While medical textbooks and the literature promoted by pro-choice advocates attempt to neutralize or sanitize the language defining abortion, pro-life advocates usually stress both the violence inherent in the abortion process, and the nature of the unborn upon which the violence is perpetrated. The viability line may reflect the biological facts and truths of fetal development, but it does not address the question of when human life or personhood begins. Although there are differences within the pro-life camp concerning when personhood begins (conception? implantation? viability?) and exactly what grounds, if any, can ever justify an abortion, pro-life advocates are united in their assessment that the "rights" of the unborn should not be pushed aside solely based upon the premise that the "rights" of the woman supersede and take priority over fetal "rights." Their literature abounds with explicit affirmations concerning the value and worth of all prenatal life, from conception to birth. Hence, the Ohio Right to Life defines abortion in the strongest emotive terms:

> Abortion ends a pregnancy by destroying and removing the developing *child* [italics mine] even in utero or while the *child* is being born (Partial Birth Abortion). Abortion is an act of violence that kills an unborn *child* . . ."

Obviously, language that identifies an embryo or fetus as a "child" sharply contrasts with the neutral language found in most pro-choice literature. We will reflect on what might be said biblically about prenatal development and personhood subsequently, but for now our point is to clarify and illustrate the widely divergent ways that abortion is understood. The divergence is further illustrated in the way that proponents articulate their understanding of abortion methods. A brief overview of the literature describing abortion procedures further highlights the wide differences in the way that prenatal life is understood and articulated:

First Trimester Abortions (90% of all abortions)

Suction Aspiration/Suction Abortion

Pro-choice: After an injection to numb the cervix, a soft flexible tube connected to an aspirating machine is inserted into the uterus and the uterine contents are removed.

Pro-life: A suction tube (27 times stronger than a home vacuum cleaner) is inserted into the womb, and a powerful suction tears the baby apart limb from limb and sucks it from the womb along with the placenta. The baby's remains are deposited into an attached waste bottle.

Dilation and Curettage (D&C)

Pro-choice: A procedure used usually in the third month of pregnancy involves a loop-sharp knife used to scrape the wall of the uterus, cutting the fetus and placenta into smaller parts and pulling them out of the woman's body through the cervix.

Pro-life: A ring forceps is inserted into the womb and the baby is extracted piece by piece. Then a sharp knife is used to scrape away any of the baby or placenta that remains. Profuse bleeding usually occurs.

Second Trimester Abortions (About 140,000 abortions yearly)

Dilation and Evacuation

Pro-choice: Because the bones are larger and stronger after 14 weeks, the doctor must use a type of pliers to pull the fetus into small parts for removal through the cervix.

Pro-life: After 14 weeks the unborn child is dismembered with plier-like forceps. The instrument seizes a body part, and with a twist tears it from the baby's body. In order to assure that all parts have been removed it is reassembled outside the womb.

Saline/Prostaglandin Injection

Pro-choice: The doctor can inject saline or prostaglandin into the amniotic fluid surrounding the fetus. These solutions are poisonous and eventually kill the fetus. These methods require that one give birth to a dead fetus.

Pro-life: A concentrated salt solution is injected into the amniotic fluid. The baby breathes and swallows it and dies an hour later of acute salt poisoning. The mother then delivers a dead, burned baby.

Third Trimester Abortions (about 3,000 abortions a year use this procedure)

Dilation and Extraction (a.k.a. Partial Birth Abortion)

Pro-choice: Late term abortion is a rare procedure where the doctor uses large forceps to grasp a leg and pull it down into the vagina feet first. After the body is delivered the fetal skull is lodged at the cervical opening, where an incision is made in the skull and a suction device is inserted to evacuate the skull. This enables the fetus to easily pass through the cervix.

Pro-life: Since the late-term baby is stronger, it is difficult to tear the baby apart through a D & E procedure. The baby's legs are pulled by forceps through the birth canal delivering the baby, except the head. A suction device is then inserted to suction out the baby's brains so the skull will easily collapse, and a dead baby is delivered.[12]

The descriptive language varies based upon the value assigned to the prenatal life that is being destroyed. Since pro-choice advocates do not believe that the unborn should be viewed as human persons, their descriptions of abortion procedures are focused more on the safety of the procedure for the woman, with little or no regard for the well-being of the fetus. It is critical that both patient and physician dehumanize the fetus so as to desensitize any compassionate regard for the life being destroyed. Certainly, in the first few weeks of pregnancy a woman may be convinced that the mass of cells called a blastocyst has little resemblance to a developing baby within her. However, by the third trimester it would be difficult to deny that the fetus is anything other than human. But it is financially expedient for the abortion clinic to define abortion as simply the removal of unwanted tissue, and not the execution of an unborn baby.

On the other hand, pro-lifers are often accused of being more pro-birth than pro-life. Not only do many within the pro-life movement fail to exhibit a high regard for human life, regardless of age and circumstances, many seem to lose interest in children after birth. This observation is intended to remind the movement "that the value worth defending is not birthing, but persons. Attitudes and policies that foster birth,

> On the other hand, pro-lifers are often accused of being more pro-birth than pro-life.

but do little for disadvantaged children once they are born, may promote an abstract principle, 'pro-lifeness,' but they can neglect the human persons that the pro-life principle is intended to nourish."[13] Until we are able to fit our convictions on abortion

> "The value worth defending is not birthing, but persons."

into a coherent scheme of values that translate into a more consistent counter to the prevalent trend of devaluing human life, our rhetoric may ring hollow in a world whose ultimate value is personal freedom and rights. The crisis of an unwanted pregnancy must be met with a countercultural ethos that values both the woman in crisis and the life developing within her. The faith community must articulate a message of compassion and mercy, not just a litany of arguments designed to win the debate. Friesen asks some perceptive questions, if the church thought of itself as a "pilgrim people," proposing an alternative way, i.e., the way of the cross:

> The faith community must articulate a message of compassion and mercy, not just a litany of arguments designed to win the debate.

But what would happen if the church were to model an alternative non-violent politics of solidarity with the weak and the marginalized that still respects the dignity and the humanity of those positions of power who violate the weak? How should such a model look if, in responding to the issue of abortion, the church were motivated less by the abstraction "right to life" and more by its identification with the unborn as well as with the often isolated and vulnerable women who seek abortions? How can the church minister and serve out of a deep compassion for the vulnerable and plight of prospective mothers who cannot see how to care for a child, whether because of poverty, physical danger to their lives, pregnancies resulting from rape or incest, or feeling abandoned and alone with no one to care for and nurture a child?[14]

> *Whereas the proabortionists have devalued the life of the unborn, the pro-life camp has often ignored the plight of pregnant mothers.*

Whereas the proabortionists have devalued the life of the unborn, the pro-life camp has often ignored the plight of pregnant mothers. We must avoid these extremes.

Is there any way that both sides can come together to pursue at least a reduction of the staggering number of deaths due to abortions? Even though recent trends suggest a slight decline in the number of abortions in the United States, the numbers are still alarming. Since the famous *Roe v. Wade* decision in 1973, abortions have consistently remained at 1.3–1.5 million each year.[15] To give some perspective, in 2002, 42,850 people died in traffic deaths. However, in American abortion clinics approximately every two weeks the same number of human fetuses die. In a so-called civilized society, far more human deaths are caused by induced abortion than by any other cause. Approximately 25 percent of all pregnancies end in abortion. One estimate for the number

> *In a so-called civilized society, far more human deaths are caused by induced abortion than by any other cause.*

of abortions occurring in 2002 placed the United States third in the world for the number of abortions (1,313,000), behind China (10,000,000) and Russia (2,140,000).[16] Worldwide, the estimates are 46 million abortions or 22 percent of 210 million pregnancies. Women who seek an abortion are more likely to be white, between the ages of 20-29 (55%), and not married (80%).

These statistics indicate that abortion has become woven into the very fabric of the American way of life. Even though both sides of the debate seem to "agree that abortions are

> *Abortion has become woven into the very fabric of the American way of life.*

undesirable, a crude solution to problems that would better be solved by other means," David and Sidney Callahan have identified a crucial distinction between pro-choice and pro-life advocates:

> Put simply, for many who are pro-choice, abortion is a necessary evil, one that must be tolerated and supported until such time as better sex education, more effective contraception, and a more just social order make possible fewer troubled pregnancies. . . . By contrast, the pro-life group believes that a better future cannot be achieved unless we begin now to live the ideals that we want to achieve, unless we are prepared to make present sacrifices toward future goals, and unless aggression toward the fetus is denied, however high the individual cost at denying it. The acceptance of reality as it is implicitly legitimates the '*status quo*,' undercuts efforts to bring about social change, and sanctions violence as an acceptable method of coping with problems.[17]

It is doubtful that meaningful dialogue will ever take place as long as the discussion is framed in terms of a conflict of "rights": i.e., the "right to choose" versus the "right to life." As Hauerwas has effectively argued, the church must move beyond issues associated with "rights" in its moral discussion.[18] An ethic grounded in "rights" is simply the extension of the current radical trend to make the privacy of the individual of ultimate value. Decisions about abortion are, therefore, often based on calculating self-interest and individual well-being. This point is well articulated by Duane Friesen:

> *An ethic grounded in "rights" is simply the extension of the current radical trend to make the privacy of the individual of ultimate value.*

> An ethic of self-interest, in which individual well-being (convenience, self-realization, success, and self-fulfillment) is the ultimate value, undermines communities that nurture cooperation and the larger corporate goods and values. Consumer capitalism and a market economy has had the effect of

'socializing' us to think in terms of calculating self-interest. . . . Individualistic consumerism evades commitment to the weak and the marginalized and to the larger common good. Politics in North America has degenerated into cynical appeals to self-interest.[19]

Ironically, those who argue for the "rights" of the individual to choose abortion have no hesitation to restrict "rights" when it comes to issues such as gun control, environmental policies, and affirmative action, which restrictions are deemed appropriate for the welfare of the social order.[20] As long as the privacy of the individual and the related notion of personal "rights" are given priority, there will never be any kind of moral consensus on this or any other moral issue. As noted by Wennberg:

. . . both the Old and New Testaments roundly condemn the killing of the innocent, but never introduce the notion of a right to life. For in the biblical tradition it is not that someone's killing me violates my right to life so much as it violates God's sovereignty over life and his authority to determine under what circumstances it can be taken.[21]

Bevere has perceptively pointed out that pro-choice advocates often come across as extolling freedom of choice or the autonomous self to make decisions as the foundation of ethical virtue. It is not the choice that is made, but rather the exercise of one's freedom to choose that seems to be given the ultimate value. Here, the stress on freedom of choice extols the sovereignty of the individual to make decisions as an isolated agent not bound by community standards or ethical restrictions, except as perceived or devised by the individual. Such reasoning clearly "makes the question of abortion or no abortion simply a matter of one's personal preference."[22]

It is therefore difficult to understand how many pro-choice advocates can acknowledge that while access to abortions should not be restricted, abortion is nevertheless not heralded as a morally good thing. If the "right to choose" is the ultimate value, then on what basis can any choice a woman makes to abort be judged good or bad? As Bevere concludes: ". . . the pro-abortion argument continually wants to lead us back, not to abortion itself as a good or bad thing, but the free decision itself. Thus, it must be concluded that the pro-abortion argument is one that is based on the issue of choice itself, not the issue of abortion."[23] Once "freedom of choice" is made, an ultimate moral value, regardless of the choice made, it is difficult to see how our claim to autonomy and freedom becomes anything more than a guise to promote our own selfish desires at the expense of another or the common good.

When the church articulates its message concerning abortion in terms of the "rights of the unborn," we have allowed secular forces to shape the rhetorical tone of the debate. From a biblical perspective, personal rights are not assigned ultimate value. Jesus envisioned that the one who would follow him "must deny himself and take up his cross" (Matt 16:24). Paul models such an ethic when he refused to avail himself of certain "rights" in order not to hinder the impact of

> When the church articulates its message concerning abortion in terms of the "rights of the unborn," we have allowed secular forces to shape the rhetorical tone of the debate. The language of "rights" has little to do with the ethics of the Kingdom.

the gospel (1 Cor 9:1-15). The language of "rights" has little to do with the ethics of the Kingdom. In fact, it is doubtful that our rights-oriented culture can even appreciate the biblical precedent of a community of people willing to give up their own rights for the care of others, including the unborn. Within this community life is understood as a "gift" not a "right." The implications for the abortion debate are noted by Bevere:

> If indeed life is a gift from God, what human being has the audacity to refuse the gift? To acknowledge the giftedness of life is to continue to acknowledge, unlike those who want to argue for one's personal autonomy over one's body, that our continued existence, and the continued existence of the world is in God's hands, not ours. To accept the gift of life is to accept God's sovereignty.[24]

While such a suggestion may not have persuasive power within the judicial process, we must avoid faulty theology in our effort to persuade the powers that be. The most powerful witness the church could present on the value and worth of the unborn is a consistent pro-life commitment to all people the world seems ready to discard as dispensable. The church needs to model an alternative vision of life that finds solidarity with the weak, the marginalized, and vulnerable. In addition, the church needs to offer an alternative to secularized individualism that reduces life to slogans promoting rights and self-interest. In the meantime, compassionate Christians should support all public policy initiatives that contribute to the prevention or discouragement of abortion.[25]

Teaching on Abortion in Scripture

Neither the Old Testament nor the New Testament says anything at all about abortion. Texts that are sometimes offered as proof-texts against abortion prove, when carefully considered, to be unhelpful.[26] Both pro-life and pro-choice sides cite Exodus 21:22-25:

> And when men fight and they strike a pregnant woman and her fetus comes out and there is no (mortal) harm, he will certainly be fined according to what the woman's husband determines. He will give it in accordance with the judges. But if there is (mortal) harm, you will repay life for life. (translation by Fiensy)

The question here is to whom does the mortal harm refer? If it refers to the fetus, then one could be put to death for accidentally causing a miscarriage and death of a fetus. If it refers to the mother, then the death of a fetus causes no punishment (or at most only a fine). Only the death of the mother results in life for life. The New International Version translates this to indicate that the mortal harm refers to the fetus, but the Revised Standard Version translates it in such a way that the mortal harm refers to the mother. Simply put, there is no way clearly to settle the issue based on the Hebrew language alone.

Another text cited by pro-life groups is Psalm 139:13-16:

> You created my innermost parts.
>   You shaped me in my mother's womb. . . .
> My bones were not hidden from you
>   when I was made in secret.
> I was intricately woven in the lower parts of the earth.
>   You saw my formless (body) . . . (translation by Fiensy).

This Psalm, which has as its theme God's omnipresence, is mainly teaching that there is no place that God is not. He is even in the womb as we are forming. As a matter of fact, God the creator was in the womb creating us as he created the first man and woman. The passage of Scripture does not say anything directly about abortion or personhood of the fetus, but it does highlight God as creator within the womb.

Although texts such as Psalm 139 and others (Jer 1:5; Gal 1:15) do allude to God's knowledge of persons while they are yet in the womb, these texts do not indicate whether aborting a fetus would be wrong. We must face the simple fact that no biblical text speaks directly and explicitly about abortion as either permissible or sinful. Rather, we must reflect on biblical principles to help us decide this issue.

> *We must face the simple fact that no biblical text speaks directly and explicitly about abortion as either permissible or sinful.*

Abortion in Early Christian Teaching

The lack of reference to abortion in the Old and New Testaments[27] was not due to the fact that abortion techniques had not yet been invented. On the contrary, Greek surgeons had long before the New Testament era developed several methods of terminating pregnancy. One could use purely mechanical methods that included striking the womb with a heavy blow or tightly wrapping the womb. A more sophisticated mechanical method was to insert a blade into the uterus to cut up the fetus and then a copper needle or blunted hook to rip out the body parts (Tertullian, *On the Soul*, 25).[28]

In addition to mechanical methods of abortion, the surgeons could use medicinal techniques. These included inserting drugs directly into the vagina to kill the fetus or using oral poisons that were strong enough eventually to kill the fetus but not strong enough, it was hoped, to kill the mother.[29]

Needless to say, women often died from such procedures, either from hemorrhaging or from taking too much oral poison. One sociologist of religion has even opined that Christianity's rise can partly be explained by its more humane treatment of women (in forbidding abortion).[30]

Not only was abortion a common practice in antiquity among the Greeks and Romans, it found powerful support from two of Greece's most famous philosophers: Plato and Aristotle. Both required in their ideal states abortions for all women after a certain fixed age. Among the Romans it was an increasingly popular practice, reaching its peak in the early empire.[31]

Christians (like Jews) rejected abortion as an immoral act. The earliest statement comes from the Didache 2:2, a Syrian Christian

> Christians (like Jews) rejected abortion as an immoral act.

work dating from the end of the first century or the beginning of the second century, "You will not murder a child in an abortion (φθορα[32]) nor will you kill one that has been born (in infanticide)." The same teaching, using this exact wording, is given in the Epistle of Barnabas 19:5, a document also from the late first to early second century, written probably in Alexandria, Egypt. Thus both Syrian and Egyptian Christians at a very early date strongly opposed abortion (and infanticide).

The second-century Christian apologist, Athenagoras, from Athens wrote even more strongly condemning abortion: ". . . we say that those women who use drugs to bring on abortion commit murder and will have to give an account to God for the abortion. . ." (*Plea for All Christians*, 35).[33] The same firm opposition to abortion was repeated by numerous Christian authors in the first three centuries of church history.[34]

The church's teaching on abortion was clear and universal and stood in stark contrast to the general practice among pagans. To be fair, some pagans, notably the Stoic philosophers, also rejected abortion, but, in the main, society accepted and practiced it as a means of birth control. Christians, Jews, and a few enlightened pagans stood in the minority in opposing and denouncing this practice. When Christians rejected abortion (and infanticide), they did so on the grounds that God is the creator, and therefore human life is not ours to take.

> The church's teaching on abortion was clear and universal and stood in stark contrast to the general practice among pagans.

Reflections on Abortion Based on Biblical Principles

Debates today among Christian ethicists focus on when a fetus becomes a person. One can find virtually all options advanced and defended: at fertilization, at implantation (when the fertilized egg attaches to the wall of the womb), at the "quickening" (when the child moves in the womb), at viability, at birth, and at independence.[35] Perhaps the debate though focuses mostly on four positions:

One position is that which considers human life as a person at conception. Thus abortion at any stage of development is murder.

Further, human beings do not merely develop in the womb, it is observed, but throughout their lives. Thus one cannot argue that a life is not fully a person until fully developed. Stephen Schwarz has perceptively argued: "If by 'person' we mean

> Debates today among Christian ethicists focus on when a fetus becomes a person.

'functioning person,' for example, a normal adult making a complex decision or reading a book, then clearly a child in the womb, or just born, or even at age one, is only potentially such a person. A baby is a potential functioning person; but he is that only because he has the actual being of a person."[36]

A second position is that a developing fetal life only becomes a person when it breathes since the Old Testament seems to identify personhood with the Hebrew word *nephesh* (נֶפֶשׁ) as in Genesis 2:7: "God breathed into his nostrils and he became a living *nephesh*." Thus since a fetus in the womb cannot/does not breathe, it cannot be a person.[37]

Third, some maintain that a certain level of consciousness and intelligence is necessary to claim personhood. Thus not only are fetuses not persons but also newborns, those in a vegetative state, the profoundly retarded, and the comatose, according to this view. By this position neither abortion, infanticide, nor certain types of euthanasia would be murder since the above types of life are not human persons.[38]

Fourth, some Christian ethicists of late argue on the basis of potential personhood. Well-meaning thinkers may not be able to agree as to when a fetus becomes a person but all can agree that it is *at least* a potential person. As argued by Wennberg: "If we judge that the image of God is the capacity, whether potential or actualized, for moral, spiritual, and rational agency (as I am inclined to do), then we are well on our way to accepting the potentiality principle."[39] A potential person is one that will eventually grow into a person, given time, protection, and nutrition. This view maintains that both potential persons and fully developed persons should be assigned a moral standing, and their lives preserved and protected.[40]

The last position probably offers the best hope for appealing to all sides. Debates about when a fetus becomes a person are useless since the pro-choice and pro-life groups cannot agree and probably will never agree. R. Hays develops this position with the consideration of the fetus as God's creation. It is more appropriate for

Christians to think about whether abortion violates our relationship with God the creator rather than whether abortion constitutes the civil crime of murder. As Hays argues:

> To terminate a pregnancy is not only to commit an act of violence but also to assume responsibility for destroying a work of God, "from whom are all things and for whom we exist" (1 Cor 8:6). . . . Whether we accord "personhood" to the unborn child or not, he or she is a manifestation of new life that has come forth from God.[41]

The precise identification of the moment of human personhood is in some ways irrelevant. The zygote is a new life which will become a human being if it is not one already. As noted by John Harvey:

> *The precise identification of the moment of human personhood is in some ways irrelevant.*

> This development from embryo to fetus, newborn babe, child, adolescent, adult, and eventually octogenarian, is simply an ordered serial development of different stages in the complete cycle of human life. It is potentiality becoming actuality. Each unique living human being is constantly changing every single second throughout his or her cycle of life. A human being is unchangeable and complete only at the moment of death.[42]

To end this life because it is inconvenient to us is at least immoral (even if one wants to argue that it is not murder).

What about therapeutic abortions or abortions done when the mother's life is threatened by the pregnancy? What about pregnancies from rape or incest? These are difficult questions to which one can give the following advice. First, the principle should be: Do not endanger the life of one fully formed by one not fully formed.[43] Thus if the mother's life is in jeopardy, a therapeutic abortion should be performed. On the other hand, pregnancies from rape or incest should not be terminated. After all, regardless of the tragic circumstances precipitating the pregnancy, a high value should be placed on fetal and neonatal life, and therefore every means exerted to preserve and protect the life of the innocent. For those who find the trauma of keeping the child too great, there are thousands of married but infertile couples longing for the opportunity to adopt. Although public policy does little to encourage adoption, the church should provide the needed information as an alternative to abortion. As Mother Teresa contended, "We are fighting abortion by adoption."

Second, we should confess that there can be some very difficult cases that may require the prayer and collective wisdom of the wider Christian community. For example, as tragic as it may be, severe abnormalities discovered through antenatal screening and amniocentesis by no means necessitate the conclusion that a severely handicapped person should be killed *for their own good*. It is commonly heard that the issue is not the *sanctity of* life but the *quality of life*, and it is therefore determined that a severely handicapped person would be better off dead. Obviously the question arises concerning who can make such a determination. It may be that the real reason why some are so willing to sacrifice the life of those severely handicapped is not to relieve an unbearable burden for the child but to remove an unbearable personal burden. But it may be that the true measure of our humanity and civilization can best be attested by the respect and care given to those most vulnerable among us. Hauerwas also reminds the Christian community of our vocation as an alternative community especially exhibited in how we treat the mentally handicapped:

> It may be that the true measure of our humanity and civilization can best be attested by the respect and care given to those most vulnerable among us.

> The mentally handicapped remind us that their condition is the condition of us all insofar as we are faithful followers of Christ. The church is not a collection of individuals, but a people on a journey who are known by the time they take to help one another along the way. The mentally handicapped constitute such time, as we know that God would not have us try to make the world better if such efforts mean leaving them behind. They are the way we must learn to walk in the journey that God has given us called Kingdom. They are God's imagination, to the extent we become one with them, we become God's imagination for the world.[44]

People in crisis who feel alone and abandoned may not evaluate the issues as those not in that situation. Thus the church's ethical responsibility is not simply to teach what is right in this matter but to give encouragement and support to those in crisis.

Postscript

As a woman and a nurse over time I have changed my view about abortion. As a nursing student I believed abortion was a woman's choice and a right. After becoming pregnant and delivering my son, I addressed the issue of abortion in a new light. There was no doubt my son was a person, full of life the moment he was born. If he had been born a minute earlier, an hour earlier, a day earlier, or a month earlier, he would have been the same person, full of life. I realized there was no logical stopping point. He was more than a piece of tissue that could be destroyed without consequence.

I was in the position of other women who seriously contemplate abortion. In fact, I was scheduled to have the abortion. Thankfully, I did not keep the appointment presented in the introduction of this chapter. I have not suffered the pain many women endure in the aftermath of an abortion. However, I have reflected many times how my life may have changed if I had kept the appointment.

I seriously doubt our marriage would have survived. I definitely would have missed the blessings my husband and I received from rearing our son. Family, friends, and others would have missed the opportunity to witness the development of this life into a Christian physician whose life has impacted multiple other lives.

Like one woman lamented after aborting the only baby she was to conceive, I could have today been "nobody's anything." My mother, father, brother, and grandparents are deceased. If my marriage had failed, I would also be "nobody's anything"—especially nobody's mother.

Notes

[1] Frederica Mathewes-Green's, *Real Choices: Listening to Women, Looking for Alternatives to Abortion* (Ben Lomond, CA: Conciliar Press, 1997), research found that rather than financial needs, child-care woes, or career implications, her discussion with postabortion women found that the central driving force behind abortions involves the network of relationships in which women find themselves embedded. If women cannot find the love and support from their most intimate circle of relationships (e.g., parents, siblings, friends, husband, or boyfriend), that encourage her to carry her pregnancy to term, she is likely to seek an abortion.

[2] Glen H. Stassen and David P. Gushee, *Kingdom Ethics: Following Jesus in Contemporary Context* (Downers Grove, IL: InterVarsity, 2003), 231.

[3] As this chapter is being written there is an attempt by Republicans in Congress to invoke the Laci Peterson murder case to enact the first federal law to endow a fetus with legal rights separate from the expectant mother (*Associated Press*, May 19, 2003).

[4]Kathleen S. Berger, *The Developing Person: Through Childhood and Adolescence*, 5th ed. (New York: Worth Press, 2000) 118.

[5]A helpful collection of essays that constructively looks at all sides of the debate may be found in the book edited by Louis P. Pojman and Francis J. Beckwith, *The Abortion Controversy* (Boston: Jones and Bartlett, 1994). In May 1993 the editors debated the subject on the campus of Taylor University. Their book is an attempt to bring together the "best arguments by those on all sides of the debate."

[6]Allan R. Bevere, "Abortion: Philosophical and Theological Considerations," *Ashland Theological Journal* 28 (1996) 51.

[7]See David K. Clark and Robert V. Rakestraw, eds., *Readings in Christian Ethics*, vol. 2 (Grand Rapids: Baker, 1996) 22.

[8]See, e.g., Keith Moore and T.V.N. Persaud, *The Developing Human: Clinically Oriented Embryology*, 6th ed. (Philadelphia: W.B. Saunders, 1998) 3; Darlene Como, ed., *Mosby's Medical, Nursing, and Allied Health Dictionary*, 6th ed. (St. Louis: A Harcourt Health Sciences Co., 2000) 6; John H. Dirckx, ed., *Stedmans Concise Medical Dictionary for the Health Professions* (Baltimore: Williams and Wilkins, 1997) A-6.

[9]Moore and Persaud, *The Developing Human*, 109.

[10]In Doe v. Bolton the court ruled that abortion could be performed after fetal viability if the operating physician judged the procedure necessary to protect the life or health of the woman. However, the term "health" need not entail a life-threatening situation. Health may be related to any physical conditions, emotional frame of mind, psychological factors, familial conditions, age, or any other issues that may be deemed as affecting the well-being of the woman seeking an abortion.

[11]See their web site at: http://www.ohiolife.org/abortion/index.asp.

[12]For pro-choice see: http://www.womenscenter.org/procedur.htm, http://www.fwhc.org/abortionab-procedures.htm; for pro-life see: http://www.theprolifeoffice.org/abortion.htm, http://www.prolife.com.htm.

[13]Clark and Rakestraw, *Readings in Christian Ethics*, 24-25.

[14]Duane K. Friesen, *Artists, Citizens, Philosophers: Seeking the Peace of the City* (Scottdale, PA: Herald Press, 2000) 134-135.

[15]The following statistics are drawn from the Alan Gottmacher Institute and the Centers for Disease Control and Prevention (DCD). See also statistics compiled by Wm. Robert Johnston (http://www.johnstonesarchive.net/policy/abortion); and the various articles on abortions compiled at http://www.religioustolerance.org.

[16]See http://www.johnstonsarchive.net/policy/abortion/wrjp3345d.html.

[17]David Callahan and Sidney Callahan, "Breaking through the Stereotypes," in *The Abortion Controversy*, 9.

[18]Stanley Hauerwas, "Abortion, Theologically Understood," in *The Church and Abortion: In Search of New Ground for Response*, ed. by Paul Stallsworth (Nashville: Abingdon, 1993) 50-52.

[19]Friesen, *Artists, Citizens, Philosophers*, 134.

[20]As noted by Friesen, ibid., 238.

[21]Robert N. Wennberg, "The Right to Life: Three Theories," in *Readings in Christian Ethics*, 2:38.

[22]Bevere, "Abortion," 46.

[23]Ibid.

[24]Ibid., 51.

[25]Stassen and Gushee, *Kingdom Ethics*, 236, offer an overview of public initiatives related to abortion that will contribute to a reduction of abortions: ". . . the development and distribution of better nonabortive contraceptives, efforts to combat rape, sexual abuse, incest and other sexual violations of women, strong emphases on sexual morality and responsibility for both men and women, broadening availability of high-quality and affordable day care, altering business practices to include more job sharing and other arrangements conducive to balancing work and family obligations, making sterilization and contraceptive products a routine part of insurance coverage, major initiatives against the grinding poverty that still characterizes the lives of millions and leads to the kind of hopelessness that undermines personal responsibility, improved adoption services and laws, and finally, support for all relevant government and nongovernmental services to pregnant women, new mothers and their children."

[26]See the list cited with critique in R. Hays, *The Moral Vision of the New Testament* (San Francisco: Harper, 1996) 446-448; Glen Stassen and David P. Gushee, *Kingdom Ethics*, 215-236; and R.B. Ward, "Is the Fetus a Person? The Bible's

View," http:www.rcrc.org/religion/es2/comp.html. The list includes Exod. 21:22-25; Psalm 139:13-16; Luke 1:44; Galatians 5:20 (the word *pharmakeion*); and Matt. 19:14.

[27]M.J. Gorman, "Why Is the New Testament Silent about Abortion?" *Christianity Today* (Jan 11, 1993) 27-29, argues that abortion is not mentioned in the New Testament because the New Testament is not a complete manual of ethics. The New Testament's silence on abortion tells us abortion was not an issue in earliest Christianity. R.B. Ward, "Is the Fetus a Person?" has quite the opposite conclusion based on the New Testament's silence: The New Testament writers did not regard abortion as murder.

[28]See M.J. Gorman, *Abortion and the Early Church* (Downers Grove, IL: InterVarsity, 1982) 16-18; R. Stark, *The Rise of Christianity* (San Francisco: Harper, 1996) 119.

[29]Gorman, *Abortion in the Early Church*, 15-16.

[30]Stark, *The Rise of Christianity*, 120, 122-124. The endangerment to women must be placed in its larger context of the infanticide especially of female infants.

[31]Gorman, *Abortion in the Early Church*, 19-32.

[32]See F.W. Danker, *A Greek-English Lexicon of the New Testament and Other Early Christian Literature* (Chicago: University of America, 2000) 1055, for the word φθορα as abortion.

[33]Translation of Athenagoras by B.P. Pratten in *Ante-Nicean Fathers*, ed. by A. Roberts and J.

Donaldsen (Peabody, MA: Hendricksen, 1949 [1885]) 2:147.

[34]See *Apocalypse of Peter* (early second century), 21-34; Clement of Alexandria (A.D. 200) *The Tutor* 2.10.96.1; Tertullian (A.D. 200) *Apology* 9.6, and *On the Soul* 26.4-5; Minucius Felix (A.D. 200) *Octavius* 30; The Council of Elvira (A.D. 3-5) *Canon* 63; Council of Ancyra (A.D. 314) *Canon* 21. See on this especially Gorman, *Abortion in the Early Church*, 47-65; and Stark, *Rise of Christianity*, 125.

[35]See E.D. Cook, "Abortion," in *New Dictionary of Christian Ethics and Pastoral Theology*, ed. by D.J. Atkinson and D.H. Field (Downers Grove, IL: InterVarsity, 1995) 131-134.

[36]Stephen Schwarz, "Personhood Begins at Conception," in *The Abortion* Controversy, 248; see also Stassen & Gushee, *Kingdom Ethics*, 223, for a summary of this view.

[37]See Ward, "Is the Fetus a Person?"

[38]For a summary of this view, see Stassen and Gushee, *Kingdom Ethics*, 222.

[39]Wennberg, "The Right to Life," 45.

[40]This view is summarized with approval in Stassen and Gushee, *Kingdom Ethics*, 223.

[41]Hays, *Moral Vision*, 450.

[42]John Collins Harvey, "Distinctly Human: The When, Where, & How of Life's Beginnings," *Commonweal* (February 8, 2002) 5.

[43]Compare Mishnah Oholoth 7:6.

[44]Stanley Hauerwas, *Dispatches from The Front: Theological Engagements with the Secular* (Durham: Duke University Press, 1994) 185.

Bibliography

Gorman, M.J. *Abortion and the Early Church*. Downers Grove, IL: InterVarsity, 1982.

This work is perhaps the most complete collection of early Christian views on abortion.

Hays, R. *The Moral Vision of the New Testament*. San Francisco: Harper, 1996.

Selected as one of the best books on religion in the twentieth century, this work presents a balanced assessment of several ethical issues as well as ethical method.

Pojman, Louis P., and Francis J. Beckwith. *The Abortion Controversy: A Reader.* Boston: Jones and Bartlett, 1994).

Undoubtedly the best anthology covering all sides of the debate. For those interested in the philosophical debate over abortion it is essential reading.

Stallsworth, Paul, ed. *The Church and Abortion: In Search of New Ground for Response.* Nashville: Abingdon Press, 1993.

This book moves the volatile discussion on abortion away from the political agenda and the framework of "rights" to the theological foundations on which the church might approach the issue.

Stassen, Glen H., and David P. Gushee. *Kingdom Ethics: Following Jesus in Contemporary Context.* Downers Grove, IL: InterVarsity, 2003.

This work offers a fresh look at many ethical issues including abortion.

BIOMEDICAL ISSUES FACING THE MODERN CHURCH

David W. Musick, Ph.D.

Introduction

A Modern Psalm

Medical Science is my shepherd;
I shall not want.
It maketh me to lie down in hospital beds;
It leadeth me beside the marvels of technology.
It restoreth my brain waves;
It maintains men in a persistent vegetative state for its name's sake.
Yea, though I walk through the valley of the shadow of death,
I will find no end to life;
For thou art with me;
Thy respirator and heart machine they sustain me.
Thou preparest intravenous feeding for me in the presence of irreversible disability;
Thou anointest my head with oil;
My cup runneth on and on and on and on.
Surely coma and unconsciousness shall follow me all the days of my continued breathing;
And I will dwell in the intensive care unit forever.

—*Robert Fraser, date unknown*

As Christians in the modern world, we find ourselves confronted with (and often perplexed by) different types of ethical dilemmas, particularly in the realm of medicine and health care. Nearly every day, it seems, we hear or read a story in the media about new life-sustaining therapies or procedures. Or we hear of a new research project (e.g., stem cell research) that involves vulnerable patients and/or controversial methods. The technological advances that have taken place in medical care during the past thirty to forty years are stunning and dramatic. Yet, as illustrated by the "modern psalm" above, such advances do not always seem to have positive outcomes.

What is an ethical dilemma? It is a situation where one is confronted with a course of action or a choice between options that seems difficult, mutually exclusive, or both. We are increasingly expected to make decisions about whether we (or someone we love) should have every type of medical treatment available regardless of cost. Many of these treatments are brand new, and some are even experimental in nature. Or we may be asked for an opinion as to the

> An ethical dilemma is a situation where one is confronted with a course of action or a choice between options that seems difficult, mutually exclusive, or both.

morality of taking certain courses of action in the conduct of biomedical research. For example, should medical researchers use cells from discarded human placenta in research? What is acceptable and what is not? As the church enters the twenty-first century, it is confronted with an amazing assortment of these types of issues; and often the consequences of our decisions are "life and death."

Ethics has been described as "the science of duty."[1] For the Christian, this means that questions about our own health care and what steps we should or should not take, given a particular set of circumstances, are ultimately related to the revelation of God's will. In other words, when confronted with an ethical dilemma, the issue for the Christian is simply this: What would God have me do? Davis provides insight into how we should approach this question:

> When confronted with an ethical dilemma, the issue for the Christian is simply this: What would God have me do?

The teachings of Scripture are the final court of appeal for ethics. Human reason, church tradition, and the natural and social sciences may aid moral reflection, but divine revelation, found in the canonical Scriptures of the Old and New Testaments, constitutes the 'bottom line' of the decision-making process.[2]

As we shall see, however, there are not always easy answers to our questions; the Bible does not necessarily address complicated biomedical issues via a chapter and verse directive. Nevertheless, relevant biblical principles (as well as prayer and the counsel of those who possess godly wisdom) may be called upon for guidance in these circumstances. The purpose

> The Bible does not necessarily address complicated biomedical issues via a chapter and verse directive.

of this chapter is to provide the reader with an overview of the most prominent biomedical ethics issues facing the church early in the twenty-first century, and to describe how biblical principles can help us in our decisions about these issues. Because there is so much material available on these topics, the chapter must by necessity be very general. My sincere hope is that these issues can be introduced and approached within the framework provided by biblical principles, so that the reader, whether as a loved one making decisions for a debilitated family member or as a spiritual guide to those seeking counsel on such matters, may subsequently be prepared to deal with biomedical ethical dilemmas when the time comes.

A brief introduction to the field of bioethics will be helpful. First, a word about semantics is in order. In the voluminous literature related to biomedical ethics, several distinct but related terms are used. The terms "ethical," "moral," and "legal" are closely related but deserve fuller description. "Ethical" is the broadest of these terms and is generally viewed as a systematic approach to analyzing questions that arise from conflicting points of view about a given issue. The term "moral" is most often associated with individual behavior, where such behavior is considered to be right or wrong. The term "legal" is the narrowest of the three terms, and includes only those aspects of morality that have been mutually agreed upon, made binding on a particular group or society, and are accompanied by sanctions for violation of codified "rules of law." Given these general definitions, it is possible to describe scenarios where one's behavior would be considered moral, yet not legal; and ethical analysis would be applied to such a scenario in order to make decisions about a recommended course of action. For example, Christians have often disagreed about such issues as capital punishment, abortion, and warfare; both sides claim positions that are moral and bibically derived, yet not necessarily in agreement with the law. Indeed, it is here (where there is disagreement about what course of action one should or should not take on moral issues) where "ethical analysis" becomes most personal and practical.

Classic principles of biomedical ethics certainly have relevance for the reader, and a large body of material (representing many different disciplines) exists concerning these principles. Health care providers are obligated by the principles of veracity (to be truthful), beneficence (to do good), nonmalfeasance (to do no harm), autonomy (to allow patient self-determination), and justice (to support the equitable distribution of

> *Health care providers are obligated by the principles of veracity, beneficence, nonmalfeasance, autonomy, and justice.*

health care resources). These principles are interwoven into the training and decision-making processes of health care practitioners and ethicists alike. The primary criticism of this "principle-based" approach has been that they are somewhat abstract and difficult to apply to individual patient cases.

Biomedical ethics issues have also been classified into three distinct categories:[3] *clinical* ethics (where analysis focuses on dilemmas which arise at the patient's bedside and affect patient outcomes); *corporate* or *business* ethics (where analysis focuses on payment for services, health care systems, and interprofessional relationships); and, *community* ethics (where analysis focuses on political issues such as resource allocation, legislation affecting disabled and/or elderly persons, and other social policy issues). This chapter will touch on issues that have implications in all three of these categories.

In my view, the biomedical ethics issues that are most urgent for the thoughtful consideration of the modern church are as follows:

1. *Reproductive and Life-Saving Technologies* (surrogate parenthood, cloning, organ transplantation)
2. *The Role of Human Genetics in Health Care* (the human genome project, gene therapy, stem cell research)
3. *Patients' Rights and Responsibilities* (informed decision-making, right to privacy, access to health-related information)

Correspondingly, the biblical principles that provide a framework within which we may approach these issues are:

• The sacredness of human life (Gen 1:26-28; Gen 2:7)

- The covenant relationship between God and the Christian (Matt 16:26)
- The concept of biblical justice (Amos 5:24)

Issue One: Reproductive and Life-Saving Technologies

As mentioned in the introduction, medicine has made dramatic advances in technology during the past half century. Due in part to these advances, we now have the ability to keep people alive for an unprecedented length of time, as evidenced by data on average life expectancies in the United States (currently estimated at 74 years for males and 79 years for females[4]). Indeed, American medicine now operates within the parameters of what some have called the *technological imperative*,[5] or the near automatic use of technology in whatever situation it is deemed possible. But in our rush to use technology, have we forgotten to spend sufficient time engaged in considering whether any and all applications of technology are good? In other words, because something is *possible* to do, does it necessarily follow that it *ought* to be done in every circumstance?

> Because something is possible to do, does it necessarily follow that it ought to be done in every circumstance?

Nowhere is this question more pressing than in the realm of technology used to aid human reproduction and to prolong life. Three issues that reflect the rapid advance of medical technology, and associated ethical dilemmas, come to mind immediately: surrogate parenthood, cloning technologies, and organ transplantation. In these three areas, we can readily see how advancing technology creates heretofore unheard-of ethical dilemmas that must be carefully scrutinized from a Christian perspective.

Surrogacy involves the idea of substituting one person in the role of another. So, for example, in certain situations a surrogate decision-maker may be asked to decide about a course of medical treatment for someone who is unable to make decisions on their own. Surrogate parenting involves another person taking the place of the biological mother, typically so that an infertile couple (with a variety of traditional and alternative connotations surrounding the term "couple") can have a child of their own. These types of arrangements in recent years have involved all kinds of scenarios, including:

Assisted reproductive technologies: the use of various types of technological means to achieve pregnancy, including artificial insemination by husband (AIH); artificial insemination by a donor, either known or unknown to the married couple (AID); in vitro fertilization (IVF) and several variations, wherein human embryos are produced either in a petri dish or within a female's fallopian tubes, and then implanted into the woman who will carry out the pregnancy.

Cryo-preservation is a long-term variant of assisted reproductive technology involving the freezing of human zygotes or embryos in various stages of development for later implantation in the female who will carry the child to term.

Surrogate motherhood: the phenomenon of women who are asked to carry an embryo to term and give birth on behalf of someone else; this usually involves payment for their efforts and a host of complicated issues involving the legal rights of the various parties involved.

Sex Selection: the phenomenon of using assisted reproductive techniques or other means (e.g., amniocentesis followed by pregnancy termination) to control the sex of the yet-to-be-born child.

Each of these techniques involves the use of artificial means to achieve human reproduction. These techniques are often presented to the public as the means by which physicians and scientists offer their services to help people who wish to become parents but are unable to do so via the traditional means. Accordingly, these procedures are often viewed as at least noble, if not exactly charitable, since the cost of such procedures is normally quite high.

Cloning technologies are alternative reproductive methods that have recently burst into the limelight in a dramatic fashion. Essentially, to clone something is to produce an identical copy of it by using its DNA. Plants and animals have been successfully cloned within the past decade by means of genetic engineering techniques (e.g., the 1996 successful cloning of "Dolly the sheep" in Britain). Some feel that scientists are close to achieving the level of sophistication necessary to clone human beings. To summarize a complicated process, it is theorized that creating a cloned human being would essentially involve the following steps: DNA is taken from a cell of the human who is to be copied; DNA is also removed from an egg in a lab and replaced with the donor's DNA. The altered egg is then placed in the uterus of the mother, where it is hoped that it will grow to a healthy genetic "copy." One pseudo-scientific group called

Clonaid claimed in December 2002 to have cloned a baby for an infertile couple;[6] however, as of this writing their claims have not been proven and are widely dismissed as propaganda designed to attract more potential members to the Raelian religious cult. While cloning technology is virtually unregulated in the United States at present, a federal ban by the U.S. House of Representatives on the pursuit of cloning technology involving human beings is currently in effect.[7] An important distinction is often made between "therapeutic" and "reproductive" cloning techniques, with the former referring to techniques used to support clinical care of patients by growing replacement tissue and/or organs and the latter referring to efforts to reproduce an entire member of a species.

Reproductive cloning techniques are very unsophisticated at this point, with a failure rate in animals of up to 98%. Nevertheless, several independent groups of scientists may be working toward the ability to clone a human being. These efforts are nearly always described as being motivated by humanitarian ideals, e.g., helping infertile couples achieve their reproductive goals, or helping parents of deceased infants to "replace" them. Such efforts are nearly universally opposed at present on moral grounds by a broad spectrum of governmental, scientific, and citizen groups.

Finally, as we consider the use of technology to save or prolong human life, we hear frequently of *organ transplantation*. This is the term used to describe a variety of techniques whereby tissue, organs, or both are transferred from either one human body to another or from one species to another. This involves the use of materials grafted from both animals and humans. So, for example, defective heart valves in humans are often replaced with the heart valves of pigs; the use of animal organs to replace human organs is known as xenotransplantation. Transplantation of a variety of tissues and organs include procedures involving the heart, lungs, corneas, liver, kidney, blood, plasma, joints, bones, and skin. Included in this general category might also be reference to assistive devices, such as artificial hearts and/or other forms of replacement material and technology designed to supplement or entirely replace existing parts of the human body.

The use of transplantation techniques is not usually controversial from an ethical standpoint, except in cases involving patients who oppose them on religious grounds (e.g., Jehovah's Witnesses who oppose blood transfusions). But ethical dilemmas often occur in the context of deciding who should have *access* to available organs; the *allocation* of available organs; what type of *consent* is needed from donors; and the *financing* of such procedures, including financial incentives for donors.[8] For example, studies have shown that organs are more available to patients who have better financial resources, who are well-known public figures, and who are not members of ethnic or minority groups.

It is apparent that there are many more patients who need transplanted organs to survive than there are available organs to give them. Given that fact, what process should be followed in making decisions about who gets the organs and who doesn't? Answers to that question are often complex and hotly debated among patients, their families, physicians, hospital administrators, insurance executives, politicians, and medical ethicists. Various approaches to organ donation and allocation have been implemented, either at a national or regional level; the most prominent is UNOS, the United Network of Organ Sharing. Systems of organ allocation are based on a variety of criteria related to the degree of patient illness and other factors. For many involved, the degree of desperation to obtain a life-saving organ leads to ethically questionable procurement procedures such as the buying and selling of organs, or the harvesting of organs from persons either not legally dead or newly-deceased. The issue of when actual physiological death occurs has been prominent in recent years, with debate often spurred by an interest in obtaining transplantable organs. The apparent willingness of at least some medical practitioners to engage in questionable practices has led one scholar to observe that, in the past decade, a dramatic shift in thinking about organ procurement has taken place:

> . . . an approach to organ acquisition that was once almost universally condemned by medical professionals engaged in transplantation, medical ethicists and politicians is now openly debated and . . . is soon to be implemented . . . are doctors and others associated with transplantation medicine leading public reconsideration of ethical positions, or are they merely responding to changing societal attitudes?[9]

In summary, there are many compelling and complex ethical dilemmas surrounding the use of technology, both in terms of human reproduction and the extension of human life via organ transplantation. We have barely scratched the surface here. But what does the Bible tell us about these issues?

Genesis 1 and 2: God and the Sacredness of Human Life

So God created man in his own image, in the image of God he created him; male and female he created them (Gen 1:27).

The LORD God formed the man from the dust of the ground and breathed into his nostrils the breath of life, and the man became a living being (Gen 2:7).

A basic biblical principle that provides part of the framework for the Christian understanding of bioethics issues is that God is the author of life. The witness of Scripture is that human life (and indeed all creation) is sacred because it comes from the hand of a benevolent, creator God. Since God is the author/creator of life, decisions concerning reproductive and life-sustaining technologies should be made by the Christian within that overarching framework.

> A basic biblical principle that provides part of the framework for the Christian understanding of bioethics issues is that God is the author of life.

There have been various opinions expressed by both Catholic and Protestant theologians concerning the previously described artificial techniques used to assist with reproduction. It is necessary for the Christian to think about procreation within the framework of marriage, another human institution established by God within Scripture ("For this reason a man will leave his father and mother and be united with his wife, and they will become one flesh," Gen 2:24). It is only by thinking seriously about the divine purpose in human creation, marriage, and sexuality that we can consider all of the ethical ramifications of the use of technology in aiding human reproduction.

Generally speaking, the use of artificial means to assist human reproduction within the confines of the marital relationship has been accepted within the Protestant tradition as ethically sound. However, the introduction of "third party" arrangements within the confines of the marital relationship (e.g., surrogate motherhood, artificial insemination by anonymous donors) have been considered less acceptable and/or consistent with Christian tradition and respect for the sanctity of human life. And, where those means of artificial reproduction involve the actual creation and/or destruction of human embryos, Christians have most often stated firm opposition. Such actions are viewed by many as a form of "playing God," defined as an unwarranted intrusion into the realm of the basic building blocks of life (as in the case of cloning); or the destruction of human life itself (as in the destruction of embryos, the sex selection of children, and abortion). Conservative Christian tradition has stipulated that life is a gift from God

> Life is a gift from God to be viewed as sacred because it is from God and shall return to God.

and is to be viewed as sacred because it is from God and shall return to God. Christians have often argued that there must be limits on the use of reproductive technology, even for purposes that are considered by some to be noble, for fear of usurping the authority of God in granting the gift of life.

Regarding the use of life-saving technology via organ transplantation, consensus appears to exist among Christian traditions that such procedures are morally acceptable as long as the dignity and inherent worth of each individual (both organ donors and recipients) is upheld. The recent trend toward commercialization within the organ transplant marketplace, however, is inconsistent with a Christian view. The buying and selling of organs for profit serves to dehumanize and devalue the worth of the individual and is in opposition to the principle of the inherent sacredness of life granted by the creator God.

Part of the reason for ethical controversy surrounding organ allocation is the well-documented fact that organs are scarce. While it would be presumptuous to suggest that all Christians have a moral obligation to become organ donors, it is nevertheless important to point out that a concerted effort on the part of the Church to persuade its members to become organ donors would likely do much to relieve the shortage. The altruistic approach to solving this problem, as opposed to the commercial approach involving buying and selling organs, is ethically preferred. And studies have shown that bereavement on the part of loved ones is lessened somewhat by the fact that organ donation takes place. Survivors often report feeling assisted in their grief recovery by the knowledge that organ donation helps others have life; this knowledge often helps them make sense of the circumstances surrounding the loss of a loved one.

In summary, the biblical principle of the sacredness of human life compels the Christian to think seriously about the use of technology in the realm of human reproduction and sustaining of life. To the extent that such technology is used in a manner that does not usurp the authority of God the creator, or does not serve to dehumanize the individuals involved, it is likely acceptable to most Protestant traditions.

Issue Two: The Role of Human Genetics in Health Care

The structure of the human DNA molecule was discovered in the 1950s. Thus, the door was opened for scientists to recombine genetic material across organisms for the purpose of creating new entities. The *mapping of the human genome*, or the identification of all of the approximately 30,000 strands of human DNA, was begun in earnest by the United States government in 1990.[10] The ultimate goals of this ambitious project are 1) to identify the genetic components of disease and 2) to suggest medical applications for disease prevention and treatment that currently do not exist. Advances in genetic markers for various diseases since that time have been widely publicized and debated, particularly with reference to the various ethical, legal, and social issues involved. In fact, one section of the federal government's human genome project web site (ELSI) is devoted to consideration of the nonbiological aspects of this work, and to describing how various funded research projects have explored those issues.

As with nearly any type of technology, it is apparent that genetic technologies can be used for purposes that are viewed as morally good or morally questionable. Certainly the identification of the genetic characteristics of given diseases, with the resulting opportunity to develop better treatments, would be viewed positively by most people. However, the use of human embryos in research is morally questionable, and patient records containing information about genetic predisposition to certain diseases by a given individual could be used negatively. For example, health or life insurance companies could deny coverage for people who have the genetic potential to develop diseases in the future, or manufacturing companies could deny employment to individuals who might develop diseases and contribute to lower productivity. Concern has been expressed about the potential characterization of certain groups of people (e.g., racial or ethnic minorities) as "genetically inferior," paving the way for resulting discriminatory practices. And, there is controversy about the patenting of the human genome by private companies. The sequencing of human DNA represents "a broad array of commercial opportunities" in such areas as clinical medicine, agriculture, industrial processes, environmental biotechnology, and the use of DNA fingerprinting.[11]

One of the most exciting, yet ethically troublesome, aspects of the human genome project concerns *gene therapy*, or the treatment of disease by methods involving the replacement of defective, diseased genes with healthy genes. This technology involves the development of new genes in laboratories and the introduction of them into patients via the use of a virus. Research is underway into gene therapy and its application to such chronic illnesses as cancer and Alzheimer's disease. Advocates state that the potential exists via gene therapy to provide cures for these and many other diseases, as well as to reverse such conditions as paralysis due to spinal cord injury. Such methods are very new, highly experimental, very expensive, and accompanied by controversy. Ethical dilemmas associated with gene therapy often focus on the recruitment of patients who serve as research subjects, the process of informed consent for participation by those patients, and the financial arrangements of the various parties involved. There have been several well-publicized deaths from gene therapy protocols, including the death of 18-year old Jesse Gelsinger at the University of Pennsylvania in September 1999.[12] Side effects of gene therapy are often related to the virus used to carry the new gene into the patient. Gene therapy research was suspended nationally for a time as a result of the Gelsinger case, and again more recently by unanticipated side effects involving gene therapy trials with children in Europe.[13]

Related to genetic issues in bioethics is another issue, that of *stem cell research*. Stem cells are defined as "undifferentiated, primitive cells in the bone marrow that have the ability both to multiply and to differentiate into specific blood cells."[14] In other words, stem cells are the basic cells from which subsequent human development takes place. There are two categories of stem cells: *embryonic* stem cells (cells that can replicate indefinitely, transform into other types of cells, and serve as a continuous source of new cells); and *adult* or somatic stem cells (undifferentiated cells found in a tissue or organ that can renew themselves and differentiate to yield the major specialized cell types of the tissue).[15] The primary difference between these types of stem cells pertains to their potential use. The primary role of an adult stem cell is to maintain and repair the tissue in which they are found. The primary role of an embryonic stem cell is to become more developed cells. The embryonic stem cell is often viewed as a "building block" cell. Normally, embryonic stem cells are derived from an egg fertilization process that takes place in the laboratory and not from a fertilization process occurring within a woman's body. Both types of stem cells have been used in research to determine whether diseased tissues can be successfully replaced or replenished with tissues grown by use of stem cells. For example, studies have shown that blood transfusions using blood taken from the placenta and/or umbilical cord of a mother is rich in stem cells and more clinically effective. And bone marrow transplants are thought to be successful largely because they involve stem cells.

The ethical controversy pertaining to stem cells is largely focused on the moral status of embryos and whether it is ethical to destroy human embryos as part of the harvesting process used to obtain stem cells. Stem cells can also be obtained from the remains of aborted human fetuses, a practice morally objectionable to many people. It is important to note that much remains unknown about whether adult or embryonic stem cells are actually more effective in treating disease and, if so, why. Adult stem cell lines have already been used for clinical benefit to patients with such diseases as diabetes, Parkinson's disease, and heart disease. In fact, there is more research evidence at the present time to support the use of adult stem cells for medical therapeutic purposes than for embryonic stem cells. However, proponents of using embryonic stem cells indicate that "non-embryonic stem cells are less able to differentiate into multiple cell types or be sustained in the laboratory over an extended period of time—rendering them less medically promising than embryonic stem cells."[16]

Finally, it must be noted that stem cell research and human cloning are closely related. Techniques of therapeutic cloning involve the removal of stem cells from the pre-embryo with the intent of producing tissue or a whole organ for transplant back into the person who supplied the DNA. The goal of this procedure is to produce an identical tissue or organ for transplant. This technique is advocated as superior to receiving organ transplants from other people in that it would minimize waiting times for organs; minimize or eliminate the potential for organ rejection; and eliminate the need for immunosuppressant drugs. However, these techniques are in the very early stages in the laboratory with little to no proof of utility.

We can readily see the dazzling array of scientific advances in the area of human genetics. But are all of these techniques ethical? How does our Christian perspective inform our thinking on these matters?

The Covenant Relationship between God and the Christian

Let us make man in our image. . . . and let them rule over the fish of the sea and the birds of the air (Gen 1:26).

What is man that you are mindful of him? . . . you made him a little lower than the heavenly beings . . . and made him ruler over the works of your hands (Ps 8:4-6).

Now we know that if the earthly tent we live in is destroyed, we have a building from God, an eternal house in heaven, not built by human hands (2 Cor 5:1).

For he was looking forward to the city with foundations, whose architect and builder is God (Heb 11:10).

A second biblical principle that provides part of the framework for the Christian understanding of bioethics issues is the covenant relationship between God and man. The Bible makes it clear that man is created by God and that God desires to have a relationship with those among his created beings who wish to know him in return. God seeks to enter into relationship with man, and the nature of that relationship is defined by a covenant, or an agreement between him and us. The nature of that agreement is that God has created us; has redeemed us from the penalty of sin and death; seeks our best interest in the midst of a sinful, fallen world; and wants us to walk with him in obedience to his divine truth. When we understand human life in this context, it radically redefines the meaning of human existence and leads to new insight into why we are here and where we are ultimately headed. All of our knowledge about medical science, therefore, must be understood within the context of this covenant relationship with

> "Now we know that if the earthly tent we live in is destroyed, we have a building from God, . . . not built by human hands"

God. Knowledge of any particular subject is useful only to the extent that it is informed by godly wisdom. And wisdom is defined as that which we can know in relationship to God the creator.

In many respects, the current state of ethical discourse is a reflection of man's pursuit of human knowledge apart from godly wisdom. Do we have the right to "play God" and insert ourselves into such matters as the actual creation of life itself? While we are probably still very far away from seeing a human being actually cloned, it is not unreasonable to assume that science will eventually reach this goal. The present distinction between therapeutic and reproductive human cloning is somewhat artificial. We are on the verge of unimaginable scientific achievements. But are these achievements good for mankind, as so many scientists proclaim, or will they lead to unalterable changes in the conduct of human existence?

> The current state of ethical discourse is a reflection of man's pursuit of human knowledge apart from godly wisdom.

So much of what we decide is moral in these matters really depends on our viewpoint concerning life and its purpose. If the present life is the ultimate goal of human existence, with no possibility of an afterlife, then why not do anything to preserve and improve it? But if our relationship to God and our eternal destiny are what ultimately matter the most, perhaps at least some of the techniques being advocated as part of today's "brave new genetic world" should be questioned. For example, research involving embryonic stem cells compels us to decide whether a consistent ethic of the sacredness of human life affects our views on the destruction of human embryos for any purpose (no matter how noble).

Within the context of a covenant relationship with God, it appears that such practices as cloning and some forms of stem cell research (particularly those involving the destruction of embryos) are ethically questionable from a Christian perspective. The covenant relationship with God sets the boundaries beyond which we dare not go. Human embryos deserve the respect and protection provided for them by the Judeo-Christian tradition; they should not be viewed as a

> If our relationship to God and our eternal destiny are what ultimately matter the most, perhaps at least some of these new medical techniques should be questioned.

means to an end. And, human beings should be viewed as more than simply a collection of genetic parts, markers, or categories (a dehumanizing and reductionistic philosophy that is pervasive within the scientific community). The covenant relationship between God and man clearly demonstrates that he does

> Human embryos deserve the respect and protection provided for them by the Judeo-Christian tradition; they should not be viewed as a means to an end.

not view us in this way at all. While the scientific study of human life and all of its complexities can certainly be proper and good, such study must only be undertaken within the overall constraints of what scriptural principles allow.

It is equally troubling to view genetics as a means to an end because we must ask "to what end?" The witness of Scripture reveals that God is the ultimate source of human life and destiny. The question of when a human being becomes fully human (i.e., at what point in the developmental process) is a genuine one. We simply cannot know the answer to this question, nor were we meant to know. This responsibility belongs to the creator, not the created. To interfere in the design of the creator not only usurps his authority and risks damage to the covenantal relationship between God and man, it may also lead to eventual imbalances in the genetic diversity intended by the creator.

In summary, the biblical principle of the covenant relationship between God and man requires us to think seriously about the ethical aspects of genetic techniques. To the extent that such techniques interfere with the designs of the creator and the conditions of our relationship with him, they are unacceptable to the Christian.

Issue Three: Patients' Rights and Responsibilities

In light of the advances described previously, a third important issue for our consideration pertains to the role of patients in our modern health care system. With few exceptions, gone are the days when we can simply walk into a physician's office, be seen by the same doctor each time we are sick, and expect the doctor's staff to send a form to our insurance company so our bill can be paid. Our task as consumers has become far more complex, and recent surveys indicate widespread dissatisfaction with our current health care delivery system.[17] An important feature of today's system is the fact that responsibility for figuring out how to obtain necessary care has been shifted to the consumer. Included in this responsibility is the need for each of us to be fully informed of our rights and responsibilities as patients.

Informed consent is a doctrine intended to ensure that patients have the right to agree to participate in medical care only after they have been fully informed as to the nature of the treatment, alternative treatments, and potential risks as well as benefits of possible treatments. Given the highly experimental nature of many of the technological procedures previously described, informed consent is an important issue not only in routine care but particularly in cases where technology of various kinds are to be used to sustain life; or in cases where patients are asked to participate in clinical research trials involving the investigation of new drugs, medical devices, or procedures.

Briefly, there are four aspects of informed consent that are important to consider: competence, disclosure, comprehension, and voluntariness.[18] *Competence* basically refers to a person's capacity to make decisions. A patient may be fully or partially competent to make his/her own decisions about treatment or may be deemed to be incompetent, thus requiring decisions to be made by a surrogate decision-maker. Legal procedures must be strictly followed in order to determine the competence of a patient. *Disclosure* refers to the provision of all relevant information about a patient's medical condition to the patient or other decision-maker, so that he/she can make fully informed decisions. Disclosure of all potential risks and harms of a given medical treatment or intervention must be provided, particularly where procedures are experimental or part of a research protocol. Common criticisms of the process typically followed to obtain informed consent from patients is that the language used (most notably on consent forms) is not easily understandable, that the person explaining the procedure to the patient may not be fully aware of all risks and benefits involved, or that the person explaining the procedure is unwilling to take the time to explain the information adequately. *Comprehension* refers to the ability of a patient to understand the information provided to him or her about medical treatment and is closely related to competence. Often the use of technological means to prolong life takes place in a setting where time is of the essence and decisions must be made rapidly. Such circumstances are often emotional and may lead to situations where full comprehension on the part of patients (or their family members) is not achieved. *Voluntariness* refers to the ability of a patient to make a fully informed decision or choice about treatment without undue influence, pressure, or coercion from anyone.

Because of well-publicized lapses in the system of obtaining informed consent from patients (or surrogate decision-makers), with resulting harms done to patients unwittingly involved in medical experimentation, the U.S. government has established a system of institutional review boards (IRBs). The purpose of the IRB system is to review medical treatment protocols that involve research and/or experimentation of new therapies on humans as well as animals.[19] These review boards primarily function through a process of peer review that requires strict attention to informed consent, sound research design prior to launching clinical trials, and periodic external review of results.

Related to the need to be fully informed and provide consent for all aspects of treatment and/or patient-oriented research, other aspects of this issue are the *right to privacy* and *control of access to health-related information*. Most notably, a major shift to computerized patient records has taken place within modern health care. While many operating efficiencies are felt to occur with the use of computers, great risk exists pertaining to unauthorized use of computerized health information about patients—in other words, about us. A recent report by the Institute of Medicine summarizes this issue succinctly:

> The computerization of most types of record keeping, as well as the recent well-publicized cases of inappropriate access by computer hackers, has increased concerns about the misuse of personal information.[20]

Concerns about the use of computer technology include a lack of standards about how to exchange medical data across entities or geographic locations; a lack of consistent security features for computerized systems; and the use of record numbers that are accessible to nonauthorized parties and can be used to identify patients.

Today's health care system leaves patients vulnerable to having their basic rights violated in many ways. Does the Bible address this issue? If so, how?

Amos 5:24 and God's Justice

But let justice roll on like a river, righteousness like a never-failing stream! (Amos 5:24).

A third biblical principle provides part of the framework for the Christian understanding of bioethics issues, that of biblical justice. The issues surrounding privacy concerns, right of access to health information, and informed consent can be viewed within this concept. In spite of the existence of a complex system designed to provide legal justice for criminals and their victims, the biblical doctrine of justice is much neglected in modern American culture. Biblical justice is defined as the active pursuit of equality for all people, in recognition of their inherent dignity and worth. Aptly defined,

> Biblical justice is defined as the active pursuit of equality for all people, in recognition of their inherent dignity and worth.

Justice in the biblical sense is achieved when each person has what she or he needs to survive, to develop and thrive, and to give back to the community. It recognizes the right of each person to share in the goods of creation to that extent. Equality of opportunity is not adequate to define true biblical justice.[21]

Informed consent is specifically designed to provide equal protection to all patients, regardless of their economic status, ethnic group, or any other characteristics. The history of this doctrine reveals a gradual evolution in the thinking of medical professionals and researchers, from a paternalistic approach that revealed little to patients to today's model that encourages the complete exchange of information between doctor and patient. To neglect to inform patients, including research subjects, of all risks associated with a given research protocol as well as their right to refuse participation or treatment is clearly unethical and implicitly inconsistent with the biblical justice principle. This still happens, in spite of a federally mandated system designed to prevent it. Some have described the IRB system as inherently flawed, due to its being based on peer review; such review is tantamount to self-regulation and (according to critics) seriously compromised by financial conflict of interest. Christians must work toward justice in all spheres, including this one. All institutional review boards have one or two positions open to lay persons. This presents an opportunity for Christians to become involved in working for biblical justice for all.

The same principle of biblical justice can be applied to the issues of privacy of health-related information. The use of such information to discriminate in any manner (due to genetic or other health information found within patient files) clearly violates the justice principle. Steps should be taken to ensure that unauthorized access to private health information is prohibited.

It appears that little Christian influence has taken place in the realm of justice issues surrounding the allocation of organs to patients who need them. A prominent theme of Scripture is the need for justice, particularly for the poor and disadvantaged. Unfortunately, in modern society access to health care (including expensive organ transplant procedures) often seems to be based primarily on financial means. Justice is not served well by such a system. And while answers to difficult questions concerning who should receive available organs are not easy, Christians should work toward a more equitable system of resource allocation that considers other factors in addition to ability to pay.

The principle of justice requires the Christian to demonstrate compassion and concern for all, with special concern for those who are poor, downtrodden, and outcast. With rare exception, this approach to caring for the less fortunate is starkly absent from the modern health care system. And it is all too easy to take advantage of people without means when it comes to seeking patients for medical experimentation and/or clinical trials. Biblical justice demands a different approach.

Conclusions

Today, we still yearn to know why we are here and where we came from.
—Stephen Hawking

This statement from one of the most brilliant scientific minds in modern history demonstrates that science, for all of its knowledge, still has much to learn about the purpose and meaning of life. Medical science can contribute to the development of biblical wisdom, but cannot replace it. New ethical challenges loom before us, and Christians today face those challenges with some degree of uncertainty. Nevertheless, our faith in God and the biblical record of his express intentions for mankind will make us aware that reliance on wisdom, and not just knowledge, will enable us to clearly navigate the turbulent waters ahead.

We began this chapter with a question. Confronted with troubling and ethical dilemmas, what course of action should the Christian take? I hope that the reader has come to realize the complexity of bioethics issues. This and other chapters in this volume make it clear that ethical dilemmas are often agonizingly difficult to deal with. Yet, attention to clearly revealed biblical principles can make such decisions easier. Biblical principles provide a guiding framework within which we can discuss specific bioethics issues facing the modern church.

> In a very real sense, the Christian response to a complex ethical dilemma is a reflection of not just what should be done, but rather "what kind of people should we be?"

In a very real sense, the Christian response to a complex ethical dilemma is a reflection of not just what should be done, but rather "what kind of people should we be?" The commitment to "act justly, love mercy and walk humbly with your God" (Micah 6: 8b) will serve the Christian well in those circumstances where ethical dilemmas are real—for us and those we love.

Notes

[1] J.F. Haas and CA Mackenzie, "The Role of Ethics in Rehabilitation Medicine: Introduction to a Series," *American Journal of Physical Medicine & Rehabilitation* 72/1 (1993) 48.

[2] J.J. Davis, *Evangelical Ethics: Issues Facing the Church Today* (Phillipsburg, NJ: Presbyterian and Reformed, 1995).

[3] Haas, "Ethics in Rehabilitation."

[4] Center for Disease Control, National Center for Health Statistics, 2002, http://www.cdc.gov/nchs/fastats/lifexpec.htm (as of Nov. 2003).

[5] A. Steinberg, "The Foundations and the Development of Modern Medical Ethics," *Journal of Assisted Reproduction and Genetics* 12 (1995) 473.

[6] "Cult Claims First Cloned Human," *Sydney Morning Herald* (December 29, 2002) http://www.smh.com.au/articles/2002/12/29/1040511243558.html (as of Nov. 2003).

[7] "House Votes to Ban Human Cloning," Cable News Network (August 1, 2001) http://www.cnn.com/2001/ALLPOLITICS/07/31/cloning.bush/ (as of Nov. 2003).

[8] A.L. Caplan and Daniel H. Coelho, eds., *The Ethics of Organ Transplants: The Current Debate* (Amherst, NY: Prometheus Books, 1998); D. Joralemon, "Shifting Ethics: Debating The Incentive Question in Organ Transplantation," *Journal of Medical Ethics* 27 (2001) 30-35.

[9] Caplan and Coelho, *Organ Transplants.*

[10]U.S. Department of Energy, Office of Science, *Human Genome Project Information* (2002) http://www.ornl.gov/hgmis/.

[11]Ibid.

[12]*University of Pennsylvania Almanac* (October 5, 1991) http://www.upenn.edu/almanac/v46/n06/deaths.html.

[13]"Regulations Split on Gene Therapy as Patient Shows Signs of Cancer," *Nature* 419 (10 October 2002) 545-546.

[14]U.S. Department of Energy, *Genome Project.*

[15]Ibid.

[16]Center for Bioethics & Human Dignity (2002) http://cbhd.org/resources/overviews/stemcell.html.

[17]"The Health Security Act Would Provide Health Care to All Americans," American Medical Student Association (2003) https://www.amsa.org/hp/mcdermott.cfm.

[18]T.A. Shannon, *An Introduction to Bioethics* (Mahwah, NJ: Paulist Press, 1997).

[19]*Guidebook on Human Subject Protections*, US Department of Health and Human Services, Office for Human Research Protections (2002) http://ohrp.osophs.dhhs.gov/irb/irb_guidebook.htm.

[20]R.S. Dick and E.B. Steen, eds., *The Computer-Based Patient Record: An Essential Technology for Health Care* (Washington, DC: National Academy Press, 1991).

[21]Canadian Catholic Conference, Center of Concern (2002) http://www.coc.org/index.html.

Bibliography

Amundsen, D.A. *Medicine, Society and Faith in the Ancient and Medieval Worlds.* Baltimore: Johns Hopkins University Press, 1996.

A collection of essays focusing on the history of medicine.

Davis, J.J. *Evangelical Ethics: Issues Facing the Church Today.* Phillipsburg, NJ: Presbyterian and Reformed, 1995.

An excellent overview of classic ethical issues in the broad sense.

Jonsen, A.R., M. Siegler, and W.J. Winslade. *Clinical Ethics.* New York: McGraw-Hill Health Professions, 1998.

A classic "how to" manual pertaining to bioethics issues.

Shannon, T.A. *An Introduction to Bioethics.* Mahwah, NJ: Paulist Press, 1997.

An excellent introduction to biomedical ethical issues.

Sulmasy, D.P. *The Healer's Calling: A Spirituality for Physicians and Other Health Care Professionals.* Mahwah, NJ: Paulist Press, 1997.

A wonderful overview of how spirituality can inform health care practice. The author is a practicing physician and Jesuit priest.

Web Sites

The Center for Bioethics and Human Dignity.
http://www.cbhd.org/ (as of Nov. 2003).
The Center for Applied Christian Ethics.
http://www.wheaton.edu/CACE/ (as of Nov. 2003).
The National Catholic Bioethics Center.
http://www.ncbcenter.org/home.html (as of Nov. 2003).
Christian Ethics Today.
http://www.christianethicstoday.com/index.htm (as of Nov. 2003).
Do No Harm: The Coalition of Americans for Research Ethics.
http://www.stemcellresearch.org (as of Nov. 2003).

TO CARE FOR THE DYING IS TO AFFIRM LIFE

Gregory W. Rutecki, M.D.

> **Acknowledgments**
>
> *To my pastors, present and past, who nurtured my spiritual insight into medical ethics with sermons that opened up Scripture. To Greg Nettle at Rivertree Christian Church whose exegesis of 2 Timothy discussed in this paper influenced my thinking. That sermon revolutionized my ministry to the dying. To Marty Voltz in Deerfield who reminds me every Sunday that God's word is a "double-edged sword" and that "we have forsaken the illusion of strength for the confession of need." His "Incarnational principle" to nourish a biblical source for care is right on! Also, his efforts to clearly preach God's word is a wonderful addition to my life.*

For we who, thanks to medicine are living longer, are living long enough to finish in protracted periods of debility, dementia, dependence, and disgrace—with medicine impotent to do more than treat the supervening acute infections that, left untreated, would allow us a merciful exit. What are we to do? Many still look to science in hope of further triumphs in the war against mortality and decay. Others, in despair here and now, want to exercise greater control over the end of life by electing death to avoid the burdens of lingering on. The failures resulting from attempts to rule over death are to be resolved by placing death still further under our own control.[1]

What is Truth? Although a fundamental question, the response has ramifications that touch everyone. For contemporaries it has become a confusing discussion since the answer has been debated,

| What is truth? |

implicitly or explicitly, from many worldview perspectives. The claims addressed involve each and every aspect of life. The dialogue has become *the* central issue for the age because, in the words of pop culture's Maximus the Gladiator, the answers will echo throughout eternity. Why? Because truth, whether in politics, medicine, or business, is *the* compass for everything valued as good, or better yet, as godly. Unfortunately, however, along a narrow way, something insidious has happened. Like Dorothy and Toto, truth is not in Kansas anymore. Or as the comedian Mort Sahl quipped with the author's paraphrase, "Washington never told a lie, Clinton never told the truth, and *we can't tell the differ-ence.*"[2] What is at stake in the search for truth in the bioethics arena is noth-ing less than answering the question as to whether beings are created in the image of God. The importance of truth claims can be underscored through a

| *What is at stake is nothing less than the question as to whether beings are created in the image of God.* |

sampling of medicine's recent queries: Does life begin at conception? Is cloning moral? And for the purposes of this chapter, can the dying choose to end their lives?

Two value systems, one absolute, the other relative, are com-peting for preeminence amidst the diversity comprising Western Culture. They are, therefore, locked in a spiritual struggle to define truth. The postmodern or relative view has freed itself from the "con-straints" of metanarratives such as the Bible. The fallout of the resultant intoxicating freedom is a tolerance of what has previously been deemed immoral. For medicine, the quest has eventuated in an inquiry concerning what it means to be human. This is a disturbing realm, one where Western culture has never dared to tread. In seek-ing to redefine membership criteria for humanity, among other things, society has begun its examination of how we die. Long-agreed-upon beliefs regarding human dignity have been challenged. The dying have been relegated to the fringes of humanity. It has now been accepted by many that the "unexamined death is no longer worth dying." Examination has evolved into pride and autonomy. How prevalent has this irreverence towards the dying become? The quote by Leon Kass that begins this chapter warns of a pervasive ethic that places death under the control of creatures, not their cre-ator. That control is euthanasia.

The correct answer to how we should die should be derived from a single source. How would the Bible respond to questions of truth in the context of dying? How would Scripture model responses for those who want to affirm God's image in those who die? This chapter will address those questions in three segments. The first will lay a foundation and is drawn from John 1:14; Matthew 14:14; and 2 Timothy 4:9-18. The texts will identify ministry. The needs of the dying will be contrasted historically with an erosion of what it means to care. The reductionism of assisted suicide can arguably be attributed to the vacuum created by an absence of care. That vacuum is now being filled by death-hastening. The devaluation of care occurred when cure became Medicine's prime directive. That change developed amidst society's demands for longer lives. Next, it will be asked how the Church can fill that vacuum. Jesus' example in the Garden of Gethsemane will be explored in this regard. It will lead to hospice as a response to the crisis of care. Other biblical examples of care, Old and New Testament, will be provided. Finally, the biblical case against assisted suicide will be presented as diametrically opposing medicine's contemporary ethic, a view that eliminates suffering by eliminating the sufferer. Examples of individuals who have affirmed life will be shared in the conclusion.

What Do the Dying Need?
Care in All Its Simplicity (2 Tim 4:9-18)

> Physicians in young America enjoyed little status. They had sparse knowledge of disease causation, and communication was primitive. They attempted to compensate for these inadequacies with highly individualized *care*, usually conducted in the patient's home. They maintained an attentive bedside vigil, often shared with clergy. Profound changes followed. . . . the modern hospital separated the seriously ill, including the well-to-do, from their *communities* and, to some extent, from *caring* families.[3]

This segment will establish the centrality of care in the biblical tradition. In so doing, it will begin to explain the desire for a hastened death, as a contingent of not caring. The truth of care and the fallout incumbent upon its absence have even become a reality to a post-Christian culture. A publication from Johns Hopkins' Medical

Press entitled, *The Lost Art of Caring*, has generated discussion in this regard.[4] Culture has noticed that medical care is not all that it's cracked up to be. Why, when today's medical establishment has conquered diseases that were lethal less than a century ago? Because cure will never replace care. God created us as beings with multiple dimensions, physical, emotional, social, and spiritual. "True" medicine does not only address the physical.[5] We must now confront medicine's purpose, since it has been distorted. Can medicine be authentic with more cure, but less care? Cure, in addressing the physical, ignores the emotional, the social, and the spiritual. Truth in the manner of dying can be found in the definition for care accepted by a given culture. Why? How society *cares* for the dying when they no longer can be *cured*, is the root cause for analysis. How a culture responds to the vulnerable tells us about its ethos. One reviewer of the aforementioned book has said,

> *Culture has noticed that medical care is not all that it's cracked up to be.*

> At the very heart of the spirit of medicine . . . is the act of a caring relationship with patients. This relationship is never an abstraction . . . and is threatened at the turn of the century by well-known factors such as technology, reductionistic [sic] science, and economic stresses . . . today's care, caring, and curing are clearly distinguished.[6]

Therefore, what is required is a definition for *care* that is scriptural.

Care from a biblical perspective should be a universal attribute of Christians. Advances in technology and the ability to cure disease does not negate the imperative to care. Care, in every nuance, from the widow to the homeless to the sick and, for our purposes, to the dying, must be integral to ministry. On the most fundamental level, care is contained in the *Incarnational Principle* (John 1:14ff.). The Word was made *flesh* and dwelled among us. That dwelling was characterized by the Word's intimate response to every human need. Whether at the calling of Nathaniel, the Samaritan woman at the well, Nicodemus's seeking, or the healings and the raisings, Jesus, as God made flesh, addressed need by personal contact. The Lord had

> *The Lord had compassion, the emotion of care, on his people first, and only then did he cure.*

compassion, the emotion of care, on his people first, and only then did he cure (Matt 14:14).[7]

It is Paul's description of ministry at the end of life in 2 Timothy 4:9-18 that will serve as a relevant model of biblical care.[8] Paul's prison experience, one into which the reality of death must have intruded every moment, speaks volumes about those who walk through the valley of the shadow of death. What do they ask for as they face the last enemy? A cloak for warmth (v. 13), the Word of God (v. 13b), and the company of believers for the sharing of intimacy and grace (v. 9,10). Paul said poignantly, "only Luke is with me" (v. 11). What is Paul saying to us? We as a community share the common experience of grace. Therefore, we should know what it is to receive what we don't deserve. In the pro-

> We all need God, and the extension of His loving-kindness comes through a community committed to filling needs.

cess of needing, we have had to learn that grace is our *only* hope. *We have forsaken the illusion of strength for the confession of need.* We all need God, and the extension of His *loving-kindness* comes through a community committed to filling needs. Can anyone think of a moment that better encapsulates need, the absence of strength, and an anguished cry than the moment of death?

Although the needs of the dying seem simple enough, the simplicity itself is deceptive. It is true that before medicine developed its

> Although the needs of the dying seem simple enough, the simplicity itself is deceptive.

impressive array of curative technologies, people modeled care for the dying. Since this contention stands in contrast to contemporary standards, it will be fleshed out. Christians must take stock of the spirit of this age, and therefore the devolution of care will be pursued.

A photographic anthology roughly covering the years 1840–1940 contained an old "black and white" picture captioned, "*Comfort in the absence of cure*," from the late 1850s.[9] Two individuals were depicted. A physician was leaning over a patient who had just died. The physician had apparently spent the night with the patient. Only the intimacy of care echoed from the picture—no need for CT scans, dialysis machines, or ventilators. The accompanying legend read, "Physician Jonathan Letterman soothes a dying patient. When this picture was taken, there was often little else a doctor could do for the very ill." I have commented elsewhere as to how foreign the photograph seemed to what I had experienced of contemporary medicine.[10]

Unfortunately, today's images portraying terminal care are different. Take the case of Joseph Sauder as an example. Mr. Sauder was a postmodern "everyman" facing death in today's hospital.[11] His illness was terminal and resulted in an irreversible coma. At the request of his family, and after appropriate consultation with his physician, Mr. Sauder was removed from life support. The discontinuation spectacle that followed became a nightmare. Mr. Sauder gasped uncomfortably for breath. The battle was witnessed only by a nurse who was left alone to "care" for Mr. Sauder during his last moments. There were no family, no friends, and no one from the medical team who seemed to really care. The nurse, who only had 18 months of prior experience, was so distraught at Mr. Sauder's predicament that he administered a lethal dose of potassium chloride killing Mr. Sauder. Arthur W. Frank addressed Mr. Sauder's death in *Not in Pain but Sill Suffering*.

> Many physicians would have stayed with their patient until death had occurred. Whatever relationships Mr. Sauder's physicians had with their patient, they defined their task as completed when the patient's death was immanent [sic]. No more medical decisions remained to be made, and their expertise was undoubtedly required elsewhere. Mr. Sauder was left with a nurse who had qualified 18 months earlier. Just dying isn't much of a medical event, as urban hospital practice goes.[12]

What has changed over the last 150 years? Marvin Olasky has described a semantic concept coined "connotative transitions."[13] The Polish writer Chester Milosz describes the same phenomenon under the rubric of semantic misunderstandings.[14] The word *care* has been emasculated in its cultural transition, i.e., stripped of biblical power. The historical exercise is necessary because the change in semantics is parallel to the loss of respect for the Bible. Society has come to understand care in a very different, more limited sense.

> *Society has come to understand care in a very different, more limited sense.*

The first edition of Webster's dictionary (1834) defined compassion as "*suffering with another* or painful sympathy."[15] This definition is consistent with Scripture. Afterwards, there was a ratcheting down in the meaning of care in the second edition of Webster's as, "the feeling or emotion when a person is moved by the suffering or the distress of another and by the desire to relieve it." Note that suffering *with* and *painful* have been replaced by feeling without action. Finally, contemporaries have stripped the definition of compassion/care to a, "deep feeling for and understanding of misery or suffering and the concomitant desire to promote its alleviation." Dr. Letterman inhabited a culture in which care and compassion required *suffering with*. Mr. Sauder died within a culture that did not understand care. Let us try a contemporary sound bite. When you care enough to send the very best, do you send flowers, a card, or better yet, model real care—by sending yourself?

Olasky also dissects the evolution of another word, *stingy*, and places it in Scriptural context. Now reserved solely for the miserly, our predecessors described individuals as stingy when they would not part with whatever they valued *most*. Olasky says that the priest and the Levite, rather than the good Samaritan, were stingy. In his words, "the priest and the Levite who passed by the beaten traveler in chapter ten of Luke's Gospel probably tithed but they were *stingy – only the good Samaritan was not*." Luke 10:25-37 is another paradigm for care. He, the Good Samaritan, "bandaged" his wounds, gave the injured his only source of transportation, then he walked alongside and provided for the man's ongoing care by a financial sacrifice. Why were the priest and Levite stingy? They did not suffer

> The minister of the gospel cannot be permitted to avoid intimacy, either with the suffering or the dying.

with, but rather experienced disguised feelings devoid of the intimacy of care. In order to avoid the label stingy, the minister of the gospel cannot be permitted to avoid intimacy, either with the suffering or the dying.

Although the story of the Good Samaritan was a parable, Jesus' life is real. Although the Law led to a distancing between leper and society, Jesus deliberately touched him when he could have healed from a distance (Mark 1:40-42). Jesus added the words, "I was sick and you looked after me" (Matt 25:36b), to the list of fundamental acts of "caring" with food, drink, shelter, clothes, and visits to prison (Matt 25:31-46). Jesus felt the pain of others who suffered and died. His own emotion at the raising of Lazarus (deeply moved, John 11:33

and 11:38; Jesus wept, John 11:35) tells us about care. One cannot help but marvel at C.S. Lewis's observation as to why Jesus wept as he confronted Lazarus's passing. Remember that the Master was well aware of being the Resurrection and the Life and therefore that he would raise Lazarus. Rather, as the Word in the first Chapter of John's Gospel, he never intended for his creation to suffer and die. Since mankind sinned and therefore brought death into the world, death has become a reality so terrible that it is the last of our enemies. Through it all, his example is sufficient. As he touched, was moved emotionally, and came *near* to heal, so should we.

What follows is a modern day parable that talks of ministry to the dying. Stanley Hauerwas has related the near-death needs of Jeffrey—a childhood leukemic. All the child asks for is to hear the story of *Charlotte's Web* read to him. Jeffrey wants to hear the part wherein Charlotte dies. What does a children's story tell us about care? What of the care required as the hour of death approaches? First there is Charlotte's own plight, "Nobody of the hundreds of people who visited the fair knew that a gray spider played the most important part of all. No one was with Charlotte when she died." Hauerwas's call to a community grounded in scriptural care followed.

> "A child's death should not imitate a spider's."

> But a child's death should not imitate a spider's. It may be that spiders are meant to live a little while and die, but we who are created for fellowship with one another and with God, cannot believe that this is all there is. It may be that spiders are destined to die alone, but as those who believe that we are destined to enjoy one another and God, we cannot allow ourselves and our loved ones so to die. We have no theodicy that can soften the pain of our death and the death of our children, but we believe that we share a common story that makes it possible for us to be with one another, especially as we die. There can be no way to remove the loneliness of the death of leukemic children unless they see witnessed in the lives of those who care for them a confidence rooted in friendship with God and with one another. That, finally, is the only response we have to the problem of the death of our children.[16]

When care is placed squarely in the context of Scripture, untarnished by connotative transitions or semantic misunderstandings, it does not ask, it does not desire, it removes loneliness and shares hope. It suffers with as Paul's brothers in Christ did with him. How these examples can be translated into ministry is the subject of the next segment.

Hospice: How We Can Show That We Care Today

So do not tell Wolterstrorff that death—the death of his son is not really so bad. Because it is. Death is awful, demonic. If you think your task as comforter is to tell me that really, all things considered, it's not so bad, you do not sit with me in my grief but place yourself far off in the distance away from me. Over there, you are of no help. What I need to hear from you is that you recognize how painful it is. I need to hear from you that you are with me in my desperation. *To comfort me you have to come close.*[17]

In an effort to discuss ministry to the dying in a more prescriptive manner, Scripture will be presented as a reminder of the prominence afforded care in the inspired Word. The message of Paul to Timothy and the Parable of the Good Samaritan are not the only occasions Scripture provides to model care. The Bible is a tapestry of care from first to last. Never presume that the Old Testament missed care and that it left that job to the New Testament. For example, God's people cared for and made Rahab an object of grace, "that you

> The Bible is a tapestry of care from first to last.

will show *kindness* to my family" (Josh 2:12), in a location slated for destruction. The curses from Mount Ebal protected the vulnerable: "cursed is the man who withholds justice from the *alien, the fatherless, or the widow*" (Deut 27:19; see also Deut 10:18). Perhaps care in the Old Testament was demonstrated most convincingly by one of Jesus' own ancestors, Ruth. In a book replete with *ḥesed*, or God's loving-kindness, Ruth became God's vehicle for grace. In the same book, the kinsman redeemer was a metaphor for grace as he recaptured covenant blessings for the disenfranchised.

Old Testament theology applied to bioethics may be contained in Deuteronomy 30:19, "This day I call heaven and earth as witnesses against you that I have set before you life and death, blessings and curses. Now choose *life*, so that you and your children may live." In the words of Carrie Earll,

> God's choice is life, and all of heaven and earth are watching to witness whether human beings will heed the eternal one's preference. . . . If God directs us to "choose life," that implies that there is always a life-affirming option to choose. . . . we need to be creatively developing and watching for alternatives to death-producing responses.[18]

Ms. Earll wrote these words as a clarion call to the evangelical community in its role of life affirmation. Let us frame the search for life-affirming responses towards the dying, as well as their community, through the life, dying, and death of our Lord Jesus. With that foundation, we can proceed to formulate contemporary life-affirming responses to the dying.

Recently, Arthur Dyck has proposed Jesus as the perfect model for a response to suffering, death, and dying.

> There is also in Christianity a more general expression that life on earth entails suffering, and in distinct ways for Christians. Beyond the suffering that results from persecution, there is suffering that results from *compassionately taking on the burdens of others.* One of the most dramatic instances in which followers of Jesus were called upon to suffer in this way occurred in the Garden of Gethsemane just prior to Jesus' arrest and crucifixion. Jesus had his disciples with Him in the garden and, as recorded, in the Gospel of Mark, He told Peter, James and John: "My soul is overwhelmed with sorrow to the point of death . . . stay here and keep watch" (Mark 14:34). The description of the enormous suffering Jesus experienced in anticipation of the torturous death to come contains an important moral imperative. Jesus expected His followers to be in prayer with Him and to be a companion to Him while He was suffering. In short, followers of Jesus owe compassion to those suffering. What happened in the Garden of Gethsemane contains a very urgent message for all who are attending the sick and the dying: Do not abandon the suffering; pray with them and for them; do not shun the suffering . . . exhibit the kind of compassionate care giving that will *incur suffering for the caregiver.*[19]

Incurring suffering for the caregiver? Notice again the consistency of painful sympathy as a result of intimacy. It should come as no surprise that Shakespeare clearly understood the message of Matthew 25:35-40. There is something about authentic care that pulls the one rendering compassion into such intimate contact with the sufferer that physical divisions blur. In the *Merchant of Venice*, a dramatic fleshing out of the "whatever you do to the least of my brethren," the intimacy of sufferer and caregiver is described as, "the quality of mercy is not strained, it droppeth as the gentle rain from heaven upon the place beneath, it is *twice blessed:* it blesseth him that *gives* and him that *takes.*"[20] In this biblical image incorporated into drama, Jesus' words have deliberately changed min-

> Authentic intimacy demands that the suffering of those in need will be felt by those who care.

isterial roles from one who ministers, to one who is ministered to, and finally to a blessing for both. In the moment of suffering, we sit so close to each other on the mourning bench that only Jesus remains. Authentic intimacy demands that the suffering of those in need will be felt by those who care. It can be no other way.

Are there vacancies on those "mourning benches"? Yes indeed there are. There are many Mr. Sauders who are alone as they face death. They wait for hospice care. There is no better example of a life-affirming response to the choice between life and death confronted by the terminal. In this regard, recent empiric study regarding care for the dying deserves careful reflection. Breitbart demonstrated that patients who were both depressed and dying were four times more likely to wish for hastened death than those terminal patients who were not depressed.[21] Another characteristic in those patients who sought a hastened death was *hopelessness*, defined as "a pessimistic cognitive style rather than an assessment of one's poor progress." Surprisingly, there was *no* correlation between a desire to hasten death and persistent physical pain. Medicine has finally succeeded in relieving the physical pain of terminal patients. Remember that Arthur Frank said earlier, "not in pain, *but still suffering!*" In fact, on June 26, 1997, the U.S. Supreme Court refused to find a constitutional right to assisted suicide. The availability of palliative care and the relief of pain were central to the judges' decision.[22] If pain and suffering had not been relieved by vigorous example, the decision may have been different. Breitbart's conclusions regarding dying, pain relief, depression, and hospice were as follows:

Given the above data and given that hospice patients very seldom persist in a desire to hasten death or in requests for physician-assisted suicide or euthanasia, one can confidently assert that hospice caregivers not only manage care very well, but also greatly alleviate suffering due to depression and hopelessness.

Can firm conclusions be drawn? When patients are near death, they have a choice between controlling the time and manner of death (by euthanasia or assisted suicide) versus dying at a time determined by a sovereign God. No longer is the choice an issue of pain control, but one of the need to relieve their depression and sense of hopelessness. People who are cared for by individuals who really do *care*, do not ask for hastened death as often. That is a profound message to the evangelical community.

If we return for a moment to care in the biblical tradition, if there is one area where this intimacy and the act of incurring suffering are intimately realized, it is in hospice. Contact there on a contemporary "mourning bench" extends to the one suffering as well as the community who suffers and grieves alongside. Nigel Cameron has commented that, "the single most significant beneficial development in medicine in our generation has been hospice care, and the rise of palliative medicine as a central specialty. It is no coincidence that this was from the start a Christian project, devised by the remarkable Dr. Cicely Saunders back in the 1960s."[23] What a wonderful place for those who care, a mirror to Paul and Jesus' specific instructions on care for the dying. All the prescriptions from Paul in 2 Timothy, and all the Gethsemane moments of pain from the Lord can be realized and ministered to in a single setting. But without hospice, what is the alternative? Unfortunately, in order to view hospice with spiritual clarity, the alternative must be confronted. Unless the Christian grasps the import of euthanasia and assisted suicide, the contemporary equivalent to death in Deuteronomy 30:19, the spiritual warfare that surrounds "how we die" cannot be fully appreciated.

An Either/Or Imperative: Whether to Care or Kill!

Thus, a change that would allow physicians to kill their patients—even within the most tightly controlled circumstances—would not be a mere addition to the physician's techniques and drugs. Rather, it would fundamentally alter the established frame of reference.[24]

Yes, assisted suicide is a fundamental alteration in a long established frame of reference. God alone is sovereign over life and death. In the Torah, he says, "It is I who put to death and give life" (Deut 32:39).[25] Sovereignty is demonstrated in 1 Samuel 2:6, "The LORD brings death and makes alive"; in Psalm 90:3, "You turn man back into dust"; as well as in other locations (Ps 104:29; Eccl 8:8). In contrast to God's sovereignty over death and suicide in Scripture have been individuals' disobedience and disgrace. Examples are Abimelech (Judg 9:52-54), Samson (Judg 16:25-30), Saul (1 Sam 31:1-6 and 1 Chr 10:1-6), Ahithophel (2 Sam 17:23), Zimri (1 Kgs 16:18-19), and Judas of course. In Abimelech's case, the evil associated with his death led to further judgment by God, "Thus God repaid the wickedness of Abimelech, which he had done to his father, in killing his seventy brothers." (Judg 9:56.)

> God alone is sovereign over life and death.

In the New Testament, Paul again offers us a biblical paradigm for placing dying completely under God's will (Phil 1:20-26). In these verses, Paul expresses the Christian perspective that maintains an important tension between living and dying. Remember that even though death is the last of all our enemies, it is not an absolute evil. Martyrdom, as one example, suggests that there can be events that are worse than death itself. How are we to explicate this tension between dying and living? Although being with Christ in heaven is the ultimate reward for the believer, death is not to be fondly desired. On the other hand, there is a spiritual reality to be considered: the wages of sin is physical death. Paul does not express his preference for dying and going to Christ versus living and continuing to preach the gospel because he knows that the decision is God's and God's alone! We are not to ask for or act in death hastening; we are to trust God's sovereign will in the manner and timing of death. We are not to assume that suffering has no place in God's economy; we are to find strength in his grace, *under all circumstances.* Finally, since there is a time to die, the tension of Philippians 1:20-26 may lead to resolution of the unnecessary extension of life through technology.

> We are not to assume that suffering has no place in God's economy.

One characteristic of the present culture, postmodernism, is a mistrust of so-called metanarratives. The Bible is such a narrative, one that encapsulates all that is important to an entire tradition. The dominant culture has devalued its timeless directives; as a result, not only has care been minimized, but so have injunctions against suicide. At one time, those dying in the manner of Mr. Sauder would have been classified as victims of homicide. The perpetrators would have been prosecuted. Unfortunately, in certain locations, judgment is no longer the norm. An experiment in physician-assisted killing that began in Holland has now extended to other countries in Europe (Belgium), select locations in Australia, parts of Switzerland (Zurich), and to one state in the U.S. (Oregon). There is an alternative to care called physician-assisted suicide, and it is a way that leads to death. The first sin represented pride: Adam decided that he could be like God. Culture's contemporary spin on pride is manifested in a desire to control death by placing it under human control. Postmoderns scoff that suffering is not a part of man's condition. Therefore, suffering is not to be endured at the end of life. Death-hastening is their solution. The directives against suicide in Scripture were relative, given they say, to an earlier, less enlightened culture. The timing of death is man's because he and his world are all there is. What is really wrong, they ask, with ending a life that will be short and uncomfortable anyway? There is much wrong with it as the following will demonstrate. When postmoderns rebel against the authority of Scripture, try to persuade them with the "corrosive" effect that assisted suicide has had on society.

> Culture's contemporary spin on pride is manifested in a desire to control death by placing it under human control.

The starting point for such arrogance has to be in Holland where death-hastening began. Study of the Netherlands has provided sobering statistics. Fifty-four percent of responding Dutch physicians have already performed either euthanasia or assisted in suicide. A further 34 percent considered that it would be conceivable for them to apply them in the future. Although 12 percent indicated that they would never perform euthanasia, two-thirds of these respondents would refer patients to colleagues who would comply with the euthanasia request. Only 4 percent of the Dutch physicians gave an outright no to either assisting patients in their deaths or referring them.[26]

In Holland, care has been replaced by an insidious alternative: eliminate suffering by eliminating the sufferer. Embarrass death by choosing it and helping it along. Evaluate the following examples of medical *care* for the dying in the Netherlands.[27] An elderly widow living alone had difficulties with activities of daily living. On a number of occasions, she asked her doctor about euthanasia. Initially, he resisted. He finally relented, but only if she agreed to tell her son. She did not want her son involved. The doctor still acceded to her request. When the physician called the son after he killed the widow, he lied and told the son that his mother died of a "cardiac arrest." That is the diagnosis that ended up on the death certificate! Next, a newborn with Down's syndrome was diagnosed with a surgically correctable blockage between the stomach and small intestine. The family was told that the problem was the first of many to come. Alternatives were not presented, and the physicians manipulated the family. The doctor hinted that it would be cruel to starve the baby to death. Without explicit parental consent, the physician killed the baby. The hospital ethicist said that the act was not really euthanasia and that the drugs administered just "helped the child along." Finally, a 56-year-old man was brought to a Dutch emergency room after a car accident. The surgeon concluded that the man's injuries were severe. Acting by himself, the physician gave the patient an injection of potassium chloride and the patient died. The family was then told that the patient died as a result of injuries sustained in the auto accident! The doctor rationalized that "death was at the door anyway," so it was justifiable to kill the patient and to lie about it. In Holland, patients no longer need to be terminal to be killed, and minors between twelve and sixteen years of age may undergo euthanasia as long as their parents consent. When patients are diagnosed with neurologic diseases, rather than have them languish and be dependent upon the care of others, they ask for their death to be hastened.

The dissonance between care and assisting in death has been described by Dr. Carlos Gomez.

> Patients trapped in the noisy solitude of Alzheimer's Disease, those dying by inches with disseminated malignancies, the crippled and the lame, the wearied sick whom we cannot cure—they all deserve the same measure of care we give to those with promising prospects. For if we fail them, Kevorkian and the experience of the Dutch will not be the odd example, but the reigning paradigm.[28]

Is assisted suicide driven by the facility of killing patients in contrast to the perceived "burdens" of care? Has our culture become

> *Has our culture become "stingy" with the time required to minister?*

"stingy" with the time required to minister? The relief of suffering requires more than the simplicity of lethal injections. Forty-six percent of the requests for assisted suicide in Oregon are rescinded as a result of palliative interventions compared to 15 percent of individuals without intervention![29] This means that attention to mood and depression can impact the desire for death. How bereft of compassion is a culture that prefers to kill patients rather than offering a chance at hospice, efforts to provide depression relief, and intimacy? Suffering can never be eliminated from the human condition, it can only be relieved by

> *Authentic care has become the new millennium's road not taken.*

suffering with. Authentic care has become the new millennium's road not taken. Unfortunately, the road that leads to death has now come to the New World.

On November 4, 1997, 60 percent of Oregonians opposed repeal of that state's *Death with Dignity Act*. Assisted suicide and euthanasia were legalized for the first time in the United States, despite lessons that should have been learned from Holland about the treatment of depression prior to assisting suicide. In fact, under law, the physician of record should document that patients seeking assistance in dying in Oregon are capable to "make and communicate health care decisions" without the burden of depression.[30] Unfortunately, the number of studies testifying to physicians' inability to diagnose and treat depression is disturbing.[31] How many patients are killed in Oregon while depressed is unknown. Where are those who can share the burdens of depression on the mourning bench?

Doctors can never be allowed to kill or to assist patients who want to end their lives. Society has to be willing to expend the cost of care as an alternative to hastening death. Dr. Gomez has commented, "Yet when this most personal of events (death) occurs in a medical context, there are aspects of it that pass beyond the control of the dying individual to professionals and to their institutional mores."[32] Institutional and dominant culture mores are intersecting. The result has been sinister, and now the dying have been added to the list of the least of my brethren.

Conclusion

Community groups and churches can help by sponsoring hospice programs and providing volunteers to relieve caregivers. My experience with churches has been fairly grim. If I call up a minister of a church a person attended for 30–40 years in the prime of her life but now she's disabled, and I ask, is there anything you can do to help this person's burden? I'd say I'm no better than 50–50 to get a favorable response. Take the last 20 members who have died in your congregation and ask their families how the Church responded. I've had patients who were furious when they received cards telling them people were praying for them. Well, why don't they come and meet me they ask? Why won't they pray with me in person while holding my hand?[33]

When it comes to answering the question of how we should die, or refining truth in choosing between life and death, everyone must commit. If dying is examined from an evangelical worldview perspective, care is "fleshed out" with examples frequently provided in Scripture. That brand of care must be personal and should lead to a suffering with that is so intimate it not only hurts caregivers, but also places them in intense proximity to the sufferers. This biblical model is today's equivalent of choosing and affirming life.

If the examined death emanates from other worldview perspectives, the prevailing sense is that death must be controlled by the dying themselves. They may request that professionals assist them in dying. Suffering, in this view, can be eliminated, but only by killing the sufferer. The story of this lethal choice began in Holland and has marched on to Oregon as well as to other locations in Europe and Australia. From the sale of plastic bags expressly to hasten death, to partial birth abortion, described as "euthanasia for a different age group,"[34] the gauntlet has been laid down. What is an individual Christian to do? What are the "life-affirming" responses? Are the choices available as a ministry for a select minority, or for all?

Charles Colson has an answer. He has watched the examples of Joni Erickson Tada, a Christian paralyzed from an accident during her teen years, and Nigel Cameron, a bioethicist who has mapped out responses. Colson says, "The (first) question: what does it mean to be human? (and) . . . the second question I hear with increasing frequency in our post-Christian culture: what difference can one

> *The problems are so huge; we feel helpless, and so we do nothing. That response is a cop-out.*

person make? The problems are so huge; we feel helpless, and so we do nothing. That response is a cop-out. Nigel Cameron and Joni Erickson Tada pressed on, confident that a sovereign God would use them, as indeed He has. They remind us that God sets each of us in a particular time and place for a precise purpose. We must strengthen our resolve, no matter the obstacles, to fulfill that purpose in a fallen world."[35] These words were introduced by the claim that bioethical dilemmas would emerge as *the* moral issues of the new millennium. It may be early to tell, but the year 2003 is already populated by contentious issues in bioethics. What it really means to be human has become an either/or, and the answers are diametrically opposed. If the guide is Scripture, the truth about what it means to be human resides in the Way, the Truth, and the Life, and in the fact that we are created in his image. This truth is the valuation for all who die. We as his redeemed may be perplexed in a post-modern world, but never despairing. To choose life by affirmation is the only answer. God redeems suffering and is sovereign over the great debates

> *To choose life by affirmation is the only answer.*

of our era, including those related to dying. Jesus suffered, suffered with, and died. His image is at stake and calls for care directed at those who face the last of our enemies.

Church-sponsored hospice groups are an excellent starting place. Support for tired caregivers who are family members of those suffering from Alzheimer's disease, for example, fits right into the paradigms developed in this chapter. Grieving with those who lose loved ones also can be ministry. The intimacy nurtured follows Paul's lead in 2 Timothy and has been proven to mitigate the depression that feeds euthanasia. The example for the lost will not be missed. When a leader in the former Soviet Union who vigorously persecuted Christians was asked why he wasn't successful in diminishing faith, he had one answer. "Because Christians never let anyone die alone"![36] The challenge is clear. The mourning benches are so very, very prevalent, but how about the workers? The contribution of each individual and every Church community will not be missed by those watching. The willing spirit alluded to in the Garden must overcome our flesh.

Notes

[1]L. Kass, "Foreword" in *Regulating Death: Euthanasia and the Case of the Netherlands*, ed. by C. Gomez (New York and Toronto: The Free Press, 1991) ix.

[2]D. Aikman, *One Word of Truth: Portrait of Alexsander Solzhenitsyn* (Mars Hill Audio, The Trinity Forum). **www.marshillaudio.org**.

[3]J.A. Benson, "Reviews and Reflections: The Lost Art of Caring," *The Pharos of Alpha and Omega, Alpha 65:1* (Winter 2002) 33. This is a peer-reviewed journal published by the National Honor Medical society. AOA is an acrostic for the Greek words, *Worthy to Serve the Suffering*.

[4]L.E. Cluff and R.H. Binstock, eds. *The Lost Art of Caring: A Challenge to Health Professionals, Families, Communities, and Society* (Baltimore: The Johns Hopkins University Press, 2001).

[5]D. Hollinger, "Curing, Caring and Beyond: Reflections for a Clinical Ethic," *Ethics and Medicine* 19 (2003) 45-53.

[6]Benson, "The Lost Art," 33.

[7]Hollinger, "Curing," 98.

[8]G.W. Rutecki, "Until Death Shall Be No More: Christian Care for the Dying," in *Bioethics and the Future of Medicine: A Christian Appraisal*, ed. by J.F. Kilner, N.M. Cameron, and D.L. Schiedermayer (Grand Rapids: Eerdmans, 1995) 274-289.

[9]"Healing Hands," *Hippocrates* (Nov/Dec 1993) 33. *Hippocrates* was a non-peer reviewed journal that had an abbreviated circulation. It is usually not kept in medical libraries and frankly has been hard to come by.

[10]Rutecki, "Until Death," 279-284.

[11]S.L. Carter, *The Culture of Disbelief* (New York: Basic Books, 1993) 247-248.

[12]A.W. Frank, "Not in Pain, but Still Suffering," *Christian Century* (October 7, 1992) 860.

[13]M. Olasky, *The Tragedy of American Compassion* (Washington, DC: Regnery Gateway, 1992).

[14]N. Davies and R. Moorhouse, *Microcosm: Portrait of a Central European City* (London: Jonathan Cape, 2002), xv.

[15]Olasky, *The Tragedy*.

[16]S. Hauerwas, *Naming the Silences: God, Medicine, and the Problem of Suffering* (Grand Rapids: Eerdmans, 1990) 148.

[17]Ibid., 151.

[18]Carrie Earll, **http://cbhd.org/resources/aps/earll.02-11-26.htm**.

[19]Arthur Dyck, "Alleviating Suffering in Dignity," *The Newsletter of the Center for Bioethics and Human Dignity* 8 (2002) 2-3.

[20]William Shakespeare, *The Merchant of Venice*, Act 4, Scene 1, lines 181-184, spoken by Portia to Shylock.

[21]W. Breitbart, B. Rosenfeld, and H. Pessin, "Depression, Hopelessness, and Desire for Hastened Death in Terminally Ill Patients with Cancer," *JAMA* 284 (2000) 2907-2911.

[22]E.J. Larson and D.W. Amundsen, *A Different Death: Euthanasia and the Christian Tradition* (Grand Rapids: InterVarsity, 1998) 221.

[23]Cameron cited in Dyck, "Alleviating Suffering," 2.

[24]Gomez, *Regulating Death*, 14.

[25]Larson and Amundsen, *A Different Death*, 31-84.

[26]J.J.M. Delden, L. Pijnenborg, and P.J. van der Maas, *The Remelink Study Two Years Later* (Hastings Center Report, 1993) 23:24-27.

[27]Gomez, *Regulating Death*, Chapter 3, beginning on page 57.

[28]Ibid., 139.

[29]L. Ganzini, H.D. Nelson, and T.A. Schmidt, "Physician's Experiences with the Oregon Death with Dignity Act," *New England Journal of Medicine* 342 (2000) 557-563.

[30]J.R. Wernon, "A Grand Illusion: Oregon's Attempt to Control Death through Physician Assisted Suicide," *Dignity, The Newsletter of the Center for Bioethics and Human Dignity* (Fall 2002) 2-4. See also K. Foley, *Don't Ask, Don't Tell* (Hastings Center Report, 1999) 29:37-42; and J. Woolfrey, *What Happens Now? Oregon and Physician Assisted Suicide* (Hastings Center Report, 1998) 28:9-17.

[31]R. Silman, T. Donahue, D. Jarjoura, and A. Ognibene, "Recognition of Depression by Internal Medicine Residents," *Journal of Community Health* 17 (1992) 143-151; see also, J. Docherty, "Barriers to the Diagnosis of Depression in Primary Care," *Journal of Clinical Psychiatry* 58 (1997) 5-10.

[32]Gomez, *Regulating Death*, 4.

[33]Larson and Amundsen, *A Different Death*, 250.

[34]D.P. Mortimer, "The New Eugenics and the Unborn: The Historical Cousinage of Eugenics and Infanticide," presented at the Center for Bioethics and Human Dignity, July 20, 2002, at the Ninth Annual Conference on Bioethics, Bannockburn, Illinois. (Audio tapes available).

[35]Charles Colson, "Undaunted: Bioethics Challenges Are Huge, but So Is God," *Christianity Today* (August 5, 2002) 64.

[36]Personal Communication with Dr. Harold O.J. Brown, Professor of Theology, Reformed Seminary, Charlotte, NC.

Bibliography

Cameron, Nigel M. de S. *The New Medicine: Life and Death after Hippocrates.* Wheaton, IL: Crossway Books, 1992.
The impact of the Hippocratic Oath on life-affirming medicine was only briefly touched upon in this chapter. The magnitude of the paradigm shift impacting medicine as a result of Post-Hippocratism, the critical outcome of the Roe v. Wade decision, is central to an understanding of life and death decisions today. This book is an insightful look at the oath and its untimely loss.

The **Center for Bioethics and Human Dignity** is an evangelical organization committed to the biblical principles surrounding life and death. They provide newsletters, yearly meetings, local meetings on life and death decision-making and have a valuable web site (**www.chbd.com**) with weekly updates on all pertinent biomedical issues.

Dyck, Arthur J. *Life's Worth: The Case against Assisted Suicide.* Grand Rapids: Eerdmans, 2002.
The quote concerning Jesus' call to the Apostles to pray with him for comfort before his death is contained in this book. The Harvard professor outlines a Christian response to the assisted-suicide crisis and staunchly maintains the evil of death hastening.

Gomez, Carlos. *Regulating Death: Euthanasia and the Case of the Netherlands.* New York and Toronto: The Free Press, 1991.
Gomez has written a shocking exposé of the first attempt to permit and later legalize euthanasia in the world. The corrosive effect of euthanasia on medicine will not be missed.

Larson, E.J., and D.W. Amundsen. *A Different Death: Euthanasia and the Christian Tradition.* Grand Rapids: InterVarsity, 1998.
This volume provides vigorous historical perspective on the Church and its response to suicide and euthanasia. It is well-written and weaves in relevant information regarding the Supreme Court and legal issues fueling the contemporary debate.